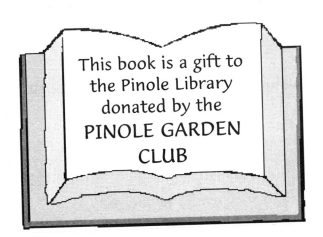

This book is a gift to
the Pinole Library
donated by the
PINOLE GARDEN
CLUB

About Island Press

Island Press is the only nonprofit organization in the United States whose principal purpose is the publication of books on environmental issues and natural resource management. We provide solutions-oriented information to professionals, public officials, business and community leaders, and concerned citizens who are shaping responses to environmental problems.

In 2000, Island Press celebrates its sixteenth anniversary as the leading provider of timely and practical books that take a multidisciplinary approach to critical environmental concerns. Our growing list of titles reflects our commitment to bringing the best of an expanding body of literature to the environmental community throughout North America and the world.

Support for Island Press is provided by The Jenifer Altman Foundation, The Bullitt Foundation, The Mary Flagler Cary Charitable Trust, The Nathan Cummings Foundation, The Geraldine R. Dodge Foundation, The Charles Engelhard Foundation, The Ford Foundation, The German Marshall Fund of the United States, The George Gund Foundation, The Vira I. Heinz Endowment, The William and Flora Hewlett Foundation, The W. Alton Jones Foundation, The John D. and Catherine T. MacArthur Foundation, The Andrew W. Mellon Foundation, The Charles Stewart Mott Foundation, The Curtis and Edith Munson Foundation, The National Fish and Wildlife Foundation, The New-Land Foundation, The Oak Foundation, The Overbrook Foundation, The David and Lucile Packard Foundation, The Pew Charitable Trusts, The Rockefeller Brothers Fund, Rockefeller Financial Services, The Winslow Foundation, and individual donors.

Sustainable
Landscape
Construction

Sustainable Landscape Construction

A Guide to Green Building Outdoors

J. William Thompson and Kim Sorvig

Drawings by Craig D. Farnsworth, ASLA

Island Press

Washington, D.C. • Covelo, California

Library of Congress Cataloging-in-Publication Data

Thompson, J. William
   Sustainable landscape construction : a guide to green building outdoors / by J. William Thompson & Kim Sorvig; with drawings by Craig D. Farnsworth.
      p. cm
Includes bibliographical references and index.
   ISBN 1-55963-646-7 (paper : acid-free paper)
1. Landscape construction. 2. Landscape protection.
3. Green products. I. Sorvig, Kim. II. Title.
TH380 .T46 2000
   712'.01—dc21
      00-008256

Disclaimer

This book reports information from designers, contractors, manufacturers, academic researchers, and many others. We have attempted to ensure that all the information herein is credible, but have performed no independent testing of these reports. Reporting such information does not constitute endorsement of any product or method. Exclusion of products or methods does not imply a negative evaluation; please see our request for updates (page xxi). All trademarks remain property of their respective owners. The authors and publishers specifically disclaim any and all liability purported to result from inclusion or exclusion of a product or method in this book.

Variations among regions and sites result in very different performance from the same products and methods, and no assurance can be given that any information reported herein is suitable for any given site. The information reported herein may contain errors and omissions, and even where complete and accurate, it is not a substitute for local expertise and professional judgment. Illustrations are not intended as ready-to-build, step-by-step instructions, but to depict concepts and processes. The authors and publisher specifically disclaim any and all liability for any situation resulting from use or attempted use of this information.

All trademarks referred to remain the property of their respective owners.

Contents

List of Illustrations

List of Tables

Acknowledgments

Research and writing for this book, as well as commissioned illustrations, were supported by a generous grant from the Graham Foundation for Advanced Studies in the Fine Arts, Chicago.

General grant support for the Center for Resource Economics/Island Press also made this book possible, and is gratefully acknowledged.

* * *

Books, like ecosystems, evolve through many interactions. Tracing the web of contributions to this work can never be complete. Thanks to everyone who responded generously to our many requests, including those whose projects, pictures, or words *aren't* included for lack of space, time, or computer compatibility.

We'd like to thank several people specifically:

The late John Lyle provided invaluable guidance in the early planning stages, and Ian McHarg has been an inspiration to us as to many others. J. B. Jackson helped with computer problems. Manuscript reviewers took on an extra burden with grace and insight: Jon Coe (CLR Design, Philadelphia); Leslie Sauer (Andropogon Associates, Philadelphia); Bruce Ferguson (University of Georgia); Pliny Fisk and Gail Vittori (Center for Maximum Potential Building Systems, Austin); Dale McClintock (Center for Resourceful Building Technology, Missoula); Mick Nickel (landscape contractor, Earth Alive Bioservices, Santa Fe); Alex Wilson (editor, Environmental Building News); and Heather Boyer and Cecilia González at Island Press.

For sustaining us, very literally, through this book on sustainability, we thank our wives: Anne Herzog ("for continuing support"—B.T.)

and Mary Sorvig (*"swa swa we forgyfa   urum gyltendum"*—K.S.). Thanks also to each other—for surviving this epic with friendship, and at least *some* sanity, intact.

Research on energy and materials-hazards was almost entirely the responsibility of Kim Sorvig. Neither his co-author nor anyone else should be blamed for errors in this material. Corrections, improved methods, or better data will be welcomed for the next edition.

Contacting the Authors

We welcome information on projects, products, or methods that fit the general theme of sustainable landscape construction. Tell us about your own work or that of others you believe is sustainable. We are also interested in unexpected results or problems with specific techniques.

Despite requesting information via the Associated Landscape Contractors of America, we have not had as much representation from landscape contractors as we would have liked, and we hope to hear from readers with that type of experience, as well as designers, landowners, and others interested in the subject.

Please e-mail all information to ksorvig@unm.edu.

Please help us keep this manageable: Start with a short verbal description, listing contact(s) for more information. Do *not* send images via e-mail. We will keep the descriptions on file and will call or e-mail the contact person when we begin updating the book. We cannot guarantee a response to each e-mail. Thank you.

Introduction

If we put our minds to it, can we gardeners, with our centuries of practical experience, help rescue species from the brink of extinction?

—Janet Marinelli, 1998
Stalking the Wild Amaranth: Gardening in the Age of Extinction

Around the world and throughout history, constructed landscapes, gardens, and parks have enriched humanity's bond to the Earth, alongside the self-sustaining, "wild" or "natural" places of the world. Today, the green places we *build* hold many of our hopes for a sustainable future. They offer green relief from an urbanizing world in which "postindustrial" society still seems bent on mechanizing the globe.

Constructed landscapes are both similar to and different from their wild relatives. Many are deliberately constructed to recall the qualities of natural places and serve the practical and spiritual needs of humanity in ways similar to wild places. Yet they remain constructed, even if less obviously so than buildings. This paradox makes it easy to assume that constructed landscapes are harmless to the larger environment. But how sustainable *is* the construction of landscapes?

Concern for the health of outdoor places is a central theme in landscape architecture and landscape contracting. It is a concern shared by many members of related disciplines such as architecture, planning, public-lands administration, and horticulture, as well as by private gardeners. In translating this concern to the materials and methods of *making* landscapes, there are both successes and problems to report. A small but growing number of landscape-makers are looking beyond the assumption that all built landscapes are ecofriendly. Their questions are still new, and the answers still evolving: how can people make environmentally responsible choices in the process of conceiving and constructing landscapes?

Such questions are of real importance. Urban and suburban development in the United States reshapes hundreds of thousands of acres of previously undeveloped land each year—in Colorado alone, 10 acres *per hour* by one estimate.[1] Worries about development usually focus on structures—tract homes, commercial strips, and industrial buildings—but the constructed *landscapes* that accompany these buildings also contribute to widespread environmental change and, sometimes, damage. When self-sustaining ecosystems are converted to built landscapes, the hidden costs may include soil loss, degradation of water, introduction of toxic and nonrenewable materials, and unsustainable energy use. This does not need to be—in fact, it needs *not* to be.

Compare an ordinary quarter-acre landscaped lot with a 2,000-square-foot house, each a mainstay of the American Dream. The landscape directly affects an area of environment five and a half times as large as the house. More important, if the landscape introduces toxic materials and invasive plants or diseases, they are free to spread; inside the house, such problems might be contained or controlled by walls, filters, or mechanical systems. In addition, many landscape practices are "non-point" sources of pollution, crossing ownership and jurisdictional lines.

Historically, some of the green of the garden has been lost in the broader battle to "control" nature. Social expectations of appearance, style, and conformity have also pushed us toward landscapes involving heavy doses of industrial-strength technology. To pretend the technology is not there, or to assume that all landscape

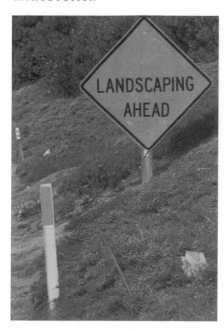

Figure i. Is this a
warning sign?
PHOTO: Kim Sorvig.

technology is equally acceptable, is to continue
the myth that gardens are 100 percent natural.
This myth, ironically, plays into the hands of
those who would happily let constructed environments replace natural ones everywhere.

Sustainable Landscape Construction reevaluates
the assumption that all built landscapes are
ecofriendly and offers practical, professional
alternatives toward more sustainable landscape
construction (including design and maintenance
issues). Techniques and materials of landscape
construction (both alternative and conventional)
are evaluated, using criteria such as nontoxicity
and renewability in manufacture, or energy savings. Projects whose success offers hope for sustainable landscape construction (of which there
are a surprising number) are described and illustrated, with sources for further information.

This book is not, however, a just-the-facts
encyclopedia. Its subject is not yet written in
stone. We feel strongly that evolving knowledge
and differing, informed opinions require something other than a cut-and-dried approach. The
book is therefore organized by principles (see
page 9, "How to Use This Book"). These pages
also explicitly include the authors' opinions, presenting a framework for decision making rather
than a single best practice.

Construction (of all sorts, not just landscape
construction) is often treated as a value-free
topic, a summation of know-how without *know-
why, know-when,* or *know-whether.* This is mistak-

enly called a "no-nonsense" attitude. Such an
approach cannot lead to *sustainable* construction,
since sustainability involves both technical and
ethical choices. Thus, although our focus is on
the practices and materials of landscape construction, we discuss values and choices throughout
the book and mention policy issues which relate
to constructed landscapes. We urge you to take
the time to consider these political, social, and
ethical issues, along with the technical ones.

The first of these value-and-policy issues is the
idea of sustainability itself.

What Is Sustainability: Politics, Ethics, and Semantics

Despite its widespread popularity, the idea of
sustainability is far from having a clear and
agreed definition. Although the core of the vision
seems simple—a lasting and nondestructive way
to live on this Earth—the questions are many. It
is important for those of us concerned with landscape construction to think clearly about the
local good or damage that we do and about the
opportunities and limits that link our site-by-site
actions to a global picture.

Probably the simplest widely used definition of
sustainability is *meeting the needs of today's population
without diminishing the ability of future populations to
meet their needs.*[2] This desirable goal has workable
precedents such as the often-quoted Great Law
of the Iroqouis Confederation, that all decisions
should consider effects unto the seventh generation. Many cultures, from the Diné (Navajo) to
the early Christians, have conserved resources
simply by frowning on excessive wealth. Sustainability in this sense means using resources
without diminishing their future availability or
quality. Even more simply, it requires living
within our ecological means.

In this book, where we say that a particular
approach can contribute to sustainability, we
mean primarily that the method or material
appears to minimize waste, pollution, and degradation of the environment. For true
sustainability, "do I need it?" choices about the
scale and appropriateness of proposed landscapes
must also play a role, as well as sacrifices in favor
of maintaining habitat and biodiversity. In these
choices, landscape professionals can (sometimes)
guide their clients and their communities.

To some degree, sustainability has become a buzzword, and fuzzy. The term is bandied about in support of widely different causes[3] and to sell products only vaguely related to ecology. Some writers have proposed different terms for the concept. "Alternative" is one of these; popular in the 1960s, it implies second-rate status, and we have chosen not to use it. "Appropriate technology" is also widely used, and it is an important part of sustainability. We prefer the term sustainability because it emphasizes *long-term* appropriateness. In the early 1990s John Lyle suggested that sustainability was not enough and that optimal design should be "regenerative"—capable of *renewing* the energy and materials of degraded ecosystems. By contrast, at least one group, the Bay Area Stormwater Management Agencies Association (BASMAA) talks about "less-toxic gardens" and "less-toxic methods" of maintaining them.[4] BASMAA, not without cause, implies that human activity will *always* have some negative impact upon nature, particularly when concentrated in large urban areas. Although we have chosen to keep the term sustainability for this book, the points raised by these alternative terms bear keeping in mind.

The limits of what we as landscape-makers can hope to contribute must also be acknowledged. The "present/future needs" definition of sustainability can be criticized for oversimplifying several key questions: Which population's needs are to be met? How large a human population can be sustained? Where do we draw the line between "needs" and desires? It would be naive of the authors or the users of this book to ignore the criticisms that have been leveled at the very idea of sustainability. Questions about sustainability have pragmatic and political effects on the construction of landscapes, as they do on almost every human endeavor in the twenty-first century.

The following questions illustrate some of the doubts about sustainability, in terms specific to built landscapes. Few if any of these questions will be resolved entirely through landscape construction:

- If nonpolluting, low-maintenance landscapes covered the globe, at the expense of wild species and places, would that be a sustainable world?

- Is there any way to avoid impoverishing the natural world without placing drastic regulatory limits on human population, land use, and resource consumption?

- For a majority of the world's population, "landscape" equates to crops, firewood, and survival. In such economies, public parks and private gardens are fantasies far beyond reach, glimpsed on TV or through closed gates. Does this mean that all landscape construction should be sacrificed to achieve a subsistence-level sustainability?

- Is stewardship of the Earth as a whole system possible without dramatic changes in often arbitrary divisions of jurisdiction over land?

For some, the answer to these questions is that sustainability is an admirable idea but can never be achieved. The authors respect the belief that sustainability is impossible, or that the idea merely disguises the seriousness of environmental degradation. (Just after reading the daily news, we may well *agree* with those opinions.) Yet with due respect, we do not feel that defeatism is warranted.[5] The critics rightly remind us that there are limits to what sustainability can or even should be. Yet within those limits, small efforts can yield important results; local results in turn can contribute to cumulative global change.

A dramatic decrease in materialism seems necessary for the Earth to sustain us in the long term. Will landscape construction be among the sacrificial luxuries? We hope that the functional value of built landscape makes it more than a luxury. The tradition of gardening for pleasure, too, has deep roots and has survived many a drought. Realistically, though, reducing the environmental costs of construction offers an alternative to no construction at all, a way of balancing a site budget that today is often overspent. The landscape professions have a special stake, and a special responsibility, in seeking a healthy environment.

We do not want to mislead anyone into thinking that changes in landscape construction can single-handedly reverse environmental

Figure ii. John Lyle's Center for Regenerative Studies sets a high standard for sustainable place-making. Many of the materials are recycled; the beautiful landscape functionally supports and renews the Center. PROJECT: J. Lyle. PHOTO: Tom Lamb.

degradation. We do feel strongly, however, that the only possibility of a sustainable future lies in initiatives from all sides, in contributions, large and small, from great numbers of individuals and groups. The landscape professions historically have made stewardship of the environment a goal, imperfectly achieved but deeply desired. To abandon this goal because our scope of influence is limited would be irresponsible; to be smug in our greenness, equally so.

Green Building: Definitions and Initiatives

Moving from sustainability in general to "green construction" in specific requires careful thought. While many of the "simple things to do to save the planet" require only substituting bad products for good ones, architectural and landscape work literally changes the face of the Earth.

There are many situations where building *anything* is a poor choice. Yet shelter is a genuine necessity for humans, and a healthy landscape is equally essential to human existence. It is not surprising that the growing number of associations that promote "green building" have struggled to define just what that means.

Many people think of the green building movement as something of a fringe activity. It is not. Certainly there is a vanguard of activists, but mainstream initiatives are gaining steam as well. One important program is the set of *industry-approved* National Building Goals, released in 1997 by the National Institute of Standards and Technology and the National Science and Technology Council. For the construction industry as a whole, these goals include fully 50 percent reduction in operation and energy costs, and in

waste and pollution, along with a 50 percent increase in durability, targeted for achievement by 2003.[6] These goals incorporate aspects of a growing movement in engineering known as "constructability"; although it emphasizes mechanical efficiency and monetary costs, constructability shares many goals with sustainability. [7]

Voluntary green building associations exist in many cities, working alongside or ahead of government environmental regulatory agencies. The most common initial goal of such groups is to provide a green seal of approval that builders can achieve by meeting energy efficiency and recycling goals, among others.[8] Associations in Austin TX and Boulder CO are notable for having both government and industry backing. Many also have links to realtors, appraisers, and lenders

who are beginning to take serious note of the market for greener design.

To be truly effective, green building programs must go beyond approving architectural products; they must also include landscape-related goals. For example, the draft for the U.S. Green Building Council's Leadership in Energy & Environmental Design (LEED) certification program awards 50 points for meeting specific environmental performance goals. Of these, 12 possible points relate directly to landscape construction (site and soil protection, infill/brownfield siting, efficient irrigation, porous paving, and so on). Another 9 points are possible for using local/renewable/recycled materials and for managing construction waste.[9] (Odd priorities are visible even here: in an early draft, a ban on smoking was mandatory for LEED certification, but site protection was optional, for extra points!)

The following definition of green construction was debated and adopted by the recently formed Santa Fe Green Building Council:

> Green construction practices reduce resource use and pollution while increasing the value derived from each resource used. Green construction protects healthy sites, restores or enhances marginal sites by working with natural processes, and contributes to regional habitat conservation. Within these parameters, green construction stimulates a stable and diverse local economy, improves local quality of life, and improves human health.[10]

The middle part of this definition, concerning site and habitat issues, is frequently ignored in defining sustainable or green practices. Writing and action about green building are often the work of architects and builders; although well-meaning toward the landscape, such definitions often show the lack of input from landscape professionals. Including site/ecosystem protection in green building is essential. A perfectly resource-green house that replaces a healthy ecosystem is a poor substitute. Badly sited, such a building destroys the site and with it, the environmental services provided to the "green" functioning of the building.

Selecting the right site, and the right location within the site, can make the difference between a building that diminishes its site and one that enhances it. Regional factors also play a large and often unconsidered role. For example, although the very green headquarters of Patagonia makes excellent use of a degraded site and is highly resource-efficient, it is located outside the Reno NV public transportation network and leaves employees little option but to drive long distances to work. Balancing these factors is difficult—and current green building definitions that exclude site issues can disguise that difficulty rather than help solve it.

Including site protection in the definition points out that structures and construction are in some senses *inherently* damaging to the larger environment. This makes green building paradoxical, and to some, unpalatable—so site issues are left out.

Ignoring site and habitat protection limits the ability to transform construction into more environmentally friendly forms. Without site protection as a goal, green building can become a little like fat-free cookies—an excuse to consume more because it's better than the other brands. Although the design and construction industries are understandably reluctant to be put on a diet, one important part of green building is *building less*. Meeting this challenge in a way that keeps both the industry *and* the environment healthy is the great challenge of the coming century. So long as green building includes site issues, it is almost always a step in the direction of meeting this challenge.

In the growing number of very successful books on green building aimed at architecture and engineering, the landscape is usually accorded only an introductory chapter or two. Too frequently, architectural writers assume that landscape is a minor subset of their profession, and that environmental evaluation of architectural materials can simply be transferred to landscape work. In researching this book, we have repeatedly found this to be far from true. Information for architects is focused on "building systems" and on component performance for *operating* the structure. This focus has clear value but requires translation to have meaning in the landscape. We hope to start that process with this book.

Sustainability: Convention, Tradition, and Innovation

In discussing design and construction in this book, we distinguish between sustainable practices and two other approaches: conventional and traditional. It is worth defining the latter two explicitly, since they contrast with sustainability in different ways. It is also important to think clearly about sustainability's relationship to innovation and "progress."

Conventional practices are modern approaches and are standard in much of the construction industry. Some of these practices are quite acceptable in terms of environmental impact or can be with minor modification. The authors expect many conventional practices to be part of a sustainable future. However, conventional construction often relies on the use of massive energy inputs, extensive transportation, the use of toxic materials, and the removal of many, if not all, existing site features. There may be rare occasions when high energy use and toxic materials serve some sustainable purpose; however, changing times and conditions (for example, rising fuel prices) make it inevitable that conventional practices will change, even if environmental issues are ignored. The uncritical assumption that conventional practices are universally acceptable is the main thing that makes them destructive.

Traditional practices, as we use the term in this book, are those surviving from premodern times, and in some cases learned from preindustrial cultures. Most rely on nonmechanized tools. Not *all* traditional land-use practices are sustainable. When applied in different climates or to different population densities than those of their origins, they can even be environmentally destructive. However, many traditional practices are extremely well adapted to their home regions. The modern focus on convenience and mechanization has displaced far too many traditions, some irreparably lost. Of those remaining, many traditional practices are worth reconsideration in the search for sustainability.

A number of the techniques and materials in this book can truly be referred to as *"innovative"*—manufactured soil or solar irrigation controllers are examples. However, many conventional practices are or were recently innovations. As many authors have pointed out, modern American culture loves newness and invention—often uncritically. Sustainability asks for deeper thought about values and choices. Neither innovation nor convention or tradition is of unquestioned value for its own sake. Sustainability, if it can ever be achieved, will have to draw on the whole range of possible practices, judging whether each one contributes to a world fit for our great-great-grandchildren.

We have tried to evaluate specific practices and materials, old and new, as fairly as possible.[11] Conventional practices are not always the bad guy, and both traditional and supposedly sustainable innovations have their share of failures. Our critiques are intended to *reaffirm* something that is close to the heart of almost everyone who makes the landscape his or her profession: *a desire to create beautiful and healthy places*. That desire can go tragically awry when old habits outweigh the new and important knowledge available today about the larger environment. This book presents some of that knowledge and

criticizes some of those habits in the confident hope of change.

We offer criticisms of some things for which we have no solutions. This is not to show that we are "greener" or more knowledgeable than everyone else—in fact, just the opposite. We hope and assume that somebody out there knows more than we do about many of the specific problems we raise. The only way solutions will be found is by many people thinking and experimenting, often about issues someone else saw but couldn't fix. We also hope that those who have solutions or suggestions will pass them on to us, for inclusion in the next edition of this book.

The Landscape Professions: NOT Construction "versus" Design

Most landscape "construction" books have, in the past, been written for designers by designers. In these books (and the courses where they serve as texts), physical labor, machinery, and tools might as well not exist. The focus of these books, despite their titles, is primarily on detail and structure in design, not on how to *build* the design at the site. There is a legitimate need for detail-design information, and the fact that construction books are widely read by designers shows how much the contractor and the designer rely on each other in their duties. We are convinced, however, that ignoring the contractor's actual work is a shortcoming in these books, perhaps reflective of a shortcoming in professional attitudes.

At the other end of the spectrum, there are many fine books on larger-scale design and planning issues. It has now been more than a quarter century since landscape architect Ian McHarg published his epochal book, *Design With Nature*. Since that time many books have dealt with ecological assessment, planning, and design. But even if these planning and design principles are sensitively followed, inappropriate *construction* methods and materials can still lead to unnecessary environmental destruction, creating significant cumulative damage. Where those books start from the broad scale (design or planning), this book has its foundation at the site-specific scale of actually constructing landscapes.

To date, information on better landscape *construction* alternatives has remained scattered and poorly documented. Much of this information is currently available only in home-owner format and is focused on maintenance issues such as reduction of pesticide use or the value of composting. This excludes many issues of importance to professionals in landscape construction and design.

In this book, we both follow and depart from precedent. Some of the information in this book is of interest primarily to one half of the landscape profession, either to contractors or to designers. Design and construction cannot truly be separated, though, and most of the issues discussed affect both groups. Changes in construction materials and methods affect what designers can specify. New ideas in design affect what contractors can build, and are expected to build. We hope to accomplish two goals: to call attention to the environmental effects and potentials of physical construction and to state the case, repeatedly, for better integration of design and construction as an essential step toward sustainable land use.

Throughout this book, we refer to "landscape professionals" and the "landscape professions." By this we mean to include landscape architects, landscape contractors, and the many others who support their work: horticulturists, arborists, nurseries, materials suppliers, grounds maintenance workers. Permaculturists, Xeriscape experts, and others are (to us, at least) part of the mix.[12] Some engineers, architects, and general contractors also deserve at least honorary membership. We have received some criticism for not directing this book exclusively at landscape architects, but feel our purpose goes beyond current professional definitions. Thinking of ourselves as members of a larger community of *professionals whose livelihood is the landscape* has great power and value, in our opinion. Breaking down barriers to cooperation is especially important for those whose goal is sustainability. The old barrier between construction and design, blue-collar and white-collar, serves no good purpose in the attempt to care holistically for the built environment.

An Evolving Effort

Like the trend toward professional concern for landscape sustainability, this book is an evolving effort. We hope it will have several editions, reflecting changes in the practice of green con-struction and changes in the relationship between green and mainstream. While we might have liked to produce the equivalent of *Architectural Graphic Standards* for sustainable landscape construction, our field is far from standardization. We have attempted to report on the state of the art and to evaluate a wide range of practices in light of green principles. However, a cookbook of how-to recipes would be presumptuous at this time in our profession's history. Detailed how-to information has seemed appropriate for only a few materials and techniques; more often, it seemed more honest to give a description, some principles, and references for following what becomes current tomorrow or the next day.

As a result, this book will not replace basic texts filled with details of retaining walls and decks, or formulas for grading and drainage. An understanding of these conventional construction skills will be required as long as landscapes are built. This book offers tools and ideas for *adapting* these conventions to new materials, new regulations, and new client demands, all driven by environmental concerns. Future landscape construction will need to be more sophisticated, not only in technique, but in careful consideration of *why* build and *what* is appropriate. We expect this sophistication to grow from a combination of innovation, convention, and rediscovered tradition, not from new technologies alone.

The time has also come to treat landscape construction not merely as a functional, value-free topic, but as part of the discussion of environmental ethics. Unlike most construction books, *Sustainable Landscape Construction* does not take a totally objective viewpoint, but it gives clearly supported opinions. This, along with its focus at the site scale, is what make this book different and, we hope, valuable today.

Who Should Use This Book?

Sustainable Landscape Construction is intended for three main audiences:

- Professionals in landscape architecture, construction, and maintenance, both in private practice and in the public sector, and their suppliers. In the book, we refer to these people together as the "landscape professions" because their collaboration is essential to sustainable landscape work.

Finding Landscapes along the Information Highway

Because landscape is both a broad subject and a term often misappropriated, searching for information about landscapes is not always easy. Here are a few suggestions for those who need to research specific topics on their own.

- Know the most **specific name(s)** for your topic. A great deal of searching, in libraries or on-line, relies on electronic "search engines" that are very literal-minded. Unfortunately, "landscape" and "environment" are terms borrowed for many things besides the physical world. Search for either, and you will get "Political Landscape," "Landscape of Ideas," and "Environment (computer systems)," to name only a few. Landscape photography and painting will also show up. More specific terms from geology, soil science, horticulture, architecture, and many other disciplines may help.

- One source of semi standardized search terms is the **Library of Congress Subject Headings (LCSH).** These are published in book form, available in most libraries, and may be available on CD-ROM. They are not currently available on the Internet, but the library is considering making such access possible. Using LCSH terms may make searching more predictable and precise on systems that follow these conventions. Because landscape spans many disciplines, however, even the terms make a long list.

- **Associations** are often excellent sources of information. *The Gale Encyclopedia of Associations* lists such groups for every imaginable subject, by name or topic. In book form, the Gale directories are available at most libraries. They are also on CD-ROM or the Internet, by very expensive subscription. Some libraries subscribe to the digital versions.

- Some **search engines** are better than others at screening out useless and unrelated sites. On the Web, many sites appear promising, but frequently disappoint. Mixed information and opinion are posted without editing, verification, or anything to indicate source reliability; sites also disappear without warning. There isn't much to do about that. We have had better luck with Google (http://google.com) than any others. Google bases its relevance rating on how many other sites *link* to the found site, indicating that someone else besides the Webmeister values the information there. Yahoo (www.yahoo.com) often seems to do better, however, at finding suppliers by product type or industry. Multiple-engine searches on the same term are also useful; Google has links to ten of them conveniently located at the bottom of its own search screen.

- Students in landscape construction and design courses, as well as some who study architecture, planning, project management, and engineering.

- Landowners and others who are concerned with the health of specific sites, ranging from individuals and businesses to neighborhood associations or conservation groups.

We hope this book will be accessible to people with various levels of experience. (Professionals will please excuse us for including basic definitions to help students and other readers.) We also hope to offer some common ground between environmentalists and builders. This is a tall order, and we welcome suggestions. (See "Contacting the Authors" on page xxi.)

How to Use This Book

Use this book to develop or improve your ability to visualize sustainable materials or methods clearly in a conceptual design. Then adapt these concepts to site-specific conditions, referring to local consultants and the resources listed for further expertise and detail.

The chapters of this book can be read in almost any order. Each focuses on a central issue, such as sustainable use of water, and on construction related to that issue. This introduction and the section "Successes and Challenges" put the remaining chapters into perspective. We suggest you read them before going on to any of the other chapters.

Principle-Focused Organization

This book is organized by *principle* rather than by technique or material. Principles are *values that people act on.* Sustainability itself is a principle. Each chapter focuses on one overarching idea that *can* and *should* be implemented in the sustainable landscape. These principles, in various forms, have guided the landscape professionals whose work is reported in this book and should guide anyone who makes, modifies, or manages a landscape. Subsections of each chapter offer specific methods to accomplish the principle.

Many of these methods can be used in concert with each other. It is not unusual, however, to find two methods of achieving the same goal that, if used simultaneously, would cancel each other. Some methods or materials also work best, or only, in certain climates. We suggest that you read each chapter as a whole, then choose among the range of techniques based on local experience in your own ecosystem.

The "principled" approach gives a clear picture of the interrelationships involved in living landscapes. Where principles overlap or complement each other (which is frequent because the landscape is a web of interacting influences), cross-references are provided for easy access to techniques or materials covered in other sections.

Abbreviations

In general, we explain any abbreviated term when it is first used. Certain government departments, however, have a huge impact on landscape construction and a great deal of knowledge about it. Abbreviations for these agencies crop up so often that defining them every time is truly tedious:

- DOT—Department of Transportation, often combined with the abbreviation for a state, such as MnDOT for Minnesota DOT, or the U.S. DOT.

- DEP or DER—for Department of Environmental Protection/Resources

- EPA—for Environmental Protection Agency; unless specified, this is federal.

- Caltrans—California's DOT.

Finally, U.S. states and Canadian provinces are abbreviated when part of a city name, using the standard two-letter postal abbreviations.

Resource Lists for Further Information

The symbol ⊃ is found throughout this book. It points you to resources related to the topic, such as organizations, suppliers, experts, websites, and publications. There is a resource section for each chapter, including contact information where appropriate. (A few listings contain only a name or title that sounds particularly relevant, but for which we have not been able to locate contact information. We would appreciate updates and corrections, as well as additions, for this list.)

In many cases, resources provide current updates on recent developments. Others provide specialized detail about techniques and materials that this book describes more broadly. Be sure to check closely related chapters for resources indirectly related to your topic.

The most general resources, such as organizations, consultants, and suppliers, are listed *first* under each resource topic. Following them are books, periodicals, and websites—some of which are obtained through the organizations ahead of them in the list. If your questions are broad or a bit fuzzy, human resources are generally best, since they can help you think through the query. If your question is fairly specific, there may be published information or a website that exactly meets your needs.

Manufacturers and suppliers of specific products have kindly provided information for many of this book's topics, but, we cannot possibly list all of them as resources, nor do we endorse individual products. Specific products are named as part of some project examples; here, too, we could not possibly illustrate projects involving every supplier. Since we cannot be all-inclusive, we have tried to be fair and to use supplier information to promote broader awareness of sustainable construction, rather than to advertise particular wares.

For these reasons, suppliers are listed in the Resources if (1) we have found them to be a helpful source of general information, *and* (2) their product, or type of product, is not yet well known. Thus, where a dozen manufacturers of roughly the same product exist, they are not listed under Resources; more likely, a magazine that carries ads from most of them would be a resource on that topic. Associations are similarly general resources and can often help in locating consultants or manufacturers.

The endnotes also serve as a listing of information sources. They are usually much more narrowly specific than the Resources listings but may contain exactly the needed specifics to answer particular questions.

For those who want or need to search electronically for landscape information, "Finding Landscapes along the Information Highway" offers some suggestions (page 9).

Individuals and Firms Mentioned in This Book

We have tried to introduce each person quoted, describing his or her background, job title, or location—but *only* at the first mention. If the information comes from a person's published work, it is footnoted. People quoted in the book, but *without* a footnote, gave their information in interviews with one of the authors. Job titles and locations are those current at the time of the interview or at the time of the project described. Names of individuals and firms are **boldface** in the index; if you are reading chapters out of order and need more introduction to a person or firm, the index may help.

We hope that *Sustainable Landscape Construction* will link readers who share interests. We hope that these links will help inspire more projects and that our next edition's list of examples will include them.

Exemplary Landscapes

This book would not exist if many people had not put sustainable principles into landscape practice already. Although a few of the ideas we discuss are still just that—ideas—we have been

able to illustrate most concepts with one or more completed landscape projects.

Listed in Appendix C, in order by the chapter in which they appear, are 105 projects discussed in this book, in which sustainability was an important basis for design and construction decisions. The list includes project location and other information, which is mentioned in the main text only when introducing a project for the first time. A firm name (usually the one most closely connected with landscape aspects of the project) is listed for each project, where known. Names of other people and firms associated with each project may also be found in the chapter where the project is described more fully.

Inevitably, some names have been omitted, especially on larger projects where the roster of names would be a chapter in itself. In a few cases, we were unable to determine who did the project. Please contact the authors to correct any factual errors in this list.

Appendix C is by no means a comprehensive list of landscape work driven by environmental principles. Space and readability required that we be selective, and many worthy projects have eluded us. Again, we hope that landscape architects and contractors, as well as landowners, may send us news of exemplary work. We also welcome lessons learned from failure, methods that could have been improved, and materials that gave unexpected results. (See "Contacting the Authors," on page xxi.)

Successes and Challenges in Green Building Outdoors

We undertake to restore indigenous communities and ecosystem function in the face of great uncertainty.

—Leslie Sauer, 1998
The Once and Future Forest

Sustainable Landscape Construction is organized around principles and illustrated with projects. Around the world, and in increasing numbers, pioneering landscape professionals and their clients have been making these principles a reality and, in some cases, inventing new approaches.

The one-hundred-plus projects chosen for this book are ones that, in our opinion, took a number of the right environmental steps and produced beautiful and intriguing results. Neither we nor the creators of these places would claim that these projects are perfectly sustainable. They simply exemplify attempts to reduce the impact of construction, while increasing the livability of the place. Our reasons for considering them successful are detailed in their descriptions. For a list of these projects, see page 323.

Success is always interwoven with challenges, and never more so than in the movement for sustainability. The listed projects give strong evidence that success in sustainable landscapes is possible. On the way to sustainability, three overarching challenges must be met and are discussed in this chapter. These are not the technical challenges that make up the rest of the book but rather are matters of the heart and mind.

But How Can Landscapes Damage the Environment?

For those of us who love landscapes, it is troubling and confusing to think that our creations damage the environment. How can a green growing place hurt the Earth? The question can be answered both in a technical way and in terms of attitudes and cultural trends.

Technical Issues: Resources and Biodiversity

Along with a generally positive report, this book also discusses materials and processes of landscape construction that contribute to ecological problems. Some are very specific, such as resource depletion when redwood or tropical hardwoods are used in quantity for consumer landscapes. Toxic materials are used in gardens both intentionally (pesticides, for example) and unintentionally (excess fertilizer that pollutes waterways, or materials like PVC that are highly valued while in use but cause serious disposal problems). Land itself is "consumed" and "wasted" by some types of conventional construction. These are the *technical* answers to the question of ecological damage from landscapes; they are detailed throughout the book.

Discussed in This Chapter

- Understanding why constructed landscapes sometimes enhance site health but other times endanger it

- Recognizing the relationships between sustainability and style

- Thinking clearly about the professional and personal attitudes that affect sustainable practice

---

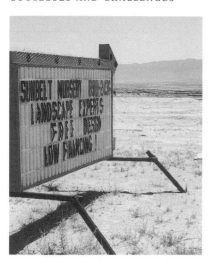

Figure 1. Conventional and cheap attitudes toward landscaping abound—and often consume or destroy natural ecosystems. PHOTO: Kim Sorvig.

Landscapes and gardens, as constructed today, also have an effect on biodiversity that can be quite negative. It may seem that gardens, especially those of enthusiastic horticulturists, are highly diverse, and in a sense this is true. Most landscapes, however, are planted with only a dozen or so species; in many schools of landscape design, this is actually taught as a way to avoid a "busy" or "cluttered" design. Furthermore, the main commercially available plant species have become increasingly standardized by mass marketing, so that diversity is reduced *between regions* as well as at the site-specific scale. Dead plants, which in self-sustaining communities form important habitat, are usually removed from gardens, further diminishing diversity.

Real biodiversity is not merely about the numbers of species, however. It is about the richness of interconnections *among* species. These interconnections take ages of coevolution to develop and cannot be recreated instantly in a garden. Plants brought together from different regions in a garden add visual diversity and may give great pleasure, but they remain akin to a diverse collection of animals in a zoo, separate and unable to interact. They do not support the great web of pollinators, predators, browsers, and symbionts that revolve around plants in their native habitats. When even a diverse *collection* replaces a biodiverse *community*, there is real ecological loss. This is a second important answer to the question of how landscapes may damage ecosystems.

From How to Why

A more fundamental question than *how* is *why* the places people make outdoors damage the outdoors. What is it that turns a heartfelt bond with plants and place into actions hurtful to the Earth? Without considering that question, any technical approach runs the risk of betraying good intentions even further.

The *why* of unsustainable landscapes lies in a confusion of cultural values that would require many books to decipher. Looking at these issues even briefly is a major departure from the standard construction text. Human feelings and beliefs about the world outside are ancient and complex. Most of us—not just contractors or designers—take them for granted. Yet these feelings and beliefs influence every choice made in the design and construction process.

Nature, or as one writer calls it, "the more-than-human world,"[1] has always been a paradox to humans. The physical earth and its plants and creatures have been sacred in too many traditions to count.[2] Yet while nature was and remains sacred, it has always been capable of destroying people, both individually and as whole communities. Controlling nature enough to survive is a goal, a dream found in the central myths of almost every culture. The question is, *how much control is enough?*

The human-built landscape draws on both halves of this paradox. The landscape-maker reveres the living gifts of nature, either for beauty or for crops. Yet landscape-making is also about controlling and subduing. An owner wants a tidy property, nothing messy or out of place; a designer chooses to limit the plant species permitted in a particular landscape; a contractor or maintenance person installs paving to control mud and dust. How much control, and how formal or controlled a style, depends in part on the individual's unconscious response to the land: Where is the balance between nature as sacred and nature as threat or nuisance?

Over many millennia, the human ability to control parts of nature has increased dramatically. Agriculture was one major step; industrialization, with its machines, synthetic chemicals, and engineered materials, was another. These forms of control are so prevalent that many modern people fail to notice them at all. In fact, many highly controlled landscapes are mistakenly considered natural: carefully trimmed lawns under the shade of planted park trees, for example. Construction books that leave out construction machinery are simply one form of a broader cultural blindness.

Not noticing "the machine in the garden" not only confuses the issue of sustainability, it also leads to an attitude of controlling things just because we can. When control is possible, it becomes expected, the way some suburban housing associations require conformity to the ideal tidy lawn. Control becomes a symbolic act. An obviously artificial garden is evidence of power, whether the power belongs to Louis XIV, to Mies van der Rohe, or to a weekend gardener. In the process, the *costs* of controlling the landscape are overlooked, assumed to be unavoidable.

It is these cumulative costs of *too much* control that turn landscape construction from an affirmation of the Earth into a disruption of the environment. The technological ways in which landscapes damage the Earth can usually be traced back to an attitude that favors too much control—the killing of many species to favor a few; the use of harder and harder materials to force space and surface into obedience; the demand for materials that require no maintenance, yet are untouched by the elements; the expectation that the floor of a landscape should be as flat and even as that of a house. Achieving heavy-handed control always demands investments of energy and materials. Especially where the desire for control is misguided, these investments may be a never-ending spiral of costs with no returns.

Even control that is *not* too costly on a small scale may become unsustainable at larger scales. The traditional land-use patterns of our preindustrial ancestors are often held up as examples for sustainability—yet they worked partly because populations were small and density low. Los Angeles County today is home to over 9 million people; neither the landscapes of the native Chumash Indians nor those of the eighteenth-century Spanish would be sustainable on today's scale. Especially in their effect on resources, energy, and biodiversity, landscapes that individually are harmless may *add up* to significant harm.

Thus many of the suggestions in this book, and about green building generally, concern changing expectations. Recognizing where our landscape expectations come from, and how deeply rooted and intertwined some of them are, is a prerequisite for properly using the techniques of sustainability. Some of these expectations change of necessity, like the increasing use of recycled materials as prices for wood and other new materials soar. Others, like the impulse to conserve the landscape as sacred, or to tidy it to show control, change only with conscious effort.

Natural "Look" and Ecological Function— A Paradox?

At the heart of landscape design are some expectations that are remarkably resistant to change: our expectations about the *appearance* of landscapes. Conventionally, aesthetic choices about the *style* of landscape are seen as unrelated to resource costs or environmental impact. But some styles require much higher investments in control than others. As sustainability focuses concern on the environmental costs of constructing landscapes, controversy over the appropriate appearance of sustainable landscapes has flared. Should a sustainable landscape look untouched by human hands—a difficult task for the contractor? Should it, at the other extreme, look like an "ecology machine," the way some sustainable houses sprout high-tech engineered appendages?

The intensely personal feelings involved in this controversy are strong evidence for the depth of human attachment to specific landscapes. Almost everyone who cares about landscapes, whether as professional, client, or amateur, has preconceptions about what the sustainable landscape ought to look like. These biases—and the unresolved differences among them—strongly affect the work of the landscape professional: how we work, and whether we get work. Because of its effect on our work, this controversy is worth exploring briefly here.

The Hand of the Designer

A common definition of "natural" is "untouched by human hands," and this idea affects the design of landscapes that serve natural or ecological purposes. Should the hand of a designer (or builder) be evident in such landscapes? Stormwater ponds, for instance, are sometimes designed to look like natural ponds with undulating edges planted with native wetland species. One example is the stormwater wetland at Fort Devens Federal Medical Center, in central Massachusetts. The work of Carol R. Johnson Associates of Boston, this carefully engineered series of ponds looks as if it has always been there.

Figure 2. Naturalistic design is strongly associated with ideas of sustainable ecological function. Stormwater wetlands at Fort Devens MA are engineered for function but also to fit in with a natural look. PROJECT: Carol R. Johnson Associates. PHOTO: Jerry Howard.

Landscape theorists like Rob Thayer, author of *Grey World, Green Heart,* have questioned whether concealing the influence of the designer makes sense. For example, applying a wild riverbank plant association verbatim to an urban drainage swale ignores the human origins of the swale, according to Thayer. Making such a constructed ecosystem look "natural" does not necessarily improve its sustainability, Thayer believes. In fact, he suggests that "sustainability requires neither the disguise nor the elimination of human influence."

On the contrary, says Thayer, because sustainable landscapes represent a higher level of complexity than "cosmetic" landscapes and incorporate ecological relationships that may be hard to observe, it is all the more important to give them "conspicuous expression and visible interpretation, and that is where the creative and artistic skills of the landscape architect are most critically needed."[3] Thayer refers to cosmetic attempts to make engineering look less engineered as "greenwash." Like many others, he sees the desire to hide the mechanical systems that support modern life as unreasoning, a NIMBY (Not In My Backyard) attitude that wants the benefits of development but none of the costs.

Other landscape thinkers agree that the mechanics or infrastructure of built landscapes should not be hidden and, in fact, should be revealed. William McElroy and Daniel Winterbottom, faculty members in the Department of Landscape Architecture at the University of Washington, have coined the phrase "infragarden" to describe a landscape that supports ecological and social values while incorporating landscape art.[4] As an example of the infragarden they cite Waterworks Gardens in Renton WA designed by environmental artist Lorna Jordan.[5] Here, fanciful grottoes and basalt slabs adorn a stormwater wetland that treats runoff from several parking lots. But according to Richard Hansen, a Colorado-based sculptor and landscape architect, the Waterworks Garden is "a bit of a shotgun wedding of environmental engineering overlaid by grottoes and other large decorative elements." Hansen argues that what is needed is "a better interweave—a sculptural presence integrated with an ecological process."

Another ecologically functional landscape that, arguably, weaves sculptural form and ecological process together is at the Water Pollution Control Laboratory in Portland OR, designed by landscape architect Robert Murase, working as part of a team of hydrologists and engineers. Runoff from a 50-acre residential and commercial neighborhood uphill of the site is directed to the pond, retaining the runoff and

Figure 3. This "infragarden" at Renton WA makes stormwater management visible and overlays it with garden art. PROJECT: Lorna Jordan. PHOTO: Daniel Winterbottom.

Figure 4. Surroundings of the Renton stormwater garden suggest that a naturalistic approach would not have fit well here. PROJECT: Lorna Jordan. PHOTO: Daniel Winterbottom.

allowing pollutants to settle out. Eventually, the water soaks into the soil or empties into the nearby Willamette River.

This utilitarian aim is expressed as sculptural form, with the upper and lower cells of the 1-acre pond formed as converging circles. A stone-lined, curving concrete flume—an abstraction of a glacial moraine or the curve of a river—juts into the upper cell. When stormwater pours into the flume from a large storm-system outfall pipe at its upper end, the stones in the flume dissipate the energy in the water and allow solids to settle out; the water then seeps into the upper cell through weepholes in the side of the flume. Stones from the flume "spill out" and form a semicircular basalt wall that defines the second, lower pond. Although the landscape fulfills important ecological functions, Murase's design conceals neither the designer's hand nor his intent to create sculptural form on the land.

"Ecorevelatory Design"

If the issue of hiding the designer's influence is one side of a coin, that of making ecological processes visible is the other. The general tendency of many highly engineered landscapes (as well as quite a number of naturalistic gardens) is to *hide* the ecological processes that go on around us. Stormwater (which, after all, is just rainwater running downhill) is one of those ecological processes. Before Murase's stormwater garden was built, the neighborhood stormwater ran in a sewer pipe and emptied directly into the Willamette River—out of sight, out of mind. The stormwater flume and pond, in essence, takes stormwater out of the murky underground realm of drains and pipes and "daylights" it, moving it to front and center in the landscape.

Ecorevelatory design is a label that has been applied to such landscapes by the University of Illinois Landscape Architecture Department.[6] The department conceived a traveling exhibit of projects, design approaches, and elements that "reveal and interpret ecological phenomena, processes and relationships."⊃ Human influence is also revealed and interpreted as one part (not necessarily harmonious) of the ecosystem, in contrast with the desire to hide all trace of human work.

The spirit of ecorevelatory design was never more simply or eloquently expressed than by John Lyle, although he did not use the term. In 1994, a visitor to Lyle's newly completed Center

Figure 5. Portland stormwater garden uses artistic form to reveal paths of runoff through the urban environment. PROJECT: Robert Murase. PHOTO: Scott Murase.

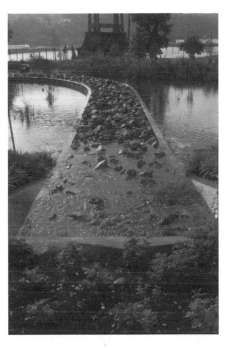

Figure 6. Portland stormwater garden combines artistry with ecological function. Flume is shown conveying stormwater after a rain. PROJECT: Robert Murase. PHOTO: Tom Liptan.

for Regenerative Studies noticed a compost pile sitting out in plain view and asked why he had not bothered to screen it. "We don't want to screen things," said Lyle. "We want to *see* things. A lot of ecological problems come from hiding the way things really work."

That, in a nutshell, is the spirit behind the Portland stormwater garden. It removes runoff from the shadowy realm of catch basins and pipes and renders it a visible component of the landscape—and by making it visible, teaches visitors to understand stormwater's place in the urban ecosystem. Threaded through this book are many other built landscapes that are equally honest about what they are and what they do.

The Portland and Renton examples each contrasts with the naturalistic landscapes to which Thayer objects. In doing so, they raise some important questions. The Portland garden's form and appearance are directly linked to the physical dynamics that govern water; it reveals these dynamics in a clearly constructed context, not a simulated stream-and-grove form. The Renton landscape allows environmental engineering to be seen (although it relies not on gravity but on a 2,000-gallons-per-minute pump), but decorates it with structures and forms from the gardenesque tradition. In neither case will vegetation be allowed to overgrow the site, nor will the water be permitted to carve its own channels. In fact, as with most built landscapes, considerable effort and expense will be spent in *preventing* these ecological processes from changing the form of the landscape. The Renton infragarden's message seems primarily about putting an artistic veneer over both the stormwater "problem" and its engineering "solution." The Portland garden relates engineering control to natural process, although at a level considerably simplified from the way those processes work in an ecosystem.

If "ecology" is taken in the scientific sense of large-scale complex biological and Earth processes of which humans are a single part, these projects, like Lyle's compost heap, are less about revealing ecology than about refusing to hide human influence. By strict definition, "ecorevelatory" would apply best to the design of nature trails, where an educational path points out elements of an existing ecosystem and, among other things, human effects on it. Does this mean that sustainable design should always look like a nature trail? Since its earliest days, ecological design has been accused of being all ecology and no design. The authors do not believe this is so. What is critical is to be clear about what is actually being revealed and why.

The hand of the designer can be as heavy on the land as a highway interchange or a strip mine. It can also be a delicate interfingering of influence, as in a Japanese garden, where the artist's touch is visible but only to thoughtful observation. (The difference, frequently, is in the contractor's level of skill, so often overlooked.) To argue that human influence should *never* be hidden, without also asking whether that influence is destructive or sustainable, is to trivialize the complexity of relations between humans and the rest of the world.

Form Follows Function in Nature, Too

There is at least one strong reason to argue against artificially maintained naturalism as the only "look" for sustainable landscapes. The "natural" appearance of an Olmsted park or a Japanese garden is maintained by considerable inputs of energy and materials. Especially where this maintenance is mechanized, those resource inputs are of concern for long-term sustainability. If hiding human influence increases this energy and material input, then revealing that influence contributes to a sustainable landscape. There is, however, strong evidence that some human landscape influences do exactly the opposite: their form actually increases the costs of maintaining them, and in some cases even prevents them from serving ecological functions.

The pipes and pumps of a stormwater system are a useful example. At some level, they substitute for the streams and wetlands of a watershed, fulfilling some functions (water transport) and failing others (aquatic habitat diversity, soil infiltration). The simplified forms of environmental engineering structures reveal, more than anything else, that ecological systems are far more multidimensional than is human engineering. Detailed study over the past two or three decades is showing more and more clearly that the complex *forms* of natural systems are essential to their functioning.

The attempt to straighten rivers and give them regular cross-sections is perhaps the most disastrous example of this form-and-function relationship. The natural river has a very irregular form: it meanders, spills across floodplains, and leaks into wetlands, giving it an ever-changing and incredibly complex shoreline. These irregularities allow the river to accommodate variations in water level and speed. Pushing the river into a tidy geometry destroys this functional capacity and results in disasters like the Mississippi flood of 1993. Reducing the irregularities of shape also decreases the variety of habitats available and cuts down on the diversity of life in the river. Putting a stream into a pipe has an even more drastic simplifying effect, at the expense of multidimensional function.

In this book, we document the fact that when

grading slopes, the stiff geometry that humans favor actually *increases* soil erosion and slope failure. We note that natural wetlands have quite specific forms and locations, and that created wetlands do not function properly unless these forms are approximated. We point out that the branching form and the spatial distribution of wild plants optimize their ability to compete for sunlight and soil resources and directly affect their ability to clean the air of pollutants. Where the hand of the designer goes too far in altering these forms, ecological function is affected, most often negatively.

Since the 1970s, the forms that make ecosystem function possible have been recognized as a specific mathematical type, called "fractals."[7] The branching patterns of trees are one example of fractal shapes. The name comes from the fact that these forms usually consist of endlessly repeated *fractions* of the whole, which create the overall form by growth over time. In the case of a tree, this basic element would be a single branch *and* its branching angle. River systems, landform surfaces, clouds, and whole plant communities follow fractal geometries because their function demands it. Human blood vessels and bronchial tubes have fractal patterns, too, which maximize delivery of blood or air; disruption of these patterns is diagnostic of serious illnesses such as cancer.[8] Similarly, straightening a river or turning an undulating hillside into a constant 3 percent slope undermines ecological *function* because it changes environmental *form*.

The forms of natural systems also have documented effects on human beings. Studies in hospitals have shown that a view of trees or other natural features improves patient recovery time and overall health when released; views of structures and machinery have no such effect. Views of natural surroundings lower blood pressure, decrease the patient's need for painkillers, and lessen the mental confusion that often goes with injury or serious illness. These benefits come from merely *seeing* the scenery, not going out into it. In fact, a photo or realistic painting of a landscape provides similar benefits, so the effect is clearly a visual one.[9] This strongly suggests that Olmsted was right: Views of naturalistic scenes have social benefits and are worth including in cities and preserving in undeveloped areas. If hard-nosed hospital administrators are increasingly paying to design buildings that give each

patient a landscape view, shouldn't landscape professionals heed this research as well?

Thus the forms that "naturalism" tries to preserve or simulate in designed landscapes are intimately linked to the ecological functioning of the landscape as well as to human health and social benefits. Because the discovery of fractal mathematics is so recent, design theorists may be forgiven for continuing to treat natural form as random or irrelevant. In presenting design attempts to mimic natural form as romanticism and nostalgia, however, they reveal their ignorance of current science. For those who are concerned with sustainability, the relationship between natural form and ecological function needs to be revisited. Although real understanding of this relationship is still developing, it is quite clear that it is far more than a backward-looking aesthetic.

The Appearance of Sustainability

So what *does* the sustainable landscape look like?

Our most honest answer is that neither we nor anyone else really knows. We can offer the following suggestions:

- The sustainable landscape does not *exclude* human presence or even human engineering; however, it does not blindly *glorify* human intervention nor equate gentle human influence with massive human domination.

- The sustainable landscape does not waste energy or resources on trying to *disguise* human influence. Rather, it *eliminates* (functionally, not just visually) influences that are destructive or disruptive. Other influences it reveals and even celebrates. In revelation and celebration, it becomes an artistic expression.

- The sustainable landscape follows natural and regional form whenever this can improve the ecological functioning of a built or restored landscape. It builds nature-mimicking forms primarily because these harbor rich diversity of life and ecological function, and secondarily because many people prefer the visual effect.

- The sustainable landscape integrates and balances human geometries with natural ones. It is not enough to allow natural form to take the leftover spaces; spatial and visual integration between nature's fractal forms and humanity's euclidean ones is essential. The means to this integration are those of the arts as well as of the sciences.

- The sustainable landscape is unlikely to be dominated by the visually simple and near sterile extremes of urban or engineered space. It is likely to incorporate elements of urban space as people transform cities and industries to a more sustainable model.

- The appearance of a naturalistic landscape often contributes to ecological function, but does not guarantee it. For this reason, neither naturalistic nor sustainable landscapes should ever be viewed as substitutes for wild places,[10] which will remain critically important no matter how "ecological" built landscapes become—or appear.

What does this mean for the practicing landscape professional? First and foremost, that the sustainable landscape will have room for creativity and diversity, perhaps even more so than the conventional styles that dominate our work today. It means, as great landscape design always has, an integration of the whole person—the supposedly opposite technical and artistic sides—in the work process. It means there will be less of a premium on the clever ability to cover up compost bins or valve-boxes, and more demand for people who can visualize and build integrally with the site. It means that fewer forms in the landscape will be oversimplified mechanical surfaces, and more will be interfingered in three dimensions, difficult to build well except by hand. It means that the appearance of the landscape will be influenced very directly by careful thought about the resources and methods used to build it. It means, we hope, a wave of creativity rising to meet one of humanity's most important challenges.

Get an Attitude

Besides appropriate techniques and materials, site protection relies on positive attitudes toward the landscape. Many conventional professionals share these attitudes, which are not the exclusive wisdom of environmental designers or specialists. It is too easy to assume that "they" (builders, engineers, contractors, conventional designers . . .)

are insensitive to landscape preservation. There certainly are such cases, like the engineer who told one of the authors that "all trees are just wood anyhow." But throughout the design and construction industries are people who know and love the outdoors and who chose their profession accordingly: civil engineers who restore wetlands, or highway contractors who can quote dozens of literary naturalists.

Sustainability is not served by an us-and-them split. Such divisions grow out of frustration, and there is no shortage of environmentally ignorant individuals who are frustrating to deal with. But to generalize that feeling too far actually decreases any hope of change.

Fundamental to protecting healthy sites is the recognition that each site is alive, unique, and connected to a web of off-site influences. By contrast, the common attitude that the site is just "unimproved land," a blank-slate location to build on, virtually guarantees site damage. Conventional concerns like practicality and keeping down costs must be balanced with respect for the health of a site. A balanced attitude, whether among team members or in an individual conscience, is a major part of any attempt to build sustainably.

Designers and construction workers alike get great satisfaction from their power to change and rearrange the site. This power, and skill in exercising it, are well deserving of pride, but can also become a "power trip." Designers can fall into the trap of arrogantly remaking the site on a whim. Cynicism and even despair are also occupational hazards, born of seeing too many good places deformed by carelessness, too many good designs denied by regulation or cost. Similarly, some construction workers begin to view site and materials as adversaries to be overcome, and they use anger to crank up the energy needed to do the job. This combative attitude is expressed when existing trees are hacked unnecessarily, or equipment is driven carelessly, or construction scrap is thrown around the site. There are strong reasons, both conventional and sustainable, to avoid any of these attitudes, which poison both professional and personal relations with the land.

Successful design firms create a "corporate culture" in which creativity steers clear of arrogance. The best contractors discourage the site-as-adversary attitude and make pride a constructive rather than destructive force. In design and construction firms, and between them, teamwork lightens the sometimes thankless task of pushing sustainability through a legal and social obstacle course. Professionals of all types work to make their *practices* sustainable. To paraphrase the basic definition, a sustainable business attitude aims for "meeting the goals of our office without diminishing the ability of other professionals to meet their goals."

The technical solutions found in this book can support, but cannot replace, an attitude that balances ecological health with human desires. This attitude, and the creative application of sustainable knowledge, thrive best in an atmosphere of collaboration, in which each team member is an important contributor to a "business ecosystem," not just a lower life-form in a vicious food chain. The dog-eat-dog image that pervades so much of American business thinking is actually a poor and inaccurate picture of the complex web of interactions in an ecosystem.[11] There is at least as much cooperation and mutual benefit in business relationships as there is competition. Recognizing that fact is essential to a sustainable society. It is particularly important for businesses that work directly in the environment, such as the landscape professions.

Take a Role in "Preconstruction"

Prior to what is conventionally considered the beginning of either design or construction work, a great deal can happen to the site. The actors in the preconstruction phase are likely to be realtors, surveyors, developers, utility companies, and in some cases government agencies who employ civil and environmental engineers. Increasingly, projects stand or fall on the input of neighborhood groups as well.

Landscape professionals have the capability of influencing most of these groups toward greater awareness of sustainable practice—but only if they form strong channels of communication and give input at the right time. Failing this, many of these same groups will act on the site, often by default, before the landscape professionals are involved. Some standard practices—including hiring a landscape consultant only at the last moment to "shrub up" an already completed design—can cause unsightly or unhealthy results

that cannot be disguised by a few plantings. Although it is not easy to win influence over the broader aspects of land-use planning, it is critically important to sustainability. The teamwork that is required between the landscape architect, the contractor, the architect (or other consultants), and the client/user is a good place to start forging connections that link to the larger community.

Build a Site-Focused Team

Like any complex activity, landscape-making benefits from collaborative effort. Many of the world's greatest and best-loved landscapes were built and nurtured by many hands over decades or even centuries, and part of their appeal lies in the traces of so much attention from so many people. It is certainly possible for one person to build an entire landscape beautifully, if the site is small enough and the time for building quite long. For larger landscapes, for those that are ecologically complex, or for ones that must be built in a hurry, teamwork is inevitable—and can work for sustainability or against it.

The minimum team for a high-quality, sustainable built landscape consists of four roles: the client, the designer, the builder, and the maintenance person. Sometimes several roles are played by one person: the client may act as designer, or do maintenance; a design-build firm may do all the work including postoccupancy maintenance. Contrary to the kind of conventional wisdom that favors narrow specialization, these overlapping arrangements can have great value in creating healthy places.

Nearly as often, each role may involve several people. The client may be one or more organizations. Some sites are owned by one entity, but *used* by other people; the input of users of a public landscape is often more important than that of the agency that "owns" it. Building codes and other regulations are often an invisible "team member" for both the designer and the contractor. Consultants and subcontractors play many roles. Lending and insuring agencies are notorious for refusing to fund "alternative" work—but can sometimes be instrumental in getting such methods approved.

What brings all this complexity together is a shared vision, a set of clearly stated goals that the whole team understands and supports. The

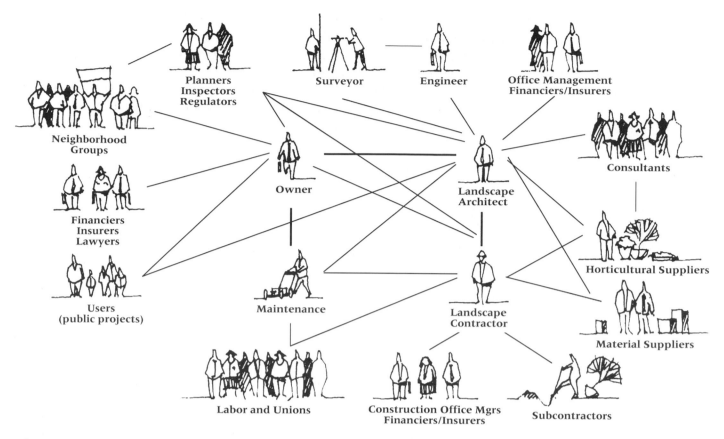

Planners
Inspectors
Regulators

Surveyor

Engineer

Office Management
Financiers/Insurers

Neighborhood
Groups

Consultants

Owner

Landscape
Architect

Financiers
Insurers
Lawyers

Horticultural Suppliers

Users
(public projects)

Maintenance

Landscape
Contractor

Material Suppliers

Labor and Unions

Construction Office Mgrs
Financiers/Insurers

Subcontractors

Figure 7. Constructing healthy and sustainable landscapes requires coordination of many specialists into a complex team.
ILLUSTRATION: Craig Farnsworth.

vision may start with a single strong personality, or may be the result of long debate leading to consensus. Unless the vision is *clear, doable, and communicated to every person involved* in the construction process, it has little hope of being realized. If the vision is some form of sustainability, clear communication is even more critical, given how woolly a word "sustainable" can be.

The architectural firm HOK recommends a *new design process* for sustainable results. The process has six phases. The last four are quite familiar: design, specification, construction, and operation/maintenance. But the first two—where the opportunities for change and cost savings are greatest—are team formation and education/goal-setting.[12]

Conventional practice tends to work against both team formation and education by insisting that each expert has a narrowly defined niche, competitively kept near secret from all the other players. Although teamwork among designers is reasonably common, including a contractor *at the design phase* is unusual. Yet nearly all designers, if

asked for their most satisfying projects, would name jobs where the contractor was a trusted collaborator. By contrast, the most frustrating projects are those that run under low-bid rules and treat a collaborative relationship as conflict of interest.

HOK minces no words in saying that overspecialization cannot achieve the quality and insight required for sustainable work. The designer cannot afford to hand near finished designs to a technical consultant. "Engineers need to be involved in the design process from the very beginning—so too must the construction professionals, including the major subcontractors, those ultimately responsible for operations, the various consultants, and in some cases key suppliers."[13] Although written with structural design in mind, this statement applies equally, if not more so, to landscapes that attempt ecological functions.

Even governmental agencies have recognized the value of teaming with contractors and suppliers. Instead of a strict low-bid process, many agencies require prequalification for all bidders. Contractors and suppliers must demonstrate certain abilities, including the quality of their work and the ability to control costs, before they qualify to bid. Environmental knowledge and care may also be criteria. A graduated series of steps, from prequalification for small projects to inclusion on the large-project list, opens this process to new firms and keeps it fair to all. At the same time, the client agency can have confidence that the low bidder for a project knows what is expected and has the skills to do the work. In this sense, the contractors become part of the team even within the limits of public-sector work.

The whole team needs to educate itself about environmental issues that will affect the project. On an effective team, the members already know, between them, most of the issues or know how to find information quickly. Equally important, they have a well-defined way of sharing their knowledge. Once the basic issues are defined and understood, goals for the project are set. These should be specific, and it should be possible to evaluate whether they were met. For example, a goal of "saving water" is too vague. "Reduce irrigation use of tap water to 40 percent of the average for nearby landscapes" is a specific goal. It is possible to test whether it has been achieved. Not all testable goals include numbers, but quantifiable goals are most easily tested. "Use no groundwater for irrigation" might be an example of a nonnumerical but testable goal.

For public lands, and for many private large projects, neighborhood input is today a legal requirement. This is changing the way that land-use decisions are made, and some conventional developers, designers, and contractors resent the change. Most landscapes, however, affect the neighbors, and public opposition that is ignored often translates to neglect, misuse, and even vandalism. Building a landscape only to have it destroyed by its users or neighbors is clearly not sustainable. We urge landscape professionals to look again at public input and see it as an opportunity. "Community-based planning" and "participatory design" are two approaches that are gaining more practitioners. The results can be quite remarkable. New York City Housing Authority landscape architect Leonard Hopper points to dramatic successes in making livable communities out of crime-ridden ones, through redesign *by* and *for* the residents. It takes commit-

ment and hard work: Philadelphia landscape firm Synterra attended over 200 community meetings in one year for a single, large public works project.

Collaborative effort may seem like a social issue, unrelated either to construction or to sustainability. In the conventional, compartmentalized mode, this is true. But that view contributes to direct and indirect waste of resources, the very opposite of sustainable practice. For example, poor coordination results in wasted site visits that consume fuel. Incorrect drawings and specs waste paper (if they are caught and corrected), and waste materials if they get built. Failing to plan for standard available sizes of materials also leads to waste. Worst of all, a built landscape that fails to meet its goals is soon an unhealthy landscape, and may take neighboring landscapes with it in decline.

The Challenges of Change

Sustainability, like construction, is often viewed as a subject in which the most important matters are all technical. Yet choices about sustainable landscape-making need the human heart as well as the mind. There is no substitute for the contented response that says "This place feels right," with intellect and emotion in agreement. To reduce sustainability to a technical puzzle is also to reduce the significance and satisfaction of our successes.

Similarly, the greatest challenges—and potentially the most serious mistakes—lie in the realm of attitude and concept, rather than in the practical matters which attitude *governs*. Those who wish to build sustainably need to think and feel deeply about their own beliefs; the serpent that leads to dominating the Earth is always lurking in the garden of our hopes. The need to understand how form follows function is far more pressing for landscapes at the end of the millennium than it was for buildings at the turn of the twentieth century. Perhaps the greatest challenge of all is reworking work: creating the team approach, the community approach that is necessary for both professional and ecological success.

Throughout the following chapters, with their focus on practical information, remember that these successes and challenges are the real themes of this book.

Resources
General

Worldwatch Institute
800-555-2028 or www.worldwatch.org
> Publishes annual State of the World report, emphasis on statistics.

Real Goods
800-762-7325 or www.realgoods.com
> Suppliers and consultants for on-site energy systems, consumer goods related to sustainability, and books on related subjects. Publishers of excellent sourcebook, newsletters, etc.

Permaculture: A Designer's Manual by Bill Mollison (1988 Tagari Publications, Australia). Widely available at U.S. booksellers.
> Hundreds of useful, mostly agriculture-focused techniques; pleasantly eccentric.

Alternatives Journal
519-888-4567, ext. 6783
> Canadian journal of environmental issues, practical and theoretical.

E magazine
815-734-1242 or www.emagazine.com/
> General magazine on environmental issues; often has articles on restoration, materials, or green construction/maintenance.

Green Disk
800-484-7616, ext. 3475
> Paperless environmental journal on disk; indexes to 70 related journals.

Cyberplaces/Architects First Source
www.cyberplaces.com
> The Links page lists hundred of links to anything about *places*—design, mapping, construction, etc.

Sustainability: SW Regional ACSA 1997 Conference Papers
Center for Research and Development, School of Architecture and Planning, University of New Mexico, Albuquerque 505-277-2903
> Four bound papers on defining and implementing sustainability in architectural contexts. See endnotes to Introduction for other sources.

Internet Addresses Useful for Sustainable Builders, Designers, and Planners by Wesley A. Groesbeck (1997 Environmental Resources Inc., Salt Lake City), 801-485-0280 or wesley.groesbeck@m.cc.utah.edu
> Lists about 400 URLs sorted by topic. Intended to be annual. Very useful, but suffers from being a paper printout of information that goes out of date rapidly.

Environmental Management Tools on the Internet by Michael Katz & Dorothy Thornton (1997 St. Lucie Press, Delray Beach FL)
> Less design/construction oriented than Groesbeck's; same values, same problems.

Landscape Architecture Bookstore
ASLA, Washington DC
800-787-2665 or www.asla.org
> Catalog of landscape titles.

Geonetwork
www.geonetwork.org/gbrc/
> Bookstore and info source. Online ordering through Amazon.com

Iris Communications
www.oikos.com or 800-346-0104
> Bookstore and info source.

Island Press
Washington DC
800-828-1302
> Not just listed because it's our publisher. Island Press has a wide-ranging list of books on applied and theoretical environmental issues.

Internet Garden Books
www.internetgarden.co.uk/frameset_1.htm
> Online source for more garden-oriented books, many with construction or environmental value.

Ecology

Landscape Ecology Principles in Landscape Architecture by Wenche Dramstad, James T. Olson, & Richard Forman (1996 Island Press)

Stalking the Wild Amaranth: Gardening in the Age of Extinction by Janet Marinelli (1998 Henry Holt)
> A clear account, by a garden-lover, of the damage and the good that gardens do.

The Urban Ecologist
Urban Ecology urbanecology@igc.apc.org
> Quarterly

Green Building

Rocky Mountain Institute
www.rmi.org
> Nonprofit research and education organization, especially strong on energy.

U.S. Green Building Council
www.usgbc.org
> Promotes green building; publications; LEED rating system still deficient in site protection.

Sustainable Design Guide by Sandra Mendler (1998 HOK Architects, Washington DC), 202-339-8700 or www.hok.com
> Revised edition soon from Wiley. Materials information also available from website.

A Building Revolution: How Ecology and Health Concerns Are Transforming Construction by D. M. Roodman & N. Lenssen (1995 Worldwatch Institute)

A Primer on Sustainable Building by Dianna L. Barnett & William D. Browning (1995 Rocky Mountain Institute) 970-927-3807

European Directory of Sustainable and Energy Efficient Building James & James Ltd.
> Annual directory.

Sustainable Building Technical Manual by D. Gottfried & A. Osso (1996)
> Purchase loose-leaf from U.S. Green Building Council. Full text also available at www.sustainable.doe.gov/

Building the National Parks: Historic Landscape Design and Construction by Linda Flint McClelland (1998 Johns Hopkins)

Building for a Future by Keith Hall (Association for Environmentally Conscious Building, UK—address unknown)

E-Build Archives CD-ROM
Searchable and indexed back issues of *Environmental Building News*. Also available: *Green Building Advisor* (interactive design and retrofit program, primarily for buildings)

Environmental Building News (EBN)
28 Birge St., Brattleboro VT 05301
800-861-0954
ebn@buildinggreen.com or www.building green.com
> Important source of news on all forms of green construction; unusual awareness of landscape issues. Publishes back issues on CD-ROM, also product catalog, bibliography, and book reviews.

Institute for Sustainable Design
http//:minerva.acc.Virginia.edu/~sustain/

Greenbuilding E-mail Discussion Group
> Send message "subscribe greenbuilding" to majordomo@crest.org

U.S. DOE/Eren Center of Excellence for Sustainable Development
www.sustainable.doe.gov/
> Excellent clearinghouse site cross-links government and private sustainability groups.

Construction

Legal Daisy Spacing: The Build-a-Planet Manual of Official World Improvements by Cristopher Winn (1985 Random House)
> Probably the world's only *funny* book on landscape construction (hey, we tried)—and insightful, too.

Associated Landscape Contractors of America (ALCA)
Herndon VA
703-736-9666 or www.alca.org

An Illustrated Guide to Landscape Design, Construction & Management by Gregory M. Pierceall (1998 Interstate Publishers, Danville IL)

An Introduction to Landscape Design and Construction by Bartholomew J. Blake (1998 Gower Publishing, Brookfield VT)

Landscape Architecture Construction by Harlow C. Landphair & Fred Klatt (1998 [3^d Ed.] Prentice-Hall, NYC)

Landscape Construction by David Sauter
(1999 Delmar Publishers, Albany NY)

Landscape Construction and Detailing by Alan Blanc (1996 McGraw-Hill)

Landscape Construction and Detailing: Articles in Landscape Architecture *Magazine, 1910–1979* by Bruce K. Ferguson (1981 Vance Bibliographies A-466, Monticello IL)

The Handbook of Landscape Architectural Construction by Maurice Nelischer (1985 [2^d Ed.] Landscape Architecture Foundation, Washington DC)

Technology

American Society of Agricultural Engineers
800-606-2304 or http://asae.org for subject index
> Publishes voluntary standards for many types of machines, methods, and materials, some of relevance to landscape work.

Why Things Bite Back: Technology and the Revenge of Unintended Consequences by Edward Tenner (1996 Vintage)
> Thought-provoking and well-documented reading on technologies that cause more trouble than they solve.

Harvard Landscape Technology website
Niall Kirkwood, Harvard Landscape Architecture
http://gsd.harvard.edu/landscapc/tcchnology/
> Information on a variety of technology issues related to landscapes.

Style and Sustainability

The Countryside Ideal: Anglo-American Images of Landscape by M.F. Bunce (1994 Routledge NYC)
> Analysis of prevailing attitudes toward the look and function of U.S. landscapes.

The Fractal Geometry of Nature by Benoit Mandelbrot (1983 W.H. Freeman)
> Clear and revolutionary analysis of natural pattern as something more than "random."

"The Experience of Sustainable Landscapes" by Robert L. Thayer Jr. (Fall 1989) *Landscape Journal* "Toward a New Garden" in *Critiques of Built Works of Landscape Architecture* by William MacElroy & Daniel Winterbottom (Fall 1997, LSU School of Landscape Architecture)
> On "infragardens."

Ecorevelatory Design exhibit
University of Illinois Dept. of Landscape Architecture
www.gis.uiuc.edu/ecorev/
611 East Lorado Taft Dr., Room 101
Champaign IL 61820
> Exhibit catalog is a special issue of *Landscape Journal*. Fifteen projects (some exemplify community-based approaches) plus eight essays.

Planning, Design, and Management

Clarence Stein Institute for Urban and Landscape Studies, Cornell University
> There are many institutes for such studies; however, this one has taken a special interest in Ebenezer Howard and garden cities as influences on sustainability.

Consortium on Sustainable Development and Planning
c/o tangotti@pratt.edu or rahder@yorku.ca

Planning Advisory Service
American Planning Association
www.planning.org.
> Subscription-based research network aids in gathering current information on planning, for sustainability and other agendas.

Design with Nature by Ian McHarg (1995 [reprint] Wiley)
The classic.

A Green History of the World: The Environment and the Collapse of Great Civilizations by Clive Ponting (1991 Penguin Books, NYC)
> Reconnects the histories of familiar civilizations and their use or abuse of environmental resources in construction, agriculture, and other endeavors.

Environmental Management Handbook by Sven-Olof Ryding (1996 IOS Press, Amsterdam, the Netherlands)
> International review of issues and technologies; intended for decision makers, summarizes technology choices.

The Living Landscape: An Ecological Approach to Landscape Planning by Frederick R. Steiner (1991 McGraw-Hill, New York)

Best Development Practices by Reid Ewing (1996 American Planning Association) www.planning.org/ Chicago: 312-431-9100
Washington DC: 202-872-0611

Conservation Design for Subdivisions by Randal G. Arendt (1996 Island Press)

Deep Design: Pathways to a Livable Future by David Wann (1996 Island Press)

Ecological Design by Sym VanDerRyn & Stuart Cowan (1996 Island Press)

Ecological Design and Planning by Frederick Steiner & George F. Thompson (1997 Wiley)

From Eco-Cities to Living Machines: Principles of Ecological Design by Nancy J. Todd & John Todd (1994 North Atlantic Books, VT)

Green Development: Integrating Ecology and Real Estate by Alex Wilson & Rocky Mountain Institute (1998 Wiley)
> A CD-ROM with case studies is also available.

Guiding Principles of Sustainable Design
(1993 National Park Service Technical Information Center, Denver, Colo.)

Landscape Planning: Environmental Applications by William Marsh (1997 [3ᵈ Ed.] Wiley)

Our Ecological Footprint: Reducing Human Impact on the Earth by M. Wackernagel & W. Rees (1996 New Society Publications, Gabriola Island, BC)

Regenerative Design for Sustainable Development by John T. Lyle (1994 Wiley)

Social Consequences of Engineering by Hayrettin Kardestuncer (1979 Boyd and Fraser, San Francisco)

The Ecology of Place by Timothy Beatley & Kristy Manning (1997 Island Press)

Time-Saver Standards for Landscape Architecture: Design and Construction Data by Charles W. Harris, Nicholas T. Dines, & Kyle D. Brown (1998 [2ᵈ Ed.] McGraw-Hill)

Earthscape: A Manual of Environmental Planning by John Ormsbee Simonds (1978 McGraw-Hill)

Construction Claims Monthly
800-274-6737 or http://xp.bpinews.com/ccm
> Newsletter of construction litigation, often related to environment.

Landscape Architecture
ASLA
636 Eye St., N.W.
Washington, D.C. 20001
800-787-2665, or www.asla.org
> Monthly. Glossy project reportage and solid information on environmental practices and issues.

Yes!
Positive Futures Network
800-937-4451 or www.futurenet.org
> Quarterly. Each issue focuses on a theme concerning sustainability; past themes include urban design; nontoxic materials; watersheds.

Environmental Design Guide
Royal Australian Institute of Architects Quarterly
2a Mugga Way, Red Hill ACT, Australia.
Center of Excellence for Sustainable Development
www.sustainable.doe.gov/buildings/gbothtoc.htm
> The "buildings" page of the CESD site. Overview of green building, statistics, success stories, ordinances, links.

Environmental Organization Web Directory
http://webdirectory.com/Science/Ecology/
Environmental_Community_Living/
Nature+Science (German)
www.nature.li/2e.htm
> Library of photos of botanical and ecological subjects.

Planners Network
http://www.plannersnetwork.org/
> A good source of contacts for policy-level issues.

Planning Commissioners Journal
www.webcom.com/pcj/welcome.html

SmartGrowth Network
www.smartgrowth.org/index.html

Sustainable Communities Network
www.sustainable.org/index.html

Virtual Library: Environment
http://earthsystems.org/Environment.shtml

Virtual Library: Landscape Architecture
www.clr.toronto.edu:1080/virtuallib/larch.html

Virtual Library: Sustainable Development
www.ulb.ac.be/ceese/meta/sustvl.html

Designer Shorts (continuing education)

Landscape Architects Registration Boards Foundation, Fairfax VA,
703-818-1300 or Mrankin@clarb.org
High percentage of courses relate to sustainability.

Greenmoney Journal
800-318-5725 or www.greenmoney.com
Quarterly. Specifically includes green building, products, and energy.

LandCadd
Eaglepoint Software,
800-678-6565, ext. 382
www.eaglepoint.com
Example of a CAD program that automates quantity and irrigation planning and simulates plant growth; can reduce waste and improve maintenance.

Teamwork

Growing a Business by Paul Hawken (1987 Fireside Books

The Ecology of Commerce by Paul Hawken (1993 Harper)
Both of Hawken's business books offer an important "ecological" alternative to the conventional dog-eat-dog view.

ProjectCenter
Evolv company 800-719-2111
Service offers web-based project sites; specs, drawings, schedule, inspection logs, etc. available to whole team at all times. Many stand-alone CAD packages can do similar data exchanges.

Community-Based Planning

Cultivating Community Success: Visions from the Heartland (1996 Heartland Center for Leadership Development)

Divided Planet: The Ecology of Rich and Poor by Tom Athanasiou (1998 University of Georgia Press, Athens)
Clear analysis of relationships between economics and a sustainable future.

Streets of Hope: The Fall and Rise of an Urban Neighborhood by Peter Medoff & Holly Sklar (1994 South End Press, Boston)

The Careless Society: Community and Its Counterfeits by John McKnight (1995 Basic Books NYC)

The Ecology of Hope: Communities Collaborate for Sustainability by Ted Bernard & Jora Young (1997 New Society)

Toward Sustainable Communities by Rachel Kaplan, Stephen Kaplan, & Robert Ryan (1998 New Society)

"Citizen Participation and Decentralization" in *Urban Politics* by B. H. Ross & Murry Stedman Jr. (1985 FE Peacock Publishers, Ithaca IL)

"Community and Consensus: Reality and Fantasy in Planning" by Howell S. Baum (1994) *Journal of Planning Education and Research*
ACSP www.uwm.edu/Org/acsp/ or 850-907-0092

"Community-based Organizations: Keys to Unity and Self-Reliance" by Raúl Yzaguirre (Sept.–Oct., 1980) *Agenda* 10(5)

"How I Turned a Critical Public into Useful Consultants" by Peter T. Johnson (Jan.–Feb. 1993) *Harvard Business Review*

"Rededicating Ourselves to Community" by Jane E. Leonard (1994) *Journal of Community Development Society* 25(1)

"Independent Community-based Social Planning" www.worldchat.com/public/hspc/sp/ingrtpln.htm

"Community-based Environmental Protection" www.epa.gov/ecocommunity/

"Community-based Resource Management" www.umich.edu/~crpgroup/
Specific to Michigan, but useful examples.

Keep Healthy Sites Healthy

The first rule of the tinkerer is to keep all the pieces.
—Aldo Leopold, quoted by E. O. Wilson, *Biophilia*, 1984

Every site resembles a living organism, and like organisms, sites vary in health. This chapter discusses what site health means and the methods for preserving it during construction. Like human health, site health is not easy to define in a simple formula. Prevention is usually more successful—and less expensive—than cure.

Landscape construction that accidentally or deliberately damages a *healthy* site is doubly wasteful. While restoration methods (Principle 2) can repair many site injuries, there is a point of no return, beyond which restoration is neither cost-effective nor ecologically sufficient. Mature trees needlessly destroyed in construction are not effectively "restored" by planting saplings, for example. Thus the first principle of sustainable landscape construction is self-evident yet easily overlooked: *Avoid harm to healthy sites.*

Protecting a healthy site requires care *throughout* the design/construction process, from the initial reconnaissance through site cleanup after construction. Sustainable *design* anticipates and integrates appropriate construction methods. The site-specific impact of *building* must influence design choices about siting, structures, and materials. The quality and coordination of such choices can make the difference between irreparable damage and minimal impact.

What Is a Healthy Site?

"Health" is one of those conditions everyone knows when they see it but which remains impossible to define completely. Despite this difficulty, it is important for both ecological and economic reasons to develop at least an operational definition of what site health means.

It is fairly easy to say when a site is *un*healthy. Sick sites are often obvious eyesores: stripped of topsoil by natural erosion or human carelessness, polluted by chemicals, supporting only a small percentage of the richness of plant and animal life found in the region, or overrun with invasive species.

Less easy to see is the connection between local, small-scale site health and the global health of the environment. Climatology researchers Jonathan Foley and Roger Pielke recently concluded that landscape changes—especially clearing and drainage of land for home-building and agriculture—are *equally* significant for global warming as carbon dioxide emissions. In

Discussed in This Chapter:

- Identifying healthy and unhealthy sites
- How site knowledge forms the basis for sustainable work
- Dealing with preconstruction impacts through teamwork
- General protection strategies applicable to any important site feature
- Protection of specific features like soil, vegetation, or water bodies
- Choice of construction equipment and construction planning

southern Florida, they found that swamp drainage over the past 100 years had raised average regional temperatures by half a degree or more and reduced summer precipitation by 10 percent—factors that lead directly to recent wildfires. [1] Clearing a single lot cannot cause widespread environmental decline—but the cumula-

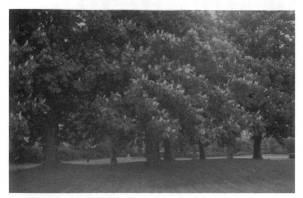

Figure 1.1. Assessing site health visually can be misleading. This site fits the conventional image of landscape health, but may use or pollute resources unsustainably. PHOTO: Kim Sorvig.

Figure 1.2. Messiness is commonly equated with ill health, but this site is growing back from flooding—an important part of a healthy lifecycle in any floodplain. PHOTO: Kim Sorvig.

Figure 1.3. This site looks healthy and probably is. Vigor and diversity (of species, spaces, edges, and communities) are good indicators of healthy landscapes. PHOTO: Kim Sorvig.

tive effect of clearing 1.39 *million* sites (the 1998 total for new U.S. housing starts)[2] is directly linked to global problems.[3]

Some site "illnesses" are brief ones, from which the site recovers rather quickly. A site that has been drowned in sediment by a flood or burned by a forest fire may look unhealthy but usually retains vitality and soon begins regrowth. In fact, many plant communities and soil types are adapted to periodic flooding or fire and depend on these events for long-term health. A site that is healthy and has plentiful resources (water, soil fertility, sunlight) can recover from minor construction damage, too.

More serious ill health results when toxic chemicals are involved, or when soil is removed, massively eroded, compacted, or paved. Some plant and animal species invade and take over the site in much the way that parasites, microbes, or even cancers invade the human body.

The cumulative effect of small, normal stresses also affects site health. Individual factors such as wind, temporary drought, or increased ultraviolet radiation can add up over time to weaken the plant life that holds a site together. Human use of a site produces new stresses. A site that had limited resources to start with may be unable to adapt to added stress.

Like healthy humans, healthy sites are productive, have vitality enough to keep growing despite some stress, and generally have a satisfying "look" and "feel." The appearance of a site can tell much about its health. However, some landscapes conventionally viewed as stylish conceal serious ill-health. Conventional landscape aesthetics are not a reliable guide to site health (see Introduction).

A healthy environment provides what have been called "environmental services," such as keeping air and water clean, improving local climate, and creating food—services on which human life depends.[4] Healthy sites also provide many of the amenities of life. Compared to landscapes cleared and flattened for convenience in construction, healthy sites have significantly higher property values (by at least 5 to 20 percent).[5]

Healthy sites are recognizable by several characteristics:

- They support a *diversity* of plant and animal life adapted to the region and linked to one another in a web of interdependence.

- They are *seldom dominated exclusively by one species,* and especially not by a species imported there by humans. (Criteria for agricultural sites are different, but crop monocultures are also considered unhealthy.)

- The community or ecosystem (soil, plants, and animals) of the site is essentially *self-maintaining,* not dependent on outside resources supplied by people.

- The living species of the site are *self-reproducing.*

- The geological portion of the site is *not changing too rapidly* to support the living community, nor is it poisoned or infertile.

- The site has sufficient vitality to *overcome* a variety of stresses.

- The community changes with age through a process called *succession.* Healthy meadow or bog may be superceded by healthy forest in a series of steps characteristic of the region. Unlike invasion by noxious species, succession is healthy. It is like the changes in a healthy human from infancy through adolescence, maturity, decline, and death—and in the case of plant communities, includes rebirth. Accelerating or holding back succession without weakening the site's health is one of the most sophisticated methods of integrating human needs with natural process (Principle 2). Excessively slow or fast succession, like unusual aging in people, can indicate ill health.

It is seldom up to a single construction or design professional to decide precisely how healthy a site is. However, if developers, designers, and contractors learn to *recognize* relatively healthy sites, such sites will be valued and protected more often, a prime goal in sustainable construction. In these professions, future success will go to those people who learn to recognize and protect healthy sites while working to restore health to damaged sites.

Do Your Homework FIRST: Knowledge as Sustainability

Although it may sound like parents nagging a schoolchild, "homework first" is critically important to protecting any site—and to avoiding

costly business mistakes. Those who think that site analysis before design or construction is expensive need to consider the costs of ignorance, which are always far greater.

There are two major kinds of homework involved in protecting a healthy site: attitude and factual knowledge. The information gained from each applies to every subsequent step of sustainable landscape work, from design through maintenance.

It is impossible to protect what you don't respect. Even for professionals who have a strong love of nature, working on a site involves carefully setting priorities and, in many cases, reeducating clients and coworkers. Attitudes about preserving natural conditions have a strong influence on design and construction priorities. Is the desire for soccer practice at home worth flattening the backyard? Is the need to impress the neighbors enough justification for using extra resources, or removing native plants to install a conventional lawn? Choices like these are never easy and require thinking back to basic attitudes about the human relationship to the landscape. The two introductory chapters include some thoughts about cultivating sustainable attitudes, as does the conclusion.

It is also impossible to protect what you do not thoroughly understand. Thus, gathering information is critical to sustainable landscape work, from the earliest preliminary studies of feasibility and appropriateness, through design and construction, and into maintenance. The two most important types of data gathering are *site reconnaissance* and technical *surveying.* Both benefit from a team effort in which information is shared and communicated clearly.

Reconnaissance to identify and evaluate site features should happen *before* design begins. (In fact, this knowledge should really be part of selecting a property to purchase or develop, though this is rare.) Much of this work is visual, just observing and noting conditions without using technical equipment. Published sources, such as soil and topography maps or land-use records, are also important in effective reconnaissance. Contractors usually carry out a separate reconnaissance just before bidding a contract. Ideally, their insights should be part of the process long before the design is finalized, though this is not conventional practice.

Surveying, which uses technical instruments

to give precision to site data, establishes site boundaries very early in any development process, usually when the land is divided for sale. Surveying may be part of reconnaissance, if precise location of major features is needed. Finally, technical surveying methods lay out the measurements for constructing a new design.

Regardless of the technique used to collect it, detailed site-specific mapping is a critical part of building sustainably. If this homework is left too late, it may be poor quality, or it may be overridden by assumptions made before good information was available. Much conventional construction is undertaken using site plans that show little more than a legal boundary, perhaps some generalized contours, and the largest existing trees. Given clearer site data, a designer can work more closely with existing topography. Good site knowledge helps a contractor work with soils or vegetation that are of differing ecological importance or present different hazards to construction.

Site-specific data has long been considered prohibitively expensive to gather using conventional survey methods. New technology, especially Global Positioning Systems (GPS, see page 34), promises to make ecologically important site information more affordable and reliable to gather, while reducing the impact of the survey process on the site. Geographic Information Systems (GIS) use computers to store, analyze, and selectively map site data, making it much more manageable and accessible. One of the most important steps that the design and construction industries can take toward sustainability is to embrace new standards of site data and use that data to inform each decision affecting a site.

Locate Features during Site Reconnaissance

The best and most vulnerable features of any site should be inventoried and located as early as possible, preferably *before* starting design. Many of these will be items of clear ecological value; others will be historic or cultural; and some may be of personal importance to the owner, client, or user group. All are likely to need protection during construction. A basic checklist includes:

- All trees, and any unusual or specimen plants
- Meadows, groves, thickets, and other identifiable vegetation communities

- Wildlife dens, breeding areas, and pathways, including seasonal ones
- Streams, wetlands, ponds, and lakes
- Soils: erodable, fragile, specially fertile areas, and geological formations
- Cultural features (archaeological, historical)
- Items or locations of personal or sentimental importance to owners or users
- Connections, links, and pathways between these features

Responsible design firms will make such an inventory the first step in their work. Analysis of the inventoried site may reveal other reasons for protecting certain features: for example, a common and none-too-beautiful tree may need to be protected because it acts as a windbreak or moderates solar gain.

Pay Special Attention to Streams, Lakes, and Wetlands

The care of water bodies is a very specialized topic (Principle 4). Because of the difficulty, expense, and legal complications involved in restoring them, it is critical to *identify* and *protect* streams, lakes, and other wetlands at the earliest possible stage. In fact, the presence of wetlands should be researched before *buying* a property for any sort of development. Many horror stories about wetlands regulation reveal an owner who didn't know, or didn't want to know, about site conditions. Despite regulation, many commercial land buyers still limit their site research to the proverbial "location, location, location." That is a mistake no designer or contractor can afford.

Once wetlands are identified, they need protection during construction. The techniques discussed in this chapter, particularly fencing to limit access, are used to safeguard wetlands as well as other site features. However, because of their biological complexity and legal status, wetlands protection often requires going well beyond generic site-protection techniques. For this reason, protection of wetlands is discussed in its own chapter (Principle 4), along with restoration, constructed wetlands, and other issues involving water.

At the site research stage, remember that wetlands

- must be delineated according to legal definitions, not just a layperson's observations.

- are highly susceptible to sediment that erodes off of adjacent land surfaces (see "Preserve Healthy Topsoil," 45).

- vary seasonally much more than most other landscape features, to the point of disappearing in dry periods.

- have life cycles and may be "healthy" or "unhealthy," affecting decisions to protect them as they are or to restore them to better condition.

- are linked to and influenced by off-site water sources, which need to be included in protection planning.

- often require the addition of a specialist to the design and construction team.

- can cause special difficulties for construction workers and machinery.

Even where no wetland exists on the site, protect the existing *drainage* patterns carefully. A featured grove or meadow, thoroughly fenced for protection, can die from flooding or drying if grading outside the fence redirects the flow of water. For sustainability, the movement of water on a site should be changed only with great care.

Tap Local Knowledge of Sites and Seasons

Contractors with many years of experience in a specific region know that weather and other seasonal changes can make or break a project, financially and practically. The same conditions dramatically affect the need for site protection. Erosion on recently graded or excavated soil may be minimal in most weather, until a summer rainsquall or seasonal high winds sweep the soil away overnight. Working on frozen or muddy soils, in addition to the practical and engineering problems, may damage a soil that would be unharmed if worked when dry. Plants may be especially susceptible to breakage, root compaction, or other mechanical damage during seasons of rapid growth or may tolerate damage better if they are dormant. The seasonal vulnerability of endangered wildlife has delayed many a public project.

For sustainable construction, at least consider whether a change in the construction *schedule* can minimize disruption. For example, in Bouctouche, New Brunswick, work on a large boardwalk for Le Pays de la Sangouine was done in

winter, with heavy machinery positioned on ice.[6] Working in the summer would have been more complicated *and* more disruptive to the river and dune-island site.

No book could possibly include the appropriate advice for protecting all sites, in all seasons, for all aspects of construction. Local contractors often have a remarkable store of seasonal and site-specific knowledge. Conventionally, this knowledge is used to plan ahead for practical matters, scheduling around periods when the site will be inaccessible. If sustainable construction and protection of site features are recognized as goals, this local knowledge is invaluable in achieving results. Local expertise is really a prerequisite to any sustainable design or construction. Large national firms can do sustainable work if they subcontract local experts and heed their influence. The tendency of large firms to standardize all procedures must not overrule adaptation to local conditions. Applied globally and in all seasons, rigid standardization is incompatible with sustainable design and construction.

Avoid Survey Damage

Although detailed site-specific mapping is often a key to reduced construction impact, the *process* of surveying a site can be the start of site degradation. Fortunately, new technology combined with new attitudes makes survey damage avoidable.

Manage Line-of-Sight Surveys

Conventional surveying relies on a clear line of sight between a known point or "datum" and any point whose position is to be determined. Optical surveying instruments, including lasers, must be able to "see" in a straight, uninterrupted line from the instrument to the point being recorded. Sonar and ultrasonic instruments, which rely on bouncing sound off a target and back to the instrument, also require a clear shot at the unknown point. To ensure clear line-of-sight connections, surveyors clear brush and small trees with machetes or similar tools, a process known as "brashing."

Depending on region, climate, and vegetation, brashing can cause anything from minor injury to long-term harm on a site. The damage is least critical in regions where vegetation grows back quickly, such as the deciduous forest. Even in these areas, brashing, like careless pruning, can spread plant disease and may affect the diversity of site vegetation, both in species and age distribution. In bioregions with fragile vegetation (for example, high desert, coastal, alpine, or arctic), regrowth after brashing often takes decades. When vegetation is removed in a linear pattern, this opens a path for soil erosion. Conventional surveys concentrate on lines, such as property boundaries, that arbitrarily cut across slopes or watersheds, thus increasing the potential for erosion and other disruptions.

Modern surveyors plan their fieldwork carefully in advance to minimize wasted time and backtracking. The same planning skills can be applied to minimize site damage from brashing, as well as from unnecessary vehicle access during the survey. In some cases, a well-planned survey can measure around an obstacle instead of removing it. Baseline-and-offset surveying can also decrease the need for brashing under some site conditions.

Because much conventional development starts with total regrading of the site, existing site features, other than landmark-quality specimens, may seem unimportant to site crews. In the worst cases, surveyors, like other construction workers, thoughtlessly destroy any inconvenient item found on the site. If minimal site damage is an explicitly stated goal of the project, the survey team becomes an important ally in meeting that goal.

Use Alternative Survey Technology

Several methods of surveying that do not rely on line of sight are appropriate for landscape construction surveying. These include both high-tech and low-tech options.

Global Positioning

Global Positioning Systems (GPS) are a recent addition to the surveyor's toolkit and are rapidly changing surveying processes and results. GPS field equipment consists of a handheld, backpack, or vehicle-mounted unit capable of receiving signals from satellites. These satellites, originally developed by the U.S. government as aids to military and civilian aviation, continuously signal their location relative to Earth. By triangulating the locations of several satellites at one time, the receiver unit computes and records its own earth-surface location. GPS units guide commer-

cial airliners and smart-missiles, rental cars and trucking fleets, recreational hikers and wildlife managers, with new applications spreading rapidly. One of these adaptations is GPS-based surveying.

GPS surveying is frequently less costly, easier, and quicker than conventional surveying. Survey results are digital and can be fed directly into computers for mapping and analysis. If site design is done on a computer, drawings can be loaded into the GPS field unit, which then guides the surveyor through construction staking. Accurate "as-built" drawings are much easier to create with GPS than ever before. These advantages make GPS surveying a cost-effective and powerful tool.

In terms of site protection, a major advantage of GPS is that earth-surface line of sight is not required. In most cases, brashing can be entirely eliminated, and access to the site is simplified. Anywhere the surveyor can carry it, a GPS unit can record horizontal and vertical location. (Dense tree canopy, very narrow canyons, or tall buildings can occasionally block communication skyward to the satellites. In most cases, such obstructions can be worked around.)

The accuracy of GPS units varies widely. Those used for surveying are generally accurate to within less than half an inch, plus or minus. The most accurate systems are known as "real-time differential GPS." In differential systems, two GPS units are used, one mobile, and the other located at a fixed, known point. By comparing the satellite readings from the mobile unit to those taken at the known point, small deviations can be corrected. A differential system is "real-time" when the corrected data is beamed directly to the mobile unit as it is computed, rather than doing a batch of corrections on an office computer after all the fieldwork is done. Such systems are expensive ($5,000 or more, though prices are decreasing as the systems become more common).

A variety of stand-alone (nondifferential) units are also available, with accuracies ranging from a few feet to a hundred yards. For site inventory, where broadly defined areas of the site need to be quickly but roughly surveyed, such units may be accurate enough. Units costing under $200 are sold in sporting goods stores to replace orienteering compasses.

For landscape contractors and landscape architects, there are several ways to take advantage of GPS technology. One is to contract or subcontract the survey, specifying the use of GPS. A second option is to rent the equipment. Rental companies may also set up the system, calibrating it at the site, and in some cases converting the field data into CAD, COGO, or GIS files. If rental with setup is available, the actual fieldwork can be done by someone knowledgeable about the project but not trained in surveying—for example, a botanist could produce a very accurate tree inventory, a designer could walk and map desirable paths, or a contractor could locate construction hazards. A third option for those whose work relies heavily on accurate site information is to purchase GPS equipment and be trained in its use.

PROJECT EXAMPLES USING GPS

Design Workshop, a landscape architecture firm with offices in Denver and Aspen CO and Tempe AZ, has used GPS on several projects where accuracy, environmental sensitivity, and speed of site analysis were important. At McDowell Mountain Ranch (Scottsdale AZ), new trails for this planned community had to be integrated with regional trails. Scottsdale's environmental laws are strict: Impact had to be minimized, but maximizing trail experiences was also an important goal. Starting with rough sketches on a topo map, landscape architect Stuart Watada leased a handheld GPS unit to refine trail locations and, at the same time, collect data on vegetation and other features visited by the trails. Design Work shop uses an inexpensive GPS unit to field-verify potential homesites at large developments. They have also found GPS an invaluable tool for early site planning in countries such as Bolivia, where no published survey information is available.

For Anchorage (AK) Botanic Gardens, Jeff Dillon of Land Design North had GPS survey data collected by University of Alaska engineering students. Existing vegetation and other site features were thus incorporated directly and accurately into design work. Dillon has also used GPS to lay out miles of ski trails in Anchorage parks.

Ohio State University's Center for Mapping has developed a "GPS van" that can produce a digital map of an area, linked to video images, simply by driving through or around the site. A GPS unit pinpoints the location at which each reading or image was taken, and onboard com-

Figure 1.4. GPS units, often backpack sized, make surveying quicker, easier, and potentially less destructive to site vegetation. PHOTO: Magellan Corporation.⊃

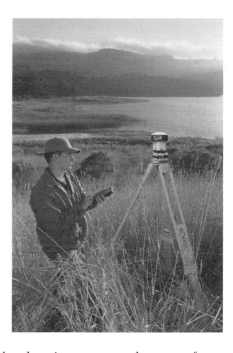

Figure 1.5. GPS comes in many sizes and forms. On an open site like this, line-of-sight instruments might cause little problem, but GPS still offers exceptional ease of use. PHOTO: Used with permission of Sokkia Corporation.

puters compile the data into a map almost as fast as the van can drive. Combining GPS and stereo-photo methods, the van can locate any item it can "see" to an accuracy of ± 14 centimeters (5 inches). OSU researchers have even used GPS to control the blade of a bulldozer. An onboard computer containing the existing and proposed topography allows semiautomated grading with an accuracy of a few centimeters.

GPS has been welcomed in conservation work. Rob Corey, a landscape architect with the Natural Resource Conservation Service (formerly

U.S. Soil Conservation Service), produces "virtual landscape animations" that allow users to visualize land-use changes and then compute environmental-impact statistics from the images. GPS is important in collecting the data on which Corey's innovative system is based. It is also a tool for The Nature Conservancy's Parks in Peril program in Latin America, helping landscape architect Brian Houseal and colleagues to establish accurate legal boundaries for nature preserves and to locate endangered plant communities. This new information greatly increases the Conservancy's ability to win protection for remote, ecologically critical sites.

LASER 3-D SITE IMAGING

The newest entry in high-tech surveying is the Cyrax system, which scans sites and buildings with a laser. Much like radar, it measures points by the time a reflected signal takes to return to the instrument. At its optimal range of about 50 yards, the Cyrax system can register detail as small as half a millimeter. Points collected in this way form a three-dimensional digital model of whatever the scanner "sees." Although it relies on line of sight, the need for physical access to the site is decreased. Thus, the Cyrax system can be used with less potential for site damage than conventional surveying. Its primary advantage, however, is its extreme accuracy, and the fact that a 3-D model is generated immediately.

Scans of a site or building taken from different angles can be "stitched" together by the software and can also be tied to survey datum points. Each scan may require fifteen minutes to an hour, with another hour for processing the whole model.

This system has been available commercially since 1998. Whether it would be useful in landscape surveys—for example, of a woodland or other densely vegetated site—is unknown. If it can accurately model major vegetation across a site, it could have immense value for ecological data gathering. At first glance, however, it seems better suited to scanning buildings, topography of open or cleared sites, or engineering structures. (Caltrans, California's highway department, has tested it for inspecting overpasses.)

At about $150,000 for the system with software, few landscape professionals are likely to buy a Cyrax system outright. The manufacturer maintains a list of firms that offer surveying services using the system. For some types of projects where exceptional detail is required, such as historic landscapes, a complete digital model might have real advantages. If Cyrax follows the trend of most technological innovations, its price may drop enough to become a tool for more ordinary site surveying. Meanwhile, GPS is currently a far more realistic option for landscape surveying.

LOW-TECH, NONLINE-OF-SIGHT TOOLS

While GPS looks to satellite technology to free itself from line-of-sight limitations, a much simpler method relies on the oldest of all leveling tools: water. The tube-level, or hose-level, is available in several forms. Like a surveyor's transit, it determines vertical level only, requiring separate distance measurements to make a complete survey. For projects where sight-line clearing must be minimized, and for some types of construction layout, it is an inexpensive and valuable tool.

If a clear tube is bent in a **U** shape and partially filled with water, the water surfaces in each of the arms of the **U** will always lie at the same level. In a hose-level, the **U**-shaped tube is replaced with 20 feet or more of flexible tubing. The waterline at one end of the tubing is held at a known elevation, and the water at the other end of the tube adjusts to exactly the same level.

Hose-levels can be used around blind corners, eliminating the need for a clear sight line, and can function at considerable distances across rough ground. They speed construction layout because no calculation is required: the two water lines are simply the same level. While laser equipment provides a similar function, it is more costly and requires line-of-sight clearance.

Some manufacturers have added electronic sensors to the traditional tube-level, so that an audible signal is sounded when the ends of the tube are aligned. This and other refinements make it possible for one person to use a hose-level more efficiently. Even these enhanced versions cost only about $50. If a site is free of visual obstructions, line-of-sight tools are more convenient for most surveying. But where clearing would be costly and intrusive, simple tools offer improved site protection at cost-effective rates.

Another remarkably simple surveying tool is the A-frame level, which has been in use since ancient Egypt. Three light-weight boards are nailed together in the form of a rough capital A, and a mark is made at the center of the cross-arm. A weighted string, like a plumb line, is hung from the top of the A. When the two "feet" of the A are level, the string intersects the cross-arm exactly at the center mark. The tool is walked across the land like old-fashioned drafting dividers, quickly establishing a series of level points. For terracing and other erosion control work, the A-frame can set up level earthworks without any math calculations at all—and with no need for line-of-sight clearance.

Minimize Utility Damage

Many modern landscapes are crisscrossed with buried and overhead utilities. Although some of these systems are invisible, constructing and maintaining them seriously alters the landscapes through which they pass.

Systems such as irrigation, site lighting, and storm-drainage lines are part of landscape construction, their functions landscape-specific. Other utility systems, like sewage, power, phone, and cable TV, serve the buildings on the property. The site may also be impacted by systems that serve larger communities (main power, sewer, or phone lines, for example), or commercial interests (oil and gas pipelines), along with easements for such systems.

In the narrowest sense, landscape construction has little influence except over landscape-specific utilities. However, landscape architects and contractors working together on public works projects have had significant effects on utility impact, as shown by the projects discussed in the next two sections. The difference between planning carefully for utilities and dismissing them as necessary evils can be like night and day and is an important aspect of site protection.

Make Maximum Use of Narrow Easements and Trenches

Access is required to construct, maintain, replace, and repair utilities. To provide this access, public utility easements are much wider than the width of the actual pipeline or cable. Significant decreases in site impact can be achieved by reconsidering how utility access is provided. Rural utility easements may well cut across country, requiring their own cleared access roads. In urban areas, utilities must frequently dig up buried lines and keep street trees clear of overhead wires. Ways to decrease the impact

Figure 1.6. The Egyptian A-frame is a simple, site-friendly way of establishing level and is the fastest way to lay out points along a contour line.
PHOTO: Kim Sorvig.

of access in each case are discussed in the following section.

According to the Edison Electric Institute, no one keeps national records of the total length or land area occupied by utility easements. Pacific Gas and Electric, as a single example, has 14,000 miles of electrical transmission lines. A 50-foot-wide easement uses about 6 acres per mile. At this common width, PG&E's transmission lines alone could require as much as 80,000 acres. Add to this the other types of utilities, and multiply it across the continent, and it is clear that the size and maintenance of utility easements have a major impact on landscape health nationally. Utilities are recognizing the potential for lessening these impacts and for creating habitat corridors in easements. The Edison Institute, for example, publishes EPA-approved guidelines for maintaining easements. ⊃

REDUCE CLEARING FOR ACCESS ROADS

Access roads are required when a utility line does not follow existing transportation corridors. Main branches of utility systems, as well as lines passing through rural areas or urban parks, often have their own dedicated access roads. The road may run on top of a pipeline or may follow overhead wires.

The cleared easement itself can often be narrowed, especially if wide turnarounds for maintenance or construction vehicles are provided at strategic points. Using the smallest and lightest possible vehicles and machinery for maintenance can also decrease the access space required. Decisions about machinery use are made at many levels, from corporate purchasing offices to the job supervisor renting extra equipment for an emergency. Landscape professionals have a variety of opportunities to influence these decisions.

Special construction techniques, such as trenchers that lay pipe or cable behind them as they go, can cut easement width dramatically. At Loantaka Brook Reservation in Morris County NJ, landscape architects Andropogon Associates challenged both conventional routing design and conventional construction methods for a gas pipeline cutting through mature beech-oak forest. By working with the contractor to devise space-saving methods of pipe installation, Andropogon succeeded in reducing a proposed 50-foot right-of-way to 34 feet. Moreover, by using a tracked loader specially adapted for the project, the contractors were able to replace slabs of vegetation-rich soil along the pipeline trench, guaranteeing revegetation.

Another least-destructive routing was accomplished in Loudon County VA when a major developer crossed park authority property to install a sewer line. Two landscape architecture firms, HOH Associates and Rhodeside and Harwell, persuaded the county sanitation authority to reduce the construction width of the sewer line from its standard 75 feet to 35 feet. Working with an arborist and an engineer, their approach avoided a radical scar through a scenic woodland.

Figure 1.7. This easement, following landscape-oriented guidelines developed in Loudon County VA, is being built less than half as wide as the utility's standard. Note the site-protection fence. PROJECT: Park Authority, HOH Associates, and Rhodeside & Harwell. PHOTO: Doug Hays.

The three main guidelines for the project were the following:

- Keep construction and final easements to a maximum width of 35 feet.

- Eliminate long, straight utility swaths. Follow topography and natural features to avoid uninterrupted lines longer than 1,000 linear feet. (This principle is particularly important in steep or forested areas.)

- Keep openings into or out of woodlands—the points of greatest visual impact—as narrow as possible. Into this project, the opening into the woods was pinched to 10 feet.

These principles proved so successful that they were followed on subsequent sanitary sewer lines in Loudon County.

Utility easements should, wherever possible, be thought of and constructed as multifunctional space. Combining an easement with a public road, trail, or "bike-path" is a common example used in the Morris County project discussed above. In fact, combining utility easements with trails is an increasingly common way for park systems to pay for needed services. The Washington and Old Dominion trail in northern Virginia combines four major functions and "recycles" an older right-of-way in the process. What began as a disused rail corridor first became a power-line easement. A paved trail was added, managed by the regional park authority. Later, a sewer line and fiber-optic cable were also installed under the trail. Annual leasing fees of $250,000 pay for trail maintenance.[7] The resulting trail is a delightful and much needed recreation corridor for area residents. By sharing functions, more can be achieved with less site disruption.

Utility corridors can share with wildlife, too. Their linear and interconnecting patterns can be beneficial as wildlife corridors and habitat—*if* they are not ruthlessly cleared of all vegetation. Clearing costs money and energy and destroys habitat, but mowing (or spraying) the entire right-of-way is still common practice. Even where a certain width of easement is legally required, clearing within that width can be selective. Where easements are extrawide to allow for future expansion, clear only the area in actual use. Leave the access road grassed to reduce runoff and erosion. Except for the road itself, shrubs or small trees can be allowed to remain. As long as the road is kept drivable, clearing the location of a specific repair when it occurs is often cost-effective, compared with ongoing clearance of the whole easement.

Keep Urban Utilities Accessible

In addition to sharing space with wildlife or bicyclists, carefully designed utilities can also share space with each other. Landscape contractors frequently lay irrigation tubing and low-voltage lighting cables in the same trench to save on costs and labor. The same concept applied to municipal utilities can save energy, simplify maintenance, and reduce the space required for easements. Excavation costs money and energy, during both initial construction and subsequent maintenance. Shared-trench construction, since it reduces excavation, should be considered as part of sustainable construction.

Not all utilities are suited for shared trenches. In particular, natural gas cannot run in the same trench as any electrical utility, including phone, cable-TV, and low-voltage wires. The bending radius required for large pipes may make it impractical to route them together with other utilities; consider designing the more flexible system to follow the less flexible. Similarly, gravity-flow systems have strict limits on slopes and lengths of run; other systems might follow the layout for a gravity system.

Shared trenching is most likely to work for "main" supply lines, because the starting and ending points of different utilities seldom coincide. For example, streetlights and fire hydrants are spaced differently along a street but are supplied by main lines running parallel to the street that might be shared. With careful planning, some kinds of utility fixtures can be located together (streetlights sharing poles with electric lines, for example), thus reducing both the materials used and the space required. Such arrangements require clear cooperative agreements between utility companies for maintenance, future expansion, and similar issues.

Easy access to buried utilities can save materials and energy otherwise wasted. Locating utilities under roads saves easement space, but digging through asphalt or concrete pavement to repair the utility line is costly and disruptive. The patched pavement is frequently inferior to the

original construction, and excavated material contributes to solid-waste problems.

A European solution relies on interlocking pavers (like bricks with jigsaw-puzzle edges). Europeans call these concrete block pavers, or CBPs. Laid without mortar, they provide a strong paved surface that can be removed and replaced for access to buried utilities. Although the initial cost is higher than sheet paving, lifetime savings on labor alone may justify the cost of unit pavers. From a sustainability perspective, the fact that interlocking pavers can be pulled up and replaced repeatedly (or reused elsewhere) means that almost no material waste is involved. To excavate through solid paving requires relatively heavy machinery, but to remove and replace unit pavers, smaller machinery or even manual labor is used. This has the potential not only to save energy but also to decrease the width of access required. Lest anyone worry about strength, interlocking pavers support huge commercial aircraft at Hong Kong's new international airport, Chek Lap Kok.

Interlocking pavers offer other practical and aesthetic advantages over the standard unbroken sheet of asphalt or concrete. Different colors can be used to designate pedestrian crossings or even make elaborate mosaics: for example, a miniature baseball diamond in multicolored block greets baseball fans at Anaheim CA's Edison Field. Streets surfaced with interlocking pavers give a traditional, cobblestone look to the mixed-use, limited-vehicle streetscapes advocated by New Urbanist designers; an example is Riverside

Figure 1.8. Interlocking pavers set on sand are easily removed and replaced for utility access, saving energy, cost, and waste. Some pavers also permit water infiltration. PHOTO: Courtesy Interlocking Concrete Pavement Institute/David R. Smith.⊃

Village in Atlanta, by progressive land management firm Post Properties.

Compared to mechanized asphalt or concrete street-paving methods, interlocking blocks may seem too labor intensive. However, European companies like Optimas⊃ have developed small forklift-like tractors that can pick up and place the pavers about eighty at a time, along with a system of tools for preparing the sand bed and edging. The same machine can pull up groups of pavers about 3 feet square when maintenance is required, setting them aside for quick replacement. If ease of maintenance is included, interlocking blocks may actually be less labor intensive than sheet paving over their whole life cycle.

One potential drawback, easily remedied, is that the edging required to keep interlocking pavers from moving sideways is often made of PVC. We believe that PVC should be phased out of landscape use wherever possible (see page 221). Many alternative materials for edging exist.

Plant the Right Street Trees, and Prune Them Right

In urban areas where overhead utility lines follow the streets, they frequently conflict with trees, with the result that the trees are pruned away from the lines. Most of the trees affected are street trees, planted along roadsides at public expense and increasingly important to environmental quality in urban areas. Utility crews have been notorious for butchering trees near their lines, a practice that fortunately is changing.

Prevention is the preferred solution. For new construction, utility lines should be placed where they will not conflict with trees, and new plantings beneath utility lines should use ornamental species that will not grow tall enough to touch the lines.

Where existing or poorly selected trees do conflict with utilities, thinning the tree *selectively* is in everyone's best interest, including the utility company. The temptation to lop the entire top of the tree like a hedge (also called pollarding) results in increased costs as well as environmental damage. Although lopping is initially quick and cheap, and requires little skilled labor, the tree will sucker vigorously at every cut, producing a dense thicket of branches. These fast-growing shoots soon threaten the utility lines again and must be trimmed every year or two. (A particularly destructive form of lopping is done with a huge, tractor-mounted circular saw. As the tractor drives along the shoulder of a road, an arm extends the saw to the edge of the right-of-way and buzz-cuts everything in its path.)

Selective thinning, by contrast, carefully removes branches that extend toward the wires. Far fewer cuts are made, and aggressive sprouting does not occur. For many species, thinning once every five years or even less frequently is sufficient to protect the utility. Taking this into account, thinning is usually at least as cost-effective in the long run as lopping. The savings in transportation energy is likely to exceed the financial savings, since distance is a major factor in tree-work along utility corridors. Thinning is far less stressful on the tree, and much less likely to spread disease. Although not symmetrical, selective thinning done well is hard to see. Thus, without extra financial cost, thinning prolongs the life of valued trees, maintains their healthy ability to filter air and provide shade, and reduces the energy expended on line maintenance.

Increased awareness of financial costs and of environmental issues has led many utility companies to contract their tree maintenance with knowledgeable arborists.⊃Public disgust with the ugliness and ill health of butchered trees, as well as outrage at the destruction of tax-financed street trees, has helped change older practices. Both landscape contractors and landscape archi-

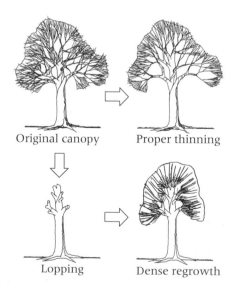

Original canopy   Proper thinning

Lopping   Dense regrowth

Figure 1.9. Dense tree canopies should be selectively thinned (top) to solve utility, shade, or view problems. Lopping, or "pollarding," (bottom) disfigures the tree, and regrowth is denser than before. ILLUSTRATION: Craig Farnsworth.

tects are in a position to continue this trend toward more sustainable utility maintenance.

Look Ahead to Make New Utility Technologies Less Intrusive

Cellular and wireless telecommunications utilities are posing a new landscape construction challenge. More than 22,000 transmission towers are already in place, and industry analysts expect another 125,000 or more as cellular companies battle for profitable markets.[8] Federal regulation has limited the ability of local communities to control this newest utility system, which should be a matter of concern to environmentally conscious professionals. With growing demand for transmission and relay towers, both structures and access roads are proliferating.

Because they rely on height to function, cellular transmission facilities cannot be buried like electrical or phone lines and are hard to integrate with the landscape. Disguising the towers as trees, as was done in one California project,[9] is not the solution, but this equipment seems likely to be even more intrusive than conventional overhead lines. One cellular tower may serve an area equivalent to hundreds of old-fashioned utility poles, and in this sense saves resources. At the present time, however, towers are not *replacing* poles, but are built *in addition*. Ideally, a wireless system could eliminate most poles and miles of wiring, using only small towers. Realistically, given the critical role of wireless communication in the exploding electronic society, common easements and shared towers for telecommunications should be a policy goal that landscape professionals actively pursue.⊃

One recently developed system, not yet in widespread use, is based on the "cable microcell integrator," or CMI, a box antenna so small it hangs from existing cable-TV wires. About four of these CMIs can replace a tower system, often at a cost savings of 30 percent to 50 percent. From a resource-efficiency standpoint, these systems share infrastructure with cable TV, which already has nearly 97 percent coverage in the United States. In addition to saving resources and costs, the system (manufactured by Sanders, Nashua NH) would have much less visual impact in the landscape than new towers. Educating designers and engineers that there are practical alternatives to new towers is one of the main challenges.[10] In the rapidly changing communica-

tions technology market, we hope that this or other less intrusive and more resource-efficient designs will replace the conventional and rather blindered belief that towers are an unavoidable necessity.

Specify and Lobby for "Alternative" Utility Systems

Because utilities are shared services, their location, use, and maintenance are strongly influenced by legal agreements. Those who are concerned with sustainable construction can use such agreements to encourage environmental care.

Many subdivisions have covenants requiring all utilities to be buried. Such covenants could be expanded to include requirements for shared trenches, limited easement widths, and selective clearance and pruning. In cases where service is provided or controlled by a community association, maintenance contracts may also be an effective way of ensuring that utility damage is kept to the minimum consistent with reliable service.

Codes and regulations governing public utilities are most frequently part of municipal, county, or state law. Many of these regulations date from a period in which the only concerns were mechanical efficiency, cost savings, and safety. (Recent cellular regulations continue the tendency to favor utilities over the public or the environment. They forbid community zoning to control tower locations.) The sustainability of utility infrastructure is now a growing concern and is properly considered an aspect of public health and safety. Infrastructure requires energy-intensive upkeep; as energy costs rise, deferred maintenance undermines safety standards. As construction, design, and planning professionals

Figure 1.10. Cellphone towers in increasing numbers mar the landscape visually and harm wildlife; access roads cause environmental disruption. PHOTO: Kim Sorvig.

become more aware of these issues, laws will need to be changed to support, rather than impede, sustainable systems.

Current laws tend to favor centralized utilities, which require extensive infrastructure networks for distribution (electricity or natural gas) or collection (sewage, crude oil). Especially where distances are great and few people are served per mile of infrastructure, these networks are a major cost in materials, energy, and maintenance. Constructing them laces whole regions with environmental disruption, temporary or permanent. The larger the infrastructure, the greater the operational losses (leakage from pipes, voltage drop from cables). Where there is an on-site alternative, transmission through a long-distance infrastructure is a costly and potentially unsustainable approach.

Many alternative systems are local: for example, photovoltaic panels generate power at the point of use; constructed wetlands treat waste on-site. These "near-the-need" systems can eliminate distribution/collection infrastructure entirely, at least in theory. On-site power generation eliminates losses in transit (voltage drop *loses* 10 percent of U.S. electricity in transit from generating station to user).[11] Similarly, on-site sewage treatment can eliminate the huge amount of water used merely to flush the waste through a municipal system. Some alternative systems have infrastructure but are fairly flexible: for example, some sewage systems rely on pressure rather than gravity to move the waste and can follow any topography in small trenches.

Two promising alternatives to utility power are expected to be commercially available by early 2001: fuel cells, which produce electricity by reacting hydrogen and oxygen; and microturbines, which are generators fueled by natural gas. These power sources are about the size of a washing-machine and are expected to cost under $5,000 for the power needs of even the most electricity-hungry American home. Fuel cells are about 40 percent efficient (compared to less than 30 percent for central power plants); when "waste" heat from the fuel cell is used to heat water or steam, they are as much as 80 percent efficient. Even a director of the Edison Electric Institute, a utility company group, has said that the era of big central power generation plants "is

certainly over." Widespread adoption of these on-site energy sources will have marked effects on landscape design and construction. Eliminating power lines may be a real possibility. If the power units are portable enough to ride in a pickup bed, a great deal of gas-powered construction and maintenance equipment (and the pollution that goes with it) could become history.[12]

The policy bias against alternative, localized systems has decreased slowly over the past several decades, and an increasing number of professionals now design and build such systems. Several projects and landscape products that rely on alternative utilities are described in the sections on Constructed Wetlands (page 165) and "Use Solar Lighting" (page 263).

Physically Protect Site during Construction

Construction, even appropriate and sustainable construction, is a forceful process. The forces used in construction, whether small and cumulative or large and intense, can easily damage a site. Unintentionally backing a few yards too far with heavy equipment can irreparably damage fragile site features; so can a work-crew's thoughtlessly placed hand-warming fire. The best way to prevent damage is by physically keeping construction activity out of protected areas. While some site-protection issues affect only large-scale landscape construction, many of the approaches discussed here are effective even for small residential projects.

In addition to protection against utility work and surveying damage, which must often be done *before* design or construction actually starts, careful decisions about what to protect must be made throughout the design process. As a goal, aim to keep clearing, grading, and other site disruption minimized: one model development guideline recommends that clearing extend no further than 10 feet from the building footprint, and that construction access coincide with permanent roadways.[13] Although this may need adjustment in some regions, it is an appropriate goal for site protection. These protection goals, often backed up by covenants, actually raise property values; developers who think of site protection as a hindrance to business, or merely as lip service, are behind the times. (For an example, see discussion of Dewees Island covenants, page 56.)

Clearly Designate Protected Areas

Based on the site inventory, all areas that are to remain undisturbed should be clearly marked on the plan *and* on site. This may require additional fieldwork, especially if the initial inventory was generalized. Inventories are often done "by eye" and show features and locations that are approximate.

It is important to mark the protected areas on *all* construction plans. This should ideally be done by the designer before bidding begins for the construction contract. Site-protection requirements affect the contractor's procedures and costs. Requirements added after the bid is accepted are more likely to cause disagreements and to be disregarded. All sheets of the plan should include the protected areas, so that sub-contractors (who may only see the irrigation plan, for example) are clearly informed. Copies for the supervisor, the crew, and the office should *all* include these markings, as should any change-orders. With CAD software, producing such documents is reasonably simple.

Areas to be protected are best staked out during a site walk at which the designer, contractor, and client are all present. This allows decisions to be made in the field to protect *that* tree and *this* piece of meadow. Especially if the site plan is conventional and lacks detail, on-site communication is much clearer and simpler than trying to work strictly on paper. As soon as the protected areas are located in the field, they must be fenced.

Fence Protected Areas and Maintain throughout Construction

There is no substitute for temporary fencing to protect landscape features. Even conscientious crews can be tired and inattentive. Snow-fence, or the newer bright plastic mesh fencing, will not physically stop a vehicle or even a determined pedestrian, but it provides a tangible and visible boundary, reminding construction workers to keep clear. More than one specimen tree has been saved by the sound of snow-fence snapping as heavy equipment backed into it. Remember that tree root systems, though invisible, need to be part of protection planning (see Figure 3.18);

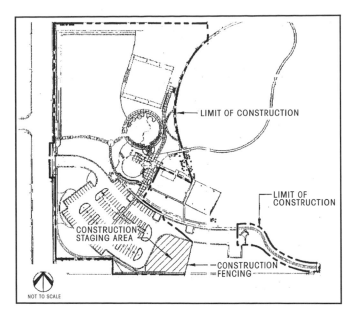

Figure 1.11. Fencing, protected zones, and staging areas should always be clearly marked on all plans. PLAN: Design Workshop.

Figure 1.12. Fencing to protect site features is critical and should remain throughout construction. Much plastic fencing used today is at least partially recycled. PHOTO: Dawn Biggs.

contrary to popular belief, roots don't extend straight down! To prevent overreaching by back-hoes and loaders, place fencing 6 feet or more beyond the edge of the area to be protected.

Fencing must be erected before *any* other work begins, including site clearing. On densely over-grown sites, it may be very inconvenient to place fencing before clearance begins, but the risk of not doing so is great. At the least, fluorescent marker paint or flagging should be used around (not on) protected features to guide preliminary clearing, followed immediately by fencing.

Protection fencing should remain until all work and cleanup are complete. At the very least, fencing must remain in place until all heavy machines (including delivery vehicles) have left the site. Reuse or recycle all site fencing.

With few exceptions, all fenced areas should be *completely* off-limits. This includes foot traffic as well as machines. A footpath cut by a dozen trips with a loaded wheelbarrow can compact some soil types enough to kill the roots of plants. Where there is foot access, there is also the risk that crew members dump buckets, or mix and spill gas or chemicals. It is better to plan site-protection fencing so that there is no reason for any access during the entire construction period.

Limit On-Site Stockpiling, Parking, Etc.

Even outside fenced protection zones, the whole site needs protection from some common construction activities. This protection is best accomplished by designating areas for certain uses, enforced by careful supervision. Specific areas should be established for activities such as the following:

- Chemical mixing and disposal (even "harmless" chemicals can damage soils when concentrated).

- On-site parking (construction equipment, large or small, *and* private transportation). Repeated parking compacts soils. Oil and gas leaks contaminate soils.

- Fires (if permitted at all, must be contained and well away from vegetation).

- Cutting and drilling inorganic materials (metal, plastic, concrete, some stone, and treated wood). Dust can contaminate soils, affecting pH and plant growth.

- Stockpiling of supplies (heavy weight can compact soil; chemicals can leak).

The need to stockpile materials on-site can sometimes be reduced by "just-in-time delivery." A widespread practice in manufacturing, this requires suppliers to deliver materials just when they are needed for use. It is not always possible to arrange construction materials purchases in this way; however, where it is possible, reduced stockpiling can limit site damage and can have economic benefits (including fewer opportunities for loss, theft, or damage of materials stored on-site).

Choose Staging Areas Carefully

Locations designated for construction activities are often called staging areas. These may be equal in size to, or even larger than, the area of actual construction. Although staging areas limit damage to other parts of the site, they do so by serving as sacrifice zones where soil compaction, spills, and other damage are concentrated. Any vegetation is cleared or simply crushed, and soil damage is common. A thoughtfully planned staging area avoids treating the entire site as disposable (a worst-case situation that is unfortunately still common). By carefully locating the staging area and keeping its size to a minimum, overall site damage can be decreased.

Some staging areas are *larger* than the area actually used for construction purposes, particularly if there is a requirement to maintain uninterrupted traffic (pedestrian or vehicular) throughout construction. Where a busy road or path exists on the site, uninterrupted traffic is often a high priority, especially for businesses. If a satisfactory detour can be established without expanding the staging area, ecological as well as monetary costs can be reduced.

Figure 1.13. Staging areas (this one is for a fairly small road project) can permanently damage an expanse larger than the site of actual work. PHOTO: Kim Sorvig.

The ideal staging area, from a sustainability perspective, is a location such as a future driveway, patio, plaza, or tennis court that is already designed to be permanently "hard" landscape. In some cases, it is possible to use existing roads or parking areas adjacent to the site. These have the advantage of a hard surface: dust and mud from staging areas can be a serious problem, both on-site and for neighbors. If existing surfaces are used for staging, be certain that construction equipment is not too heavy for the pavement. In urban areas, getting permission for staging areas on public streets and neighboring lots is a major but worthwhile undertaking.

Before an unpaved staging area is used, topsoil should be removed and stockpiled (page 77). Unless the staging area is to become hardscape, it must be restored and revegetated once the project is complete, using stockpiled topsoil and appropriate restoration techniques (Principle 2). Soil compaction, the crushing of soil pore space until neither water nor air nor roots can penetrate, is almost inevitable in staging areas. Because of this, staging should be well away from important trees. Tilling to loosen the compacted soil is usually necessary as part of restoration.

On large sites, it may be necessary to plan access roads into the site. Where possible, construction access should use existing roads or follow future permanent roadbeds. Temporary construction roads can be considered extensions of the staging area. Their overall area should be minimized as far as possible. This must be balanced against total distance covered by machinery, an energy-efficiency concern. Within reason, the number of trips across the site should also be minimized. Crossing streams or wetlands should be avoided; special restoration will be required if crossings are unavoidable (Principle 4). Temporary roads generally require topsoil removal and restoration, as do staging areas.

Access needs are strongly influenced by the size of machinery used. Consider extra-small machinery (page 235), and plan for the effects of working space (see Figure 10.2).

Preserve Healthy Topsoil

Topsoil, the top few inches in which 70 to 100 percent of all root activity occurs,[14] is a living part of every site, composed of billions of life-giving organisms interacting with organic materials and mineral components. Protecting the soil of a site during construction is one of the most fundamental sustainability practices—and one of the most easily overlooked. When not protected adequately, soils are easily damaged and must be restored (Principle 2). This costs both money and scarce resources, and should be avoided wherever possible.

"In 1978, 80 million tons of soil were eroded from construction sites, and 169 million tons from roads and roadsides. . . . Nearly 90 percent of this takes place on land under development."[15] The rate of erosion from construction sites is *2,000 times* (or more) greater than normal rates on healthy vegetated sites (see Figure 6.22), equivalent to the worst erosion from mine sites. Although there has been some improvement in development practices since the time of these statistics, soil erosion caused by conventional carelessness is still a serious problem. Agriculture, mining, and forestry also cause major soil erosion—but as with all sustainability issues, each industry must do its part, not point fingers at others.

Saying that soil is alive is no poetic exaggeration. It is difficult to imagine the microscopic life teeming in healthy soil, but estimated numbers can help form a picture.[16] In just 1 pound of soil, there are more than 460 billion organisms; in a cubic yard of soil, something like 740 trillion; and in an acre covered with one foot of soil, the truly mind-numbing figure of 1 quintillion living things. This counts earthworms, but nothing larger. The vast majority are bacteria and actinomycetes, with significant numbers of fungi, algae, and protozoa. Even in a single gram (0.03 ounce) of soil, these organisms number in the millions; with bacteria, in the billions. It has been said that if the nonliving part of Earth's soil mantle were somehow vaporized, leaving the living organisms undisturbed, the shape of the land would not change noticeably. Thus, treating soil "like dirt" is truly life-threatening behavior.

Avoid Soil Compaction

The structure of any healthy soil is permeable, with spaces between solid particles where water, air, and soil organisms can move. Soil compaction occurs when weight on the soil surface collapses these spaces, creating a hard, solid mass. Compaction can result whether the weight occurs as a single intense force or as small repeated forces such as persistent foot traffic. Water, air, and roots may be completely unable to penetrate compacted soil, reducing or destroying its capacity to sustain life. The susceptibility of soils to compaction varies greatly by soil type and is an important reason for knowing the soils of each site before beginning work.

The sections on staging areas (page 441 on the choice of construction machinery (page 50) discuss specific ways to decrease the danger of soil compaction. Compacted soil may already exist on the site because of previous land-use patterns. Compacted areas will need to be tilled and often will require adding amendments to restore fertility and porosity.

Protect Healthy Native Soils from Unnecessary "Improvement"

Soil is conventionally viewed simply as *more* or *less* fertile, with the goal always to "amend" or "improve" the soil toward the more fertile condition. For sustainability, think of different *types* of soil fertility, not just different *levels*—that is, some soils have the appropriate type of fertility for rich grassland, while other soils have the right fertility for desert plants. This is not strictly a scientific concept but does point out that fertility is directly linked to characteristics of ecosystems. Complex interactions between available minerals and a host of organisms (from microbes to grazing herds, from fungi to trees) are specific to each region, site, and soil type. Fertility is also influenced by how *long* this soil-creating interaction has been happening, and in what climate. Looked at in this way, raising the chemical fertility level of the desert soil may be an "improvement" if the goal is to grow grass but is *detrimental* to the type of fertility that sustains native vegetation and animals.

Increased fertility can be inimical to native plants in biomes other than deserts. At Freedom Parkway in Atlanta, where a highway landscape was designed for all-native plantings, an overzealous contractor was found to be fertilizing soil intended for common broomsedge (*Andropogon virginicus*) and other natives that thrive on depleted soils. Added fertilizer was only hastening the growth of invasive weeds.[17]

The usual reason for changing soil fertility is almost always the desire to alter the plant community, usually toward agricultural crops or horticultural ornamentals. This is an important sustainability topic for two reasons. The energy and materials used to change the soil may be too energy-intensive to be considered sustainable. Second, changing the ecosystem may have unsustainable results. Some soil amendments, especially heavily processed ones, can concentrate in runoff and cause serious water pollution, even though they are beneficial to soils. Especially when the existing soil is an undamaged local type, "improving" the soil may have negative effects. Appropriate uses of amendments in site *restoration* are discussed on page 79.

It is also important to recognize that air pollution has deposited significant amounts of extra nutrients (especially nitrogen and sulfur) in many "untouched" soils. The conventional impulse to add still more fertilizer is doubly wasteful in such cases. Even compost, which is almost universally a good idea for soil management, needs to be used with care on healthy native soils. It should not be imported from dramatically different sites. For instance, composted grassland vegetation will not support the best microorganisms for forest soils. Compost made from vegetation *similar* to what is being reestablished may *aid* the process with appropriate seeds and microbes. The balance of woody, dry, and green matter, as well as its age, should be matched to the litter found on healthy sites. Leafy compost decomposes more rapidly than the compost layer in woodlands, which contains a great deal of fallen wood. Replacing a layer of twigs and rotting logs with fully rotted and sieved commercial compost may satisfy a desire to tidy the site, but this actually changes the nutrient status for the worse.

Exotic plantings (for whose benefit the soil is usually improved) displace native species if planted over an entire site. Exotic specimen plants can bring a great deal of pleasure and beauty in a landscape, but when they begin to outnumber native plants, loss of habitat, climate deterioration, and other serious problems can result.

For these reasons, a sustainable approach to creating landscapes must protect healthy soils and limit the "improvement" of soil to carefully chosen areas. Specimen plantings that require high soil fertility can be grouped together in locations where they provide the most impact and pleasure. The remainder of the site can then retain unamended soils, an unirrigated water regime, and native plants. This design approach (based on a water-conserving system known as Xeriscape, detailed on page 159) is likely to reduce resource and energy use, pollution associated with manufacturing and transporting soil amendments, and ecosystem disruption caused by overuse of nonnative plant species.

Amending only selected areas of soil is not a new technique. Planting beds and vegetable gardens are often selectively amended. Some extra planning and care are required of the contractor. Selective soil amendment is highly compatible with the sustainability goal of using small, light equipment and may in fact help protect the site from compaction. Closely targeted soil fertilization using GPS (above) and computer-driven tractors is now an experimental technique in agriculture. Drip irrigation can also deliver exact amounts of liquid fertilizer to precise locations.

There are many situations that cause the loss of soil fertility and create conditions where soil improvement *is* appropriate. Among these are contamination, depletion by poor agricultural or horticultural practice, and damage by mechanical forces, including construction itself. Soil Survey maps show large regions, especially in and around urban areas, where the soil type is "Made Land," the result of conventional construction processes. Made Land is usually at least part subsoil, generally compacted, and often contains construction rubble. Surprisingly, even this unpromising stuff can be restored (see page 79).

Amending and improving soils that have been damaged or have lost fertility are important goals of site restoration. The energy costs of transporting soil amendments to these sites must still be weighed carefully, and overfertilization must be avoided. But these issues are frequently offset by the benefits of restoring even a modest-sized piece of the earth. Restoring damaged soil can re-create habitat, stop erosion, and even break down some kinds of pollutants. Unlike the questionable "improvement" of healthy native soils, restoring damaged soils to match their regional norms is almost always a sustainable practice. See Chapter 2 for discussion of site restoration.

Save Every Possible Existing Tree—Even Just One

Existing trees are among the most valuable features a site can have, from both ecological and real-estate perspectives. Experienced realtors always note mature trees as a selling point (sometimes with comically differing opinions on the meaning of mature). A well-maintained *mature* landscape is reported[18] to increase the value of property by up to 75 percent. Yet damage to trees during construction is common and often fatal; one study estimates such losses for a single medium-sized U.S. city at $800,000 annually.[19] This problem is entirely preventable, though often overlooked. For sustainable landscape construction, prevention is a must.

Get Professional Evaluation of the Health of Existing Trees

The many species of trees vary widely in life span. Individual trees also vary in health, affected by soil nutrition, disease, and physical injury. Ideally, clearing for construction would remove only those trees that were already in poor health or near the end of their expected life span (even leaving some of these for wildlife habitat). Although this ideal is seldom fully achieved in practice, careful planning can greatly reduce the number of healthy trees destroyed. Success requires evaluating the site's vegetation in detail.

If possible, existing trees should be mapped and their health evaluated before either design or construction begins, as part of the surveying and site inventory process. Both design (the siting of new features) and construction methods (access and staging) affect the need for clearance. Designing a new structure to fit beautifully among ancient trees is of little use if construction requires removing those trees for access. Site-protecting construction methods, such as limiting heavy equipment, should drive the design on sites with high-quality vegetation.

A professional arborist or tree surgeon is the best person to evaluate the health and expected life of trees. Thorough evaluation requires knowing the characteristics and life span of the species and the hidden signs of weak health. In some cases, determining the health of specimen trees may require climbing them with tree surgeon's equipment. Although a designer, a surveyor or contractor, or even the owner may be able to make a rough visual assessment of the condition of trees on the site, they generally do not have the specialized knowledge and equipment required to make a reliable evaluation.

The cost of an arborist's evaluation, which conventional developers often avoid, is small compared to the value of trees saved (see Table 3.2). Consulting cost can be lowered by limiting the number of trees evaluated. To do this in a way that contributes to sustainability, set a "construction envelope," an area inside which all construction must occur, including access and staging (further discussed on page 55). Outside the envelope, *all* trees and other site features are to remain undisturbed; thus, it is only necessary to evaluate in detail the trees *inside* the envelope. Laid out during site inventory, or at the early stages of conceptual design, an envelope can reduce *both* costs and environmental damage. Some developers, recognizing that sustainable design and protected landscape can dramatically raise property value, lay out building envelopes for every lot prior to selling.

Although trees are the most prominent vegetation on most sites, the health of other vegetation may be equally important in some regions. Large cacti and shrubs, meadows, hedgerows, windbreaks, and groves strongly affect both the character and the ecological functioning of the site. The health, life span, and growing requirements of such features may also require professional evaluation. In some such cases, a botanist, forester, or range management expert may be the appropriate consultant.

Figure 1.14. Bloedel Reserve's eerie beauty relies on retaining stumps and logs in the moss garden. Death and decay are part of every landscape, important for habitat and for nutrient cycling. PROJECT: Richard Haag et al. PHOTO: Kim Sorvig.

One caution: Arborists usually offer pesticide-spraying services. Those who make a substantial portion of their profits from spraying can be like doctors who are too quick to recommend expensive, heavy-duty medicine. Cultivate working relationships with arborists who respect preventative approaches to tree health and who practice Integrated Pest Management (see page 280).

Evaluating trees and other plants is usually easier and more accurate when done during the growing season. Judging a plant's condition when it is leafless and dormant is not impossible but requires extra skill. A dormant evaluation is better than none, but where possible, plan ahead for this task to occur at the proper local season.

Remove Trees Early, if at All

Where it cannot be avoided, tree removal should usually be one of the first construction tasks, along with fencing of protected areas. Although competent tree surgeons can drop a tree piece by piece in a very restricted space, there is always the risk of damage by falling timber. After construction, felling may destroy new work. Large branches or trunks can leave deep gashes in the soil where they fall, and stump removal leaves a crater, so it is better to complete these tasks before site grading.

Removing the felled logs raises several sustainability questions. In "sustainable forestry," logs are winched out of the forest using cables to avoid the need for tractor access. This limits soil compaction and clearing and is often practical for landscape construction.

REMEMBER THE HEALTH BENEFITS OF DEATH

An important option, requiring the agreement of the designer and the client, is not to remove dead trees, logs, or stumps at all. (Those in danger of falling must of course be trimmed or felled, but may be left lying.) Standing snags, in particular, are home to many species of wildlife. In an undisturbed natural system, decomposing wood fertilizes the soil and nurtures young trees. These benefits are lost when dead trees are removed.

Stump and root removal, in particular, has conventionally been done with heavy equipment, extremely strong chemicals, and dynamite. Cost and environmental damage from these methods make leaving dead timber in place even more attractive. Clearly, not all landscape design styles or construction methods can integrate relic timber. Richard Haag's mysterious, stump-strewn moss garden at the Bloedel Reserve near Seattle proves that a sustainable approach can produce great beauty from what is conventionally considered an obstacle.

Fence All Protected Trees Thoroughly

Around trees it is especially critical to exclude all traffic and to prohibit stockpiling, parking, and toxic materials. One common mistake is to pile excavated soil under a tree "temporarily." This can kill many species.

There is no foolproof way of knowing where an existing tree's roots lie. The horizontal zone of root spread "is not a neat and tidy radially circular or concentric pattern, but one that is strictly determined by the path of favorable subsurface conditions."[20] For this reason, rule-of-thumb practices have been developed but should always be considered the *minimum* area to fence and protect. One such guesstimation is that most of a tree's roots lie within the "dripline," an imaginary line formed by projecting the edge of the tree's canopy onto the ground. (See Figure 3.18.) The *actual* root zone is irregular and often two or more times the diameter of the dripline, although the likelihood of damage to major root masses decreases with distance from the trunk. For most trees, especially very old, very large, or shallow-rooted ones, the protected area should be increased by at least 50 percent beyond the dripline.

Species like aspen, sassafras, or sumac spread in circular groves by underground runners. The runners extend far beyond the dripline of any individual trunk, joining what appear to be many trees into one plant (a "clone"). Damage to roots near one trunk can spread to other trunks. If possible, groves of any species should be fenced as a group, enclosing an area *twice the diameter of the grove* if there is any reasonable way to do so. This is especially important, however, with clonal species.

Trees that "weep" or trail branches near the ground may require an extra buffer space beyond the branches. Similarly, tall machinery used near trees is responsible for many unnecessarily broken branches.

Build with Great Care under Trees

People love the sheltered space under a tree or within a grove, which by definition is within the dripline. This presents a special challenge. Seating, gazebos, and other construction close to trees are important features of gardens. Such construction should be lightweight, should make little or no change in drainage or permeability, and should be set without foundations, or on the least intrusive foundation possible, such as pilings. Work should be done by hand, since even the smallest lawn tractor can compact soil around roots or injure the tree's bark. (So-called lawn-mower disease—scrapes on the trunk caused by carelessly operating machinery too close—is a leading killer of trees in horticultural settings.)

Pliny Fisk, of the Center for Maximum Potential Building Systems in Austin TX, has developed a way to place even large buildings very close to trees by using a highly unconventional foundation system. Taking the piling concept one step further, Fisk uses auger-like soil anchors *as the foundation*. These can be screwed into the soil with little disruption. If an addition adds more weight to the building, properly designed anchor foundations can be screwed in deeper to provide the holding power to support the remodeled structure. Once it is no longer needed, the whole foundation can be unscrewed, leaving none of the long-term disruption of abandoned masonry foundations. Based on similar concepts, a commercial system called Pinned Foundations is gaining popularity, especially for wetlands use (see page 142 and Figure 6.17). These removable foundation systems should be seriously considered for many landscape structures.

Working closely around existing plants requires craftsmanship and care. Some conventional construction crews treat existing plants as

Figure 1.15. Sitting under trees seems to be an innate human desire. Furniture or construction under trees must use minimal foundations (if any); erosion from constant use is a concern, but paving is risky unless very porous. PHOTO: Kim Sorvig.

inanimate obstructions rather than living specimens. Although gradually changing for the better, this attitude is a real hazard to existing plants and is part of widespread cultural carelessness toward nature. It is not uncommon to see construction workers hack off branches they feel are in their way, rather than tying them back. Instead of careful pruning where branches really have to be removed, bare-handed ripping and tearing leave jagged stubs that invite disease. Experienced contractors take the extra care required to build quality landscapes around existing trees, knowing that there is a payback in their profits and their reputation, as well as in a healthier environment.

Avoid Grade Changes near Trees

Ideally, no cutting, filling, or tilling of soil should occur within the protected area around existing trees. On some projects, however, financial and other pressures may mean a choice between grading around a tree or removing it entirely. It is critical to keep such changes to a minimum; consulting an arborist is wise in such cases. As a rule of thumb, no more than 6 inches of soil can be added or removed within the dripline. (Even this is too much if it applies to the *entire* dripline area.) Trees "breathe" in large part through their roots, which take up oxygen as well as water and nutrients. Building up the soil can smother the roots, while removal of soil exposes them. If a lowered soil level causes water to collect around the trunk, many tree species will eventually drown.

Sometimes it is impossible to avoid grade changes around existing trees without abandoning construction altogether. In such cases, special soil-retaining structures called tree wells and tree walls can be built to give the tree a chance at survival. These structures enclose the dripline (or more), keeping the soil and the tree at their original levels while the new grade steps up or down at the edges. On a slope, a well or wall may be semicircular, either protruding from the new slope or cut into it. Many decorative variations on the basic circular shape are possible. Drainage into and out of these structures must be carefully designed and constructed.

Don't Half-Save a Tree

Unless most of the above guidelines are followed, leaving a tree on a drastically changed site and expecting it to survive is mere pretense. Some species are more adaptable than others, but most require rigorous protection. Unless a competent arborist is involved, it is better to err on the side of extra protection. Heavy equipment, repeated parking, and grade changes (including "temporary" piles of excavation) are stresses that few trees can tolerate in their root zone without shortening their life span. Many ignorant or disreputable developers have "left" (rather than protected) a large tree on-site, only to have it die within a year or two. By that time, the developer has made the sale and can deny all responsibility, and in any case it is too late; the magnificent old tree can only be replaced, if at all, with a nursery sapling. Nothing about such a practice is sustainable.

Use Appropriate Construction Machinery

Mechanical construction equipment is a part of most landscape projects. Available equipment varies widely in size, weight, energy consumption, and clean or pollution-prone operation. Each of these factors affects the site directly and influences the need for staging and access areas. Careful choices of equipment are essential in sustainable construction, especially for site protection.

Don't Assume a Need for Heavy Equipment

Most experienced contractors have encountered at least one project where machinery other than handheld power tools was impossible to use: a back garden for a row house, where access was strictly through the house, or a terraced landscape too steep to drive onto without extreme risk. In these situations, a can-do attitude finds ingenious ways to complete the work without heavy machines. The same approach can serve a sustainable construction agenda.

Many of the world's most admired construction projects have relied on limited machinery. Thorncrown Chapel, in Eureka Springs AR, was deliberately designed by architect Fay Jones to be constructed with materials no larger than two men could carry.[21] This deliberate decision kept the chapel and surrounding forest in intimate contact, a prime quality of this beloved building. Fallingwater and many other Frank Lloyd Wright buildings were constructed without heavy machinery.[22] Other modern, low-mechanized projects include Staten Island Blue Belt and Mill Brook in Portland ME (Principle 4). Many preindustrial landscapes and buildings, entirely constructed with hand labor and nonmechanized tools, are the basis for ideals of design. The enduring quality, health, and popularity of these places can be attributed at least partly to the appropriate technology used in their construction.

For many conventional construction workers, using powerful, heavy equipment has become a "we can, so we do" assumption. It is easier, when planning a fleet of landscape construction machinery to purchase the biggest, most powerful tools, on the assumption that they can do any job, large or small. From a sustainability perspective, it is more important to match the size and power of the machine to the job and the site. Mechanical overkill has many costs that are not accurately reflected by the monetary price of purchasing or operating a machine.

The larger and heavier the machine, the greater its turning radius, and as a result, the more cleared area it requires for working and staging. Heavier machinery also means greater soil compaction: the weight of the machine is concentrated through the relatively small area of wheel or track in contact with the ground. The bottom surface of an average-sized car or small truck, for example, is about 16,500 square inches; four ordinary tires put about 140 square inches on the ground. Thus the pressure per square inch on the tires is over 100 times greater than if the same weight were placed directly on the ground. This increases the likelihood not only of soil compaction but of vegetation loss and soil erosion. Balloon tires and tracks are designed to decrease the per-square-inch pressure on the ground.

Even on paved roads, AASHTO (American Association of State Highway and Transportation Officials) estimates that a tenfold increase in vehicle weight results in 5,000 times the damage to the road.[23] A dump truck with dual rear axles, at about 30,000 pounds, wears down the road 5,000 times more than a private car at 3,000 pounds. This is due to the high ground pressure exerted by the truck. (For fuel efficiency comparisons, see page 241, "Energy Use: Transportation.")

In Table 1.1, note that some vehicles, especially tracked ones, have lower ground pressure than a person exerts when walking. (Wheels or tracks

Figure 1.16. Thorncrown Chapel is a national treasure, in part because nonmechanized construction preserved its relationship to the woods. PROJECT: E. Fay Jones. PHOTO: Stephen Schreiber.

churn the soil, however, so walking is still less damaging in many cases.) In general, damage to soil is reduced by any decrease in mechanical power and ground pressure. Often, reductions can be made without compromising the ability to do the work. In other cases, the benefits of doing the work must be balanced against the damage done by heavier machinery.

Table 1.1
Ground Pressure of Vehicles and Pedestrians

Vehicle Type	Ground Pressure (psi)
Mars Sojourner	0.14
Tracked all-terrain vehicle (recreational or small work ATV)	1.0
Cuthbertson tracked LandRover	1.9
Person standing, flat shoes*	2.5 to 3.0
12.5 ton Rolligon timber hauler (loaded)	3.2
Person walking or running	3–12
Low Ground Pressure vehicle (legal definition, Canada)	5 or less
Passenger cars	8–12
Person standing, in "sensible" heels	9–12
Bulldozer, military tank	10–80
Work trucks	18–36
Spike heels (weight on toes and heels)	26–33
120 lbs. on single quarter-inch-square spike heel	1,920

*Based on 40 to 75 sq. in. (both shoes), weight between 100 and 220 lbs. Pressures increase when pushing off to walk or run.

Use the Lightest Machinery Available

To match the tool to the job, it is worthwhile to consider both traditional construction tools and newly refined modern machinery. Many of the former accomplish construction tasks without relying on internal-combustion engines at all. The latter have miniaturized and improved the powered machine in search of efficiency. Both approaches can reduce the weight, access clearance, and energy requirements of the job.

In many cities of the eastern United States, there are sidewalks made of huge slabs of granite, up to 12 feet square. These were hoisted into place and set with remarkable accuracy using a tripod of poles and a block and tackle. Most of the stonework in the great gardens of Japan and China was constructed with similar tools. This system of hoisting and placing heavy objects is cheap, simple, portable, and energy-efficient. Control in placing boulders and similar objects is actually more precise with these hand-powered tools than with a crane, loader, or backhoe. Using power lifting tools delicately requires unusual skill on the part of the operator.

Heavy objects do not always require moving with a tractor or forklift. The traditional pole sling, carried on two people's shoulders with the weight centered between them, is a remarkably efficient lifting and carrying tool. Widely used in Asia, and in Europe and America until the 1800s, two- and four-person slings are an energy-efficient way of moving objects weighing several hundred pounds. They are especially useful for irregular-shaped items, where the main difficulty is not the weight, but getting a handhold. On awkward slopes, a sling or similar device may offer access where wheeled carriers cannot go.

Come-along

Plank & roller

Cant dog

Tripod with block & tackle

Pole sling

Figure 1.17. Traditional ways of moving heavy objects still work in landscape construction (often more flexibly than modern machines) and can reduce environmental costs. ILLUSTRATION: Craig Farnsworth, based partly on R. Daskam (Dubé & Campbell ⊃ Principle 6).

"Ball-carts" for ball-and-burlap trees are available in a variety of sizes. Low-slung like a furniture mover's dolly, ball-carts are also good for moving boulders and other heavy, irregular objects. Victorian horticulturists moved trees with root balls nearly 6 feet across in special tree-moving frames. Drawn by horses or large crews of workers, these frames were practical only on fairly flat land and are now considered antique curiosities.

Roller-panels can also move large, heavy irregular objects. Usually aluminum, these have a frame several feet long and a foot or more wide, with rollers every few inches—a modern equivalent of the rollers that helped build the Egyptian pyramids.

Winches and "come-alongs" can also drag heavy landscape construction materials into place, directly across the ground, on a ball-cart or roller, or hoisted by pulleys. Powered and hand-cranked winches are available for moving objects up to several tons. The Appropriate Technology movement has invented several innovative ways for a winch to replace a tractor in pulling a plow or tiller across a field. As long as fossil fuels remain artificially cheap, these tools are unlikely to replace conventional use of trucks and tractors, but they are far more energy-efficient and avoid most soil compaction.

Not all modern equipment is "heavy." Since the 1980s, construction machinery has become available in smaller and more efficient sizes. Tractors, backhoes, trenchers, and other common landscape machines are often half the size and weight of their 1970s counterparts. Powered wheelbarrows, walk-behind forklifts, and small "site dumpers" are available. The small machines are not only more maneuverable and lighter on the soil, their decreased weight increases their fuel efficiency as well. The design of the smaller equipment originated in Japan and Europe, where work space and fuel availability are much more limited than in the United States, enforces an energy-conservative approach. Several of these mini-heavy machines are illustrated in Figures 7.1 to 7.6, in the section on fuel consumption.

For the 18-acre Mill Brook restoration in southern Maine, the team (a landscape architect, a forester, and wetland scientists) were determined to find the least destructive methods of reclaiming a sensitive site. Noting that "stan-

Figure 1.18. A modern version of the pole sling, from tool supplier A. M. Leonard, enhances the advantages of hand labor. PHOTO: A. M. Leonard.⊃

dard methods of large-scale soil installation using bulldozers, excavators, etc. often trample or bury vegetation in the process," the team identified a machine that was being used to spread recycled soil products and mulch onto steep slopes and reforestation areas. Advantages of this "air spreader" include not only minimal disturbance but an even application of soil that followed the

Figure 1.19. Col. Greenwood's Treelifter (1844) allowed one worker to transplant a 30-foot-tall tree. The "ship's wheel" cranked the axle, pulling up the lifting chains. In transit, the axle rotated independent of the chains. ILLUSTRATION: From "The Tree-Lifter," London 1844. Thanks to Tim Brotzman, Brotzman's Nursery, Madison OH.

existing contours of the ground.[24] For a restoration project on Staten Island, NYC, small "power wagons" by Honda were found effective in transporting boulders down an erodable embankment for placement in a streambed. Other small mechanized equipment may be *more* effective than heavy machinery on sensitive sites.

Hand-*carried* motorized equipment should also be considered in sustainable construction. When a machine is too heavy to be carried by one or two people, it is typically mounted on wheels or tracks and made self-propelling. The ability to move under power is necessary for trenching, grading, plowing, and for carrying very heavy objects. But in other tools, such as backhoes, augers, cranes, small mowers, or cement-mixers, powered transportation is *not* essential to the machine's main purpose. Running a relatively small tool by connecting it to an engine large enough to move a tractor is not fuel-efficient and may result in increased pollution. As sustainability becomes a stronger imperative in construction, the extra fuel and weight of self-propelled machinery will very likely be reserved for tools that truly require it.

A two-person motorized auger for digging postholes is a good example of a hand-carried machine. The handheld auger may be slightly slower than a tractor-mounted one but can dramatically reduce soil compaction and the need for clearing. A muscle-powered posthole digger is still more energy-efficient, but in some soils it is unacceptably hard to use. From an appropriate-technology standpoint, the two-person motorized auger is often a good compromise. Small engines, however, must be compared to larger engines on a case-by-case basis, since both fuel efficiency and pollution rates vary.

Similarly, not all heavy equipment is equally unsustainable in all uses. Given a suitable staging area, a crane may be used to "fly" heavy materials into a site, avoiding the need for trucks, barrows, or other wheeled machines that would otherwise cross the site repeatedly. Concrete pumping systems are often used in this way. Standing on an already paved or damaged area, such equipment can lift materials over protected parts of the site. Whether this should be considered "sustainable" depends on both the energy efficiency of the individual machine and the importance of preserving existing site features.

Related Design and Planning Issues

The pursuit of sustainability requires teamwork, and the issues involved often cross the conventional boundaries between design, construction, and maintenance. Many of the approaches discussed in this chapter refer to design choices that link to construction methods. The following are some areas of site protection where, in practice, the designer, planner, and owner have more influence than the construction professional.

Site Selection

Landowners (and designers if they are involved in the identification of suitable sites for proposed projects) can dramatically affect the protection of healthy sites by simply *choosing other places to build*. In particular, prime agricultural soils are of exceptional importance to any sustainable society. Many communities limit building on these types of land in order to ensure continued crop production. Agricultural lands also provide habitat for many nonagricultural plant and animal species and can serve as migratory corridors. The financial drive to subdivide such land is powerful but short-sighted since it diminishes society's food reserves. Neither designers nor contractors have much direct influence on individual decisions to subdivide and develop, but they *can* support planning approaches and political initiatives that encourage development on more appropriate land types.

Among these appropriate types of land for development, two stand out. One is the "hurt site," or "brownfield," where land damaged by previous use can be restored and put to new use. This approach, discussed in detail in Principle 2, decreases the demand for development on healthy sites. A second, sometimes overlapping idea is called "in-fill development." This approach encourages development of the many leftover spaces found in most urban areas. Skill, commitment, political backing, and innovation by designers and contractors support these land-saving strategies.

Since McHarg's *Design with Nature* became influential in the 1970s, many types of broad-scale planning have been used to protect an endless range of land types—including steep hillsides, fire-prone forests, and coastal beaches—from inappropriate development. Without appropriate site selection at both regional and individual scales, the construction techniques described in this book cannot be truly sustainable and can in fact cause great damage. Site selection and even unpopular limitations on the right to use certain categories of land are an essential part of progress toward sustainability.

"Building Envelopes"

Even if the site selection process is a "done deal" before the designer is hired, there are still ways to limit the disturbance of a healthy site. One of the most useful is the building envelope concept. This concept is based on careful site inventory, the designer first lays out an area of the site within which all construction will be contained. This "envelope" is located to take advantage of the site's best features and to avoid damaging fragile areas and is sized to include the square footage of the new construction as well as a carefully limited work zone for construction use. Everything outside the envelope is treated as a protected area during construction (see page 42). This limits the disruption of healthy areas of the site, especially if the envelope can be located on the least healthy, already disrupted areas.

Some subdivisions, like Desert Highlands in Scottsdale AZ, also use the envelope as part of protective covenants that each landowner agrees to respect. Gage Davis Associates' design guidelines specify that the area of envelope immediately surrounding the house may contain nonnative plants and constructed landscape features. Outside the envelope, only native plantings are permitted. This approach balances the resident's desire for personalized outdoor space with the goal of preserving the native landscape as a community feature. A clear and smooth transition links the constructed landscape within the envelope to the relatively unaltered landscape outside its boundaries. The zoned transition is highly compatible with water-saving Xeriscape principles (page 56). This idea was used at the similarly named High Desert in Albuquerque, by Design Workshop.

Reasonable Grading and Clearing Regulations

Grading and clearing are regulated by law in many communities, but this can be two-edged. One study found that only 40 percent of communities studied had an inspection or confirmation

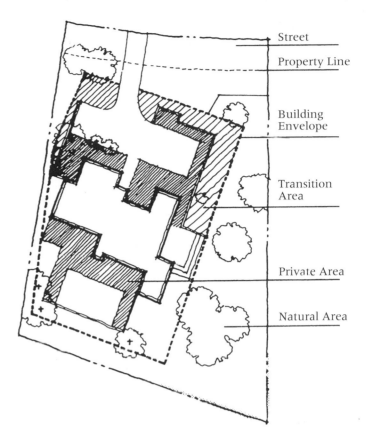

Figure 1.20. Development "envelopes" can help integrate new construction with protected landscapes. PROJECT: Design Workshop. GRAPHIC: High Desert Investment Corporation.

requirement to enforce their regulations; less than 20 percent set specific, measurable targets for how much of the site could be cleared.[25] Tree and woodland protection ordinances are common in Europe, protecting specimen trees and forested areas from destruction.

Grading limits can be too specific, resulting in site damage. Many communities set a steepest allowable slope; such regulations often force excess grading. For example, making a gentle slope between a structure and a woodland takes more horizontal distance than making a steep slope. The extra length of gentle slopes often requires removal of trees or features that could be saved with a steeper grade, given more flexible regulations.

In general, regulations of this sort should be performance-based: they should set a clear goal, such as preserving a specific percentage of the vegetated area on a site, but avoid narrowly regulating the *methods* used to meet the goal.

Covenants for Site Protection

Covenants can protect much more than the building envelope. Because they are contracts between private parties, they can be more specific or more flexible than governmental zoning laws. Covenants and conservation easements can be used to protect a traditional land use, a specific view or landmark, a habitat for particular species, or the character of a neighborhood or region. They can also be used preventatively to prohibit certain types of development or construction. "Reversion clauses," which give the land back to the community or the donor if misused, can add teeth to covenants.

Dewees Island, a residential development off the South Carolina coast, has been called by *Environmental Building News* "a model of what development can and should be."[26] The covenants used at Dewees Island will seem aggressive, even extreme, to those who think of themselves as "bottom-line" advocates—yet the project's return on investment will be *double* the original investors' expectations. With less than half the lots sold, the investors have already made their expected return. Clearly, something is being done right when good for the environment proves good for business.

The Dewees covenants

- limit the total disturbance per site to 7,500 square feet, including house footprint, all paving, and utility easements. Houses may not total more than 5,000 square feet, nor stand over 40 feet tall.

- require restoration of any temporary disturbance.

- prohibit removal of any tree over 24 inches in diameter and require permit review for removal of *any* vegetation.

- require the use of native plants from a list of 136 species.

- limit driveways to 12 feet wide and require all roads, driveways, and paths to be surfaced with sand, crushed shell, or wood chips.

- allow only collected rainwater for use as irrigation.

- permit only organic fertilizers and pest control, except for developmentwide mosquito control that follows Integrated Pest Management, using biological controls such as purple martins and bats first and pesticides only if unavoidable.

- prohibit solid lumber larger than 2 × 12, metal or plastic siding, asphalt or fiberglass shingles, several types of insulation materials, and high-VOC paints and varnishes.

- require a construction waste management plan, including sorted recycling of building materials.

- prohibit garbage disposals and trash compactors as obstacles to recycling.

- provide for constructed wetlands for each house.

These covenants pull together many of the recommendations made in this book. Together with conservation easements, they have protected 65 percent of Dewees Island's 1,200 acres. A transfer fee of 1.5 percent on all lot sales supports the environmental and community programs. Contrary to accusations that this type of development only applies to high-end homes, the developer has invested in ongoing public education programs in low-income communities nearby. Although covenants usually start out in wealthy developments, many of them can, do, and should trickle down into zoning standards that benefit whole regions.

Zones within Constructed Landscapes

In any well-designed landscape, compatible uses and features are grouped in patterns that encourage efficient use of space. Xeriscape explicitly extends this principle to place plants with similar water requirements together for irrigation efficiency. Maintenance is another consideration, and designing zones of similar landscape maintenance can result in savings of time, energy, and materials. These principles are discussed in chapters on water and maintenance, but they have relevance to site protection, too. Landscapes that combine similar uses into carefully designed zones can accomplish more with the same area—leaving more of the site undisturbed.

Specifying Site Protection in Contracts

Cooperation between owner, designer, and contractor is the best way to achieve effective site protection. By selecting contractors who are responsive and cooperative, and cultivating a strong working relationship, designers and landowners can do much to ensure a healthy site.

In some cases, especially public-sector projects, selection of the contractor is strictly by lowest bidder. Since the cheapest methods of construction frequently rely on wholesale clearance of the site, low-bid selection is often a guarantee of site damage. Especially in such situations, the designer must rely on clear, strong specifications to gain an acceptable level of site protection. (We hope that as sustainability grows in importance, better site protection will become part of *standard* specifications, local and national building codes, and covenants attached to land deeds.)

Among the most important items to specify are the following:

- Explicit methods of determining what areas are to be protected.

- Physical fencing of protected areas, in place before construction begins and removed at the latest possible date.

- Strict limits on the activities noted on page 42.

Since damage to existing landscape features, especially living plants, is usually irreversible, specifications *must* include financial motivation for the contractor to protect existing features. A positive approach is to offer an incentive, a bonus that the contractor can earn if final inspection shows the protected features remain undamaged. A liquidated damages clause setting financial penalties for damage can have a similar effect. Without such financial motivation, site-protection specifications lack teeth and will be ignored by contractors who are ignorant or unconcerned about sustainability. It is often cheaper for a contractor to buy nursery stock and "replace" a mature tree than to pay a crew extra to work carefully around it. Contractual language and financial penalties can only go so far in overcoming this problem. Selecting and working closely with a contractor whose work is conscientious are far more preferable. Fortunately, more and more contractors are becoming convinced of the value of sustainable practices and have the skills to protect construction sites from unnecessary damage.

Coordination and Follow-Up

Protecting a healthy site requires coordination. Like a bad haircut, damage to a healthy site can't just be glued back in place. It will have to grow back, perhaps with the help of expensive restoration techniques, always with a requirement for time. Planning, surveying, design, physical protection, machinery use, cleanup, maintenance, and monitoring all play a role in keeping healthy sites healthy.

Because design, construction, and maintenance are conventionally organized as separate professions, monitoring and follow-up are often neglected. As discussed in the Introduction, a team effort is the best way to sustain those increasingly rare sites that have retained their health in today's stressed environment.

Resources
Surveying and Mapping

American Society for Photogrammetry and Remote Sensing
310-493-0290 or asprs@asprs.org
  Mapping, GIS, GPS, and related topics; membership.

National Society of Professional Surveyors
301-493-0200
  Publications, referrals to surveying firms.

GPS suppliers
Magellan, 408-615-5236
Sokkia, 913-492-7585
Trimble Navigation, 800-874-6253

Tube-level
Zircon Corp., Campbell CA
800-245-9265 or www.zircon.com/
  Commercial version of tube-level with audible signal when level.

Navtech Books and Software
800-628-0885
  GPS books, software, educational items, booklists, etc.

GPS Made Easy: Using Global Positioning Systems in the Outdoors by Lawrence Letham (1996 The Mountaineers, Seattle)
  Instructions on using simple GPS for hiking, as well as field data collection and basic site reconnaissance. Glossary, supplier and book lists.

GPS Satellite Surveying by Alfred Leick (1995 Wiley)
  Textbook; covers GPS history, applications, and mathematics.

GPS: A Guide to the Next Utility
(1989 Trimble Navigation) 800-874-6253
  Introductory volume on GPS.

GPS World
Advanstar Publishers 908-549-3000
> Monthly. Rated listings of GPS models and new applications.

Cyrax 3-D laser surveying
Cyra Technology Oakland CA
www.cyra.com or 510-633-5000
info@cyra.com

Site Inventory

"Getting to Know a Place: Site Evaluation as a Starting Point for Green Design" by Alex Wilson (March 1998) *Environmental Building News*

USGS topographic maps
www.usgs.gov or 1-888-MAP-DEAL
USGS
> Web site lists available maps and related products, finds map sellers by region.

EPA Ecoregions maps
www.epa.gov/OST/standards/ecomap.html
www.epa.gov/grdwebpg/bailey/index.html
> Clear, detailed color maps showing regions of the United States based on ecological rather than political similarities. These boundaries are critical to many aspects of sustainability.

American Digital Cartography
800-236-7973 or www.adci.com
> Digital maps, including non-topo types, such as urban maps showing road and street widths.

Maptech
800-627-7236 or www.maptech.com
> Digital USGS maps. Terrain Navigator software, plus CD-ROMs with 200 USGS topographic maps per disk. Automates calculations of regional distances and elevations; draws topographic sections.

Guide to a Plant Inventory at a Historic Property by Margaret Coffin and Kristin Baker (1998 Olmsted Center for Landscape Preservation, Boston)
> Landscape history can be essential in deciding the goals of restoration.

Advances in Historical Ecology by William L. Balée (1998 Columbia Univ. Press, NYC)

Archaeologies of Landscape: Contemporary Perspectives by Wendy Ashmore and Arthur B. Knapp (1999 Blackwell Publishers, Malden MA)

Breaking Ground: Examining the Vision and Practice of Historic Landscape Restoration (1999 Old Salem Winston-Salem NC)

Cultural Landscape Bibliography by Katherine Ahern, Leslie H. Blythe and Robert R. Page (1992 U.S. National Park Service Cultural Landscape Program, Washington DC)

Earth Patterns: Essays in Landscape Archaeology by William M. Kelso and Rachel Most (1990 University Press of VA, Charlottesville VA)

Enduring Roots: Encounters with Trees, History, and the

American Landscape by Gayle B. Samuels (1999 Rutgers University, New Brunswick NJ)

Historic Landscape Directory: A Source Book of Agencies, Organizations, and Institutions by Lauren Meier and Sarah S. Boasberg (1991 U.S. National Park Service Preservation Assistance Division and U.S. ICOMOS Historic Landscapes Committee, Washington DC)

History on the Ground by M. W. Beresford (1998 Sutton Pub., Stroud UK)

Landscape Assessment: Values, Perceptions and Resources by Ervin H. Zube, Robert O. Brush and Julius Guy Fabos (1975 Halsted [Wiley])

Landscapes and Gardens for Historic Buildings by Rudy J. and Joy P. Favretti (1997 [2d Ed.] Alta Mira Press, Walnut Creek CA)

Landscapes in History by Philip Pregill and Nancy Volkman (1998 [2d Ed] Wiley)

Preserving Historic Landscapes: An Annotated Bibliography by Lauren Meier and Betsy Chittenden (1990 U.S. National Park Service Preservation Assistance Division, Washington DC)

The Landscape of Man: Shaping the Environment from Prehistory to the Present Day by Geoffrey Jellicoe and Susan Jellicoe (1995 [3d Ed.] Thames and Hudson)

Site Protection

Soil Mat Lifter
Monroe Ecological Services
990 Old Sumneytown Pike
Heartlesville PA 19430
610-287-0671
> A commercial version of the forest-sod-lifting machine described on page 45.

Caring for Our Land by Carol Greene (Enslow Publishers, Hillside NJ)

Checklist for Sustainable Landscape Management by J. D. van Mansvelt and M. J. van der Lubbe (1999 Elsevier) (European Union report AIR3-CT93-1210)

Connectivity in Landscape Ecology by Karl-Friedrich Schreiber (1987 Conference Proceeding of the International Association of Landscape Ecology) (1988 F. Schöningh., Paderborn, Germany)

Developing a Land Conservation Strategy by George D. Davis and Thomas R. Duffus (1987 Adirondack Land Trust, Elizabethtown NY)

Greenline Parks: Land Conservation Trends for the Eighties and Beyond by Marjorie R. Corbett and Michael S. Batcher (1983 National Parks and Conservation Association, 1701 18th St. NW, Washington DC 20009)

Landscape Ecology: Theory and Application by Zeev Naveh

and Arthur S. Lieberman (1994 [2ᵈ Ed.] Springer-Verlag)

Landscape Protection Bibliography by Mary A. Vance (1988 Vance Bibliographies *A 949*, Monticello IL)

Making Educated Decisions: A Landscape Preservation Bibliography by Charles A. Birnbaum, Cheryl Wagner, and Jean S. Jones (1994 U.S. National Park Service Preservation Assistance Division, Washington DC)

Preparing a Landscaping Ordinance, Report no. 431 by Wendelyn A. Martz and Marya Morris (1990 American Planning Association Planning Advisory Service, Chicago IL)

Protected Landscapes: A Guide for Policy-makers and Planners by P. II. C. Lucas (1992 International Union for Conservation of Nature, Chapman and Hall NYC)

Protected Landscapes : The United Kingdom Experience by Duncan Poore and Judy Poore (1987 Great Britain Countryside Commission, Manchester UK)

Saving America's Countryside: A Guide to Rural Conservation by Samuel N. Stokes, A. Elizabeth Watson, and Shelley S. Mastran (1997 [2ᵈ Ed.]) Johns Hopkins)

Saving the Prairie, Two Days at a Time (1974 Save the Tallgrass Prairie, Inc., Shawnee Mission KS)

The Economic Valuation of Landscape Change by José Manuel L. Santos (1998 Edward Elgar publ. Northampton MA)

The Economics of Landscape and Wildlife Conservation by Stephan Dabbert (1998 CAB International, NYC)

The Funny Thing about Landscape: Cautionary *Tales for Environmentalists* by Jay Appleton (1991 Book Guild, Lewes UK)

The Legal Landscape by Richard C. Smardon and James Karp (1993 Van Nostrand-Reinhold)

Wilderness by Design: Landscape Architecture and the National Park Service by Ethan Carr (1998 University of Nebraska Press, Lincoln)

Land Development Checklist for Environmental Concerns by Greater Grand Rapids Home Builders Association, Grand Rapids MI (Address unknown.)

U.S. Landscape Ordinances: An Annotated Reference Handbook by Buck Abbey (publisher unknown). Info or order call 212-850-6336.

"Land Conservation"
www.mayolawfirm.com/Conservation/home.html
  Mayo Law Firm site lists books, legal decisions, nonprofits and trusts, links on legal aspects of land conservation.

Site Protection: Vegetation

Preventing Construction Damage to Municipal Trees
Milwaukee Forestry Division

841 North Broadway, Room 804
Milwaukee WI 53202
  Detailed manual including sample specifications; for sale by the City.

Trees and Development: A Technical Guide to Preservation of Trees During Land Development by Nelda Matheny and James R. Clark (1998 International Society of Arboriculture, POB 3129, Champaign IL 61826; 217-355-9411 or www.ag.uiuc.edu/~isa)

Trees and Building Sites: Proceedings of an International Workshop on Trees and Buildings by Dan Neely & Gary Watson (Conference proceedings, May 31-June 2, 1995, International Society of Arboriculture)

Vancouver Tree By-laws
City of Vancouver BC
www.city.vancouver.bc.ca/commsvcs/planning
  Example of a thorough law governing protection of trees during construction.

Vegetation: Consultants

Certified Arborists List
International Society of Arborists
www.ag.uiuc.edu/~isa/arborists/arborist.html\

Vegetation: Native Plants

Guide to the Standard Floras of the World by D. G. Frodin (1990 Cambridge Univ. Press)

Native Plant Revegetation Guide for Colorado
Colorado State Parks
http://elbert.state.co.us/cnap/publications
  Probably applicable to much of the Rockies.

The Landscape Restoration Handbook by Donald F. Harker (1999 [2ᵈ Ed.] Lewis Publishers [CRC Press] 800-272-7737)
  Extensive maps and species lists for native plants; covers the whole United States.

National Biological Information Infrastructure
www.nbii.gov/
  Gateway to government and private sources of data about biodiversity, native plants, and most other biology data.

Invasive Plants, Changing the Landscape of America: Factbook
U.S. Government Printing Office
www.access.gpo.gov/su_docs/sale.html
202-512-1800 or

National Strategy for Invasive Plant Management
http://refuges.fws.gov/FICMNEWFiles/NatlWeedStrategyTOC.html
  www.nbii.gov/ also has information and links on a limited number of invasive species.

Edison Electric Institute
www.eei.org

Information on electric utilities, with a clear industry slant. Guidelines for easement maintenance.

Utility Impact

Interlocking Concrete Pavement Institute
Washington DC
202-712-9036 or icpi@bostromdc.com
> Publishes *Interlocking Concrete Pavement Magazine*, quarterly trade journal. Information on all aspects of interlocking pavers and machinery for handling them; ads list suppliers and contractors.

Cellular Tower Coalition
www.cellulartower.com
> Alternatives to communications towers are discussed on several Web sites, which is somewhat ironic. This one has excellent links and news.

Cellular Telecommunications Industry Association
www.wow-com.com/professional/siting/index.com
> Industry views; the FCC also has a site, www.fcc.gov.

EMR Alliance
www.cruzio.com
> Health concerns of electromagnetic radiation.

Municipal Research and Services Center
www.mrsc.org/legal/telecomm/tcapage.htm
> Among other issues, concerns about cell towers have been raised in this professional discussion group.

Energy Generation

Home Power
> Bi-monthly magazine

Tools

Hand Tools for Landscape and Arboriculture
A. M. Leonard
Piqua OH
800-543-8955 or www.amleo.com
> Wide range of horticulture, arboriculture, and landscape tools, machinery, books, and supplies. See also Resources for Principle 7.

Heal Injured Sites

And they shall build the old wastes and repair the waste cities, the desolation of many generations.

—Isaiah 61:4

In a consumer society, landscape development too often becomes a form of consumption. As development sprawls outward along an ever-expanding urban fringe, forests are leveled and farms destroyed to make way for cul-de-sacs, backyards, business parks, and, of course, acres and acres of parking.

This paradigm must be rethought before this continent is paved from sea to shining sea. Instead of *consuming* virgin landscape to make a place to live and work, start to think in terms of *recycling* existing sites. In particular, degraded sites in cities and older suburbs can be rendered fit again for new uses. At the same time, managed growth must preserve the farms, forests, and natural areas surrounding the cities.

There are various tested models of growth management, of which the Oregon model of greenbelts or "urban growth boundaries" around cities is probably the best known. Such initiatives lie, of course, in the realm of politics and land-use planning, not landscape construction. But landscape construction that recycles existing sites has its own role to play in reinhabiting waste places and making them as attractive to live in as they once were.

The focus of Chapter 1 was methods of protecting undamaged sites and of minimizing damage to them. The techniques in this chapter are useful in restoring sites (or portions of sites) damaged by prior use or during the process of construction. These techniques may occasionally apply to healthy landscapes, too, but are most important because they offer help for abused landscapes—what most of us would consider wastelands. Fortunately, landscapes, like people, have a remarkable ability to heal, and numerous precedents exist for turning even wastelands into gardens.

Turn Wastelands into Gardens

Urban and suburban landscapes may be degraded in various ways, from minor damage to Superfund sites. For this book, we consider three levels of damage (in order of severity), recognizing that there is some overlap:

- Derelict sites—damage to health and structure, but not particularly toxic
- Brownfields, including contained landfills
- Toxic waste sites

Discussed in This Chapter:

- Types of sites requiring restoration
- Evaluating whether restoration is appropriate
- Social and organizational aspects of site restoration
- Structural restoration techniques
- Restoring soil to health
- Using plants in site restoration
- Getting professional help for heavy-duty site toxicity

Derelict Sites

Every community has its derelict sites that, while not actually toxic, may be stripped of topsoil, littered with debris, and capable of supporting only noxious weeds. Buildings or paving covers some of these sites. From a real-estate point of view the structures "improve" the site, but from an ecological perspective they form compacted or impervious surfaces. As such, derelict sites cause harm without necessarily harboring toxic waste: they prevent recharging of aquifers and seal off the soil, supporting neither oxygen-replenishing plants nor wildlife habitat. For derelict sites, revitalizing the soil may be enough to return the site to a condition where normal gardening techniques work once more. Removal or retrofitting of excess structures to increase the area of available habitat is also a realistic and promising approach to these damaged but low-toxicity sites.

Brownfields

Brownfields are polluted lands—"the neglected sites of the postindustrial landscape," in the words of Niall Kirkwood, landscape architecture professor at the Harvard Graduate School of Design. Brownfield sites suffer from polluted soil or groundwater or both; one type of brownfield is the landfill, where pollution-prone materials are deliberately stockpiled. The EPA defines brownfields as "abandoned, idled or under-used industrial/commercial facilities where expansion or redevelopment is complicated by real or perceived environmental contamination."[1]

Landscape construction can play an active role in reclaiming these sites, usually in conjunction

Figure 2.1. Brownfields take up large areas in most modern cities. Neither society nor the environment can afford this waste, and restoring the potentially toxic sites is a priority and a challenge. PHOTO: Eric Carman.

with engineering solutions. Damage is greater than found on derelict sites and requires special techniques for reclamation. In addition to significant structural repair, these techniques include the use of special plants that actively remove toxins ("phytoremediation") and newly developed techniques of "manufacturing" soils.

Kirkwood believes cleaning up brownfields could return landscape architecture to the original precepts of the profession: "the nineteenth-century vision that the landscape is the body and the lungs of the city. A lot of Frederick Law Olmsted's work," says Kirkwood, "was really environmental engineering—or what used to be called sanitary engineering. His Emerald Necklace [in Boston] is essentially a drainage project. At the end of this century landscape architects have the opportunity to look back and reconsider our roots in issues of health, infrastructure, and open space—the Olmstedian concept of regenerating the city."

Recognition of brownfields' potential value, both for the environment and for the landscape professions, has been slow to dawn but is growing rapidly today. Until recently, redevelopment of these abandoned, polluted industrial sites has been stymied by various concerns. Brownfield owners were liable for any site contamination, even if it existed long before they purchased the site. Recently, however, federal and state governments have moved to streamline regulations governing brownfield redevelopment. Such states as Massachusetts have initiated their own brownfields-cleanup programs, and banks have begun lending money for sites that were previously deemed untouchable. In March 1998 the *New York Times* reported that a small army of consultants is emerging to address the 6,500 brownfields in and around New York City alone. Nationally, some 450,000 such sites are waiting to be returned to some productive use—and funding is increasingly available for this purpose.

Toxic Sites

Finally, there are sites such as those covered by the EPA's Superfund. On these toxic sites, landscape construction is not the primary solution to site damage. Only after highly technical remediation of the site by environmental engineering might surface landscape construction be appropriate. Remediation and restoration of sites at this level are outside the scope of this book. For this category of injured sites, this chapter offers sources of technical information and referral to consultants.

Balance the Environmental Costs and Benefits of Restoration

Restoring landscapes costs money, energy, labor, and time. Hindsight is clear: Avoiding contamination in the first place would have been much cheaper. But faced with undeniably injured landscapes, choices must be made. There are both economic and ecological limits to what can be restored. There are places where only full restoration to preindustrial conditions is worth doing, and others where any remediation is better than nothing. Not all technologies are appropriate for all restoration sites, or for the communities in which they exist. As with most sustainable practices, site-specific is the key concept. The following guidelines may help in decision making.

Site Restoration Is Usually Appropriate if:

- Disturbance is the result of human land use or changes in land use (construction, grazing, mining, logging, dumping, abandoned structures or sites, off-road vehicles, regional economic decline, etc.).

- Use of the *restored* site can prevent the need to develop or disturb a *healthy* site.

- "Recruitment" (regrowth and spread from natural sources such as relic seeds in existing soil) can be a major part of the strategy.

- Restoration costs are likely to yield long-term savings by stopping erosion, rebuilding productive soils, buffering or treating noise or air/water pollution, or protecting threatened species.

- Restoration is legally required, especially as a condition for permitting a particular land use, with costs to be borne by the parties who profit (e.g., mining restoration).

- The site has strong cultural significance, as in national and historic parks, or was significant prior to becoming degraded.

- Degraded wetlands, estuaries, or aquifer recharge zones are involved.

Site Restoration *May* Be Worth Considering if:

- Disturbance is a result of disaster "provoked" by humans (landslides due to abuses of soil, topography, or drainage; floods due to failed "flood control," etc.).

- Restoration will yield economic or aesthetic results valued by people (but of no particular ecological value).

- Restoration work can be used to create jobs and educate workers or to support a local industry (a native-plant nursery, for example).

- Restoration work can involve community participation, increasing community cohesion and identity.

- Restoration can educate community members about sustainability through the planning and fieldwork processes or through activities at the completed site.

Site Restoration Is Usually Not Practical or Appropriate if:

- Disturbance is the result of natural processes not accelerated by humans.

- The site is so small that outside influences will overwhelm the restoration effort.

- The true cause of disturbance is off-site, and there is no likelihood of cooperation from the owner of the source site.

- The so-called "restoration" is cosmetic (disguising a persistent problem, not-selfmaintaining).

- Restoration requires major use of materials, such as wild-dug plants or imported topsoil, whose removal damages other sites.

- Restoration cannot be expected to sustain itself without long-term intensive maintenance, irrigation, or similar intervention. (Maintenance during the 1–2 year establishment period should be expected; minor periodic maintenance over a longer period may also be needed.)

- Restoration defers the real problem onto another site or into the future (in which case, it is probably cosmetic).

- Restoration may attract poaching, destructive/motorized site access, illegal use, or other problems, unless these can be monitored and prevented.

- Costs of restoration is excessively high, even when figured as life-cycle costs and taking environmental services, intangibles, and job creation into account.

Involve the Community in Site Restoration

Abandonment of defunct industries and deteriorated neighborhoods has created a desperate need to turn old sites to new uses. A case in point is the city of Baltimore's plan to demolish 800 vacant rowhouses in two inner-city neighborhoods. Only a quarter of the resulting sites would be developed as housing; most would be transformed into open greenspace. The challenge, in Baltimore and elsewhere, is to effect this transformation in as affordable and as environmentally sound a manner as possible.

Clearly, such transformations rely on both social and technical solutions. To understand the technical approach, which is where landscape construction is usually most involved, it is essential to know the social *context* in which these techniques are invented, communicated, and used. As infill development and neighborhood revitalization become more common steps toward sustainability, we expect that a growing percentage of the landscape professional's clients will be community groups, rather than top-down agency or commercial entities. The techniques appropriate in community-based recycling of derelict spaces will include both conventional and unusual ones, and the contractor or designer who wants to be part of this process will need to learn and adapt.

Know the Site's History

The concept of restoring something implies going back to an original condition. For something as complex as a landscape, knowing what condition was "original" is not always simple. Sites are living, changing entities; both natural succession and human land-use change most sites over time.

It is important to distinguish between *historic* restoration, which attempts to re-create the site at a particular point in time, and *environmental*

restoration, which attempts to restore site health. Both forms of restoration have their purpose and overlap significantly. However, health is a much more dynamic goal than period restoration. Consider the human equivalent: the health of a sixty-year-old can be restored; the sixty-year-old cannot be restored to being sixteen. (Landscapes can be set back in time much more than people can, but the re-creation is never exact.)

A person who recovers from ill health continues, once healthy, to age and change. So does an environmentally restored landscape. Suppose a forested site was developed, abused, and left derelict. Restoring it to health would primarily mean restoring its ability to support life. The restored parcel might look like a meadow and still be "restored" in terms of health. It might also, given many years, use its restored health to grow back to forest. People could, of course, also choose to restore its health by planting forest trees. That would restore it both environmentally and historically. Thus, restoration requires both knowledge (What was the site before? How did it develop?) and decision (Should the site be restored to its condition in 1800, or in 1492? Is the goal health or history?). In both knowledge and decision making, the local community's input can be indispensable.

No matter what kind of restoration is set as a goal, the knowledge on which such a decision is based almost always includes history. This includes knowledge of natural processes, as well as knowledge of human land use. For this reason, we have included a number of resources to help gauge the historical influences on a site.⊃ Conventionally associated only with historic preservation, these resources are essential in understanding how an injured or drastically altered site got that way, which is prerequisite to deciding what to do to restore it. Environmental and historic restoration may be separate goals; but the environmental past of a site is seldom separate from human influences. This is especially true of the derelict lands most in need of restoration, since they are usually the result of human abuse or neglect.

Start an Urban Barn Raising

Abandoned lands contribute heavily to the plight of older cities. Transforming these lands, regenerating or restoring them, is crucial to restoring the human communities that have been abandoned or banished on these unpromising sites. One individual who has a vision of how this restoration might occur is Karl Linn. Landscape architect, psychologist, and social activist, Linn shares widespread concern about the decline of inner cities. Shrunken populations (some of them, like Baltimore, still shrinking) result in tracts of derelict land where factories and older housing stock have been torn down. While teaching at the University of Pennsylvania and the New Jersey Institute of Technology, Linn worked with inner-city residents to construct "neighborhood commons" that functioned as parks and playgrounds. Conventional, horticultural approaches to regreening the inner city have largely failed, relying on expensively installed and maintained specimen plantings in very limited areas. Drawing on the experience of grassroots groups like New York City's Green Guerillas, Linn has explored other approaches.

Linn proposed that derelict tracts be turned into urban farms or wildflower meadows, at least in the interim until further development. His methods rely primarily on natural plant succession, with help from humans, to improve the soil and transform neighborhood appearance. Linn envisioned Newark (which many people stigmatize as America's most squalid city) becoming "the Garden City of the Garden State of New Jersey." Bringing together Newark's vast acreage of urban land with an ecological vision of sustainable urban habitat could serve as a model for communities around the world. Linn's vision, not yet implemented in Newark, is expressed in his brief text, *From Rubble to Restoration: Sustainable Habitats Through Urban Agriculture.* Published nearly two decades ago by the Earth Island Institute, it is still pertinent.⊃ Now based in Berkeley CA, Linn has been working with community groups to create city gardens and farms in the Bay Area.

Linn's approach to restoration, and other approaches that are community-based, are critically important to the success of urban restoration in particular. They parallel environmental protection efforts in less-developed countries, where participation of local and indigenous people has proved vital to success.[2] Clearly, they also link with the community garden concept, a well-established movement in many parts of the world.

Follow the Lead of Community Garden Groups

One group Linn works with is the San Francisco League of Urban Gardeners (SLUG), one of the country's most active community gardening groups. SLUG's work crews have constructed numerous neighborhood gardens, plus San Francisco's only working farm, the 4-acre St. Mary's Urban Youth Farm in low-income Hunter's Point. St. Mary's has utterly transformed a seemingly blighted inner-city site.

Because the site (adjacent to a housing project) had been used by contractors for dumping, it was littered with spoil dirt and waste concrete. Old refrigerators, wrecked cars, and household garbage had found their way to the site as well. SLUG workers filled several 16-foot-long dumpsters with this debris and broke ground for the urban farm. Today the site features thirty raised garden beds for the residents' use and for distribution to food kitchens in other low-income communities. There are approximately 100 fruit trees. Gardens provide herbs for a cottage industry line of salad vinegars, made by local residents. A composting operation at the farm will produce and sell garden mulch from yard waste collected throughout San Francisco. While many urban Americans struggle to understand even the concept of food production, St. Mary's Urban Youth Farm is busy doing it.

Grassroots rehabilitation of derelict sites by the community garden movement is quiet but widespread, a potent force for site restoration. Community gardening organizations are based on the

Figure 2.2. St. Mary's Farm relinks urban residents with the land and their own skills. Most cities could benefit from similar community landscapes; where soil is not toxic, they produce food as well as social activity. PROJECT: SLUG. PHOTO: Karl Linn.

thesis (quite foreign to this supermarket culture) that food should be grown in cities close to where people live. Community gardens already account for thousands of gardens around the United States, most of them in major cities. In Philadelphia alone, there are approximately 2,000 such gardens.

In some European cities the land devoted to "allotment" gardens is significant. A 1980 survey in England and Wales found only two main types of *urban* soils: sterile soils disturbed by construction, engineering, and dumping and the fertile soils of community gardens. The survey described allotment garden soils as "man-made humus soils which have an abnormally thick A horizon of dark well-structured topsoil from particularly deep cultivation (double digging) coupled with heavy organic manuring."[3] The survey is dramatic evidence that humans can play an important role in reinstating site health in urban areas.

Much can be learned from community gardeners about building soil on degraded urban sites. The two most common approaches are compost (including composted manure) and "green manure" crops that add organic matter, improve soil texture, and aid drainage. Details of these techniques are discussed in the following section.

Despite their immense value, urban community gardens are seldom safe from development pressure. New York Mayor Rudolph Giuliani recently coerced community garden and environmental groups into paying $4.2 million to ransom 11 acres of gardens they had revived from

Figure 2.3. Peralta Community Art Gardens in Berkeley CA is a decorative meeting place made by neighbors from leftover land and materials. PROJECT: Community & Karl Linn. PHOTO: Karl Linn.

trash-strewn abandoned lots. Giuliani equated the gardeners' efforts to hold on to the lots with communism and did his best to create conflict with people on the eight-year waiting list for public housing. Like the environment-versus-jobs ploy, setting community landscapes against community housing is the worst sort of dishonesty and shortsightedness.[4]

Invest in a Garden Festival Restoration

Urban barn raisings and community gardens are grassroots approaches to healing derelict sites. A more capital-intensive and ambitious but nevertheless valid approach is that of the European garden festival, by which abused sites (both derelict and brownfield) are redeveloped as large, themed public gardens. Festival gardens are open for a period of months, after which the garden infrastructure is "recycled" as parks, open space for housing, and for other uses. Essentially, such festivals use landscape design and ornamental planting as a catalyst for reinvestment. Starting in Germany after World War II, garden festivals were effective in rehabilitating bombed-out cities to productive use. The concept was then exported to other European sites, including Britain's urban and industrial brownfields.[5] Despite high costs, they show how much can be accomplished quickly when a society decides to reinvest in its damaged sites.

Nearly all of the British garden festivals were constructed on industrially degraded sites. Portions of the Liverpool Garden Festival of the 1980s, for example, were built on lifeless spoil tips from coal mining and on inner-city garbage dumps. The "Nature in the City" portion of that festival, devoted to showcasing the native plants of Britain, was built on a mountain of garbage that covered some 18 acres and stood more than 100 feet high—the highest point in the entire site.[6] "The people of Liverpool through the event were made aware," wrote one festival designer, "that you could transform a totally useless, severely polluted area of land into a major visitor attraction of international standing."[7]

One recent example of a British garden festival developed on a brownfield site was Ebbw Vale in South Wales. The 57-hectare (141-acre) site of this festival had been an air-polluting steel mill, long since defunct. Once the mill was demolished and the adjacent mine shafts capped, the Welsh Development Agency reclaimed the site at a cost of £20 million. The festival garden included such amenities as a 5-million-gallon lake and a 120-foot waterfall. Some 33,000 trees and shrubs and 550,000 flowers and other plants were brought in. *Landscape Design* magazine described the site this way: "Where there used to be satanic mills and furnaces there is now a fantastic array of lakes, gardens, floral displays, marquees, exhibitions, and fun rides." After the six-month duration of the festival, the festival's landscape infrastructure was earmarked for the development of a business park.[8]

The garden festivals, although a very effective concept for the rehabilitation of degraded sites, are costly and may fail to meet ecological goals. As fast-track projects they require the installation of semimature trees and other plantings, trucked in from distant nurseries for quick effect. Like other social issues affecting the landscape reconstruction, the decision about speed of restoration is seldom a simple one. Instant landscape, however, is clearly a manifestation of a commodity-driven society. Emphasizing speed strongly affects the choice of techniques available and may rule out the gradual approaches of community-based reclamation. Instant plantings also can *mis*educate festival visitors: paradoxically, they obscure any understanding of natural plant succession on the site over time. By contrast, if a community accepts the concept that built landscapes grow and evolve, it has an expanded range of cost-effective and ecologically sound methods available in reclaiming derelict sites.

Educating the public about landscape ecological processes is integral to the Earth Center in South Yorkshire, England. Although it is on the scale of a garden festival, its stated mission is "to promote understanding of sustainable development and to help people become involved in the process of achieving it in their own lives." A theme park aimed at presenting concepts of sustainable development in a stimulating and entertaining way, the Earth Center is—appropriately enough—built on a brownfield site, a pair of abandoned collieries (coal mines) on the River Don near the town of Doncaster. It is the biggest landscape project in the United Kingdom based on sustainable principles—"to demonstrate," in the words of Andrew Grant, the landscape architect, "how regenerating land can provide rich opportunities for play, production of food, wildlife, and general public enjoyment."[9]

In designing the Earth Center, according to Director of Sustainability Dan Epstein, only con-cepts justifiable in terms of sustainability were accepted. At the heart of the Earth Center's policy for materials specification was the use of local materials, suppliers, and labor. This minimized environmental costs of transporting materials from distant sites—and bolstered the local economy. Many materials came from the site itself: For pedestrian paving, the design team used burnt coal shale—a pinkish by-product of the coal-washing activities that had taken place at the collieries—producing an attractive surfacing at very little cost.[10]

The planting scheme at the Earth Center was the antithesis of the "instant landscape." Instead, "the Earth Center landscape is designed to make people look at, think about, and react to the issues that affect our future landscapes," says Andrew Grant. "It is to be a visual and ecological response to the process of regeneration on this site, and is deliberately planned to evolve and redefine its character well into the next century."[11] The process of plant succession is front and center here. Accepting that the appearance of the landscape will change over time contrasts both with the instant landscape approach and with the attempt to "freeze" landscapes in a certain stage of development through labor-intensive maintenance and repeated applications of chemicals.

Despite their different methods, the Earth Center and the garden festivals have one thing in common: a public celebration of the ability to regenerate blighted landscapes.

Figure 2.4. The Earth Center, a Yorkshire UK "environmental theme park," demonstrates many of the techniques noted in this book, including water harvesting, on-site sewage processing, and recycled building materials. PROJECT and PHOTO: Center staff.

Make a Virtue of the Necessity for Landfills

Landfills, unlike many other brownfields, are created deliberately and at taxpayer expense. They serve one necessary purpose—containing the enormous quantities of waste generated by resource consumption—but can become a land-use problem themselves if simply filled up and closed. The government agencies responsible for landfills can often collaborate with other agencies to get an important second use out of closed landfill sites. Restoring these sites for public use may be cheaper than acquiring urban land for parks and recreation facilities. Not only does landfill restoration get a second use from the land, it solves the problem of dumps as eyesores. (A future based on recycling and reduction of use, in which huge dumps were a thing of the past, would clearly be even better. This process is

beginning in some cities. Until then, landfill restoration fulfills a real need.)

Many examples of parks on landfills already exist around the United States. One large urban example is Danehy Park: at 55 acres, it added 20 percent to the total open space for Cambridge MA. The popular park, which features a variety of turf and naturalized areas, also incorporated at least one recycled material—ground glass—in its construction. The ADA-accessible path around the park was created from "glassphalt," a mix of asphalt and ground glass. (See page 204 and Figure 6.12.)

Landfills have been given new lives as golf courses in Charlotte NC, Phoenix AZ, and St. Petersburg FL, among other places. Perhaps the most spectacular of these golf-on-garbage courses—and at 425 acres, the largest—is Harborside International on Chicago's South Side. It comprises two eighteen-hole courses together with a 45-acre practice facility and a golf academy. Harborside lies on a raised plateau in the flat Illinois landscape, built up of fly ash from an adjacent garbage incinerator shut down by the federal Clean Air Act. To create new land atop the landfill, a recycled product was used: processed sewage sludge from nearby Chicago Metropolitan Water Reclamation District facilities. Few visitors would guess, however, that anything but the very finest materials were used to construct Harborside, a public links-style course with amenities more typical of a private club. Certainly, no one could fail to be moved by the beauty of its sinuous greens meandering through tawny grassed mounds and steep hillocks where fescue and rye, unmown, wave in the unfailing breeze. Harborside has won several awards, including the 1996 Superior Achievement for Excellence award from the American Academy of Environmental Engineering.

One hot-off-the-press landfill project serves as a particularly potent example of how many functions—ecological, social, and economic—a well-reclaimed site can serve. Camp Dresser & McKee (CDM) has parlayed its experience with Danehy Park into several other landfill-closure projects, says its vice president, John Kissida. CDM has developed landfills as office parks, sports fields, and major parking facilities. One project, however, stands out for its integration of functions: the 57-acre landfill at Yarmouth MA, on Cape

Figure 2.5. Danehy Park, once a landfill, is a popular public landscape in Cambridge MA, and incorporates art made from recycled materials. PROJECT: Camp Dresser McKee/City of Cambridge. PHOTO: John Kissida.

Figure 2.6. Harborside International golf course makes beautiful reuse of a landfill. Industrial buildings in the background show the context of this massive site restoration. PROJECT: Nugent Associates. PHOTO: Sally Hughes.

Cod. Federal and state regulators forced the closure of the forty-year-old dump, which, among other problems, was located in one of Cape Cod's scarce aquifer recharge zones.

Through a community-based, participatory process, CDM got unanimous town approval for $12 million to create a golf course, park, bike path, and the modern replacement for the dump—a combined residential and construction/demolition waste and recycling facility. Revenues from the construction waste facility offset the cost by over $1 million in the first year; a state grant, a no-interest state landfill closure loan, and revenue from the golf course, plus phased construction, brought the economic costs even lower. The first sewage effluent reuse project in Massachusetts, under strict purity guidelines to protect the underlying aquifer, provides nearly half the water (and fertilizer nutrients) for the golf course—a matter of considerable importance on the Cape, which has limited potable water supplies.

Yarmouth is an impressive example of multifunctionality in site restoration. What is even more important, perhaps, is that it is *not* utterly unusual—many other restoration projects have taken the same approach in different, site-specific ways. We are convinced that this kind of synergy, among public and private entities and between ecosystems and human efforts, is the last best chance of the industrialized world to adapt to sustainability.

Recognize Agricultural and Rural Restoration

Urban and industrial restoration projects are often dramatic, gaining media coverage because they restore lost services to downtrodden neighborhoods. In terms of sheer acreage, however, there is probably more restoration activity *outside* the city. Some of this, associated with mining, deals with sites very similar to urban industrial land, but often at a huge scale. Reforestation of recent or historic timber clear-cuts can involve small armies of workers, as can rangeland restoration after overgrazing.[12] And although agricultural fields may seem benign, many have suffered fertility and topsoil loss, or worse abuse. They too are candidates for restoration, especially where they were created by draining a wetland. (Wetlands restoration is discussed in Principle 4.)

These site restoration projects have much in common with their urban cousins but differ because of their scale and location. When hundreds or even thousands of acres are being restored, cost and practicality require simple methods. Some, like broadcast seeding, or prescribed burns in place of weeding or thinning, produce a naturalistic result. Other mass techniques, like forestry methods of inserting seedlings with a single shovel-cut at a rate of hundreds per day, result in a functional landscape, a forest restored for its next crop. Both these outcomes are accepted as appropriate to rural areas, where a highly designed landscape restoration might not fit.

Landscape architects and contractors may not often do this kind of large-scale, nonurban restoration, but they should be aware of it. Range management, reforestation, and mine reclamation specialists have an extensive repertoire of practical knowledge that can be invaluable, with some modification, on the kind of sites typically associated with landscape construction. The County Extension is often a good place to find regional expertise in large-scale restoration.

Use Techniques Appropriate to Both Community and Site

As the previous sections illustrate, there is a very wide range of approaches to site restoration. Tiny lots may be repaired by the loving hands of a few volunteers. Where abandonment of a major industry has left gaps in the community as big as a city park or shopping mall, significant funding and professional work are required. Thus, the techniques described in the next section must be adapted to the community as well as to the site.

Abandoned land often goes hand in hand with meager resources: such a community needs simple, inexpensive methods, cooperation, and patience. Compost and planting to restore some health to the soil may be the only options that are initially feasible. A surprising amount can be done with well-planned volunteer labor, however, and some of the more intensive approaches can be scaled down. Inventive ways of funding such projects have been found by programs like the Massachusetts Heritage State Parks program or Philadelphia's linkage of public-art money to vacant site restoration.

Larger-scale restoration often involves the agencies of the larger community—municipal, state, or federal. Creativity and inventiveness apply in these projects, too, but methods and funding are inevitably different. It is more difficult, as an official agency or a nonresident investor, to win the local support that makes did-it-ourselves projects so powerful. Nonetheless, truly public projects can take on problems too big for individual neighborhoods, and many succeed extremely well. It is critical to avoid moving in and taking over. Also important is making site-specific adjustments to public standards set in distant offices. We urge anyone involved in such projects to incorporate community-based planning and participatory design into their work. The results of community choice linked to the methods available with serious reinvestment can be truly uplifting.

Thus the following list of techniques includes a range of approaches adaptable to various site and community needs and finances. Many successes in restoration have resulted from communities borrowing ideas from other places and improvising to suit their own situation.

Restore Landscape Structurally

Although healthy soil and vegetation are the most evident goals of site restoration, it is often necessary to deal first with *structural* damage to the site. This includes site topography and drainage, which may have been damaged by inappropriate grading or by erosion. It also includes the presence of impervious structures that interfere with environmental functions. The unique structural issues of capped landfills, and techniques for surface restoration of landfill sites, are also discussed in this section. Many emerging restoration methods address the damage caused when structural forms fail to integrate with ecological dynamics.

Figure 2.7. Conventional grading insists on uniform, planar slopes. Until recently, objections to this approach have been aesthetic, but recent research shows environmental disadvantages, too. PHOTO: H. J. Schor.

Figure 2.8. Landform grading creates forms that resist erosion by being in equilibrium and that provide increased habitat diversity and aesthetic appeal. Lifetime cost of creating and maintaining these forms is less than for conventional grading. PROJECT and PHOTO: H. J. Schor.

Restore Environmentally Appropriate Grading

Grading changes the surface shape of the Earth. Conventional thinking assumes that such changes are purely a matter of human convenience and aesthetics. But recent evidence, both scholarly and practical, shows that Earth-surface forms are a critical functional part of the environment. Partly because modern society tends to see all natural patterns as "random," the irregularities of landform surfaces are conventionally viewed as unimportant, even as nuisances. Nothing could be further from the truth.

Most conventional grading is based on straight lines, in plan or section or both. Such grading patterns produce level or near-level surfaces for human use and unvarying slopes on the "in-between" areas (such as road cuts or embankments).

Until recently, the acceptability of such large planar slopes was seldom questioned. Their grim shapes often raise public outcry because they are ugly, but engineers overrule these concerns with arguments about safety, slope failure, erosion, and cost. All of these, conventional thinking insists, require the mathematically regular patterns of conventional grading. The evidence suggests otherwise. Two possible alternatives are discussed in this section.

GRADE TO FOLLOW REGIONAL LANDFORMS

Horst Schor, whose Anaheim CA consulting firm specializes in what he calls "landform grading," began working on the issue while a senior vice president of the Anaheim Hills development company. Schor's interest in landforms stemmed from one-too-many denied planning permits.

"We, like every other developer," he says, "were taking natural (hilly) terrain and transforming it into rigid, mathematical shapes for building. It was a practice based on the idea: We've always done it that way." Public resistance to the stark ugliness of the results was a heated issue in Anaheim, and Schor himself didn't like the looks of the engineered slopes.

His solution was to study and photograph natural hill forms across the world and then to retrain his team of designers, engineers, surveyors, and contractors to construct landforms based on natural patterns. The bulldozer operator turned out to be the critical person in the process. When instructions down the chain of command failed to produce the intended results, Schor writes, "We finally had to go into the field and call a bulldozer operator off his machine, show him the drawings and photos and explain the ideas. 'Sure, I can do that. Why didn't you say that in the first place?'" was the response.[13]

The resulting slopes were carefully engineered but looked natural. Still, engineers and planning agencies were doubtful, if not hostile, at first. The engineers in particular predicted that the naturalistic slopes would cause *increased* erosion. Schor proved them wrong by landform-grading an experimental hillslope 70 feet high. On this experimental site, all the artificial drains and pipes usually required by code were deliberately left out. After three years of unusually heavy rains and no maintenance, the landformed slopes were in perfect uneroded condition. Similar-sized conventional slopes were gullied and severely damaged by the same rains.[14] In California, where developed land is regularly washed away in landslides, Schor's grading practices had immediate practical appeal and won acceptance both from professionals and from the public.

Schor has carefully documented the comparative cost of conventional and landform grading.[15] Because the idea is new, the first time a contractor is asked to do landform grading, the costs of learning (and of resistance to learning) can push costs up as much as 15 percent, in both the design and the construction phases. Once the learning curve is overcome, however, surveying costs average only 1 to 5 percent more than conventional methods, and design costs, 1 to 3 percent more. Construction costs (once the contractor is experienced) are typically only 1

percent higher than conventional grading. (GPS surveying may help; see page 34.)

Offsetting these costs are strong benefits. Construction costs were *reduced* by 20 percent on one project because landform grading required much less earthmoving in total. Contractors often like doing landform grading because it does not require extremely tight geometric control. For the developer, residential density is equal to conventionally graded sites (commercial sites, which demand huge level pads, may be 1 percent fewer over the whole site). Costly delays due to public opposition can be avoided. Buyers perceive landform grading as more attractive than conventional engineered surroundings, which can result in quicker return on investment, or higher values for the completed properties, or both.

Landform grading has been shown to decrease erosion and fits well with scientific theory about the geomorphologic evolution of natural slopes.[16] It clearly helps blend restored land with undisturbed areas. It seems likely that compared to flattened slopes, landformed slopes will revegetate more quickly and cost-effectively, since they offer a diversity of concave and convex, shaded and sunny, exposed and sheltered plant habitats.

Because of its combination of ecological and social benefits, landform grading deserves to be a major part of sustainable construction practice. It is applicable both to site restoration and to work at the edges of protected healthy sites. Whether it becomes a widespread standard, as the authors feel it should, depends in large part on educating construction, design, and planning professionals about it. "A willingness and an open mind to depart from old concepts are essential elements," says Schor. "Approving agencies must also be brought into the information dissemination process."[17]

Like porous paving (page 184) or bioengineering (page 100), landform grading remains underused despite nearly twenty years of well-documented results. Rethinking, retraining, and overcoming entrenched resistance are one-time hurdles that need to be surmounted in each firm, agency, or community. (Schor uses clay models of typical landforms, along with slides of natural hillsides, to help both design and field workers get a feel for the desired results.) A more general change is also required for these promising sustainable technologies to succeed: Slightly increased up-front costs must be viewed as investments with rich, long-term pay-offs, rather than as immediate gouges in the monetary bottom line.

GRADE LONG SLOPES IN STEPS

Another effective approach that avoids some problems of conventional grading is called the "stepped slope" method. Used on highway slopes in hilly topography from California to Appalachia, the stepped approach may also be applicable to other grading situations. Essentially, stepped slopes are small horizontal benches that are constructed as the slope is being graded—a modern version of the terraced slopes that has been used for centuries by traditional societies to practice agriculture on hillsides.

As water collects on each bench and begins to flow, it drops to the step below, dissipating its energy. Because it flows more slowly and puddles on each step, water falling on the slope has more time to infiltrate the soil, aiding plant establishment. Over time, the risers of the steps do erode, but this only deposits loose soil on the benches below and serves as a rooting medium for seeds. Once plants have revegetated and stabilized the slope, the steps will be difficult to detect.[18]

The steps are typically cut at about 2-foot vertical intervals; their width is in proportion to the slope ratio. The steps are cut with a bulldozer as the excavation is made. The steps should be cut with the dozer traveling in alternate directions so that material does not pile up at one end of the slope.[19] It is critical that the "tops" of the steps be truly level, or slope back into the hillside. Otherwise, erosion can actually be speeded.

An important benefit of the stepped-slope approach is that it typically costs no more than conventional construction methods. In fact, on some projects costs are reduced because the slopes are not fine graded after excavation. Change-orders have added the stepped-slope approach to contracts at no increase in price, according to one engineer with the Federal Highway Administration.[20]

Although designed to erode, stepped slopes must be able to stand long enough for vegetation to become established. John Haynes, an erosion-control specialist, has extensive experience with stepped slopes for Caltrans (California's highway department). Haynes has found that compost and mulch provide a means of protecting the soil while providing a nutrient source (see page 72). The steepness of many California highway cuts has not been an obstacle to the use of compost; Caltrans has applied wood-chip mulch on slopes up to 1.25:1. Vegetation, established in the protection of mulch, is important in stabilizing stepped slopes.

GRADE SUBSOIL, NOT TOPSOIL

Whatever form grading takes, always grade the *subsoil* to change site topography. Differences between subsoil and topsoil are discussed on page 77; topsoil should usually be stockpiled and reapplied to graded or otherwise altered areas. The top surface of the regraded subsoil must be several inches lower than the designed finish grade. This difference, usually about 6 inches, allows for topsoil to be respread; note that topsoil may expand or compact during stockpiling and replacement. The completed site has a blanket of topsoil over the structural subsoil. Avoid mixing subsoil into the topsoil blanket during spreading.

A common problem of subsoils, including many urban soils, is compaction. Probably the best single volume on problems and amelioration of urban soil is soil scientist Phillip Craul's *Urban Soil in Landscape Design*, which describes ways of ameliorating compaction. These include deep water-jetting and air injection, in which compressed air or water is injected to fracture the compressed soil; the fractures are then backfilled with some dry material such as vermiculite.[21] Applying humic acid will also loosen some soils.

Another approach—deep plowing or subsoiling, a technique used in agriculture for the destruction of clay pans—is applicable to urban soils. When pulled at a given depth by a farm tractor, the plow shatters the compacted soil, creating large pore spaces that aid water drainage, aeration, and root penetration. Two caveats: Subsoiling is not a permanent fix (it must be repeated every two to three years), and it cannot be used around trees and shrubs because of damage to the root systems.[22]

A related approach is the use of a backhoe to loosen the profile on construction sites; this approach loosens the soil more thoroughly than deep plowing or subsoiling. This technique must be carried out as construction nears completion but before the respreading of topsoil and final grading.[23]

NOTE: REGRADING AND WETLANDS

Poor grading often creates areas of standing water. If these ponding areas have persisted for a number of years, it may be important to find out whether they are legally classed as wetlands. Even if no regulatory situation exists, ponded water may be a desirable site feature or can become one with design help. Normally, however, badly engineered grading should be corrected as part of restoration.

Grading to eliminate *naturally* swampy or marshy ground is never sustainable and in most cases is illegal under the Wetlands Protection Act. Filling of wetlands, once an accepted practice, is a good example of how concerns for sustainability are changing landscape construction.

Remove Damaging Structures

Design and construction professionals are increasingly likely to find themselves called upon to *remove* existing structures as part of land restoration. Most structures have environmental costs: they are designed to keep out water and wildlife and to block or absorb sunshine. These costs are offset by human benefits when a structure is in active use. The same structure, abandoned or poorly used, has most of the costs without the benefits. Derelict houses in declining cities are just one example of how unwanted or failed structures hinder sustainable site use. On a much larger scale, the Army Corps of Engineers will soon *demolish* dams on rivers in Maine and Washington because they disrupt river wildlife, especially the economically valuable salmon.

Instead of removing some structures, it may be possible to use bioengineering methods to clothe them with plantable surfaces (Principle 3). These surfaces, including ecoroofs and greenwalls, can provide the air and water quality benefits of vegetation. They also replace hot, sterile structural surfaces with habitat area.

REMOVE EXCESS PAVING

Paved surfaces, in the United States at least, almost seem to grow by themselves, and a net *decrease* in paved area on a site or in a region has been nearly inconceivable to conventional thinkers. However, when a closed factory is renovated as shops, or a single firm takes over what was once several offices, parking needs may decrease. The formulas used by city planners to set the number of parking spaces required per structure frequently produce paved lots of which no more than a quarter is ever filled at one time (see page 174). Many writers on sustainability envision major reductions in single-occupant vehicles.[24] Changes like these will call for the restoration of paved areas.

Even where the demand for paved space has not decreased, pavement removal may be necessary. Where land is affected by increased runoff and erosion or by extremes of flooding and drought, successful restoration may depend on removing excess hard surfaces. For parking still in use, porous pavement may replace all or part of the impervious surface, and biofiltration may be used to cope with runoff on-site (see page 182).

On the Upper Charles River just outside Boston, impervious surfaces have been removed on a grand scale. Here, in the early 1990s, the Metropolitan District Commission (MDC) decided

Figure 2.9. The Upper Charles River was the site of miles of illegal paving. Note the ironic No Dumping sign. PHOTO: Carol R. Johnson Associates.

Figure 2.10. The site shown in Figure 2.9, with paving, trash, and signage replaced by restored vegetation and public access. PROJECT: Carol R. Johnson Associates. PHOTO: Dan Driscoll.

to reclaim several miles of abandoned, overgrown riverbank and turn it into a public greenway. There was just one problem: For years, businesses adjacent to the river had encroached on the banks, mostly by building impromptu parking lots. One stretch of the river contained ninety-two such encroachments. The MDC, with landscape architects Carol R. Johnson Associates, forced the encroachers to pay for pavement removal, soil rehabilitation, and planting. As of this writing, 3.5 miles of the Upper Charles riverbanks have been restored, with more to follow.[25] There is no doubt that the removal of these paved areas benefits the health of the riverbanks. Equally important, it has returned the land to its rightful use—a green riparian park for the enjoyment of Boston's citizens.

Reducing runoff at the *top* of a watershed is usually more effective than trying to combat erosion with expensive engineering *downstream*. Ownership boundaries often hamper this approach, however. The pursuit of sustainability is likely to increase the pressure for watershed-wide cooperative control of stormwater, including removal or replacement of impervious paving on upstream sites.

In restoration, what is *under* the paved surface is equally important as the pavement itself. Standard paving specifications require the removal of all organic soils and the placement of gravel "base course." These materials are highly compacted and chemically infertile. For revegetation, base course must be removed along with the asphalt or concrete surfacing, and the subsoil then tested and amended before planting can be successful.

When paving is removed, conventional practice (or simply habit) is to dump the removed materials. Sustainability requires better practices. Both asphalt and concrete can be recycled (Principle 6) using high- or low-tech methods, and rubble is potentially reusable in some cases. Base-course aggregate is so cheap at present that it is seldom reused. Sieving the aggregate could in theory make it equivalent to newly mined gravel; where transportation costs are high, on-site reuse may become practical.

REPLACE OVERENGINEERED DRAINAGE STRUCTURES

Conventional drainage practice focuses on quickly getting water away from desirable structures (especially buildings and roads), often at the expense of adjacent land and aquifers. Water that is considered "excess" is piped or shunted into ditches for delivery to a surface body of

Figure 2.11. Rigid structures protect only the soil they can shield from water. Along the hard edges, erosive undercutting is actually increased. PHOTO: Kim Sorvig.

water. This deprives the land of infiltrated rainfall and increases the eroding, sediment-carrying and flooding power of the runoff. The true source of these problems may be the engineered structures themselves. Restoration of downstream lands and water bodies may not be possible without removing the structures.

Many "hard" erosion and flood control structures deflect and concentrate the force of the water onto other surfaces. Usually these surfaces are the soft soils just beyond the edges of the hardened structure, which erode quickly and undermine the structure, causing its collapse. In extreme climates, many municipally funded concrete drainage structures break down from undercutting and weathering *many years before* the bond issue debt is paid off.[26]

Where poorly planned grading *dams* natural drainage, stagnant water may produce anaerobic soil conditions and drowned plants. Examples are often seen along interstate highways. Where the road is raised on fill, cutting off drainage in surrounding low places, eerie dead forests stand like ghosts of misdeeds past.

Drainage methods that infiltrate more and harden less are the best candidates for restoration and sustainability. These include bioengineering and appropriate planting (Principle 3), the use of porous paving materials and infiltration structures (Principle 5), and nonconventional or landform grading (page 70). In all of these cases, removal of damaging structures may be the first step in restoration.

Create Landscapes on Landfills

Landfills are structurally unique in the built environment. Sealed on all sides to isolate the polluting materials abandoned in them, they are huge containers buried in the landscape, containers that cannot be moved and must not be punctured. These structural characteristics have resulted in some inventive techniques for restoring the surfaces over landfills. Some of these techniques are also applicable to other sites where buried obstacles or toxics lie close to the surface.

As old landfills close, they present remarkable opportunities for every community to develop new open space. "If you cap the landfill correctly, you've got a park," says veteran landfill restoration specialist Bill Young. Old landfills are continually closing. They present blank slates for what might be called "the postconsumer landscape": golf courses, wildlife preserves, and community parks built on "recycled" land. Developing landfills relieves the pressure to develop virgin sites for these uses.

Recycling land is no substitute for waste-stream reduction, even though it helps protect other sites and makes wastelands useable again. Landfill closure as presently conceived in North America is at best a transitional step, better than abandonment but not truly sustainable. Entombing garbage within a clay liner, cut off from water and air, preventing natural processes of decay, is fundamentally questionable. As solid-waste authorities find more effective resource-recovery and recycling methods—or, for that matter, as consumers buy fewer throwaway products—landfills and landfill restoration may fade into history. These are social and technological issues far beyond the scope of this book. What *is* within the realm of landscape construction is the ability to make the most of the new site created atop the cap. Reclaiming this habitat, even temporarily, can make a significant contribution to the environment.

Although the technology of capping and sealing landfills is now well developed (and regulated), the options for developing and planting the cap are still wide open. The question of where to get the massive amounts of topsoil needed for covering and planting a landfill is discussed under "Manufactured Soil," page 86. Structurally, landfills present one important landscape construction problem: Are plant roots a threat to the capped structure of the landfill?

Trees versus the Cap?

Trees have long been taboo on landfills because of the supposed danger of their roots punching through the clay cap, allowing dangerous gases to escape and rainwater to enter the landfill. (In fact, laws in some states ban trees from landfills.) Conventionally, landfills are planted with unvarying swaths of turf. Recent research suggests strong reasons to change this practice.

The lack of trees and shrubs severely limits the landfill's potential for wildlife habitat/corridors, not to mention visual variety. Another compelling reason to plant trees (or allow them to colonize) is to reduce landscape maintenance. Local trees will colonize almost any site unless actively prevented; after all, the process of succession will produce forest on bare sites in most regions of North America. Preventing trees on landfills entails some combination of mowing and herbicides, both of which carry energy and pollution costs. Devoting at least part of the site to trees reduces the need for these practices. Trees also have potential for erosion control, a serious issue on landfills, where typical 3:1 slopes may be 250 feet high.

The thickness and construction of landfill caps are strictly regulated. Penetration of a properly constructed clay or plastic cap is highly unlikely because (1) the density of the capping material physically prevents root penetration, while anaerobic conditions in and below the cap kill roots, and (2) tree roots are concentrated in the surface layers of most soils, usually no more than 3 feet deep.[27]

These findings are supported by a British study, "The Potential for Woodland Establishment on Landfill Sites," which responded to a 1986 directive from the U.K. Department of the Environment that trees should not be planted on landfills. The study concluded that tree roots do not exert enough pressure to penetrate an engineered cap, and that there is no empirical evidence that roots breach caps. As a result, the directive was rescinded.[28] Further supporting these findings, no problems have been reported from the closed landfill sites of "festival gardens" that include trees.

The benefits of trees on landfills rather clearly outweigh potential problems. Methods from the following case studies should be adapted to fit each site.

Fresh Kills

One of the world's largest dump sites, at 2,400 acres, is Staten Island's Fresh Kills landfill (the name, ironically, means fresh brook). Of more interest than sheer size is the fact that Fresh Kills has been scientifically monitored, providing hard data on the safety and cost-effectiveness of restoration methods used there.

In the late 1980s the New York City sanitation department devoted 6 already-capped acres of the landfill to a series of planting test plots. One goal was to determine whether the landfill could support anything approaching the indigenous vegetation of Staten Island, which of course includes many species of trees. Like its British counterparts (above), this research questioned conventional wisdom about keeping trees off landfills. On such a vast site as Fresh Kills, excluding trees had larger than usual implications for wildlife, appearance, erosion, and cost.

Bill Young (who then worked for the city) and horticulturist John McLaughlin began at Fresh Kills by creating undulating dune-like slopes that mimicked the native coastal landscape of the island. (Compare this approach to landform grading, page 70.) By contrast, most landfills are engineered to uniform 3:1 slopes, interrupted every 50 feet by wide flat benches.

The designers worked with the city parks department to rescue plants from sites slated for development elsewhere on Staten Island. In all, 3,000 shrubs were planted along with 523 native trees. Native perennial grasses and wildflowers were seeded throughout the site.

Trees do need to be irrigated, at least during the establishment period, and landfill sites do not always have access to sources of clean water. Young advocates irrigating with leachate (water that drains from the landfill and may pick up contaminants). This proposal was controversial, but leachate at Fresh Kills was tested and found to be within toxicity thresholds set by the EPA. Admittedly, the leachate could not be allowed to flow off the landfill to nearby watercourses but would have to be recirculated on-site. Young notes that irrigating with leachate would be much more feasible in the United States if such toxic items as batteries and household cleansers could be eliminated from the landfill. Increasingly, landfills do require that such materials be sorted out (for reasons other than watering trees).

Once Fresh Kills was planted, a team of restoration ecologists from Rutgers University was hired to monitor the plantings. They found moderate tree growth and excellent shrub growth in the test plots. Woody plants on the plots provided much-needed perching sites for birds, who reciprocated by dispersing seeds, helping to plant other areas with volunteer trees. This cost-effective planting strategy is called "habitat islands." Surprisingly effective, seed dispersal from the habitat islands boosted the number of woody species from eighteen to fifty. Of the added species, fourteen were trees.

Perhaps the most important finding from the Rutgers Fresh Kills study, however, was that the tree roots did *not* affect the clay cap.[29] Upon excavation of selected trees, the Rutgers team found that successful trees developed wide, shallow root systems. Ecologist Steven N. Handel, leader of the Rutgers team, reported: "None of the trees breached the cap, and in fact, exhibited startling deviation from genetic traits by confining all roots to the thin mantle of overburden [the planting soil on top of the cap]." The fact that the trees were planted directly in a sand/compost mix, with neither imported topsoil nor excavated "tree pits," may have encouraged horizontal rooting. Handel's finding matches research at other landfill sites; in fact, there is no record of a tree ever penetrating a clay cap.

SUGGESTED PRACTICES FOR LANDFILL SITES

1. *Involve a landscape architect early in the design process.* Solid-waste-disposal facilities are often huge complexes. Particularly where the end-use of the site will be a park or other amenity, overlapping systems must be sensitively intertwined. Landscape architects (or similar holistic site designers) should be on the initial design team, along with waste-management specialists and engineers, to ensure well-integrated environmental and human benefits.

2. *Stockpile soil for reapplication on the completed landfill.* Prior to site development, strip all topsoil and stockpile it (see page 77). To protect soil organisms, plan topsoil removal to minimize the time in stockpile. Also worthwhile for such large projects is separately stockpiling the next foot or so of A-horizon soil. Reapply stockpiled soil to recreate these horizons on the capped landfill.

3. *Grade the site using landform or stepped-slope methods.*

4. *Plant in uniform soil cover, not in pits.* Any situation where soil composition varies markedly can constrict roots and might force them into the cap.

5. *Plant trees for erosion control and habitat.* Turfgrass is the best material where landfills are restored as active recreation areas. Native

grasses and wildflowers are also satisfactory for landfill plantings. However, there is no functional reason why trees do not belong on landfills as well, and they offer both ecological and cost benefits.

6. *Try bare-root stock or an on-site nursery.* The nursery will allow the seedlings to acclimate themselves to the landfill's microclimate and soils. Commercially grown trees, aside from being expensive, may not survive landfill conditions as well as field-hardened stock.[30] Bare-root stock can sometimes be obtained at very low cost from the local U.S. Forest Service office or similar agency. These sources tend to mix native and nonnative species in their offerings, a factor that should be carefully evaluated.

7. *Plant trees as "habitat islands," from which no-cost seedlings can spread.* For more information, refer to the Rutgers study cited on page 76.

8. *If additional soil is needed, consider manufactured soil.* See below.

Restore Damaged Soils On-Site

Once structural problems have been corrected, or if they are not an issue, restoring health to the soil is an important next step in most site restoration. Compaction may need to be reversed, or soil that has been hauled away or allowed to erode may need to be replaced—erosion rates on construction sites are disastrously high if not controlled (see Figure 6.22).

Urban soils in particular are generally problematic, almost by definition: "a soil material having a non-agricultural, manmade surface layer more than 50 centimeters [20 inches] thick that has been produced by mixing, filling, or contamination of land surfaces in urban and suburban areas."[31] Such soils are called "made land" for good reason.

Methods of re-creating healthy soil range from simply adding proper amounts of organic material to completely replacing lost soil with "manufactured soil" mix. Unless the site has been stripped of all soil, sustainability is best served by methods that rebuild the soil on-site. Only in rare occasions should soil materials be imported in quantity, and never at the expense of another site.

Avoid "Topsoiling"

One of the most common—and most questionable—practices in contemporary landscape construction is "topsoiling"—trucking in fresh topsoil for planting areas in new construction. Some sites may truly lack topsoil, due to prior abuse. But more commonly, the rationalization for importing soil is that on-site soils are thought to lack the fertility necessary for lush plant growth—or simply that during the building process, it seems easier to strip off the topsoil and haul it away than to stockpile it on-site.

In most urban areas, there are companies that specialize in collecting the topsoil from land under development and reselling it as "new" topsoil for *other* developments—amounting to a game of musical soils. The excuse is often made that since a site under development is being disturbed anyway, making off with its topsoil is no crime and saves the soil from complete destruction. The energy and pollution costs of transporting bulk soils, however, make good on-site soil management during construction the preferred alternative in all but the rarest cases.

Importing soil also carries an *unseen* environmental cost—in many cases, topsoil is stripped from productive farmland for development use. In an era of diminishing farmland, this practice is rapidly becoming unconscionable. "I feel strongly that landscape architects should never use the word 'topsoil' in specifications," says Cornelia Oberlander, a landscape architect in Vancouver BC.

Fortunately, alternatives to importing topsoil do exist. The preferred option wherever feasible is to save whatever topsoil exists on-site and reapply it as a means of restoring the damage done during construction. Where more severe or long-term damage has left the site without any topsoil, other related soil restoration methods are required; these are discussed in later sections.

Stockpile Existing Topsoil

The depth of topsoil varies widely depending on the soil type, from an inch or less in the desert Southwest to several feet in the most fertile farmland. (For sustainability, neither extremely poor nor very rich soils are the best candidates for construction sites, and rich soils in particular are often protected as prime agricultural land.) Below the topsoil is subsoil, which contains far fewer organic materials and soil organisms than

Figure 2.12. In this test pit, living organic topsoil contrasts clearly with light-colored subsoil. A precious resource, topsoil is created from subsoil only by major resource inputs, either from humans or from time. PHOTO: National Resource Conservation Service.

does the topsoil. Subsoil can be thought of as primarily structural, whereas topsoil is alive.

The best way to preserve topsoil is to leave it strictly alone. But, construction usually means that some areas are disturbed, no matter how carefully these are minimized by good planning and design. Prior to construction, topsoil should be scooped off of all parts of the site that will be built on, as well as access paths and staging areas. As a practical rule of thumb, the top 6 inches are removed, but in unusually poor or unusually fertile soils this may vary.

Stockpile this topsoil on-site in piles covered with breathable material. This slows drying, keeps down dust, excludes windblown weed seeds, and avoids mud, sedimentation, and erosion. On large projects, stockpiles are sometimes planted with a quick-growing crop of erosion-preventing ground cover, such as vetch or annual ryegrass.

Inevitably, many of the organisms in stockpiled soil die from lack of oxygen, drying, or other factors. Stockpiling over periods of more than a month are particularly likely to kill the microorganisms on which soil health depends. (Cases where construction cannot be phased to avoid long stockpiling are one of the few times when selling the topsoil may be justified.) These concerns have led to the reevaluation of how to protect topsoil that must be moved during construction.[32] Nonetheless, stockpiling is clearly better than simply destroying the topsoil. In order to keep the soil organisms in the topsoil alive, observe the following suggestions.[33] The local Soil Survey (now the Natural Resource Conservation Service) or county Extension office

may also provide advice or contacts on keeping stockpiled soil healthy.

1. Make several small piles, not one large one.

2. Depth of piled soil should be no more than 6 feet for sandy soils and 4 feet for clay soils.

3. Keep the piles moderately damp.

4. Protect the piles from wind and water erosion by covering or planting.

5. Handle the soil as little as possible, and stockpile for as short a time as possible.

On large projects, the guidelines present a challenge of logistics and space. Nonetheless, studies by the California Department of Transportation have shown in no uncertain terms that topsoil reapplication works. Test slopes on which topsoil was reapplied after highway construction had 250 percent better plant growth after three years compared to fill slopes that had no topsoil—even when the latter had an equivalent application of all nutrients, seeds, and erosion-control materials.[34] Under the even more demanding conditions of mine reclamation, "high sodium content, nutrient deficiencies, toxicities, and soil-water relationships were mostly alleviated by replacing topsoil." There are limits, however: the same study found that 2 inches of replaced topsoil produced up to 70 percent as much grass regrowth as did 30 inches.[35]

One possibility to preserve topsoil and the seed bank found in healthy soil is to treat it like sod. A classic example is the use of a modified front-end loader bucket to scoop up huge sheets of intact soil and plants, pioneered by Andropogon Associates for the Algonquin pipeline in Morristown NJ.[36] A similar machine is now commercially available.⊃ Small plugs of seed-bearing soil are commonly used to plant wetlands (see page 144).

Balance Cut and Fill

Transporting soil is costly, both in money and in energy (see page 241). Balancing cut and fill, so that no soil needs to be trucked in or carted off the site, is standard practice for large engineering projects. This concept can contribute to sustainability and should be considered in the design and construction of all sites. Many construction projects, however, create large new impermeable surfaces (buildings, pavement), resulting in more topsoil than should be respread on the remaining areas. Rather than placing topsoil to a depth that does not benefit plants on-site, it *may* be appropriate to truck the excess to another site where soil remediation is required. Because of the energy costs involved in transport, and because not all soils are equal in chemistry or fertility, trucking topsoil from site to site should be a last resort in sustainable construction. It is far preferable, wherever possible, to limit the creation of impermeable surfaces and to avoid contamination and other conditions that require remediation of soils.

In roadway construction, strictly balanced cut and fill can lead to raising or lowering the roadbed far beyond what is needed for safety. Although energy and cost savings result from not hauling the soil, excessively raised or lowered roads tend to disrupt natural drainage patterns on the site and may require increased maintenance. Sustainable construction should *first* minimize the *total* amount of grading and then come as close as possible to balancing cut and fill on the site.

"Amend" Soil—But with Restraint

Wherever possible, an effort should be made to find a place on or near the construction site to stockpile existing soil. But there are cases, particularly on abused urban sites, where there is little or no topsoil worthy of the name; it was stripped away long ago or covered up by rubble and fill. Many damaged sites meet the definition (page 77) of "made land," also known simply as "urban soil." Even in the worst cases, however, the existing soil, properly amended, may be better than any commercially available "landscape" soil, according to Simon Leake, an Australian soils scientist.[37]

Some of the most unpromising soils may actually be much more viable than expected. For example, urban renewal has left a heritage of large tracts of land strewn with brick rubble. Research in Great Britain suggests that such sites may be amended to quite suitable planting medium, particularly if the bricks have lain on the site for a period of years. Soil-forming processes work on the raw bricks and mortar to form a kind of stony soil.[38]

Researchers R. A. Dutton and A. D. Bradshaw analyzed samples of brick rubble from demolition sites in inner-city Liverpool and Belfast. In terms of soil texture at least, they found decomposing rubble comparable to topsoil. Drainage and aeration are excellent. Nutritionally, rubble soils are unbalanced. Nitrogen is typically deficient, although it quickly builds up if nitrogen-fixing plants such as legumes colonize the site. (Acid rain and some forms of air pollution contain nitrates that also increase the nitrogen content of soil.) Phosphorous—remnant skeletons of prehistoric organisms—is present in the clay from which the bricks were made. Potassium and magnesium are also abundant in the clay. Calcium, an important nutrient and controller of pH, is readily available in the mortar rubble. Physically and chemically, brick rubble lends itself to colonization by plants, even though stoniness coupled with nitrogen deficiency may initially restrict plant growth.

Other types of rubble, especially broken concrete, do not include the nutrients derived from clay and can add so much calcium that the soil becomes alkaline. Concrete rubble is also much harder and denser than mortar rubble and would in most cases break down more slowly. Although brick and mortar and concrete are probably the most widespread components of construction or demolition debris found on-site, many others, such as plastics, metals, woods (treated and untreated), paints and sealants, and petroleum fuels, can be present in widely varied proportions. Soil restoration requires site-specific testing, even when debris is not a factor, to decide what amendments to add. The unpredictable and spotty patterns in which debris may be scattered on a site make testing more complicated *and* more necessary.

Gardens on rubble are not easily created or even feasible in all cases. The above research does suggest, however, that removing *existing* debris from derelict land may not be the only way, or even the best way, to rehabilitate a site. (This applies only to existing debris: responsible contractors must avoid leaving new trash behind them, by reducing waste, recycling and reusing scrap on-site, and by appropriate disposal of any remaining debris.) Rubble-strewn lots are just one example of a seemingly hopeless urban situation where biological processes and human practices together can bring life back to damaged sites.

Materials and Energy for Soil Amendment

A wide range of materials is marketed for improving soils, and many of them are appropriate for use where the existing soil is badly damaged. As noted on page 45, however, it is possible to amend soil too much. As landscape architect Leslie Sauer puts it in *The Once and Future Forest*, "Researchers have shown repeatedly that fertilizer benefits weeds." Decreasing fertility and changing pH often favor native species.[39] Avoiding overfertilization is especially important when relatively undisturbed and healthy native soils are involved. In general, the goal of soil restoration should be to produce a soil with chemistry and fertility similar to those found in healthy regional soils. There is usually enough variety in regional soils to allow for most reasonable landscape purposes.

Experts are not fully in agreement on the appropriateness of soil amendments, and indeed these practices are site- or region-specific. Here, however, are some general guidelines:[40]

- Compost (rotted vegetative material) is the most universally valuable of all soil components, a paradoxical substance that helps sandy soils hold water and clay soils release it. Landscape uses of compost are discussed in the section that follows.

- Sand is often specified to improve drainage of clay soils; however, so much sand has to be added to most clays that this is not practical. At least one third of the final result must be sand, meaning that for an existing volume of clay, half that volume must be added. Smaller amounts of sand can actually bind the soil together, as it does in adobe bricks. Add compost instead.

- Remember the farmer's adage; "Sand on clay, money thrown away; clay on sand, money in hand." As long as it is well mixed, clay added to sandy soil can readily improve its *structure*, but compost is a better choice for *both* sandy and clay soils.

- Gypsum is useful only on unusually calcium-deficient soils or those affected by salt. Most western U.S. soils are already too alkaline to benefit from gypsum.

- Wood ash is useful on acid soils in the eastern and southern United States, but it can increase existing pH and salt problems in western soils.

- Peat moss is widely specified as a soil amendment. Because it is harvested from wetlands in vast quantities and shipped long distances, many experts consider its use entirely unsustainable. Use compost instead, from local leaf litter or similar materials.

- Analyze soil before fertilizing. In many areas, soils contain extra nutrients from acid rain and air pollution. Because of this, adding fertilizer may be unnecessary or even harmful. A major nutrient from pollution is nitrogen, and high nitrogen in many cases encourages weeds.

- Some soils, especially if irrigated in areas of high evaporation, may have high salt content. Be sure not to add to this with salty fertilizers, which include fresh cattle and poultry manure, as well as ammonium nitrate and other high-nitrogen mixes.

- The microbes that decompose organic material require nitrogen. Amendments that are high in carbon and low in nitrogen (a C:N ratio higher than 20:1) cause microbes to *take* nitrogen from the soil to fuel their work of decomposition. This can make nitrogen unavailable to plants until decomposition is finished. Amendments with high C:N ratios include horse manure, dairy (but not beef) cattle manure, straw, wood chips, and some composts if not well matured. Such amendments may be good for high-nitrogen soils or for woodland soils where leaf and twig litter naturally composts slowly. Elsewhere they should be used with caution.

- Many plants live cooperatively or symbiotically with other organisms in the soil. Roots of such plants work in cooperation with mycorrhizae (fungi that process certain nutrients and exchange them with the plant). If the correct type of symbiotic organism is not present in the soil, these plants cannot survive. Mycorrhizal "inoculants" are commercially available for some species. They should be used with caution and expertise, however, since the wrong mycorrhizae can displace beneficial ones native to the soil.

- Apart from composts, one potentially valuable way to increase available moisture is to add superabsorbent polymer granules to the soil. One pound of such granules can absorb nearly 50 gallons of water; an almost bizarre amount of water disappears into the dry polymer when first mixed. Polymers have been used successfully to reduce irrigation needs as part of backfill mixes. Bare-root or live-stake bioengineering materials (Principle 3) can be dipped into a slurry of the water-absorbent material before planting. Although there is some concern about polymers holding salts, they have been widely accepted both in horticulture and in dryland reforestation.⊃

Embodied energy and potential toxicity of soil amendments vary widely. Some amendments are simple and relatively unprocessed materials like sand, clay, topsoil from other sites, compost, or manure. Such materials are only toxic if contaminated, but energy to "mine" the materials and transport them to the site can be significant. As noted earlier, topsoil should rarely be imported or exported. Toxicity by overusing fresh manure is a possibility. Other materials used for amending soil are processed, ranging from ones that require only simple processing, such as limestone, to completely artificial chemical fertilizers or water-holding polymers. A responsible approach to sustainable construction does not simply reject these materials because they are artificial or processed. Rather, each material must be analyzed for embodied energy, toxicity, and related concerns and used accordingly.

Even if soil-amending materials are energy-efficient and nontoxic, widespread change in a site's soils may have undesirable effects on the ecosystem. Anyone who has overwatered or over-fertilized a houseplant will understand this problem. In some regions of "poor" soils, increased soil fertility actually *decreases* the health and hardiness of native plant species. At the same time, it makes the soil more hospitable to weeds that are not picky about soil type. The result is unsatisfactory both horticulturally and ecologically and increases maintenance problems.

To repeat an important point: The goal of soil restoration should usually be to bring damaged soil back to conditions similar to other healthy soils in the region. In landscape use, this implies design based on native plants. Dramatically increased soil fertility should be reserved for the limited number of exotics planted as special accents in such designs.

Use Greenwaste and Other Composts

Applying compost to private yards or community garden plots may be everyday practice, but is anyone actually using compost in large-scale landscape construction? Yes. In fact, some of the very largest landscape projects—highway rights-of-way—routinely employ or are testing composted materials. A 1997 study by the University of Florida found that thirty-four of the fifty state Departments of Transportation use compost on roadsides routinely or experimentally.[41]

For large-scale projects, compost is usually applied hydraulically in a slurry, often mixed with uncomposted home and agricultural greenwaste. The range of composted materials is almost endless: grass clippings and leaves from suburban backyards; poultry and livestock manure; brewer's waste; biosolids (composted sludge) from municipal sewage; trees chipped after felling; farm by-products such as walnut shells and peach pits; and chopped wood waste from demolished buildings.

The range of applications is equally wide: as a soil amendment, as mulch or topdressing, for erosion control, and as a component in planting-soil mixes. Frequently noted benefits from compost include the following:

- Better plant growth due to addition of organic matter, slow-release nutrients, and microbial populations; compost nutrients are already balanced for reuse by plants and soil organisms.

- Effective erosion control and slope stabilization, as well as improved water-holding and drainage.

- Fewer weeds and reduced use of herbicides and chemical fertilizers (where used as mulch, which also protects the soil surface).

With compost, says Caltrans' Haynes, "you're effecting some real soil improvement, since we often install landscape plantings in subsoil or parent material." Although the term "improvement" is often used too casually about landscape practices, in the case of compost, it is truly valid.

The Minnesota DOT (MnDOT) has had compost as a standard specification for the past nine years and has completely discontinued the practice of bringing in topsoil or peat moss. MnDOT uses 20,000 cubic yards of compost annually on roadsides, largely in the planting of trees and shrubs. DOTs in California, Florida, Illinois, Maine, North Carolina, Washington, and Massachusetts also report substantial—and successful—

applications of compost. Caltrans' wide use of compost fits California state policy of diverting recyclable materials from landfills. "It just makes too much sense not to do it," says Haynes.

These agencies have tested the performance of compost against results obtained from peat, humus, bark, topsoil, or fertilizer. Compost compares favorably in almost every trial. Caltrans' has found compost to be as effective for slope protection as erosion-control blankets. The Maine DOT has found that turf grown on a 50/50 mix of compost and subsoil resists erosion better than grass grown on straight loam topsoil. (New plantings were heavily mulched with a coarsely textured compost to stabilize the soil surface.[42]) In short, compost has immense value on almost every landscape project.

AVAILABILITY AND QUALITY OF COMPOST

In most urban areas there is a glut of yard waste—grass clippings, leaves, pruned branches, and removed trees. (If processed into boards, the volume of woodlike wastes is enough to replace all wood harvested for timber; see Figure 6.19.) In the past, this valuable organic matter was trucked to landfills, a practice that persists in some municipalities. Leaves and grass have made up as much as 18 percent of landfill volume, with another 7 percent composed of soil, rocks, and woody landscape waste.[43] Thus *one quarter* of landfill volume could be eliminated by simply making good use of these organic materials. As landfills in many parts of the country have begun to bulge at the seams, the value of greenwaste has been recognized. California legislation passed in the 1990s required communities to reduce the volume of waste going to landfills by 50 percent by the year 2000. Separating yard waste is a fairly easy way to meet these goals, and the practice is becoming more widespread.

Certain municipalities around the country, such as Cleveland OH, have a history of composting yard waste.[44] Christmas trees, agricultural by-products such as fruit pits and nut shells, scrap wood, and food wastes from food services and restaurants are also frequently composted. (In Vancouver BC, one composting firm makes a high-quality compost entirely from restaurant wastes. Landscape architect Cornelia Oberlander's use of this product is discussed on page 114.)

Despite the large volume of raw greenwastes generated by most communities, availability and consistent quality remain issues in large-scale landscape applications of compost. Several state DOTs have found it difficult to obtain compost in the quantities required for highway projects. In Texas, for example, rates of application have sometimes been affected by availability. The New Hampshire DOT has found that product quality varies greatly from one town to the next. For similar reasons, Caltrans has had to import compost from out of state. Trucking compost from far-flung locations means hauling charges, which, due to the volume of the material, can be substantial—particularly in such large and sparsely populated states as Colorado, Nebraska, Texas, and Wyoming.[45] In such cases, the environmental costs of energy use and air pollution must be carefully weighed against the benefits of compost. When long-term improved health of plantings, reduced erosion, reduced chemical use, and decreased volume disposed in landfills are all considered, however, transporting compost may still be environmentally viable, despite financial cost. As the compost industry evolves, high-quality compost is likely to be available in quantity in more and more communities.

Specifications that spell out the characteristics of quality compost to suppliers are important in ensuring that a safe and consistent product is delivered to the construction site. Fortunately, model specifications do exist. One is the *Suggested Compost Parameters & Compost Use Guidelines* developed by the Composting Council.⊃

Contamination and the maturity of the compost itself are the most common quality issues. The presence of contaminants—weed seed, heavy metals, salts—should be limited by the specification. Some substances, such as small pieces of plastic or glass, pose no horticultural problem, and some soils experts favor ground glass as an ingredient in creating soils from recycled materials (see "Manufactured Soil," page 86). Of course, foreign objects that may cause injury to construction workers, to users of the site, or to wildlife must be eliminated.

If the compost is not fully mature—that is, if it is still decomposing—it can leach nitrogen from the soil to fuel its continuing breakdown process. This robs plants of soil nitrogen. To avoid such problems, the Washington DOT now requires producers to provide maturity-testing kits with compost deliveries so that DOT personnel may field-test compost if they suspect it is not mature.[46]

In addition to monitoring maturity, there are some special concerns when using compost on relatively healthy and undisturbed soils. These are noted on page 46.

The technology of composting is well established; there is no problem in turning raw materials into compost. At present, there is more raw material potentially available than is actually collected or processed. In many areas, increased demand for compost would actually help municipal governments fund the facilities for increased compost production. Landscape professionals and the landscape industry should make a commitment to putting this valuable product to use.

On-Site Use of Yard Waste

Although municipal composting and the use of compost in construction are desirable, most U.S. yards would be healthier if yard waste were composted and reapplied *on-site* (see page 281). As with most environmental technologies, on-site reuse also saves transportation and its associated costs. If garden maintenance (and agriculture) becomes more sustainable, it is possible that current sources of greenwaste may decrease. In the meantime, however, municipal compost should be a mainstay in reclaiming damaged soils.

Green Manure Crops

A related soil restoration approach is called green manure—soil-enriching plants that farmers have known about for millennia. Grown on the site for one or more seasons, they are then tilled into the soil to become compost. Most of the plants used are leguminous (in the pea family). Their roots have the ability to fix nitrogen, which becomes available to later plantings as the green manure breaks down. For regionally appropriate green-manure practices, contact a local agricultural school or the County Extension. Be sure to pick species that are not likely to become invasive—a few leguminous crop plants, such as alfalfa, spread aggressively in some climates.

Watch for Lead in Soils

A persistent problem for community gardens on derelict urban land is lead in the soil. Although lead is no longer used in consumer paints or in gasoline, it may remain a soil problem because it is not biodegradable. Older buildings painted with lead-based paints, heavily traveled roadways, or service stations may have contaminated adjacent sites. Former industrial locations should always be researched carefully for processes involving pollutants that may remain in the soil.

Community garden sites where food crops will be grown should *always* undergo a soil test. If such a test shows lead at levels lower than 500 parts per million (ppm), the Ohio State University Extension recommends incorporating organic material such as compost or manure into the soil at the rate of one third by volume. This amounts to 12–16 cubic feet of organic material for a 100-square-foot garden plot. If lead levels are higher, the extension service recommends building raised beds that separate the planting medium from the contaminated soil.[47]

Raised beds are typically 9 to 18 inches tall, except when built at table-like heights for handicapped gardeners. They are convenient, in many ways easier to maintain than plantings at ground level, and are a traditional method of intensive vegetable cultivation in Europe. Where bed depth is less than 12 inches, some pollutants may migrate upward unless a floor separates contaminated soil from the planting mix. Get expert advice or build taller beds.

Whenever chemical residues are found, reconsider whether to use the garden for food plants—decorative gardens are also an appropriate use of community allotments.

Heal the Soil with Biosolids

The urban environment produces many by-products in need of recycling. In restoring landscapes and keeping them fertile, few recycled products are more appropriate for use than biosolids—processed from municipal sewage (yes, *sewage*)—yet none is so underutilized. Many fears and misconceptions surround its use. Certainly, some concern is legitimate where food production is involved, but for most other types of landscapes, biosolids are too valuable to waste.⊃

Many traditional societies around the world still prize this composted human waste as a natural fertilizer. Small-scale, on-site treatment, using composting toilets, constructed wetlands, and other alternative systems, is common—but not common enough—even in industrialized countries like Japan and Sweden. Such systems reduce the toxic contamination and the infrastructure costs associated with centralized sewer systems. In modern societies, however, sewage is too easily piped away underground, out of sight and out of almost everyone's mind.

At the other end of the sewage pipe, treatment plants must either dump the treated sewage or process it into useful soil amendments. Since the 1920s, an increasing number of people have realized that disposing of sewage is neither cost-effective nor environmentally intelligent. In 1926, the Milwaukee Metropolitan Sewerage District began marketing the granddaddy of U.S. biosolids products, and still the best known, Milorganite.

A full-fledged biosolids industry emerged after the 1988 federal ban on dumping municipal sludge in the oceans. The ban left few disposal options for wastewater treatment facilities; they could dump the sludge on landfills or incinerate it—both expensive and environmentally questionable. Since 1988, biosolids products with names like Biogrow, GroCo, Nutramulch, and Technagro have become increasingly available from municipal treatment facilities and private contractors around the country.

One result of increased availability is that the cost of biosolids has dropped in many areas—from $120 to $42 per ton in Florida between 1990 and 1994, for example.[48] Some wastewater plant operators, under pressure to dispose of a never-ending flow of municipal sludge, may even be willing to supply biosolids at no cost for landscape projects.

Not everyone concerned with the environment supports the use of biosolids. Despite extensive standards set by the U.S. Environmental Protection Agency, some biosolids contain heavy metals and other contaminants dumped ignorantly or maliciously into sewer systems. These contaminants are of particular concern if biosolids are applied to food-producing fields. The EPA standards set levels of these contaminants that many experts consider very low risk, even for food crops, but not everyone accepts these definitions. Certainly, the 1998 proposal to allow foods fertilized with biosolids to be labeled "organic" raised serious public objection. Ironically, other common manufactured fertilizers, for which there are *no* standards, have recently been shown to include concentrated toxic wastes merely relabeled as fertilizer[49] and arguably pose a far greater health threat than do

biosolids. (See "Toxics as 'Fertilizer,'" page 223.) It is the authors' belief that when produced and used in accordance with EPA standards, biosolids are highly appropriate for *landscape* use, with the possible exception of aquifer recharge zones or previously little-disturbed, near-natural sites.

Biosolids are soil conditioners, similar in many ways to compost, that increase water retention and help retain nutrients in the soil. They improve soil tilth, permitting easier root penetration. They boost fertility, with significant amounts of such nutrients as nitrogen, phosphorus, and potassium, as well as beneficial trace metals. Used as a mulch, particularly when mixed with wood chips or yard waste, they are effective in erosion control. Biosolids, then, are a multipurpose, low-cost soil amendment.

How safe are biosolids? The EPA, in Part 503 of the Code of Federal Regulations, recognizes two main classes of biosolids, A and B.[50] Both classes are removed from wastewater during treatment and subjected to a process known as digestion. This reduces pathogen levels by 90–99 percent. Heavy metal content is reduced to levels specified by the EPA. At this stage, biosolids are rated as class B. Application of class-B biosolids to a site requires a state permit and some degree of site monitoring for up to a year.

Class-A biosolids are additionally subjected to extensive composting, heat-drying, or irradiation. This further sterilizes the product and decreases the odor. Although class-A biosolids cannot be guaranteed to be odor-free, odors are rarely a problem. Sea World of Ohio, which uses a class-A product called Technagro on flower beds next to public walkways, takes the precaution of stockpiling the material for two weeks to allow any lingering odors to dissipate before application.

Biosolids use does require certain cautions. Pathogens are seldom the issue; however, the chemical composition of sludge varies greatly from one treatment plant to another. Because lime is used to stabilize sludge at some facilities, the pH ranges up to 11, far too alkaline for most organisms. Soluble salts are not uncommon; nitrates and heavy metal contaminants may be a problem in some products. According to one noted soils scientist, these contaminants can build up with repeated application, although they seem to dissipate if application stops for several years.[51] Two forms of site remediation discussed later in this chapter use plants (phytore-mediation) or microbes (bioremediation) to remove very similar contaminants from soil. These methods might provide a way of completely removing chemical contaminants from biosolids, either before or after they are applied to landscapes.

Anita Bahe, while a doctoral candidate at North Carolina State University, undertook a study of biosolids applications on three golf courses in the Carolinas. She found that while metal concentration in grass tissue did increase, it was still within a range considered acceptable by the EPA. On the basis of her study, Bahe is enthusiastic about the potential for biosolids applications to urban turf.[52]

The point is not that biosolids are risk-free; that claim cannot be made for commercial fertilizers either. Properly applied, biosolids solve two major environmental problems—sewage disposal and soil fertility—with minimal health or environmental risk. One caveat: Quality compliance may vary from one *producer* to another; some may let standards slip between annual inspections. Bob Rubin, a professor of agricultural engineering at North Carolina State University who has conducted extensive research in landscape applications of biosolids, recommends that buyers and specifiers call the appropriate state regulatory agency and ask a few key questions: What facilities in the state are producing class-A pathogen-free biosolids? Has the agency done any analysis of the levels of nutrients, salts, metals, and other elements in that product? Which producers have consistently remained in compliance with state and EPA guidelines? Such information is available in every state, says Rubin, and helps in locating producers of quality products.

Satisfactory biosolids products may not yet be available in every locality. As recently as 1996, Caltrans was unable to find a local biosolid that John Haynes could use confidently in southern California. He had to import Biogrow from Arizona. More recently, Haynes reports that local, high-quality material is now available. The main reason for tapping local or regional sources is, of course, the cost of transport (roughly $1 per ton per mile, according to Haynes; see also energy costs, page 241). Biosolids costing only $20 to $40 dollars a ton may still be almost as expensive as conventional mulches when they have to be trucked long distances. If California is any indication, however, the biosolids industry is developing so rapidly that products should be available in most localities in the near future.

BIOSOLIDS PROJECT EXAMPLES

It's enough to make many contractors blanch: applying biosolids on the lawn at the residence of the First Family of the United States. Nevertheless, the White House has used biosolids. In the late 1980s, 825 tons of ComPro—which consists of biosolids from Washington DC's sewage composted with lime and wood chips—were applied to solve compaction on the South Lawn. The head White House groundskeeper reported no problems with the material. A few blocks away, 6,000 tons of biosolids were applied to the National Mall in 1976 to establish the Constitution Gardens. The grounds of the Washington Monument, the lawns of Mount Vernon, and the gardens at Dumbarton Oaks are other sites in the nation's capital on which biosolids have been put to good use.

One Washington-area landscape architect, James Urban, views biosolids as inexpensive soil additives that can help restore nutrient-poor, compacted city soils—in lieu of hauling away such soil and replacing it with topsoil stripped from a site in the country. Urban specified ComPro for the soil mix at the National Geographic Society headquarters in Washington DC. (Despite what humorists might predict, Washington's sewage is relatively benign; it has few of the heavy metals that plague the wastewater of historically industrial cities like Boston.)

The Seattle Department of Parks and Recreation used class-B biosolids in 1995 to restore Discovery Park, a 500-acre expanse degraded by years of logging and farming. Landscape architect Barbara Swift and project manager Kevin Stoops used biosolids from the King County wastewater treatment plant. On a 14-acre demonstration area, 2 inches of biosolids were spread on the surface and tilled to a depth of 15 inches. The presence of class-B material required posting signs and fencing the area for one year. Stoops notes that the odors of the material dissipated fairly quickly when exposed to air and sunlight. Late in the process, as a truckload of biosolids was being dumped at the site, the winds changed and blew into a neighborhood only a block away. When residents complained about the smell, the city suspended work until the wind shifted again and, as an additional precaution, switched to

85

GroCo, a class-A mixture of biosolids and yard waste, for the remainder of the application.

Seeded with grass, the site now exhibits very luxuriant growth, says Stoops. Because Parks and Recreation obtained the biosolids free from the wastewater plant, it realized enormous cost savings over other fertilizers and soil amendments.[53] Stoops sums up his experience with biosolids by saying, "It's a product the county needs to get rid of. It's not a waste product that needs to be hidden away."

In general, Washington State appears to be ahead of other states in biosolids application—Seattle's world-famous Gas Works Park, for example, was treated with class-B biosolids in the mid-1970s. In 1988 the state banned the disposal of sludge on landfills, spurring a search for more productive uses. Current Washington projects include Mountains to the Sound, a greenway initiative along Interstate 90 that uses King County biosolids to revegetate highly visible logged slopes and logging roads along a scenic mountain corridor. The city of Everett, moreover, is testing biosolids in a wetland restoration project.

Not surprisingly, attempts to use biosolids in the landscape often encounter resistance, some related to health issues and the primal fear of solid wastes as a source of pathogens. Although several state highway departments routinely use biosolids on rights-of-way, for example, the Kentucky DOT has been apprehensive about biosolids' potential for fouling the water supply, and the Minnesota DOT uses biosolids only in pilot projects. When the Wyoming DOT tried to use biosolids on a large roadside reconstruction project, they encountered a backlash that forced them to end its use—even though the biosolids in question tested well below EPA standards for both pathogens and heavy metals. States like Massachusetts are moving confidently ahead with biosolids, while in Nebraska, farmers use it as fast as it is made.[54]

A darker form of resistance to biosolids emerges from entrenched conventional interests. Producers of wood mulch and fertilizers see any form of compost as cutting into their markets, and at least one attempt to legislate roadside use of biosolids was "shot down by chemical industry lobbyists."[55] Special-interest resistance is in some ways one more reason in favor of biosolids. Public and professional education are the keys to appropriate use of this material.

Lynn William Horn is a Tacoma WA landscape architect who has been specifying biosolids for more than ten years. He uses a class-A product, Nutramulch, on playing fields and planting beds around state fairgrounds, office buildings, and upscale residences. He views biosolids as "an excellent alternative for landscape architects to be using. Without question, we should be using them more." When contractors attempt to substitute other soil amendments on a project, Horn tells them, "I don't want a substitute. This is a recycled product. I'm putting something back into the earth."

Manufactured Soil

What of those abused sites that have no topsoil at all? As noted earlier, many sites have fill and rubble where topsoil should be. Landfills and highway cuts are the most extreme example of soilless sites, and their size alone prohibits importing topsoil. To cover the 2,400 acres of New York's Fresh Kills landfill with as little as 12 inches of soil would require 104,551,200 cubic feet, or nearly 5,000,000 tons. The question, clearly, is where to get that much topsoil. ("Excuse me, can you spare 5 million tons?")

That question can be answered by another: What could be more appropriate than recycling discarded materials to reconstruct a dump site? Manufactured soil does exactly that—and not only on landfills.

Although its seems an oxymoron, manufactured soil is technically quite feasible. It may even be the ecologically responsible option in situations like those just cited. The various constituents of soil—its mineral, organic, and chemical components—can be assembled mostly if not entirely from recycled materials. (Similarly, the "potting soils" familiar to home gardeners often combine inorganic materials like perlite and vermiculite with organic materials like peat or compost.) Like many landscape technologies, this mix provides a welcome for microorganisms and plants that complete the "manufacturing."

Soils scientist Phil Craul is the author of *Urban Soils*, a teacher at Harvard's Graduate School of Design, and a leading interpreter of soils science to landscape professionals. Craul has consulted on many projects using manufactured soils and has also written guidelines for specifying them. Here is Craul's definition of manufactured soil, or, as he calls it, "sustainable" soil:

Sustainable soil is comprised entirely of recyclable products alone or in a mixture with derelict soil material, the latter of which is useless without supplementation. It contains few, if any, non-renewable resources.[56]

Although soil can be manufactured "from scratch," soil components are usually available on or adjacent to even the most abused sites. Examples include the following:

- Sand from river dredgings, or recycled ground glass

- Derelict soil material such as selected mine tailings

- Fine-ground till from the bottom layers of glacial deposits

- Dehydrated washings from aggregate plants

- Certain smokestack fly ashes

- Any composted/recycled organic material[57]

All the soils for derelict sites that Craul has produced so far have contained *some* recycled materials, but his current passion involves manufacturing soils *entirely* from such materials. The soils he envisions would *not* include sand specifically mined for the purpose, but only the types of materials listed above. In most cities, says Craul, "you've got all the components you need for making soil—and it's all recycled."

Craul came to the idea of using glass in 1991, when he read in a soils journal of a proposal to devise agricultural soils for space colonies on the moon. The dust on the lunar surface, noted the article, resembles ground glass and, as such, could serve as a silica matrix for man-made soils. "If they can use that stuff on the moon," mused Craul, "why can't we use ground glass as a matrix here on Earth?" He soon learned that others were thinking along similar lines. A landfill near Syracuse NY is covered with a drainage layer of ground glass, and Washington State encourages the use of ground glass as a substitute for sand in residential septic fields. "So there's a movement afoot," says Craul. However, the design of manufactured soils is such a new field that few professionals are experienced in it.

Craul has yet to implement a project using completely recycled soil but has proposed to demonstrate it in grounds restoration of the Washington Monument, collaborating with Sasaki Associates of Watertown MA. Craul also points out that the restoration of derelict inner-city districts, which have little, if any, topsoil, will require massive soil inputs. Manufactured soils could make such projects much more feasible economically and ecologically.

PROJECTS

A pioneering use of manufactured soil is on Spectacle Island in Boston Harbor. The island serves as a landfill for contaminated spoil excavated to build the Boston Central Artery tunnel—2 million cubic yards of it so far. Once completed and capped with clay, plans call for transforming the island into a city park accessible by ferry. Toward this end, the site is being covered with a layer of topsoil—a great deal of topsoil. In fact, Craul and Boston landscape architects Brown & Rowe calculated that 582,000 cubic yards of topsoil would be needed to cover the 105-acre island. To find that much soil, says Craul, "We would have had to strip the topsoil from all the remaining farms in Suffolk County," which neighbors Boston.

Instead, Craul elected to manufacture topsoil. He started with an ingredient available right on the island: stone grit, derived from the glacial till of which the island is composed. Other materials were barged over from the mainland: coarse sand quarried in New Hampshire and compost. Obtaining the inert till and sand proved relatively straightforward. The compost was another matter: 21,000 cubic yards would be needed, by Craul's calculation. The Rochester NH firm of

Figure 2.13. At Spectacle Island, the foreground has been planted using manufactured soil. In the background, construction spoil from Boston Tunnel are dumped and graded. PROJECT: P. Craul with Brown & Rowe. PHOTO: Brown & Rowe.

AllGro was contracted to supply compost, which was supposed to be made of a mixture of 70 percent brewery waste and 30 percent biosolids.

The brewery waste ran out during the first phase of soil application, and AllGro began sending 100 percent biosolids, the most commonly available compost. Because of the volume of compost needed, AllGro had to contract for much of it from other processors in the region—municipal wastewater plants, for example. Soon shipments of compost began showing up at the site containing large sticks and wood chips—low-cost bulking agents that, as the wood decomposes, cause the soil to settle inconsistently. Such fluctuations in quality are symptomatic of the growing pains of the composting industry. Far from arguing against manufactured soils or the use of compost, they argue in favor of better specifications for compost and for ongoing monitoring of what arrives at the construction site.

Spectacle Island is unfinished, but the completed mountain of spoil has been seeded with grasses—which, judging from their luxuriant growth, love the manufactured soil. It is gradually being planted with native trees and shrubs.

Not far away is another project in the Craul portfolio, recently completed in a much more central location: Boston Common. After the Common was excavated to repair an underground parking garage, the project designers, Sasaki Associates, brought Craul on board to re-create the soil. With over 6 inches of coarse sand and various membranes and caps designed to prevent leaks, Craul laid 2 feet of soil composed of brewer's waste, composted biosolids, wood chips, and sand. That part of the Commons was fenced for two years to let the turf establish itself.

Other projects for which Craul has designed soils include the South Cove at Battery Park City in Manhattan and the J. Paul Getty Center in Los Angeles.

At Fresh Kills, Young and McLaughlin also manufactured soils, experimenting with ratios of between 3 and 4 parts sand to 1 part compost and varying depths from 12–30 inches. The project made use of salvaged materials: discarded Christmas trees were chipped to provide part of the mulch needed to cover the site.

Suggested Practices for Soil Restoration

- Cardinal principle: Wherever possible, avoid bringing in fresh topsoil to a construction site.

- Don't overimprove soils; aim to approximate fertility levels of the best soils in the local region. Use regional plant species, tolerant of poor soils, as alternatives to soil amendment and irrigation.

- Wherever possible, remove the topsoil from areas on which construction will occur. Stockpile it on-site and respread as soon as possible.

- Where there is only fill dirt on-site, amend that to create a viable soil rather than bring in new soil. Build the soil by adding compost and other recycled materials or by planting restorative plants. Where necessary, consult with a soils scientist to develop a soils specification appropriate to your site.

- Wherever soil amendments and erosion control materials are needed, specify recycled local materials, if possible.

- Get over your inhibitions about biosolids, and help your clients get over theirs. Promote this material (within the limits noted earlier) as a viable way of turning waste into a resource.

- Become knowledgeable about the different grades of biosolids available regionally. Locate reliable producers (through the appropriate state agency), and specify their products. Use class-A to avoid odor and class-B for less public sites.

- Where there is no soil on the site, or if on-site soil must be removed due to contamination, consider manufactured soil.

- Once restored, ensure that good maintenance practices are used (Principle 10). Irrigation and fertilization can *damage* soil fertility if inappropriately applied.

Restore Regionally Appropriate Vegetation

Restoring the health of site soils is often seen as essential to reestablishing healthy vegetation, but the process is two-way. Vegetation interacts with mineral earth and with climate to produce regional soil types.

Without appropriate revegetation, few sites can properly be called restored. Over the past several decades, landscape architects have become increasingly familiar with the use of native plants, both for restoration work and in garden design. This new design focus places new demands on landscape contractors. Although a few contractors and nurseries specialize in native plants, a majority of *construction* professionals still need to develop the knowledge and skill to work successfully with native plant material.

Site restoration is not just about the replanting of appropriate species—it is also about the control and removal of ecologically inappropriate plants. Some derelict sites are quite green but are covered with an unhealthy mix of weedy plants. Restoring such a site requires attention to changed soil, grading, and drainage patterns that may have invited the weedy species. Standard construction methods and equipment are not always well adapted to creating site conditions that favor native plants (often quite different than the conditions favored by human users). Thoroughly eradicating aggressive introduced plants also requires methods not common in conventional work.

There are many books on site restoration using native species.⊃Because this type of construction is specific both to region and to the type of site damage that must be restored, no single book or resource can detail all the necessary practices. The following is an overview of the main issues that affect construction professionals.

Remove Invasive Plants and Restore Native Succession

In purely economic terms, invasive plants, imported by people and allowed to overrun fields and forests, do tens of billions of dollars worth of damage annually in the United States. The federal government's National Invasive Plant Man-

agement Strategy, drafted in 1996, estimates that 4,600 acres of public lands *per day* are lost to noxious weeds in the western half of the United States alone, reducing both economic yield and ecological viability of these lands.⊃ Removal of these invasives, and restoration of a diverse native plant community, is expected to be the largest public works project *ever* undertaken. It is a task that could largely have been prevented, with hindsight, if horticultural and agricultural plant introductions had been more carefully screened for invasive characteristics.[58]

Removing invasive plants is hard work. One mower manufacturer provides as advertising a list of "the toughest weeds in America." Of these, fully 50 percent were introduced from Asia or Europe, while many of the others have become weeds only after being accidentally or deliberately transported outside their original range.[59]

Invasive nonnative plants can be either the cause or the result of damage to a site and figure prominently in most restoration projects. (For discussion of what constitutes a native and how they are used in new planting, see "What is a Native?" page 124.) Invasion by weedy plants is often a sign of other disturbance, such as overgrazing, soil erosion, declining water table, or pollution. Correcting these problems is essential to restoring a healthy plant community. Some invasives, however, actively displace all other species and must be physically removed before the soil or desirable plants have any chance of recovery. Design and construction professionals concerned with sustainability can expect to see removal of invasives and reintroduction of native species as an increasingly important source of work. Both aspects of this work require new knowledge and new practices.

Conventional plant removal, called "grubbing," tends to be a hit-or-miss process in which the largest plants are ripped out with heavy equipment or sawed down. Eliminating invasive plants is not so simple: these species are among the world's most vigorous. Many can resprout from a small piece of root left behind in the soil or can multiply explosively from a few seeds. Ridding an area of invasives may require careful hand labor, such as forking the soil, to remove roots or tubers. Some invasives can be eliminated by changing soil conditions to favor native plants, a method that requires unusually careful analysis of soil nutrients and knowledge of plant metabolism. In the case of truly damaging invasives, selective use of herbicides may

Figure 2.14. This entire NM floodplain (est. 100 acres) is covered exclusively with two nonnative invaders: salt cedar and Russian olive. Native plants and animals are virtually banished from this once-diverse ecosystem. (Single-lane road at lower right shows scale.) PHOTO: Kim Sorvig.

be essential. Workers on such projects will need to be familiar with the more advanced techniques of herbicide application, such as ultra-low-volume and targeted application. Considerable plant identification skill will be necessary. It is also likely that full eradication of invasive species will require repeat visits in different growing seasons to complete the job. Most of these practices are unfamiliar to conventional construction crews.

Replanting a diverse and appropriate native plant cover also requires new skills and knowledge from construction professionals. While horticultural plants are commonly selected because they transplant or propagate easily by simple methods, success with native plants can require a very broad range of nursery skills. To give a single example, many native species can grow only in cooperation with specific microbial or fungal organisms around their roots. Seeding such plants requires inoculating the seeds with the proper organisms; in transplanting, soil containing these organisms must be included in the planting mix.

In contrast to horticultural care for *individual* plants, native plant restoration usually involves management of *communities* and management of *succession*. Briefly, a plant community is a group of species that grows closely, and often cooperatively, together. Usually, they support an identifiable community of animals. The plant community undergoes succession, which means a series of changes in the composition of the community over time. Succession is considered to "start" from bare ground, whether exposed by natural events like fires or landslides or cleared by humans. Small nonwoody plants are usually the pioneers on bare ground, especially if the soil is poor. Over time, these will be crowded out by shrubs, small trees, and eventually (if soil fertility, water, and sun permit) forest. Ecologists originally considered the forest or other "climax community" as the end of succession, but more recent work shows that succession is frequently set back a stage, or even restarted, on a given site. This idea is extremely useful in site management.

The stages of succession (for example, the change from a meadow to shrubland) are fairly distinct for most regional vegetation. Each stage requires certain conditions before it can develop, and each can be set back by other conditions. As an example, for woodlands to take over from shrubs often requires a high level of organic matter, left in the soil by earlier meadow and shrubland plants. Many tree species are also adapted to germinate only in shade, which must be provided by their forerunners in succession, the shrubs. Thus, providing shade and organic soil might be human *management strategies* for hastening the succession toward its forested phase. Similarly, changing the pH of the soil, or burning a meadow annually, can be used to set back succession, so that woody plants cannot occupy meadow territory. These ways of managing succession were widely used by preagricultural cultures—for example, burning the Great Plains to favor grass for the buffalo on which the people relied. The same methods are being adopted for restoration and management of landscapes today.

Some stages of succession are more socially desirable than others: many people favor meadows and woods over the big-shrub stage called "oldfields," for example. It is crucial to note that although native shrubs may be "invaders" in a native meadow, this is an entirely different process than the invasion of an ecosystem by imported species. As just outlined, native invaders are frequently set back by natural disasters or by aging of the community; in the process, other native species have their day again. When imported invasives take over, all other plants may be permanently suppressed, to the point of extinction. For example, the floodplain in Figure 2.14 will never see native cottonwoods again unless massive human effort eradicates the imported tamarisk and Russian olive that have overrun it.

Those who develop the skills necessary to do successful site restoration, including work with native plants, are likely to be in demand as sustainability grows in importance. For most designers and contractors, collaboration with a native-plant nursery is the most practical route to this knowledge.

Follow Field-Based Planting Patterns

Restoration planting needs to be based on *patterns* of plant growth that occur naturally in the regions. Natural plant patterns are often seen as random, disorderly, and too irregular to reproduce (compare to similar issues in landform grading, page 70). In addition, many designers, influenced by avant-garde artistic theories, have developed deep-seated prejudice against any "mimicry of nature." As discussed in "Successes and Challenges," nature-mimicry *as cosmetics* over socially objectionable structures is a questionable practice. However, practical experience indicates that *pattern* is as important as species selection, soil condition, or microclimate to the long-term health of plant communities.[60] In fact, the idea that plants grow in communities is a critical recognition of the importance of pattern in self-sustaining landscapes. In site restoration, by definition, getting the pattern right is the only appropriate course.

Leslie Sauer, in her book on forest restoration, *The Once and Future Forest*, urges, "Plant in patterns that you have observed on the site or in analogous habitats."[61] Sauer and her colleague at Andropogon, Carol Franklin, have for years taught a simple method of using these patterns: field-sketched minimaps showing the growth patterns of regional trees and shrubs. Select a little-disturbed grove of trees pace off distances and draw, on graph paper, a roughly scaled plan of the major plants. The plan is like a designer's planting plan, but derived from naturally occurring patterns. It should show the approximate trunk size of each tree and a dotted line representing the tree's canopy—which will seldom, if ever, be perfectly round, since trees growing in groups compete for space and sunlight. Once you have a small file of these plant patterns, use them as models on which to base designed and constructed plantings. Contrary to at least one aspect of Robert Thayer's theories on the subject of naturalistic design (see page 16), these patterns are important to the survival and ecological function of plant communities.

Construction professionals and nursery employees are frequently the people responsible for taking the planting plan and creating it on-site. Conventional attitudes encourage these workers to believe that accurately following the planting layout is optional, and that "close enough for convenience" is acceptable. For those firms concerned with sustainable construction, careful adherence to well-patterned plans is a must. Although it is easier to locate and measure points along straight lines, planting crews need to relearn the skills of laying out irregular, but not random, patterns.

Match Plants to Restoration Purposes

In restoration work, plants serve both the general purposes of stabilizing and enriching soil, and more specific purposes like reattracting wildlife or processing toxic materials from the soil (called phytoremediation, see page 91).

PLANTS FOR WILDLIFE RESTORATION

The desire to reintroduce wildlife into damaged habitat is a frequent motive for land restoration. Plants and wildlife in any region are a coevolved community and depend on one another for survival. In addition, some plants (or their fruits) may attract *undesirable* wildlife, either pests like rats or desirable animals too wild to coexist well at close quarters with humans such as bears.

For wildlife restoration, both plant species and planting patterns take on extra importance due to wildlife preferences. A simple and well-documented example: The three North American bluebird species are attracted to sassafras, cherry, dogwood, and cedar (juniper) trees. However, bluebirds are reluctant to nest unless surrounded by a clearing nearly 100 feet across, which forms a barrier to their most aggressive competitor, the house wren.[62] Thus, a large dense grove of their favorite species would fail to attract nesting bluebirds, whereas a single tree planted in a meadow might succeed.

Restoration projects intended to attract wildlife must be designed with detailed knowledge of the whole community and consideration for human impact. Constructing such landscapes offers unique challenges for the right contractor, who must work closely with the designer, scientific specialists, and the client to achieve success.

PHYTOREMEDIATION FOR BROWNFIELDS CLEANUP

Correctly chosen, plants can be active workers in the remediation of many kinds of pollution. This approach is called phytoremediation. It has great but largely untapped potential for the hundreds of thousands of brownfields that litter the North American landscape.

In innovative phytoremediation efforts, the United States is lagging far behind Europe. A few environmental artists have created interesting artworks aimed at cleaning up toxic sites. New York sculptor Mel Chin conceived the idea in 1989 of turning a contaminated site into a garden that he called a "revival field." Chin teamed up with U.S. Department of Agriculture agronomist Rufus Chaney, who was experimenting with processes by which plants absorb pollutants from the soil. Because little was then known about how to increase the uptake of toxins by plants,

Chaney suggested that Chin's artwork be configured so that it could serve as a scientific testing ground.

Chin's site was the Pig's Eye landfill in St. Paul MN, which was contaminated with the heavy metals cadmium and zinc. On the landfill Chin and his team created Revival Field, a 3,600-square-foot garden, in the spring of 1991. The design was a circle within a square. Walkways formed an X and contained ninety-six test plots where various plants were grown. Three years of digging up the plants each spring to analyze their metal content showed Chaney that alpine pennycress was best at extracting zinc and cadmium. In 1993 Chin and Chaney collaborated in a residential area near a zinc smelter in Palmerton PA, and in 1998 Chin began work on a third such garden in Baltimore.[63]

Such environmental artworks as Revival Field raise awareness of the need to rehabilitate toxic sites. But an estimated 450,000 brownfields remain to be reclaimed, and not all are suitable for art projects. More prosaic methods also have to be employed. Unfortunately, this typically means viewing the cleanup as an engineering problem, ignoring biological or horticultural possibilities. Some of the approaches that have been tried on brownfields—sealing the entire site with paving, or encasing the soil in concrete, for example—are not just prosaic, they are brutal. Other, more high-tech approaches include vitrifying the soil (turning it to glass with high-voltage electrical probes) or excavating the site and trucking the soil off to a processing plant, where it is cleansed by chemical and mechanical processes and re-

turned. Even if these approaches are effective, they greatly increase the price tag of the reclamation process. Encasement and vitrification also raise serious environmental questions.

These costs and questions make phytoremediation preferable where feasible over more engineered methods for cleansing toxic sites, in our opinion. Large-scale planting is the kind of work that landscape professionals are well qualified to do. Considered as an alternative to harsher engineering methods, phytoremediation appears to offer significant benefits to the environment, to the public, and to the landscape industry.

Although phytoremediation is a new term, and although its use on brownfields is still largely experimental, its basic principles are more familiar in another setting: constructed wetlands for stormwater and wastewater treatment (see page 73). In wetlands, aquatic plants take up pollutants and cleanse the water, often exceeding standards required of conventional treatment. The pollutants typically remain in the plants, which must be periodically harvested as toxins build up in their tissues. In many cases, the toxic materials have industrial value and can be reclaimed. Constructed wetlands could, in fact, be called aquatic phytoremediation, since the same processes are at work. A related development is the use of plants to extract gold and nickel from marginal ores, called phytomining.

Today, phytoremediation is being developed for a whole range of sites affected by substances considerably more toxic than the stormwater or sewage typically treated in wetlands. Briefly, phytoremediation is

Figure 2.15. Phytoremediation of a petroleum-contaminated site in Wisconsin. The left photo shows willows at planting; the right, after one year. PROJECT: Geraghty & Miller. PHOTO: Eric Carman.

- useful for treating a wide variety of environmental contaminants: crude oil, solvents, pesticides, landfill leachates, and such metals as chromium, mercury, and lead.

- best used for relatively low concentrations located in upper soil layers.

- aesthetically pleasing.

- solar-powered, unlike energy-intensive mechanical methods.

- far cheaper to install, maintain, and operate than other methods of site decontamination, although slower.

"Public acceptance of a phytoremediation project on a site can be very high, in part because of the park-like aesthetics, shade, dust control, and bird and wildlife habitat," notes Steve Rock, an engineer with the EPA's National Risk Management Laboratory. "There is a widespread intuitive agreement that a site covered in vegetation is less hazardous than a bare abandoned lot. When the plants are growing the site is apparently being cleaned."[64] Of course, healthy growth is not a perfect indicator of site health and must be backed by instrumented monitoring to ensure full and safe results.

Phytoremediation operates through three principal mechanisms: extraction, containment, or degradation of the contaminants.

1. *Extraction* involves species that take up and accumulate contaminants in their shoots and leaves as in the stormwater example cited earlier. (Phytoremediation experts like to compare a plant to a solar-powered pump that brings the contaminants up out of the soil.) The plant is then harvested, thereby removing the contaminant from the site. The plant tissue may then be dried, burned, or composted under controlled conditions, sometimes reclaiming the extracted chemical from the ash for reuse by industry.

2. *Containment* uses plants to immobilize the contaminants. Certain trees, for example, can sequester large concentrations of metals in their root systems. Although harvesting and carting away whole trees and their roots are impractical, the contaminants at least no longer circulate within the environment.

3. *Degradation* is a process in which contaminants—principally hydrocarbons and other organic compounds—are broken down or digested so that they are no longer toxic. This degradation may occur in the rhizosphere (root zone) through the action of microbes or fungi symbiotic with the plant; it may also result from chemical effects of the root zone, or enzymes exuded by the roots. Another mechanism for degradation is the plant itself. Some plants take in organic toxins and, by using some chemical elements of these poisons as food, detoxify them. Degradation may also convert a chemical from a water- or fat-soluble form (easily taken up by animals and people) to insoluble forms that pose little danger.

Phytoremediation is no cure-all. For one thing, it will not be effective on every contaminated site—particularly the profoundly contaminated sites of the Superfund variety. Phytoremediation's effectiveness is generally limited to sites with lower overall concentrations of pollutants as well as shallower distribution of pollutants in the soil and groundwater. Most phytoremediation plants also seem to require a soil-chelating chemical (one that binds the metal to itself, allowing the plant to take it up). However, recent genetic research appears to have isolated a gene from a relative of alpine pennycress, *Arabidopsis thaliana,* that allows that species to produce its own chelating chemical—and this gene could be bred into other plants.[65]

The science of phytoremediation is in its infancy. Its experimental status, and the lack of a long-term track record, may cause regulators to view the practice with some suspicion, and installations must be approved on a site-by-site basis. Certainly, valid questions have yet to be answered. What happens in the food chain if wildlife consume leaves or shoots of phytoremediation plants? How is air quality affected if plants pull pollutants out of the soil and release them via evapotranspiration? More research is needed to answer such questions.

There are, as yet, no brownfield sites on which phytoremediation is part of a planting design for *permanent* future site development—yet this, surely, is a direction in which phytoremediation needs to go. Alan Christensen, a landscape architect from American Fork UT who has studied brownfield remediation techniques, puts it this way: "What if you could plant trees to get rid of the contamination, and at the same time use the trees as landscape buffers or to create shade for parking lots and buildings? That would save a lot of money on future landscape installation costs. Up to this point no one has pursued that idea on any site in the United States—and it's a waste not to." (The National Park Service is currently planning a pilot project in Charleston SC that will incorporate phytoremediation as part of the long-term planting design for the park.)

Is it really feasible to use those same pollution-cleansing plants to provide color, texture, and all the other design attributes of plants? The number of plants that can remediate a specific contaminant is limited; there may not be, for example, any tree that can degrade cadmium, let alone a frost-hardy shade tree with yellow flowers. If the contaminant is highly toxic, and if the plant processes the poison by exuding it on leaves or bark, permanent public plantings would be unthinkable. Capacities and hazards differ for every contaminant or plant species. We would urge more designers and contractors to examine the possibilities; only widespread field studies of permanent phytoremediation plantings can test its potential. Widespread test projects are the only way to understand what kinds of phytoremediation sites work as parks and recreation areas.

BIOREMEDIATION

A strategy related to phytoremediation is bioremediation: the use of soil bacteria and other microorganisms to cleanse pollution from soil or water. Like phytoremediation, it is a low-tech, environmentally sound approach that harnesses a benign force of nature—the enzymes that occur in certain microorganisms—to biodegrade pollution.

Whereas phytoremediation is still in the experimental stage, bioremediation has already become a mainstream approach to the cleanup of toxic sites. It is widely used to clean up petroleum spills. Other substances for which bioremediation has proved successful include uranium, selenium, vinyl chloride, benzene, phenol, creosote and pentachlorophenol wood preservatives, naphthalene moth repellent, toluene and other solvents, oil, gas, transmission fluid, brake fluid, PCBs, explosives residue, and herbicides. Especially if the chemical bears a

resemblance to natural substances, there is a good chance that a microbe can be found—or genetically engineered—to metabolize it.

It has been known for decades that the soil contains microbes with the ability to degrade chemicals. Until recently, however, a lack of practical field experience has kept them from being widely used. This lack is gradually being remedied as more government agencies and for-profit consultants enter the field.

A widespread environmental problem is petroleum product leakage from old, corroded, underground storage tanks. Minnesota's DOT uses bioremediation in the form of "biomounds" for routine remediation of contamination from gasoline, diesel, and used motor oil, according to senior environmental engineer Brian Kamnikar of MnDOT. The simple secret of bioremediation, according to Kamnikar, is that indigenous soil bacteria treat petroleum as a free lunch—a source of energy for the bacteria. MnDOT enhances this natural biodegradation by mounding up the contaminated soil (hence the name biomounds) and amending it with nutrients (typically sheep manure) to accelerate the soil's natural processes. To be most effective, bioremediation must be an aerobic process, which requires getting as much oxygen as possible to the microbes. MnDOT adds moistened wood chips to reduce the bulk density of the soil, keep oxygen flowing through the mound, and provide moisture, which promotes bacterial activity.

Soil tests have shown biomounds to be quite effective, and MnDOT has successfully reused the decontaminated soil as topsoil on highway-construction projects—thereby completing the cycle by returning the resource to productive use.[66]

At the federal level the EPA is actively promoting bioremediation and has published the results of its field testing. At least one nonprofit group, the National Ground Water Association, offers courses in what it refers to as "natural attenuation" of soil and groundwater pollution. Finally, a number of bioremediation consultants have sprung up, advertising their services on the Internet and elsewhere. (By spreading timely information, the Net has played a significant role in the growth of bioremediation.) We find it encouraging that alternatives to high-tech chemical or mechanical remediation are quickly gaining acceptance.

Bioremediation is not a panacea for all hazardous wastes; for example, wastes that contain heavy metals will kill the bacteria capable of metabolizing organic pollutants in the waste. Bioremediation is generally used to treat dispersed, dilute soil contamination. In soils that air cannot readily penetrate, anaerobic conditions can hinder the process. There are some relatively simple methods for aerating soil, such as using blowers or compressors to pump oxygen into the earth.[67]

From the point of view of a landowner or government agency, perhaps the greatest appeal of bioremediation is its low cost. According to one summary on the Internet, "The cost of restoring the burgeoning global inventory of contaminated ecosystems is virtually incalculable. As a result, government, industry and the public have recognized the need for more cost-effective alternatives to traditional physical and chemical methods of contaminant remediation. Bioremediation . . . is a safe, effective, and economic alternative to traditional methods of remediation."[68]

Like many sustainable strategies, bioremediation is based on services that the environment has always provided. A 1999 study found that bacteria living in lake- and stream-bottom mud can remove 35–85 percent of two carcinogenic water pollutants.[69] As emphasized in the section on soil preservation (page 45), microorganisms exist by the billions in soil and are among the best-known defenses against pollution. Bioremediation is simply advancing human ability to make specific use of what the Earth has been doing for eons.

Get Specialist Help for Tanks and Toxic Wastes

The removal of hazardous and buried structures like fuel-storage tanks, and the remediation of heavily contaminated soils, are very specialized tasks. This work requires both special permits and special skills. It is critical to long-term sustainability that these tasks be thoughtfully planned and skillfully carried out.

While we have discussed some relatively nontechnical methods that may apply to some brownfields, any site remediation involving toxic materials is likely to require input from environmental engineers. The degree of engineering involvement *should* correspond to the severity of contamination. However, current regulatory control of site remediation is written and adminis-

Figure 2.16. Restoration of mines, heavy industry, and Superfund sites requires specialized engineering, but should not exclude landscape concerns such as habitat and visual fit with surroundings. PHOTO: New Mexico Department of Mining and Minerals.

tered largely by engineers and sometimes excludes biological solutions. It is critically important to balance both types of approach in ways that meet safety requirements, minimize financial costs, and truly restore the site (rather than making it "idiot-proof" and ecologically dead).

Landscape professionals can work to educate both their engineering colleagues and the public about biological approaches to site remediation, but this must be done thoughtfully and diplomatically. No purpose is served by insisting on "natural solutions" that fail and tarnish the credibility of more carefully site-specific approaches. Although bias against biological solutions is frustrating at times, the landscape professional *must* know when engineering help is truly the most appropriate solution. Among the following resources are several that can help you understand the issues and find a specialist contractor; Resources for Principle 6 also offer information on identifying toxic materials.

Resources

Site Restoration

Earth Island Institute
300 Broadway, Suite 28, San Francisco CA 94133
415-788-3666
   Publishes Karl Linn's booklet, *From Rubble to Restoration.*

Society for Ecological Restoration
http://ser.org

Excellent source of detailed information on all facets of site restoration. Library of publications; links to consultants.

Beyond Preservation: Restoring and Inventing Landscapes by A. Dwight Baldwin, Judith De Luce & Carl Pletsch (1994 University of Minnesota, Minneapolis)

Environmental Remediation
Construction Industry Institute
http://construction-institute.org/ or 512-232-2000
RS48-1. Inexpensive overview of three detailed CII publications on site contamination management.

Land Planning and Design for Land Reclamation Bibliography by Bruce K. Ferguson (1982 Vance Bibliographies, Monticello IL)

Landscape and Surface Mining: Ecological Guidelines for Reclamation by Gerhard Darmer & Norman L. Dietrich (1992 Van Nostrand Reinhold)

Practical Handbook of Disturbed Land Revegetation by Frank F. Munshower (1994 Lewis Publishers [CRC Press] 800-272-7737)

Restoring Our Earth by Laurence P. Pringle (1987 Enslow Publishers, Hillside NJ)

The Ecology of Woodland Creation by Richard Ferris-Kaan (1995 British Ecological Society; Wiley)

The Once and Future Forest by Leslie Sauer (1998 Island Press)
Excellent source on restoration, focused on eastern forests.

The Tallgrass Restoration Handbook by Stephen Packard & Cornelia Mutel (1997 Island Press)

NOAA Landscape Restoration National Oceanographic and Atmospheric Administration
www.csc.noaa.gov/lcr/
Good information; shows how strong the link is between landscape, oceans, and atmosphere.

Brownfields

Dealing with Dereliction: The Redevelopment of the Lower Swansea Valley by Rosemary D. F. Bromley & Graham Humphrys (1979 University College of Swansea, Swansea UK)

Derelict Britain by John Barr (1969 Penguin)

Derelict Properties: Scale and Scope of an Urban Environmental Problem by Craig E. Colten (1995 Illinois Department of Energy and Natural Resources, Springfield)

Brownfield Center at Carnegie Mellon
http://funnelweb.utcc.utk.edu/~adoshi/

Brownfields Action Plan Page
www.brownfield.org/Action/action.htm

Brownfields—Center of Excellence for Sustainable Development: Land-Use Planning Strategies
http://webdevvh6.nrel.gov/landuse/brownf.html

Brownfields—GAO report
Government Accounting Office www.gao.gov/AIndexFY98/abstracts/rc98087.htm
Economics, grants for reuse of brownfields.

Brownfields—Wisconsin
Wisconsin Environmental News Report
www.wienviro.com/70514a.htm
Describes one large federally funded cleanup and has links to related sites.

Green Pages—Global Directory for Environmental Technology
http://eco-web.com/
Listing of 4,000 products and services internationally related to waste management as well as energy; organizations, some articles on the subject.

Regional Brownfield Reuse Initiative Pilot Proposal
ECO Services International
www.mrpc.org/mrpcoedp/regional.htm

Grading

H. J. Schor Consulting
626 N. Pioneer Dr.
Anaheim CA 92805
714-778-3767
Landform grading consultation for mines, development; author of articles on topic.

"Erosion Measurements on a Smooth and Stepped Highway Slope" by John Haynes (Caltrans Engineering Services Center, Sacramento CA, 916-227-7109)

"Stepped Slopes: An Effective Answer to Roadside Erosion" by John Haynes (Feb 1990 *Landscape Architect and Specifier News*)

"Overview of Engineering Techniques to Reduce Grading" California Coastal Commission
http://ceres.ca.gov/coastalcomm/web/landform/attach3.html

Compost and Mulch

Clean Washington Center
999 Third Avenue, Ste. 1060
Seattle WA 98104
206-464-7040
Standards and information on composting.

Composting Council
4424 Montgomery Ave., Ste. 102
Bethesda MD 20814
301-913-2885
Standards and information on composting.

Compost Utilization by Departments of Transportation in the United States by Donna Mitchell (1997 University of Florida Depts. of Environmental Horticulture and Soil and Water Science, Gainesville)

Composting
Ohio State University Extension factsheet
700 Ackerman Road, Ste. 235
Columbus OH 43202-1578
www.ag.ohio-state.edu/

Australia Mulch Network
http://argo.net.au/jiaren/mulchnet.subpage.html
    Interesting way of matching mulch supply with users.

Biosolids

Northwest Biosolids Management Association
Washington State, 206-684-1145
    Source of information on Washington's innovations in biosolids
    use.

Water Environment Federation
Alexandria VA 703-684-2400
    Health and regulatory aspects of biosolids.

Biosolids Recycling: Beneficial Technology for a Better Environment (EPA 832-R-94-009)
U.S. EPA
National Center for Environmental Publications and
Information
POB 42419
Cincinnati OH 45242
800-490-9198 or 513-489-8695
    Primer on biosolids use in the landscape.

Soils

Urban Soil in Landscape Design by Phillip Craul (1992 Wiley)
    Detailed and complete source; specific to landscape, rather than
    other aspects of soil science.

Soil Survey
Natural Resource Conservation Service (formerly Soil
Conservation Service)
Contact local office; Federal depository libraries also
hold *Soil Survey* books
    Soil types of almost all U.S. regions identified, mapped over air-
    photos, and explained. Essential resource for capacities of local
    soils, incl. bearing strength, infiltration rates, and vegetation
    suitability.

Soil Amendments and Manufactured Soil

Western Polyacrylamide
POB 1377
Jay OK 74346
918-253-8922
    Manufacturer of superabsorbent soil amendment. Has studies on
    effectiveness.

Worm's Way
 800-274-9676 or www.wormsway.com
    Catalog sales of soilless, hydroponic, and other growing media and
    low-toxic pest control products, tools.

"Designing Sustainable Soil" by Phillip Craul, 1997, in
Opportunities in Sustainable Development ASLA; Margarita

Hill, editor, Washington DC, 800-787-2665 or
www.asla.org

Manufactured Loam Using Compost Material by Michael S.
Switzenbaum, Phillip J. Craul, & Tom Ryan (1996 University of Massachusetts Transportation Center,
Amherst)
    Book of specifications—one of several developed independently
    around the country—an apparent groundswell (pardon the pun)
    of interest.

"Developing Biosolids Compost Specifications" by
Phillip J. Craul & Michael S. Switzenbaum (Dec. 1996
BioCycle magazine)

Phytoremediation

A Citizen's Guide to Phytoremediation
US EPA
National Center for Environmental Publications and
Information
POB 42419
Cincinnati OH 45242
800-490-9198 or 513-489-8695

"Plants to the Rescue" by A. Maureen Rouhi (January
13, 1997 *Chemical & Engineering News*)

Phytoremediation Bibliography
www.rtdf.org/phytodoc.htm
    Currently lists 1,171 journal articles, abstracts, and books.

*Phytoremediation: Using Plants to Remove Pollutants from the
Environment* by Ilya Raskin American Society of Plant
Physiologists
www.aspp.org/pubaff/phytorem.htm or 301-251-0560
    Good primer on phytoremediation.

Bioremediation

"Munching Microbes"
Purdue University engineering dept.
    Describes bioremediation research and projects.

Bioremediation and Groundwater information
Environment Canada, Groundwater Assessment &
Restoration Project
http://gw2.cciw.ca/internet/bioremediation/
whatis.html
    Actually several good pages; not easy to navigate their menus.
    http://gw2.cciw.ca/internet/bioremediation/ has links on biore-
    mediation. http://gw2.cciw.ca/internet/ is menu of groundwater
    items.

U.S. EPA
http://clu-in.com
    Actively promotes and reports bioremediation field testing.

Soil and Groundwater Cleanup magazine
204 W. Kansas, Ste. 103
Independence, MO 64050
816-254-2128
    February/March 1998 issue focused entirely on phytoremediation.

Favor Living, Flexible Materials

He that plants trees loves others besides himself.

—Thomas Fuller, 1732

A quiet revolt is underway against conventional approaches to erosion control. Known as biotechnical erosion control or bioengineering, it uses *plants*, sometimes in conjunction with mechanical methods, to *build living structures* at the vulnerable interfaces between soil and water, especially on steep slopes, stream banks, and shorelines. Although a specialist consultant should almost always lead any bioengineering project, basic knowledge of these methods is more and more a critical part of the repertoire of every landscape professional.

Rigid structures of concrete and steel as the technology of choice for controlling erosion are twentieth century inventions that are barely a century old. By contrast, bioengineering is a modern adaptation of an age-old green technology. For centuries before the industrial revolution, constructed banks were held in place by grading and terracing, by pervious walls of local stone, and by the root systems of plants.[1] These tested systems have been rejected by conventional engineering, which has insisted that rigid structures were always cheaper, more durable, safer, and mathematically more predictable.

Detailed observation has shown, however, that these claims obscure the problems *caused* by rigid erosion- and flood-control structures. Hard, engineered structures certainly have their place, but as a one-size-fits-all standard they can trigger the problems they were designed to solve. Concrete ditches and pipes transform the precious resource of rainwater into a problem to be whisked away. Wherever stormwater is shunted away, it becomes a concentrated and destructive force and fails to nourish the ground or replenish the water table. Hard structures, especially in floodplains, preempt the wildlife habitat that belongs there. Engineered for "safety," but usually posted with "Danger" signs, these lifeless, armor-plated canyons traverse most cities.

The alternative is to use the dynamic, flexible strength of living things as a way of building resilient and healthy landscape structures. Closely related to the sustainable use of water (Principle 4), live surfaces may also be applied to building walls and roofs. Bioengineering and its close relatives require a new—or renewed—respect and knowledge about an essential component of the landscape: living vegetation.

Discussed in This Chapter:

- Controlling slope erosion with the strength of living plants

- Using "greenwalls" to retain slopes and clothe buildings in growth

- Revitalizing wasted acreage on the skyline with planted ecoroofs

- Designing and building appropriate structures for sustainable planting

- Selection, substitution, and handling to ensure plant survival

- The use of native plant species for sustainability

Hold Slopes in Place with Biotechnical Erosion Control

Biotechnical erosion control (BEC) includes a wide array of applications. Almost all make use of the remarkable ability of some plants to sprout from a fresh cut twig stuck in the soil. The most vigorous of these are willows, poplars, or dogwood (the authors have seen poplar fenceposts sprouting leaves). These and a few other species are the most commonly used materials of bioengineering. When cut, they have neither roots nor leaves, making them almost as convenient to work with as very small boards or stakes—yet they are alive, and within days or weeks begin to weave new roots deeply into the soil.

Perhaps the purest form of BEC is *soil bioengineering*, a simple system in which live woody cuttings and branches provide both structure and growth. Mulch and natural or synthetic fabrics also play a major role, preventing surface erosion until the cuttings leaf out. Once the cuttings take root—usually within one growing season—they provide long-term stability for the slope and are self-repairing and self-maintaining.

BEC does not rule out the use of hard structures. Inert structures made of concrete, wood, metal, or plastic—through and around which lush plants may grow, and through which water drains gradually but freely—are an important part of bioengineering for certain extreme conditions. In this book, these live-plus-hard structures are discussed under the heading of "greenwalls" (see page 105). A whole menu of green structural approaches are gaining acceptance in this country among public agencies (especially state transportation departments) and other clients.

Biotechnical methods recall one of the themes of this book—that many supposedly outdated traditional techniques need to be reexamined and, in some cases, reintroduced to replace conventional landscape technologies. Twig-and-wattling and other uses of plants for erosion control have been in use for millennia in widely different cultures, but their modern application in the United States seems to have begun in the 1930s by such agencies as the Works Progress Administration and the Civilian Conservation Corps, whose workers repaired gullies and restored stream banks with native stone and cuttings from local plants.[2] Bioengineering was pursued most energetically, however, in the German-speaking countries. Bioengineering applications in North America seem to have begun in earnest in the 1970s as an approach imported from Europe; specialized supplies for some forms of bioengineering are still imported.

Soil bioengineering is useful for repairing gullies and controlling shallow landslides and slumps, on wet soils or dry, on cut or fill. It is probably most widely used for stabilizing stream banks (Principle 4, page 146).

Here are some of the advantages that bioengineering provides:

- A flexible, self-sustaining, self-repairing, structure.

- Cheaper installation and maintenance than hard structures, in many cases.

- Greater strength than standard surface plantings, due to deep burial of cuttings, and interwoven stems, roots, and geotextiles.

- A practical alternative where heavy equipment cannot be used.

- Wildlife habitat, air and water quality filtering, and other functions of plants.

Bind the Soil with Living Plants

Soil bioengineering uses fast-rooting cuttings in a number of ways:

- *Live stakes* (sturdy cuttings 1 inch or more in diameter) can be tamped directly into the slope with a mallet, typically 2 to 3 feet apart. Driving them into the soil increases the friction among soil particles, helping the soil mass stay together—similar to inserting rebar in concrete. Not only do the live stakes provide initial structural slope protection, but as they take root, the root systems strengthen the slope's resistance to failure, and the cuttings will later leaf out above ground to intercept some stormwater before it hits (and erodes) the ground.

- *Wattles* and *brushmattresses* ("woven" pads of live branches) are staked to slopes for coverage.

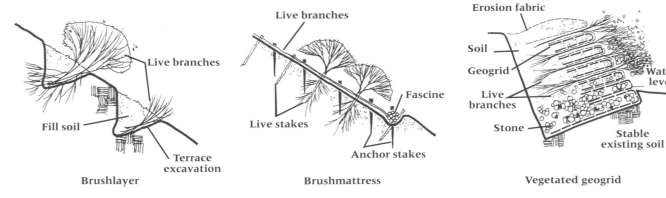

Brushlayer

Live branches

Live branches

Fill soil

Terrace excavation

Brushmattress

Live branches

Fascine

Live stakes

Anchor stakes

Vegetated geogrid

Erosion fabric

Soil

Geogrid

Live branches

Stone

Water level

Stable existing soil

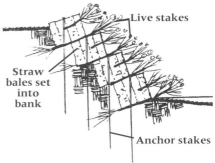

Live stakes

Straw bales set into bank

Anchor stakes

Bales with live staking

Figure 3.1. Bioengineering holds soil with structural assemblages that later root. Correctly installed, these resilient solutions often outperform rigid structures at less cost. ILLUSTRATION: Craig Farnsworth, based on Robbin Sotir and Stan Jones.

- *Fascines* (tied, linear bundles of branches or whips) are buried lengthwise in trenches along contours to reduce surface erosion and stabilize slopes. (Some companies refer to these as wattles, too, but fascine is the preferred term.)

- *Brush layering* places branches perpendicular to the contour on excavated terraces. The terraces are then backfilled with soil, covering the branches except for the tips. When the branches take root, the tips leaf out.

- *Live crib walls,* boxlike structures of interlocking live logs or other timbers backfilled with alternating layers of soil and branch cuttings, can be used to stabilize the toe of a slope. Roots of cuttings extend into the slope, providing structural support.

Control Surface Erosion with Mats and Mulches

In new BEC installations, the entire surface of the newly installed slope needs some form of cover until plants can take root and start protecting the soil. For most situations, the options are two: one uses erosion-control nets, blankets, and mats; the other relies on organic mulches. Both work primarily by blunting the force of raindrops, which dig into bare soil surfaces; both also

Figure 3.2. Lakeshore stabilization at Whiskeytown CA. Soil wraps are being constructed on top of brush-layers. PROJECT: Salix Applied Earthcare. PHOTO: John McCullah.

Figure 3.3. Three weeks later, at the site shown in Figure 3.2, willow twigs are sprouting between wrapped soil layers. The willows will be at water level once the lake is refilled. PROJECT: Salix Applied Earthcare. PHOTO: John McCullah.

absorb some water. Both have proven quite effective in preventing erosion; but mulching, in most cases, is by far the cheaper alternative—and has the added environmental advantage that it may be composed of recycled organics. Given time, mats of organic materials break down, too, and in effect become mulch. Mulch can slow runoff moving across the surface, but the structure and weight of a mat may be more effective under such conditions.

Mats and Blankets

Many BEC practitioners use mats and blankets for surface cover. A variety of products is available. When choosing among these, consider how persistent the material will be once installed. Some products are completely biodegradable (i.e., they will compost themselves and disappear once plant cover becomes established). Others have synthetic components that will remain in the environment, helping to stabilize the soil on a long-term basis.

Biodegradable products are usually the better option for ecologically sensitive sites. They are typically made of fibers such as jute, straw, wood, excelsior, coconut fiber (coire), or a combination of these. Even the pins and stakes needed to secure the blankets to the slope are now being made of degradable materials: North American Green's Bio-STAKE and Eco-STAKE, made of lumber scraps, are examples.⊃ Like mulches, the biodegradable products add a certain amount of organic nutrients to the soil over time.

For extremely steep or erodable slopes, some practitioners consider it important to use products bound together with synthetic fibers that will hold the soil after the natural materials have decomposed (see "Project Examples" on page 113). If using such materials, especially ones incorporating a plastic mesh, it is important to ensure that the mesh is not a trap for birds or mammals. If the mesh opening could go around an animal's neck or leg, the mesh should not be too strong for an animal of that size to break free. This also applies to biodegradable mesh, though it weakens over time and eventually disappears.

At least one BEC practitioner views all blankets and mats with some suspicion. "Landscape architects, like engineers, are too ready to use manufactured products," says John Haynes of Caltrans. "All these products have their niche and can be very effective in the proper application; but some of them are pretty darn expensive. We need to be looking at locally available, inexpensive materials for use in erosion control." For large-scale highway construction projects, even an inexpensive brand of blanket would cost $15,000 per acre, whereas tackified straw mulch from local sources would cost only $1,500 per acre to accomplish the same end.

Mulches and Composts for Slope Stabilization

Except on unusual soils or extreme conditions, mulches and similar stabilizers perform as well as mats, at much less cost. These materials include composts made from almost any organic material, biosolids, and proprietary "soil tackifiers" applied directly to the soil or mixed with straw or other fibers. Loose wood chips will also protect a surface against rainfall as long as running water is not channeled under them. In general, for surface erosion control, all types of mulching material are best applied as a slurry, using a hydroseeding machine.

Tackifiers of guar gum are environmentally preferable to asphalt-based ones, since asphalt fumes are moderately toxic, and as a petroleum product it can contaminate soil. Polymer tackifiers have various formulas; each should be evaluated for biodegradability.

The many uses of compost are discussed in more detail in Principle 2. Further information on these practices is available from Caltrans.⊃

Evaluate and Monitor Each Site Carefully

When is bioengineering appropriate for a project? Landscape architect Andrea Lucas of Berkeley CA, who has used BEC techniques on many projects, recommends it for any slope that is steep and subject to excessive runoff. "If you see a long, cut slope with rills occurring," says Lucas, "this is the perfect place to reduce runoff velocities by adding contour wattles and contour straw rolls." Hillsides that have already been planted with standard techniques but continue to erode are also prime candidates, as are the banks of streams and lakes (page 146). Extremely steep slopes or abrupt grade changes may require a greenwall, the bioengineered version of a retaining wall (page 106).

Looking back on her experience with bioengineering, Lucas recalls it initially being presented to her as a foolproof miracle cure. Despite continued enthusiasm, Lucas warns against taking that view. As part of her research for a graduate degree at the University of California at Berkeley, she visited bioengineered stream banks in California. Every bank had eroded at least 20 percent after the bioengineering was installed. This does not mean that BEC is invalid, says Lucas, but that, like most landscapes, every BEC installation requires some monitoring and maintenance for the first few years—patching unexpected gullies in particular. Monitoring, evaluating, and adjusting new installations not only makes the difference between success and failure—it is the best way to gain expertise for the next project.

Bioengineering cannot always be expected to stand alone against major off-site influences, such as expanded upstream pavement and increased runoff. Bioengineering provides structural solutions as part of a watershedwide water and erosion management plan. Bioengineering adds living and structural strength to eroding slopes. In addition, it makes these surfaces rougher, more irregular, and more absorbent than conventionally engineered slopes. This roughness and irregularity relate directly to the concepts of landform grading (page 70), Permaculture (page 171), and near-the-source solutions (page 136). Used together, these concepts reinforce each other.

A growing body of information on bioengineering techniques is available in English, including computer programs for planning. One of the foremost authors of bioengineering books, as well as an active consultant (see Project Example, Figure 3.6), is Robbin Sotir, of Marietta GA. Sotir emphasizes that even though bioengineering is straightforward in concept, success depends on adjusting to complex and site-specific conditions and requires well-honed ecological expertise. Lucas seconds this: "As a designer or practitioner you need to respond to each site individually," she says. "Along with the specific plants you choose, soils, compaction, slope angle, amount of sunlight, runoff forces that the site must weather—all affect the design." Sotir, who has tirelessly championed bioengineering in the United States, has seen many

enthusiastic do-it-yourself bioengineering projects fail because seasonal or regional conditions were overlooked, plants were misidentified, or cuttings were harvested at the wrong time.

Bioengineering is more expensive than hydroseeding or standard landscape plantings, though usually cheaper than hard alternatives. Compared to simple planting, it often involves more grading, filling, or extradeep plantings. Some can be done with machinery, but many methods are hand-labor intensive. Where labor is scarce or high priced, bioengineering becomes less competitive with other systems. Bioengineering is also knowledge intensive, requiring an experienced bioengineering practitioner to provide design services and on-site supervision throughout project installation. Nevertheless, says Lucas, bioengineering "may be cheaper, depending on what your alternatives are. It's always cheaper than building a concrete wall."

One way to evaluate the effectiveness of a specific BEC product or approach is to observe a completed installation that has been in place for one or more growing seasons. Many erosion-control manufacturers or consultants can provide a list of projects and contacts in your area. There are also hundreds of demonstration projects sponsored by the federal government. Unfortunately, their locations and other particulars may be scattered among various agencies and therefore hard to ferret out. The examples below and in Principle 4 give some idea of the diversity of existing installations.

PROJECT EXAMPLES

One of the most encouraging developments in BEC is that state highway departments are beginning to experiment with it. John Haynes has used BEC techniques for several years on state highway projects. In 1993, on a road construction site with highly erodable soils near Redding CA, he compared various approaches on test plots. On one 1.5:1 slope, Haynes employed brush-layering: willow cuttings were laid at the rate of twenty stems per yard on terraces created by a bulldozer. The bulldozer then backfilled the slopes, allowing the tips of the stems to protrude.

Four weeks into the project, a major storm hit northern California, dumping about 15 inches of rain on the test site. The rain caused some slopes treated with erosion-control fabrics to fail, but

Figure 3.4. Brush-layer installation can be done by hand or aided by equipment. PROJECT and PHOTO: Biohabitats Inc.

Figure 3.5. Fabric anchored with logs, live-stakes, and fast-sprouting grass, in place only a few weeks when this storm struck, survived with no losses. PROJECT and PHOTO: Andrea Lucas.

slopes reinforced with willow cuttings held. The only damage they suffered was gullying—a problem that could have been avoided, Haynes believes, if he had specified a 6-inch layer of cuttings (about three times as many as were used in the test). The results of the test plots are summarized in the *Proceedings of the 1994 IECA Conference*, available from the International Erosion Control Association.Ↄ

Brush-layering was also employed to stabilize the site of a large mudslide near Pacifica CA, above a residential area with slopes from 2.5:1 to 1.5:1. Andrea Lucas collaborated on the project with BEC pioneer and author Andrew Leiser.Ↄ As at the Redding site, workers constructed terraces on which they layered nonrooted native willow cuttings harvested from the local area. The team then backfilled the terraces to re-create the contours of the original slope. Next, Lucas planted rooted pine and cypress seedlings native to the area and seeded the slope with an erosion-control mix of grasses and herbaceous perennials and annuals. Although installed during California's rainy season, the work immediately reduced sediment transport dramatically, Lucas reports. The project continues to perform well today.

Gullies and watercourses respond well to bioengineered repairs. Securing fill in a drainage channel is particularly difficult because the soil tends to liquefy during storms and flow downhill. At Sanders Ranch in Moraga CA, one drainage ditch, though lined with pieces of concrete, was eroding ever deeper with each

rainstorm. Lucas began stabilizing it by reconstituting the channel bottom with "burritos"—fill soil that her crew wrapped with geotextile. At the edges of the burritos, the crew buried live willow brush with only the tips exposed. These locally gathered cuttings quickly rooted, tying fill, geotextile, and existing subsoil together into a strong flexible channel.

Lucas's crew then seeded the side banks with a fast-growing annual grass and a perennial native bunchgrass, covered with the same geotextile blankets. Into this they drove stout willow "live stakes" 2 to 3 feet deep. As an added precaution the geotextiles were pinned to the ground with cables to withstand stormflows of up to 10 feet per second.

Lucas notes that BEC projects must be secure enough to withstand stormflows as soon as they are constructed. Sure enough, a storm struck one month after installation during an El Niño winter—and the system held. The grasses then sprang up and covered the slope with a carpet of green, holding the soil with their root systems. Within a year, the willows had grown taller than the grasses, further anchoring the slope.

Robbin Sotir has built scores of projects all over the United States, including the desert Southwest. In addition to the technical side of her work, she has been the negotiator in adversarial projects where community groups have had to threaten to block a project in order to get vegetation and wildlife issues addressed, and she has for years been educating the public about alternatives to standard engineering. The Crestwood project in Houston TX is an excellent example of the way bioengineering *combines* techniques to fit the site, or even the specialized conditions within a site.

The Buffalo Bayou (a ship channel leading to the Port of Houston) was eroding the 20-foot banks below the Crestwood condominiums. Virtually all the techniques diagrammed in Figure 3.1 were used to stabilize this bank. At the toe of the slope, rubble wrapped in erosion-control fabric provided a strong footing above and below mean water level. Above that, the main slope was held with vegetated geogrid—soil wrapped in fabric and/or stronger plastic grid sheets, and planted with layers of branches between the supported soil layers. Fascines as well as bare-root plantings were used to make transitions: between the rubble toe and the geogrid system, and also along the top of the slope where stabilization ended. The slope has been carefully monitored since construction and shows no sign of moving. Sediment from the bayou is trapped by vegetation and deposited at the toe, gradually building even more strength.

BEC is increasingly being employed in high-profile locations. In the late 1990s it was used to stabilize the banks of Walden Pond near Concord MA, where Henry David Thoreau lived and wrote. As a popular swimming spot and the destination of 80,000 visitors annually, the pond was suffering from severe edge and bank erosion. Cellular containment systems (a honeycomb material described on page 105), live-staking, and coconut mats were used to reconstruct 3,800 feet of pond edge, bank, and path. The project (by Walker Kluesing Design Group of Cambridge MA) won an award from the Boston Society of Landscape Architects in 1998.

Suggested Practices for Bioengineering

- Soil bioengineering must be tailored carefully to site, plant species, and environmental conditions.

- Successful bioengineering requires an experienced practitioner.

- Vegetative systems may need supplemental retaining structures on extremely steep slopes (see Greenwalls, below).

- Bioengineering methods may be limited on rocky or gravelly slopes lacking soil for plant growth, or in extremely arid regions.

- Where possible, obtain cuttings of native species from the immediate locale. (Be sure to obtain the property owner's permission. Do not harvest on ecologically sensitive sites.)

- Limit the removal of vegetation on-site. Stockpile and protect topsoil and protect exposed areas during construction.

- Build to withstand stormflows immediately, or divert or drain runoff while the project is newly in the ground.

- Maintain bioengineering like any other planted work, for at least a one-year establishment period.[3]

Make Vertical Structures "Habitat-able" with Greenwalls

What can hold up a truck, protect a prince, foil graffiti—and clean the air? It's not the Incredible Hulk, it's the greenwall.

On near-vertical slopes, soil bioengineering by itself may not be enough stabilization, and some nonliving retaining structure may be required.[4]

Figure 3.6. Bioengineering techniques form a flexible tool kit, often used in combination, as in stabilizing this bank at Crestwood (Houston TX). Note the large stump, left, as added protection, visible in the before, during, and after photos. PROJECT and PHOTOS: Robbin B. Sotir.

In cases like these, bioengineering uses structural supports through and over which plants can grow. In various forms, these achieve strong structures with a green face. Closely related to the ecoroof concept, greenwalls are part of the larger family of bioengineering techniques that rely on flexible, living materials for functional purposes.

Jon Coe (CLR Design, Philadelphia) is a persuasive advocate of greenwalls, which fit his firm's specialty, zoo exhibit design. But Coe sees much wider possibilities for the greenwall. "To keep structures clean and shiny," he says, "contemporary technology spends inordinate effort to stifle biological succession on built surfaces. What if we set out to design structures that *welcomed* plant growth?"

Advantages of Greenwalls

Greenwalls offer compelling alternatives to landscape structures of cast-in-place concrete, metal, or wood. A vegetated surface suits many aesthetic preferences; it deadens and diffuses noise, makes graffiti impossible, cuts heat and glare, holds or slows rainwater, traps air pollutants, and processes carbon dioxide, while providing food and shelter for wildlife. Most greenwalls use small, light elements, installed without heavy equipment. Many require reduced materials, no formwork, and for some types no footings, saving money and resources. Most deal flexibly with unstable soils, settling, deflection—even earthquakes. Careful attention to irrigation and microclimate is richly repaid. Various designs are discussed below, with examples from residential to heavy-duty.

Types of Greenwalls

Greenwall systems have been based on many concepts. Not all are commercially available in the United States; some can be built with on-site materials. The main structural *concepts* include the following:

- *Block*—engineered with gaps where plants root *through* the wall.

- *Crib wall*—concrete or wood elements stacked log-cabin style. A related stackable unit looks like giant jacks from a child's game.

- Frame—interlocking circle- or diamond-shaped units stacked like masonry (mostly in Europe and Japan). Also used flat to "blanket" water channels. For parking, Grasscrete is a similar concept.

- *Trough*—stackable soil-filled tubs (retaining or freestanding).

- *Gabion*—wire baskets filled with stones to provide a strong but permeable wall or dam.

- *Mesh*—like mini-gabions, holding a thin layer of soil to a surface.

- *Cell*—flexible, strong honeycombs filled with soil. Closely related are plastic turf support systems like Grasspave.

- *Sandbag*—geotextiles wrapped around soil, formally called "vegetated geogrid."

Geotextiles are woven or feltlike synthetic fabrics also used for their filtration capacities. *Geogrids* are products that look almost exactly like plastic construction fencing, with open-square grid patterns. Geogrid is also (confusingly) a trademark for a type of cellular honeycomb. Several good publications give further detail on methods and definitions.⊃

Bioengineering weaves together living woody plants for structural strength; inert materials are usually secondary. Greenwalls contrast with other closely-related methods in one important way: They derive their strength *primarily* from the inert part of the system; planting protects the surface and adds some strength. Both have advantages and are often combined.

The best greenwalls are part of a systematic whole-site design. With many materials to choose from, it is essential to get technical assistance from manufacturers and bioengineering specialists.

Greenwalls are as effective as conventional structures for slope retention in almost all situations. Planted surfaces offer habitat, making greenwalls much more attractive for many sites (as well as the ecological advantages of plant cover). For example, precast open-front crib walls with vegetation growing through the openings blend seamlessly into the landscape while holding nearly vertical slopes.

Newly planted greenwalls require maintenance, like all other plantings. Wherever

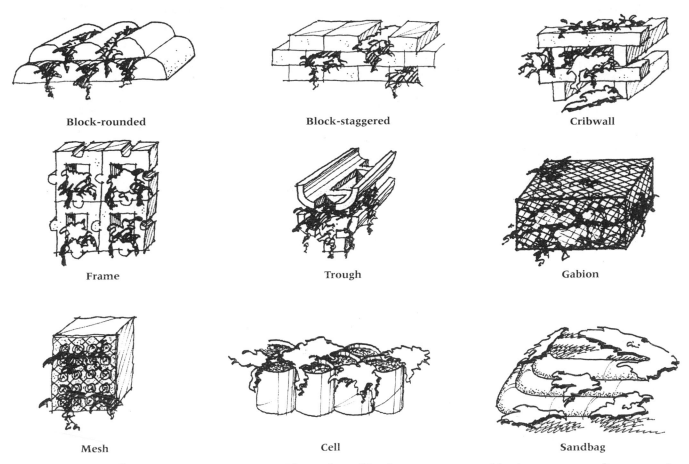

Block-rounded **Block-staggered** **Cribwall**

Frame **Trough** **Gabion**

Mesh **Cell** **Sandbag**

Figure 3.7. Greenwalls combine bioengineering with a variety of hard structures; several basic concepts are diagrammed here. ILLUSTRATION: Craig Farnsworth.

planting spaces are created, there is the risk that invasive weeds will move in before plantings are established, or if plantings fail. At least a year's monitoring and maintenance should be planned for any new greenwall. Mulching and other preventive measures against weedy invasion should be carefully considered. Once weeds are present, hand removal or selective herbicide use may be unavoidable. With proper design and vigorously established plantings, however, a mature greenwall can require less maintenance than hard surfaces—especially if graffiti is an issue.

Greenwall structural systems, discussed here for outdoor use, can be used indoors, for example, in zoos or botanical exhibits or for indoor air quality and other benefits. Lighting, watering, and fertilization need adjustment as with other forms of indoor horticulture.

As a general rule, any structure used to stabilize a slope should not be monolithic but rather an open system around and through which plants may root and establish themselves.

Ample evidence suggests that there is no longer any excuse in landscape construction for impervious, monolithic retaining walls of concrete or any other material.

Plantable Masonry Structures

The simplest plantable retaining structure is a drystone wall, usually lower than 6 feet in height, constructed against the toe of a slope. The wall is built by stacking local stones on top of one another, in a single course one rock wide—which can require considerable skill.[5] If rocks are readily available near the site, building such a wall is particularly attractive.

For taller structures, gabions (rocks encased in rectangles of heavy galvanized steel wire) are an alternative to stone walls. Usually, the empty basket is set up and filled on-site; moving prefilled gabions requires heavy equipment. Typical 3-foot-high gabions may be stacked in a battered arrangement, tilted into the slope. Although gabions have been criticized as unattractive, soil

Figure 3.8. Gabions cause fewer problems than impervious walls because they allow water to seep through. Over time or by design, gabions can support vegetation. PHOTO: Kim Sorvig.

Figure 3.9. The Evergreen trough greenwall serves both as retaining wall and as noise-wall on Philadelphia's Blue Route (I-476). PROJECT and PHOTO: Synterra Ltd.

can be added, inserting and establishing vegetation over the gabion.[6]

A somewhat more sophisticated retaining structure is a crib wall—an open-faced, interlocking structure of wood or concrete beams assembled log-cabin style and embedded in the slope. Normally, crib walls are battered to improve stability, although vertical crib walls may also be specified with appropriate foundations. The beauty of the crib wall is that there are ample openings between the beams through which plants grow. The American Wood Preservers Institute has developed standard designs for crib walls; however, the authors share widespread concern over landscape use of toxic treated wood (see page 221 for details on this issue). As mentioned earlier, live crib walls may be assembled in the field from living logs, then filled with soil and fast-rooting cuttings.[7] These are far preferable to treated lumber.

Where walls must be extremely high or nearly vertical, concrete may be a better choice. Concrete "logs" resemble parking wheel-stops in size and shape and are notched for stacking. Short walls of this kind can be built with hand labor.

THE EVERGREEN TROUGH

Imagine earth-filled concrete troughs with slab legs in a tapering stack up to 60 feet tall. Holes in the bottom of each trough connect the soil fill to the next trough, forming a continuous soil core throughout the wall and allowing moisture to reach each level. The Evergreen system has the narrowest footprint of any greenwall plantable on both faces for noise or security (an example surrounds the Jordanian royal palace). They can

be freestanding; to retain soil or rock faces, Evergreen units stack against the surface. Philadelphia's Synterra used a 600-foot Evergreen wall along the Blue Route expressway. The affected neighborhoods favored the appearance of the greenwalls, and after testing, PennDOT went on to use Evergreen walls elsewhere, according to Synterra principal Bill Wilson. The National Park Service used Evergreen to naturalize huge earthworks at the Cumberland Gap tunnel.

Trough units are 16 feet long, weighing up to 3.5 tons without soil. Unlike other greenwall systems, they can only be installed with heavy equipment.

Tessenderlo Group, a large international chemical manufacturer based in Brussels, has produced a greenwall structure that appears from photographs to be similar to the Evergreen wall—but made of recycled PVC. This product is known as EKOL and is in use in Europe as a sound wall.⊃ It would certainly be lighter for installation than the concrete troughs. Our concerns about PVC as a material make it hard to evaluate this idea; however, recycling that keeps PVC out of landfills and does not require new manufacturing of this controversial plastic may be a good thing.

GREENING THE BLOCK WALL

Any wall can be draped with trailing or climbing plants, especially if terraced. A true greenwall has plants growing *on its surface*, which requires soil spaces. There are two ways of achieving this: leaving out blocks in each course or rounding the corners of each block.

Leaving out a block every so often in laying the wall is the approach taken by so-called S-blocks, a system like many greenwall products that originates in Europe, distributed by various U.S. licensees. The S or Z shape and the weight of the blocks lock one course to the next, allowing blocks to be left out without loss of strength. S-blocks require poured footings and must slope at least ten degrees off vertical. In earthquake-prone California, these walls withstand Richter-7 tremors, settling tighter after the quake.

Verdura blocks, recently patented by Soil Retention Structures (Oceanside CA), are small troughlike blocks with elliptical front faces; planting spaces occur at the rounded corners, into the soil trough behind. Up to 50 feet tall, Verdura block walls have an interesting fish-scale texture, until covered by growth. A similar system, known as Hercules (St. Louis MO), uses a face shaped like an m, which allows planting at both sides and in the middle of each face.

Standard block systems, like Keystone, Anchor, or Rockwood, are plantable if terraced. Attempts to put planting "pockets" on the face of such blocks (without root access through the wall) have not been successful, resulting in root-bound plants and awkward irrigation.

Many block systems are anchored by overlapping geogrid sheets, pinned to the blocks and buried in the soil behind the wall. This is a variation on the sandbag system, described in more detail on page 109. Geogrid anchors, with or without block facings, are standard fare in heavy-duty civil engineering, giving them a clear track record for stability.

Flexible Soil Support Systems

An entirely different concept for greenwalls relies on flexible materials rather than masonry to make soil stand upright. Mesh, honeycomb, or fabric, these flexible materials are filled with soil. The weight of the soil prevents the support material from moving, and in turn, the support keeps the soil from slumping.

EXPERIMENTS WITH MESH

Bill Bohnhoff, landscape architect and owner of Invisible Structures, notes that turf can grow in soil less than an inch deep. Invisible Structures manufactures landscape products from recycled plastic, including Grasspave and Slopetame, a mesh of 2-inch-diameter rings held in a flexible

grid. The grid is usually pinned to the top of a slope and rolled down. The rings are filled with soil on-site or "prevegetated" in a greenhouse. Bohnhoff speculates that the grid could be hung vertically if anchored to a structural backing. It could also cover a sandbag system with a kind of reinforced sod.

An ultrathin greenwall made of wire mesh is used in Europe under the name System Krismer. The mesh is pinned to rock, concrete, or soil, and filled with soil-gravel mix using hydroseeding equipment. Krismer products are apparently not available in the United States. Another mesh system, Terratrel, from Reinforced Earth Co., is normally used for temporary soil retention but might be adapted for greenwalls.

SANDBAG VARIATIONS

At zoos in Seattle and Rochester, Jon Coe has developed a simple, cost-effective greenwall. Reinforcing fabric is laid down wider than the wall's footprint, usually without footings. A 1-foot layer of soil is placed on the fabric; the extra width is then folded over the soil. More layers of fabric folded around soil are added, stepped to the final height. Soil weight holds the fabric, and the fabric holds the steep front face of the soil. If the height:width ratio exceeds about 2:3, fabric is pinned to the ground or a structure. Stronger geogrid may be wrapped around one or more fabric-lined "bags" for extra strength. The face of the wall is seeded or turfed; woody seedlings or cuttings are planted through the geogrid or fabric. At Seattle's Woodland Park, grass covered the wall immediately, with arctic willow taking over by the third year.

Coe layers geogrid and porous mat together or uses Enkamat Type S, which fuses grid and mat into a single sheet. He avoids "the ziggurat look" of a stepped face for two reasons. In zoos, kids who climb the steps risk falling off—and being eaten. Second, sharply stepped angles in the wall can produce plant-killing air pockets between the fabric-wrapped soil and the sod or roots. So Coe's workers soak the finished wall, then beat the face flat with shovels.

Atlanta landscape architect Kevin Kleinhelter used a similar system for Post Properties, whose management emphatically values landscape as a prime client attraction. One of Post's Atlanta GA developments needed a steep slope stabilized, but massive concrete retaining walls didn't fit. Instead, Kleinhelter used Tensar's Sierra system,

109

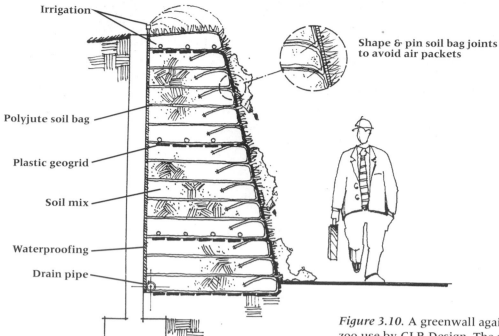

Irrigation

Polyjute soil bag

Plastic geogrid

Soil mix

Waterproofing

Drain pipe

Shape & pin soil bag joints
to avoid air packets

Figure 3.10. A greenwall against a structure, designed for zoo use by CLR Design. The same concept used for bank stabilization is called vegetated geogrid (Figure 3.1). ILLUSTRATION: Craig Farnsworth, based on Jon Coe.

combining geogrid stabilization with plantable-mat surfaces.

Naturalistic greenwalls suit zoos or historic themes, such as a CLR exhibit based on the sod-covered Kodiak Island pit-house. In other settings, greenwalls could be ornamental, patterned with colored sedums or blooming displays. One limitation: any fabric-reinforced system relies on the weight of fill and needs a wide footprint. For this reason, they are best used where the slope is fill (or to cover built walls). If used on cut slopes, significant additional excavation is required, affecting existing vegetation and offsetting the benefits of the greenwall.

CELLULAR CONTAINMENT

Honeycombs of heavy polyethylene sheet are shipped folded flat, expanding when pulled like crepe-paper holiday decorations. Once staked at the edges, the expanded cell sheet is strong enough to walk on as workers fill cells with soil. Each cell is about 8 inches square, available in 2-inch to 8-inch depths.

A single layer of cells can be laid over an existing slope for stabilization; filled with gravel, it substitutes for paving. Cells are available with perforated sidewalls used to stabilize stream crossings. To make a greenwall, cell sheets are laid horizontally on top of one another, stepping upward as steeply as 4V:1H. All but the edge cells are filled with gravel; edge cells, exposed by the stepping structure, are filled with planting soil. The polyethylene edge of each layer remains exposed but is quickly covered by plants.

At Crystal Cove State Historic Park, near Newport Beach CA, greenwalls showed their versatility. Landscape architect Steve Musillami was faced with creek and beach erosion undercutting the Pacific Coast Highway in a historically certified landscape. Geoweb by Presto, one of many geocell products, replaced the road's original vegetated fill slope. Filling the planted cells with local "duff" soil produced a healthy mix of native plants from seed. By steepening the slope, Musillami was able to widen the creekbed to accommodate the real source of the problem: increased runoff from upstream development. The landscape architect's solution went far beyond the riprap suggested by highway engineers—and did it in record time. The cell material, according to Musillami, easily installs to curves, without massive formwork or heavy equipment. Presto cites a similar creekbed project flooded 10 feet deep without damage.

Some greenwalls can benefit from underdrains; Musillami used one to return water to the

Figure 3.11. Cellular containment materials are flexible honeycombs filled with soil or gravel. A single layer can form a drivable surface; stacked as shown, cells form a greenwall. PHOTO: Webtec.

Figure 3.12. Green-walls can reduce the "footprint" or horizontal extent of a high bank by steepening it. This approach protects Crystal Cove State Park (CA) from increased upstream runoff—shown during and after construction. PRO-JECT: California State Parks, Steve Musillami. PHOTO: Alan Tang.

stream. At Minnesota's Grass Lake, state highway engineers underdrained a cellular greenwall to keep potentially polluted road runoff out of the lake. The engineers noted that the geocell (Terracell by Webtec) avoided disruptive excavation, resisted road salts better than concrete, and was safer for vehicle impact in accidents.

Design Issues

Many design choices go into a successful greenwall. Be sure to consider the following:

- Microclimate on any vertical surface depends on compass orientation and is usually severe—hot/sunny, cold/shady, or alternating daily.

- Irrigation can be sprayed onto the wall, channeled down from the top, or (using drippers) run on or behind the face.

- Soil mix and plant selection are critical.

- Especially if the greenwall covers a building, plan scrupulously for maintenance of the underlying structure.

- Costs are often 25–50 percent less than cast-in-place concrete, but they can only truly be compared design by design.

- Be sure to plan for maintenance during plant establishment.

- For similar purposes on the *roofs* of structures, use the ecoroof concept.

Turn Barren Roof Spaces into Ecoroofs

"If we are to survive in our cities . . . we need roof gardens," says landscape architect Cornelia Oberlander.

Every contemporary city has, in the words of Toronto environmental designer and author Michael Hough, "hundreds of acres of rooftops that for the most part lie desolate and forgotten." Conjuring the image of a city in decline, Hough's description is true even of economically vibrant cities: at ground level, they are lively, but at roof level, lifeless. Conventional roofs are impervious to water and exposed to high winds; they cause severe microclimates by absorbing or reflecting heat. No wonder they are nearly barren of life and resistant to environmental improvement. Every square foot of sterile roof corresponds to a square foot of life missing from the ground surface.

The ecoroof, a concept pioneered in Europe, offers new possibilities for integrating buildings into the living environment. These ecological roof gardens involve large planted areas, specialized soil substitutes, and little or no reengineering of the existing roof. Landscape professionals have a real opportunity to be involved in this type of construction.

Environmental Benefits of Ecoroofs

Roof gardens—at least as they are conventionally conceived—do not adequately address the problem of sterile roof expanses. Hough, in fact, raises serious questions about the conventional roof garden—its "creation and survival depends not on natural determinants but on technology and high energy inputs." Among these costs: beefing up the structure of a building to withstand the added weight of soils, shrubs, and even trees; imported soil that must be lifted to great heights; extra irrigation and maintenance for plantings to withstand exposure and drying winds. Conventional roof gardens, for Hough, are a prime example of the amounts of wasted energy and effort required in the contemporary city to combat an unrewarding environment.[8] They may be delightful to the favored few who have access to them, but they do little for the urban environment as a whole.

But what if there were a roof garden type requiring little or no modification to a building's structural system and hardly any irrigation or maintenance, but that covered urban roofs with a living carpet of vegetation? Such an approach would go a long way toward reclaiming this for- gotten area of the city as productive environment.

Fortunately, such gardens do exist. Variously known as ecoroofs, green roofs, or *extensive* roof gardens (as opposed to conventional *intensive* roof gardens), this new model of a roof garden has emerged from the crowded cities of northern Europe and is catching on in other countries. Ecoroofs typically cover the entire roof of a building with a continuous layer of growing medium, as thin as 50 millimeters (about 2 inches), that supports low-maintenance vegetation. In concept they are a lightweight modern version of the sod roof, a centuries-old tradition in Scandinavia. They are not intended to be walked upon and generally do not feature pedestrian access.

Ecoroofs require little additional load-bearing capacity and may be retrofitted to many existing buildings with no modification in their structural systems. They do not require flat roofs as do conventional roof gardens but may be installed on roofs with slopes of up to thirty degrees. In contrast to conventional roof gardens, whose gardenesque plantings require irrigation, fertilization, and intensive maintenance, ecoroofs typically require little or no irrigation (at least in temperate climates) and no fertilizer.

Like greenwalls, ecoroofs can be invaded by aggressive species, especially if poor establishment or maintenance leaves bare soil exposed. Many of these invaders are weedy aliens that cause problems wherever they grow. However, most ecoroofs approximate a meadow, which usually is an early stage of succession, naturally

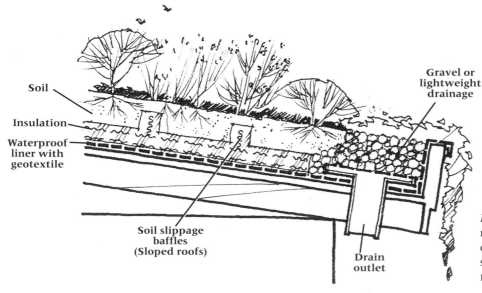

Soil

Insulation

Waterproof liner with geotextile

Soil slippage baffles (Sloped roofs)

Gravel or lightweight drainage

Drain outlet

Figure 3.13. Unlike conventional roof gardens, ecoroofs are light enough to retrofit on existing structures. ILLUSTRATION: Craig Farnsworth, based on Re-Natur.

modest, yet the environmental benefits are considerable:

- Improves the building's thermal insulation.
- Reduces the urban "heat island" effect, by absorbing less heat.
- Produces oxygen, absorbs carbon dioxide, and filters air pollution.
- Stores carbon.
- Provides wildlife habitat, especially for birds.
- Absorbs up to 75 percent of rain falling on it, thus slowing stormwater runoff.[9]

Project Examples

Ecoroofs are becoming fairly common in parts of Europe, principally in Germany, the Netherlands, and Switzerland. The Amsterdam airport has incorporated an extensive green roof into the design of its terminal building. Some cities in Germany now require ecoroofs on flat-roofed industrial buildings. As early as 1989, 1 million square meters (10.8 million sq ft) of low-maintenance green roofs were under construction in Germany.[10]

Ecover, a manufacturer of biodegradable laundry products, built a large ecoroof on their headquarters in Oostmalle, Belgium, in 1992. Billed as "the world's first ecological factory," the facility lends credibility to the firm's environmentally benign products. The Ecover plant is—even by the standards of progressive northern Europe—a remarkably green building in all respects, not least in its roof, which consists of 5,000 square meters of native grasses and wildflowers.[11] Ecover's home page contains information about the project.⊃

Ecover's grass roof has a perlite insulation layer underneath a rubber waterproofing layer. Covered with a thin layer of soil mix and planted with meadow grasses, the roof acts as an efficient temperature regulator summer and winter. In the summer, particularly, the grass absorbs a great deal of the sun's heat; during the night, the dew falls on the grass, vaporizing to provide cooling next morning. To irrigate the grass roof in the summer, Ecover uses treated effluent from an on-site sewage treatment pond. Many birds—including a falcon, unusual in an industrial area—regularly alight on the roof; some even nest, according to Ecover spokesperson Peter Malaise. He reports that maintenance require-

Figure 3.14. Ecoroofs are an update on traditional sod roofs—an example of revisiting past technologies to meet sustainability goals. PHOTO: Kim Sorvig.

Figure 3.15. In northern Europe, large-scale urban greenroofs like this one are fairly common. PROJECT and PHOTO: Re-Natur.

Figure 3.16. The ecoroof atop Ecover's headquarters helps meet the company's goal of a green factory producing green products. PROJECT and PHOTO: Ecover.

replaced in most regions by shrub or tree communities. The shallow, nutrient-poor soil mixes used on ecoroofs prevent shrubs and trees from thriving for long—but not from sprouting in the first place. Although a few woody ground covers fit right in, removing woody seedlings is a maintenance task that must be planned for any green roof.

The requirements of an ecoroof are relatively

ments are minimal: mowing twice a year and weeding volunteer tree and shrub seedlings as needed.

This pioneering project has not been without its problems. Early on, leaks occurred owing to the faulty adhesion of the waterproofing sheet to the roof panels. The soil substrate layer has proved to be too thin, leading to burned roots in full summer. In retrospect, plant selection should have included more xerophytic species—drought-tolerant plants that grow directly on traditional European roofs and stone walls even without substrate.

Driven by dense existing development and increasingly rare urban open space, European countries are forging ahead with ecoroofs and learning by their mistakes. Meanwhile, the green-roof movement in North America is in its infancy. A few groundbreaking (or ground-mending!) projects have been built. One is atop Library Square in Vancouver BC. This high-rise building was designed by Moshe Safde; its eco-roof was designed by Cornelia Oberlander to be viewed from the surrounding office and residential towers. There is no pedestrian access. The plants were chosen for beauty and low mainte-nance—green and blue fescue grasses and deep green kinnikinick (*Arctostaphylos uva-ursi*), a ground cover, planted in a pattern suggesting the Fraser River flowing through British Columbia's mountains. The garden never requires cutting or fertilizing; the only maintenance needed is raking at the end of the winter. It does require irrigation by low-intensity spray heads.

The growing medium is lightweight—at 14 inches deep, it weighs 60 pounds per cubic foot

saturated, according to Oberlander—and is com-posed of one-third sand, one-third pumice, and one-third Humus Builder, a compost product made of food waste, collected from Vancouver-area restaurants by a local firm. (Oberlander notes that, at $20 per cubic yard, the compost is not cheap, but it saves fertilizing.) The medium's light weight was important for the structural cal-culations of the building, which did not have to be upgraded to accommodate the garden.

An ecoroof on a much humbler scale is to be found atop the home garage of Tom Liptan, a stormwater specialist at Portland's Bureau of Environmental Services, and a "stormwater nerd" by his own admission. He combined the two roles by turning the relatively flat 10-by-18-foot roof of the garage into a stormwater experiment. Liptan's tiny project might seem loopy, but it had a higher purpose. Liptan was testing his convic-tion that ecoroofs, retrofitted on office buildings in Portland, could sponge up some of the city's perpetual rain, thereby reducing flooding, storm-sewer overflows, and related problems.

Since the garage's wood frame was very light, Liptan first had to brace it to support additional weight. For waterproofing Liptan used inexpen-sive plastic sheeting, over which he shoveled two inches of soil that he dug out of his own yard, mixed with compost. In this soil base he planted a variety of sedums but also allowed volunteer grasses and other species to take root.

Liptan's frequent monitoring has shown that even this simple, inexpensive ecoroof is effective in capturing stormwater. From a storm of 0.4 inches of rain (approximately 40 gallons of rain-water on the 180-square-foot roof), only 3 gal-lons of runoff reached the ground. After a 2-inch storm, runoff continued to flow from the roof, slowly, for two days. During periods of heavy rainfall, Liptan's ecoroof becomes saturated and cannot hold any more runoff. Overall, however, it retains 15 to 90 percent of the rain that falls on it (depending on intensity). Plants have thrived on the roof despite the lack of any irrigation.

Ecoroof Materials and Approaches

Ecoroofs are generally similar in their underpin-nings to conventional roof gardens. Like other roof gardens, ecoroofs feature the following layers: a waterproof membrane, a layer of insula-tion, a drainage layer, and the growing medium, sometimes referred to as the "substrate." (There is some flexibility in these elements. Insulation may

Figure 3.17. Even small-scale ecoroofs decrease runoff, support habitat, and clean the air. Tom Liptan replaced his conventional garage roof with this one. PROJECT and PHOTO: Tom Liptan.

be above or underneath the waterproof membrane. Where the roof pitches five degrees or more, a drainage layer is not needed.) Typically, a protective layer of PVC is placed between the substrate and the layer beneath to protect against roots penetrating the waterproofing layer. (Given PVC's environmental difficulties, substitutes for this purpose should be found.) On steeper roofs, greenwall techniques could be adapted to holding the growing medium on the roof.

In their soil conditions ecoroofs differ markedly from conventional roof gardens, which rely on significant depths of high-quality soil. Ecoroofs generally make do with poor and relatively thin growing medium, adequate for wildflowers. Growing media specifically manufactured for green roofs are available in Europe. Grodan, a lightweight medium produced in Denmark from volcanic rock, has been widely used for more than twenty years in green-roof retrofits, usually avoiding structural upgrades. Such products are not yet available in the United States. Lacking premanufactured products, designers may develop their own growing media, as Oberlander did for Library Square. Author Ted Osmundson suggests using a mix of 45 percent expanded shale (a lightweight material that is widely available) with 45 percent sand and 10 percent humus.⊃

No one substrate is suitable for all sites, however. Perhaps the most bare-bones approach is pure sand planted with stonecrop, a species of sedum, successfully employed to create green roofs in Berlin. Rubble and other on-site materials may also be crushed and used as the basis of substrate, thereby avoiding the double environmental cost of hauling the rubble away to a landfill and hauling in fresh materials. Crushed brick waste and concrete are among the materials (mixed with organic materials) that have been used in Europe to produce perfectly viable substrates.

What plants do well in the thin, nutrient-poor substrates of an ecoroof? Begin by looking at plants that spontaneously colonize local hard surfaces, including roofs that were never intended to support plant life. For example, many roofs covered with a layer of gravel are colonized over time with mosses and stonecrop.[12] Develop a list of such drought-resistant plants for ecoroofs from the regional flora. A xerophytic plant palette reduces the need for irrigation; in fact, many authorities stress that irrigation is

Table 3.1
Ecoroof Costs (based on European experience)

Materials	$/sq ft
Fleece layers	0.45
Root protection mats	0.74
Waterproof seal	0.74
Soil mixture	0.60
Plants and seed	0.30
Total	**$2.83***
Additional Options	
Heat insulation	$1.49
Drainage layer	$0.52

*Plus incidentals: sealants, clamps, connectors, edge lumber, etc. Contractor fees not included.
    Source: Based on Beckman, Stephanie, et al., *Greening Our Cities: An Analysis of the Benefits and Barriers Associated with Green Roofs* (Portland: Oregon State University, 1997) p. 44.

unnecessary for ecoroofs unless there is an extended dry spell.

Ecoroofs are a landscape form that has been well tested in Europe. Green roofs would greatly improve the urban environment of North American cities. The time is ripe for landscape professionals and architects to begin to understand the technical requirements of this new garden form.

SUGGESTED PRACTICES FOR ECOROOFS

- Think of *every* building as a candidate for an ecoroof, especially buildings with large roof expanses.

- Understand waterproofing, insulation, and other structural requirements.

- Specify lightweight growing medium from locally available ingredients. (See "Manufactured Soil" page 86.) Where feasible, use recycled ingredients such as ground glass. Do not make the mix too fertile. Use the shallowest soil layer that will support herbaceous plants.

- Select drought-tolerant, shallow-rooted plants that grow well in your area.

- In most regions, rely on average rainfall alone. If irrigation is a must, use greywater, treated effluent, or water harvesting (Principle 4).

PRINCIPLE 3

Construct *For* and *With* Plants

Much of the "hard" construction of any landscape is created to support or control plants. Landscape plants represent a significant financial investment, whether purchased from a nursery, transplanted, or protected on-site. Healthy plants, and the construction that keeps them that way, are essential to the functional, ecological, and aesthetic success of a built landscape.

Plant-friendly construction methods are not new; conscientious designers and contractors have used them for years to avoid financial losses. What *is* new is the realization that all plants, including horticultural plantings, are critical to a sustainable future. Construction *for* plants, as well as handling and maintenance standards, are more important than ever.

In stark contrast, *careless* plantings are too costly in money, materials, and energy to be called sustainable. Many plants of all sizes are unavoidably removed during construction—damaging any more by carelessness or poor planning is utterly wasteful. The city of Milwaukee WI, for example, estimates that its *annual* loss to street trees, caused by poor construction practices, exceeds $800,000.[13] Milwaukee publishes a very thorough manual including sample specifications to help avoid this destruction.⊃

The purchase cost of a landscape plant is far outweighed by the value it adds to the built environment. The Michigan School of Forestry has estimated the value of a single mature tree at $162,000—based solely on the quantifiable services it provides, such as cleaning the air water and controlling soil erosion.[14] Other values, such as providing habitat for wild birds, or aesthetic and historic worth, are hard to put in dollars but cannot be disregarded. Computer software, and a manual for legally defensible tree appraisal, can help; the Council of Tree & Landscape Appraisers (CTLA) offers such aids.⊃ Contact the International Society of Arboriculture for regional experts.⊃

Table 3.2 compares initial costs of landscape plantings against some estimates of their true worth. These figures vary by region as well as species and age; historic and cultural values are also reflected.

A study by Cornell ecologist David Pimentel estimates the economic value of environmental services provided by nature to humans at $320 billion for the United States, and $2.9 trillion globally—*not* including the value of agricultural crops.[15] Plants clearly provide a significant portion of this amount. A U.S. Forest Service scientist estimates that urban forests save the United States about $4 billion annually by moderating climate, and thus cutting heating and cooling bills.[16]

Plants obviously contribute greatly to sustainable environments. The construction that sustains or restrains these plants must be designed and built *with plants in mind*. Knowledge is the key to successful use of plants, both general knowledge of the principles of plant biology and specific knowledge of site conditions and the needs of particular species. To ensure that built landscapes thrive, and that native plants protected on-site remain healthy, botanical expertise on the team is essential.

While much of the responsibility for landscape plants rests with the landscape architect or horticulturist who does the planting design, the landscape contractor's expertise is also critical.

- The contractor is typically responsible for all *handling* of the plants: transporting them from the nursery, planting them, and if necessary storing them on-site.

- The contractor may have to *guarantee* that plantings survive, or pay to replace them, so it is in his or her interest to select, handle, and maintain plantings properly.

- Careless *hard construction* practices, such as compacting soil or burying debris in planting pits, can influence the health of plantings.

- Successful contractors need to be prepared to build *innovative* planting structures designed for sustainability.

Contractors frequently must substitute for plants that are not available as specified. Unless the "or-equal" substitute is a variety well suited to site conditions and functional demands, it may never thrive, wasting the cost and effort of planting it. Substitutions made just because they are cheaply available can ruin a well-designed planting scheme. When *native* plants are specified, but cheaper, easier-to-find nonnative relatives are substituted, this is not a minor change; not only the aesthetics but the ecological results

116

Table 3.2
Comparison of Costs and Values of Landscape Plantings

Service, Value, or Cost	Amount	Notes
Purchase or replace nursery stock up to 6" caliper size	$25 to $750	Varies regionally; based on informal survey of nurseries
Cost to install and establish one tree	$75 to $3,000	Through second year; based on CTLA rule of thumb, 2–3 × initial cost of tree
Annual maintenance investment, one tree	$0 to $75	Informal estimate of likely costs
Oversize replacement (> 6")	9" = $955 to $5,725 36" = $15,270 to $91,620	CTLA, $15 to 90 per sq. inch of trunk cross-section area
Oxygen production, one mature tree	$32,000	Mich. Forestry
Air pollution control, one mature tree	$62,000	Mich. Forestry
Water cycling and purification, one mature tree	$37,500	Mich. Forestry
Erosion control, one mature tree	$32,000	Mich. Forestry
Energy saving (heating and cooling adjacent structure), one mature tree	$26,000	50 years × Annual $520 (40% of EPA heating/cooling national average; equiv. 10.7 million Btu savings per home)
Insurance limit for one tree under ordinary property-owner policy	$500	Informal survey of several policies
Litigation value of one tree destroyed	$15,000	1981 Arlington VA U.S. Tax Court case on record
Annual losses of trees caused by construction in Milwaukee WI	$800,000	Hauer, R.J., R.W. Miller, and D.M. Ouimet. 1994. "Street Tree Decline and Construction Damage." *Journal of Arboriculture* 20(2): 94–97.
Annual energy savings of entire U.S. urban forest	$4,000,000,000	Rowan Rowntree, USFS—no other information: cited at http://www.treelink.org

are affected, usually for the worse. Substituting plants properly is generally much more complicated than substituting hard materials or mechanical systems (see page 123). The contractor should *always* consult both the designer and a reputable nursery if substitution is necessary.

Construction professionals should not assume, however, that the designer never makes mistakes about planting design. Planting structures such as raised beds, planter boxes, or street-tree pits require buildable, maintainable, well-dimensioned designs, and the contractor's experience with

such structures may be considerable. From the pre-bid meeting through the last change-order, the contractor has opportunities to spot problems that the designer may not have noted, or that are site-specific. Challenging the design may be tricky, but a team approach focused on survival of the plantings is the best path to achieving results.

The following sections give some guidelines about structures and handling for plants.⊃ These guidelines will help most plants survive, decreasing the costs of replacement and maintenance and contributing to sustainability. However, it is always best to modify such general rules in light of local or regional experience. Unusual climate conditions, soils, and plant species may require additional or different care.

Follow Up-to-Date Planting Structure Guidelines

Alan Blanc, a British lecturer and author on landscape construction, had a sense of humor about his topic. His term for street-tree pits built too small for their occupants was "dog-graves" (really tiny ones were "chihuahua-graves"). The image is a bit morbid, but appropriate. Without adequate soil *volume* for roots and nutrients, and adequate *surface* for water and air to pass through, even the toughest plant is doomed to die, leaving the pit empty and gravelike.[17]

Especially for those plants grown in structures—notably street trees and anything in a container or planter—conditions are extra stressful. Conventional tree-planting specifications, in use for the past century, appear to be more concerned with squeezing plants into the minimum space than with keeping the plants healthy. Space has monetary value, and when it comes to a choice between an extra foot of sidewalk and an extra foot of planter width, even the conventional specifications are often ignored. Because clients demand maximized space for people and vehicles, as well as maximized buildable and rentable area, the landscape design and construction industries continue to build lethal, undersized planting structures. Sustainable prac-

tice does not waste trees where they cannot survive, and it makes survivable space for plants a priority.

STREET-TREE STRUCTURES

Inadequate planting structures, particularly ones with too little soil volume, are the leading cause of an epidemic of urban street-tree deaths. The average life span of urban trees has been estimated to be as short as two years, and few experts give them longer than ten years to live.[18] These are trees that could live fifty years or more in suburban settings or in the wild. Clearly, this is an economic and environmental disaster. As one expert puts it, "Elaborate and expensive designs are produced and installed only to have the plant materials succumb to some malady even before the grower's guarantee expires."[19]

What is "adequate" soil space for a tree? A widely accepted *minimum* is 300 cubic feet, that is, a pit 10 feet by 10 feet by 3 feet deep. This is much more than many street trees ever get, yet it is truly adequate only for trees whose mature trunk diameter (DBH) is less than 6 inches. For a 24 inch DBH tree, about 1,500 cubic feet of soil are recommended—a pit about 22' feet by 22 feet by 3 feet deep. (Increased *depth* is not of much value to most plants, since root growth stays mainly in the top foot of soil.)

This relationship between the amount of tree canopy and the root-supporting soil volume is

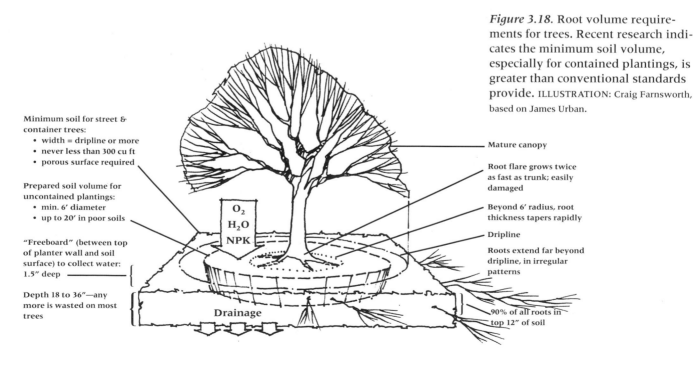

Figure 3.18. Root volume requirements for trees. Recent research indicates the minimum soil volume, especially for contained plantings, is greater than conventional standards provide. ILLUSTRATION: Craig Farnsworth, based on James Urban.

Minimum soil for street & container trees:
- width = dripline or more
- never less than 300 cu ft
- porous surface required

Prepared soil volume for uncontained plantings:
- min. 6' diameter
- up to 20' in poor soils

"Freeboard" (between top of planter wall and soil surface) to collect water: 1.5" deep

Depth 18 to 36"—any more is wasted on most trees

O₂ H₂O NPK

Drainage

Mature canopy

Root flare grows twice as fast as trunk; easily damaged

Beyond 6' radius, root thickness tapers rapidly

Dripline

Roots extend far beyond dripline, in irregular patterns

90% of all roots in top 12" of soil

"the most critical factor in determining long-term tree health," according to James Urban, a landscape architect from Annapolis MD who has become a national expert on planting conditions and tree survival.[20] The relationship can be expressed by another useful rule of thumb: *The volume of root space (cu. ft.) is roughly1.5 times the area under the mature canopy (sq. ft.).* (See Figure 3.18.) Some plants probably use more than this in the wild, and many can survive on less. However, as a general principle, the *more the root volume is reduced* from this ideal, the *more stress* the plant must cope with, and thus, the *more maintenance* it is likely to require. Stress and increased maintenance are costly and ultimately unsustainable.

Note that just as the aboveground volume of plants may be domed, columnar, or pyramidal, so the root volume may vary in shape. A narrow columnar tree does not necessarily have a deep, narrow root system. The common idea of the dripline is handy but seldom accurately represents the actual extent of the roots. The dripline is still a useful visual aid. Because plant roots taper and fork quickly as they grow away from the trunk, the dripline usually covers the majority of the largest roots. The tiny root hairs far beyond the dripline are still the place where much water and nutrients are taken up, but protecting the main roots is critical.

Available root volume may be even less than it appears at the surface. Utility lines frequently run through tree pits; steam lines are particularly lethal, but all utility lines steal space from already inadequate root volume. Flared footings, bedrock, and other invisible barriers may cut off more of the pit volume. Many trees survive only by sending roots immense distances, following any line of weakness and permeability in the urban soil. Not only does this stress the tree, it can result in heaved sidewalks, broken planters, and clogged sewers—conditions that most contractors have had to deal with. (Contrary to popular belief, few trees will attack foundations, and then only in the most stressful conditions.) The conventional view of this problem is biased toward protecting the structures, which unnecessarily destroys many trees as a result.

Only a relatively small number of tree species are capable of such structural damage. Even with these species, the problem does not occur if the tree is given adequate root space. Most of the "problem" species are "gross feeders" whose roots follow the soil surface, thus requiring a broader planting area than other species. In new construction, such trees should not be planted unless extra distance from structures is available. In existing situations where these species have been ignorantly planted, compromise should be sought before destroying the tree.

There are proprietary products that form a physical or chemical barrier to stop the spread of roots. But unless the plant can spread in other directions, the barrier is merely another reduction of root space, producing the same stresses discussed above. Spreading in another direction may cause new problems elsewhere. These barriers are usually short-term solutions at best, and especially for sustainable construction they should be considered a last resort. Avoid placing structures and vigorous-rooted trees too close together. Make sure that water, irrigation, stormwater, and sewer pipes are solid and do not leak within a plant's root zone, attracting roots toward the leak and eventually into the pipe.

Reduced root volume can have several effects, found in almost all container plantings, from potted petunias to street trees. The most striking example is *bonsai*, in which pruning the roots is used as a way to dwarf the aboveground plant. Bonsai can be kept alive and healthy for hundreds of years, but only with devoted maintenance of a sort seldom available for landscape plantings. (Bonsai are regularly turned out of their pots for root care; don't try this with the average street tree!)

Without adequate space or intensive maintenance, plants may be not only dwarfed but also short-lived. The stress of inadequate planting space makes these trees highly vulnerable to pests, diseases, and even storm injury.

Research by James Urban, Henry Arnold, Nina Bassuk, and others has produced serious changes in industry standards for tree planting, especially in containers or limited spaces. (See page 122 for planting standards for open, uncontained areas.) Despite publication of the new standards in *Architectural Graphic Standards* and other references, many horticulturists, landscape architects, and contractors are still using outdated planting details.

Besides significant increases in recommended volume per tree, the new standards have introduced two new methods of designing street-tree

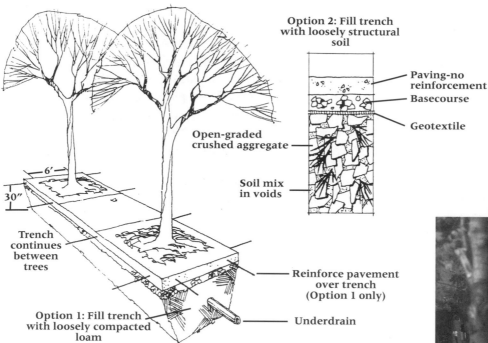

Option 2: Fill trench
with loosely structural
soil

Paving-no
reinforcement

Basecourse

Geotextile

Open-graded
crushed aggregate

Soil mix
in voids

6'

30"

Trench
continues
between
trees

Reinforce pavement
over trench
(Option 1 only)

Option 1: Fill trench
with loosely compacted
loam

Underdrain

Figure 3.19. Continuous trench plantings gain enough root space to survive in urban settings. The trench may be filled with loam (reinforced paving is required) or with structural soil. (See Figure 3.22.) ILLUSTRATION: Craig Farnsworth, based on James Urban, Nina Bassuk, et al.

Figure 3.20. Continuous trench plantings can unify a streetscape. Paver joints are open to admit air and water. PROJECT and PHOTO: Henry Arnold.

pits: the "continuous trench" structure and the "root path trench."

Soil under pavement is deliberately compacted for engineering support of the sidewalk or traffic lane. This subsoil creates a wall around the conventional pit, often as hard as concrete. The continuous trench stretches from tree to tree, under paving strengthened by reinforcement. This design greatly increases the soil volume available to each tree. It also requires slightly different details of sidewalk construction, which any experienced contractor can readily learn. Variations on the design are used for plazas, sidewalk plantings, and other urban situations.

The root path trench system leads the roots out of the pit in small radial trenches, about 4 inches wide by 12 inches deep. Each trench contains a drainlike product, a plastic "waffle" core wrapped in geotextile, which brings both water and air through the length of the trench. Sur-

rounded by good planting soil, this air and water source provides the conditions roots need to grow, and thus the roots follow the trench. The surrounding soil must be good enough for them to spread eventually but does not need to be replaced wholesale with planting mix.

"Structural Soil" for Urban Plantings

Structural soil sounds either totally obvious or totally contradictory, but it is an important new development in planting structure design. Developed by Cornell University's Urban Horticulture Institute, structural soil uses crushed rock for strength, with soil filling the spaces in the gravel.⊃ This produces a material that is strong enough to support paving like base course yet, even when compacted to full strength, has space for plant roots to grow through.

The gravel must be angular crushed stone, not round river gravel, so that it "locks" together

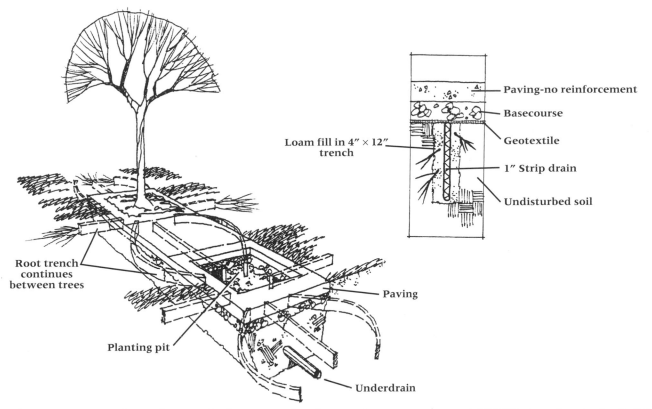

Figure 3.21. Root path trenches require less excavation than continuous trenches, yet provide air and water "paths" that lead root growth. Pavement reinforcing is also eliminated. ILLUSTRATION: Craig Farnsworth, based on James Urban.

when compacted. It must also be "open-graded" (also called "no-fines"), meaning that all the stones are sorted by sieving and are very close to the same size. This ensures that the pore spaces between stones remain open, leaving room for the soil mix. (This concept is identical to that of porous paving, which uses no-fines aggregate, bonded with asphalt or concrete, leaving the pores open for drainage; see page 184. A similar concept is called "air-entrained soil" by Henry Arnold.)

UHI's specification for structural soil starts with 100 pounds crushed stone, sized from 3/4 to 1 1/2 inches. To this are added 20 pounds clay-loam and 0.03 pounds (0.5 ounce) artificial copolymer (hydrogel) that tackifies the mix. Moisture content should be about 10 percent. Moisture and tackiness keep the soil from sifting out of the gravel mix while being placed. The mix is placed in 6 inch layers and compacted to 95 percent, which is sufficient to support all but the most industrial of paved surfaces. Because of the soil-filled voids, however, roots can grow through this structural mass.

Figure 3.22. Structural soil resists compaction by incorporating crushed stone; soil fills voids, providing space for roots, air, and water. PHOTO: J. Grabosky.

Structural soil is best used in conjunction with a continuous planting bed such as Urban's. Reinforced paving is not required when using structural soil. The surface of the bed open to rain and air should be at least 6 feet wide; this is often covered with mulch or alternatively with interlocking pavers that are removed over time as the tree grows. In some climates, underdrainage may be needed to ensure that the structural soil bed does not become a water-holding reservoir.

Structural soil has been successfully tested in New York, Ohio, and Massachusetts. It is not known, however, how this system would fare in hot dry climates. Even where irrigation can be provided, the heat-holding capacity of the gravel in the mix may be harmful to some species. Since the gravel is incapable of holding water, the total volume of water available in 1 cubic foot of structural soil is vastly less than the water-holding capacity of 1 cubic foot of ordinary soil. This has implications for maintenance of plants during drought and for overall water resource use.

Urban plantings are an important part of the environment in which an increasing percentage of people live. These new planting systems offer considerably better survival rates than conventional ones. However, the main reason that such systems are needed is a social one: the value of urban land is so inflated that landowners refuse to allow adequate space for plantings. Special systems like the trench and structural soil cost resources that could be avoided if more generous space-planning were common in the urban landscape. From a resource perspective, changing social expectations to recognize trees as an essential part of healthy urban places would be more sustainable than merely squeezing plants in by means of special engineering.

Planters, Raised Beds, and Containers

Any plant grown in a container or planter is under more stress than is the same species planted in the ground. The limited soil volume in the container tends to dry out, heat up, or freeze quickly and can easily become waterlogged or deficient in nutrients. Containers are most often set on hard surfaces, which stress the plant with excess heat. These stresses make container plants particularly hard to sustain, whether in a plaza or a roof garden. Subjected to extremes of climate, plants that are *also* stressed by undersized planting structures seldom survive.

Container plants require water and air. If the container has a large enough exposed permeable surface and "freeboard" (see Figure 3.18), it may collect enough rainfall to sustain the plantings. Otherwise, irrigation is required. Container plantings without an adequate irrigation system are generally an unsustainable waste. Drainage for excess water must also be built in.

Similarly, plants that require maintenance they will never get cannot be part of a sustainable landscape. Container plantings not only tend to increase the maintenance needs of plants, but also are frequently located in inaccessible places, making maintenance nearly impossible. Contractors, with their practical experience, are often in a position to help landscape designers avoid such costly mistakes.

When designing or constructing any sort of container structure for plants, extreme care is required. Otherwise, the result will be loss of plants and waste of materials, which are at odds with the goal of sustainable landscape construction.

Updated Standards for Uncontained Plantings, Too

Since roughly 1900, the standard details for planting trees and shrubs remained unchanged. But today, even where container situations are not involved, these standards have changed.[21] Unfortunately, the old standards are still frequently reproduced from old books, cut and pasted onto blueprints, and taught in university courses.

In particular, the recommended size and shape of planting holes have changed. An older standard of "twice the width of the root ball" is now considered a minimum. In good soils, a shallow pit just 6 inches deeper than the root ball but at least 6 feet wide is now preferred. In poor, clayey, or compacted soils, the width of the pit increases dramatically, to 15 or 20 feet.

The bottom and sides of the pit must be roughened, so that existing and filled soil will bind together. Clay soils, in particular, will "glaze" when dug, making a surface that stops roots as effectively as a pot and creating "virtual container" conditions. Soil for filling the pit should be amended with compost or other organic matter up to about 5 percent by weight. Making the soil too rich can discourage the roots from leaving the pit—and voilà, virtual container again. Mycorrhizae (fungi that live symbiotically with plant roots) are increasingly recognized as an important part of the planting mix and are purchased commercially or incorporated from native leaf litter and soil. The finished surface of the planting should form a saucer to collect water, but not so deep that too much is collected for too long.

One other major change in conventional practice is that many experts now believe that staking and wrapping the trunk of trees should be avoided. In addition, the tree should be oriented in the same direction it was growing in the nursery. This is not just a reference to the old horticultural jokes about "green side up." Rather, it means marking the north side of each tree in the nursery, and turning that side northward when planting it on-site.

Select Sustainable Species (and Substitutes)

Landscape architects select plants for aesthetic and practical reasons, ranging from color and flowering season to capacity as a windbreak or shade tree. When sustainability is a goal, these reasons must be balanced carefully with the environmental costs of planting and maintaining the plant. Resource costs can vary greatly between different species. When a contractor must *substitute* because the specified plant is unavailable, a basic understanding of the ecological issues about planting helps guide the decision.

Every species of plant evolved in, and is adapted to, a fairly specific region with its own range of soils and climate. Individual species are also "coevolved" to depend on other species of plants, animals, insects, fungi, and microbes in their environmental community. Some species are very narrowly limited to exact growing conditions, while others, informally known to plant ecologists as "wides," are adaptable within a broad range of conditions in the wild.

When people plant landscapes, they must help their plants to survive in one of two basic ways. The conventional approach is to provide the conditions that each plant requires—watering, shading, warming, and sometimes cooling the garden environment to match the conditions of the place where the plant evolved. The second approach is to select plants that are adapted to areas where conditions are similar to the new landscape. These plants tend to be able to survive in the new location with little maintenance. Because of this, the second approach is generally more compatible with the goal of sustainability.

One way of being sure that landscape plants will be adapted to the new location is to select species that grow nearby without human assistance—the *native* plants of a region. There is some controversy over how to define "native" (see page 124), and the maintenance performance of different species is not conclusively documented. Nonetheless, a growing number of professionals have found that landscapes based *primarily* on native species save water and other resources. This is not an argument for using natives *exclusively*. Exotic or nonnative species, adapted to similar conditions, are used in many regional gardens as specimen or accent plants.

It is critical to understand that few if any plants, including natives, are "no-maintenance" in a built landscape. Even the most hardy natives are stressed by being transplanted. Isolated from the diversity of their coevolved ecosystem, and placed in close contact with human activity and human chemical substances, even native plants require care to overcome these pressures. This care is especially important during an establishment period of one or two years after planting. After that time, natives require less maintenance than most exotics—but not zero maintenance. The only zero maintenance landscape is solid concrete, and even that will begin to break down after about thirty years.

Because they are adapted to a range of conditions, wide species are among the easiest to match to new sites. Many of the most commonly available horticultural species are wides, because they are able to survive in many settings. However, some of these species adapt *so* easily to new conditions that they can become invasive, disrupting native ecosystems and causing the extinction of unique regional species. The loss of regional species and ecosystems, like the high maintenance of poorly adapted imports, is a serious sustainability issue. It is also a tragedy for design, since the results are homogenous around the globe.

What does this have to do with the landscape professional? Native plants, ironically, are not as easily available in nurseries as globe-trotting imports to which gardeners are more accustomed. As a result, it may take *more* work to locate a native species. It may also be harder to find an appropriate substitution when the specified plant simply can't be found. Some natives require specialized planting techniques. Contractors and designers committed to sustainable landscape

Figure 3.23. Native-plant gardens conserve resources and link users to their region; this one also harvests rainwater. Skilled designers like Judith Phillips find unique beauty in locally adapted plants. PROJECT and PHOTO: Judith Phillips, Bernardo Beach Nursery.

construction *must* be prepared to go the extra mile and, in particular, to communicate extremely clearly about substitutions.

In general, if a specified plant is native, the substitution should also be native to the same region. If a suitably similar native can't be found, then the substitution should be well adapted to survive without extremes of artificial maintenance. Nonnative species that are invasive under local conditions should *never* be specified for outdoor use. (Nursery catalogs often refer to "naturalizing species"; their ability to naturalize is an environmental problem if they spread rapidly and aggressively.)

Trying to match these sustainability concerns to the desired form, color, flowering season, and so on is not easy. In some regions, such as the desert Southwest, no other substitutable species may exist. In such cases, we believe that the design should change to achieve sustainability, not the other way around. Those who have mastered the art of native-plant gardening produce stunningly beautiful landscapes that eloquently tell the story of their region. This regional awareness in turn contributes to sustainable attitudes about specific places.

What Is a Native?

At first glance, it would seem simple to define which plants are native to a region and which are not: a native is one that grows someplace naturally and always has—right? But this apparently simple issue has stirred one of horticulture's hottest controversies in the 1990s.[22] This book is

not the place to throw more fuel on that fire, but native plants are an important part of sustainable landscape construction. Without respecting native species, it is difficult to protect or create self-sustaining, diverse plant communities.

Several criteria can be used to distinguish native plants, but no single one will define them:

- The species *reproduces* in the region, without human intervention.

- The species *survives* in the region without human care (irrigation, fertilization, removal of competitors, or other maintenance).

- The plant shows distinctive *local variations* that it lacks when growing in other regions.

- The species *coevolved* with and depends for survival on the other plant and animal species of the region.

- The plant (or its ancestors) was not transported to the region by humans, purposefully or accidentally.

The basic concept of a native plant is not overly complicated. It has practical value in maintaining healthy ecosystems, not to mention a sense of regional place. However, scholarly and geographic certainty about what is native is hard to achieve, and controversy has been surprisingly bitter. Landscape professionals can benefit from considering some of the difficulties in pinning down the concept.

- Plants do extend their ranges without human help, dispersed by wind, tides, or animals. However, like species extinction or soil erosion, dispersion is a naturally occurring process that has been dramatically and selectively speeded by human actions.

- Prehistoric and precolonial people frequently managed the plant communities around them; for example, using fire to keep grasslands from being overtaken by shrubs and trees. However, the "managed" species, both those favored and those hindered by management, usually remained parts of the native plant community; only their balance was changed.

- Prehistoric and precolonial people also introduced seed from distant regions, usually for food. Relatively few of the imported crop plants colonized aggressively or survived without cultivation, unlike the many weedy invaders imported by colonial settlers.

- Defining the region can be difficult. For example, red fir (*Abies magnifica*) is found in the Sierra Nevada, at elevations of 6,000–9,000 feet. Saying that the species is native to the Sierras, which few would dispute, is still risky: there are many areas in the Sierras above or below the species' altitude range, where it would never grow well. Stating that a species is native to a *political* region (e.g., a state) can be even more misleading. The red fir is also considered an *Oregon* native, since it grows in the southern edge of the Cascade Mountains, yet its current range includes less than 5 percent of Oregon's land area.[23]

- The "range" of a plant is really a snapshot in time. During the most recent Ice Age, the red fir grew at much lower elevations and further south than it does today and may have been totally absent from the areas where it now thrives.

None of these points, in our opinion, seriously discredits the idea that coevolved, self-sustaining plant communities are critical to sustainability and should be planted and protected at every opportunity. The alternative is an anything-goes horticulture favored by critics of the native-plant movement. Historically, that type of horticulture is responsible for many of the 400 species of invasive plants now threatening vast areas of U.S. ecosystems (see page 89). A working definition of native, even if not perfectly precise, is appropriate—and necessary—for sustainable landscape construction.

For landscape purposes, the most appropriate snapshot or baseline for native plants is fairly clear: just before colonization and industrialization began their trend toward unhealthy and unsustainable environments. In the United States, for example, this list would include those plants growing here between the end of the Ice Age and the arrival of European settlers. This is clearly not a "pure" historical or botanical yardstick. Rather, it is a value-driven choice reflecting the goal of reestablishing *self-maintaining* plant communities that conserve environmental resources.

From a practical landscape perspective, there is no need for a vendetta against nonnative plants. Only those nonnatives that are invasive should be eradicated and/or prohibited. The remainder should be used sparingly, with consideration for their higher resource demands and lower value to coevolved regional species.

Handle with Care

Besides requiring appropriate structures and conditions to support them, landscape plants need careful handling during the unnatural process of moving and planting them. This is almost always the contractor's responsibility. Observing a few guidelines can cut losses—financial losses for the contractor, and waste that affects sustainability on a larger scale.

These guidelines are relatively common knowledge—conventional nurseries and contractors follow them for business reasons. When sustainability is a goal, these points increase in importance.

Energy and materials costs involved in preparing, transporting, and planting nursery stock may be estimated roughly using data in in Principle 7.

CHOICE OF NURSERY STOCK

Landscape plants are supplied by nurseries in temporary containers, balled in burlap (B&B), or bare-root. They may also be transplanted directly from one on-site location to another. The choice between these forms of landscape stock significantly affects the amount of energy and labor used and the survival rate of the plantings, all of which are environmental issues worth considering.

- Bare-root stock must be protected from drying; even a few minutes exposure to air and sunshine can kill exposed roots. Use moist sawdust or wet paper, often covered with plastic, to hold in moisture.

- Handle bare-root plants while dormant; this restricts the period for planting. Refrigerated storage, used to keep plants dormant longer into spring, has serious energy costs.

- Bare-root plants are the least expensive financially; resources for containers are not consumed. They have reasonable survival rates, especially when plants are fairly small.

- Containers and burlapped root balls protect plants during moving and transplanting, with generally higher survival rates than those shipped without this protection. This is offset by resource costs of containers and extra weight for transportation. Be sure the ball or container size complies with or exceeds minimum industry standards.

- Most containers are plastic; some are metal or wood. Resource issues, including toxicity for some plastics, are discussed in Principle 6.

- Large mature plants, in great demand for landscape use, are always B&B or container; they cannot survive as bare-root. Large specimens represent long growing time and, like old-growth forests, are becoming rare and expensive.

- On-site transplanting may save plants located in construction zones. Hand-dug transplants are usually bare-root. Root balls of transplants can be burlapped; this requires skill, and the work must be done in season.

- "Tree-spades," large truck-mounted machines that lift trees, soil and all, provide the only option to save most mature trees. They represent significant energy costs and may risk compacting soil very near the new planting pit.

- All plantings, regardless of how they are prepared or moved, require significant time to recover from "planting shock." The larger and older the plant, the more severe the shock. Smaller stock recovers more quickly and may catch up in size with larger plantings that take extra seasons to resume full growth.

Moving and Storage

- Highway speeds generate wind, which along with sunshine and high temperature can wither the plants rapidly. Plants that have been recently dug or repotted are especially susceptible.

- In winter, windchill affects plants in transport and may create freeze-dry or frost conditions even when temperatures are not below freezing.

- Plants in transport should *always* be completely covered with tarps; in summer,

spray the truckload with water before putting on the tarp.

- Chemical antitranspirants can be sprayed on the leaves to slow water loss into the air, both summer and winter.

- An enclosed delivery van, covered truck, or semitrailer is excellent protection and can double as an on-site storage shed. Enclosed vehicles *must* be ventilated to prevent overheating in the sun, especially while parked.

- Ideally, deliver and plant landscape plants all in one day. Realistically, weather, available labor, and incomplete hard construction require careful on-site storage, partially shaded and protected from wind.

- For longer storage, or in hot, dry, or very cold weather, consult a nursery professional. "Heel in" roots or root balls with loose soil or moist sawdust, water regularly, and mist leaves.

Planting Practices

- Both designer and contractor should ensure that planting specifications comply, *at a minimum*, with up-to-date industry standards. These include the structural requirements discussed in this chapter.

- For bare-root plants, it is critical that the roots be spread out in the planting pit. Placing the plant on a cone of soil aids this process.

- Dipping bare roots in a slurry of finely powdered superabsorbent polymer has proven valuable in increasing water availability during the critical period after planting.[24]

- Rough handling of container and B&B plants cracks soil away from roots and must be minimized. Never lift B&Bs by stem or trunk; use the wire cage or nursery hooks.

- Most contractors are aware that the container must be removed at planting, but it is not uncommon to see dying plants buried in their containers.

- Plastic and metal containers may be carefully slid off the root ball, sterilized, and reused. If containers must be cut off, try to recycle them.

- Remove any wire from B&Bs, which may endanger wildlife and future gardeners.

- Cut back a few inches of burlap around the trunk. Some professionals find that leaving the burlap in place at the trunk helps stabilize the newly planted tree for the first year, after which it should be removed.

- For large stock, wood boxes are sometimes used. Disassemble and reuse the wood (but not in new plant boxes, because of potential for spreading diseases).

- Strangling roots of container-bound plants should be loosened or cut before planting.

- If included, sod, bulbs, seeds, and potted herbaceous stock must be selected, handled, and maintained with care equal to that given larger plants.

- Set plants at the same depth in soil as indicated by the "nursery line," visible as a color change on the trunk. In especially heavy clay or compacted urban soils, provide drainage and/or soil amendments, rather than merely "planting high." Collect water toward or drain water away from the plant by re-grading the surroundings, *not* by burying the plant deeper or shallower.

- Completely fill soil around roots. Air pockets are a common cause of death in new plantings. To avoid them, water the plant immediately and thoroughly.

- Use root stimulants and vitamins, especially vitamin B, to help the plant recover from stresses of being moved; apply immediately at planting.

- It is usually better not to *fertilize* the plant until it has established new roots. This requires an extra trip to the site, so conventional contractors usually fertilize at the time of planting. Only local experience with soils, climate, and plant species can determine the best fertilization practices.

- Mulch the planting bed surface about 3 inches deep to help hold water, but keep mulch several inches from the trunk itself.

WILDFLOWERS

Meadowlike plantings of wildflowers have become very popular as part of a naturalistic, low-maintenance gardening style. Many but not all commercial wildflower mixes are composed of native species; work with local suppliers and carefully evaluate the species included.

Homeowners and professionals often assume that "wild" flowers require no maintenance. As with other native plantings, this is not true.

- For most sites, soils prepared for wildflowers should *not* be tilled deeply. Loosen the top inch of soil for planting. Deeper tilling releases dormant weed seed to compete with planted wildflowers.

- Don't bury the seed too deeply. Follow recommendations of the supplier. Many wildflower seeds should simply be broadcast, then rolled or tramped in.

- Use mesh or, for some plant species, mulch to protect the seed from birds during germination.

- Keep the seed evenly moist during germination, even for dryland species.

One wildflower supplier points out that the main cause of failure is *impatience*, followed by incorrect site evaluation, improper soil preparation, and inadequate early maintenance.[25] These reminders apply equally to all plantings, not just wildflowers.

Maintaining New Plantings

Even with careful planting, many landscape plants die within their first year or two. Some of these losses are unavoidable, but many are due to inadequate maintenance. Watering, pruning, protection from extreme weather, and monitoring for pests and disease are especially important during the "establishment period," the first one or two growth seasons after planting. Yet this is the time when these tasks are *least* likely to be done, at least in landscapes built under contract.

Unlike planting done by the homeowner, the landscape contractor's planting on residential or commercial sites is often completed long before the buildings are occupied. Between the time of planting and the date when the client takes occupancy, *no one* may remember to do maintenance. The structures seldom suffer from this oversight, but for new plantings, it can literally be a matter of life or death. Watering, particularly critical just after planting, may be forgotten; the plumbing may not be hooked up, or the irrigation system may not be programmed. Post-move confusion may keep the client from doing anything for the landscape for weeks after occupancy. The result: dead or stressed plants, remedial maintenance costs, and the loss of the "environmental services" that the plantings were supposed to provide. These sorts of waste are unacceptable in landscapes designed for sustainability.

To avoid this undesirable situation, contractor, designer, and client must plan in advance for maintenance responsibility. Some landscape design firms provide a written landscape maintenance schedule as part of their services; a few even include doing scheduled maintenance as part of the contract.

Each client has specific needs and abilities—when the client's occupancy begins, whether the client or hired groundskeepers will do maintenance—but the common factor is a transition period when responsibility passes from the contractor to the client or the client's maintenance person. Since the landscape construction contractor is already familiar with the plantings, and is in many cases responsible for guaranteeing them, that contractor is in the best position to ensure the plant's survival during the establishment period. It is the authors' conclusion that planting contracts should include complete maintenance services *for the first two growing seasons after planting*. By that time, the guarantee on plants has been fulfilled, the client is usually in occupancy, and the contractor can hand over an established maintenance program to the client or bid to continue the service.

To cover two growing seasons, the maintenance contract for spring plantings must run eighteen months; for fall plantings, twenty-four. Including such long-term maintenance requirements in the construction contract is not common practice. It would certainly increase the initial cost to the client and would require landscape construction contractors to do (or subcontract) horticultural maintenance. Lack of maintenance, however, is the most common cause of unsatisfactory landscape performance. Such failures are costly in dollars and in environmental wastefulness. Good maintenance *during* the establishment period almost always decreases maintenance needs *after* that period by

establishing strong plants from the start. It is a form of preventive medicine for landscapes. Planning and paying for competent maintenance up front is a cost-effective investment in sustainability (Principle 10).

ORGANIC MAINTENANCE

"Organic" or "natural" gardening has become well known and popular in the past few decades, both for chemical-free production of food crops and for decorative gardening. It is beyond the scope of this book to detail these maintenance practices, for which many excellent reference works are available (⊃ page 286). Not all of these home-oriented practices can easily be used with large-scale landscapes or paid labor. However, decreasing the use of toxic chemicals in *all* landscapes is clearly a major part of sustainability. The energy costs of synthesizing, transporting, and applying them are also of concern in moving toward a healthier long-term environment.

The conventional separation between landscape construction and landscape maintenance sometimes blurs the importance of this issue for designers and contractors. Likewise, many professionals who maintain commercial and institutional landscapes continue to opt for machinery and chemicals. The authors strongly believe that the design, construction, and maintenance of built landscapes at all scales benefit from keeping organic gardening principles in mind.

Count on Plants to Sustain

Plants are the only truly "productive" organisms on Earth, the ones that can trap solar energy in the form of photosynthesized food. All the rest of the world's creatures rely on plants, with rare and bizarre exceptions such as sulfur-eating, geyser-dwelling microorganisms. One plant species in eight is on the verge of extinction, globally, while in the United States, nearly one third of all known species are threatened.[26] The destruction of rain forests and oceanic algae are two well-known threats to global sustainability. What is less widely considered is that every tree damaged in "developing" land contributes to the same problems—and every tree planted offsets them, however slightly.

Planted trees serve many functions that can decrease other resource use. They can perform a number of functions better than any technological equivalent yet invented, notably in bioengineering and in cleaning up air, water, and soil pollutants. They take in the greenhouse gas carbon dioxide, potentially balancing some of the release of that gas by industrial and transportation fuel combustion. (This concept, dubbed "carbon banking," may soon make it more *profitable* to conserve standing forests than to log them.) Because of their essential role in making life possible, as well as the social and financial costs of raising them, cultivated plants are too valuable to abuse. Sustainability requires that the very best of human horticultural knowledge become a universal standard for landscape work.

Resources
Bioengineering

Geosynthetic Institute (GSI)
Drexel University
Philadelphia PA
610-522-8440 or robert.koerner@coe.drexel.edu
Academic and industry membership group, research and education on geotextiles and geogrids.

Bestmann Green Systems
Salem MA
508-741-1166
Suppliers and consultants for erosion control and bioengineering.

Robbin B. Sotir and Associates
Marietta GA
770-424-0719 or www.sotir.com
Consultant and author on bioengineering.

Bioengineering for Land Reclamation and Conservation by H. Schiechtl (1980 University of Alberta, Edmonton AB, Canada)

Biotechnical and Soil Bioengineering Slope Stabilization: A Practical Guide for Erosion Control by Donald Gray & Robbin Sotir (1996 Wiley)

Biotechnical Slope Protection and Erosion Control by Andrew Leiser (1982 Van Nostrand Reinhold)

Soil Bioengineering for Upland Slope Protection and Erosion Reduction by Natural Resource Conservation Service, (1992 National Technical Information Service, 5285 Port Royal Road, Springfield VA 22161, 703-487-4650)

Use of Vegetation in Civil Engineering by N. J. Coppin & I. G. Richards (1990 Construction Industry Researach and Information Association; Butterworths Publ., Boston MA)

Vegetation in Civil and Landscape Engineering by D. H. Bache & I. A. MacAskill (1984 Granada publ., NYC)

Erosion Control

"A Soft Approach to Erosion Control" by James L. Sipes (February 1999 *Landscape Architecture*)

Bioengineering, Wetlands, Erosion Control, and Ecological Restoration; The Bioengineering Group, Inc.
Salem MA
978-740-0096
or www.bioengineering.com/links.htm
Web site links to information about bioengineering (many already included here).

International Erosion Control Association
Steamboat Springs CO
800-455-4322; 970-879-8010; www.ieca.org
Professional organization for erosion control.

Use of Organics in Erosion Control by John Haynes (Caltrans Engineering Services Center, Sacramento CA, 916-227-7109)

Erosion Control Magazine
International Erosion Control Association Santa Barbara CA
805-681-1300

ECMDS 4.1 (Erosion Control Materials Design Software)
North American Green
800-772-2040 or www.nagreen.com.
Also erosion control suppliers/consultants.

ErosionDraw 2.0
Salix Applied Earthcare
800-403-0474 or http://erosiondraw.com
Software includes Best Management Practice lists and standard detail drawings.

MOSES (Modular Operational Soil Erosion System)
National Soil Erosion Research Lab
West Lafayette IN
317-494-8695
Calculates soil erosion under a wide variety of site conditions and uses.

Greenwalls and Ecoroofs

Re-Natur Gmbh
24601 Ruhwinkel, Germany
www.re-natur.de/index.htm or 011-49-4323-901012
Consultant with twenty years experience in ecoroofs, wastewater treatment with constructed wetlands, and biological pest control. Web site is in German and English. Catalog available.

"The Vertical World of Greenwalls" by Kim Sorvig (1999 *Landscape Architecture*)
Project examples and further information on greenwalls.

Ecover
www.ecover.com
Organic household product manufacturer, with large ecoroof.

Roof Gardens: History, Design, and Construction by Theodore Osmundson (1999 W.W. Norton)

Building Green: A Guide to Using Plants on Roofs, Walls, and Pavements (no date) London Ecology Unit, Bedford House, 125 Camden High Street, London NW1 7JR UK, 44-171-267-9034)

Greenwalls: Cell type

AGH Industries (TX) 800-434-4743

Fluid Systems (Aurora IL) 800-346-9107
Presto Products (Appleton WI) 920-738-1118

RK Manufacturing (Ridgeland MS) 800-957-5575

Webtec (Charlotte NC) 800-438-0027

Greenwalls: Mesh type

Invisible Structures Inc. (Aurora CO) 800-233-1510

Reinforced Earth Co. 800-446-5700

Greenwalls: Plantable block

Hokanson Block (Sacramento CA) 916-452-5233

Modular Concrete Systems (Vista CA) 800-321-5699

Soil Retention Systems (Oceanside CA) 760-966-6090

Hercules/St. Louis Retaining Wall (St. Louis MO) 314-389-6416

   Hokanson and MCS are licensees of the "S-block" system. SRS currently serves only the southwestern United States.

Greenwalls: Grid/textile-wrapped

Akzo Nobel Geosynthetics (Enka NC) 828-665-5057

Huesker Geotextiles (Charlotte NC) 800-942-9418

Tensar Earth Technologies (Atlanta GA) 800-836-7271

Greenwalls: Trough type

EKOL trough recycled greenwall

Group Tessenderlo
Rue de Trône 130
1050 Bruxelles
www.tessenderlo.com
   Greenwall/noise-wall made of recycled PVC. Not marketed in United States(?).

Evergreen Wall Systems (trough)
Norcross, GA
770-840-7060
   Concrete trough greenwall/noise-wall system.

Plants: Valuation

Council of Tree and Landscape Appraisers (CTLA) 916-753-4042
   Consultant references, plus appraisal formulas and methods.

Building Greener Neighborhoods: Trees as Part of the Plan (1996 National Association of Home Builders 800-223-2665)

Guide for Plant Appraisal (Council of Tree and Landscape Appraisers [CTLA])
   Methods and formulas for legally defensible valuation of landscape features. Ninth edition due soon.

Tree Appraisal Species Values
www.forestry.uga.edu/docs/for96-06.html
   Example of a regional (GA) list of values assigned to species. Typically these lists devalue natives.

Plantings

Urban Forestry and Landscape Professional and Volunteer Organizations
www.ag.uiuc.edu/~forestry/guide/
   Excellent list of organizations related to urban landscapes.

Irrigation and Green Industry Network
www.igin.com or 323-878-0771
   "Virtual Trade Show" of urban forestry and landscape professional groups.

Urban Forestry bibliography
Dr. G. Kuchelmeister
Tree City Initiative (Illertissen, Germany)
Tel: 49-7303-43776
http://ag.arizona.edu/OALS/ALN/aln42/
   Lists thirty-five books specifically on urban forestry and the value and effects of urban trees.

Plant Materials in Urban Design: A Selected Bibliography by J. Wayne Pratt (1986 Vance Bibliographies A 1575, Monticello IL)

Plantings: Native Plants

Cooperative Extension
USDA, county government, and/or local agricultural college
www.reeusda.gov/
   For each state or region; often an excellent source of local expertise on plants and other landscape issues.

Landscaping with Native Trees by Guy Strenberg & Jim Wilson (1995 Chapters Publ. Ltd., 2031 Shelburne Rd, Shelburne VT 05482)
   For eastern United States. Guides for other areas, check local bookstores and botanic gardens. Check whether entry for each species lists its origins; many garden books steadfastly refuse to inform on this topic.

Plants for Natural Gardens: Southwestern Native and Adaptive Trees, Shrubs, Wildflowers, and Grasses by Judith Phillips (1995 Museum of New Mexico Press, Santa Fe)

A good source for a region much neglected by horticulture writers.

Landscaping with Wildflowers: An Environmental Approach to Gardening by Jim Wilson (1993 Houghton Mifflin)

Native Trees, Shrubs, and Vines for Urban and Rural America by Gary Hightshoe (1988 Van Nostrand Reinhold)

The Native Plant Primer by Carole Ottesen (1995 Crown/Random House)

The Natural Habitat Garden by Ken Druse & Margaret Roach (1994 Clarkson N. Potter)
   Good information in coffee-table format; Druse's other books are also excellent and show how much exciting design can be done with what some call "boring weeds."

The Wild Lawn Handbook: Alternatives to the Traditional Front Lawn by Stevie Daniels (1995 Macmillan)

Plantings: Structures

"Sidewalk Design for Tree Survival" by Matthew Evans, Nina Bassuk, & Peter Trowbridge (March 1990 *Landscape Architecture*)

"Selected Literature: Root Control Methods" by Dr. Kim D. Coder (March 1998 University of Georgia Extension)
   www.forestry.uga.edu/efr/olddocs/newdocs/html/for98-013.html

Horticultural Products

Green Net: Company-Product-Service Database
http://206.214.55.166/green/db/

Horticultural manufacturers list
www.yetmans.mb.ca/manufacturers.html

Respect the Waters of Life

*A mighty mercy on which life depends, for all its glittering shifts
water is constant.*

—Donald Culross Peattie, 1950

Water covers nearly 70 percent of the globe, and makes up almost 99 percent of the human body. Essential to life, it is also a powerful force of change and destruction. Despite its global presence, far less than 1 percent of it is freshwater suitable for sustaining land animals and plants.[1] In Ambrose Bierce's wonderful phrase, "Water occupies 2/3 of a world made for Man—who has no gills."[2]

Besides regional and seasonal water *scarcity*, water *quality* is threatened by pollution. Even in such apparently waterlogged and water-surrounded places as Florida, scarcity of fresh clean water is a serious issue.[3]

Construction affects water and water quality in many ways. By changing natural patterns of water movement, structures and surface grading/paving can change water from a life-giving force to a destructive one. Carefully planned landscape construction, however, can compensate for some of these changes. During construction work, sediments and pollutants enter water on or near the site. Collecting and distributing water for human use also affects the site's hydrology—and that of its neighbors.

Water is well known as a poetic metaphor for patient, slippery, flowing power, gentle yet unstoppable. Yet the conventions of engineering have frequently taken a confrontational stance toward water—as if it could be pinned down by brute force. As recently as a 1996 text on landscape construction, students were being indoctrinated with ideas such as "Water causes scouring action when left uncontrolled."[4] Ironically, scouring and other destructive actions of water are more often than not the result of human attempts at *controlling* water, upstream hardening that drastically increases the speed or volume of flow. Unlike hard construction materials, water *never* responds well to heavy-handed methods. It must be worked *with*, like plants, people, or any living thing.

This chapter looks at ways of protecting the most critical resource of all.

Work with the Site's Water Regime

Water is more a system than a substance. Using water sustainably and protecting natural water

---

Discussed in This Chapter:

- Understanding natural water patterns
- Protecting surface water features, such as wetlands, lakes, and streams
- Restoring water bodies that have been damaged
- Special techniques for balancing human water needs with regional conditions
    - "Harvesting" and storing water
    - Getting more out of each drop with greywater
    - Efficient irrigation
    - Vegetative water purification

bodies begin with an understanding of this system. Although it is possible to think of a pond as an object, its boundaries are muddy, and its connections to other objects are many. The pond, though perhaps the *simplest* form of surface water, cannot be properly protected just by fencing it, the way a tree or a historic sculpture might be protected. Protecting water features means understanding their links to larger patterns.

For this reason, water protection is given a separate place in this book, rather than treating it as part of site protection. The techniques discussed in Principle 1 are *part* of protecting water on-site. What differs is how these techniques are applied to the web of water called the hydrological cycle, a web that extends from rivers and wetlands through evaporation and rainfall. In this web, surface waters are linked to one another, to underground aquifers and springs, to water vapor and precipitation, and ultimately to the oceans. Protecting any part of this system is valuable in itself and also contributes to conserving the health of the whole. For maximum benefit, protection of water bodies needs coordination throughout each watershed or river basin.

Respect Natural Drainage Patterns

Because river geometry is complex, many people still think of stream channels as random in shape and location. Nothing could be further from the truth. Each channel where water runs, and each pocket where it collects, match the quantity and speed of water that normally flows through it. A similar relationship between shape and capacity is clear in roadway design, where the factors are fairly simple: a four-lane avenue with distinct turn lanes can handle more and faster traffic than a two-lane street where turning cars wait in traffic. Likewise, the shape of any landscape feature touched by water is dynamically related to the way water flows through that feature. So is its location. For construction, the important point is this: Change the shape and you change the performance of the water. In practical terms, performance means how much soaks in to benefit soil and plants and how much runs off or collects. Too much or too little of either can dramatically change the site, sometimes overnight, sometimes over many invisible years.

Three major factors interact to determine how water performs on a site:

- the *quantity* of water itself,

- the *material(s)* over which it runs, and

- the *shape*, particularly the steepness, of the surface on which flow occurs.

A small quantity of water running on a porous soil at a gentle slope will mostly be absorbed into the soil. On the same material and slope, a large quantity (from a huge storm or from hard surfaces upstream) will erode the soft soil quickly. Surfaces stabilized by vegetation erode more slowly, as do hard surfaces. Hard materials are vulnerable, however, where they meet softer soils.

Construction can change any of these three factors. Soil materials are compacted, loosened, and amended; grades are changed, and plant cover removed or altered. In addition, any waterproof or impervious surfaces shed water, increasing the quantity of water moving across the site. Once the dynamic balance among the three factors is changed in any part of the system, all the links in the water web must readjust toward a new balance. This readjustment happens gradually all the time in natural watersheds and is a key concept in construction where water is concerned.

The only way to plan for adjustment in the way water moves on a site is to understand local patterns that have evolved over centuries. This is site-specific and region-specific, but there are several key questions to ask. If you cannot answer these yourself, or you don't understand what they imply about changes proposed on your site, get specialist help. Water is too important to ignore.

1. From where does water come to the site, and where does it go from the site? Even standing water has a source and a destination, if only rain and evaporation.

2. Does runoff on the site move in sheets across the soil or quickly collect in gullies and channels? Are the surfaces hard or porous, and where does water spill from one kind of surface to another?

3. Where does standing water accumulate, and why? How are standing water and moving water linked on the site?

4. On a regional scale, what are the shapes of river systems? Do they branch like trees at acute angles or like the "arms" of a trellis, making sudden right-angle changes in direction? Large-scale patterns often indicate that geology is shaping the drainage, making it hard to construct new channels "against the grain."

If there is any kind of stream, creek, or river on the site, or affecting it, the following questions also need answers:

1. Does the channel meander (bend from side to side)? This indicates a stream that is slowing and dissipating excess force. The force may be due to steep slopes or to increased volume from upstream. Straightening the meanders is ill-advised; forceful flow will cause erosion and flooding until meanders are reestablished. Working upstream from meanders involves different conditions and methods than working downstream.

2. Is the stream cutting away its banks or depositing soil? High volume and speed are indicated when the stream cuts. Slowing, and expanding into a larger channel, will drop sediment. Planting or stabilizing areas of cut requires a different approach than the ones used in areas of deposition.

Besides answering such questions in the present, it is important to respond to changes over time. Upstream, development may increase the rate of runoff, or agriculture and industry may divert water. An example of a response to upstream development is the Crystal Cove project (page 110). Downstream changes are less likely to affect the site, although well-drilling can affect whole regions. If the landowner (or a watershed association) monitors proposals for development and water use, such changes can be prevented by design and planning.

Accept Regional Limitations of Water Supply

Conventional water management imports and exports water over very long distances. It is not uncommon for municipal or agricultural water to be brought a hundred miles by pipe or ditch. Water is diverted from regions, particularly undeveloped mountain areas, that are said to have "excess" water in order to supply the demand of locations that have used up their

locally available supply. Water is also impounded in reservoirs before it can "wastefully" run away downstream. Clearly, this affects the ecosystem from which the water is taken, or to which it no longer flows, sometimes dramatically. From a sustainability perspective, the smaller the quantity of water and the shorter the distance diverted from natural flows, the less likely the harm.

Regional water management may seem a planning issue, remote from site-specific construction. However, the demand for imported water is affected by where and how people build. Conventional water features, like fountains, ponds, and artificial waterfalls, can be great sources of pleasure, but ostentatious designs waste water— often imported, purified water. Modern recirculating technology, combined with traditional designs that get stunning effects from tiny amounts of water, offers responsible ways of using water for pleasure in sustainable landscapes.

Demand for water is also affected by the choice of plants that make up constructed landscapes. The need to minimize the import/export of water is one of the main arguments for gardening with native plants (page 123). In a few regions, such as the desert Southwest and near-polar parts of Alaska and Canada, the truly native plant list may not include plants for every use. For example, in the high desert, there are simply no native "shade trees" except along watercourses; upland trees are small and shrubby. Using the native cottonwood on the dry mesas around

Figure 4.1. This Guadalajara convent garden makes elegant, sparing use of water for tranquility. Roof drains replenish the pool. PROJECT: Arqs. Alfonso Peniche-Banisteros and Ricardo Aldana-Amaya. PHOTO: Kim Sorvig.

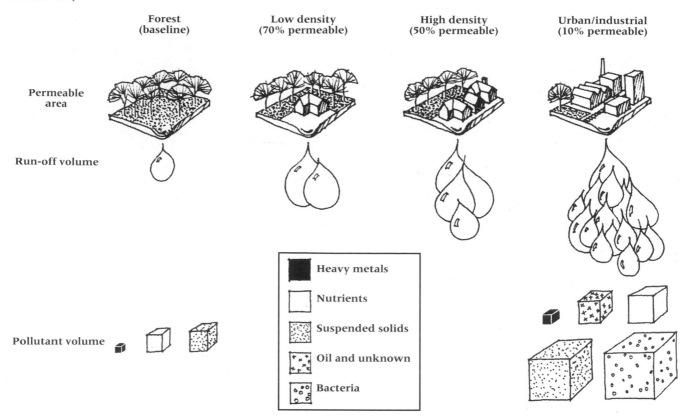

Figure 4.2. As impervious development reduces infiltration, the volume of runoff increases dramatically, as does pollution. Even nutrients, harmless in forest runoff, become serious problems at higher concentrations. ILLUSTRATION: Craig Farnsworth, based on data from W. Groesbeck.

Albuquerque requires imported water, even though the plant is technically "native." The Indians of the region created shade structures (ramadas) out of brushwood. Many beautiful Southwest landscapes have adapted this idea instead of shade trees. In doing so, they are truly respecting the regional water regime.

Deal with Stormwater near Where It Falls

When rain cannot infiltrate the ground where it falls, it turns into runoff. Although runoff is a source of water for most natural streams, lakes, and wetlands, excessive runoff causes problems for humans through flooding and erosion. With increased runoff comes a dramatic increase in water pollution as well. Loss of infiltration capacity due to development is one of the single most serious barriers to sustainability.

Many techniques are available for controlling run-off, but their success depends on one simple principle: Control runoff near its source. The further runoff travels, the faster it moves, and the more of it accumulates to move together in a steady flow. Speed and volume, as noted

earlier, give water its erosive force, as well as the ability to carry sediment over long distances. As a result, controlling water quality and runoff damage "is most easily and economically achieved if stormwater management *starts at the point that water contacts the earth.*"[5]

Many of the specific techniques in this and other chapters have their roots in this close-to-the-source strategy. These include bioswales (page 182) and water-harvesting (page 154). For filtering and dispersing water, or for collecting and using it, a single large centralized collector almost always adds pipes, pumps, and other hardware that a dispersed, close-to-source system does not require. Like water, other systems such as sewage treatment (page 165) or power generation (page 41 and 265) are most resource-efficient if *decentralized*—that is, close to the resource or to the point of use, or both.

In water management, there are two reasons why this principle is not followed. One is that a landowner may have no influence on upstream neighbors and must deal with runoff that they have neglected. For this, there is no simple cure.

The other reason, however, is that conventional practice favors massive design solutions instead of multiple small ones; for instance, a single dam instead of a series of check-dams along the length of an eroding gully. The conventional wisdom is that the larger structures offer an economy of scale. Particularly in the case of runoff control, this is a false economy and considers only capital costs, ignoring performance and maintenance. Several small infiltration devices (French drains, for example) located in the upper part of a water-shed are more effective than a single large one in a lower location. At the lower spot, fast-moving water will not infiltrate as effectively, and the sediment it carries will clog the gravel in the drainage structure much more quickly.

Where runoff is controlled early, slower speeds and lower volumes also allow the flexible materials of bioengineering to be used effectively (Principle 3). These "low-tech" solutions are sometimes dismissed by engineers because calculating their performance numerically is more complex than calculating for hard structures. However, bioengineering has a modern track record of being at least as effective as hard, massive control structures and a pedigree that stretches back to ancient cultures on several continents.

Designers, contractors, and even some engineers are increasingly recognizing that "small and close to the source" is the key to sustainable water management. The principle applies both to permanently designed features like weirs and detention basins and to temporary water-control installations like silt-fencing or bale barriers. Treating runoff like many small flows, and slowing each one so that it infiltrates right there, is an important strategy in dealing with water on-site.

One study suggests that, at least in the eastern United States, every gallon of water properly managed on-site saves at least $2 in engineering costs downstream.[6] This "avoided cost analysis" makes it financially feasible for communities to invest in or offer incentives for good close-to-the-source water management construction.

These three general strategies—know the patterns, accept regional supply, and deal with water near its source—play a role in applying most of the more specific techniques discussed in the rest of this chapter.

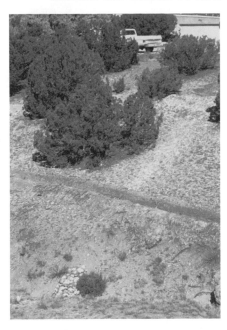

Figure 4.3. Contour-line infiltration trenches, plus check-dams in gully at bottom, stop erosion and raise soil moisture in this Permaculture project in arid NM. PROJECT: Arina Pittman. PHOTO: Kim Sorvig.

Figure 4.4. More effective than a single massive dam, series of small check-dams stop and infiltrate water throughout a stream or gully. Only the highest floods overflow spillways. PHOTO: New Mexico Department of Mining and Minerals.

Figure 4.5. Straw bales pinned to the ground provide temporary control of erosion and sedimentation. PHOTO: New Mexico Department of Mining and Minerals.

Understand, Protect, and Restore Natural Wetlands

Among the many kinds of sites a landscape professional may work on, wetlands may well be the most unique and challenging. Part land, part water, wetlands are often in the news yet often misunderstood. Conventional landscape work, not long ago, needed no knowledge of what wetlands were, how to recognize them, or how they functioned. Today, even though the majority of wetland work is still done by specialists, almost everyone in the construction-related industries knows: Watch out for wetlands. Landscape professionals need to go further, since the health of wetlands is closely linked to the sustainability of human land use.

Despite controversy over their legal definition, it is not difficult to understand what a wetland is. According to international wetlands consultant Donald Hammer, wetlands are places that are *wet enough long enough* each year to produce *oxygen-poor soils* favoring *specially-adapted plant species*. Contrary to popular misconceptions, wetlands are not constantly wet. They are transitional zones, or "ecotones," between land and water, both spatially (edges where land meets water) and over time (land and water sharing the same surface at different times of year). Understanding this shifting and transitional character is essential to working with wetlands. Misunderstanding this, or trying to force wetlands to fit an unvarying stable-state concept, is one source of the bitter controversy over wetlands regulation.

Wetlands are a critical link in the web of water. That they are also crucial to food webs and habitat diversity should come as no surprise. Wetlands in the United States are home to 190 amphibian species, 270 birds, and 5,000 plants, many of which can survive only in wetlands. Of all U.S. endangered species, 26 percent of the plants and 45 percent of the animals are wetlands species.[7]

Recognize "Services" Provided by Wetlands

The many ways wetlands serve humanity are enough to warrant their protection:

1. They act as filters, purifying the water that flows through them, trapping sediment, giving plants and microorganisms a chance to biodegrade many pollutants, and transforming others through the special chemistry of anaerobic soils.

2. They are often hidden gateways to groundwater, porous areas through which surface water can seep into aquifers.

3. They are overflow basins where floodwaters spread out, slow down, and lose their destructive force.

4. They provide some of the richest and most diverse ecosystems on Earth, influencing fisheries and many other economic products. Estuaries, the type of wetlands where freshwater and saltwater meet, are particularly productive.

5. Many types of wetlands have high recreational and aesthetic value. Enlightened developers are increasing the value of their properties by including protected wetlands as amenities.

Wetlands have been providing these "services" to humans since prehistory. Compared to modern technological solutions, wetlands are often the most cost-effective alternative for flood and erosion control, wastewater treatment, and pollution handling. For example, stone revetments to control coastal erosion cost

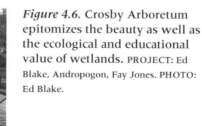

Figure 4.6. Crosby Arboretum epitomizes the beauty as well as the ecological and educational value of wetlands. PROJECT: Ed Blake, Andropogon, Fay Jones. PHOTO: Ed Blake.

Figure 4.7. Under construction, Crosby Arboretum shows the awkward conditions and sensitive work typical of wetlands restoration or construction. Piling foundations for Fay Jones's visitor's center are just visible at right rear. PROJECT: Ed Blake, Andropogon, Fay Jones. PHOTO: Ed Blake.

$150 per lineal foot in 1982; Ed Garbisch of Environmental Concern, one of the first wetlands specialists, could provide the same function with a strip of salt marsh created for $15 to $25 per lineal foot.[8] For sewage effluent treatment, wetlands frequently cost one tenth of conventional facilities and are simpler and cheaper to maintain and operate.[9]

A wonderful example of what can be accomplished by focusing on wetlands is the Crosby Arboretum in Picayune MS. Architect Fay Jones, curator Ed Blake, and landscape architects Andropogon, of Philadelphia, made the wetlands accessible to visitors through carefully planned construction. The result carries a message of hope for sustainable construction on unusual sites—and is a supremely beautiful place as well.

Know the Issues before Working in or near Wetlands

The general rule of "homework first" is especially critical for sustainable construction involving wetlands. Wetlands are a resource, and sustainable development, design, and construction benefit from the thoughtful use of this resource. Careful planning is required in order to avoid diminishing or endangering the resource for the future.

To work successfully in or around wetlands, both ecological and legal understanding is essential. In-depth treatment of either subject is beyond the scope of this book, but major issues are summarized here.

UNDERSTANDING AND RECOGNIZING WETLANDS

Scientists recognize more than a hundred types of wetlands, including marshes, swamps, bogs, mangroves, and seasonally flooded bottomland forests.[10] While most design and construction professionals can learn to recognize whether a landscape includes some sort of wetland, classifying the types of wetland and understanding their workings usually requires specialist advice. An ideal team would include a wetland ecologist, a hydrologist, a soils specialist, a wetlands botanist, and a landscape architect with strong engineering skills.[11] Wildlife specialists, a geologist, and experts in environmental education, recreation, and cultural archaeology may be important on some projects. Much of this expertise is available at little or no charge through governmental and educational institutions.

To restore or create a wetland, the best basis is observation of natural wetlands in the region. This is no place for aesthetic theories that dictate that designers must never mimic nature. Wetlands consultant Hammer emphasizes that "the created wetland must closely imitate natural systems adapted to that region if it is to succeed without excessive operating and maintenance costs."[12] Self-maintenance is directly related to diversity of species and habitat and to the varied and irregular physical forms that permit this diversity.

Several general points about wetlands are critical to the success of specific protection and restoration methods:

1. Wetland plants *tolerate* flooding, but more and deeper water is not always better. Like all plants, wetland species require air and sunlight and must usually have at least their leaves above water. Species that grow underwater require clear water to get sunlight to their leaves. Many wetland plants need both flooding and drier conditions *alternating* through their life cycle. Although they tolerate flooding that would kill dryland plants, wetland species can be stressed and killed by too deep or too long inundation.

2. In natural wetlands, alternating flooded and drained conditions control nutrient availability, set up conditions for germination of desired species, and influence wildlife behavior. Alternating flood and dry states keep many weedy invaders out—especially important in newly planted wetlands. Thus, in building and managing wetlands, the ability to control water level precisely, and to drain the wetland seasonally, are essential. In general, the best way to control water level is with a "stop-log" or "flash-board" system, in which boards or logs set into a vertical channel in the dam create an adjustable spillway. Valves only control the volume of flow, but the stop-log spillway sets the water level directly and simply.

3. Any wetland is a temporary feature in the natural landscape. Ecological succession changes wetlands to drier and drier communities, as sediment and humus fill the basin and create soil. When humans protect, restore, or create wetlands, management practices must offset this natural pattern of

succession, or the wetland will disappear over time.

4. Essential information for managing, restoring, or creating wetlands includes the source(s) of water supply; the "hydroperiod" of seasonal water-level changes; the soil type(s); the plant species; the adjacent land uses, especially upstream; and the objectives for the project.

5. Wetlands, like most natural systems, usually serve multiple functions. If a wetland is created to "replace" or "mitigate" the destruction of an existing wetland, it is critical that the replacement matches *all* the functions of the original. For other wetland construction, a single function may be primary, but a small additional investment in secondary functions usually offers a large return. For example, the constructed wastewater-treatment wetlands of places as diverse as Arcata CA and Minot ND include wildlife habitat, environmental education, and similar "secondary" functions. Among other benefits, these have gained public acceptance and thus have avoided costly complaints and even lawsuits.

LEGAL AND POLITICAL ISSUES

Historically, most states have lost at least half of their precolonial area of wetlands, and in several states, 90 percent or more have been destroyed.[13] Wetlands received their first protection under U.S. law in the 1970s, although hunting groups had been restoring wetlands earlier, out of concern for decreasing numbers of waterfowl. A variety of state and federal laws, notably section 404 of the Clean Water Act and the Swampbuster regulations on farming, have responded to new knowledge of the values of wetlands and to concern about their rapid loss. For the twenty years before wetlands regulation began, 700 square miles of wetland were destroyed *per year*, or nearly 450,000 acres (180,000 hectares) annually. That rate dropped to 300,000 acres annually soon after regulation began, and today it is about 100,000 acres.

Regulation has achieved important reductions in the rate of loss, but construction professionals should be aware of two concerns that still remain. The first is that although present losses are slowing, past losses are far from being restored. The second is that the main success in slowing wetlands loss has been through agricultural regulations, while losses due to development and construction have declined very little and now make up 80 percent of the total.[14]

For these reasons, protection of wetlands remains a priority in working toward sustainability, on a par with protection of rain forests. Because 80 percent of the wetlands lost today are due to development, the construction industry and landscape professionals especially need to do everything possible to reduce the impact of development activities on wetlands.

Filling and draining wetlands, which was once common practice, is largely prohibited, and erosion and sedimentation precautions are also required. These measures have been quite unpopular with conventional developers, who see the laws as restricting their freedom to build on what were once cheap lands. Some conventional contractors have adopted the developers' attitude, complaining that they are no longer free to do their job without worrying about wetlands. While the frustration of having to work with new regulations is understandable, wetlands are too important to sustainability to allow negative attitudes to destroy them.

There are, however, strong arguments to be made that too many conflicting laws and definitions exist, and in fact the focus of much current legislation is to make wetlands regulation more consistent nationally, more responsive to regional differences, and more straightforward. Legal definitions for delineating wetlands are moving closer to Hammer's (page 138), while developers and the public are learning to understand and recognize these transitional areas *before* damage and regulatory penalties happen. Although there have been horror stories about making mountains out of mud-puddles, wetlands protection deserves the support of everyone concerned with sustainability.

WETLANDS "CREATION" AND BROKERING

Legislation protecting wetlands often includes a provision allowing wetlands to be destroyed if they are replaced on another site. This process is called "mitigation." Brokering (also called "mitigation banking") goes one step further and allows developers to buy and sell the rights to destroy wetlands, trading mitigation rights across projects.

Some mitigation wetlands have succeeded in

replacing wildlife and plant habitat, water filtering, and recreational and amenity value. Others, as reported in a series of studies in several states, replace less area than was destroyed and create a completely different type of wetland (23 percent of the replacements were essentially "tanks," the steep-sided ponds built for livestock on ranches). Only half are ever monitored for function at all. Permits, justified by these inadequate "replacements," allowed the destruction of endangered species habitat "in most states evaluated."[15] Despite successes, there is still controversy whether even the best created wetland is interchangeable with a natural one.

A major concern about re-created wetlands is whether they can function as aquifer recharge zones. Aquifers are porous underground reservoirs held between impervious soil or rock layers that prevent water from escaping. For an aquifer to recharge, water must get from the surface into the porous layer. Places where the porous layer reaches the surface are called recharge zones. Where these coincide with low areas of topography, water can collect and infiltrate slowly— and many such low areas are wetlands. Unless a wetland is re-created in very similar conditions, it is likely to function like a tank, unconnected to groundwater and offering no recharge.

Wetlands are also related in complex but logical ways to surface drainage patterns. Although some wetlands are fed strictly by rainwater or groundwater, far more wetlands rely on a stream or river to deliver water. Wetlands linked to flowing water serve as flood dispersal basins. Susan Galatowitsch, assistant professor at Iowa State's Landscape Architecture Department, points out that (at least in prairie regions) a wetland's surface area must be at least 0.5 percent of the area of its watershed before it is effective for flood control.[16]

Especially for recharge and flood control, replacing a wetland with another of different size, location, or type may fail to replace the original wetland's functions. Without replacing function, mitigation becomes primarily decorative and in some ways disguises the damage being done.

Proponents of brokering argue that the system allows regional planning, focuses on restoring the most valuable wetlands, combines replacement wetlands rather than having them created piece-meal by each developer, and provides a profit motive for protecting and replacing wetlands.[17]

By the EPA's own analysis, wetlands brokering seldom recreates the functions or values of the destroyed wetland.[18] Rather, it is driven by what land the developer can acquire cheaply enough to make the trade worthwhile. Brokering is often a feature of highway construction, where the difficulties of locating a road and the extreme value placed on road-building combine to make wetlands removal very attractive. These criteria are not necessarily at odds with relocating the wetlands to ecologically appropriate sites, but in practice, they act against it.

Proposals for mitigation banking are often linked to a call for stricter attention to function-for-function replacement. However, even advocates of wetlands creation and brokering acknowledge that "our ability to replace functional values, with a few exceptions, is limited because of our poor understanding of these functions . . . [and even] existing information has often not been used . . ."[19]

Thus the authors are not certain that creating wetlands to replace others lost to construction is a sustainable practice. It is unclear whether current technology can create a fully functional wetland on dryland sites (wastewater-treatment wetlands excepted). *Restoring* wetlands on sites where they previously existed has a much higher chance of success. Simply in terms of energy and materials, *conserving* an existing wetland is more efficient than either creating or restoring it. What is clear is that protection of these important ecosystems is always the preferred alternative.

Protect Wetlands during Construction

Many of the techniques described for general site protection (Principle 1) are used in protecting wetlands. The main difference in applying these techniques is that wetlands, and especially wetlands associated with streams or rivers, will almost certainly stretch off-site in one or more directions. This requires extra care and ingenuity when restricting access to the wetland. Nonetheless, preventing construction traffic from entering or crossing wetlands is very important.

If there is no alternative to crossing a stream or wetland, temporary access that can be removed without damage on completion must be provided. Some work can be carried out from boats and other specialized equipment.⊃

(Launch or landing sites will still need protection and/or restoration.) If land vehicles must cross a wetland, protect the bottom soils from being churned by wheels, tracks—or feet. This is usually accomplished by temporary bridges, planks, or mats or by removable wire or fabric structures filled with gravel. Dumping gravel directly into the wetland forms a passage but is hard to remove when the job is over.

The banks of any water body are especially susceptible to damage. Protect the banks well beyond the actual crossing. Temporary shoring may be an option in some situations. Banks throughout the project may require protection because they are attractive to both people and animals. Expect to rebuild and replant the banks at the end of the project.

Any runoff created by construction should be prevented from entering the wetland or at least filtered through straw bales, sediment fencing, or other standard erosion and sedimentation (E&S) controls. Natural rates of erosion can be increased by a factor of 2,000 on construction sites, unless controlled (Figure 6.22); the soil carried off construction sites often washes into water bodies. Polluted runoff is a particular threat, especially to streams and ponds. However, according to Dawn Biggs, a Virginia landscape architect with strong experience in wetland and stream management, the filtering and buffering functions of wetlands make them remarkably resilient in removing chemical impurities from the water (see discussion of bioremediation, page 97 for related information). Overwhelming the wetland with dense sediment, and the mechanical disturbance of wetland soils that opens the way for invasive species, may be more serious threats than some kinds of water pollution.

Even a wetland that is protected from access can have its soils drastically disturbed as a result of adjacent construction. On some projects, certain stages of work can lead to temporary danger of flooding. For example, extreme runoff can result from a storm just after clearing the site or between paving a parking lot and planting vegetative buffers around it. Since flooding can cause major washouts and damage, care should be taken to prevent the extra volume of water from rushing into the wetland. Even wetlands designed to hold floodwater need an establishment period during which gradually increasing

amounts of stormwater are directed into the wetland. It may be critical to deal with problems of the whole watershed before attempting to protect or restore a wetland.

WETLANDS REQUIRE DIFFERENT PROTECTION STRATEGIES

In addition to general site protection, the unique ecological, structural, and legal conditions of wetlands bring other protection strategies into play.

- Soil compaction risk is much greater on saturated soils than on dry ones, in general.

- Any obviously wet zone should have a generous buffer around it, above and beyond what would be fenced for a dry site feature.

- It is particularly important to plan for seasonal variations that affect water bodies, such as seasonal precipitation, water table, and flooding. These, as well as tidal motion, can dramatically change the size and shape of a water body or a wetland over the course of a construction project.

Use Low-Impact Construction if Building in Wetlands

Nature centers, as well as water recreation facilities and other special projects, may require construction *in* a wetland. Such cases involve specialized construction techniques and materials.

Work in standing water is likely to stir up sediments from the bottom. Sedimentation curtains, hung from a string of floats, are used to keep the muddied water within the construction zone, and out of the water beyond. These function similarly to filter-fencing on land, except that they form a boundary between two areas of water.

Structures built in or at the edge of wetlands are best supported by foundations that have a small footprint. Pilings are commonly used, as is a newly patented system called "pinned foundations," described on page 143 (see Figure 6.17). The small footprint minimizes disruption of the wetland, permits water motion around the structure, and overcomes the limits of unstable wetland soils.

Pilings are available in many forms and materials. Tubular forms driven into the soil and filled with concrete are common, as are wood pilings. Rot resistance is important in wetlands construction but must not be achieved by the use of toxic preservatives that can leach into the water; however, ACZA preservative has been successfully used (see page 221). Some woods, such as elm, are rot-resistant if they *remain* underwater. These species cannot resist alternate wet and dry situations (such as fencing or decking) but may be extremely useful as pilings. Ancient ports built their docks of such woods, and pilings hundreds of years old have been found in near-perfect condition so long as they were not exposed to air. But not all species of naturally rot-resistant wood will function well when submerged.

Recycled "plastic lumber" has also been used for some waterside construction. Plastic lumber has great value for waterside construction, despite some structural strength limitations (see page 207). It is waterproof, rotproof, and cannot leach into water, making it a good choice for construction in wetlands.

Boardwalks have traditionally been used for pathways into wetlands. Again, treated lumber should not be used because of the potential for leaching, contaminating the water, and potentially killing wildlife.[20] Well-designed boardwalks leave spaces between boards, permitting both water and light to pass through to the area under the walkway. This is important both for maintaining the water balance in the wetland and to ensure that aquatic life is not excluded from the boardwalk areas by lack of light.

The work of several landscape firms in wet Washington State shows the range of tactics used to give the public dry-footed access into wetlands where disturbance is prohibited by law.[21] At Juanita Bay Park, landscape architects Jongejan Gerrard McNeal used two different methods of supporting boardwalks. One, which required considerable skill by the contractor, was to lay logs across the wetlands as grade beams. The contractor had to match the variable thickness of the logs to the ground surface, without digging, in order to keep the upper surfaces level. The second system, where the ground was even wetter, was to drive 2-inch steel pipe into the bog soils as pilings. By using small-diameter pilings, heavy equipment was avoided: one worker with an air-hammer and scaffolding was able to install the pipes. Cross-tie pipes were added for stability, plus 4 × 12 beams. Both support structures were decked with ACZA-treated lumber. The boardwalks were designed to clear the ground by 18 inches so that visitors would think twice about stepping off.

Figure 4.8. Boardwalks, such as this one at Spring Peeper marsh in the Minnesota Arboretum, can make an art form of the necessity for minimum disturbance in wetlands. PROJECT and PHOTO: Fred Rozumalski.

An innovative foundation system with great promise for sensitive sites is the "pinned foundation," from the company of the same name in Gig Harbor WA. Metal brackets are attached either to grade beams or to short wooden posts, neither of which extend down into the soil. Through slots in the brackets, the pins (4- to 8-foot-long sections of galvanized pipe) are driven at several diagonal angles down into the soil. The pins are locked into the slots by the weight of the structure. They can be driven in with hand tools or a small jackhammer, thus eliminating any heavy machinery. They can also be pulled up, adjusted, or removed with minimal site disturbance. These foundations can be placed closer to existing trees than can more conventional pilings. The system, illustrated in Figure 6.17, is reminiscent of the auger-foundation method developed by Pliny Fisk and noted on page 49.

Finally, of course, there are floating boardwalks. Some are created from unusual materials, such as Styrofoam-stuffed used tires. These must be properly sealed to prevent waterlogging or degrading into the wetland. Floating walkways have the advantage that they can be assembled in segments, off-site; one section is placed from the bank, providing a platform for placing the next, and so on. Assuming the segments are sized for a crew to move by hand, very little disruption of the site occurs. A system like this was used by another Washington firm, Bruce Dees & Associates, at the Hood Canal Wetlands Project.

Restore Damaged Wetlands

Wetlands that have been damaged or drained by prior land use can be restored. Many of these techniques also apply to postconstruction restoration of small areas of wetlands or to creating new wetlands. The difference is that using the techniques on the site of an existing but damaged wetland takes advantage of the original links to aquifers and to other surface water, as well as remnant soils and a seed bank of dormant wetland species. The restored wetland is much more likely to function as a recharge zone or flood basin than is a wetland created at a site of convenience.

The first step in restoring a wetland may be to reestablish water flows and levels. Determining the appropriate level may be simple, if the original level was carefully noted before construction began. In many cases, though, there will be no record of the original level, and specialist help will be required to decide what level to use. Wetlands drained for agriculture may primarily require removing or altering drainage structures to restore wetland hydrology, with plants and animals soon reestablishing themselves.

On other sites, a dam or dike may be needed. This is usually constructed of earth; a core of clay may be needed, and welded wire mesh is often buried in the center to prevent burrowing animals from breaching the dam. Structures in the dike control normal water level and permit flood overflow. The water level is most easily set with the stop-log device described on page 138. The flood

spillway is a separate element. It should be designed to accommodate the ten-year-storm event for wetlands under 20 acres. A grassed spillway, reinforced with geotextile, is preferable to concrete in cost, functionality, and appearance.[22]

Once the surface level and the rate of water flow are known, grading may be needed to shape the basin in which the wetland lies. The basin should not be steep-sided, even if deep water exists in the center. A broad shallow basin offers the widest area and diversity of plantable shore.

Grading must be unusually accurate, because precise water depth is critical to the survival of wetland plants. Since the water surface is always horizontal, it is the basin bottom that determines water depth. Zones of different depth support diversity of species. It is generally easier to manage the water level if each zone has a horizontal bottom rather than a sloping one; this terraced form keeps water depth consistent throughout each zone. A very small slope (as little as 0.05 percent) can cause a major difference in depth over 100 yards, so that the same plants cannot survive throughout the zone.[23]

If the site is graded, wetlands soil should be stockpiled *underwater* to preserve seeds, tubers, and anaerobic chemical conditions. Some artificially created wetlands require a seal or liner of bentonite clay or waterproof sheet. The liner is covered with 16 to 24 inches of soil for planting. Either an artificial liner or a natural impervious surface can be punctured by careless construction work, causing the wetland to fail.

Figure 4.9. The t-shaped opening in this wetland structure sets the water level. Small rises in level flow out through the stem of the t; if major flooding raises the level higher, the top of the t permits faster drainage. PROJECT and PHOTO: Rick Scaffidi, EQR.

Figure 4.10. Wetland plants survive only in specific water depths, requiring terraced design and careful grading, as at Lake Terrace Convention Center, Hattiesburg MS. PROJECT and PHOTO: Ed Blake.

Another reason for care during grading is that soil disturbance invites invasion by aggressive aquatic plants like giant reed (*Phragmites* sp.) or purple loosestrife. Unlike many other invaders, these will not be deterred by fluctuating flooding and drying. Once established, these invaders can be difficult or impossible to weed out and will actively displace native species. Since invasive species are responsible for the decline of many existing wetlands, creating a haven for them defeats the purpose of restoration. Outside their native regions, these species should not be planted deliberately except where climate or other strong control keeps them from spreading. In general, select wetland species native to the region and suited to the specific type of wetland.[24]

Specialized planting techniques are used to place wetland species. Only a few species float freely in the water; most must be rooted in the bottom even if their leaves or flowers are above the surface. When replanting areas of an existing wetland, plants or seeds are often weighted and dropped into the water from a boat, a technique that seems to have mixed success. Where possible, flooding the wetland and then draining it to produce muddy planting conditions is good for the plants and permits access on foot or with specialized machinery. Tubers, seedlings, and live-stake cuttings may be planted in the mud. Furrows, cut in the basin across the direction of water flow, can speed planting. In soft soils or where wildlife are feeding, plantings may need to be anchored and protected with erosion control matting or biodegradable mesh.

When a wetland is restored on a site where wetlands previously existed, planting may not be necessary. Seed of wetland plants can survive for a decade or more in drained or filled soils and still germinate once wetland conditions are restored. Soil "cores" collected from nearby wetlands are sometimes used to seed a restored or new wetland. Extreme care must be used in collecting cores to prevent damage to the donor site. Small cores (a few inches across) should be dug in a scattered pattern, leaving a large border of undisturbed soil from which the cored space can grow back.

Managing water level is critical to plant establishment. After planting, the water level needs to be adjusted to match the speed of plant growth, keeping the leaves of most species just above water. Like dry land plants, aquatics have an

Table 4.1
Plants to Avoid (or Use Very Cautiously) in Wetlands

Botanical Name	Common Name(s)
Eichornia crassipes	water hyacinth
Lysimachia spp.	purple loosestrife
Melaleuca quinquenervia	melaleuca, bottlebrush
Phalaris arundinacea	reed canary grass
Phragmites australis	giant reed
Salix spp.	willows (some shrub and tree forms)
Tamarix spp.	tamarisk, saltcedar
Typha latifolia and *T. angustifolia*	cattail

establishment period during which they are extra vulnerable to stress. Hammer describes water management schedules for various newly established wetland types, in some cases filling and draining the wetland weekly. After establishment (two to five years) management needs decrease, annual or seasonal manipulation of water levels is still common.[25]

The final aspect of restoring wetlands is monitoring and adjusting the results. Flows and levels, plant and animal establishment, and water quality may all need to be recorded. Final adjustments of grade at the inlet and outlet may need to be made after observation through the seasons. Responsibility for these adjustments must be carefully spelled out in specifications if projects are to be successful at a reasonable bid price. Wetlands construction exemplifies many of the aspects of teamwork, coordination, and inclusion of long-term maintenance that are essential to many other kinds of sustainable landscape work.

Detailed and site-specific planning is essential to the success of wetland design, construction, and maintenance. Few wetland creation and restoration techniques should be attempted without specialist help.⊃

PROJECT EXAMPLE

Las Vegas doesn't seem like a wetland sort of place to most visitors (although many do take a soaking). But the Las Vegas Wash, which empties into Lake Mead, had 2,000 acres or more of wetlands as recently as the 1970s. Used for sewage effluent discharge, the Wash today has lost all but 10 percent of those wetlands. Meanwhile, it receives as much as 1,600 tons of sediment per day.

Figure 4.11. At Spring Peeper marsh, lines of color-coded stakes show water-depth contours and coincide with vegetation changes. Wetlands are prime sites for education and interpretation. PROJECT and PHOTO: Fred Rozumalski.

Las Vegas drinks from Lake Mead, and in 1998 the EPA found bacterial pollution and traces of rocket fuel in the lake. Although it wouldn't take rocket science to figure that declining wetlands, sewage, and drinking water spell trouble, this discovery galvanized the county government into action. Early in 1999, it unveiled a plan to build fifteen erosion-control dams with wetlands behind each one, laced with trails that one politician expects to attract a million visitors a year. At the same time, the restored Wash will restore clean drinking water to Vegas residents (at least those who don't subscribe to W.C. Fields' ideas on drinking water). Called Clark County Wetlands Park, these reconstructed wetlands will also have interpretive exhibits and a small visitors center and theater. Interior Secretary Bruce Babbitt has called the plan "a model for the West."[26]

Another wetland, the Spring Peeper marsh at the Minnesota Arboretum near Minneapolis, recently won an ASLA award for its original education efforts. The bad news is that wetlands are so rare and misunderstood that they need interpretation; the good news is that they attract and educate people so successfully.

Restore Rivers and Streams to Full Health

Eroding streambanks are an environmental problem that is close to many people's backyards. In neighborhoods all over North America, streams have been degraded by two main forces: the channelization, culverting, and burial of streams to make them fit into human development patterns; and the massively increased stormwater runoff that results from roofs, paving, and other impervious aspects of urbanization. In many communities, degraded streams have become prime candidates for community projects by groups like Save Our Streams and Friends of Trashed Rivers.

Anyone who wants to restore a stream must understand that restoration is much more complex than simply stabilizing an eroding stream bank. Holistic restoration takes into account the stream's entire watershed and the ways in which water entering the stream has been affected by development. According to Tom Schueler, the executive director of the Center for Watershed Protection, simply repairing the bank—even if this is done by the most environmentally progressive methods—may be little more than a short-term fix. "A lot of people have been doing that kind of work because, quite frankly, it makes for great before-and-after pictures," says Schueler. "I don't mean to imply that it's just cosmetic, but that alone is not stream restoration. It's stream-bank stabilization."

Keith Bowers is a landscape architect whose design-build firm, Biohabitats (Towson MD), has increasingly worked in stream restoration in the last five years. "Stream restoration doesn't start in the stream channel," Bowers is fond of saying. "It starts in the watershed. If you just patch a stream, that improvement may be blown away in the next big storm. You have to recapture some of that off-site flow and try to release it slowly." (Capturing and slowly releasing water is a function of wetlands; thus, restoring upstream wetlands may be essential to restoring a stream. These systems are closely linked and tend to affect whole human communities; best results are achieved by looking at and involving the whole watershed and all the communities in it.[27])

The overall goal, says Bowers, is to "get the water into the ground as fast as possible in as many places as possible," through infiltration. These measures are easiest to apply in new design, but apply to retrofits, too. In older developments where extensive paved surfaces already exist and cannot be redesigned, control stormwater runoff *before* it enters the stream. Retention basins or other control devices must be put in place prior to restoring the stream banks;

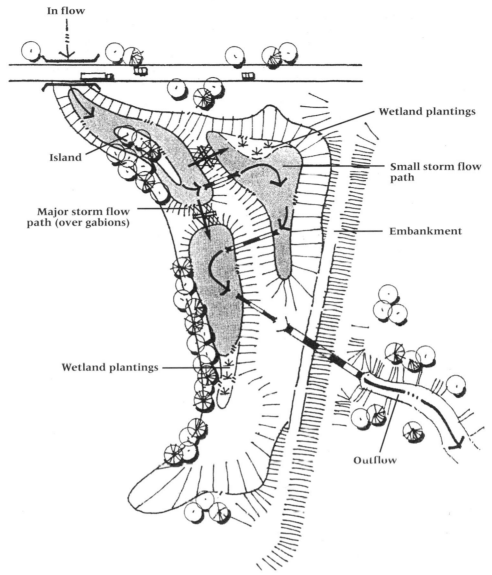

In flow

Island

Major storm flow
path (over gabions)

Wetland plantings

Wetland plantings

Small storm flow
path

Embankment

Outflow

Figure 4.12. Ponds at the headwaters of Wheaton Branch hold stormwater, infiltrating part and slowly releasing it into the stream. ILLUSTRATION: Craig Farnsworth, based on Center for Watershed Protection and Loiederman Associates.

otherwise, stream-bank-erosion problems will return periodically.

For aspiring neighborhood stream restorers, the process entails a considerable learning curve. Fortunately, many learning aids exist: a growing how-to literature, courses and workshops, and environmental action groups. Most groups would agree with the Center for Watershed Protection that much of the real work of stream restoration takes place outside the stream corridor itself and involves regional design and policy measures that reduce impervious surfaces and recapture storm-flows: for example, narrower streets, porous paving, or elimination of curbs and gutters (see Principle 5).

It is often valuable to install an infiltration pond or stormwater wetland near the headwa-ters of the stream. Such ponds are designed to contain stormwater as it first sheets off imper-vious surfaces and to infiltrate most of it, releasing a more stable, predictable flow of water downstream. Without such a pond or ponds, a sudden "flush" of stormwater can wash out the careful bank restoration. The Center for Water-shed Protection calls the construction of such ponds "a watershed manager's most reliable tool . . . to successfully improve a stream's overall operating health."[28]

University of Georgia landscape architecture professor Bruce Ferguson, one of the country's leading stormwater experts, emphasizes that flood-control basins must be selectively sited or they can do active damage. A watershedwide plan is the only way to determine the proper locations for ponds and other infiltration or retention devices. Basins that slow floodwaters at random or uniform locations throughout the watershed fail on two counts: Flow from these ponds may join downstream to create a delayed flood; and storm runoff still by-passes "base flows," in which streams are gradually replenished by water that has infiltrated into soil and slowly reemerged in the stream. To avoid both problems, runoff must be infiltrated, not just held back, and it must soak into the drier soils at the top of the watershed, not at the bottom.

Local policy has long required detention basins on every developed site. However, Ferguson cites several studies that found that this site-by-site approach produced excessive numbers of basins located in the wrong places. Unless properly located and designed for infiltration, these detention basins actually can *increase* flooding downstream and seldom reduce stormflows to predevelopment levels.[29]

Thus, for headwater ponds to be reliable tools, they must be sited with an eye to the whole watershed, and they must infiltrate, rather than just detain, stormwater. This fits the general definition of a wetland, and in fact ponds can be designed as diverse wetlands rather than simple holding tanks. Convincing engineers and regulators to go beyond neat conventional tanks can be a challenge, though more people in such positions are becoming aware of the benefits of wetlands. It is even more difficult to develop statutes that manage stormwater by watershed, ignoring private property boundaries.

Ponds can be installed at the headwaters of the stream or at strategic points along it (such as at large parking areas) and generally require a spillway fitted with a weir or drop structure to control any water that flows into the stream. For a more diverse wetland, the fixed weir may be replaced with a level-adjusting stop-log.

With stormwater infiltrating and base flows normalized, the restoration of the stream itself can be addressed. The purpose of restoring the stream banks is to bring back at least some semblance of the structure, function, and dynamics that existed in the stream before development. This often requires some regrading of the stream banks or even reconfiguration of the streambed itself.

Two general patterns of stream dysfunction may be encountered: the *incised channel*, where erosion cuts (incises) deeper and deeper into the bed, and *aggrading channel*, in which the stream is filled with silt, becoming broad and shallow without pools or riffles. Incised channels generally reflect increased volume of flow or increased speed, which occurs if a culvert or other construction deepens the level of the streambed someplace downstream. Aggrading streams reflect water slowing and dropping its sediment load; either a blockage downstream or an increased amount of sediment from upstream erosion may be responsible. (In the project examples on page 150, Maguire Avenue on Staten Island was incised, while Wheaton Branch in Maryland was aggrading.)

The two forms of dysfunction require differing restoration approaches; determining the proper method may call for a stream-restoration consultant. In general, an incised channel needs to have the volume and speed of flow decreased and the banks strengthened. An aggrading channel has been a site where the current suddenly slowed, dropping sediment; cleaning out the deposits and creating a more steady flow may be needed. The source of the sediment (often an incised channel upstream) may require repairs, too.

Bank erosion is one of the most commonly encountered problems, and there are several approaches to solving it. A conventional approach is to dump riprap or river rock down the banks. Although riprap may solve some immediate erosion problem, it may accelerate trouble upstream or downstream because the real cause—excess runoff—has not been addressed. Nor does riprap provide resting and feeding places for fish that vegetated streambanks provide. Finally, dumped riprap is generally unsightly, neither neatly engineered nor beautifully naturalistic. (Strategically placed boulders, particularly in the streambed itself, can help restore a stream's natural structure of pools and riffles.) Because of the problems inherent in riprap, most restorationists recommend returning plant cover to stream banks as a means of holding the soil. This is essentially bioengineering in a specialized, partly submerged use. As in other forms of bioengineering (Principle 3), hard structures such as crib walls or gabions may be required if banks are extremely steep or are collapsing. (An unusual approach, described on page 205, combines used rubber tires with tree saplings to rescue a collapsing bank.)

An increasingly popular approach to stabilizing stream banks is to use tree branches, roots, or even entire trunks. As California restorationist Ann Riley puts it, "Instead of rushing out to your bank erosion site with rock, rush out to it with some dead tree branches or even a dead tree."[30] The Missouri Department of Conservation has perfected tree-trunk revetments in which whole trees are cabled along stream banks. The trees usually come from development or road-building sites and reuse salvaged materials that would otherwise be trucked to the municipal dump. Root masses from storm-toppled trees are also used.

Most of the materials and methods described in the section on bioengineering are useful for stream restoration. A range of products is available from such suppliers as Bestman Green Systems.◌ Biodegradable fabric blankets are widely used to hold stream banks and streambeds in place until plant growth can be established. At the toe of the bank, where water and soil meet, rolls or "biologs" made of coconut fiber have proved effective. It should be noted, however, that for extensive bank restorations ready-made products can be expensive. The Departments of Architecture and Landscape Architecture at the University of Oregon found this out when stabilizing a stream bank on campus. Their solution was to put students to work assembling and installing cost-effective biologs of their own making. This may be an option for cash-strapped community groups and for contractors in some situations.

Other bioengineering methods have proved effective in bank restoration. One technique that Ann Riley and many others recommend is that of live willow or cottonwood cuttings driven into the banks to provide the same structure for a bank that rebar does for concrete. Riley calls these "the underused workhorses of restoration" and says that they are capable of holding a bank in place better than riprap. Another University of Oregon project first "walled" the bank with straw bales, then drove live-stakes through the bales to root.

Willow cuttings were used in a recent restoration project on a highway embankment in Portland OR for the Oregon Department of Transportation. Bioengineering consultant Robbin Sotir used plants alone (mostly willow cuttings from the contractor's property) to stabilize the banks while providing excellent wildlife and aquatic habitat. Such techniques are attractive

Figure 4.13. Tree trunks, complete with root wads, form revetments to slow scour at the outside of a stream curve. They also create habitat. PROJECT and PHOTO: Biohabitats Inc.

Figure 4.14. University of Oregon landscape students fabricated "soil burritos" of fabric, soil, and chicken wire for a campus restoration, demonstrating a simple, inexpensive method. PROJECT and PHOTO: Professor Stan Jones.

Figure 4.15. Students installing "burritos" and brush layer to stabilize stream bank. PROJECT and PHOTO: Professor Stan Jones.

Figure 4.16. Straw bale and live-stake wall reinforces riverbank at University Oregon's Center for Landscape Studies. PROJECT and PHOTO: Professor Stan Jones.

for several reasons, including that materials are available at little or no cost. One disadvantage is that, especially for steep banks that are subject to heavy rains and flooding, an experienced consultant is required to spend considerable time designing and supervising the process. Unable to find a qualified consultant locally, the DOT had to bring Sotir all the way from Georgia for the duration of the project, driving up costs accordingly. The bioengineered solution, which resisted a major flood in 1996, was still probably more cost-effective than repeated hard-engineering failures.

PROJECT EXAMPLES

Wheaton Branch in Silver Spring MD, just outside Washington DC, typifies the history that requires stream restoration. As Silver Spring developed with the usual impervious surfaces, the little stream that had meandered through its woodlands became the recipient of direct runoff from area roads, parking lots, and a regional shopping mall. Wheaton Branch's highly urbanized watershed is 55 percent impervious. When it rained, county environmental planner Pamela Rowe recalls, stormwater would cascade down the bed of the stream; after years of such torrents, Wheaton Branch degenerated into a broad, shallow channel with eroding banks and scant streamside vegetation. "It had a moonscape look," remembers Rowe. The natural cobbles in its bed were buried beneath inches of silt, and aquatic life was reduced to two pollution-tolerant species. This situation is not uncommon, according to Ann Riley: "Conventional stream and river practices [create] community blight where natural resources once existed."[31]

Nowadays, visitors to Wheaton Branch see a very different scene. A restored Wheaton Branch meanders between densely vegetated banks, stabilized by a variety of techniques including whole trees buried, roots outward, in the bank. The complex branching of the roots slows water passing through and around them. The water runs clear, revealing that the cobbles in the streambed are scoured clean. Plentiful small fish and crayfish dart in the pools and riffles created during the restoration.

Wheaton Branch is the first phase of a larger, ongoing restoration of Sligo Creek, of which it is a tributary. This project is the work of an interdisciplinary team from the Metropolitan Washington Council of Governments, the Maryland-National Capital Park and Planning Commission, the Department of Environmental Protection, and other public agencies. At least in its organizational complexity, the larger Sligo Creek project may be, in the words of the Center for Watershed Protection, "perhaps the most comprehensive urban stream restoration yet attempted."

What makes Sligo Creek exemplary is that rather than simply repairing or "patching" eroded stream banks and leaving it at that, the restoration team is addressing all the channels and tributaries in the stream's entire 13.3-square-mile watershed. Moreover, the completed Wheaton Branch restoration followed in a single project all the steps that the Center for Watershed Protection considers essential, from controlling runoff at the headwaters of the stream to restocking the restored channel with fish.

The project began with the construction of three interconnected ponds that detain the runoff for up to thirty-six hours and allow pollutants and sediments to settle out. Thereafter, a concrete weir with gate valves gradually releases the water into the stream channel. The next crucial step was the complete reconstruction of the channel downstream from the ponds: reconfiguring the streambed with stone "wing deflectors," log weirs, and other means; rebuilding and reinforcing the banks; and revegetating the riparian zone with a total of nineteen shrub and tree species. Finally, fish were reintroduced with the help of a bucket brigade of neighborhood volunteers. Preliminary monitoring indicates that aquatic life—perhaps the best indicator of water quality—is flourishing.

Despite the very visible improvements, the Wheaton Branch project has been criticized for starting from the premise that runoff from parking lots and other impervious surfaces was a given. An almost opposite approach, which focuses on restoring the infiltration capacity of the developed areas of the watershed, was used for Nine Mile Run in Pittsburgh PA.[32] Here the hypothesis is that *stream* restoration will result primarily from *upland* improvements, such as reducing paved area, sending runoff to vegetated buffers, and other methods of restoring permeability to an overdeveloped watershed. This project began with a three-day meeting of designers and other experts, hosted by the Rocky

Mountain Institute and the Studio for Creative Inquiry. Their charge was to brainstorm methods for retrofit and redevelopment in the city that would deal with stormwater at its sources. No redesign of the stream itself was included—that will come later, after the conceptual methods developed at the meeting are applied throughout the watershed. Because its focus is on changing the urban problems that lead to stream degradation, and because results at the stream bank will emerge very slowly, this project bears watching.⊃

Different as they are, these two projects represent a national movement to approach stream restoration in a more comprehensive, holistic manner. Driving this movement are state and federal regulations mandating reductions of non-point-source pollution (in sheet runoff) as well as point-source pollution from sanitary and storm sewers. (The Pittsburgh region's sewer authority stands to be fined $275 million if it does not reduce sewer overflows, for instance.) Both runoff and storm-sewer flows directly affect streams, and the old piecemeal approaches to stream restoration are, in many cases, simply not working. Truly holistic restoration will need both the whole-channel work of Wheaton Branch and the infiltration retrofitting of Nine Mile Creek.

Hydrologist Dave Rosgen, of Colorado-based Wildland Hydrology, seems to have become a guru of sorts to those interested in stream restoration. He is the author of a profusely illustrated book classifying the many different types of streams according to morphology.⊃ At the risk of oversimplifying, Rosgen's scientifically based approach to restoration is essentially about restoring a stream by re-creating its natural dimension, pattern, and profile. Rosgen's general premise is that the restoration of a disturbed channel should begin by asking the question, What stream type should this be? In practice, such restoration may involve excavating an entirely new stream channel for a disturbed stream. This may require more room than is available in many dense urban situations. However, if the approach of Nine Mile Run is taken, the end result should approximate a predevelopment stream, even at the expense of removing structural interference. Rosgen's methods are central to understanding and assessing what might be called each stream's essential nature.

Figure 4.17. Stone deflector in restored Wheaton Branch unobtrusively guards the stream bank from floods. PRO-JECT: Washington Council of Governments. PHOTO: Walt Callahan.

The degree to which this essential pattern can be restored varies from site to site. As with many other site features, we doubt that a stream's ecological functions can be entirely restored until it closely approximates the self-maintaining patterns of streams that have not been degraded.

Those involved in the restoration of Wheaton Branch were fortunate in having room around the stream to excavate extensive ponds and to reconfigure the streambed. Many urban and suburban situations are too built up to allow such options. A recent restoration project in the borough of Staten Island demonstrates just how challenging it can be to bring back a degraded stream corridor to anything resembling its original ecological structure and function.

A common problem in restoring urban streams is that the entire stream corridor is not available for repair—much of it being buried in underground storm sewers and culverts. Sweet Brook, one of the major streams on Staten Island, is a case in point. It alternates between aboveground fragments of its natural channel and underground storm sewers. One quarter-mile segment of Sweet Brook flows above ground through a wooded valley alongside Sweetbrook Road, but its water supply pours out of a storm-sewer culvert. Directly upstream, manhole covers are the only aboveground evidence that the stream exists, and, at the downstream end of the little valley, Sweet Brook empties into another culvert. The valley is "a little remnant—an island in an otherwise man-made environment," says Dana Gumb of the New York City Department of Environmental Protection.

The difficulty in restoring any urban or suburban stream lies in the "hardening" of the surrounding watershed—the stream's headwaters in particular. Like Wheaton Branch, a highly impervious watershed had reduced Sweet Brook to a broad, shallow channel with eroding banks, exposed tree roots, and little aquatic life. Receiving far more cubic feet per second of water from the culvert than its narrow channel could possibly handle, the stream regularly flooded its little valley, tearing out a pedestrian bridge and turning Sweetbrook Road into a linear lake. Unhappy residents had to travel by boat. The streambed turned black from motor oil, street runoff, and "septic influence" (a euphemism for sewage overflowing into the storm drain). Conditions were not helped by people who used the valley for dumping everything from construction rubble to old bathtubs.

In 1995 the DEP moved to restore the quarter-mile segment as part of its Staten Island Bluebelt program, a watershed-scale effort aimed at restoring Staten Island's remaining streams, ponds, and wetlands to their natural functions: conveying, storing, and filtering stormwater. Funding for the Bluebelt program comes from a multi-billion-dollar storm-sewer initiative to prevent flooding in parts of southern Staten Island. Bluebelt planners have been able to piggyback watershed-restoration projects onto the island's well-funded sewer initiative by arguing that restoring the natural systems to convey some of the stormwater is actually cheaper than installing pipes throughout the entire island. "Ecological-restoration advocates often have to walk around hat in hand to get funding," says Gumb. "The glory of this program is that we're doing something that is not only environmentally compatible but economically sound—so that we can sell the idea [of watershed restoration] to the bean counters in the city government."

But what form was the restoration of Sweet Brook to assume? Most of the current principles of the stream-restoration movement—begin at the level of the watershed, control runoff at the headwaters, excavate a new "natural" channel—simply were not options in Sweet Brook's tight, urbanized situation. Even though the stream was part of a 12,000-acre watershed, there was not even room to construct a retention basin directly upstream to slow the stormwater.

Something nevertheless had to be done to mitigate the sheer quantity of stormwater that poured out of the culvert; without that, all the effort of restoring the stream channel would soon be literally down the drain. Fortunately, as part of the flood-control initiative, Sweetbrook Road was earmarked for a sewer—actually, two 12 × 12 storm sewers that would parallel the streambed. The plan was to keep the base flow of the stream in the natural channel while diverting all storm-flows in excess of 160 cubic feet per second into the sewers by means of a device known as a flow splitter.

Another hurdle had to be faced: Although the little valley was designated open space (a protective zoning overlay for unique natural areas on this part of Staten Island), the midsection of the valley was the property of four homeowners. DEP landscape architect Dean Cavallaro, the on-site project manager, had to visit each of the owners and build trust for a restoration process that would introduce heavy earth-moving machinery into their front or back yards. Fortunately, the negotiations were made easier by incentives that the DEP was able to offer the homeowners. These included rebuilding concrete retaining walls that repeated floods had rendered very unstable—and facing them with local field-stone in the bargain.

With the newly installed sewers temporarily diverting the base flow, restoration of the stream corridor went forward. Consultants included restoration ecologists. The streambed was excavated down to its original grade and the resulting sediment used to rebuild the eroded stream banks. Stones and concrete rubble were picked out of the streambed and used for stabilizing the banks. (Asphalt rubble, because of its potential effect on water quality, was plucked out and carted off-site.) Pools and riffles—essential for aquatic habitat—were constructed by the consultants; the rocks brought in to construct the riffles, although taken from a site in neighboring Brooklyn, are from the same glacial moraine as that on Staten Island.

The plant list was carefully compiled for fidelity to the native plant community of Staten Island, even including plants long since lost from the island: the fern *Polypodium vulgare*, for example. Exact faithfulness to the original community was considered crucial. When 200 beech trees arrived on site, they looked suspicious; a tree expert confirmed that they were European beeches—which, says Cavallaro, "poisoned the whole concept" of an all-native planting. Even though a hundred of the beeches had been planted Cavallaro required the nursery to take them back and replace them with bona fide American beeches. With planting, the nine-month construction process came to fruition.

The total cost of the 6-acre corridor restoration: $1.1 million, half of which went for constructing a total of ten new walls. Is a quarter-mile segment of stream between two pipes worth this effort and expense? "Whether such projects are worth the investment is widely debated," says Richard Claytor, the principal engineer with the Center for Watershed Protection. But Claytor points out that stream restorations in fragmented watersheds are not all that uncommon. As an example he cites Strawberry Creek on the Berkeley CA campus. This is probably the most visible stream restoration in the country—yet it too, says Claytor, is in pipes above and below the restored, "daylighted" segment.

Claytor concedes that Sweet Brook is "less valuable than a continuous stream. Aquatic exchange of plant and animal species is severely limited, so it has limited value from a biological standpoint. But it has great value as an educational resource: It sharpens nearby residents' ability to appreciate the watershed."

Gumb has no doubt that the city is getting its money's worth. In addition to it being a lovely green area, "We look to this project as a model," he says, "of how we can fit the restoration of these segments of the watershed into the process of sewer construction—and make these watercourses attractive community amenities. It's a revelation to many of our sewer-construction personnel that they don't have to be ugly."

Sweet Brook typifies the many streams that are partly buried. Another Staten Island Bluebelt segment suffered a different malady common to urban streams: channelization. A portion of a stream along Maguire Avenue had effectively been turned into a drainage ditch for the road. Typical of the long-term incompatibility of hard engineering with stream systems, a 250-foot stretch of this channel had eroded and undercut Maguire Avenue, causing the road to cave in. The stream channel, squeezed between the road and an adjacent property, left no room for maneuvering.

Figure 4.18. Tons of accumulated sediment were removed from Sweet Brook and used to fertilize the restored banks. PROJECT: New York DEP. PHOTO: Dean Cavallaro.

Figure 4.19. Sweet Brook after restoration, just downstream from the location is shown in Figure 4.18. PROJECT: New York DEP. PHOTO: Dean Cavallaro.

Cavallaro's restoration consultant for this project was Creative Habitats of White Plains NY. To prevent another collapse of the road, it was essential to stabilize the stream's vertical banks. This was accomplished by bioengineering methods. Massive stone-filled wire gabions were installed beneath Maguire Avenue. (Gabions are the method of last resort in bank stabilization, according to restorationist Ann Riley, but can be appropriate in situations like this.) On the more visible opposite bank a dry-laid fieldstone wall was built. Boulders were laid in the streambed to slow the stormwater. As a stable medium for plantings along both banks, biologs—rolls of coconut fiber supplied by Creative Habitats—were installed. (In the restoration industry consultants are often suppliers of restoration products. This is not necessarily a conflict of interest—unless, perhaps, the consultant specifies only his or her own products.)

The end result at Maguire Avenue is a project Cavallaro considers very successful. A year after the retrofit was installed, it had surpassed his expectations: plants had almost completely covered the banks, and all of the boulders were still in place.

Because a considerable learning curve faces anyone who wants to enter the stream-restoration field, landscape architects may be wise to follow Cavallaro's example and hire a competent consultant. These abound in many parts of the

Figure 4.20. Erosion undercut pavement at Maguire Avenue and prevented plants from reestablishing. PROJECT: New York DEP. PHOTO: Dean Cavallaro.

Figure 4.21. Maguire Avenue after installation of gabions, boulders to deflect culvert outflow, and plantings. PROJECT: New York DEP. PHOTO: Dean Cavallaro.

country because of the boom in stream-restoration projects. "Throw a rock up in the air and you'll hit one" in California, says Vincent Resh, a professor of environmental science at the University of California at Berkeley who helped restore Strawberry Creek. The problem, according to Resh, is one of competency; all consultants are not equally qualified. He advises caution in retaining one.

How does a community group or project manager locate a competent restoration consultant? One place to start is with the listings in the Products & Services Directory from the International Erosion Control Association➲; look under the heading "Shoreline and Stream-bank Stabilization." Cavallaro followed a more complicated but ultimately successful process. He first called other government agencies, environmental planners, plant nurseries, and fellow landscape architects and compiled a list of consultants in his region. He then called each of these consultants and asked for brochures and before-and-after photographs of completed projects. Finally, he visited several of their completed projects before selecting Creative Habitats.

Collect and Conserve Water

Besides being potentially destructive, water is a valuable commodity to humans, and conserving it makes economic sense. By reducing human use of water, natural water systems are also protected. It is increasingly common, especially in the western United States, to see conflicts between diverting water for human use and leaving it in-stream to support aquatic life. Today's in-stream flow advocates may be primarily interested in sport fishing; in the long term, there is much more at stake if rivers or aquifers dry up from overuse. Not only biodiversity and habitat but human survival depend on water, much of it diverted from distant sources. Conserving water, through a wide range of techniques, is necessary in its own right, essential to protection of wetlands and streams, and important in keeping water supplies clean.

Harvest Water from Roofs and Landscapes

Water-harvesting is the collection and storage of rainwater from roofs, paved surfaces, and the landscape. At one time traditional in the United States, it is a classic example of the principle of dealing with rainwater near where it falls. In 1997 the president of the American Rainwater Catchment Systems Association estimated that there were about 250,000 roof systems in the United States[33]; they are common in Australia and on many Caribbean islands. Homes built around 1900 in the United States often had water-harvesting systems supplying a cistern in the basement.

Harvesting from a ground surface catchment area has an even longer history and is an example of how industrialized societies can learn to be more sustainable by studying allegedly "backward" times and cultures. Ancient Israelites, the Chinese, the Pueblo and other Indians of the American Southwest, and Australians (both aboriginal and recent settlers) have used such water-harvesting systems to survive. Most techniques consist of variations on terracing, usually at a small scale. Low stone walls or check-dams hold back and infiltrate water at strategic points in a watershed, causing fertile sediment to deposit a moist planting bed even in some of the most arid environments on Earth. Shallow ditches roughly following contours (often called "key lines") arc also used to gather erosive sheet flows into series of small hillside ponds.

The results of arid-land water-harvesting can be startling: stopping gully erosion, raising the water table, and greening the desert without artificial irrigation. In recent years, these techniques have been revived and somewhat systematized by Australian author Bill Mollison, under the name Permaculture. Permaculture is an agriculturally focused system of sustainable construction, and many of its techniques are adaptable to landscape construction. Water harvesting is only one of the techniques considered by Permaculturists.[34]

Evaporation and precipitation "distill" rainwater, so it is free of many of the pollutants found in surface water. It holds few minerals, making it "soft" water, and escapes the chlorine and flourine of municipal systems. Unless it is contaminated by materials on the collecting surface, its purity makes it desirable drinking water and also ideal for many species of plants.

Choosing the best materials for rainwater-harvest depends on the ultimate use of the water. In roof systems, stainless steel, tile, terra-cotta, and slate arc frequently used. Lead is found in some color coatings, solder and fasteners, making them inadvisable for collector roofs, and metals may also leach from galvanized roofing. Where rain is frequent and plentiful, as in the Caribbean, limestone roofs—which sweeten the water— are used. In any less-wet climate, the porous surface of the stone would collect impurities and grow algae, bacteria, or mold. Shingles (asphalt or wood) share the problems of porosity, and if treated with preservative should not be used on collector roofs.

Any paved surface can be a water-harvesting collector, but not for drinking water. Asphalt can produce contaminants, but most other paving materials are relatively inert. Paved surfaces may have pollutant residues, from air pollution as well as spills from automotive sources, Dumpsters, and industrial processes. Paved non-vehicular surfaces are generally suitable for water-harvesting; vehicular paving with light traffic is often clean enough, too. Runoff from potentially polluted surfaces (driveways, Dumpster pads,

Figure 4.22. Rainwater from a roof drain is caught in a gravel basin and routed to furrows in the garden at Denver offices of designer Bill Wenk. PROJECT and PHOTO: Bill Wenk.

etc.) should be routed through a vegetated biofilter before flowing to final use. Because of their linear shape, bioswales are mostly associated with road and parking lot runoff and are discussed in detail in Principle 5, page 182. However, they may be useful for infiltrating and decontaminating runoff from other sources and may be part of water-harvesting systems intended for irrigation. Lawns, unless maintained with excessive pesticides, also serve as collecting surfaces, although like any porous surface they yield less runoff.

Perhaps the simplest form of water harvesting for landscape use is simply grading the site to drain toward planted beds or ponds. Permaculturist Ben Haggard of Tesuque NM used this approach for the landscape of New Mexico's first Energy Star–compliant house. In a region where annual precipitation averages about 12 inches, this system supports mature shade and fruit trees without using supplemental water.

The volume of water collected by any surface—paved, roofed, or planted—can be calculated using standard engineering formulas. Water-harvesting calculations treat the resulting volume as a *resource*, instead of the conventional idea that runoff is a nuisance to be disposed of. The same formulas make it possible to size the basins into which harvested water may be directed. Without careful planning, the collected water may drown some plants while parching others. Planting beds, which are low points in such a design, must be sized to prevent water standing in them and drowning the plants. If a pond is to collect water, it needs to be sized so that heavy rains do not overfill it and provided with spillways to avoid washout.

Most of the research on water-harvesting is directed at using the water to drink. For landscape irrigation, purity need not be as high as for potable water, although heavy metals and lead should still be avoided. Because landscape watering can use two to three times as much water as indoor uses combined, collecting enough to supply the entire irrigation demand may be difficult or costly. Nonethless, as a backup system, reducing the amounts pumped from groundwater or purchased from municipal sources, water-harvesting can still make good sense. At the University of Arizona's Casa del Agua in Tucson, and at the Environmental Showcase Home maintained in Phoenix by Arizona Public Service, harvested water supplements greywater to meet irrigation needs.[35] Water harvesting is also extensively used at the Lady Bird Johnson Wildflower Center in Texas.

Water-harvesting captures the water that falls on impervious surfaces and keeps it from running off. Used as irrigation, it is applied slowly to the site and infiltrates "close to the source." It may, as in the following example, moderate both peak flows and seasonal fluctuations in water availability. The collected water is held back from flows downstream, so intense water-harvesting in an area could cut down in-stream flow, as can sending harvested water into the sewer system after use. Infiltration of harvested water avoids this problem where water is plentiful, but it may still be a concern in arid regions. Local small-

scale water-harvesting that ultimately results in infiltrating the captured water on-site appears to have far more benefits than drawbacks for a sustainable community.

PROJECT EXAMPLE

Parque da Cidade in Oporto, Portugal, offers an intriguing example of contemporary water-harvesting. The park's designers faced a major design problem of maintaining the water level in a manmade lake throughout Portugal's six-month dry season. Project engineers initially specified a plastic liner for the lake bottom on the premise that the sandy soil would not hold water. An alternative strategy was developed by project manager and landscape architect Sidonio Pardal, working with a hydrologist. He sited approximately fifty infiltration basins throughout the park. Some are grassy swales; others are lined with granite, salvaged from around the city. The basins interrupt overland flow during Portugal's rainy season (October to March) and collect rainwater that slowly infiltrates into the ground. Water collected during the rainy season reaches the lake when it is most needed—Pardal estimates that the trip from any one of the infiltration basins takes months. Almost no drains or pipes were used, in contrast to modern engineering practice; speeding up water movement was not desirable at all. In similarly wet/dry climates such as California's, this approach to water-harvesting could have considerable value.

Infiltrate Water Simply On-Site

As recently as the mid-1990s, devices for water infiltration were given little mention among conventional landscape architects and were often ignored in teaching. A focus on *getting rid of* water, through pipes and other systems, virtually displaced the many varieties of water infiltration devices, such as the so-called French drain. European texts on landscape construction were well ahead of most U.S. counterparts on this subject, an exception being Ferguson's work. For example, a standard British text from the *1970s* contains no fewer than four detail drawings for infiltration devices, plus calculations showing how large a land area each can drain in normal soils.[36] It is no coincidence that the infiltration example described above is from Europe.

On-site infiltration may be overlooked

Figure 4.23. Collected on the Portland Water Pollution Control Lab's roof, water spouts from scuppers in rhythmic jets. PROJECT: Robert Murase. PHOTO: Tom Liptan.

because it is so simple. It relies on two basic principles: slowing or holding the water flow and increasing soil permeability. Both are easier to achieve close to the source of water, since either large volumes or fast flow is harder to hold, and greater volume takes extreme porosity to infiltrate quickly.

Many of the methods discussed in other sections of this book are applicable to on-site infiltration, even though they fulfill other purposes. Bioswales (page 182) use vegetation and gentle gradients to slow water. Wetlands, whether natural, restored, or constructed for wastewater treatment (this chapter), slow and hold water due to topography and vegetation; they frequently are major sites of infiltration. Porous paving over a reservoir is a prime example of on-site infiltration (page 184). Water-harvesting, while it may be used with storage tanks, often has direct infiltration as its goal. Check dams, terracing, key-line trenches, and many other techniques of bioengineering and Permaculture hold water in small, even tiny, reservoirs from which it soaks into the soil. Conventional retention basins do the same thing, though generally on an overcentralized scale.

Two structures especially designed for infiltration are the French drain and the "soakaway." Conventional construction recognizes these but treats them as minor tools in the arsenal of water control. For sustainability, they warrant much more frequent use.

The French drain is simply a pit or trench, filled with rubble or gravel. The size of the rubble should be graded, large at the bottom to small near the top. Over the smallest gravel, several inches of soil are placed to match the original grade. Modern variants can be made considerably more efficient by lining the pit or trench with filter fabric, which permits water to move through the rubble fill, while keeping out the sediment that would eventually fill the voids.

This brings up an important reason why such drains were rejected by conventional designers: prior to the invention of filter fabric, French drains had to be dug up and cleaned of silt, or replaced, every few years. Conventional concrete catch basins can also be overwhelmed by silt, but are somewhat easier to clean. Silting, however, really indicates that the structure is serving an area that is being eroded more quickly than it should. Often the reason for this is that a single

drain is built too far from the origins of the water flow, causing volume and speed to concentrate and start eroding. A single drain for a large area may seem economical, but only in terms of initial costs. Shorter flow-lines, and vegetated surfaces for the flow, significantly cut maintenance costs due to siltation.

Soakaways are quite similar to French drains but usually receive water from a small pipe rather than overland flow. Some soakaways are rubble-filled; others, called dry wells, are empty. Dry wells have unmortared stone walls and an earth floor through which infiltration occurs. They hold a larger volume of water than the rubble-filled types. Unlike the French drain, these structures are usually covered with a grate or manhole cover. If the incoming water is very silty, a conventional silt trap can be added on the upstream side of the soakaway.

In soils with ordinary drainage and for the rainfall typical of Britain, a 60-cubic-foot-capacity soakaway can infiltrate runoff for about 2,200 square feet (1.6 m³ for 200 m²). With a capacity of 400 cubic feet (11 m³), a larger soakaway could serve almost 10,000 square feet (900 m²), an area almost 100 feet square.[37] Where the "design storm" delivers less rainfall at once than is the case in the United Kingdom, the same size structure could serve somewhat larger areas. However, this gives an idea of the small scale appropriate to these infiltration methods. For larger areas, terraces or check-dams may be simpler and cheaper, since many of them can be built for the cost of one dry well.

Like other wells, dry wells on certain sites may pose the danger of someone falling into them. Given the ability of filter fabric to keep the pore spaces of rubble fill clear of silt, the filled soakaway (a synonym for French drain) may be a better choice.

A number of commercially available drainage systems use the principle of a core with large voids (usually waffle-like plastic), wrapped in filter fabric. In effect, they provide a French drain in the shape of a pipe and can be very useful for collecting sediment-laden water, filtering it, and dispersing it for infiltration. Old-fashioned perforated pipe serves some of the same purposes, but may clog with sediment. These filter drains are an important part of some updated tree-planting standards (Principle 3).

A number of high-tech storm-sewer fittings

have recently arrived on the market and can remove sediment from large urban piped systems by creating a vortex in the water flow, or by similar methods. These are doubtless valuable in taming the damage caused by conventional engineered water controls and can also remove the trash that is washed or thrown into urban catch basins. However, their long-term sustainability seems dubious, since simple, small-scale, on-site infiltration methods will prevent the problems these water machines are designed to solve. As a temporary step in improving water quality downstream from engineered stormwater systems, they can be used in the service of sustainability.

Store Water for Later Use

Harvested water can be stored in tanks above or below ground, or in ponds, as just noted. Ponds lose a great deal to evaporation in arid climates, but they can be used for raising fish, for solar collectors with a heat pump, for slowing flood flows, or for decorative landscape features. As simple holding space for irrigation water, they are inefficient, and they are not suitable for drinking water.

Tanks are available ready-made in metal, fiberglass, plastic, or precast concrete. They can also be built on-site from stone or ferrocement (thin cement over steel reinforcing mesh) or of wood, though water-resistant woods like redwood are often unsustainably harvested. If located above ground, they should be opaque, since sunlight will promote the growth of algae in the water. Buried tanks generally must be heavier models; they have the advantage of being protected from freezing. Not all tank materials are suitable for drinking water, and their energy and toxicity in manufacture should be considered as well (see Principles 6 and 7).

Use Pumps if Needed

Where possible, gravity-flow water systems are the most energy-efficient. However, harvested rainwater is normally stored at a level below the surface it was collected from; if this is a roof, gravity flow into the same building's plumbing is unlikely, and from underground tanks, virtually impossible. Careful placement of storage tanks fed by roof collection might make gravity *irrigation* possible, since most landscapes are by definition at ground level. However, it is difficult to achieve the water pressure required for modern irrigation using gravity. The height of the tank determines the "head" of pressure developed in the system.

For these reasons, water-harvesting often requires pumps. Water-pumping is one of the most efficient uses for solar electricity (photovoltaics, see page 265). Solar power is widely used in agricultural water-pumping and in remote campgrounds. For water supply, it is cheaper to store water than to store electricity— that is, pump to a high storage tank during sunny periods, supplying users by gravity, rather than pumping on demand using storage batteries. Decorative fountain pumps could certainly be solar powered; the intensity of sunshine could regulate the volume pumped, creating a climate-responsive fountain. For a solar pump to operate constantly, it needs a battery system.

There are many types of pump design. From a sustainability perspective, the main things to look for are low energy usage (the wattage and amperage are usually listed on the label) and a good service life with low maintenance. Many suppliers offer pumps specifically designed for compatibility with solar power. A pump running on DC power can be operated directly from solar panels without an inverter, keeping the system simple. Real Goods now offers kits with matched solar panels and pumps of varying sizes.⊃

Filter and Purify Collected Water for Drinking

Collected water may need to be purified for some purposes, although for landscape use this is not routinely necessary and may be wasteful. Water is purified by physical filtration, ultraviolet light, or the use of chemicals. For sustainability, the use of chemicals should be a last resort and is undesirable for irrigation because of negative effects on soils and plants.

Physical filtration can be a simple screen or sand filter that removes coarse particles or a high-tech ceramic filter. Ceramic filters are commonly sold for camping (see Real Goods⊃) and can remove bacteria and even viruses, down to sizes smaller than one micron. Similar systems can be installed at the faucet. For drinking/ cooking water, it may make sense not to treat it in storage, but to filter it as it is used. Filters require either cleaning or replacement periodically, or both. Roof-washers (there are many designs) are used as a kind of prefilter for drinking-water harvesting systems. Before allowing water into the storage tank, roof-washers divert the first few gallons of stormwater, which carry dust and contaminants from the roof surface.

Solar power is a trusted technology for purifying water supplies in the Third World, and at some U.S. campgrounds far from municipal water. Photovoltaic power can be used to run standard ultraviolet purification systems, though these can require significant energy—80 kWh per year or more.[38] Filter the water first to remove particles that can hide microorganisms from the UV light. With carefully designed storage, perhaps in dual tanks, water can be pumped and purified during the day, eliminating the need for electrical storage batteries.

A related application is a floating swimming-pool purification system manufactured by Floatron. This unit ionizes the water in which it floats, eliminating the need for chlorination. A 12-inch unit can treat a 50,000-gallon tank continuously.

Irrigate Intelligently and Sparingly

Irrigation means the addition of water above and beyond normal precipitation. Although some irrigation techniques save water compared to other forms of irrigation, all irrigation requires extra water. The *baseline* for evaluating the ecological costs and benefits of irrigation should always be the unirrigated landscape and the natural water regime of the site.

This does not mean that irrigation should be excluded from sustainable design. Rather, it means that irrigation should be used where it can really produce outstanding results in a resource-efficient way. Truly saving water requires considering all options, from irrigating with surplus water to eliminating irrigation for most or all of the landscape. Comparing the relative efficiency of different irrigation systems is not, by itself, sufficient to make a landscape sustainable.

Landscape irrigation consumes about 75 percent of residential water use in arid regions during the hot summer months.[39] Much of this water is from municipal supplies, treated and purified to drinking-water standards that are unnecessary for most irrigation. Clearly, sustainability is not served by wasting treated water. There is a critical need to reduce the overall amount of water used for irrigation. A combina-

tion of design, appropriate hardware components, and maintenance can cut down on water use through increased efficiency rather than by doing without irrigation altogether.

Water efficiency is not just a matter of technology, though. "The most important feature of a water-conserving landscape is the preservation of as many existing [native] trees and shrubs as possible."[40] Thus the issues and techniques raised in Principle 1 are critical to water conservation. This constant interlinkage of good practices that benefit other good practices cannot be overemphasized.

XERISCAPE AND LOW-WATER LANDSCAPES

Xeriscape is an approach to water conservation based on designing and constructing landscapes that use water efficiently. This system, trademarked by the Denver Water Department and the National Xeriscape Council,[41] promotes seven basic principles that correspond to many of the themes of this book:

1. Planning and design
2. Soil analysis and improvement
3. Practical areas of turf
4. Appropriate plants
5. Efficient irrigation
6. Mulching
7. Proper maintenance

These principles (which, taken individually, are not new to gardeners) are all essential to the system. Xeriscape's central concept, however, is that plants with like water requirements are grouped together, and that water-intensive plants are reserved for areas where they will have maximum effect. Exotic, water-hungry specimen trees might be used at focal points in the landscape near a residence. A small and drought-tolerant lawn might be used in the same way, as a special feature. Moving away from the house, however, planting zones would contain more drought-tolerant plants. On larger properties, only a reasonably sized garden would contain plants requiring irrigation; outside that zone, the native landscape would predominate. In the native zone, any planting would be done with species that could survive with no watering once established.

Clearly, this concept offers far greater water savings than does irrigating the entire lot, no matter how efficiently. Combined with efficient irrigation technology for the small watered areas, Xeriscape gardens live up to their name: xeric means dry.

Like native-plant use in general, Xeriscape requires changes in attitude about landscapes. The new attitude encourages people to see well-adapted plants as pleasing and beautiful rather than assuming that only certain horticultural varieties have any merit, and that all other plants are scruffy weeds. Xeriscape encourages attention to the qualities that make a place unique. The authors feel that this attitude is critically important to sustainability, especially if the sustainable landscape is to be beautiful as well as merely functional.

A simple approach to water efficiency, emphasized by Xeriscape and many other systems, is the use of organic mulch. (Inorganic mulches, like gravel, can hold some water in the soil, but lack other benefits of composted mulches.) In addition to increasing soil fertility, applying 2–4 inches of mulch over a garden bed dramatically decreases water loss through evaporation and drying of the soil. Where regular mulching can be expected as part of maintenance, design for reduced water use. This is discussed further in the chapter on maintenance, Principle 10.

As a general rule, soil improved after specific soil testing can produce healthier plants while demanding or wasting far less water. Before increasing site irrigation, the ability of existing soil to store water and release it to plants should be carefully tested and maximized. See page 79 on soil amendments, recalling that excessive soil "improvements" can be counterproductive in some regions.

WATER-EFFICIENT IRRIGATION TECHNOLOGY

The three main forms of irrigation are flood, spray, and drip. Flooding a field or bed with water requires the least equipment but is labor-intensive and not very flexible at directing water from one bed to the next. Spray can use simple hoses and fittings, which are easily moved and aimed, although dragging hoses is many a gardener's complaint. As a result, buried pipe with fixed spray heads and automated sequential controllers have become popular. Drip irrigation uses drippers or emitters to deliver water to a precise point on the ground, or even underground. Like buried spray systems, it requires considerable pipe runs but can easily be automated.

Comparisons of water efficiency between these three systems are relatively straightforward. Flood and spray systems lose significant amounts of water to evaporation, and spray systems waste water by overspraying unless very carefully installed and maintained. Microspray systems have also been developed; these suffer less loss but are not as efficient as drippers. Drip systems can save up to 90 percent of the water used by flood and spray systems, and they usually save at least 30 percent. Instead of going to waste, nearly 95 percent of the water supplied by a drip system is delivered where plants can use it.[42]

Drip systems are particularly good at keeping soil evenly moist. Waterlogging, from poorly adjusted sprinklers or other causes, is deadly to most plants. Even when the majority of the soil is not waterlogged, soil pores filled with water can become anaerobic. Drip systems deliver water so accurately that these conditions can be avoided—albeit with a lot of fine-tuning. Alternating dry and saturated soil, also common with flood or spray systems, stresses many plant species and can result in hard or salty crusts building up on the soil surface.

Drip was initially developed in Israel for agricultural use under extreme conditions. However, it is not only for arid climates. In virtually any region, consistent, well-aerated moisture tends to produce healthier growth in many species, as well as heavier yields for food plants and profuse bloom on ornamentals. Exceptions are some dryland natives, such as piñon (*Pinus edulis*), which need to dry out between waterings or are easily overwatered. Some trees also need larger volumes of water, requiring a large number of emitters in that zone. Careful design, adjustment, and monitoring (and a good controller) can make drip compatible with these cases; flooding once a month may just be simpler.

Irrigation systems can be water-efficient only if the amount of moisture required by plantings is accurately calculated. A factor called the evapotranspiration reference rate (ET_o) is used for this purpose, representing the amount of water used by an "average" plant per day. ET_o varies by region and season; in arid regions it is often published daily in local newspapers. For California, it is available on-line; irrigation programs like ET-

Calc can compute it.⊃ Multiplied by factors for actual plant species, density of planting, groupings in a zone, and special microclimate conditions like wind or shade, ET₀ gives a far more accurate estimate of watering needs than rule-of-thumb or trial-and-error methods. Based on this estimate and knowledge of how much water one head or dripper puts out per minute, the number and spacing of fittings can be designed, and the run-time for each zone can be determined. Getting all these factors in balance is what a good irrigation designer does. For sustainable, water-conscious irrigation, this is a must.

Other comparisons among irrigation systems, such as ease of maintenance, are difficult to make. Drip systems are harder to bury successfully; the dripper pipes, which must be near the surface to deliver water, tend to heave up out of the ground, possibly due to frost action. Some models clog easily if buried. However, self-cleaning emitters are available in many brands. Even self-cleaning drippers exposed to strong sunshine may become caked with mineral salts evaporated out of the water. Buried under lawns, drippers may need to run very frequently (every few hours) for a very short time, to keep grass roots from growing into the emitters.[43] Filters and pressure regulators are more important for drip systems than for spray irrigation. Spray heads can clog but can more easily be cleaned than emitters, which must often be replaced if clogged. However, spray systems have moving parts, while drippers do not. Risers and pop-up heads are easily broken or damaged. A buried drip system, by contrast, is completely below ground and unlikely to be damaged by surface traffic or vandalism.

Unburied drip systems can be an unsightly sprawl of piping. However, for full efficiency, surface drippers should be covered by mulching anyhow. As long as the owner is committed to regular mulching as a part of maintenance, drip systems tend to stay invisible. By leaving them on the surface, pipes remain accessible and somewhat adjustable as plants grow or are replaced. No other fully automatic irrigation system can easily be moved, so this is an advantage. Some landscape professionals believe that combining microspray with drip gives certain advantages: a humid microenvironment at the soil surface, microbe populations on periodically wetted leaves, and water to help break down surface mulch. The authors would welcome further information on this theory.

At present, the authors are convinced that if irrigation is truly necessary, well-designed, controlled, and maintained drip is the most environmentally responsible way to do it. Because of this, some further information on drip systems follows.

DRIP IRRIGATION EQUIPMENT

The design of irrigation is a fairly specialized field, and many landscape architects subcontract this work. Drip technology continues to evolve, and different models and types of drippers are available. Without duplicating the many references and computer programs available on irrigation design, some broad principles with implications for sustainability are worth summarizing. The following are based on the work of Robert Kourik, a consultant and author on irrigation.[44]⊃

- In-line emitters (built into the supply tube every few inches) are most reliable.

- Other drip types are useful for some conditions, including emitters that punch in to the supply tube wall or connect via small "spaghetti tube," and porous or "leaky" pipe types, in which water oozes through the whole wall of the tube.

- Pressure-compensating emitters adjust for supply pressure, topography, and pressure drop over distance and thus increase efficiency.

- Self-cleaning emitters are preferred for obvious reasons.

- Filters are essential, upstream from all valves, even with self-cleaning drippers. The so-called Y-filter is preferred over straight-in-line designs, because it provides a larger filter surface and simplifies draining/cleaning the filter, which can even be automated.

- Pressure regulators are best installed one per valve, downstream from the valve.

- Backflow preventers are required on all irrigation and may be especially important where harvested water or greywater (see page 165) supplement tap water.

Drip irrigation relies strongly on "zoning"—the Xeriscape concept that groups plants with similar water requirements. Although much has been made of the ability of drip systems to deliver water to individual plants exactly as needed, in landscapes (as opposed to containers) the system actually waters a zone. Putting each *plant* on an individualized watering schedule would require a separate valve and pipe system per plant.

In fact, the idea of individualized water delivery has misled many designers into placing a single dripper per plant, a system that Kourik refers to as "water bondage." Kourik recommends that emitters should be on a grid throughout each zone, producing a uniform watering of that area.[45] Some zones might contain only one or two trees and ground-cover; the trees would have many emitters apiece, while the ground cover might have one dripper per half a dozen plants. Grid spacing also needs to be adjusted for the rate of percolation and spread in the local soil type.

CONTROLLERS AND SENSORS FOR EFFICIENT IRRIGATION

Even when irrigation hardware is highly efficient, immense waste of water can occur if the system runs at inappropriate times or past the point of ground saturation. Few people can remember to turn irrigation on and off at precisely the right times, and in fact the best times for residential irrigation are often when people are asleep or not home. To avoid these problems, programmable controllers are an important tool with the potential to contribute significantly to sustainable irrigation regimes.

Automated irrigation has become an expectation, a must-have, for American landscapes; many landscape contractors say, with resignation, that landscape is a sideline to their irrigation business. As such, the controllers that run these systems are familiar to most people. Setting a controller can be as simple as dialing in an on-off time or as complex as recording summer reruns on a fancy VCR.

For sustainability, a flexible controller is advantageous. Good controllers have a fairly large number of valve stations (six or more) and can be programmed for time, date, day of week, number of days, odd/even days, and sequences of the above (often two sequences can be stored). They accept input from sensors, have a battery to retain programming if power fails, and a default program that ensures some water to each zone if custom programming is lost.

Controllers are, however, no better than their programming. This seemingly self-evident statement is not entirely simple. Programming requires the ability to predict and respond to conditions. Predicting what the day-to-day weather will do to water needs is no easier than predicting the weather itself. Using ET_o calculations (described on page 160) can approximate water needs, but these can be programmed in many ways, some quite wasteful. Almost everyone has seen automatic sprinkler systems watering during rainstorms, for example. Large, complex commercial and institutional irrigation systems are often the worst offenders. Wes Groesbeck, author of *Resource Guide to Sustainable Landscapes and Gardens*, tells of "stealing holy water" by pumping from the gutter 8,000 gallons a month wasted by a neighborhood church's irrigation system; he saved 31 percent of his usual water bill.[46]

Sensors, working together with controllers, can reduce this kind of waste dramatically, making their use appropriate for sustainable landscapes. Rain sensors are optional with many brands of controller and override the watering calendar if it is raining. Wind sensors can keep spray-type irrigation from being blown away (a problem avoided by drip irrigation). An ideal system for water efficiency might include soil moisture sensors in each zone (one per valve), as well as pressure sensors that could detect broken heads or pipes and flag that section for repair. At least some irrigation manufacturers offer each of the above sensor types. Sensors of many other kinds currently used in laboratories may also find landscape applications in the future. As water costs rise, and penalties for waste are imposed by more and more cities, the costs of a sensor system may make economic sense even to conventionally minded clients. The entire state of Florida, and cities in a number of other states, require rain sensors today, and more jurisdictions are certain to follow suit.

Well-designed sensors are energy-efficient. For example, Netafim markets a battery-operated controller that relies on a moisture sensor to turn the system on only when needed. Without the sensor, battery life would be unacceptably short. With the sensor, the battery is good for 1,000 irrigation cycles before replacement.⊃

Even with a good controller and sensors, the valve system must be capable of responding in a specific, not general, way. Each Xeriscape zone, where plants share requirements, really needs its own valve. If plants with unlike water needs are served by the same valve, some are always over- or underwatered. This is not good for the plants and is ultimately wasteful. It is a false economy to install controllers with too few stations to match all the landscape zones. A landscape with too many zones for a good controller may need to be redesigned with closer attention to Xeriscape principles.

Energy Efficiency of Irrigation Systems

Controllers, sensors, and the valves they operate all require electricity. A few models run on 9V batteries, large or small. Manufacturers like Altec (formerly Solatrol), Photocomm, Hardie, and Heliotrope-General have developed systems that supply irrigation power from the sun. These controllers take advantage of the greatest benefit of photovoltaic power: flexible location. Solar-powered irrigation controllers have proved popular with streets and highways agencies for irrigating road medians and other nonelectrified areas. One large California developer, McMillin Properties, installs Photocomm solar controllers temporarily at new sites to run irrigation systems during the vulnerable period before utility power is turned on. Solar power units can be located close to their valves, decreasing wire runs and thus reducing both voltage-drop and materials costs.

Solar irrigation controllers are available both for retrofitting existing irrigation systems and for new construction. Differences in the type of solenoid used to operate the valves determine which kind can be used and what results can be achieved. Existing systems most commonly use solenoids that are held open by a constant electrical current and close when the current stops. Supplying this constant current has until recently been possible only with utility power; solar panels could not generate enough electricity. So-called latching solenoids are much more energy-efficient because they are opened by a brief pulse of energy and closed by a second pulse. Whether a latching solenoid can be retrofitted to a standard valve depends on the model of each.

Photocomm incorporates an inverter in their photovoltaic unit. Photoelectric DC power is converted to 12V or 24V AC, which can power most standard irrigation systems. Developed at the instigation of Tucson landscape architect Mark Novak, the system uses solar panels of varying sizes; the power units look like medium-sized transformer or phone equipment boxes.

Altec's LEIT (Light Energized Irrigation Technology) system uses extreme low-voltage latching solenoids. To use LEIT on an existing system, all solenoids must be replaced. A pulse of 3.5V energy is enough to operate the high-efficiency valves and moisture sensors. Solar-generated power is stored within the parking-meter-sized controller, avoiding the need for separate storage batteries. Because it is so low-voltage, the system will operate in light conditions equivalent to a bad winter day in Alaska. The controller has a wide variety of programmed cycles, as well as an internal log of its own operations. An option called LEIT-LINK allows remote-control operation of any number of controllers by FM radio. By saving the fuel energy normally used in visiting each controller site, LEIT-LINK may be the most energy-efficient of all irrigation systems.

Costs of solar systems are significant, sometimes as much as two or three times the cost of conventional controllers. They are most cost-effective for new, rather than retrofitted, work. Depending on the site, savings may well pay for these costs. The savings are primarily from installation, operating, and maintenance costs, not from the electrical bill, but may still represent energy savings.

At one time, Solatrol advertised its solar-powered irrigation controller with a photomontage of irrigation on the moon. Theoretically, this clever image is possible now that lunar water has been discovered. However, it also is a reminder that solar-powered irrigation makes it easy to bring

Figure 4.24. This large Photocomm solar irrigation controller uses an inverter to provide 110V AC to standard valves.
PHOTO: Photocomm/Golden Genesis Co. ⊃.

Figure 4.25. Small, solar-powered, and radio-controlled Altec irrigation controllers can save electricity as well as fuel used in site visits. PHOTO: Altec Co.⊃.

irrigation to truly remote sites, where irrigation may be quite inappropriate to sustainability. Used with good judgment, however, solar irrigation can significantly increase the efficiency of irrigation.

MATERIALS EFFICIENCY OF IRRIGATION SYSTEMS

Like any other materials, the pipes, valves, and other components of irrigation systems "embody" energy used in their manufacture. This concept is discussed in Principle 7 and relates to other environmental impacts, such as toxic materials, introduced in Principle 6. In the long-term view of sustainability, it is important to consider the relative energy and material costs of different landscape hardware, including irrigation.

Irrigation is a significant user of PVC and other plastics. PVC in particular is a controversial material in the discussion of sustainability (see page 221). Organochloride materials, of which PVC is one, are highly toxic during manufacture and disposal. Many environmental experts have called for phasing them out except for essential uses. Solvents for PVC and other plastics pose health risks for installers. Thus, irrigation designers and contractors have a stake in careful consideration of how these materials are used.

There are two main ways of reducing the impact of materials: by reducing the amount of material used and by using materials that have low embodied energy. The ability to reuse or recycle materials also reduces their overall energy and environmental costs.

The irrigation system that uses least *materials* is simple flooding. In old-fashioned agriculture, this was done with nothing more than small soil channels cut with a hoe. However, the potential for waste of water, and the labor-intensiveness of the process, offset the savings in materials.

Although it is popular to bury them, spray irrigation, and to a lesser extent drip systems, can be based on a single supply hose that is moved around the landscape. Crawler sprinklers were once the only "automated" systems and are still common for home use. Large parks sometimes use movable metal pipes for irrigation. Although this uses less piping than a fixed-placement buried system, it also involves labor costs that may be unacceptably high. Home-owners do not like to move hoses around constantly, and the large-scale metal pipes require tractors to move them.

Buried systems eliminate much labor and allow the water-saving use of controllers. However, they crisscross the site with pipes, which must connect every spray or drip fitting to a valve and water source. If the controller is at a distance from the valve-box, a wire run must join the two. Material costs for subsurface drip have been reported as 10 to 15 percent greater than those for a sprinkler-type buried system; in this case, costs are probably a reasonable reflection of resource consumption. Installation, however, was reported by the same author to be 10 percent less for buried drip than for buried spray irrigation with its more complex assemblies of risers, pop-ups, and so on.[47]

Embodied energy of plastic pipe has been estimated at about 20,000 Btu per foot, and as mentioned earlier, may also have other environmental impacts because of the toxicity of ingredients in some plastics. Copper wire ranges from 500 to 1,700 Btu per foot, depending on gauge. (See Table 7.16.) These factors, along with monetary cost, make it important to lay out irrigation systems as efficiently as possible. The problem of connecting a set of points, such as irrigation-head locations, with a minimum total length of connectors, such as pipes, is a classic example of a mathematical riddle called the Random Walk. New research has recently proposed computerized solutions to the Random Walk.[48] These might be adapted to optimizing materials use in irrigation, combined with existing software that helps size pipes and avoid extremes of pressure drop.

Intelligent irrigation has a role to play in sustainable landscapes. The new generation of controllers and sensors, combined with materials-conscious system design and appropriate planting, offers considerable increases in "bang for the gallon." Given the life-giving value of water, it is well worth the time of landscape professionals to work for improvements in society's use of irrigation.

REUSE GREYWATER

Greywater is the term for all "used" household water except that from toilets. If biodegradable soaps are used, laundry wastewater may be included. (Some definitions also exclude kitchen sink water, for fear of food particles in it.) Greywater systems use separate plumbing from the "blackwater" sewage pipes, allowing the greywater to be reused. Greywater typically amounts to 60 percent or more of the household wastewater; using it "twice" can be a significant saving of water.[49] Although some systems use greywater to flush toilets, the most common use is for landscape irrigation.

Concerns have been raised about health and safety when using greywater, and it is not legal under building codes in some areas. However, Australian researchers concluded that there was little evidence for the spread of disease if greywater irrigates ornamental landscapes.[50] Few disease organisms will survive in greywater once applied to the soil. In 1992 California established a U.S. precedent in its building code by allowing untreated greywater for landscape irrigation.

Greywater should be applied directly to the soil, and most standards require that it never "daylights"—that is, the water is applied underground or under mulch, where people cannot come in direct contact with it. Application from ordinary hoses, flooding, and broadcast sprinklers could expose people to potential pathogens and could leave a residue on plants. Driplines installed on the soil surface and covered with several inches of mulch are the best no-daylight way to irrigate with greywater. Alternatively, they can be buried in the top 3–6 inches of soil. Deeper burial puts the water at a level below the roots of plants that need it and below the soil organisms that are most effective at breaking down the impurities from the water. (For these reasons, many experts believe that the California code requirement for burial to 9 inches is a mistake.[51]) As a precaution, greywater should not be used for edible gardens. If used with a drip irrigation system, greywater should be filtered to remove suspended and dissolved materials that could clog the drip emitters.

Home-owners must be informed about and willing to take on the maintenance of a greywater system. Filters and tanks need periodic cleaning. The household must usually adapt to alternative cleaning solutions; paints, solvents, and other likely toxic materials must be kept out of the greywater. Powdered detergents high in sodium, bleaches, boron, and softeners need to be avoided, since these can build up in the soil. Acid-loving plants also tend not to thrive on greywater, according to Sacramento's *Water Conservation News*.

An even greater water saving is possible by eliminating water-flushed toilets entirely. By substituting a composting toilet (see page 281), *all* the wastewater is greywater. Especially in arid climates, this may be a more sustainable solution than using water to flush, and then building a constructed wetland to purify the water again. These options must, as always, be evaluated using site-specific and user-specific criteria.

Purify Water with Constructed Wetlands

Constructed wetlands are beautiful water-gardens with a new ecological twist: They transform sewage effluent into a rich growing medium for plants—and the plants, in turn, filter the effluent, turning it into water fit for swimming and fishing. Natural wetlands have provided similar services to humans since prehistory, yet people still find the concept novel—half treatment mechanism, half nature center. In fact, constructed wetlands form a bridge between two main issues of this chapter: sparing use of the water supply and restoration of wetlands and other water bodies.

As Alex Wilson, editor of *Environmental Building News*, notes, "Constructed wetlands can become valuable assets to the landscape around buildings, especially if we call them 'flower beds.'

It is quite conceivable that within a few years it will be landscape professionals who deal with wastewater treatment, not sanitary engineers."[52]

Constructed wetlands are more widespread than many people realize. When the subject comes up, the famous wetland at Arcata CA is typically the only one mentioned; there are, however, at least 500 functioning wetlands systems in the United States constructed expressly for the treatment of wastewater, and more are under construction. As a testament to the efficacy of these wetlands, the EPA is actively promoting their spread as an alternative to conventional sewage treatment.

The technology of constructed wetlands is fairly straightforward, although various configurations of treatment systems exist. The modern wetland for sewage treatment originated in Germany in the 1960s and was introduced to the United States in the 1980s. Essentially, a constructed wetland is a shallow pond, often divided into "cells." Wastewater flows over a substrate of gravel or similar material supporting vegetation. The roots of the plants and the many microorganisms that live in the root zone filter and absorb pollutants. The process is passive, in the sense that mechanical equipment (other than a pump) is not involved.

Standards for waste treatment recognize three levels: *Primary* treatment removes solids, *secondary* treatment removes most of the remaining pathogens, and *tertiary* treatment "pol-

ishes" the effluent. "Tertiary-treated effluent" is water clean enough to swim in, irrigate with, or discharge into lakes or streams, often exceeding standards for municipal drinking water. Wetlands are perfectly capable of providing all three stages of treatment, but most constructed wetlands in the United States are specifically for tertiary treatment only. A fair number do provide secondary treatment, and a primary-treatment wetland on the border between California and Baja California was proposed by students of visionary landscape architect John Lyle.[53] At this time, however, no U.S. constructed wetland provides primary treatment. Solids are removed before reaching the wetland by a pretreatment unit that may be as simple as an ordinary septic tank. For larger systems, mechanical primary systems like those found in conventional sewage-treatment plants are used.

There are two design options for constructed wetlands: (1) subsurface-flow, in which water flows beneath a layer of gravel through which emergent wetland plants grow, and (2) surface flow, in which water is visible among the wetland plants, closely resembling a natural wetland. Subsurface-flow wetlands are often recommended for applications near housing or office buildings. This is because water is never at the surface, and some designers take this to mean less risk of mosquito breeding, odor, or human contact with the effluent. Wetlands expert Donald Hammer, however, states that the

Figure 4.26. Treatment wetlands in raised beds are the focal point of gardens at the Albuquerque home of green architect Paul Lusk. PROJECT: Paul Lusk. PHOTO: Kim Sorvig.

Figure 4.27. The "business end" of any treatment wetland is the root zone and the billions of microorganisms that live in its complex geometry. PROJECT: City of Albuquerque and MFG. PHOTO: Michael D. Marcus.

attempt to hide the effluent under gravel has led to systems that are less reliable than surface-flow designs. As he puts it, "The latest designs . . . are quite simply [returning to the initial concept] that patterned constructed wetlands after natural wetlands. [These] have proven to be the least costly to build, have higher removal efficiencies for a wider variety of pollutants, [and] are less costly and complex to operate."[54] Surface flow also provides greater wildlife habitat and tends to be more feasible in the poorer communities that have most to gain from a simple waste-treatment system. As far as the authors can determine, however, both designs are legitimate alternatives and should be compared for site-specific advantages.

A typical subsurface system is 1 to 3 feet deep, with impervious (plastic lined or concrete) bottom and sides, filled with gravel and planted with wetland species. With the wastewater out of sight below gravel, small-scale subsurface-treatment wetlands are easily integrated into the landscapes of housing, parks, and office complexes. One prototype of a subsurface wetland, at Indian Creek Nature Center in Cedar Rapids IA, lives up to Alex Wilson's image as a "flower bed." Designed by North American Wetland Engineering of Forest Lake MN, the wetland treats all sewage from the visitor's center. The wetland has become locally popular for its show of aquatic plants and wildflowers. It is clearly not an objectionable feature—the deck overlooking the wetland is a favorite place to hold weddings.[55]

Despite some people's reluctance to do so, surface-flow constructed wetlands can also be installed quite close to public or private buildings—for example, at the Crosby Arboretum in southern Mississippi. A small pond system provides *secondary* and *tertiary* treatment for the site's

Figure 4.28. Increasing clarity is visible in water from Arcata CA's constructed wetlands, sampled at progressive stages of wastewater treatment. From left: inflow to system, outflows from oxidation pond, treatment marsh, and enhancement marsh. PHOTO: Professor Joe Meyer, University of Wyoming.

two public rest rooms. It was designed by Mississippi-based scientist Bill Wolverton, a pioneer in the natural treatment of sewage. When the director of the arboretum, landscape architect Ed Blake, saw Wolverton's design concept—a standard engineer's rectangle—he asked, "Can we loosen this up a bit?" With Wolverton's consent, Blake reconfigured the treatment pond as a naturalistic river meander. The resulting pond fits seamlessly into the landscape of the arboretum and is a site amenity in full view of all visitors—who learn from interpretive guides that the pond treats on-site sewage.

Constructed wetlands can fulfill many functions in addition to water purification. Two wetlands built several years apart by the town of Gilbert AZ (a suburb of Phoenix) make an excellent case study of the *process* by which multifunction design is achieved. The wetlands are fine examples of their type, but more important, the variations on public perception and team

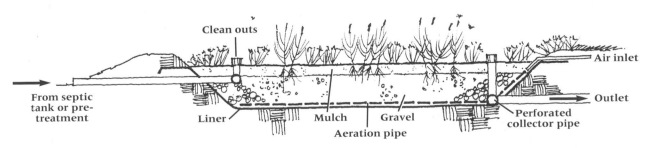

Figure 4.29. Constructed wetland (subsurface type; surface-flow type would have water instead of mulch at surface). Treatment wetlands discharge to infiltration basins, irrigation systems, leach fields, surface water, or tanks. ILLUSTRATION: Craig Farnsworth, based on North American Wetland Engineering P.A.

Figure 4.30. Indian Creek Nature Center illustrates Alex Wilson's vision of constructed wetlands doubling as flower beds. PROJECT and PHOTO: North American Wetland Engineering P.A.

Figure 4.31. Cooper Road Ponds treat wastewater, support waterfowl, and attract bird watchers. The square ponds were already excavated when landscape architects were called in. PROJECT: Jones & Stokes. PHOTO: Joe Donaldson, ASLA.

approach between the two projects are a valuable lesson.

Comparing the two projects is made easier because the multidisciplinary Sacramento CA firm of Jones & Stokes worked on both, but in different capacities. Landscape architects Joe Donaldson and Sheri Brown were involved in habitat restoration and interpretive exhibit design for both projects. Donaldson in particular speaks of wetlands as the kind of experience that invigorates professional practice because of attention and feedback from the public.

In the early 1990s, Gilbert's wastewater reclamation agency built the Cooper Road Recharge Ponds, a series of shallow ponds designed for the single engineering purpose of recharging groundwater, using water from a secondary-treatment plant. After the boxy, functional ponds were already laid out, the town saw an opportunity to create urban habitat for birds, bats, and other fauna and was able to get funding from the state Game and Fish department. Jones & Stokes was hired at this point to enhance the habitat value of the ponds. With assistance from desert-plants purveyor Wild Seed and community volunteers, Donaldson planted riparian and marsh plants around the ponds' banks, as well as upland species on the levees around the ponds. Although not able to alter the basic layout of the ponds, Donaldson and Brown constructed nesting boxes and inserted a viewing area with interpretive exhibits and a *ramada* (shade structure) for visitors. Despite their initial functionalist

layout, the Cooper Road Ponds have garnered a Governor's Pride award for environmental leadership, as well as the Arizona Planning Association's 1994 Best Project Award.

Perhaps more important for the continuing story, the habitat and its interpretation won the approval of Gilbert residents. When the opportunity arose for another recharge facility in a 130-acre park, the town again turned to Jones & Stokes, with one important difference: this time, landscape and restoration specialists managed the multidisciplinary team from the start. Engineers, as well as local landscape architect Carol F. Shuler, became part of the team.

The result of this public support and consistent planning is clear. Named by the town as the Riparian Reserve, the park is a highly visible feature, next to the public library and at the intersection of two main bike paths. Permanent marshes, wildlife islands, roosting structures, and varied wetland and upland planting are included, managed as an urban wildlife sanctuary. At nearly 70 acres, the recharge ponds are a significant return of lost habitat. Xeriscape design principles, and botanic-garden-like exhibits of rare Sonoran Desert plant communities, make this an educational center as well as a recreational center. This was possible because the public had been convinced: Multifunction wetlands have much greater value than single-function ponds.

One issue raised by the Gilbert ponds is that of access. Interestingly enough, there is no consistent standard from one locale to another

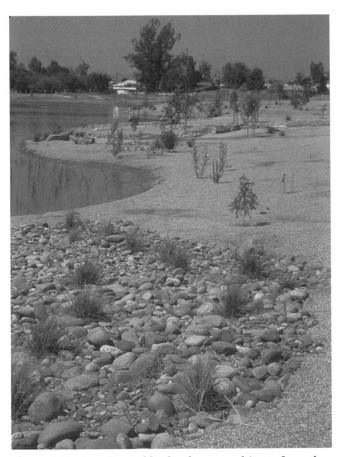

Figure 4.32. Coordinated by landscape architects from the start, Gilbert AZ's Riparian Reserve will go beyond its Cooper Road predecessor to create a full-fledged public park. PROJECT: Jones & Stokes. PHOTO: Joe Donaldson, ASLA.

regarding access around wastewater ponds. Some facilities allow visitor access around ponds treated to a much lower level than the Cooper Road ponds (secondary treatment). Those ponds are fenced to prevent visitors from making contact with the water. At the Riparian Reserve, the town weighed the benefits of education and recreation against the risks of liability. Since this facility infiltrates tertiary-treated water, the balance was clearly in favor of public access. Similarly careful planning could open many more wetlands to amenity use.

The principle of respecting water comes full circle, like the hydrological cycle itself. When water is wasted, shoved aside as a problem, or contaminated, both humans and the environment suffer. When humans work thoughtfully with water, it repays them in health, in livable surroundings, and in recreation and learning.

Resources

Wetlands

Management of Lakes and Ponds by (1985 Krieger Publishing Company)

Shoreline Protection Study: A Report to the Wisconsin State Legislature (1996 Wisconsin) Dept. of Natural Resources, Madison

Enhancement of Ecologic and Aesthetic Values of Wetlands Associated with Interstate Highways by Carl A. Carlozzi & Kenneth L. Bergstrom (1971 University of Massachusetts Water Resources Research Center, Amherst)
   Old publication, but addresses specific wetlands affected by highways.

The Future of Wetlands: Assessing Visual-Cultural Values by Richard C. Smardon (1983 Allanheld Osmun, Totowa NJ)

Wetlands Restoration

Marsh Master II amphibious work vehicle
Coast Machinery 504-753-1323
   1,500 lb. load with 1 psi ground pressure.

Wetland Planting Guide for the Northeastern United States by Gwendolyn A. Thunhorst & Dawn Biggs (1993 Environmental Concern, St. Michaels MD)

Creating Freshwater Wetlands by Donald A. Hammer (1997 [2nd ed.] Lewis Publishers [CRC Press] 800-272-7737

Lakes and Ponds by J. T. Tourbier & R. Westmacott (1992 [2nd ed.] Urban Land Institute)

Mitigation Banking: Theory and Practice by L. Marsh, D. Porter & D. Salvesen (1996 Island Press)

Riparian/Wetland Research Expertise Directory (SW USA) by Barbara Tellman, University of Arizona, Tucson & Roy Jennison, U.S. Forest Service, Ft. Collins CO (1995) Contact bjt@ccit.arizona.edu
   Printed or database. A similar directory covering the University of California system is online at www.nceas.ucsb.edu/expl, maintained by Jeff Woled, UC Davis.

Statewide Wetlands Strategies: A Guide to Protecting and Managing the Resource by many contributors (1992 Island Press)

Wetlands by William J. Mitsch & James G. Gosselink (1986 Van Nostrand Reinhold)

Wetlands: Mitigating and Regulating Development Impacts by D. Salvesen (1994 [2nd ed.] Urban Land Institute)

Wetlands Restoration Links by State
www.epa.gov/owow/wetlands/restore/links/
   Lists agencies involved in wetlands restoration nationwide.

Construction in Wetlands

Nonintrusive foundations
Pin Foundations Inc.
Gig Harbor WA
253-858-8809 or 206-858-8809
www.pinfoundations.com
> See illustration under Plastic Lumber. Web site has product descriptions, design/installation information.

Stream Restoration

Wildland Hydrology
1481 Stevens Lake Rd
Pagosa Springs CO 81147
970-264-712
> Courses and publications, consulting.

Applied River Morphology by Dave Rosgen (1996 Wildland Hydrology)

Nine Mile Run Briefing Book (draft) by Rocky Mountain Institute & Studio for Creative Inquiry 1998, 970-927-3807 or 412-268-3673

Restoring Streams in Cities by Ann Riley (1998 Island Press)

"Streambank and Shoreline Protection," Chapter 16 of *Engineering Field Handbook* (1996) Natural Resources Conservation Service, POB 2890, Washington DC 20013, 202-720-9155

Water Bioengineering Techniques for Watercourse, Bank and Shoreline Protection by H. M. Schiechtl & R. Stern (1997 Blackwell Science)

"Bioengineering for Stream-Bank Stabilization"
Rutgers University Continuing Professional Education
Cook College
POB 231
New Brunswick NJ 08903
908-932-9271
> Three-day, hands-on course.

Stormwater

Center for Urban Water Resources Management
Derek Booth, Dir.
Dept. of Civil Engineering
University of Washington,
Seattle WA 206-543-7923

Center for Watershed Protection
8391 Main St.
Ellicott City MD 21043 410-461-8323
> Information on BMPs for stormwater control, watershed-based zoning, vegetative stream buffers, and permeable parking.

Permaculture Institute
Bill Roley
640 Diamond St.
Laguna Beach CA 92651

Water Resources Protection Technology by (1981 Urban Land Institute)

Introduction to Stormwater by Bruce K. Ferguson (1998 Wiley)

Land Development Provisions to Protect Georgia Water Quality by David Nichols et al. (1997 University of Georgia School of Environmental Design and GA Dept. of Natural Resources)
> Good sample guidelines, translatable to most regions.

Model Development Principles to Protect Our Streams, Lakes, and Wetlands by Tom Schueler (1998 Center for Watershed Protection)

Site Planning for Urban Stream Protection by Tom Schueler (1995 Center for Watershed Protection)

Start at the Source by Tom Richman (January 1997 Bay Area Stormwater Management Agencies Association, Oakland CA 510-622-2326)

Stormwater Infiltration by Bruce K. Ferguson (1994 Lewis Publishers [CRC Press] 800-272-7737)

Stormwater Strategies: Community Responses to Runoff Pollution by P. Lehner, G. Clarke, D. Cameron, & A. G. Frank (no date, Natural Resource Defense Council NYC)
> Case studies.

Urban Watershed Protection Reference Guide bibliography (1996 Center for Watershed Protection)

Watershed Protection Techniques (Center for Watershed Protection)
> Quarterly: case studies and methods illustrated; summer 1995 issue focused on urban stream restoration, with extensive annotated bibliography of guidebooks and manuals.

"The Failure of Detention and the Future of Stormwater Design" by Bruce K. Ferguson (Dec. 1991 *Landscape Architecture*)
> Documents that stormwater detention does not work except with regionally coordinated location, and that infiltration is preferable.

Winning Projects: Stormwater Design Award Competition 1996 and 1997 (Rosemary Furfey, Portland OR Metro Growth Management Services Dept.,
600 NE Grand Ave., Portland OR 97232
furfeyr@metro.dst.or.us)

Watershed Academy
www.epa.gov/owow/watershed/wacademy/its.html
> Publications and courses on watershed management.

Stormwater management and design software
Scientific Software Group
Washington DC
703-620-9214 or www.scisoftware.com

Water Harvesting, Storage, and Purification

Real Goods
800-762-7325 or www.realgoods.com

The Home Water Supply: How to Find, Filter, Store, and Conserve It by Stu Campbell (1983 Storey Communications/Garden Way, Pownal VT)
> Pragmatic and thorough guide to water supply, from geological sources to cisterns, pumps, and purification. Relatively conventional "homesteader" attitudes, some not very green.

Planning, Design, and Management

Water in the Garden: Design and Installation of Ponds, Fountains, Streams, and Waterfalls by James Allison (1991 Little Brown)
> Conventional water features; many are adaptable to sustainability goals.

Elements and Total Concept of Urban Waterscape Design by Henshubu (?) (1990 Grafiksha, Tokyo)

Waterstained Landscapes: Seeing and Shaping Regionally Distinctive Places by Joan Woodward (2000 Johns Hopkins)

Greywater

Building Professional's Greywater Guide by Art Ludwig (1995 Oasis Design, Santa Barbara CA, 805-967-3222)
> Detailed decision-making criteria pro and con; conceptual system layouts; analysis of detergents for compatibility.

Gray Water Use in the Landscape by Robert Kourik (1991 Metamorphic Press, POB 1841, Santa Rosa CA 95402)

Xeriscape, Permaculture, and Related Strategies

Consumptive Water Use by Landscape Plants: A Brief Sourcelist for Landscape Architects by Anthony G. White (1980 Vance Bibliographies A-319, Monticello IL)

Drought-tolerant Plants: Waterwise Gardening for Every Climate by Jane Taylor (1993 Prentice-Hall)

Southwestern Landscaping That Saves Energy and Water by E. Gregory McPherson & Charles M. Sacamano (1989 University of Arizona Cooperative Extension, Pub. 8929, Tucson)

Taylor's Guide to Water-saving Gardening (1990 Taylor's Guides [Houghton Mifflin])

Water Conservation in Landscape Design & Management by Gary O. Robinette (1984 Van Nostrand Reinhold)

Water-conserving Gardens and Landscapes by John M. O'Keefe (1992 Storey Communications/ Garden Way, Pownal VT)
> Includes plant selection list, drip irrigation guide, region/zone maps.

Water-efficient Landscape Guidelines by Richard E. Bennett & Michael S. Hazinski (1993 American Waterworks Association, Denver CO www.waterwiser.org/)

Waterwise Gardening by Kathryn Stechert Black (1989 Sunset Books; Lane Pub. Co., Menlo Park CA)

Water-wise Gardening by Peter Robinson (1999 American Horticulture Society guides; DK Pub.)

Water-wise Gardening: America's Backyard Revolution by Thomas Christopher (1994 Simon & Schuster)

Xeriscape, Water-conserving Gardens by Carol Kopolow (1994 National Agricultural Library, publ. no. AT 94-01, Beltsville MD)

Indigenous Permaculture Center
Traditional Native American Farmers Association
505-983-2712

Permaculture Drylands Institute
Santa Fe NM
pdrylands@aol.com

Irrigation

The Irrigation Association
Fairfax VA
703-573-3551 or www.irrigation.org/ia/
> Web site, referrals to members, product search engine, and forum for posting questions; ag, turf, and landscape irrigation.

American Society of Irrigation Consultants (ASIC)
www.igin.com/asic

Water Wiser Clearinghouse
American Waterworks Association
Denver CO
www.waterwiser.org/

Drip Irrigation for Every Landscape and All Climates by Robert Kourik (1992 Metamorphic Press, POB 1841, Santa Rosa CA 95402)

The Complete Irrigation Workbook: Design, Installation, Maintenance, and Water Management by Larry Keesen & Cindy Code (1995 Franzak & Foster, Cleveland OH)

Irrigation Business & Technology
The Irrigation Association, Fairfax VA
703-573-3551 or www.irrigation.org/ia/
> An irrigation trade magazine that "tries to be proactive" about environmental issues.

CIMIS (California Irrigation Management Information System)
California Department of Water Resource and the University of California at Davis
www.ceresgroup.com/col/weather/cimis/
916-756-0778
> ET statistics for California by county.

Glenn Hilton company
www.glenhilton.com/links.html
> Links to many suppliers and organizations related to irrigation.

Irrigation Industry Links
http://jessstryker.com/industry.htm#suppliers

Irrigation Product Manufacturers list
http://apphost.infosrc.com/ia/search/products/pfind.htm

PRINCIPLE 4

Irrigation Suppliers list
http://apphost.infosrc.com/ia/search/products/
products.dbm

US Water News
www.mother.com/waternews/

ET Calc
Irrigation Management Group
Union City CA
    Irrigation scheduling and design software.

Landscape Irrigation Science degree
Cal Poly Pomona 909-869-2084
    First U.S. accredited program.

Controllers and Sensors

IRRIGATION CONTROLLERS AND SENSORS
Weathermatic (Garland TX) www.weathermatic.com
Glenn Hilton (Richmond VA) www.glenhilton.com
Tucor (Wexford PA) www.tucor.com
    Three companies offering advanced sensors and controllers.

SOLAR CONTROLLERS FOR IRRIGATION
Altec 619-229-3750

Photocomm 800-223-9580

Heliotrope 800-552-8838

Hardie Irrigation 714-643-6861

Constructed Wetlands

"Waste as a Resource" in *Regenerative Design for Sustainable Development* by John Lyle (1994 Wiley)
    Good introduction to the subject.

Constructed Wetlands for Wastewater Treatment by Donald A. Hammer (1989 Lewis Publishers [CRC Press] 800-272-7737)
    In-depth look at wetlands technology.

Constructed Wetlands for Wastewater Treatment and Wildlife Habitat (1993 US EPA [EPA832-R-93-005])
    Seventeen case studies; well-illustrated introduction to systems operating in the United States.

Constructed Wetlands for Water Quality Improvement by Gerald A. Moshiri (1993 Lewis Publishers [CRC Press] 800-272-7737)

Constructed Wetlands in the Sustainable Landscape by Craig Campbell & Michael Ogden (1999 Wiley)
    Authors are principals of Southwest Wetlands and pioneered wetlands in desert United States.

Constructed wetlands bibliography
US EPA
www.epa.gov/owow/wetlands/construc/sources.html
    Lists about fifty books and articles on constructed wetlands.

Pave Less

Little by little, roads eat away at the hearts of mountains.
—Gary Lawless, *First Sight of Land*, 1990

The United States paves more area each year than the Roman Empire did in its entire existence. In the 1990s the average was about 30,000 linear miles per year. The U.S. Department of Transportation counts a total of 8,177,823 "lane miles" of public highway, as of 1996.[1] Assuming the standard 12-foot lane width, plus an average of 4 feet for shoulder and other auxiliary areas, 1 lane mile equals 84,480 square feet, or nearly 2 acres. The total—almost 16 million acres—is more than enough paved area to cover Massachusetts, Connecticut, Rhode Island, New Jersey, and Delaware. Add to this an estimated 105,200,000 parking spaces in the United States, covering another 434,680 acres.[2] It is easy to see that paving is an environmental issue of colossal proportions.[3] The U.S. road network is "perhaps the biggest object ever built."[4]

Widespread paving is a very recent phenomenon. Even a century ago, the normal condition of city streets was a muddy morass (recall, for example, Sherlock Holmes' deductions from clay on urban trouser cuffs); many rural roads were still "paved" with logs. All that changed in the mid-1800s, when macadam (compacted stone bound with asphalt) was introduced by a Scottish contemporary of the fictional detective. The past 100 years have seen paving cover unprecedented areas. By the early 1970s, paving was referred to as "the nation's biggest publicly endowed business."[5]

For all its popularity and functionality, paving has been implicated in a wide range of ecological problems. Most paving materials create surface stability by excluding water from the soil, and this impermeability causes a number of difficul-ties. Soil absorbs rainfall and nurtures flora, fauna, and humans, but impervious surfaces increase runoff, causing erosion and flooding, depleting soil water, and contributing to siltation and water pollution. Modern construction has created such vast nonporous areas that many communities are being forced to limit the creation of new impervious surfaces.

Parking lots, for example, constitute an ever-increasing blight on the American landscape. As metropolitan areas sprawl farther and farther from transit-friendly cores, surface parking becomes the common denominator of the urban fabric. From the air, parking is *the most visible*

Discussed in This Chapter:

- Planning and policy strategies to reduce paving requirements

- Design options to decrease paving area and its site impact

- Techniques for infiltrating more of the runoff from pavement

- Infiltration to reduce pollution potential of pavement runoff

- Porous and partially porous paving materials

- When it's most appropriate *not* to pave

- Reducing the heat-sink effect of paved areas

feature of many communities. This hardening of the American landscape results in a net reduction in the biologically productive surface of the Earth as acres of pavement replace cornfields, meadows, forest, or desert. Moreover, "paving the planet" (as it has been called) consumes non-renewable resources both in building the lots and in the fuel required to truck the materials to the site. Asphalt, the material for most parking lots, is a complex mix of hydrocarbons, the mixing and application of which is an air-polluting act in itself. One indicator of this is that asphalt has been shown to have adverse health effects on workers exposed to its fumes.[6]

Parking lots can directly affect microclimates and the overall climates of cities. Since the advent of widespread use of the automobile in the United States, summer temperatures in urban areas have increased so that now they are two to eight degrees Fahrenheit hotter than in surrounding rural areas.[7] Because surface parking is the prime land use in most American cities, parking areas are a major factor, if not *the* main factor, in this "heat island" effect in American cities—not to mention spiraling land costs.

Low-speed roads—residential streets in suburbs, in particular—are often wider and more impervious than necessary. Thirty-six feet or more is a typical width, making the streets the largest single impervious surface in the subdivision. The total width of the average residential street has increased by 50 percent since World War II.[8] Why are they so unreasonably wide? Blanket application of standards for high-speed, high-volume state highways to low-speed, low-volume streets has created unwanted and unneeded pavement in thousands of neighborhoods. Overbuilding of roads has serious sustainability (and safety) implications and has recently been challenged by several national engineering organizations.

The most egregious impacts of these veritable rivers and seas of paving have to do with stormwater.[9] Conventional parking lots, for example, seal off the absorptive quality of soils, preventing rainwater from soaking into the ground and replenishing crucial groundwater resources. With every rain, parking lots' subsurface drainage systems send erosive torrents of runoff cascading into local streams. Erosion, sedimentation, extremes of flooding and drought, and habitat loss are among the results.

There are many practical and well-tested alternatives to overpaving. Many have been known for almost as long as the automobile—yet they are ignored by conventional practice predicated on ever-increasing road speed, volume, and "convenience." Society's demands, for which highway and parking engineers alone cannot be blamed, are changing, however. From the Federal Highway Administration to the Institute of Transportation Engineers, official research and design standards are focusing on the benefits of better integration of roads with community, ecosystem, and scenery. Today, overpaving remains one area of landscape design and construction where the *main* culprit is outdated, unthinking habit—stoutly defended by industries with vested interests and by a society addicted to cars.

Planning and Design Issues for Reducing Paving

Although this chapter focuses on ways of building parking lots and streets that ameliorate their environmental impacts, the crying need in North America is to *reduce the overall paved areas that are built*. This constitutes an enormous challenge to planners, designers, and policy makers for the simple reason that parking is generally regarded as a universal good, even a necessity. American cities are increasingly built around automobile use, which means that destinations are spread out so that walking from, say, your house to the grocery store is no longer possible.

Many urbanists are now suggesting a fresh look at pre–World War II patterns of development—walkable communities effectively served by mass transit. This concept goes against many national habits but is being successfully promoted by groups like Walkable Communities, the Congress of New Urbanism, and others. This movement is sometimes called neotraditionalism, because it takes its planning and design models from livable older communities, rather than accepting suburban sprawl or urban jam. Not surprisingly, New Urbanism's traditional design models treated streets as public spaces for *people* and kept automotive space to a minimum.

A related planning approach attempts to rein in the effects of sprawl and encourage infill development. This method can increase urban density, thus reducing the need for paving. A well-known (if sometimes controversial) U.S.

example is Portland OR. In 1976, Portland politicians and planners took the unprecedented step of drawing an urban growth boundary (UGB) around greater Portland and prohibiting expansion beyond it. The UGB has not completely abolished sprawl—Portland housing prices have risen, and the city still has its strip malls and cookie-cutter subdivisions. The boundary restrains these, however, just 3–18 miles from downtown. The entire metro area, moreover, is tied together by an exemplary light-rail system that converges on Portland's compact, walkable downtown.

Several specific site planning policies are valuable for avoiding unnecessary paving and decreasing the negative effects of existing pavement.[10] These include:

- *Density zoning.* Local policy that uses overall density (a number of units per acre, or a percentage of acreage devoted to structures) works better than minimum lot sizes, because it allows flexible adaptation to site topography.

- *Cluster development.* Placing several buildings together surrounded by open space, rather than each in the center of its separate lot, can greatly reduce infrastructure costs, including paving.

- *Combined land uses.* Zoning that allows residences and workplaces to coexist makes walking, biking, or public transit much easier for workers. This is often a matter of removing barriers to coexistence from existing zoning laws.

- *Impervious surface limits.* Set a maximum percentage of site area that can be impervious. This must include both paved and roofed areas, existing and new. Where this level is set to 10 percent or lower, streams and other hydrological features of the area can be considered protected. Above 10 percent, impacts are serious enough to require mitigation; and where 30 percent of the area is impervious, degradation of the ecosystem is almost inevitable. In urban areas already far over this threshold, incentive programs for reducing impervious cover can be effective.

- Street width limits. Techniques discussed on page 177 often require changed laws.

- Planted islands in turnarounds. Paving the center of a turnaround is of no use to drivers and can be replaced by permeable, planted surfaces as a matter of policy.

- Pollutant collector isolation. These include paving at gas stations, car washes, Dumpster pads, and other point sources of concentrated pollutants. Isolating runoff from these sources keeps the flow on ordinary streets much cleaner.

- Storm drain inlet labelling. Knowledge of where pavement runoff goes can decrease public dumping of pollutants onto pavement and into drains.

Paving less begins at the policy level. Some of the above policies are aimed at existing problems, but the most important ones are forward looking. The central intent of these policies must be to establish growth management policies that encourage denser patterns of development and decrease automobile dependency. Construction methods can help, but only a concerted effort can create compact cities. Decreased paving will primarily be the *result* (though also occasionally the cause) of more people traveling by foot, bicycle, rail, or bus.

Put New Development on a "Parking Diet"

Even in cities that are fundamentally automobile-oriented (which includes most of the places Americans live and work), there are ways of reducing parking. In 1996 Olympia WA completed a large-scale research effort, the Impervious Surface Reduction Study, aimed at reducing the need for new parking and decreasing the environmental impacts of new or existing paving. The study began by carefully documenting the effects of runoff from roads and parking on Olympia's water quality and quantity and ended by articulating a set of strategies with the truly remarkable goal of *smaller and fewer parking lots in future developments* throughout the city.

How does Olympia propose to accomplish this intent, which flies in the face of current development practices? A central strategy is to get developers to *size parking lots to reflect real needs.* Olympia's study uncovered a fact that applies across the United States: Developers routinely *oversupply* parking to meet a single "peak day" (or even peak hour) projection—the needs of retailers at the height of the Christmas rush, for example. In Olympia, large retailers and other developers built parking *51 percent above nonpeak needs*. Retailers fear that without this excess, customers will be turned away for lack of parking during peak shopping periods. In Olympia, this fear proved to be groundless. On those peak shopping dates, the study team surveyed thirty-one parking areas, representing fifteen different commercial uses. Eighteen of the lots had less than 75 percent occupancy rates *during their peak periods*.

Armed with data that showed that more impervious surfaces than anyone needed were being built, Olympia formed new policy recommendations.[11] One is *to encourage cooperative or shared parking*. This combines the parking area required for land uses with different hours of operation—a church and an office, for example, or a movie theater and a paint store. Shared parking works best for long-term tenants whose parking needs do not fluctuate much over time. It may require legal agreements between neighboring tenants; local governments can promote such agreements and should take an active role. Shared parking is already working in some cities, Oakland CA among them, according to the Institute of Transportation Engineers, which promotes shared parking.[12] ⊃

An important related principle is to enforce the *maximum* amount of parking that may be provided for any land use. Typically, local governments enforce parking requirements for development as a *minimum* number—apparently based on the notion that parking is an unqualified good and should never fall below a certain amount. Many developers and designers, who have struggled to fit required parking spaces into a lot at the expense of other amenities, would welcome an enforced-maximum approach. Other developers, however, use minimum parking ratios as license to overpave. Suburban office parking is routinely oversupplied by one-third.[13] Another study found that townhouse developers commonly provide the actual spaces required, *plus 103 percent—fully double what anyone needs*.

Handicapped parking contributes significantly to overpaving, with required ratios apparently based more on the heated politics of accessability than on actual numbers of disabled users. It is not uncommon to see twenty vacant oversized handicapped spaces in an otherwise full one-hundred-space lot.

The Center for Watershed Protection recommends that parking codes impose a maximum number of spaces that may be built at a project of a given size, unless compelling data clearly justify more parking spaces.[14] ⊃ Oympia's new parking code requires developers to build according to median parking ratios that reflect day-to-day use.

Mass transit lowers parking demand by reducing the number of vehicles driven to the site and parked. For developments close to a bus or rail stop, local regulations should reduce the number of parking spaces. Granted, this may be a controversial proposition; getting U.S. car users to switch to mass transit has never been easy. In addition to Olympia, a number of other communities have nevertheless encouraged or even required developers to reduce parking when mass transit is available; these include Chicago, Hartford CT, Montgomery County MD, and Albuquerque NM.[15] When Portland OR added 20,000 new seats to its sports stadium, it did not add a single parking space, because a light-rail stop was available at the stadium. (Excellent mass transit is obviously essential to such a solution.)

On a smaller scale, Seattle landscape architects Berger Partnership prescribed a "parking diet" for the Washington Department of Ecology headquarters in Lacey WA. The client's original proposal called for 1,150 parking spaces, nearly one for each of the department's 1,200 employees. This would have claimed some 4.5 acres, more than twice the footprint of the building itself. In the final design, parking used just over 1 acre. This was accomplished by slashing the number of spaces to 900, and stacking them in a land-saving parking garage. The new design challenged employees to adjust their ways of getting to work but also served, in the words of partner Tom Berger, as "a model for what the Department of Ecology should expect from other planners." Besides cutting runoff, the reduced footprint for parking made it easier to put the main building close to bus and foot access. In the garage, the closest spaces were reserved for carpoolers; not even the director got a free space. Still, the furthest spaces in the garage were closer than most surface parking would have been. The system seems to be working, and state officials call the experiment a success.[16]

The ongoing goal of *reducing the total amount of new parking that is built* is largely a task for local government. Planners and designers can and should advocate such policies and, where possible, implement them for new development. Questioning assumptions about the need for parking is becoming more feasible, as the previous examples show. It still requires careful and persuasive planning.

Fortunately, there is an expanding literature available on strategies for reducing parking. The Institute of Transportation Engineers provides information on shared parking, and the Center for Watershed Protection and Olympia WA are eager to share what they have learned.⊃

Legalize Narrower Streets and "Traffic Calming"

Road standards can be even more difficult to update than those concerned with parking. Overengineered roadways, and the standards that enforce overbuilding, have many of the same environmental impacts as excessive parking. Over-sized roads also have negative effects on traffic safety and diminish the quality of life for communities through which they pass. A new approach to roadway design, called traffic calming, is gaining acceptance in the United States; in Europe, Canada, and Australia, it has a thirty year track record. Traffic calming originated from safety concerns; it also has significant potential to reduce environmental damage from roads, especially where it results in narrower roadways.

Conventional street and road statutes, although often imposed by local agencies, tend to be carbon copies of state and federal requirements more suitable for major highways. Ironically, at the Federal Highway Administration, the Institute of Transportation Engineers, and many state agencies, progressive research has cast real doubt on older requirements for extrawide, straight, and flat roads. Updated standards are available or will soon be, including the FHWA's computerized Interactive Highway Safety Design Model, but many local governments continue to enforce design standards that are decades out of date.⊃ These standards are often presented to the public as cut-and-dried matters of safety. However, the assumption that bigger roads are always safer (like the assumption that more parking is always better) is increasingly being questioned, even by otherwise conventional agencies and professional organizations.

Where did bigger-is-safer come from? Throughout the recent past, American society has demanded that highway engineers give absolute and exclusive priority to ever-increasing speed and "convenience," meaning that an exploding number of private cars should always be able to drive door-to-door at full speed. This single-minded focus on increasing speed and capacity has disguised several crucial safety issues. Current research shows that the real cause of most accidents, and especially of serious-injury accidents, is speed itself, and that wide, straight, flat roadways encourage drivers to speed. Conventional engineering has struggled to make speeding as safe as it can be, which is not actually very safe at all.

Traffic calming takes a different approach. In the words of Robert A. White, a Norwich VT landscape architect who consults on traffic calming, "measures that reduce lane width, introduce roadside 'friction' features like street trees, and prominently define pedestrian crossing points can [significantly reduce] roadway speeds—from 20 percent to 50 percent reductions depending on the technique and location. It has been shown that similar safety improvements can reduce crashes by as much as 80 percent, and those that do occur tend to be less severe."[17]

Traffic calming relies on the innate good sense of most drivers, rather than on fear of punishment. "Most drivers adjust their speed more readily in response to road and traffic conditions than to speed limit signs and the often remote possibility of enforcement penalties. . . . 85 percent of drivers tend to adopt a sensible speed for prevailing road conditions. [Drivers] unconsciously respond . . . to the physical cues presented to them."[18] Thus, making a road narrower (or even making it *look* narrower by using grassed shoulders or roadside shrubs) is something highway designers can do to get drivers to observe safe speeds.

Robert White, along with hundreds of other experts in this emerging field, considers traffic calming as "a set of roadway design tools and principles where the road and its context can be placed in better balance and where *community values* as they relate to traffic management are more fully represented and integrated into the actual roadway design." Integrating community values means that streets and roads once again become multipurpose spaces: narrower side roads release space for bike lanes, walkways, and bridle paths; in residential neighborhoods and small business districts, streets become truly public space; on scenic highways, conflicts between tourists and local drivers are reduced.[19] Traffic calming provides practical methods of achieving these neotraditional goals. For freeways and major highways, conventional design and exclusive use by automobiles remain appropriate. However, for any road where access cannot be limited, the multiple-user approach is safer, less disruptive to environment or community, and frequently cheaper. This approach has been recognized by TEA-21, the renewed "intermodal" or multiuse federal transportation funding act, which can provide grants for traffic calming projects.

Traffic calming is the target of bitter attack from special-interest positions. The American Road and Transportation Builders Association (ARTB), for instance, takes the position that *despite a 63 percent increase in federal funding* for highway construction between 1993 and 1999, "environmental and community extremists" are out to deprive road-builders of their livelihood.[20] Although ARTB and similar associations represent a part of the construction industry, contractors and designers concerned with sustainability need not feel too much sympathy for the poor starving highway-construction lobby. These groups are among the worst environmental dinosaurs, and their arguments are simply a new twist on the famous "What's good for General Motors is good for the USA." Like developers who produce 50 to 100 percent more parking than necessary, the ARTB treats paving as an unqualified good—which it clearly is for ARTB pocketbooks.

The authors encourage landscape professionals to learn more about emerging and up-to-date approaches to roadway design.⊃ While the safety and community benefits of traffic calming are outside the scope of this book, they are clearly of concern to landscape professionals—especially those who are tired of being steamrollered by outdated arguments in favor of overbuilt roads.

ENVIRONMENTAL BENEFITS OF NARROWER STREETS

One of the main techniques of traffic calming, and the one with the clearest *environmental* benefits, is narrowing traffic lanes. In some cases, the narrowing is visual, an illusion created by painted lane markers, but still effective for slowing traffic to safer speeds. But to have an environmental effect, the narrowing must be physical, reducing the amount of paving material

used and decreasing the impervious surface created. Road narrowing is most applicable to two types of roads: rural two-lane highways and residential neighborhood streets.

For rural roads, recent research by the Federal Highway Administration's Turner-Fairbank Highway Research Center has shown that "9-feet lane widths have lower accident rates than 10-feet lanes with narrow shoulders, at least partly due to reduced vehicle speeds." Ten-foot lanes increase speed and the risk of driver error; adding a narrow shoulder cannot compensate for the increased risk. The report suggests that it is *safer* to retain the 9-foot lanes of existing roads unless a community can afford dramatic widening of both the roadway and the shoulders.[21] Retaining the narrower road also saves construction and maintenance costs, and because older roads tended to follow topography, avoids the environmental destruction common to much so-called road improvement.

Residential streets have been the focus of much traffic calming study, and narrowing streets is widely recommended. Conventional standards frequently call for two 12-foot lanes plus 6-foot shoulders, totaling 36 feet. National engineering organizations now suggest that residential streets can be as narrow as 22 feet in neighborhoods that generate fewer than 500 daily trips (about fifty homes).[22]

Compared to the 36-foot-wide standard, a 22-foot-wide street saves nearly *1.75 acres* (75,000 square feet) of paving *per mile*. Assuming a city block of 700 feet by 500 feet, or about 8 acres, the 22-foot-wide street on all sides saves nearly an acre. That land savings can be used for open space, stormwater or wetland functions, or additional lots. At the same time, the narrowed streets reduce infrastructure costs both for paving and for utilities.

In most states the local governments have the option to permit narrower streets, and communities such as Bucks County PA and Boulder CO have implemented narrower streets with success. One of the most important achievements of New Urbanist communities like Seaside FL and the Kentlands, near Washington DC, is that they incorporate much narrower streets than is the nationwide norm.

Unfortunately, in many localities, narrow streets are still *illegal* under local codes and DOT requirements. These laws have varied origins,

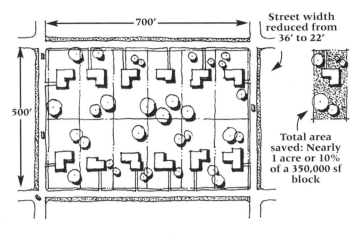

Figure 5.1. One acre of developable or protected land is saved by reducing street width from 36 feet to 22 feet around an 8-acre city block. ILLUSTRATION: Craig Farnsworth.

700'

Street width reduced from 36' to 22'

500'

Total area saved: Nearly 1 acre or 10% of a 350,000 sf block

from boosterism that portrayed broad streets as patriotic and sanitary to concerns about emergency access. Traffic calming in fact causes little delay for police and ambulances; delays for larger fire trucks average 5 to 20 seconds,[23] compared to delays of 10 to 20 *minutes* commonly caused by sprawl development.[24] Given that traffic calming also reduces the frequency and severity of the accidents to which emergency vehicles must respond, the overall effect on public safety is definitely positive. Challenges to narrowed streets on the basis of the "right to drive" or "right to park" are entirely outweighed by the overall public benefit; even some drivers' groups say these attacks on traffic calming smack of conspiracy theory and lack credibility.[25]

Standards that ban well-designed narrow streets are outdated and should be seriously reconsidered by state and local traffic planners and engineers. Appropriately narrow streets have multiple values, not least restoring a sense of community to places now deadened by the dominance of the car. For sustainability, the major issue is the effect of needless impervious surfaces on stormwater runoff. For this reason, The Center for Watershed Protection recommends narrower streets as Principle Number One in its model development principles for new communities.⊃

On Sensitive Sites, Scatter the Parking

One problem with parking lots, and especially overbuilt expanses, is that they require clearing the site of trees and leveling the land-forms. A design approach that is appropriate for forested

and other sensitive sites is to *scatter the parking throughout the site*. This minimizes cutting trees or disturbing other important features. The Simmons Mattress Company outside of Atlanta used this strategy successfully for 200 parking spaces. Instead of the typical monolithic lot, landscape architects Robert E. Marvin & Associates created "woodland parking" throughout the forest, shoehorning one to three parking spaces at a time off a sinuous one-way driveway. Not only does this approach require much less cutting of trees and disturbance of the forest floor, it allows stormwater from the slender roadway and scattered parking spaces to run directly onto the woodland floor (there are no curbs or gutters) and soak in.

Scattered parking is an approach that requires much more detailed siting and staking of the parking spaces. It also requires extra care during construction and strongly suggests the use of smaller, lighter machinery for grading. Landscape contractors who are willing to forgo the convenience of grading a single large space will gain the satisfaction of seeing very attractive results and knowing that environmental impact has been reduced. They are also likely to gain a reputation that brings them repeat business and an edge over more conventional competitors.

One objection to the scattered approach is that, because the parking is so dispersed, an employee may have to walk farther from her or his car to the building. The authors say: Get over it! Like the right-to-drive arguments mentioned earlier, this objection has little merit. Dispersed parking should be tried at many more low-density sites

Figure 5.2. Narrow streets enhance livability of older cities, especially in Europe. Recent U.S. developments use narrowed streets to save land and infrastructure costs and to protect watersheds. PHOTO: Kim Sorvig.

where trees or other site features need to be preserved.

In general, even where preservation of site features is *not* a major issue, it is advisable to break up parking lots into smaller units so that each parking area can drain to an adjacent unpaved area. By reducing the distance that runoff flows, and infiltrating it near its origin, this system protects the site's water regime. The concept is discussed in more detail on page 136.

Just Say No to Some Paving Demands

This concept is self-evident yet almost radical: *Not all parking areas need to be paved.* In fact, many lightly used parking lots would be better (from a water-quality standpoint) if they were surfaced with a more permeable material.

Here and there, a few communities are beginning to realize this. In the upscale suburban community of Medford Village NJ, widespread use is made of the most humble paving material in the world—gravel. Professor Bruce Ferguson, an expert on stormwater management, says that this material, properly called crushed stone or crushed aggregate, was largely abandoned as a result of the overengineering of parking lots since about the 1930s. Seeing crushed stone used with consistency and sensitivity in the center of historic Medford, Ferguson "really concluded that gravel pavements had a future."

Although it may be porous, not just any gravel will do. Technically, "gravel" is rounded small stones, washed by a river; as a paving substitute, it is highly unstable. Crushed stone, which will interlock under pressure, is preferable for this reason, despite the extra energy costs of producing it. In specifying crushed stone, Ferguson notes, there is a trade-off between a coarser grade, which drains more readily, and a finer grade, which is more walkable and accessible to the disabled. Either grade can be sorted so the particles are all nearly the same size. This is called "open-graded" or "no-fines" aggregate. Open-grading improves drainage and reduces dust and is also an important step in making porous asphalt or porous concrete (see page 184). Crushed oyster and clam shells are used in some regions in a similar way.

Open-graded crushed stone has been used since the 1970s in Medford Village to fit a townshipwide stormwater infiltration plan by environmental planner Ian McHarg. It substitutes for paving on entire parking lots and many residential driveways. Because it is best suited for relatively low traffic, it is commonly used in parking-stalls, served by an asphalt travel lane, with adjacent grassed swales to handle overflow from large storms.

Like most materials, crushed stone should be used selectively. For clay soil types, gravel surfaces and the soils underneath them can become highly compacted under heavy traffic volumes.[26]

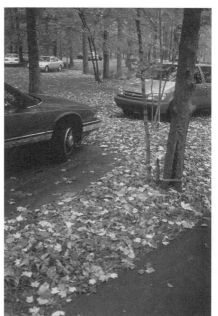

Figure 5.3. Dispersed parking for Simmons Mattress headquarters reduced disruption and infiltrates runoff near its source. PROJECT: Robert Marvin Associates. PHOTO: Bruce Ferguson.

Figure 5.4. Plan of Simmons headquarters' dispersed parking shows small graded and paved areas integrated with the existing site, rather than one large flattened area. ILLUSTRATION: Craig Farnsworth, based on Ferguson.

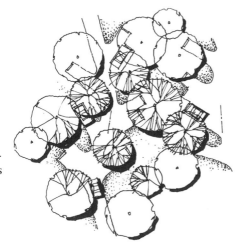

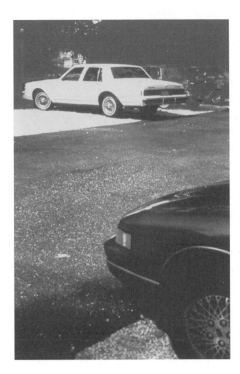

Figure 5.5. Crushed stone is a simple permeable parking surface suitable for many locations and used on expensive estates. Stone must be angular to lock into a firm surface. Note the asphalt driving lane. PROJECT: Medford NJ. PHOTO: Bruce Ferguson.

Because compaction equals imperviousness, compacted gravel would have little stormwater advantage over asphalt. To absorb and spread the load, 6 inches of aggregate is a minimum depth. Use a filter fabric or geotextile under the stone to keep it from mixing into the soil below. The surface layer will almost always become compacted as cars displace and pack the top stones; raking the surface by hand each year will restore porosity.

Two of the product types discussed under greenwalls (page 105) can also be used to stabilize gravel surfaces as pavement substitutes. These are the cellular containment products and various meshes similar to those used for grass paving (see page 186).

Stone chips or screenings are widely used for pedestrian surfaces in parks. Many famous European gardens, such as the Tuileries in Paris, incorporate such materials. Henry Arnold used the same surface, supported by "air-entrained (structural) soil" at Metrotech plaza in Brooklyn.

For pedestrian paths and other very low-use areas, organic materials such as bark chips or mulch can be used as a surface. In some cases a cellular or mesh support system might be combined with these materials. They must be maintained and replenished; some but not all are acceptable for handicapped access when properly designed.

Use Techniques That Reduce Runoff from Paving

Although the authors support planning and design efforts to reduce the total amount of new parking, some new parking is inevitable. The environmental impacts of those new streets and parking lots can and should be limited by appropriate choice of materials and methods.

A good starting point for this discussion—in opposition to the prevailing tendency to pave every piece of ground in sight—is "Haag's Theory of Softness." Propounded by Seattle landscape architect Richard Haag, this simple principle states that *no ground surface should be any harder than absolutely necessary for its function.* Paving, for instance, should not be used where crushed stone will do, nor crushed stone where a path of bark chips is sufficient. Many conventional paved areas are much harder than function requires them to be.

The concept of softness does not necessarily mean that paving is malleable—porous concrete, for example, is quite hard. The same principle can be restated with permeability equated to softness: *No ground surface should be any more impervious than necessary.* Even if the paving itself remains hard, approaches like eliminating gutters and curbs, infiltrating stormwater in planted areas, or using porous pavement can legitimately be thought of as "softer" than conventional engineering.

Figure 5.6. Stone screenings over air-entrained soil at Metrotech in Brooklyn create a permeable surface with the feel of traditional French public spaces. PROJECT and PHOTO: Henry Arnold.

Make Gutters and Curbs Permeable

In many cities and towns, municipal standards require a concrete curb and gutter along both sides of a residential street, regardless of the number of houses served. One problem with such a system is that it *collects and concentrates pollutants* that cars deposit on the road surface. Conventional road drainage usually dumps these into the nearest stream.

A better strategy is to allow stormwater to flow over grass or other vegetation. There is considerable evidence that many pollutants are either degraded or contained by vegetation. In most residential neighborhoods it makes sense *not* to add curbs and gutters—a seemingly simple design strategy, but one that may require a variance from the municipality. If curbs are absolutely required, add multiple openings in the curb that allow the water to flow through it. Gutters of brick laid on sand can also infiltrate a considerable amount of precipitation.

Infiltrate Road and Parking-Lot Runoff in Bioswales

Beyond (or instead of) the curb, install grassed or vegetated areas called bioswales—linear, planted drainage channels. A typical bioswale moves stormwater runoff as *slowly* as possible along a gentle incline, keeping the rain on the site as long as possible and allowing it to soak into the ground—contrary to conventional engineering practice. At the lowest point of the swale there is usually a raised drain inlet that empties any overflow (during particularly heavy storms) into the nearest waterway. This is insurance, however, since well-designed bioswales are capable of infiltrating most or all of the rain from normal showers. Along with the infiltrating function, bioswales cleanse runoff via their plants and soil microbes (compare phytoremediation, page 97).

Bioswales for road drainage are becoming common practice in the Pacific Northwest and are mandated in some counties. One challenge is to design them to enhance the streetscape rather than look like ditches. At the Heritage planned-unit development in Vancouver WA, more than 5 acres of bioswales were configured as roadside park and handsome plantings. The project won a merit award in 1997 from the Portland/Vancouver Metro Area's Stormwater Design Award Competition.⊃

Bioswales function particularly well in parking lots, which generate runoff laden with pollutants that drip from cars and collect on the parking-lot surface. In addition to their decontamination functions, these bioswales create a place for lush plantings amid the parked cars.

A desire to purify stormwater led to bioswales at the Oregon Museum of Science and Industry (OMSI) in Portland. This demonstration project shows that bioswale infiltration works even in the rainy Pacific Northwest climate and features seven bioswales where the raised parking-lot medians would typically be. The OMSI bioswales improve water quality by filtering pollutants from the museum's 800 parking spaces before the runoff enters the Willamette River. This is quite different from the conventional goal of getting the water off-site as quickly as possible via catch basins and underground storm sewers that do nothing to protect the rivers into which they empty.

Designed by Murase Associates, OMSI's bioswales exemplify the definitions given above. Graded to a very gentle incline, they retain water rather than hurry it out of sight. River rocks and small wooden check dams placed at 30-foot intervals cause the water to pond, giving it time to soak into the soil. Wetland plants—cattails, bulrushes, yellow iris, and others, mostly natives—further slow the water while biologically breaking down pollutants. Contaminants that escape this gauntlet are captured in the topsoil, where they are attacked by soil microorganisms. Thus filtered, the stormwater seeps through the subsoil into the underlying water table. Raised drain inlets at the lowest points of the swales take any overflow into the Willamette, but in practice rainwater rarely gets that far.

The city's Bureau of Environmental Services asked OMSI to build the bioswales in 1990. Tom Liptan, a landscape architect with the bureau, had become aware of pioneering work on grassed bioswales at the University of Washington and felt that the idea should be tried in Portland. OMSI management supported the concept. "Stormwater should be part of the landscape architect's design palette," says Liptan. "We need to be much more involved in the water that falls on a site than most of us are currently." Liptan notes that conventional details for parking lots *raise* the landscaped area above the curb, usually mounded so that any rainfall runs off onto the pavement—the antithesis of the bioswale.

OMSI's first step was to direct the project engi-

Figure 5.7. Bioswale at OMSI filters, slows, and infiltrates runoff from parking. Raised grate overflows to storm sewers only in very heavy storms. PROJECT: Robert Murase. ILLUSTRATION: Jeff Foster, Portland Bureau of Environmental Services.

neer to pitch the lot so that it would drain inward—toward the medians between parking rows, where the swales would be. This was critical because most parking lots are pitched *away* from the median strips. Murase Associates designed the richly planted swales, using native plants in lieu of turf, as an "exhibit" to tell the story of the water that falls on the site. The Murase team convinced the engineers to cut approximately 2 feet off each parking stall (only 16.5 feet for a full-sized car); the saved space let them widen the swales. The outcome, according to a computer model of the site, is that the swales hold runoff *longer* than the engineer had calculated; they will fully infiltrate 0.83 inches of rainfall in a twenty-four-hour period. This is sufficient for 75 percent of all the rains that fall on Portland annually, says Liptan. The computer model estimates that the swale's topsoil captures 60 percent of suspended solids in the runoff; with a few improvements Liptan expects a pollutant capture of 90 percent. The parking design recently won an honor award from an Oregon consortium of municipal governments.

Not surprisingly, the question visitors to OMSI most often ask is whether the swales are a breeding ground for mosquitoes. "They don't hold water," is Liptan's response. "The water drains into the soil quickly enough that mosquitoes are not an issue." But this may not be true on all sites, Liptan cautions; much depends on the soil and its permeability.

Most encouraging for the future of such projects, the OMSI parking-lot design saved $78,000, compared to a conventional lot with its expensive catch basins and drainage system. This cost savings has helped Bob Murase market the bioswale concept to several clients in the Portland area. One is the Bureau of Environmental Services itself, which practiced what it had been preaching and installed bioswales at its new Water Pollution Control Center (see page 17). There, bioswales capture runoff from both the parking lot and the roof of the laboratory. The building has no gutters; instead, scuppers extend from the roof, and with each rain these send water spurting in graceful trajectories to land in a rock-lined bioswale several feet from the edge of the building. The Water Pollution Control Laboratory has already won two important awards, one regional and one national.

Whether or not a road or parking area incorporates a bioswale or similar system, it is a good idea to break up paved areas so that they drain directly to an unpaved area rather than to a storm drain. Directly connected impervious areas (DCIAs—paved surfaces that drain straight from one to the next) should be minimized in design.[27] Although storm drains may be necessary for many parking lots to cope with heavy rains, it is important that the "first flush" of rain off a parking area go to a grassed or vegetated area. This is because the first flush carries pollutants that have been deposited

Figure 5.8. Small weirs and plants in the OMSI bioswale make water infiltrate rather than erode. PROJECT: Robert Murase. PHOTO: Tom Liptan.

by cars. If stormwater is routed first to a bioswale, and enters a drain system only if ponding is deep enough to reach an overflow outlet, most of the first-flush pollutants will be contained in the bioswale.

Use Porous Paving Materials

Another way to decrease the stormwater impacts of paving is to make the pavement more permeable so that infiltration occurs *through the surface of the paving itself.* (Nonporous alternative paving materials, such as soil cement, can conserve resources but do not address the sustainability issues specific to impervious paving. These are noted, with other resource issues, in Principle 6.)

POROUS ASPHALT AND CONCRETE

Porous paving combines surface stability with permeability. Since the 1970s, landscape professionals have been pioneers in its development and use. These materials are gaining acceptance, but unfortunately are not as well known as they deserve to be. Considering how often the profession is involved in (and frustrated by) pavement design, familiarity with these materials is a must for being part of the solution rather than part of the problem.

Porous asphalt and porous concrete are similar materials that go by a variety of names: no-fines paving, pervious paving, permeable paving, and percrete (for "percolating concrete"). Stone aggregate is held together with either asphalt or Portland cement as a binder; some high-tech versions have used epoxies to bind the stone. The aggregate must be angular crushed stone, usually three-eighths inch in size, carefully sorted to exclude all the fines (sand-sized particles) that normally fill the voids between the larger aggregate. Without fines, the voids make the material porous. (The same concept is used to create root space in structural soil, described on page 120.) Specify this stone as open-graded or no-fines crushed aggregate.

Whether held together with asphalt or cement, porous paving is strong enough for parking, pedestrian use, and some road surfaces. The asphalt version was originally developed for airport runways, where it prevents dangerous surface ponding. Many state highway departments have adopted it for road surfacing, and asphalt plants routinely carry it, specified as "open-graded mix," "popcorn mix," or "porous friction coat." As a surface over conventional paving, it gets water off the road quickly (the focus of conventional pavement engineering) but does nothing to solve runoff, erosion, or soil water problems.

In order to affect these issues, the porous surface material must be underlaid with a bed, or "reservoir," of larger aggregate surrounded by filter fabric. The reservoir supports the porous surface and holds precipitation until it can percolate into the soil. The bottom and sides of the reservoir are lined with filtering geotextile. The reservoir may be as shallow as 9 inches on some well-drained soils. Using crushed rock open-graded to about 2 inchs in size, almost 40 percent of the reservoir's total volume will be voids capable of holding water. A "choker course" of half-inch gravel is laid on top of the larger stone to even up the top of the reservoir. Heavy equipment must make the minimum possible number of trips across the excavation and must drive on previously placed layers of stone, not on the excavated surface. The filter-fabric edges must be used like erosion-control fencing to keep all sediment out of the reservoir. The porous surface above the reservoir is then laid, using either asphalt or concrete as a binder.⊃

For porous asphalt, binder is about 6 percent of the aggregate's dry weight, and the porous course is about 3 inchs thick. It will withstand freezing and thawing and is slightly flexible. In hot weather, vehicle tires that repeatedly take the same path may rut the surface. Thus, in warm climates, and where traffic is in and out constantly, porous concrete may be a better choice.

Porous concrete uses Portland cement binder in a ratio of 4.0 or 4.5 parts aggregate to 1.0 part cement by weight. This layer is usually 5 inches thick for ordinary vehicular traffic, and thicker for heavier use. Porous concrete is frequently laid directly on compacted soils in areas with very good soil drainage. It will withstand heavier and more repeated loads than the asphalt version and does not soften under heat. However, it is susceptible to freeze-thaw damage. A larger reservoir, which ensures that no water is left in the porous paving itself, can help prevent freeze-thaw damage in the pavement. Air-entrained concrete can also combat freeze-thaw problems, although concrete additives are frowned on by many in the green building movement.

Both the mixture and the timing of porous concrete must be carefully controlled. The contractor must keep the water:cement ratio to the narrow range of between 0.34 and 0.40. With too much water, the cement runs off the aggregate and seals the bottom of the layer; with too little, bonding of the material is weak. Porous concrete must be placed within sixty minutes of mixing, finished immediately, and covered with plastic sheeting within twenty minutes of placement, to cure for three to ten days.

The technique of porous asphalt over a reservoir was first researched in the 1970s by Edmund Thelan and Fielding Howe of Philadelphia (the latter a practicing landscape architect). Since then, firms such as Cahill & Associates, Resource Technologies, and Andropogon Associates⊃ have not only completed significant porous designs but have won several awards for them. An example easily accessible to the public is at the Morris Arboretum, in Philadelphia.

Ecologically, reservoir porous paving reduces both runoff volume and the concentration of overland flow. This decreases disruption of the site's groundwater recharge capacities, as well as slows downstream erosion and siltation. While water is percolating through the porous reservoir, significant amounts of waterborne pollutants are also filtered out or neutralized by soil organisms.

In addition to its ecological advantages, porous paving can save construction, real estate, and maintenance costs. As such, it is a clear example that working with natural systems yields economic benefits. The cost advantages of porous paving derive from its serving two purposes at once—or perhaps more precisely, in the same place. Porous paved surfaces absorb rainfall near where it falls, making the storm drainage system for the site significantly smaller and simpler. Considered strictly as a paving material, porous paving may cost 10 percent more than conventional asphalt. However, because it doubles as a stormwater system and eliminates storm drains, it may be 12 to 38 percent cheaper overall.

A second, greater savings occurs where a porous paving reservoir system substitutes for open stormwater detention, retention, or infiltration basins. The land area otherwise required for the basins is freed for other uses—to create more buildable space, which can offset several times the added paving cost; or to conserve natural features of the site, which would otherwise have been destroyed. In Lower Merion PA, Cahill & Associates were able to create porous tennis courts over reservoirs, an amenity that met stormwater management regulations.

A third advantage is reduced maintenance costs, particularly where snow removal is significant. Snow that falls on porous paving tends to melt quickly and drain into the pores. Only after heavy snowfall will any removal be required, and dangerous surface icing can be virtually eliminated.

Soil around any porous installation must percolate at a minimum rate of a half-inch per hour and should contain no more than 30 percent clay. The bottom of the reservoir must be at least 3 feet above bedrock or the water table to allow unimpeded drainage. If clay lenses or other impermeable barriers exist on the site, the reservoir must either be well above them or be deep enough to reach permeable soils. On sites that slope 3 percent or more, the paved areas should be terraced so that the bottom of each reservoir remains relatively level.

The size and depth of the reservoir must be designed to fit site conditions: soil permeability, slope, and the local design storm. (Cahill & Associates uses a computer program to do this.) The reservoir must be sized to accommodate the water generated by the design storm and to hold it long enough to percolate into that specific soil. If the site is sloped, drainage from the upper end requires extra depth at the lower end. Some conditions may require underdrains or overflow pipes set to catch water at the point the reservoir is full.

Runoff from roofs and nonporous pavement may also be directed into the reservoir, assuming it is sized accordingly. This water is thus directed into the groundwater recharge cycle. Sediment-bearing runoff, such as flow from wooded areas, should not discharge directly onto porous paving. It may, however, be channeled or piped into the reservoir via bioswales, sediment traps, or filter fabric.

With all its advantages, why hasn't porous paving become a standard material? The primary reason appears to be resistance from some members of the engineering and regulatory community. Porous paving goes against conventional "pave-and-pipe" notions of stormwater management, which emphasize keeping water out of the soil and getting it off-site. Moreover, successful design requires more sophisticated site-specific data than the standardized pipe-sizing process; in particular, soil, bedrock, and groundwater characteristics must be tested and respected. As with any new technology, porous paving has a learning curve and requires educating both clients and colleagues.

Among concerns raised by engineers and planners, the fear of clogging is most common. Unfortunately, some "tests" of porous paving were reportedly built on unsuitable soils and at toe-of-slope locations where clogging was virtually assured. Yet most researchers have found that proper design, installation, and maintenance can prevent any loss of porosity over time. In one test, an inch of loose fine material was applied to a porous concrete surface. The pavement never became less porous than turf, and full porosity was easily restored by cleaning with a device called a hydrovac.[28] Porous asphalt may lose surface porosity in areas deformed by traffic; drilling the compacted areas with a small bit can restore much of its performance. A relatively minor loss of porosity occurs in all porous materials over the first four to six years and should be assumed in design calculations; even after this loss, the porous surface is still able to deal with most normal regional precipitation.[29]

Underdrains, overflow drains, and edge drains have been installed on some systems in case the reservoir should ever clog and cease to percolate. Cahill & Associates states that in more than twenty-five years of experience with porous paving, these added features have had only one real purpose: not to deal with clogging, but to act as "insurance" to convince skeptical planning commissions.

Most designers familiar with the material recommend porous paving, especially asphalt, for areas of lighter traffic where repetitious movement will not be severe. Employee parking, with once-a-day in and out, is an example. The main traffic lanes are paved with ordinary asphalt in such designs. Porous paving can also be used for many light vehicles, such as golf carts or bicycles, for pedestrians, and for sports surfaces.

Because this material has such great potential to diminish the environmental problems associated with paving, we believe that research into improved binders would be well worth the effort. The World Trade Center in New York is reportedly roofed with a porous pavement in which the aggregate is bound with epoxy. If a porous-pavement binder with improved strength, flexibility without permanent deformation, and resistance to temperature extremes could be developed at reasonable cost, many of the conflicts between transportation and the environment would become dramatically easier to resolve.

PAVE WITH GRASS

Among the most permeable parking surfaces are grassed paving systems that allow turfgrass to grow through an open cell of concrete or plastic that transfers the weight of vehicles to an underlying base course. A variety of commercial products is available, including large sheets of plastic mesh, precast open concrete blocks, and form systems for casting concrete cells in place.

The environmental benefits of grassed paving can be considerable. According to one manufacturer's study, every 1,000 square feet of grass paving infiltrates nearly 7,000 gallons per 10 inches of rainfall, which would otherwise be runoff; converts enough carbon dioxide to oxygen to supply twenty-two adults for a year; provides significant cooling (equated to 1.7 tons of air conditioning annually); and, in the case of this manufacturer, recycles more than 400 pounds of plastic in the product itself.[30]

Grassed paving is somewhat limited in its applications because grass will not survive constant daily traffic. (Grass stays healthy if not used for parking more than about one day a week—less in dry climates.) Grassed paving is typically used for emergency fire lanes or for temporary overflow parking. But as the Olympia study documented, many more parking areas receive temporary use than is generally supposed. Sports arenas, for example, are typically used on one or two days a week; the entire stadium parking lot could be grassed, greatly reducing the need for storm drains (see project examples on page 188). Grassed paving could probably be used much more widely than it is at present.

Where there is demand for grass parking to be used more than the grass can withstand, an active operating plan may increase its capacity. A large grass-paved area can be divided into two or more subareas, using fences or barriers (permanent or temporary). By alternately using and resting the subareas, each can be given a chance to recover from wear. This works especially well

Figure 5.9. Porous concrete, shown here, and porous asphalt support vehicles but permit water to infiltrate rapidly. PHOTO: Florida Concrete and Products Association/Dennis Graeber.

for overflow parking where, for example, the *whole* area is needed only occasionally, but filling the lot to *half* capacity is fairly common. Base the plan on realistic, not speculative, numbers.

Grassed paving systems do not have to be filled with sod. A number of ground covers, such as thyme or chamomile, will flourish in some climates. Fine gravel, oyster shells, or other permeable materials can substitute for grass where frequent parking is expected (or in climates in which grass does not readily grow). Such materials provide the strength and permeability of the grassed paving system without worrying about the health of the grass. At least one paving-systems company, Invisible Structures, manufactures a system, designed to be filled with a gravel mixture (Gravelpave). This system was employed in 1999 as part of a demonstration project for the headquarters of the Riverside/Corona Resource Conservation District in Riverside CA⊃. (Gravelpave is only one of the innovative materials used at the center; others include car stops made of recycled tires.)

A drawback of grassed paving is its cost, which can be higher than that of solid asphalt or concrete parking lots. In fact, the Olympia WA study found that concrete grass pavers average two to four times the per square foot cost of asphalt. A parking area with 20 percent of the lot in grassed pavers would cost approximately 60 percent

more to install than an equal all-asphalt area. But the Olympia study found that permeable paving systems are less costly than asphalt to maintain over time.[31] Moreover, the initial expense of grassed pavers may be deceptive because it does not take into account the *reduced* need for storm drains and sewers. When subtracting the cost of such drains, the overall cost of grassed systems may actually be lower than conventional, impervious paving.

Three general types of grassed paving systems exist:

1. *Poured-in-place* systems such as Bomanite's Grasscrete consist of steel-reinforced concrete. These are typically the most expensive systems, and installation requires skilled workers.

2. *Precast concrete pavers*, like poured-in-place concrete, provide rigid structural support. Typical pavers are heavy and require some type of equipment for hauling and lifting. In some ways these are similar to interlocking concrete pavers (page 39). Both types of concrete systems tend to have a latticed or checkered appearance, with the concrete grid framing areas of grass. This can be very attractive in some designs and may help make it clear that the area is for parking.

3. A large number of the available systems are *plastic pavers.* Although they do not have concrete's rigidity, these pavers are flexible and conform to irregular surfaces. They appear to support grass growth better than the thick-walled concrete cells if moisture is scarce. Plastic grid systems come closest to disappearing entirely under the grass, giving

Figure 5.10. Gravelpave² uses recycled plastic grids to stabilize gravel. Similar plastic or concrete grids strengthen grassed paving or combat slope erosion. PHOTO: Invisible Structures⊃.

the appearance of ordinary lawn. Some of the products are manufactured from 100 percent recycled plastic such as film canisters and milk cartons.[32] Invisible Structures, founded by Denver landscape architect Bill Bonhoff, makes all its products of recycled plastics. Invisible Structures' grass pavers have been tested up to 5,700 psi bearing strength when filled, and the empty plastic structure will support over 2,000 psi.

In general, it is better to use a mix of sand and water-absorbent polymer as grass-paver growing medium than to use topsoil. Topsoil usually is loamy or clayey and will compact. A sandy fill is also most permeable. The ultimate porosity of the system depends strongly on the native soil underneath it. Over clay or loam soils, 50 to 80 percent of rainfall may run off (compared to 95 percent from hard pavement); over sandy soils, runoff from grass paving can be as little as 15 percent.

A key requirement of grassed paving is maintenance. This includes mowing, which is important because tall grass that is matted down by vehicles can decrease the perviousness of the system. (Also, people are less likely to park on the infiltration system if it does not appear stable and well cared for.[33]) Invisible Structures states that snow can be plowed off their systems if inch-thick skids are attached to the snowplow blade. An irrigation system is also recommended even in areas of high rainfall to counter the stresses of compaction, shallow rooting space, oil drips, heating of concrete cells, and "wicking" of water from soil by the concrete.[34] Maintenance costs appear to be comparable to or less than those for conventional pavement, although maintenance comparisons between different types of grassed paving are hard to make. Durability is likely to vary with soil type and climate.

In choosing between different grassed systems, evaluate ease and weight of installation, durability, grass growth and maintenance issues (preferably by comparison of projects in your regions), and finished appearance.

Grassed Paving: Project Examples

Periodic "event parking" is an appropriate use for grassed paving; the city of Miami uses a grassed paving system for the new parking stalls at the Orange Bowl. The driving lanes are conventional asphalt.

"Overall, it's working out really well," says Enrique Nuñez, a landscape architect with the Miami Department of Community Planning and Revitalization who was involved in the design and implementation of the parking. The paving system for the project was a recycled-plastic product. Nuñez confirms that the grass pavers have helped to eliminate runoff, although the site does have a conventional stormwater system as a backup.

If—as the Olympia study discovered—much retail parking is used only at peak periods, then large chunks of the parking at malls and shopping centers are appropriate for grassed paving. Although mall developers rarely seize this opportunity, Westfarms Mall in Farmington CT did. When the mall proposed adding 4.7 acres of parking, primarily to accommodate the Christmas rush, the local zoning board pointed to a requirement that a certain portion of any developed site remain in greenspace. A grassed paving system of recycled-plastic pavers enabled Westfarms Mall to get its parking while meeting the greenspace quota, and without enlarging existing storm drains. Although this particular project incorporated tree plantings, too, grassed paving is certainly a minimal form of greenspace, and the authors cannot recommend it as a way to *get around* planted-area regulations. In general, it is preferable *not* to build for rare peak-demand levels, as discussed at the beginning of this chapter. Converting excess *existing* parking, used only at peak hours, to grassed paving would be more appropriate; removing the excess altogether, better yet.

Olympia WA tested the effectiveness of grassed paving in 1996 as part of that city's search for ways to reduce impervious surfaces and promote the infiltration of rainwater. The demonstration project was a public school parking lot from which storm runoff regularly flooded an adjacent athletic field. An 8-foot-wide, 2.5-foot-deep infiltration trench was dug along the edge of the lot and backfilled with porous sandy gravel. Honeycomb-like cellular containment units, filled with a mix of gravel and soil, bear the weight of parked cars while allowing rainwater to percolate into the trench. For quick vegetative cover, turf was installed over the infiltration system. The soil mix was designed not to percolate so fast that the grass would lack water to survive.

Postconstruction evaluation of the system was

Figure 5.11. Overflow parking at Westfarms Mall uses Grasspave² instead of impervious asphalt. PHOTO: Invisible Structures⊃.

Figure 5.12. Traditional granite setts being laid on sand in Philadelphia's historic district. Joints are somewhat permeable if not mortared. PHOTO: Kim Sorvig.

done for forty-eight days, of which thirty-four were rainy. Ponding on the athletic field occurred on only six of these days, which the city inspectors say is a marked improvement. People tended not to park on the area, which the study attributes to an aversion to driving on grass. City parks and recreation vehicles did drive over the turf without any significant damage; tire tracks were found on several occasions, none that irreparably damaged the lawn. There was no compaction of the backfill that would affect infiltration.[35] Probably a more effective, but more costly, solution would have been to rehabilitate the whole parking surface that was generating the runoff.

Unit Pavers on Permeable Subgrade

Another potentially permeable surface uses unit pavers (pavers set as individual pieces, rather than a continuous sheet like poured concrete). Because the pavers themselves are not permeable, the key to this approach is that they *must be laid on sand, crushed stone, stone screenings, or some other permeable material.* (Obviously, if brick is set on concrete—as it so commonly is—then the resulting surface is no more permeable than the concrete itself.)

Unit pavers are time-honored materials in many older cities: the brick that makes the undulating historic sidewalks in Washington DC or Philadelphia so appealing; the hexagonal pavers used in New York and other northeastern cities; or even flagstone, granite setts, or cobblestones. (One of the recurring themes of this book is that traditional materials are still quite viable and often more ecologically sound than newer "conventional" approaches.) Interlocking concrete

Figure 5.13. In small-scale, low-traffic areas, unit pavers can even support wildflowers. PROJECT: R & V Sorvig. PHOTO: Kim Sorvig.

unit pavers (ICP) in many styles and colors also provide some percolation. (Because permeability is not their primary environmental benefit, ICP systems are discussed in Principle 1.) Some ICP units are cast with spacers on each edge that automatically create extrawide joints, while maintaining paver-to-paver contact for stability. These "spaced" ICP systems are probably the most permeable of any unit paver; the closely related precast grass pavers are more permeable than ICP systems.

Because the percolation actually takes place in the joints between the pavers, the width and the material of the joints become critical. A study done at Cornell University in the 1980s produced some important findings for the design of side-walks and other pedestrian areas, parking lots, and even streets constructed with unit pavers.[36] The Cornell study recommends:

1. Use wide joints (one-quarter inch is probably the maximum without reducing stability) or small pavers, either of which maximizes total joint area.

2. Use thicker pavers to compensate for loss of rigidity, if necessary.

3. Use permeable joint-filler materials. Coarse sharp sand bound with bitumen (a sort of miniaturized porous asphalt) was found to be the most permeable.

4. After initial installation, settling of the paving occurs; brush in more coarse joint-filler material, rather than allow finer debris to accumulate and block the pore space.

5. Where possible, leave joints lower than the walking surface; this increases the infiltration rate by creating tiny "reservoirs" between the pavers.

6. Make the base course beneath the pavers as coarse as possible to prevent water being retained in the surface layer.

7. Do not compact the base course excessively, or vibrate the whole sidewalk after construction. Similarly, the National Concrete Masonry Association recommends *not* compacting sand under interlocking concrete pavers.

As with porous paving, unit paver permeability may decline over time as joints become compacted by traffic and filled with debris. It appears that the decline levels off after about five years, leaving considerable permeability over the life of the installation.

For landscape architect Henry Arnold, the major benefit of such systems is that they permit easy percolation to the roots of trees and other plants, making for healthier plantings and cutting costs for irrigation. As an example, Arnold used colored concrete unit pavers set on a bed of finely crushed stone in downtown Atlanta's Peachtree Plaza. This beautiful walking surface collects and infiltrates water, helping to irrigate nearby plantings.

Cool Asphalt with Planting and Albedo

Conventional parking lots, as noted earlier, are a major contributor to the heat islands in American cities. Black asphalt is particularly heat-absorbing. Concrete and some other light-colored hard paving materials reflect more sunlight and therefore absorb less heat. Dark brick and stone, as well as some colored concrete, may be almost as heat-absorbent as asphalt.

Grassed paving is significantly less absorptive of heat than is any hard surface. If the climate is not too hot to support grass, this alternative paving can cut heat retention. Although not tested, it also seems logical that porous paving, because it contains voids, and because it often overlays a reservoir of moisture, might be cooler than conventional paving.

Reducing the *amount* of paving should always be the first consideration where heat is an issue. Where a hard-surfaced lot is essential for a project, however, the EPA recommends two ways of reducing the heat increases from paving.[37] The first is to plant shade trees—a seemingly simple move. However, more and more urban trees are small, almost dwarf species, which never grow to give real shade. Leaf litter of large, overhanging trees is sometimes seen as a cleanup problem, and this perception has led to city tree ordinances that actually ban many useful shade trees. Vine-covered trellises can be an alternative, but the magnificent street trees of well-planned cities shade more area more economically.

The second EPA approach is to increase the reflectiveness—or "albedo"—of pavement and thus reduce its heat-absorption capacity. (Too much reflectance equals glare, and must also be avoided.) Albedo-increasing methods have mostly been targeted to black asphalt, perhaps somewhat unfairly, since other dark materials also hold heat. However, given the prevalence of asphalt (nearly 75 percent of all U.S. paving is asphalt), and the fact that its oily composition makes it hard to paint or stain, methods of lightening the surface of asphalt paving take on particular importance for sustainability.

Fortunately, asphalt can be lightened in several ways. One is to specify that the mix include light-colored stone, both aggregate and fines. Although the asphalt binder will initially coat any aggregate, making it black, surface wear exposes the aggregate. Many conventional "blacktop" roads are in fact the color of the local aggregate. It is important that neither construction workers nor maintenance staff apply the conventional pure black "wearing coat," which is often routinely applied because it makes the surface look new and tidy. Light-colored aggregate can be used for porous as well as nonporous asphalt, unlike some color-coating systems.

Color-coating asphalt developed in large part as a decorative system but has promising environmental possibilities. Slurry seals, composed of sand, cement, and acrylic-polymer binders, have been developed to adhere to the slightly oily surface of asphalt. These can give asphalt a surface of almost any color, and when light colors are used, will make asphalt paving less heat-absorptive.[38] Companies that manufacture, distribute, and install these coatings use them in conjunction with metal templates that, pressed into the hot asphalt by a vibratory roller, produce surface patterns like brick or cobblestone, even custom logos and other artwork. Both patterning and coating can be done by ordinary laborers. Normal cracking of the asphalt is reduced because the areas compressed by the template act as expansion joints, and because the coating seals out water. The first installations in the United States, made in the early 1990s, have not reached the end of their life spans and have required much less routine maintenance than conventional asphalt.⊃

The main environmental reason to consider these coatings is to reduce heat absorption. To the extent that these coatings reduce the maintenance and extend the life of asphalt paving, they save resources. They may also solve one of the problems of sheet asphalt, which is the difficulty of repairing trenches dug for utilities: using the templates, trenches can be recoated to match the original work. Coatings do not address the problem of solid asphalt as an impervious surface, nor the health problems that exposure to hot asphalt can create (see page 313, Appendix A). However, they provide an attractive paving surface similar to patterned concrete at 50 to 80 percent the cost of high-end concrete systems like Bomanite. The coatings add 30 to 50 percent to the price of plain asphalt.[39]

In addition to coatings, there is now a way of coloring asphalt in the hot mix. Supplied by Asphacolor (Madera CA), this relatively new

Figure 5.14. Henry Arnold has used open-jointed unit pavers at large plazas in Atlanta GA, Brooklyn NY, and Newport NJ, usually with extra aeration vents. PROJECT and PHOTO: Henry Arnold.

process was used to provide colored paving for Los Angeles' Union Station. Heat-island reduction was not apparently a deliberate goal of this project but would occur incidentally.

Bagged colorant is batch-mixed with the asphalt and aggregate at the plant; as with coatings, almost any color can be produced. Compared to ordinary asphalt, mixing is slightly slower, more coordination is required, and extra cleanup is necessary before mixing other colors or conventional mixes. Costs are somewhat higher than the coating systems, even when colored asphalt is reserved for the top 1.0- to 1.5-inch layer, but still less than colored concrete. Because it is integral to the mix, the Asphacolor process may wear longer than coatings. It offers some interesting design possibilities in combination with contrasting colored aggregate and is the only way that *porous* asphalt could be colored.⊃

Given society's massive demand for paving, and the fact that asphalt is one of the cheapest ways of meeting that demand, asphalt is likely to remain a major component of the built environment for a long time to come. Being able to achieve colored asphalt more cheaply than colored concrete may change the marketplace for asphalt, which as an industry is used to competing solely on cheap cost and simple installation. Whether these decorative systems can make asphalt paving significantly more sustainable remains to be seen. However, they clearly affect the heat-island problem and may somewhat decrease resource consumption for asphalt. Used in conjunction with methods for reducing runoff described in this chapter, high-albedo asphalt has a role to play in reducing the environmental impact of paving.

The state and local agencies that regulate parking are slowly recognizing the legitimacy of permeable pavement and other sustainable alternatives to conventional paving. Monitoring and reporting on existing projects have begun to establish these materials as reliable. A greater hurdle, however, may be educating the public. It will take many successful examples of alternative parking to win the acceptance of the average motorist. As stressed throughout the book, the technical solutions to sustainability problems can only succeed if they are paralleled by social changes. Creative and high-quality work by landscape designers and contractors is one of the best

hopes for raising public awareness and acceptance of new methods. Museums, nature centers, and educational institutions, as well as national and regional parks, have environmental goals and offer high-profile opportunities to showcase sustainable methods. Sustainability is also a concern in more and more corporate boardrooms; projects for such clients offer avenues to educate the public.

Resources

Overpaving

Asphalt Nation: How the Automobile Took Over America and How We Can Take It Back by Jane H. Kay (1997 Crown/Random House)
Overview of history of paving in the United States; despite the title, not focused only on asphalt.

Paving

Portland Cement Association
Skokie IL
708-966-6200
Publishes and consults on concrete use.

Porous paving

Andropogon Associates. 215-487-0700

Cahill & Associates 215-696-4150

Florida Concrete & Products Association 407-895-9333

National Aggregate Association. 301-587-1400

National Asphalt Paving Association
301-731-4748
Consultants and associations with experience in porous asphalt and/or porous concrete.

SF-Rima wide-joint unit pavers
SF Concrete Technology
Mississauga, Ontario
888-347-7873
Unit pavers held apart and sturdy by joint-spacers on all sides.

Grasspave, Gravelpave
Invisible Structures, Inc.
Aurora CO
800-233-1510
Recycled-plastic, porous alternatives to paving; notable for being owned and run by a landscape architect.

Impervious Surface Reduction Study (Cedar Wells, Dir., Olympia WA Public Works Dept., 360-753-8454)

"Grass Paving Systems" by James Sipes & Mack Roberts (June 1994 *Landscape Architecture*)

"Porous Paving" by Kim Sorvig (Feb 1993 *Landscape Architecture*)
Article introducing porous asphalt and concrete.

Figure 5.15. Decorative color coatings for asphalt can lighten the surface, decreasing heat-island effects. Integral color, mixed into hot asphalt, is also becoming available.
PHOTO: StreetPrint, Scott Hind.

"Parking Supply Management" (1997 Federal Transit Administration www.fta.dot.gov/)
> The specific page for this document is /fta/library/planning/tdmstatus/ftarpksp.htm

"Shared Parking Planning Guidelines" (1995 Institute of Transportation Engineers, Washington DC, 202-554-8050 or www.ite.org/)
Highway construction statistics (Bureau of Transportation Statistics)
> Numbers and databases on all modes of transportation in the United States.

"Impervious Surface Coverage" by Chester Arnold & James Gibbons (Spring 1996 *Journal of the American Planning Association*)

International Parking Institute
www.parking.org
> Answers to common questions about parking.

Parking Spaces by Mark Childs (1999 McGraw-Hill)

Riverside/Corona CA conservation district
www.rcrcd.com
> Innovative planning and technologies of interest.

Garden Paths: A New Way to Solve Practical Problems in the Garden by Gordon Hayward (1998 *Taylor's guides* [Houghton Mifflin])

Bioswales

Vegetated Swales
> Viewable at www.asla.org

Roadway Design

Greenways: A Guide to Planning, Design, and Development by Loring Schwartz (1996 Island Press)

Interactive Highway Safety Design Model
FHWA Turner-Fairbanks Highway Research Center
www.tfhrc.gov
> Software simulates and evaluates two-lane road design, driver behavior, speeds, etc., interactively for better design. Incorporates traffic calming concepts. Due for release 2001.

Lying Lightly on the Land by Timothy Davis and Joseph Roas, Curators (National Building Museum, Historic American Engineering Record, and Federal Lands Highway Office www.nbm.org or 202-272-2564)
> Exhibit on park road design and construction. Alternatives to overengineered roads.

Traffic Calming

Traffic Calming Library
Institute of Transportation Engineers
http://dev.issinet.com/ite/traffic/
> Searchable library of articles on traffic calming—issues, methods, devices, law, etc.

Heat Islands

ASPHALT COLOR COATING
DecoAsphalt (CA) www.decoasphalt.com
877-332-6277 or
Integrated Paving Concepts (Canada) 604-574-7510 or
www.streetprint.com/
> Asphalt patterning and coating systems with potential for albedo use.

ASPHALT: INTEGRAL COLORANTS
Asphacolor
Madera CA
800-258-7679 or asphacolor@mail.telis.org

Cooling Our Communities: A Guidebook on Tree Planting and Light-colored Surfacing by Hashem Akbari (1992 Lawrence Berkeley Laboratory report LBL-31587, U.S. Government Printing Office www.access.gpo.gov/su_docs/sale.html or 202-512-1800 or orders@gpo.gov)

Consider Origin and Fate of Materials

Nature resolves everything into its component elements, but annihilates nothing.

—Lucretius, 57 B.C.

One theme of this book is that inappropriate landscape design and construction—such as overpaving or invasive plantings—damage sites. In some cases, however, a landscape that seems perfectly harmonious with its site can impact the environment far *beyond* its boundaries. Pliny Fisk, codirector of the Center for Maximum Potential Building Systems in Austin TX, illustrates it this way: "One can disturb a site to the least possible degree and be causing utter havoc on Earth at the same time—because of what you're *bringing to* that site. Let's say that landscape architects are going to do a large paved area and they decide to use granite pavers quarried in Minnesota. There's a good chance that the granite is shipped to Italy, sliced up, sent back and delivered to Houston, or wherever the building site is. That's an incredible imposition on the well-being of this planet."[1]

Fisk is referring, of course, to the energy costs (and concomitant air pollution) required to move that granite around the globe. The *materials* used in landscapes have many such impacts. Extraction of raw materials for making landscape products has environmental and energy costs. Products that are themselves quite clean may orginate in air- or water-polluting factories far from the landscape site. Even the debris hauled off site has an impact—the energy costs of its removal and the land area taken up by landfill use.

While designers have become increasingly vocal about the need for more sustainable design, the majority of landscape projects still specify virgin materials. "Such landscapes, no matter how sensitive they are to the ecology of a site, are still destructive," says Kathleen Baughman, a landscape designer in Portland OR, "for they pro-

mote the continued environmental degradation associated with resource extraction."[2]

Almost every construction material is extracted from somewhere. Some extraction processes are more destructive than others; some products are renewable or reusable. The hidden costs can be high, from the nonrenewable petroleum products used in asphalt to the destruction of rain forests for tropical hardwoods—or, for that matter, the felling of domestic redwood forests to produce decks and site furniture. This chapter focuses on recognizing these hidden costs of landscape materials and the hazards they can pose for landowners and for landscape workers, as well as for the larger environment.

Realistic alternatives do exist: local materials, reused or recycled materials, and even materials

---

Discussed in This Chapter:

- Eight basic guidelines to simplify the choice of sustainable materials

- Using on-site and local resources

- Recycled products for the landscape

- Recycling construction materials

- Recognizing and avoiding toxic materials in landscape construction

- Impacts of transportation, mining, and other general processes

---

already found on the site. The acceptability and availability of these materials are growing rapidly: a 1998 contest to win a custom home built of "top-of-the line products manufactured from recyclables" attracted *seven times* as many entries as the previous year's contest.[3] Alternative materials are viewed by many landscape professionals not as limitations, but as opportunities. Not only do these materials impose a lesser burden on the planet, they are also spurring some of the most creative and innovative landscape work being done today.

Some Simple Guidelines

As a simple set of operational rules, consider this short list of principles from Maurice Nelischer, a landscape architect in Guelph, Ontario:

1. Whenever possible, specify locally produced products.

2. Use less-processed materials (rough-sawn or air-dried lumber, for instance, instead of finished kiln-dried boards).

3. When specifying materials, perform a rough audit of the energy required to mine, produce, ship, and install them. See Principle 7.

4. Explore the availability of recycled materials. Specify reusable materials—for example, stone, brick, or concrete pavers rather than poured concrete.

5. Avoid petroleum-based materials whenever possible. Asphalt and many plastics are indispensable in a few uses, but not for every purpose.[4]

While by no means inclusive, these guidelines offer a starting point for better choices of landscape materials. Here are some additions to the list:

6. Use durable materials with high carbon content (such as wood): the carbon "locked up" in these materials offsets the release of greenhouse gas carbon dioxide (CO_2) from other sources. (Fisk speaks of "balancing" a project's materials for CO_2.)

7. Protect existing vegetation, use new plantings or bioengineering: living plants take up CO_2,

offsetting greenhouse gases from manufacturing.

8. Minimize use of materials that are toxic, either on-site or during manufacture or disposal. (Appendix A lists forty-nine basic construction materials and summarizes hazards associated with each.)

Let Reuse Be Reinspiration

Recycling is more than just a practical way of saving energy and resources. Clearly, it is worth doing for simple pragmatic reasons. But like necessity, it can be a source of invention and creativity, inspiring both designers and users of landscapes.

The uniqueness of specific places has been diluted by modern communication and transportation, until many people feel adrift in a featureless landscape of convenience. Reusing cast-off materials is a link to other people and places and gives a sense of continuity that many people deeply want. The results may be as quiet as the "character" a site gains from worn, used stone or as obvious as an old tractor planted with petunias. Large or small, tasteful or garish, reused materials have an identity that is hard to buy new.

Use Local, Salvaged, or Recycled Materials

The simplest single way to cut down the impact of the materials used in construction is to obtain them locally. Trucking 1 ton of material 1 mile typically uses between 2,000 and 6,000 Btu; air freight can easily be twenty times this energy-costly.[5] Fuel consumption for transporting materials from afar, as in Fisk's example above, can be far greater than the energy used to extract and manufacture the items themselves.

Not only is this an energy cost worth reducing, but fuel combustion is also a primary source of pollution and greenhouse gases. For every mile that a supplier is closer to the site, nonrenewable fuel resources are saved, and emissions that cause health problems and contribute to global warming are reduced. Current figures are rough, but it appears that research in these areas is approaching a major milestone—the ability to assign accurate energy and emissions costs to specific materials and to plan accordingly (Principle 7).

Some materials are easier to obtain locally than others. Steel, for example, is produced in a few centralized factories, while cement or brick are frequently manufactured in more localized operations. In some cases, production efficiency requires centralization; buying from your local steel mill is not an option in most locations. For other materials, such as lumber, it may be possible to find a local supplier, but conventional business practices (such as supplying most U.S. lumber from the Pacific Northwest or Georgia) keep the costs of local materials artificially high. Distant or foreign ownership of local material production can also distort costs. Monetary cost is often a misleading indicator of energy and other environmental costs, and sustainability requires new ways of estimating the true costs of materials.

Salvaged or reused materials are generally obtained locally and have the additional advantage of serving twice for roughly the same energy cost. Clearly, some salvage methods use so much energy that the materials offer no real environmental savings, but usually the bulldoze-and-dump approach uses even more. Salvage work is typically done with hand tools or small power tools, so that the ratio of renewable human energy to nonrenewable mechanical energy is high.

Recycled materials are *remanufactured* between their first and second use. In general, the authors support recycling, but careful analysis is required to know which materials are environmentally cost-effective to recycle. Although it is one of the most popular causes endorsed for sustainability, some forms of recycling do not save enough energy to be environmentally sound. Materials like aluminum can be remanufactured at only a fraction of the energy cost of new production; for other materials, the savings is much smaller. Add to this the necessity to collect and transport

Figure 6.1. Landscapes that reuse neglected materials can be a much-needed source of pride and identity in a homogenizing world. PHOTO: Kim Sorvig.

Figure 6.2. "Recycling" a power turbine into a picnic umbrella (New Zealand) saves no materials but humanizes a massive postindustrial artifact. At this scale, reuse and recycling can be both whimsical and transformative. PHOTO: Kim Sorvig.

materials for recycling, and the net energy savings may vanish. For some materials and some uses, recycling can only produce a second-rate class of material; this is called "downcycling." An example is plastics that are pure enough for medicine and food containers; in most cases, recycled plastics of the same sort are not usable for such purposes. Recycling, like salvage and reuse, does keep materials out of landfills; sometimes this is reason enough to continue recycling a material when energy savings are borderline.

In some cases recycling and reuse may *converge*. For example, yard waste currently makes up about one-fifth of the municipal solid waste stream; many states and municipalities now ban it from their landfills (see page 81). If used as a perfectly viable mulch and soil builder, greenwaste is seldom considered "recycled" in the same sense as a recycled plastic planter. Yet in a way, greenwaste uses the landscape as the *medium* of recycling. The concept of *renewability* also relates directly to the landscape: Only products that can be grown can truly be called renewable. Wood is the only really renewable construction product, with the exception of a few plant-based paints and varnishes.[6] Renewability depends on proper management of forests or fields so that these can continue to produce the resource.

Sustainable use of materials has many complexities, and the well-known slogan "Reduce, Reuse, Recycle" needs to be taken as a list *in priority order*. Using less materials, reusing them in their present form, and finally recycling them is a sustainable path. When recycling, or even reuse, becomes an excuse to continue using more and more materials, or to use materials with extremely poor environmental records, it makes a mockery of hopes for sustainability. Likewise, using a locally produced but highly toxic material is of little environmental benefit.

For better or worse, the environmental choice of materials is seldom cut and dried. As Sandra Mendler points out in HOK's *Sustainable Design Guide*, these choices are likely to become easier the more the profession practices them. "Much of the history of building in the nineteenth century is one of trial and error as people struggled to understand [newly industrialized materials and methods]. . . . It took about 100 years to arrive at a generally accepted set of 'rules' to deal with basic issues of safety in 'modern' buildings. . . . We must now move forward by focusing on sustainable design as our nineteenth-century predecessors emphasized life safety."[7]

Use On-Site Materials

If using local materials follows the "close-to-the-source" principle, then the closest source is the site itself. The great majority of materials for traditional construction—soil, wood, or rock—was taken from the site or very nearby. Limitations on locally available materials played a strong role in the development of regional technologies and design styles. For example, the high deserts of the southwestern United States and Mexico have tall trees only in limited mountain areas. This led directly to the use of adobe—earth from within the building's footprint, in many cases—as the

Figure 6.3. Stone from site excavation, reused in walls and paving at Club de Golf Malinalco, makes a stunning argument for inventive use of site "waste." PROJECT: Mario Schjetnan. PHOTO: courtesy Grupo de Diseño Urbano.

main building material in these regions, with timber reserved for roof beams and door and window lintels.

Far from being just a constraint, these local materials awakened a creative design response that has become one of the most popular and imitated styles today. A wide range of on-site materials may be productively reused in the landscape—if the designer takes the time to look and consider them creatively. In an era when the homogenizing effects of industrial, Modernist design are widely regretted, creative use of local materials offers not only environmental benefits, but the basis for artistic rebirth.

BOULDERS, STONE, BRICK, AND TIMBER

Many sites harbor hard materials—stone, either cut or rough, bricks, and sometimes lumber as well as earth and plants. Mario Schjetnan, a landscape architect from Mexico City, made extraordinary reuse of on-site volcanic stone at

the Malinalco golf club south of the capital. In this case, the stone—some of it sizeable boulders—was unearthed during excavation for the golf course, and the original plan was to reinter it at great cost. Schjetnan suggested instead that the stone be used to construct a massive stone wall used to define the entry, and a spacious entrance plaza built entirely of smaller stones. The project won an honor award from the American Society of Landscape Architects in 1998. (Another Mexican example that makes a feature of on-site volcanic stone is Luis Barragan's famous Pedregal.)

The stones at Malinalco were put in place by hand—a very labor-intensive process. This approach may not be replicable in more developed nations with high labor costs; social issues are part of the mix in any construction, and designers and builders must evolve ingenious reuses that fit their own societies.

On-site rubble can be used in developed

Figure 6.4. Salvaged during demolition, roof-tiles form curbs and gutters and fill gabion-like planted walls in this urban garden in Oslo, Norway. Crushed tile surfaces paths and serves as concrete aggregate. Stone, too, is second-hand. PROJECT: Snøhetta Landskapsarkitekter. PHOTO: Rainer Stange.

Figure 6.5. Broken concrete, reused in slabs or crushed as aggregate, demonstrate John Lyle's concepts at the Center for Regenerative Studies. PROJECT and PHOTO: John Lyle.

countries, too. In Oslo, Norway, the demolition of some old buildings in the midst of apartment buildings permitted the creation of a garden court. Landscape architect Rainer Stange transformed roof tiles and other rubble into retaining walls to bridge level-changes in the gardens. The walls also offer a ghostly reflection of the former buildings in this historic area, emphasizing the recycling concept. Steps were made of reused stone curbs. Tiles and other salvaged materials such as hubcaps fill plantable gabions, while for contrast, the clean high-tech look of metal trellises ties the space together. Careful selection of climbing plants, one species per wall, helps orient users to this charmingly offbeat garden.[8]

Rubble from demolished buildings or parking can be reconstituted as paving surfaces. At the Institute for Regenerative Studies, concrete rubble was pieced together and cemented to form the basis of a new driveway and parking area. This significantly cut requirements for new cement.

Elsewhere in this book, we argue for removing old paving and structures and restoring the soil underneath, but where the structure can be adapted, or where energy costs of removal are high, it may make more ecological sense to leave such structures in place and simply work around them. An example is Monnens Addis Design in Berkeley CA, where a defunct warehouse was rehabilitated as a graphic-design studio. The owners of the business wanted a garden, but the only available spot was the former warehouse's loading dock, covered with a concrete slab 8 inches thick. The landscape architect for the project, Jeffrey Miller, chose an unusual strategy: instead of demolishing the slab, he built the garden atop it.

Cost was an obvious factor in this decision; transporting and dumping demolition debris have become a significant expense in most cities, as local landfills reach capacity and dump sites migrate farther and farther away. But beyond this pragmatic consideration, Miller is a believer in the use of on-site materials. "I've found that if you can leave things where they are," he says, "you're not spreading more junk around the planet."

Miller did have to punch through the slab to create planting pits for four weeping acacia trees, one queen palm, and two species of bamboo. To cut the pits, Miller brought in a subcontractor with a diamond-blade saw. Miller even used the rubble from the holes by piling it against the building to create raised, planted seating areas. First compacting the rubble by mechanically vibrating it, he then filled any voids in the mounds with gravel and sand, and finally added 18 inches of soil. The striking results can be seen in Figure 6.8.

ADOBE, SOIL CEMENT, AND OTHER EARTHEN MATERIALS

Mud, that most elemental of materials, has been the basis of building methods in dozens of cultures, not just the familiar Santa Fe style. Ironically, architects and historians are more likely to be aware of this than most landscape architects and contractors whose profession is building with earth. Although scarcely familiar in the contemporary landscape, earth-building techniques are intimately linked to landscape history.

A few landscape architects use earth structures today. Those who know earth-building appreciate its sculptural, geomorphic flexibility, plus the unparalleled intimacy that it creates, site-specific and understated. Albuquerque landscape architects Baker Morrow and Bill Hays have used adobe blocks for garden shelters, walls, seating, and even patio pavement. In New Mexico's dry climate, adobe will last nearly twenty years without even a coping. Russell Beatty, a California landscape architect, has used the related rammed-earth technique for garden walls. The firm of Cochran and Delaney used rammed-earth walls based on South African tradition in their African Healing Garden in San Francisco. Although earth-building is almost never taught in landscape courses, it is an energy-efficient, nontoxic, self-recycling material worth trying.

Technically, only sun-dried bricks of earth are "adobe," although the term is widely used for any kind of earth-building. Other kinds of earth-building include "puddled" or "coursed" adobe, a poured-in-place approach. Rammed earth is made by tamping a form full of relatively dry, cement-stabilized earth; "pressed" adobe is blocks made by a similar ramming method; and "stabilized" adobe is the old-fashioned sun-dried kind, with a little asphalt emulsion added to the mud. *Adobe quemado* is a porous, low-fired brick, made on-site, typical of Mexico and parts of Arizona.

Historically, the earliest Persian gardens were probably earth-walled; almost certainly, so were

Figure 6.6. This unpromising site for Monnens Addis Design (Berkeley CA) was reborn as a garden—without major demolition. PHOTO: Jeffrey Miller.

Figure 6.7. The Monnens Addis renovation in progress. PROJECT: Miller Co. PHOTO: Jeffrey Miller.

Figure 6.8. The finished Monnens Addis garden gives no hint of its former derelict status. PROJECT: Miller Co. PHOTO: Jeffrey Miller.

Figure 6.9. Adobe is one of the most flexible materials to work with, and it inspires site-specific construction that celebrates existing features like this tree. PHOTO: Kim Sorvig.

Figure 6.10. Earthen landscape construction graces hundreds of historic sites, including Japan's most refined gardens. PHOTO: Kim Sorvig.

the Hanging Gardens of Babylon. North Africa and the Arab world have a vibrant tradition of mud-building with arches, domes, and incised decoration. The Great Wall of China is cored with rammed earth, and many of Japan's most sophisticated gardens are walled in mud, often whitewashed. Even in rainy climates of Europe, each country has its earthen architecture: "cob" and "wattle-and-daub" in England, *leichtlehm* in Germany, or *pise* in France; some of these came to the colonies, where examples still survive.

Soil cement (ordinary soil mixed with a few percent Portland cement) was widely used for everything from paths to dams by the New Deal builders of National Parks and other public works; most are still in good shape today. Several companies offer binders or stabilizers that, mixed with soil, produce paving. These soil-based materials blend aesthetically with the existing site, and at least some stabilizers are plant-derived; however, the result is an impervious surface, with many of the same runoff problems as asphalt or concrete.

Many but not all types of soil can be used for earth-building. High organic content and shrink-swell soils should be avoided. The National Bureau of Standards even has a formula: 17 percent clay, 25 percent silt, 19 percent coarse (angular) sand, and 42 percent fine sand. More than 30 percent clay causes shrinkage cracks; added straw can help for cracking and adds slight tensile strength. About 10 percent water is the right consistency for forming adobes, while

rammed-earth is better at 7 percent or so. Stabilization uses either asphalt (about 4 percent) or cement (usually not more than 6 percent) to slow water absorption and surface erosion of the blocks. The compressive strength of adobes ranges from 300 to 600 psi; adobes are strong enough for arches, overhangs, and carving. Rammed earth is considerably stronger.

Construction with adobes is wonderfully flexible. Just about any item can be embedded (from tiles to mailboxes) or flowed around—existing trees are often simply given space by adobe builders. The material seems to evoke artistic improvisation.

To shelter a free-standing landscape wall, an Asian- or Spanish-style tile coping that projects beyond the wall face is best. Capping the wall with concrete actually accelerates erosion of the softer wall below. A waterproof foundation is also advisable. Traditionally, though, permanence in earth construction is achieved using the technique that makes Taos Pueblo the oldest continuously inhabited structure in North America: a new skin of mud plaster every couple of years. Retaining walls of adobe are possible, but should be carefully engineered; rebar reinforcement, a rigid foundation, and drainage behind the rear face are usually incorporated.

One interesting variation on adobe is the on-site firing technique invented by Iranian-born architect Nader Khalili. By placing simple oil-fired burners inside a domed adobe house (or, in the case of a landscape wall, under a ceramic-fiber blanket), the whole structure is fired and glazed, like huge tiles. Khalili has also experimented with a self-hardening sandbag technique for walls and other resource-efficient building methods.⊃

Adobe has the distinction of being both the most expensive building material (if made commercially and trucked to the site for custom housing) and the cheapest—if done by an owner-builder, by hand, on-site. In terms of energy costs, one study showed that for 1.5 gallons of gasoline, a dozen standard bricks can be fired and transported to a site—or ninety adobes can be made using an on-site machine. Each of the adobes has the same volume as a dozen common bricks, so adobe made this way is ninety times as energy-efficient. Hand-pressed adobes require so little fuel energy that they hardly register on the embodied energy scale.

Unstabilized earth-built structures also demonstrate a characteristic quite appropriate for sustainable thinking: As long as they are maintained and used, they are lasting and solid, but once abandoned, they slowly return to the earth.

Earth-building does pose one significant problem for sustainability: The sandy loam soils that work best for adobe may also be the best agricultural soils an arid region has to offer. Stabilizing adobes with cement or asphalt dramatically slows their return to the earth and takes the soil out of agricultural use for much longer, similar to fired bricks. This problem is less serious as long as the soil is taken from the footprint of the building, where it would be under an impervious roof anyhow. A large population building expansive adobe homes could threaten its own farmland, as appears to have happened in some areas of Egypt. Whether this should be blamed on adobe or on overpopulation is debatable. Ideally, only poor soils should be used for earth-building.

Find and Reuse Off-Site Salvage

When materials are not available on-site, nearby sources are worth finding. The use of municipal greenwaste and other soil products is one example (page 81). Any salvage that makes a dent in the endless stream of waste going to landfills is worthwhile. Another significant component of the waste stream—construction and demolition debris—comprises anywhere from one-quarter to one-third of municipal solid wastes. Metal, wood, glass, brick, and concrete are materials that are typically recycled; yet they are also materials that are commonly used in the landscape.[9] If they can be sourced locally, such materials can be reconfigured in artful ways in the landscape *without* putting them through a resource-intensive industrial recycling process.

STONE

Reused stone may be particularly applicable for public projects because public works departments often stockpile granite curbing and other stone elements that can be reconfigured to striking effect in the landscape. Salvaged stone was used evocatively at Parque da Cidade in Oporto, Portugal, described on page 156, for its water-harvesting design. Sidonio Pardal, the park landscape architect, reused salvaged granite obtained from public works departments to construct retaining walls and other structures, including faux ruins. One such ruin overlooks the park's lake, resembling the remains of some fabulous palace; in it are the irrigation controls for the park. Many other structures, in a variety of styles, could be constructed with salvaged curbs and other stone elements. Not all landscape designers approve of "fake" features, although reused materials seem to lend themselves to fantasy. The presence of salvaged, durable stone can lend a remarkable sense of history and place to new landscape work.

Figure 6.11. A "recycled folly" in Parque da Cidade, made of stone salvaged around the city of Oporto, Portugal. Many salvaged materials are becoming expensive because of demand for their weathered appearance. PROJECT: Sidonio Pardal. PHOTO: Lynn Miller.

TIMBER

The challenge in using any salvaged materials, of course, is not simply to make do with second-hand materials but to create visually powerful design elements and compelling places. Landscape architect Marjorie Pitz accomplished this when she constructed The Sacred Circle, a temporary (1998) AIDS memorial, in Loring Park, Minneapolis. Her budget was only $2,500. "My project involved significant structure, which made the jury wonder if it would be possible to pull it off with such a limited budget," notes Pitz. "The use of salvaged materials made it feasible."

The Sacred Circle consists of a circle of twelve "tree trunks" made of salvaged utility poles that were donated by the local utility after removal from another Pitz project site. Pitz's concept was to wrap the poles with saplings to symbolize AIDS victims cut down in their prime, but she was reluctant to cut trees that were of value to anyone. Fortunately, she was able to locate, through her network of colleagues, a farm outside Minneapolis on which a stand of willows was being removed to restore the native prairie. The property owner had lost a cousin to AIDS and was happy to see the willow saplings salvaged and reused. Finding the poles and saplings required a certain amount of scouting, compared to the more usual route of obtaining materials through a salvage dealer. Pitz's initiatives suggest ways in which landscape professionals might use salvaged materials in new and imaginative ways.

CRUSHED GLASS

Crushed glass, or cullet, is one of the most versatile of all recycled materials in the landscape. Because of its functional resemblance to sand, glass can replace sand in many applications, and its inherent beauty suits it to many decorative purposes. Cullet's many uses may be classified into three broad areas: as a replacement for sand in concrete, asphalt, and other paving; as a fill material to replace aggregate; and as an ingredient in tiles and similar products. (These require remanufacturing and are discussed on page 209). It should be noted that the glass for all landscape uses is tumbled to smooth away sharp edges.

Glass has been used successfully in the construction of pedestrian and bike paths, parking areas, and even roads. In "glassphalt," aggregates such as rock and sand are replaced by crushed glass. Successful test roads have used up to 10 percent glass content without any instability or cracking. Cullet cannot be used without other aggregates; glass is not as mechanically sound as crushed rock.[10] New York City, through a joint venture between its departments of sanitation and transportation, has made a commitment to using glassphalt in all its repaving projects.

A highly appropriate use of glassphalt is for bike/pedestrian paths. Such a path leads to the top of the artificial hill at Danehy Park in Cambridge MA, built atop a former landfill. (See page 68 for description.) The Cambridge Department of Sanitation worked with an environmental artist, Merle Ukeles, exploring artful applications of glassphalt.[11] The project combined community involvement, recycled materials, and artistic intent. Ukeles turned the hill path into an artwork that recalls sacred Indian mounds. The 22 tons of glass required for the project were mostly collected by schoolchildren and community groups. A stained-glass manufacturer in Washington State also donated ten tons of scrap stained glass, normally considered unrecyclable, and a New York manufacturer of round cosmetic mirrors donated scrap. Because the state of Massachusetts had never used glassphalt, it requested that the material be tested at New York City's glassphalt plant—unfamiliar materials often require testing to ensure they meet engineering standards, especially for public projects.[12]

One caveat in specifying glass for paving is a small potential for contamination—not from the glass itself but from lead in the rings on wine bottles, where these have not been properly extracted from the cullet. Producers are required to test periodically for contamination; in properly handled cullet, lead should not be a problem. Test projects using glass aggregate in King County WA have not detected any appreciable leaching.[13]

Recycled cullet in larger sizes can also be used as a construction aggregate or fill material. For use in drainage trenches, the Glass Aggregate Corporation makes an underdrain product, called Redpak, from cullet. It consists of cylindrical geotextile sacks filled with coarse recycled glass and placed end to end in the trench, which is then backfilled as usual. (The concept is similar to the French drain discussed in Principle 4 or the reservoirs used under porous paving, noted in Principle 5.) Geotextile sacks filled with crushed glass are also used for erosion control during landscape construction.

Using glass in trenches and sacks nullifies its inherent beauty, of course. Glass aggregate is an attractive replacement for gravel in walkways and garden borders, as was demonstrated at the Jardin Encore exposition at the 1994 Northwest Flower and Garden Show in Seattle. (See Figure 6.18.) Intriguing and partly transparent, cullet is available in a range of green, amber, and clear; more exotic blues and reds are sometimes available. The King County (WA) Commission for Marketing Recyclable Materials recommends that, for walkway applications, the glass be screened between one-quarter and one-sixteenth inch, which gives it a consistency somewhat like coarse sand.

TIRES

Worn-out rubber tires are a familiar decorative element in the vernacular landscape: Who has not seen old tires used as planters or to define a driveway in front of rural homes? Increasingly, however, scrap tires—whole, shredded, or reconstituted into entirely new products—are being put to functional uses in the landscape, such as stream-bank and slope stabilization; for constructing check-dams; as a surfacing material; for marine construction; and as an ingredient in rubberized asphalt. Increasing such uses may help deflate the monstrous U.S. national glut of billions of scrap tires, which increases by 280 million each year.[14]

Scrap tires, laid flat and buried into a slope, can created low garden terraces as shown in Figure 6.14. So long as they are not laid too high, they can be built without reinforcement.

A more widespread use of rubber tires has been made in Oklahoma. There, the state Department of Environmental Quality, concerned about stream-bank erosion and about more than 3 million waste tires stored in 200 illegal dump sites, is promoting a single solution that helps solve both problems: armoring stream banks with tires. This approach is not only a constructive reuse of waste products, but it is also lower in cost and simpler to build than riprap or concrete bank stabilization. Tires for such projects are typically obtained from local gas stations, tire dealers, and junkyards—thus minimizing transport impacts.

Figure 6.12. Glassphalt pathway at Danehy Park glitters with colored glass aggregate. Colored asphalt or concrete plus glass offers further possibilities. PROJECT: Merle Ukele. PHOTO: CDM/John Kissida.

Figure 6.13. At the Northwest Flower and Garden Show, Jardin Encore is primarily made of recycled materials, including glass, wood, and iron. A new exhibit each year promotes recycling in the landscape. PROJECT: King County Commission for Marketing Recycled Materials. PHOTO: David McDonald.

Figure 6.14. Tires and broken concrete achieve unexpected elegance as terraces at the Center for Regenerative Studies. PROJECT and PHOTO: John Lyle.

Bank construction is quite straightforward. Rows of tires are placed along the waterline lying flat, and tires that ascend the bank are placed upright. Cables are run through each row, tying the tires together, and are anchored into the ground using deadmen (buried logs) placed at 50-foot intervals and at least 50 feet from the edge of the bank. Little or no streambank grading is required. After installation, silt carried by the stream settles inside the tires, further anchoring them. Over time, most of the tires on the riverbank are buried under tons of silt, forming a new and more stable bank.

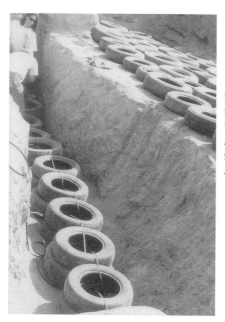

Figure 6.15. Check-dams reuse waste tires to stabilize an arroyo in Arizona. Tires in trench form a footing for dam at upper level. PROJECT and PHOTO: Stuart Hoenig and Joshua Minyard.

Figure 6.16. Strapped in place, tires form a strong flexible structure that traps sediment and eventually supports plants. Some systems incorporate live-staking. PROJECT and PHOTO: Stuart Hoenig and Joshua Minyard.

Planted trees anchor the soil to the "new" stream bank with their roots. Native black locust is the preferred species for these Oklahoma projects because it has a fast-growing fibrous root system. More than 40,000 trees have been planted in such projects statewide. At least eighteen projects have been built in Oklahoma, helping to protect roads, bridges, oil pipelines, and other infrastructure elements threatened by collapsing stream banks. Overall, about 500,000 waste tires have been used in these projects.[15]

Tire-bank projects vary from 300 feet to 4,750 feet in length and employ from two to ten rows of tires. (The number of tires depends on bank height and whether car or truck tires are used.) Cost is low, typically only $20 to $30 per linear foot of bank. For one demonstration project along Deer Creek near Weatherford OK, 1,800 feet of stream bank were stabilized with ten rows of tires at a cost of $70,000—higher than the typical per-foot cost but far lower than the estimated $550,000 for regrading and stabilizing the streambank with riprap. Installation requires little skilled labor or costly machinery. In Oklahoma, placement of the tires is typically done at no cost by work-release prison inmates. Where inmate labor is not available, such projects could conceivably be installed by community or environmental-group volunteers.

In Pima County AZ, Stuart Hoenig, a professor of agricultural and biosystems engineering at the University of Arizona, along with engineer Joshua Minyard, directed the construction of a check-dam made of 2,000 passenger-car tires. Five layers of tires were placed on their sides, held together by plastic bands, reinforced by quarry rock placed between each layer, and anchored to the side walls of the arroyo like a conventional concrete structure. The design was funded by the state and approved by the Army Corps of Engineers and the Arizona Department of Water Quality—an interesting example of the institutional acceptance of an "alternative" technology. Construction costs, including labor from the county probation service, totaled only $6,000. The dam was installed in 1997; a year later, vegetation had begun to grow in the arroyo for the first time in years, and a road upstream of the dam no longer washed out as it had previously.[16]

Tires are available baled, used much like straw bales for bulk construction. Sliced sideways like bagels, they have been laid under lawns to retain water and cut irrigation needs⊃ Tires can also be reused as flotation materials for docks, marinas, and wetland boardwalks. Topper Industries of Battle Ground WA uses discarded tires this way and finds them cheaper than other support or flotation materials. According to Topper, a floating walkway system is ideal in sensitive wetlands, because nothing leaches from tires; they are biologically inert.[17]

Other interesting products made from scrap tires are beginning to turn up on the landscape market. In New South Wales, Australia, Tyredrain Australia has patented a system for making drainage channels from half-sections of recycled tires. Among other advantages, the tire drains are much cheaper than concrete channels. Tyredrain is seeking to license the idea in other countries. In Ft. Dodge IA, Dodger Enterprises is promoting the use of whole, cut-up, and shredded tires for a variety of landscape uses. One-inch tire chips can be spread on bare soil to control wind erosion and to hold the moisture and heat needed for seed germination. Dodger also offers cutout tire sidewalls for use as rings to protect bare slopes. On slopes of 3:1 or less, the rings are simply laid down next to one another. On steeper slopes, the rings can be tied together to form a blanket. The grass grows through and between them.[18]

None of these tire structures are particularly beautiful, at least until completely overgrown. However, they are a prime example of ways in which one environmental problem can be turned to solve another. This mimics natural systems in a very fundamental way—natural systems depend on a high rate of reuse, leaving very little as "waste" in the long term.

Specify Remanufactured Materials

Recycled materials specifically for the landscape are widely available today. What distinguishes them from salvaged products is the much higher degree of manufacturing energy to recycle the material, rather than reuse it. A good introduction to the breadth of recycled landscape materials is *The Resource Guide to Sustainable Landscapes* by Wesley Groesbeck and Jan Streifel.⊃

The latest (1996) edition of this work is a 425-page catalog of products related to landscape work. More than 2,000 product listings are included, organized by CSI sections. Most, though not all, include at least some recycled

content. The book's purpose is to list "sustainable products and materials that are energy-efficient, ecologically safe, and support healthy landscapes and gardens." Suppliers, more than 1,300 of them, are listed from the English-speaking world, plus Germany and Mexico.

A quick look at the table of contents tells a great deal about the desire for sustainable materials. Among those items explicitly listed as recycled are glass-brick pavers; asphalt, rubber, and rubber-asphalt pavers and patching materials; lumber; used brick; reclaimed stone; plastic lumber; tile; resilient flooring; exterior paint and lacquer thinner; and tire structures. More than fifty exchanges and stores carrying used building materials, for profit or nonprofit, are also listed. Plastic lumber lists twenty-five manufacturers and another fifty suppliers. By comparison, in 1992 when Sorvig wrote an early landscape-related article concerning plastic lumber,[19] there were fewer than a half dozen brands, and few were available through ordinary distributors.

The *Resource Guide* offers clear proof that recycled or environmentally friendly materials are available today for almost any landscape purpose. Although the *Guide*'s criteria for what makes a product sustainable are not spelled out, no one reading this useful volume could argue that products for sustainable landscapes are merely a futurist's dream.

PLASTIC LUMBER

Plastic lumber—a simulated wood product constituted of recycled milk jugs and other everyday items—has become a familiar feature of the landscape, most commonly as plastic benches and picnic tables. To some people, plastic lumber lacks the beauty of real wood, but it has some distinct advantages.

- From an environmental point of view, a prime advantage of plastic lumber is that it is biologically inert—it does not give off toxins into the air or soil, in contrast to wood treated for outdoor use, which contains poisons. This inertness recommends it for use in such sensitive landscapes as wetlands. Boardwalks and overlooks are examples of wetland uses in which recycled plastic may be especially appropriate, and environmental permitting agencies are increasingly favoring such uses.

- The fact that plastic can last virtually forever has been a major environmental problem. Plastic lumber turns this into an advantage. It does not rot, splinter, or peel and is not subject to damage from insects. Plastic lumber never needs replacing or painting, will not bow or warp with age, and requires minimal maintenance—advantages that offset its initial cost, which is higher than that of lumber. Provided that it is kept from high heat and stabilized for UV (ultraviolet light degrades most plastics outdoors), it is very durable.

- Finally, the use of plastic lumber in the landscape provides a new, productive use for some of the immense quantities of throwaway plastic that are inundating landfills and saves trees from being cut for lumber.

Despite plastic lumber's advantages, its use was hampered for years by lack of reliable data on its strength, shear properties, and other performance criteria. That changed in 1997 when the American Society for Testing and Materials (ASTM) approved a number of testing methods to ensure uniform standards for plastic lumber.[20]

One reason standards are important is the variety of types of plastic lumber currently available. One researcher identifies three grades:

1. *Purified plastic lumber* (such as Durawood and Duratech) uses a single postconsumer plastic such as high-density polyethylene (HPDE). Other factors being equal, the use of a single plastic provides a more consistent quality. See Table 6.1 on page 220 for general types of plastic such as HDPE and their applications for landscape products.

2. *Commingled plastic lumber* (such as Hammer's Envirowood and Earth Care products) are made with two or more plastics and are generally cheaper, but the different plastics may cause variability in such physical properties as resistance to chemicals and stresses.

3. *Composites* (such as Lifecycle, Trimax, and Timbrex) are manufactured by mixing sawdust or other fibers to the plastic. The resulting composites are stiffer than pure plastic lumber, with rougher textures. In some uses, composites may absorb moisture or suffer from insect damage.[21]

Plastic lumber does have some disadvantages. The first is cost, which, on average, is two to three times as high as pine lumber. (The lower cost of plastic lumber over the *life* of the product may more than offset this, but the high initial cost may hamper bidding and frighten off clients concerned about the bottom line. For help in presenting life-cycle costs convincingly, see Table 7.18.) Second, plastic lumber is considerably heavier than wood; this may limit its use in applications like decking, where weight is a consideration. Third, plastic lumber contracts and expands to a much greater degree than wood and may deform at high temperatures. Finally, plastic lumber is much more flexible than wood. In applications like boardwalks, plastic boards must be spaced closer together than wood to minimize sagging. Its use as beams and other structural elements is questionable.

It has been said that plastic lumber is not usable for posts or other structural supports for this same reason. However, for decks overlooking the Upper Charles River outside of Boston, landscape architects Carol R. Johnson & Associates (CRJA) specified supporting piers of

Figure 6.17. Recycled plastic lumber piers support decks along the Upper Charles River near Boston. Metal "pinned foundations" cause almost no site disruption and can be removed or adjusted easily. PROJECT and PHOTO: Carol R. Johnson Associates.

recycled plastic lumber. CRJA wanted a material that would not leach chemicals into wetlands along the river, as would treated wooden piers. Bruce Leish of CRJA notes that the designers did not use plastic lumber for beams or joists for fear it would flex too much, but that the plastic piers have caused no problems.

Working with plastic lumber is generally similar to working with wood: it can be sawed, drilled, and fastened with staples or nails. However, expansion can loosen screwed or nailed joints, so nuts and bolts (or similar mechanical fasteners) are recommended. Unlike wood, most plastic lumber cannot be glued.

Plastic lumber is the most common but not the only use of recycled plastic in the landscape. Many grassed paving systems (see page 186) are made of recycled plastic. One example of such a system is Grasspave from Invisible Structures in Aurora CO, whose entire line of landscape products is recycled plastic; many other landscape product manufacturers use at least some recycled plastic.

RECYCLED GLASS TILE

In addition to the minimally processed cullet, glass can be reprocessed as an ingredient in tiles and pavers. Stoneware Tile Company (Richmond IN) manufactures colorful pavers with a minimum glass content of 70 percent. New Design (Seattle WA) uses fewer colors to make glass tiles with a rugged, weathered look. Syndesis (Los Angeles CA) manufactures tile from glass in combination with other waste products such as sawdust and metal shavings. These decorative products are becoming available at specialty stores.

Garden ornaments may also be crafted from recycled glass. These include decorative garden lanterns, manufactured by New Design. Glass block is available from recycled glass in standard shapes and sizes. Finally, limited-production art glass ornaments are hand-blown from recycled material in some small shops. To the artist's hand and eye, glass—new or recycled—remains an inspiration.

CRUMB RUBBER

Discarded tires can be used whole or with minimal processing, as described earlier. Recycled rubber products entail more intensive processing. For most of these, discarded rubber products are

Figure 6.18. Glass fish "swim" in elegant recycled tile, part of the annual recycled garden exhibit staged by King County WA. PROJECT: King County Commission for Marketing Recycled Materials. PHOTO: David McDonald.

ground into "crumb" rubber, something like coarse sand in texture, then remanufactured.

Crumb rubber has found a number of landscape uses, primarily for surfacing or paving. Rubberized asphalt mixes crumb rubber with asphalt; although more expensive than conventional asphalt, it is durable, elastic, and age resistant, reducing road maintenance costs. For playgrounds and athletic fields, several companies now process crumb rubber into resilient surfaces for athletic, safety, and playground use—either reconstituted into mats or as a loose "mulch." Resilient surfaces greatly reduce the risk of injury from falls in high-risk play areas but are fairly expensive.

Loose crumb rubber is also proving its worth as a trail-surfacing material. Polk City FL ground up 10,000 scrap tires to surface the 49-mile Withlahoochee State Trail—the first time crumb rubber has been used for a trail, according to the Rails-to-Trails Conservancy. In Georgia, a sloping 100-yard trail at Tallulah Gorge State Park was paved with ground-up tires in 1996. The manufacturer, Phoenix Recycled Products, donated the material to see how it would withstand heavy usage. Apparently the trail is resisting erosion and is wheelchair accessible. Georgia's Spalding County has ground scrap tires for a pedestrian trail at Airport Road Park; elderly park users in particular like the trail because it is smooth and easy on their feet. The county received a $100,000 waste reduction grant from the state for the experimental project.[22] Similar funding opportunities may be available in other states.

Other Recycled Materials

Plastics, glass, and rubber are certainly the most common and visible recycled materials in landscape use today. Some other products that are remanufactured are not as easily recognized but are also present. Steel and aluminum are regularly recycled in large quantities; although we have not discovered any landscape-specific products of these materials, it is certain that much of the metal used outdoors contains recycled elements. Metals are particularly good for recycling in at least one sense: the recycled material is a much closer equivalent to the virgin metal than is the case with many plastics, for instance.

Concrete is crushed and recycled as aggregate and for other uses, keeping this bulky and slow-to-degrade material out of landfills. Asphalt is also recycled; it is unique in that the recycling machinery comes to the asphalt. These large machines mill the surface off an existing road, reheat and mix the asphalt, and lay it down as new paving, virtually on the same spot. It is unclear how energy-efficient this process is, but it clearly makes good use of another material that not long ago was discarded after a short service life.

Recycle at the Job Site

Every construction job generates scrap material. Even when using salvaged and recycled products, cutting, fitting, and finishing leave a variety of unused items: cutoff boards, whole overestimated items, sawdust, surplus concrete and mortar. Construction machinery produces used blades and other parts, and sometimes used oils. Construction workers drink from disposable aluminum cans and Styrofoam cups and buy lunch-wagon meals in various wrappings.

Setting up the job site so that wastes can be sorted is a simple but effective first step for recycling construction materials. On small residential jobs, this may take little more than the kind of bins homeowners use for recycling—just a couple more of them for different materials. For large jobs, one or more dumpsters, possibly with internal partitions, may be required. Be sure to locate these in the staging area at a place where

they can be hauled out without site damage at the end of the project.

Properly sorted construction leftovers can be taken to municipal recycling centers in some regions, but others prohibit this. Some commercial recyclers will buy certain types of construction salvage. A growing number of communities have special construction recycling programs. Many of these include a site set aside for exchanging construction salvage; those who have usable excess materials leave them, and those who can use materials take them. An alternative to exchange at a physical site is a newspaper or Website listing system; those who have materials list them, and others list what materials they need. Civic-minded newspapers, sometimes in cooperation with local government, businesses, or social service organizations, donate space for these listings, so that the service is free.

Starting a construction recycling program takes time and has up-front expenses. One approach to funding such a program is analyzing the costs avoided by keeping construction materials out of landfills. Even a relatively small exchange program can keep a ton or more a week out of the local dump. Encouraging reuse and avoiding waste are goals appropriate to public–private partnerships. Contractors benefit by reducing their landfill fees; the community benefits by not paying for constant expansion of landfill space.

Evaluate Environmental Costs When Choosing Suppliers

When several sources for similar materials are available, sustainable materials choices can be confusing. Concise rules are still evolving, and making responsible choices is a big assignment. Meanwhile, we can suggest evaluating the following factors:

- *The distance between supplier and end-user,* as well as the number of intermediate deliveries involved. Does your wood come from California or Brazil? Is it sawed where it is felled, or at your supplier, or is it transported to Michigan or Michoacán for processing?

- *The mode of transport.* To continue the former example, are the logs floated to the sawmill or trucked (or are they, as some firms are reputed to do, flown whole from the forest to Japan)? If there are several stages in the supply chain, evaluate each. The difference between diesel trucks and gasoline ones, as well as between relatively fuel-efficient ships and less-efficient air or land modes, can be significant. It is not always easy to find out which mode of transport a supplier uses, but the information is worth seeking.

- *The CO_2 production involved in the material or product.* One rule of thumb is that for every billion Btu of energy consumed, an eighth of a pound of the greenhouse gas is released. This applies best to electrical power. Current research (including comprehensive work by Pliny Fisk under an EPA grant) is on the verge of a quantum leap in the availability and accuracy of this data for specific materials.⊃

- *The Embodied Energy of the product* (a concept discussed in more detail in Principle 7). Rough energy-cost numbers are shown for basic materials. Like the CO2 figures, what is currently available is a limited but useful rough approximation, likely to be updated and improved soon by ongoing research.

- *The toxicity of materials over their life cycle.* In most cases this cannot be done quantitatively, but should at least be considered in a reasoned way, based on such information as is found in Appendix A of this book.

- *The manufacturer or source.* Many manufacturers and suppliers are just as green as you are; at the other extreme, many still resist all environmental responsibility. Ask about factory safeguards and mitigation and about energy awareness. Favor those suppliers who will at least make an honest attempt to discuss these issues and who are taking appropriate steps to reduce the environmental impacts of their business.

Use Sustainably Harvested Renewables

Wood is America's renewable resource, the slogan reads. Clearly, wood is the only major construction material that is grown rather than mined. Using renewables, like recycling, is a very popular concept and, in general, worthy of sup-

port. But like recycling, even renewability has limits that must be respected.

The primary limit is the rate or speed of renewal. *Given time*, forests can and do renew themselves. Historically, the entire East Coast of the United States was logged by colonists, farmed, and then abandoned as small family farms became uneconomical. The forests of today are evidence of renewability—requiring a hundred years or so to reach their current size. For forests as well as people, time is the great healer.

If the demand for wood is too great and too impatient, the rate of harvesting outstrips the rate of regrowth. Quick harvesting limits the size of wood a forest can produce: where old-growth forests once yielded huge beams, much of today's forestry hurries to harvest 2 × 12 at best. At speedy rates of harvesting, or where destructive methods of harvesting are used, the health of the forest declines. Eventually there comes a point of no return, meaning that at least in that location, the living ability of renewal is lost. Push a renewable resource too far, and it faces at least local extinction.

In an unlogged forest, dead timber is recycled into the soil by insects, fungi, microbes, and periodic fires—a complex form of natural composting. How much new growth the forest can produce depends in part on how much of this compost is available. Removing timber removes this soil-renewing material; too much removal without some replacement depletes forest soil, just as it does in agriculture or horticulture. Perhaps the most striking example is the tropical rain forest; so much of the organic material is embodied in the living trees, and so little is stored in the soil, that carting away the timber often leaves a bricklike, near-sterile soil called laterite. If the forest is to renew itself on such soil, it would be over millennia, if at all.

For these reasons, the fact that wood is renewable does not give license for unlimited use—contrary to marketing that has often portrayed it as infinitely renewable. Renewability fits into the reduce/reuse/recycle equation as a form of recycling. As long as reduced use and salvage are the first-choice strategies, using renewables is a valuable concept.

Three major ways of managing renewable resources for long-term sustainability are emerging in today's market. These are salvaged wood, sustainable harvesting certification, and substituting waste for wood.

Salvage Wood Where Possible

Although it is still common to see mangled framing lumber on its way to landfill with other bulldozed waste, salvaging of wood during demolition is becoming more common. Wood from the 1940s or before is particularly valued; harvested from healthier, older trees, it is often denser and stronger than any new lumber sold today. Much of the wood salvage business today is aimed at high-end custom homes, marketed as antique wood at prices beyond reach for most landscape use.

Salvage for landscape use is complicated by several factors. Outdoor timbers suffer from rot, termites, and other insects; posts may be hard to extract from concrete footings. However, naturally decay-resistant landscape woods (tropical hardwoods and redwood, in particular) should be considered for salvage where at all feasible, because these species are threatened by past overuse. Similarly, preservative-treated lumber is likely to be reuseable with care and should be salvaged because there is no environmentally responsible way to dispose of it (see page 212).

Specify Sustainably Harvested and Processed Wood

As this book undergoes final editing, a major step toward sustainably harvested wood has been announced. The world's largest retailer of lumber, Home Depot, has decided the time is right to phase out all wood products from old-growth forests. By 2002, all wood sold through Home Depot's nearly 900 stores in the United States, Canada, Puerto Rico, and Chile will be from sources certified as sustainably managed. Although Home Depot is a retailer, and sells only about 10 percent of the world's total lumber, environmental groups such as the Rainforest Action Network, as well as Home Depot's own staff, predict that the move will compel the rest of the market, including contractor sales, to follow. Home Depot does not expect its prices or availability to be directly affected by the requirement for certification.[23] Some reputable sources are concerned that this program's standards for certification will be lax, undermining more rigorous certification programs, but at least on the surface mainstream acceptance of the need for certification is a positive step.

A number of organizations certify sustainable lumber. Wood is tracked from the forest or plantation through manufacturing and distribution. Certification takes into account the basic issues of harvest rate and forest health discussed earlier, as well as whether previously untouched forests are cut, or whether clear-cutting is used. Carefully managed methods like "shelter-wood cutting," which selectively takes trees to maintain health, size, and diversity of the whole forest, are usually required for certification. The use of waste-reducing sawmill tools, such as thinner blades and more efficient chippers, is often a consideration; the U.S. Forest Service estimates that such techniques can reduce wood waste by 33 percent.[24]

Since certification is a relatively new process, and because the market is clearly changing rapidly, specifiers will need to become familiar with the different certification groups and their criteria. Like the various seal-of-approval systems that have emerged for consumer goods and health foods since the 1970s, wood certification is likely to produce both reputable and superficial claims of sustainability. For this very valuable system to work, the efforts of reputable certifying groups as well as informed specifiers will be essential.

Substitute Straw and Other Wastes for Wood

A third emerging approach is that of substituting various wastes, such as straw, paper, and waste wood, for new lumber. This can take a number of forms: Direct use of straw bales as a construction material is one; plastic lumber is another, especially the composite forms that incorporate wood waste. Wallboard manufactured from straw is another example, though primarily for interior use.

U.S. production of lumber, including plywood, was about 65 million tons in 1993. That same year, almost 155 million tons of waste from straw, paper, wood, and woody materials like nutshells were available; plastic waste added another 15 million tons. Wheat and rice straw alone equaled the total tonnage of lumber produced.[25]

Clearly, if all these wastes could substitute for wood, lumber production could cease for nearly three years without being missed. Just as clearly, these substitutes cannot replace *all* uses of lumber. Besides, these wastes are also in demand for ethanol production, compost, and many other environmentally important products. However, so-called waste materials offer significant opportunities for slowing the use of timber and protecting the renewability of forests.

One example of a thoughtful waste-for-timber substitution is the way in which the AERT company (Junction TX) manages resources for plastic lumber production. AERT's product is a composite of recycled PET plastic (milk jugs and other #2 sources) with fibers from juniper. The fibers are waste after scented juniper oil is pressed from the scrubby wood. AERT is also managing the lands from which the juniper is harvested so that more valuable hardwood species will eventually reforest the areas.[26]

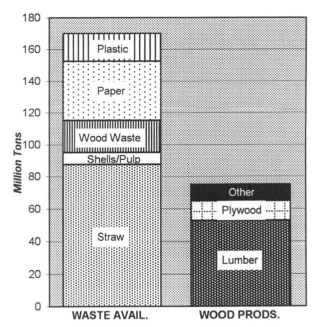

Figure 6.19. Wood products and possible substitutes, annual tonnage (based on Fisk).

Avoid Toxic and Nonrenewable Materials

Reducing material use avoids environmental costs. Reusing and recycling are ways to get more material benefit at less environmental cost. In addition, some materials must be handled correctly, and others used sparingly if at all, to avoid costly hazards to human health and to the environment.

An important addition to Nelischer's guidelines, quoted at the beginning of this chapter, is careful consideration of whether a material is hazardous, and if so under what circumstances. Toxic materials can threaten construction workers on the job, as well as anyone using the finished landscape. These materials also pose hazards to the larger environment in ways that are not always visible on-site. In many instances, the contractor or the designer can act directly to eliminate or reduce toxic exposure. In other cases, the combined influence of environmental professionals and their industries can affect the larger issues surrounding pollutants and hazardous material use.

The ways in which toxic and hazardous materials affect landscape construction differ from effects in buildings. Radon is a good example of the difference. It is an indoor hazard but a normal outdoor condition.[27] If trapped in unventilated buildings (or mines, where radon was first noticed), concentration makes radon and other "natural" substances hazardous. Such natural exposure is sometimes used to dismiss concerns about hazardous materials ("Even too much water will kill you . . ."), a posture that seldom promotes rational debate, let alone sustainability. It is critically important to know *at what point* a substance becomes toxic, and if this point is unknown, to err on the side of caution.

Responsible professionals must analyze how and where a material will be used, as well as how it is produced, transported, disposed of, or recycled. A few materials are so hazardous that their use in landscape construction is truly unsustainable. More frequently, toxicity is one important consideration among many in comparing the life cycles of materials.

Anticipate Hazards from Prior Land Uses

Sites that have never been developed for modern use seldom hold existing hazardous materials. In rare cases, site geology may produce hazards. An example is serpentine, a rock that is toxic to many plants and to humans, and that might interfere with some land uses. At Potrero Heights, a housing development on a steep hillside in San Francisco, prominent soil-filled retaining walls are in part a response to serpentine underlying the site. The initial grading plan called for excavating terraces out of bedrock; this was abandoned when the rock was found to be serpentine, which releases toxins when excavated. Such hazards, however, are uncommon.

On brownfields and other sites with a history of previous use, toxic materials may be present before landscape construction ever begins. Knowing which materials are potentially hazardous, and recognizing them in the field, require a great deal of experience. The following sections can help with the basic knowledge, but clearly not with real-world identification. If contamination is suspected, it may be best to hire a consultant, since there are few self-help methods of learning what toxic materials look like in the field.⊃

During demolition or remodeling work, existing structures may harbor hazardous materials. These can include not only landscape-specific materials, but also lead paint or asbestos from old buildings, or PCBs from abandoned utility transformers. Lead used in flashing can be found in old roofing waste, as well as in antique garden-wall copings. Because building demolition is a messy job, interior materials may well become part of the landscape. In this way, some materials that play no part in normal landscape construction can be site hazards.

If there has been *dumping* on the site, an even greater range of hazards requires alertness and planning. Illegal dumping is common in some areas and often affects remote sites with no history of previous use—sites that may look pristine at first glance. Urban sites are often illegally used as dumps, too. It is very difficult to predict what might be in these illegal dumps. In many cases it

Figure 6.21. Industrial dumping, much of it illegal, leaves highly toxic and unknown chemicals as "somebody else's problem." Landscape professionals should seek assistance with such materials. PHOTO: National Resource Conservation Service.

is merely household trash (which can still contain many toxics) that some ignoramus refused to take to a landfill. However, some illegal dumping is deliberate criminal disposal of industrial or medical hazardous waste, dumped to avoid regulation, and could be truly deadly. In addition, the owners of farms and small businesses, ignorant of the hazards, have often disposed of wastes on-site. Public awareness has decreased this kind of dumping, but it still goes on. Pesticides, oils, solvents, and batteries may have been buried in such private dumps, sometimes in quantity. Old vehicles dumped or abandoned on-site can leak many toxic materials. Neither illegal nor small-user dump sites are usually documented, unlike larger and more industrial sites.

If the site has ever been used industrially, be on the lookout for toxic materials. Soil and water can be contaminated by pollutants settling out of the air around a factory, by runoff that leaches poisons from stockpiled materials, or by tanks leaking, as well as by deliberate on-site disposal. Industrial pollution frequently spreads to neighboring sites and, in the case of air or water pollutants, can move considerable distances. Fortunately, public records usually indicate types of past land use at an industrial site. This information can be used to predict what types of hazards may be likely.

The following industrial operations are common sources of heavy metals, which are

Figure 6.20. Dumping of consumer products disfigures many otherwise healthy landscapes and may pose toxicity hazards for workers. PHOTO: National Resource Conservation Service.

some of the more dangerous contaminants in soil:

- electroplating (cadmium, chromium, nickel)
- battery production or use (cadmium, lead, nickel, zinc)
- paints and painting (cadmium, chromium)
- mining (arsenic, copper, nickel)
- metal production and products (chromium, copper, lead, mercury, zinc in brass and for galvanization)
- pesticides and preservatives (arsenic, copper, mercury)
- rubber production (zinc)
- petroleum and coal (arsenic)
- plastics (cadmium)
- fire brick (chromium)
- fly ash (copper)
- fertilizers (copper)

A number of catalysts used in manufacturing may leave traces of mercury. Nickel and lead traces can be carried and deposited by rain or air, far from their industrial sources.[28] Besides heavy metals, pollutants such as organochlorides, volatile organic compounds (VOCs), and many others may be the residue of a wide variety of industrial and household products.

While the actual remediation of highly hazardous sites is a task for specialists (see page 95), landscape architects and contractors need to know what "red flags" to watch for. Removing contaminants can add thousands of dollars to a project, and subjects workers to hazards. *Failure* to remove such pollutants can harm workers and end users, leaving owner, designer, and builder open to lawsuits. It is far cheaper and smarter to investigate the possibility of existing hazards before work begins:

- Check available records, such as land title, historic zoning maps, and other legal documents, for clues to land use over the past century. Watch for industrial uses as well as agricultural ones. Old orchards, for example, often harbor arsenic or cyanide, which was used for pest control; fields of some crops would have been sprayed with DDT prior to the U.S. ban in 1973 (even later against certain much-feared insects like tussock moth).

- Carefully inspect the site for signs of dumping. On previously undeveloped sites, refuse is usually above ground. If previous use seems likely to have generated hazardous wastes, look for signs of ground disturbance or peculiar vegetation patterns. Try to imagine where a convenient and accessible dump site would have been, and how (or whether) people might have tried to hide it.

- A wide range of field-testing kits that can give early warning of hazards is available. For example, Labware Safety Supply⊃ lists several kits that can detect lead, PCBs, or chlorine in soils; other kits can reveal an even wider range of toxics in liquid form. One test (in a kit of six to ten) costs about $5, a small price if it avoids a serious problem. The kits are advertised as requiring no special training. In five to ten minutes, they indicate—usually by an unmistakable color change—whether hazards are above or below a safety standard. While no substitute for specialist analysis, these types of tests can give a quick reading of potential hazards.

- If anything indicates serious contamination, get advice from specialists in hazardous waste mitigation. Trying to remove the wastes yourself can subject you and your client to red tape and costs at the least, and prosecution at the worst.

- If you work in areas where many contaminated sites are found, investigate whether you or your client can be insured against unforeseen costs and liabilities related to cleanup.

Lest anyone think that these "engineering" matters are too complex for landscape architects, consider the Boston firm whose principals are Nina Brown, Clarissa Rowe, and Alison Richardson. They have developed, almost accidentally, a specialty in designs for contaminated sites. In urban areas, it is hardly necessary to seek out such projects; many sites, and especially those left to the public as open space, are blessed with fruits of industry and illegal dumping. Brown & Rowe has uncovered buried car battery dumps, extensive engine-oil spills, and on one project, the threat of biological-warfare agent anthrax. Taking it all in stride, the three partners often use the site's history as an interpretive part of their designs. (They usually collaborate with environmental specialists; for example they teamed with Phillip Craul on Spectacle Island's manufactured soil, page 87.)

Be Aware of Direct Hazards from Construction

A very long list of products, which includes many building materials, is suspected of causing health problems for people. Most of the research done on this type of toxicity, however, refers to *indoor* air quality (IAQ, also called IEQ [indoor environmental quality]). Many chemicals, including some naturally occurring ones, are hazardous when trapped within walls and concentrated. Except for the most toxic ones, adequate ventilation is the main user precaution. Since landscapes are by definition open-air places, hazardous chemicals are quickly diluted by outdoor air, greatly reducing the *direct* risk to users. Many materials that are quite hazardous if used in enclosed spaces are not considered dangerous if used outdoors.

The use of toxic materials in landscapes, however, raises different questions than when those same materials are used indoors. In the early days of environmental awareness, a popular slogan decreed that "Dilution Is the Solution to Pollution." This has proved short-sighted. The very openness that lets toxic chemicals dilute into the air also means that they are free to move beyond the site. Some biodegrade, but others accumulate in ever-increasing quantities in air, water, or soil. Increased levels of global pollution parallel increasing percentages of the population suffering from allergies, respiratory diseases, and other chronic conditions.[29] The *outdoor* use of chemicals that are known to be hazardous *indoors* may contribute to regional pollution levels even if they do not pose an immediate threat to the user.

Some individuals suffer from a condition called multiple chemical sensitivity (MCS), believed to be severe allergic reaction to chronic pollution. Very small quantities of chemicals, or materials that do not affect most other people, can cause mild to severe symptoms in MCS sufferers. Many advances in knowledge about "healthy building materials" have resulted from designs for MCS sufferers. Lists of such materials are available from a number of books and on the Web; one

book even includes sample specifications organized by CSI division.◐

Relatively few *outdoor* construction materials actually cause symptoms for people with MCS. Large areas of hot asphalt are a concern, as are outdoor pesticides. The use of preemergent herbicides or broad-spectrum insecticides around foundations and under unit pavers is a landscape practice that can affect indoor air quality.[30] It is worth remembering, however, that not every material banned from indoor use by MCS considerations is inappropriate outdoors. Some MCS-safe materials are not weatherproof enough for landscape use. Nonetheless, these nontoxic materials deserve consideration in landscape construction wherever possible.

Many landscape materials are in direct contact with the soil and stand unprotected from weathering. From either soil contact or weathering, toxic materials may leach into the soil, where they are taken up by plants and make their way into the food chain. Because of such risks, some outdoor materials may need to be *more* completely nontoxic than their indoor counterparts, just as brick exposed to the weather needs to be more durable than grades for interior use.

Minimize Invisible Hazards Off-Site

In addition to on-site hazards, some materials cause environmental problems either during manufacturing or during disposal. Materials that are completely nontoxic in use may present serious problems at the beginning or end of their life cycle. For genuine sustainability, these issues cannot be ignored even though they are invisible. In fact, for most common *landscape* construction materials, research for this book lead us to believe that direct toxicity to users is a minor problem compared to hazards of extraction, manufacturing, and disposal.

Manufacturers of basic building materials, like the rest of society, have changed in response to environmental concerns. Many have developed a sincere commitment to reducing the environmental impact of their products. Others have improved their records only under the pressure of regulation. Overall, significant improvements in efficiency and pollution control have been made in most basic U.S. industries within the past few decades. These improvements have been offset, and in some cases even overwhelmed, by increased consumption of goods and depletion of resources due to population pressures.

Neither the most conscientious manufacturers nor their customers in landscape fields can completely prevent all toxic releases. Spills and accidents during transportation of hazardous materials can release toxics, as can natural disasters, sabotage, and human error. Facilities that *release* little or no pollution to the environment may still expose their own workers to serious hazards. Landscape professionals share a responsibility with other citizens to see that foreseeable pollution problems are prevented and that unforeseen problems are kept to a minimum.

Resource extraction is a related off-site issue. Timber and stone, for example, are nontoxic materials, but conventional forestry and mining practices have caused widespread environmental damage. Transportation of materials causes pollution in the form of internal combustion byproducts. These general production processes, which are very much taken for granted by society, have serious impacts that must be considered part of the environmental cost of materials.

IMPACTS OF GENERAL MANUFACTURING PROCESSES

The following processes contribute to the environmental costs of a majority of construction products. For detailed information and source citations, see Appendix A, page 295.

- *Electrical generation* is a major source of CO_2, at about 1.5 pound per kilowatt-hour (from coal). According to Amory Lovins of the Rocky Mountain Institute, converting a *single* lightbulb from incandescent to compact fluorescent of the same light output saves 57 watts of energy. Over the lifetime of the efficient bulb, this reduction in electrical use will eliminate about 1 *ton* of CO_2, 17 pounds of SO_2 (sulfur dioxide), and various quantities of other pollutants. If the electricity source is nuclear, the same bulb change would eliminate generation of 25 grams (nearly an ounce) of plutonium, a deadly by-product of nuclear reactions.[31]

- *Fuel combustion*, both for industry and for vehicles, produces volatile organic compounds (VOCs), sulfur and nitrogen compounds ("Sox and Nox"), CO_2, and carbon monoxide. Diesels produce particulates. Most fuels are mined, a process with its own impacts.

- *Petroleum production* produces both toxic and nontoxic drilling sediments and a number of air pollutants. Petroleum fuels are burned to drill and maintain wells. Oil spills, as well as poorly designed pipelines and access roads, can seriously disrupt habitat.

- *Mining* can elevate soil erosion rates up to 2,000 times what occurs in stable forested land.[32] Some kinds of mine tailings give off toxic leachates and can poison or clog waterways. Physical disruption of the site, especially by pit mining, is difficult if not impossible to restore fully.

- *Logging* elevates normal forest erosion rates by up to 500 times. Reduction of forest areas may decrease global ability to process CO_2. Burning of slash and waste produces air pollutants. Overharvesting decreases biodiversity; replanting may be inadequate to sustain a productive forest even for commerce.

- *Construction* itself elevates normal erosion rates by up to 2,000 times, causing roughly the same degree of added soil and water problems as mining.

- *Disposal* of materials not recycled can release toxic leachates from landfills and fumes from incinerators. Bulky or nondegradable materials consume landfill space that is increasingly at a premium.

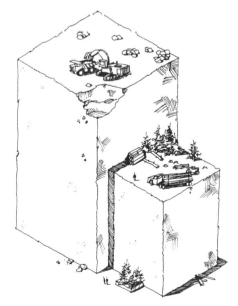

Figure 6.22. Erosion from healthy forests averages 0.0375 tons (75 pounds) per acre per year. Logging raises this 500 times, while mining and construction raise it 2,000 times. ILLUSTRATION: Craig Farnsworth.

In part because of these general impacts, and also because materials and manufacturing methods vary widely, it is important to consider the entire product life cycle when deciding which building materials to specify or what construction methods to use.

Use and Advocate Life-Cycle Analysis (LCA)

Much of the best information about the environmental impacts of building materials is based on life-cycle analysis. As its name suggests, LCA takes into account the entire cycle of production, use, and disposal/reuse. (For a graphic representing life cycles in general, see Figure 7.7.) At each stage of the life cycle, energy consumption, toxicity, resource depletion, potential for misuse, and other factors are accounted for. Comparisons are made between whole life cycles rather than between materials at the point of use. Examples include the Center for Resourceful Building Technology's *Guide to Resource Efficient Building Elements*, the AIA's *Environmental Resource Guide*, and a checklist for materials selection developed by *Environmental Building News*.[33] Each lists explicit general guidelines for determining whether a product is in tune with sustainability over its life cycle.⊃

Pliny Fisk points out that many LCA approaches are manufacturer-specific and suffer from limited data. While he supports the overall idea that materials can be understood only over the entire period from "cradle to grave," his own research is based on national statistical databases that make it possible to look at the life cycles of all materials of a specific kind, not just the products of a selection of manufacturers. A study using national data was published in the 1980s by Stein and others. This pioneering study is still often cited, but its data were collected in the late 1960s. We hope that Fisk's work, when completed, will produce up-to-date, detailed, and nationally averaged information—and that information on landscape materials will be extractable from the data.

Although LCA (which in the broad sense includes Fisk's work) is probably the best basis for materials selection, there are difficulties applying *existing* LCA studies to landscape construction. The main difficulty is that most existing research has focused on life cycles related to *buildings*. Because basic materials are used differently in landscape applications, their life cycles may not be comparable to that of the same material as a building component. In trying to make LCA information accessible to architects, many authors have also focused on building "assemblies" or components, such as structural insulated panels or complete framing systems. These assemblies are seldom relevant to landscape construction.

The authors feel that the time is ripe for landscape-specific studies of materials, covering their whole life cycles as used outdoors. Full-scale original studies of this type are well beyond the scope of this book. As a step in that direction, however, we have compiled *basic* information on toxicity (this chapter) and energy use (Principle 7). Only information related to landscape materials and processes is included. We hope that this information will encourage landscape professionals and researchers to develop life-cycle studies of landscape materials in greater depth.

Summaries of Toxicity Issues by Material Type

Almost all available publications on toxicity are organized by the technical names of chemical ingredients. In these, it is possible to look up DEHP or 1,1,1-trichloroethane, but not to find out what each is used in, much less find entries for "plastic pipe" or "oil-based paint." We have tried to remedy this situation in two ways: by giving an overview of the toxicity and hazard issues specific to landscape materials and by compiling a list of materials under names more recognizable to design and construction professionals.

This section *summarizes* the hazards and concerns associated with basic building materials used in landscape work. Many minor hazards that may be important for particular sites or clients are not noted in this section. Appendix A, page 295, describes forty-nine materials in more detail. The appendix is organized *by material* and notes the main ingredients or emissions associated with the material. Situations when a material may pose special risks (such as accidental fires or improper disposal) are also noted.

For some materials, and for most chemical ingredients that pose hazards, Material Safety Data Sheets (MSDS) from suppliers may provide more detail. Use the appendix to identify the main ingredients that pose hazards, and then read the MSDS for each ingredient. Several Websites make MSDS information available.⊃

Published information indicates that most landscape construction materials, in the forms to which end users are exposed, are *relatively* nontoxic to humans. Their toxic effects on the regional environment are not well understood. All construction materials require proper use and disposal as well as and continued improvement by manufacturers in assuring that toxic ingredients are handled safely and emissions are controlled. Alternative materials with fewer toxic effects are becoming increasingly available for many types of products.

Of the landscape materials reviewed, only two (PVC and wood preservatives) appear to be of such environmental concern that serious calls have been made to ban them outright. The controversy around hazards of these materials, along with a scandal concerning illegal toxic materials relabeled as fertilizers, is discussed in the section beginning on page 219.

Coatings, adhesives, and solvents expose users to hazardous fumes called volatile organic compounds (VOCs) during application and curing. These have been reduced considerably in recent formulas but still can harm both the user and the broader environment. More than 50 percent of all paints and coatings used in the United States are for construction work.[34] Some types of specialized outdoor paints (such as those used for pavement marking or flagging items during surveying) have unusual formulas—for example, to allow use during freezing weather. Such proprietary formulas are often kept secret, concealing possible dangers.

Postconsumer disposal, accidental fires, and spills present problems for many plastics, coatings and preservatives, adhesives, and solvents. Improper and illegal disposal is one facet of this problem; officially approved disposal has also been criticized, especially incineration of these materials or their use as fuels in cement kilns and other industrial facilities.

Many plastics, coatings and preservatives, adhesives, and solvents, as well as a few metals and fertilizers, have toxic chemical ingredients, precursors, or by-products. Factory mitigation processes control many of these risks adequately or are making progress toward doing so. Product

specifiers have many opportunities to influence suppliers toward safer production and toward complete disclosure of product and production risks.

Conventional mining and lumbering create extremely serious environmental problems (see page 217); however, these impacts vary from firm to firm, and sustainable forestry is becoming more widespread.

Plastics Used in the Landscape

Many types of plastics have landscape uses, either in construction or in landscape furniture and furnishings. The result of an unscientific survey of catalogs, home centers, and garden stores, Table 6.1 lists landscape objects according to the types of plastic from which they are made. Many other plastic landscape products are not marked with any information to allow identification of component materials.

Three Controversial Materials

If you read no other detailed listings from Appendix A, read those on PVC and wood preservatives, which are reproduced on the following page. A number of reputable organizations, including both industry and environmental groups, have called for phasing out these products from general use.[35] Although there is controversy over the idea of a complete phaseout, we agree that these materials should be used only for essential purposes, and that safe substitutes need to be developed. Landscape professionals have a responsibility to know the hazards associated with these materials and to make informed decisions about using them.

PVC is widely used in irrigation parts and pipes, lawn edging, soft "vinyl" tubing for drip irrigation and other landscape products (see Table 6.1).

Wood preservatives and pressure-treated lumber are *primarily* used to meet outdoor conditions, with landscape construction using a significant amount of these materials.

A third controversial material important in landscape use is fertilizer. As detailed next and in Appendix A, the Associated Press has reported that heavy metals, toxic chemicals, and radioactive waste are being relabeled as fertilizer—without any actual processing and with no regulation.

Table 6.1
Plastic Used for Landscape Products—An Unscientific Survey

	♳ PET	♴ HDPE	♵ PVC	♶ LLDPE	♷ PP	♸ PS	Other
Irrigation		watering cans irrigation mainline pipes hose reel carts & hose pots flexible downspouts drainage pipes	garden hoses drip tubings ("spaghetti") irrigation pipes drainage pipes extendable downspouts	drip tubings ("spaghetti") laser soaker hose & drip tubes			irrigation heads (ABS)
Furniture		floating lounge chairs picnic tables	"wicker" furniture arbor w/ benches "leather" upholstery umbrella fabric closed-cell foam floats & pool lounges		outdoor furniture		"bentwood" rocker (resin) "wicker" furniture (resin) "cast iron" furniture (resin) outdoor upholstery (acrylic)
Planters & Pots	*	planters bins planter w/ trellis fake terra-cotta pots nursery pots	trellises		fake terra-cotta pots nursery pots	*	fake terracotta pots (foam resin) propagation trays ("polymer") planters (resin) arbors (resin) planters (fiberglass)
Storage		bins			storage boxes & bags		storage sheds (resin)
Work Clothes		hard hats	work gloves rain and chemical-spray clothing work boots				
Construction Supplies		"landscape plastic," clear & black sheets tarps most plastic lumber duct tape	coated metal cable and wire mesh flagging and barricade ribbon		construction fence tarps		
Electrical			light fixtures electrical conduit junction boxes, etc. electrical tape				
Green Houses							greenhouse windows (polycarbonate) clear greenhouse fabric (polyethylene reinf. w/ nylon mesh)
Other		basketball backboards chain-link privacy slats composting bins	inflatable pools fencing, picket or rail styles, incl. posts pool toys vinyl grill covers		doormats, "jute"-look and other mailboxes		in-lawn alligator & other ornaments (resin)

*The only landscape use found for PET and PS was in pots for nursery growing.

Sources of the following information are cited in Appendix A.

Polyvinyl Chloride (PVC and CPVC)

PVC and CPVC are materials raising great contention in environmental debate. The solid polymer is relatively harmless, but other stages of PVC's life cycle raise major environmental concerns. (Polymers are multiple chains of molecules called monomers; in this case, the monomer is vinyl chloride, and the polymer, *poly*vinyl chloride.) CPVC, also known as PVDC, is a form of PVC made more heat-stable by adding extra chlorine. (Plastics industry spokespeople hotly deny much of the following information; their arguments appear hairsplitting and self-serving.⊃)

End-use issues: Chlorine compounds have been reported to leach from PVC pipe into water supply, and outgassing from some PVC products may be an indoor air quality issue. End users can also be affected by gases if PVC burns in accidental fires or, in some cases more dangerously, smolders without igniting, as when wiring insulated with PVC overheats. The state of California has recently required labeling of all vinyl garden hoses (vinyl is essentially PVC with plasticizers) as follows: "This product contains chemicals known to cause cancer and birth defects or reproductive harm. Do Not Drink From This Hose." PVC has been banned as a food-container material. PVC remains very popular despite its dangers, for several reasons. It is more rigid than many other plastics (but also easily made flexible with additives). Tensile strength is high enough to keep PVC pipes from bursting under pressure. It is easily joined by glue fittings, unlike other pipe systems, either plastic or metal. And it is relatively cheap in today's economy.

Production issues: Manufacture of PVC and CPVC poses significant problems. Ingredient vinyl chloride is a known carcinogen; incomplete polymerization can leave leachable traces of this monomer (single molecular "link" in a polymer chain) in PVC. Liquid vinyl chloride is used in gluing PVC. Despite improvements, there is still potential for release of dioxins and other highly toxic chemicals during manufacture.

"The environmental community generally wants to see a phaseout or banning of [organochloride compounds, including PVC and its ingredients] except for essential uses."[36]

General hazards: Petroleum production; mining.

Factors that reduce/offset risks: Strictly regulated manufacture has dramatically reduced production risks but cannot affect use and disposal or accidental hazards. There is no question that PVC has great practical and commercial value, but there is serious doubt that the risks are worth it.

Renewability/recyclability: PVC is not recyclable to any significant degree. Possible, but not practiced, is recycling of CPVC. Disposal is a serious problem. Burning PVC for disposal, or in accidental fires, releases chlorine compounds, dioxins, furans, and heavy metals. PVC in waste has been said to account for half of the chlorine in incineration fumes. Chlorine is a main ingredient in the organochloride and chlorofluorocarbon (CFC) groups of chemicals, which include DDT and dioxin and are strongly implicated in cancer, reproductive disorders, species loss, and ozone depletion.

Associated materials in use: Solvents used to join PVC are of concern for indoor air quality and worker health.

Alternatives: Several other plastics are less toxic in manufacture and easier to recycle or dispose of than PVC. For pipes and some other products, traditional materials like metal and clay, although less convenient and with energy and cost disadvantages, may need to be reconsidered. For garden furniture and other low-tech items, PVC should be replaced with HDPE or other plastics.

Wood Preservatives

Safety of wood preservatives has been a subject of much controversy. Questions concern safety in use; potential for accidental or deliberate burning of treated wood; leaching of preservatives into soil; production dangers; and disposal problems. As with PVC, problems of disposal appear greater than direct threats to end users.

End-use issues: As Alex Wilson, editor of *Environmental Building News*, notes, there is no getting around the fact that "preservatives are designed to kill . . . [Preventing wood decay requires] finding the right balance between toxicity to the problem organism and safety to us and the environment."[37] The EPA has established precautions for use of all wood preservatives.

Pentachlorophenol and creosote should not be used in interiors but are fairly common outdoors and are very common on recycled wood from industrial sources, such as railroad ties or utility poles. Both are highly toxic by inhalation. "Penta" is toxic through the skin, may be fatal if swallowed, and appears to be a cumulative toxin, with small doses building up to toxic levels over time as it moves in the food chain. Both are oilborne preservatives.

Chromated copper arsenic, or CCA, combines the wood-preserving properties of copper chromate and copper arsenite, both of which are highly toxic, the former also suspected carcinogenic. Close relatives are ACA (ammoniacal copper arsenate), ACZA (ammoniacal copper zinc arsenate), and ACC (acid copper chromate), all waterborne preservatives, usually applied under pressure. In most situations, these chemicals appear to bond very tightly with the wood; this is good for user safety but causes problems in disposal. Although gloves are recommended when handling CCA-treated wood, and the EPA requires cleaning off surface residues before indoor use, it is widely used for children's play structures and for decks. Manufacturers cite this as evidence of its safety, while consumer advocates see it as evidence of inadequate regulation. There is evidence that CCA can leach from treated wood into soil and water, especially under raised decks, in wetlands, or in marine facilities. It has been claimed that these leachates are quickly neutralized by the soil, but less so in aquatic systems.

Production issues: Pentachlorophenol is made by combining chlorine and phenol; both are hazardous, and phenol is derived from benzene, a very hazardous material. Creosote and its parent material, coal tar, are both toxic, presenting hazards to workers. CCA is produced from three chemicals that are each highly toxic, capable of causing death or reproductive disorders (copper oxide, arsenic pentoxide, and chromic acid); chromic acid is also explosive and flammable. Because of this, the AIA concludes that the most serious environmental hazard of CCA is the potential for spills when materials are trucked to produce it.[38] Others believe that disposal of treated wood is even more significant.

General hazards: Petroleum production and refining; mining; fuel combustion.

Factors that reduce/offset risks: Preserving wood can dramatically increase its service life, thus saving resources and the energy involved in rebuilding or repairing decayed structures. Preservative treatment allows plentiful woods to be used instead of such naturally resistant but overlogged species as redwood; in many cases, the species used with preservatives are structurally stronger than redwood.

Renewability/recyclability: Treated wood can be reused if carefully salvaged; reused wood, such as railroad ties, is common in landscape construction. Recycling or remanufacturing is unlikely, although some attempts have been made to use shredded treated lumber as fiber in composite materials. Job-site scraps and wreckage are mostly landfilled; some are incinerated. *Environmental Building News*, after several thorough reviews of the controversy, stated flatly, "At present, there is no environmentally sound way to dispose of [CCA] treated wood . . ."[39] and went so far as to call for a phased ban on CCA. Creosote-treated wood can be incinerated; penta-treated wood *may* be possible to incinerate safely under careful controls. CCA and its relatives can only be landfilled, where the preservative means they (theoretically) never break down, thus depleting landfill space. Incineration of CCA is likely to release air pollutants; even if these are captured by stack-cleaning equipment, they end up in ash, from which they are easily leached.

Associated materials in use: Metal or plastic containers, which may be too contaminated to recycle.

Alternative products: ⊃ ACQ preservative (Chemical Specialties): "Alkaline-Copper-Quat" formula is nonhazardous and has been recommended for people with chemical sensitivities. ("Quat" is quaternary ammonia.) Kodiak Inc. offers lumber pressure-treated with CDDC (copper dimethyldithiocarbamate). Osmose and Hickson, who along with Chemical Specialties are the three U.S. manufacturers of CCA, have developed alternative products but market them only in Europe where regulations on CCA make higher-priced alternatives salable.

Boron preservatives are used indoors but will not withstand wetness and may be toxic to plants. Other nontoxic preservatives based on mineral oils or pitch may be suitable for outdoor use; check with manufacturers. Further alternatives include plastic lumber for nonstructural use and naturally decay-resistant woods (some of which are endangered or scarce).

Toxics as "Fertilizer"

In 1997, the mayor of the small town of Quincy WA led an investigation for local farmers whose cattle had sickened and whose crop yields were declining. Their discovery was that toxic waste was being repackaged and sold to them as fertilizer. The Seattle Times pursued the investigation and found examples of this practice nationwide. An Oklahoma uranium-processor licenses its radioactive waste as a liquid fertilizer. Pulp mills in Washington State spread lead-laced waste on livestock grazing land. Two Oregon steel mills put a powdered waste into silos under federal hazardous waste permits and take the exact same material out of the silo for sale as fertilizer. While most industrialized nations regulate fertilizers, the United States does not, nor do most state governments.

The repackaged wastes contained cadmium, lead, arsenic, radioactive materials, and dioxins

and were not treated in any way before being sold as fertilizer. It is unclear what level or concentration of toxic materials is being sold to the unwitting public in this way. As far as has been reported, none of the major brand-name fertilizer companies are or were involved. The practice is certainly unethical, since at the very least labeling should be required. Similar concerns about treated sewage sludge have been raised, often preventing its use. Research on sludge shows that soil organisms appear to be able to detoxify much of the trace toxicity that remains in treated sludge (see page 97). Industrial toxic waste, however, seems likely to have higher concentrations of harmful materials than does sludge.[40]

As users of considerable quantities of fertilizer, landscape professionals would be well advised to keep abreast of this issue and to lobby for truth-in-packaging (at least) for all industrial materials sold as fertilizer. If concentrated toxic materials are in fact being passed off as fertilizers, it is in the landscape industry's self-interest, not to mention the interest of environmental and public health, to demand that the practice be stopped.

Priorities When Selecting Landscape Materials

We draw the following conclusions about ways for landscape professionals to lessen the environmental impact of the materials they use.

Priorities

Focus on proper *disposal, salvage, and recycling* of construction materials, *reducing fuel use*, and on *influencing manufacturers* toward nontoxic processes and accident prevention. Because relatively few outdoor materials are directly hazardous to end users, end-use issues are probably *not* the area in which professional attention can produce greatest results.

- Reuse materials creatively and create jobs and markets by doing so.

- Support technical and social efforts to reuse and recycle construction materials. ⊃ Disposal of construction materials, and failure to recycle them, are areas where real results could be achieved with fairly small changes in conventional practice.

- Analyze and reduce transportation, equipment use, and other fuel-consuming processes, through practices discussed in Principle 7. Fuel use, rather than materials hazards, probably contributes most to the total environmental impact of landscape materials.

- An increasing number of manufacturers have recognized the social and economic value of nontoxic processes and materials. Landscape professionals should support those whose claims can be clearly documented.

- Select certified sustainably harvested wood whenever possible.

- For plastics, give preference to manufacturers who label each product (better still, each distinct piece of a product) with the recycle symbol, number, and plastic type and who use mostly recycled plastic in their products.

- Use the product with the fewest known end-use effects on human health and the environment. Use products with known hazards only where no practicable alternative exists. Even minor effects may be cumulative or may interact with other pollutants. Avoid PVC and conventional wood preservatives wherever they are not absolutely essential.

- Current information, including this book, is not sufficient to give landscape materials selection a truly sound environmental basis. Information about architectural materials and indoor air quality, although more readily available, should be used cautiously as a guide to outdoor conditions.

- There is a definite need for authoritative and accessible information on *landscape* products and their environmental impacts. The landscape professions should fund production of such information, preferably in LCA or similar format. Individual landscape professionals should work to convince suppliers that accessible information is to everyone's advantage.

Resources

Recycled, Re-seen: Folk Art from the Global Scrap Heap by Charlene Cerny & Suzanne Seriff (1996 Harry N.

Abrams, Inc. and the Musuem of International Folk Art, Santa Fe NM; 800-217-7522.)
> A wonderful overview of recycling as art and as livelihood for much of the world's population. Exhibition catalog, richly illustrated. The creativity (in the items, and in the exhibit itself) is stunning, while the similarities of recycled work by widely different cultures is thought-provoking. Two chapters are devoted to landscapes made with recycled materials by folk artists.

Materials

Athena Sustainable Materials Institute
www.athenasmi.ca/
> Research organization on materials and energy.

Center for Maximum Potential Building Systems
http://www2.cmpbs.org/cmpbs/
> Pliny Fisk, codirector of the center, has exceptional information on materials, energy, and economics for sustainability.

Construction Specifications Institute
www.csinet.org/
> Research and standards on specifying materials.

A Guide to Estimating Landscape Cost by Gary O. Robinette (1983 Center for Landscape Architecture Education and Researach; Van Nostrand Reinhold)
> As a guide, this book is less dated than standard annual price summaries.

Biocycle
Emmaus PA http://grn.com/news/home/biocycle/
610-967-4135 or Biocycle@jgpress.com
> Magazine devoted to composting and recycling. The March 1998 issue discusses uses of crumb rubber.

Chemical glossary
Chemical Abstracts
www.cas.org/vocabulary/15431.html
> May be useful in understanding chemical terminology.

Sustainable Design Database
HOK Architects www.hok.com/sustainabledesign/database/welcome.html
> Excellent data on materials. Slow to load because of architectural graphic overload.

Plumbing Claims Group (polybutylene)
800-356-3496 or www.spencerclass.com
> Information on why PB is no longer manufactured in the United States

Plastics industry associations
800-2HELP90 (US) and (UK)
> Recycling code system; opposing positions on PVC and other environmental regulatory issues.

Materials Selection

American Institute of Architects *Environmental Resource Guide* by Joseph A. Demkin (1994–98 Wiley)
> Loose-leaf, with annual supplements. Exceptional detail on materials, life cycles, and energy.

EBN Product Catalog
> *Environmental Building News* annual loose-leaf directory

Environmental by Design by Kim Leclair & David
Rousseau (1992 Hartley & Marks Ltd., Vancouver BC)
Focused on interior materials and IAQ, but useful because it
includes Canadian and European products.

Green Building Resource Guide by J. Hermannsson, (1997
Taunton Press)
Primarily for buildings, but useful for CSI-format and price comparison indexes.

Guide to Resource Efficient Building Elements by Tracy
Mumma (1997 [6th Ed.] Center for Resourceful
Building Technology, Missoula MT 406-549-7678)

Resourceful Specifications: Guideline Specifications for Environmentally Considered Building Materials and Methods by
Larry Strain (1997 Siegel & Strain Architects, Emeryville
CA, info@siegelstrain.com)

Constructability Concepts File
Construction Industry Institute
http://construction-institute.org/
512-232-2000
Mainly engineering, but some related concepts on materials
efficiency and on-site remediation.

Environmental Design & Construction
Saddle Brook NJ 201-291-9001 or www.edcmag.com
Bimonthly, mostly buildings. Good annual buyers guide.

Landscape Architect and Specifier News
Landscape Communications Ltd., Santa Ana CA,
714-979-5276
Monthly trade magazine. Valuable for ads, annual product guide,
and Landscape Online (same product info, plus find-a-firm listings, etc.) Articles tend toward advertorial.

CITES (Convention on International Trade in Endangered Species)
U.S. Fish & Wildlife Service
Lists endangered timber species and other natural products that
should not be specified.

Masterspec Landscape Architecture Specifications
ARCOM Systems
800-424-5080 or www.arcomnet.com
Not specifically green, but useful.

*National Park Service Sustainable Design and Construction
Database* by Sally Small (1994 National Park Service
Technical Information Center Denver CO)

Resources for Environmental Design Index (REDI)
Iris Communications, Eugene OR
www.oikos.com
Frequently updated database of products

Materials: On-Site

EARTH-BUILDING INNOVATIONS
Nader Khalili
Cal-Earth foundation
Hesperia CA
760-244-0614 www.calearth.org

Information on site-fired earth housing and other low-tech, high-result building methods.

STABILIZED SOIL PAVEMENT
Stabilizer
Phoenix AZ 800-336-2468
Bonds soil in place for paths, etc.

Soil Stabilization Products
Merced CA, www.sspco.org
Bonds soil in place for paths, etc.

Natural Stonescapes: The Art and Craft of Stone Placement by
R. L. Dube & Frederick C. Campbell (1999 Storey Communications/Garden Way, Pownal VT)
Practical advice; cultivating a sense for unusual stone.

Materials: Recycled

RE-USE OF WHOLE TIRES
Prof. Stuart Hoenig hoenig@ece.Arizona.edu
Has long list of creative uses for old tires (1999 paper to the International Erosion Control Assn.).

University of Arizona AZ Engineering School
newsletter at http://unisci.com
Covered reuse of tires.

RECYCLED PLASTIC GREENWALLS
EKOL Belgium www.tessenderlo.com
Recycles mixed domestic plastic as park benches and tables, flower
troughs, molded paving slabs, fencing, and traffic islands, plus
"Lüft" motorway sound barriers, easily erected structures filled
with compost.

Impact-Post
800-863-6619
Plastic lumber in railroad-tie sizes.

The Resource Guide to Sustainable Landscapes by Wesley
Groesbeck & Jan Streifel (1996 Environmental
Resources, Inc., Salt Lake City UT
801-485-0280, wesley.groesbeck@m.cc.utah.edu)
Listing of some 3,000 landscape products with recycled content or
other environmental benefits.

"Caltrans & Recycled Transportation Products"
www.ciwmb.ca.gov/condemo/factsheets/ Caltrans.htm
Online article on specifying recycled materials for surface transportation.

Sustainable Wood

ProSilva Europe
http://ourworld.compuserve.com/homepages/
J_Kuper/page1_e.htm
Information on sustainable forestry and related issues from
Europe.

Ecoforestry: The Art and Science of Sustainable Forest Use by
A. Drengson & D. Taylor (1997 New Society Publ.)

Good Wood Directory
Certified Forest Products Council cfpc@ix.netcom.com
Annual.

The Forest Certification Handbook by Christopher Upton &
Stephen Bass (1996 St. Lucie Press, Delray Beach FL)

Woods of the World database
1996 Tree-Talk Inc. wow@together.net
    CD-ROM with photos, or diskettes without. Encourages use of
    plentiful but unknown woods.

Construction Waste Management

International Solid Waste Association
www.recycle.net/recycle/assn/
Copenhagen, Denmark; Tel: 45 32 96 15 88

WasteSpec: Model Specifications for Construction Waste Reduction, Reuse, and Recycling by Judith Kincaid, Cheryl
Walker & Greg Flynn (1995 Triangle J Council of Governments, POB 12276, Research Triangle Park NC
27709)

Construction Materials Recycling Guidebook by Pamela W.
Laner (1993 Metro Council of St. Paul MN 612-291-
8140)

*Residential Construction Waste Management: A Builder's
Field Guide* by Peter Yost & Eric Lund (1997 National
Assn. of Home Builders,
800-223-2665)
    Free 30-page booklet.

Hazard Identification

Soil Contamination: Think First, Dig Later!
Construction Industry Institute
http://construction-institute.org/
512-232-2000
    VC-404, 90-minute video; other reports and videos also sold.

The Home and Land Buyer's Guide to the Environment by
Barry Chalofsky (1997 Center for Urban Policy
Research, New Brunswick NJ
732-932-3133, ext. 555)

TOXICS TEST KITS
Labware Safety Supply Janesville WI
800-356-0783

Toxics A to Z: A Guide to Everyday Pollution Hazards by
John Harte, Cheryl Holdren, Richard Schneider, &
Christine Shirley (1991 University of California Press,
Berkeley)
    Lists about 100 of the most common toxic materials, plus noise,
    and discusses health effects. Lists are by common name; covers a
    few construction materials and many solvents and other ingredients.

What Remodelers Need to Know and Do About Lead by 1993
National Assn. of Home Builders, 800-223-2665)

Lab Safety Supply Inc.
www.LabSafety.com or fax-back service from 800-393-
2287
    Safety data on industrial chemicals, processes, and regulations,
    provided by this supplier of labware.

"Cement Plants and Toxics"
http://gopher.essential.org/listproc/
dioxin-l/msg02264.html

"Hazardous and Toxic Waste Management
Bibliography"
Water Quality Information Center of the National Agricultural Library
www.nal.usda.gov/wqic/Bibliographies/
    Extensive annotated bibliography on toxic wastes affecting land
    use.

"Pollution-Preventing Landscape Management"
www.epa.gov/owow/nps/mmgi/Chapter4/
ch4-6.html
    Lists ways in which landscapes contribute to pollution, and how
    to avoid these.

1996 Toxic Release Info (TRI) Public Data
www.epa.gov/opptintr/tri/pdr96/drhome.htm
    Lists events in which toxic materials have been released into the
    environment.

"Guide to Cleaner Coating Technologies"
U.S. EPA http://es.epa.gov/program/epaorgs/ord/
org-coat.html
    Clear discussion of various coatings, environmental issues, and
    alternatives.

MSDS-Search
www.msdssearch.com/
    Free Website with 1 million Material Safety Data Sheets.

U.S. EPA
www.epa.gov/epahome/search.html
    Searchable site for pollution and many other environmental
    issues.

Materials: Nontoxic or Alternative

Green Seal
Washington DC 202-331-7337
    Environmental standards for paints, caulks, adhesives, plus general environmental publications.

Soy Clean
Overland Park KS, 913-599-0800 or
www.soyclean.com
    Nontoxic paint stripper, adhesive remover, graffiti remover,
    driveway cleaner, lubricants.

Prescriptions for a Healthy House by Paula Baker, Erica
Elliott, & John Banta (1998 InWord Publishers, Santa
Fe NM)
    CSI-format listings of materials healthy enough for IAQ for chemically sensitive people.

Bio-Form nontoxic form-release agent
Leahy-Wolff Franklin Pk IL, 888-873-5327
    Described in Appendix A under "Concrete, Form-release agents."

Safer wood preservatives (ACQ)
Chemical Specialties 800-421-8661
    Other manufacturers with similar products not marketed in the
    United States: Osmose Corp. (copper citrate); Hickson Co. (Copper
    Azole); and Kodiak, Inc. (CDDC).

Life-Cycle Analysis

"The Big Picture: Life-Cycle Analysis" by Rob Goldberg
(May 1992 *Academy of Natural Sciences,* 215-299-1000 or
www.acnatsci.org)
> Good article on abuses of LCA if not kept in perspective with
> other regional factors.

Know the Costs of Energy Over Time

The law of conservation of energy tells us we can't get something for nothing, but we refuse to believe it.

—Isaac Asimov, 1988

Energy is the core of life, central to doing, living, building. Since the energy crisis of the late 1970s, design and construction professionals have been keenly aware of energy issues: energy-saving lights and appliances, efficiency standards for heating and cooling, and the ever-increasing costs of fuel for machinery. Energy efficiency can sell a property, and inefficient use of energy can sink a construction business. Yet despite energy's increasing importance in building design and construction, it is still rare to find energy conservation principles systematically applied to *landscape* construction.

The American Institute of Architects, in its *Environmental Resources Guide*, estimates that more than 30 percent of *all* the energy consumed in the United States goes into construction and upkeep of buildings.[1] Other estimates are even higher. The role that landscape construction plays in these estimates is unclear. However, if landscape construction consumes even *one-twentieth* of what building construction does, this would be 1.5 percent of the U.S. total—comparable to some estimates of energy used in constructing highways (1.64 percent) or single-family residences (1.19 percent).[2] It is well beyond the scope of this book to attempt accurate estimates of *total* energy use by the landscape industry. However, landscape construction clearly consumes enough energy to make energy analysis and energy conservation worthwhile.

Energy analysis, although its methods are still evolving, is a skill that will be as essential as cost-estimating to the designers and contractors of the very near future. As decisions about which material, what design, what machinery become

increasingly interlinked and complex, energy costing offers the clearest available baseline for these hard choices. At present, energy studies are rough-and-ready, generalized, and occasionally even misleading. In the evolution of knowledge about energy in construction, landscape professionals have real opportunities both to benefit and to contribute.

Construction "represents a huge, relatively long-duration energy investment";[3] currently,

Discussed in This Chapter:

- How energy affects landscape construction

- Ways to make better, more energy-conscious decisions about landscapes

- The difference between energy consumed in *using* a landscape ("operating energy") and energy used to *construct* a landscape (fuel energy for construction machinery and "embodied energy" in construction materials)

- The emerging field of *embodied energy analysis*, a relatively new concept whose uses (and limitations) every environmentally conscious designer and contractor needs to understand

- The use of *life-cycle costing* to make thorough long-term cost estimates (energy and/or dollars) for construction materials and methods this investment is mostly gambled rather than managed. Any landscape professional who wants to work sustainably will gain a great advantage by keeping current with emerging ways of planning for energy efficiency.

The authors hope to encourage construction, design, and planning professionals to *help develop* practical methods and reliable standards for energy evaluation. In the next edition of this book we would like to be able to report that this infant approach has grown into a mature and robust tool.

Landscape Energy Use Is Different

Throughout this book, we have pointed out differences between *building* construction and *landscape* construction, differences that have important environmental consequences. Energy use, too, differs between indoor and outdoor construction: the types and total amounts of energy used, as well as where and when energy is used. To understand why landscape professionals need to concern themselves with energy issues, it is essential to understand these differences.

Types of Energy in Construction

Since energy plays so many roles in life, it is not surprising that the word has multiple definitions. Only two or three definitions are specifically important in talking about energy in construction.

It takes energy to produce construction materials, to install them, and to operate or use the site or structure once it is completed. To discuss these uses of energy clearly, we will use the following terms: operating energy, fuel energy, and embodied energy.

Operating energy (also called end-use energy) refers to power used in day-to-day functioning of a completed project. A common example is energy for heating and cooling buildings. In landscapes, operating energy includes electricity to run the valves and controls of an irrigation system or for outdoor lighting.

Fuel energy (sometimes called inherent or specific energy) is the energy that a material can give off if it is used as a fuel. It is different from embodied energy (described next) and applies only to those materials that have practical value as fuel. For example, a piece of pine lumber weighing 1 pound might produce 2,600 Btu

(British thermal units) when burned as fuel;[4] its embodied energy (energy for felling and sawing) would be about 2,776 Btu for an unprocessed 1-pound board; planing, drying, and glue-laminating the board could bring the embodied energy to as much as 6,788 Btu per pound.[5]

Fuel energy, and the efficiency of transforming it into useful work, are factors in computing both operating and embodied energy. Fuel efficiency for construction machinery is one area in which landscape contractors can directly affect both their operating costs and the environmental impact of their work.

Embodied energy refers to the energy used to *produce* materials. Energy is required to mine or extract raw materials, to refine and combine them, shape them, and, in complex products, to assemble the parts. Between each step in the process, the material may be transported, at an energy cost. Transport from factory to construction site also uses energy. The embodied energy of materials sums up all these energy inputs, usually in terms of energy per pound of material. The energy cost of disposing of the material or recycling it is an important, but sometimes neglected, part of embodied energy. Embodied energy for a whole construction *project* totals all energy inputs for materials, processes, and waste.

Embodied energy has a number of synonyms: embedded energy, process energy (which emphasizes factory processes and often excludes transportation), and energy intensity. Energy intensity emphasizes the relative level of energy required to produce a unit (weight, volume, size, etc.) of material. The same term, unfortunately, is used by the U.S. Department of Energy and others to mean the amount of energy used to produce a *dollar's worth* of product.[6] Although this energy-per-dollar idea has its own uses, it should never be confused with energy-per-*material* figures. Architects have also used "energy intensity" to mean the per-square-foot *operating* energy of a building.[7] Because of these confusions, we feel that embodied energy is the most consistent term for energy in materials production.

Energy in Buildings vs. Energy in Landscapes

In buildings, large amounts of energy are used for *operation*; 60 percent of the running costs of the building can be saved through efficiency in heating and cooling.[8] There is a trade-off, however: improved operating efficiency usually requires up-front investment in better construc-tion and materials. Low-cost developments, for example, often skimp on insulation to keep the sale price low; increased heating and cooling bills are the result. The same trade-off occurs in energy costs: for poorly insulated houses, oper-ating energy costs are so high that total energy to *produce* the structure is only about nine times what it costs in energy to *operate* the building for a single year. By comparison, a house built to today's best efficiency standards can be operated for nearly eighteen years for the energy price of its materials; one year of operation equates to less than 6 percent of the energy embodied in construction.[9] Thus, in *building* construction, investing extra in the *embodied* energy of mate-rials such as insulation or double-pane glass gives large savings in *operating* energy.

In constructed *landscapes*, the relationship between operating and embodied energy is quite different from that of buildings. The major oper-ating energy costs of a building are either absent or greatly reduced in landscapes. Mechanical heating and cooling are rarely used outdoors, and insulation is not a consideration. As a result, if energy embodied in construction is compared to annual operating energy, the *ratio* is much larger for landscapes than for buildings. Thus, better landscape construction, at a higher cost in embodied energy, is unlikely to yield as dramatic a savings in *operating* energy for landscapes as the 60 percent for efficient buildings.

Some types of operating energy are certainly part of today's landscapes and are discussed in this book. Outdoor lighting, like its indoor equivalent, has been greatly improved for energy efficiency in the past decade. This environmentally important subject is discussed in Principle 8. Irrigation con-trollers (see page 162) have also been redesigned with operating energy efficiency in mind.

Other outdoor appliances also use energy: gas grills, poolside conveniences, gate-openers, or fountain equipment, for example. When pur-chasing or specifying such landscape items, energy efficiency seldom seems to be a main client concern. Outdoor appliances are viewed as luxuries, and there is a peculiar human tendency *not* to expect efficiency from luxury items. Nonetheless, a few manufacturers are starting to design outdoor appliances to use less energy in operation. Energy consumption figures for such items, however, are extremely scarce.

The machines used in maintaining landscapes, such as lawn mowers, chipper-shredders, and chainsaws, can be considered as operating energy costs. However, because they are similar to con-struction equipment, their energy requirements are discussed in the section on machinery and energy, page 231.

Saving Energy in the Landscape

Any net energy savings is significant in sustain-ability, and where possible, the energy consumed in using landscapes should be minimized. How-ever, the amount that can be saved through greater efficiency in landscape *operating* energy is limited. Much greater potential energy savings can be accomplished in three areas:

Site design strongly influences the operating energy efficiency of *buildings*: shade or windbreak plantings, solar orientation, rainwater manage-ment, and many other well-known techniques use landscape as part of ecological design. ⊃ These design approaches are not detailed in this book.

Careful planning of machinery use, both on-site and for transportation, can result in significant energy savings. Total machine fuel energy use on any project is strongly affected by choices: between a local supplier and a distant one, among options for bringing workers to the site, and between heavy or light equipment and hand tools. Energy consumption estimates and guide-lines for making such choices are given in the following section.

Significant savings are possible in the amount of energy represented by *landscape materials* themselves, as analyzed through embodied energy calculations and life-cycle energy costing. Each of these topics is discussed in a section of this chapter, which concludes with some energy-saving suggestions for landscape construction.

Energy for Machines, Tools, and Labor

Landscape construction makes use of a wide range of tools, from very heavy equipment to simple hand tools. Some, like the dibble or planting stick used for mass planting, have been in use since prehistoric times; others, such as bulldozers and laser levels, have come into exis-tence only in the last few decades, a mere second in the long day of human existence on this planet.

In thinking about how energy is invested in landscape work, it is important to recognize that the *tools* of landscape construction also differ from those used by building construction. Neither set of tools is better than the other; each is simply suited to specific jobs. Site work today relies on large motorized machines; building construction other than site work uses different and, in general, fewer heavy machines. A vast array of handheld power tools is used in building construction; many are too specialized or too easily damaged by weather to be used regularly outdoors. Landscape construction frequently uses simple hand tools, both because many landscape sites are remote from power supplies, and because the variability of terrain, site size, and other outdoor conditions often require the great adaptability of handwork. The differences between these two tool sets, especially in their balance of powered and nonpowered tools, means that the energy economics of landscape construction cannot be optimized by an approach based solely on architectural work.

A simple comparison makes it clear how much impact the choice of landscape equipment can have on energy consumption. A modern scraper (often called an earthmover) can move 20 cubic yards of soil a distance of 200 yards in less than two minutes. The same task would take a full day for eight workers using picks, shovels, and the kind of backpack baskets still common in the Third World. The machine, with a 450-horsepower engine, would have used 0.6 gallons of diesel fuel, or about 84,000 Btu. The eight laborers would use about 20,000 Btu to accomplish the work.[10] This represents an energy cost for the machine more than four times as high as that for human labor.

Conventional practice in industrialized countries has accepted this increased energy cost for two reasons: because speed of work is so highly valued and because true energy costs are disguised by artificially cheap fuel prices and high labor costs. There is no question that the machine is faster—almost 240 times faster. But for sustainability, other considerations compete with convenience, speed, and monetary cost. In the earth-moving example, diesel is a nonrenewable source of energy, and putting it to use usually produces various forms of pollution. The food consumed by the workers is readily renewable and all their waste is biodegradable. In addition, the scraper is composed of many tons of steel and other energy-intensive materials. Its size and weight damage the soil and limit its use to large unobstructed sites.

Few if any industrialized societies would willingly move back to the days of manual labor for all tasks. However, using manual labor is not the only way to cut energy costs. Choosing the most appropriate sources of energy and types/sizes of machinery for the job can result in significant energy savings as well as protect the environment in other ways (see page 50).

Alternatives in Generating Energy

Energy for tools used in construction, manufacturing, and homes is *generated* in a variety of ways, each with its own implications for sustainability and for the landscapes in which people live and work. The most common sources of construction power are gasoline and diesel, plus electricity generated by the local utility company from a combination of coal, hydro, and nuclear plants. Portable generators, which are gas powered, are also common at the job site, along with air compressors powered by gas or electricity. Solar (photovoltaic) and wind-generated electricity increasingly provide power to homes and some businesses, but they remain rare as power sources for construction work.

Each way of generating energy starts a chain of events leading to the final use of the energy to power a tool or machine. Some of these chains are long; for example, heat energy from coal burned at a power plant is converted into electricity, which is transmitted through utility wires, then may be used to run an electric motor to compress air that powers the actual tool on-site. Other chains are very short; internal combustion engines, for example, convert fuel energy directly into the mechanical energy of the tool. Each time energy is converted from one form to another (solar to electric, combustion to mechanical, etc.), there are losses, since no conversion is completely efficient.

For in-depth analysis, all forms of energy should ideally be measured by a common yardstick, one that allows for the energy cost of converting energy from one level to another. Such a system forms the basis of the work of Howard Odum and his associates, who can, for instance, quantify the energy value of solar radiation or of nuclear-generated electricity in terms of "fossil-fuel equivalents." Although his conclusions about the value of alternative energy sources seem dated, anyone interested in a thorough introduction to energy costs and their effects on society and the environment would do well to start with Odum's book, *Energy Basis for Man and Nature*, a classic since 1976.⊃ Odum's methods are particularly useful in putting day-to-day energy use into the perspective of long-term policy.

TOOLS AND THEIR ENERGY SOURCES

In thinking about energy and sustainability, what matters most is resource depletion and pollution that result from energy use. In many ways, this simplifies the evaluation of energy consumption by specific tools. The specific details of efficiency that affect tool design (for example, what percentage of the energy theoretically available from the explosion of gasoline actually reaches the tires of a tractor) are less important for the tool user than is the *total amount of fuel consumed* while the tool is in use. It is this total amount that affects the environment directly—and that most directly affects the pocketbook. This total use is what construction professionals need to reduce. Voting with dollars can also create a demand for more efficiently designed machines.

The tables in this chapter give rough energy usage rates for machines and tools of many kinds. To interpret these rates, the source or type of energy must be considered. We have made the following assumptions:

- Gas, diesel, and gas/oil engines consume their fuel directly. Energy use for the machine or tool is based directly on an estimate of fuel used per hour, converted for ease of comparison to one of the standard units of energy, the Btu. To convert to the metric unit, the joule, multiply Btu by 1,055.

- Electrical tools running from utility power are part of a system that, as a national average, loses about 60 percent of fuel energy during generation and transmission. At the beginning of this energy chain, 2.5 times as much fuel is burned to *produce* electricity as ever reaches the user. This does not mean that electrical tools are necessarily inefficient. It does mean that in comparing effects on the environment, electrical tools must be evalu-

ated in terms of the energy generated to support them, rather than the energy used "at the plug." The tables give an at-the-plug figure for each tool, followed by the same figure multiplied by 2.5 to include systemwide losses.

- When an on-site generator is used, its total fuel use is a better gauge of environmental impact than measuring the electricity used by the tools connected to it. A 10,000W generator used to run a 700W drill or saw is consuming fuel based on generator capacity, not on the attached tool; it is also consuming fuel while the tool is idle. Thus, for sustainability, it is important to evaluate the number of hours of fuel consumption *by the generator*, rather than try to add up the use by all the individual tools.

- Air tools should also be evaluated by the fuel usage of the compressor, especially if gas-powered or tankless, since these types of compressors run constantly. (An electric compressor with a tank runs only when tank pressure drops, which is efficient but more difficult to estimate; based on experience, assess how many minutes per hour the compressor motor actually runs.) For these reasons, we have included only compressors, not specific air tools, in the tables.

- Alternative power sources, such as solar and wind, are essentially "free," since no fuel is used or pollution generated. (Like any power-generating equipment, resources are used in *building* a PV panel or windmill; these "second order" resources are not usually considered in energy analysis, though they will eventually need to be.) If installed on a site as the first step in construction, these alternatives can sometimes provide construction power. They generate relatively low wattage and require an inverter to produce AC. Portable solar or wind power for contractor use could probably be developed. One contractor has developed a way to recharge 12V cordless tools from a solar panel on his truck; *Environmental Building News* editors advised anyone modifying tools for this purpose to wait until the warranty runs out![11]

PRINCIPLE 7

Energy Use: Heavy and Self-Propelled Machinery

Most of the equipment used in landscape work is relatively small in the overall world of heavy equipment. Usually adapted from agricultural and engineering machinery, landscape equipment looks tiny compared to truly *heavy* equipment. Mining industry trucks, for example, may weigh 200 *tons* empty and carry 300 tons; there are 3,500-horsepower excavators that move 60 tons at a scoop.[12] Nonetheless, thousands of smaller landscape construction machines do add up. Their combined energy usage, as well as their effect on the soil (see Table 1.1), makes them important targets for energy efficiency and appropriate use.

Some rough estimates of energy use by various types of machinery are given in Tables 7.1 through 7.7. Tables 7.8 through 7.10 relate energy use to processes, such as mowing, irrigation, or transportation, rather than to specific machines. Data in Tables 7.1 and 7.2 can be used for doing your own estimates. These are *rough* estimating tools only and do not reflect specific performance of specific models. More accurate information, by brand name and under specific work conditions, is available, but these rough averages may be of equal value for several rea-

sons: Fuel consumption varies with the condition and age of the equipment. Engines operate most efficiently within specific ranges of RPM and at full loads—but in the field these conditions cannot be maintained constantly. Fuel consumption also varies with such circumstances as soil hardness, surface conditions affecting traction, outdoor temperature, and elevation. Thus an average figure may be more useful than detailed specifics in *planning* for energy efficiency across a whole job.

To estimate energy consumption, it is necessary to know how much energy is burned up with each gallon of fuel and how many gallons are used to run a given machine for a time or distance. Tables 7.1 and 7.2 give rule-of-thumb figures.[13] Table 7.1 shows how much energy is released by burning each of the three most common types of motor fuels.

Nichols and Day, in their respected reference, *Moving the Earth*, give the following fuel usage factors (Table 7.2), in gallons used per horsepower per hour.[14] Based on Table 7.1, these are converted to Btu per hp/hr, which makes comparison between different engine types easier.

To use these figures, multiply the number in Table 7.2 times the machine's horsepower to determine gallons of fuel or Btu consumed per hour.[15] For example, a 30-horsepower gas-powered tractor would use 30 × 10,000 Btu for each hour of operation, or 300,000 Btu. The number of hours of machine work required for particular jobs is one type of statistic given in standard estimating references like Means or Spons. If the Means book says that the task you are estimating requires a small tractor for nine hours, total energy use for that task would be 2.7 million Btu.

These figures are for ordinary machinery and average conditions. For extremely well maintained equipment and light work, *subtract* 25 percent for diesel and 13 percent for gasoline (including 2-stroke). For poorly maintained machinery and difficult conditions, *add* up to 75 percent for diesel and 25 percent for gasoline. If manufacturer's data for a specific machine are available, Nichols and Day recommend using 80 percent of the rated full-load fuel consumption. Such information will need to be converted first from pounds to gallons, and then to Btu.[16]

Tables 7.3 through 7.7 give *rough* energy estimates for various types of heavy machinery,

Table 7.1
Fuel Type and Energy

Fuel Type	Energy Produced in Use (Btu/gallon)	Weight per Volume* (pounds/gallon)
Diesel	140,000	7
Gasoline	125,000	6
2-stroke gas-oil mix†	125,000	6

*Machinery manufacturers and engineers usually chart fuel usage in pounds per hour of operation. Use these factors to convert pounds to gallons.

†The figure for gasoline is used as a round number, since the usual gas-oil mix (50:1) is primarily gasoline.

Table 7.2
Average Fuel and Energy Consumption per Horsepower-Hour

Fuel Type	gal/hp-hr	btu/hp-hr
Diesel	.06	5,600
Gasoline	.08	10,000
2-stroke gas-oil mix	.09	11,250

234

based on the fuel consumption factors in Table 7.2. The machines listed were selected as representative of *types*—not specific models—used in landscape construction. The listing is not comprehensive and tends toward the *smaller* machines of each type. (Larger machines, less common in landscape work, may be estimated if the horsepower and the type of fuel are known, using the method just described.) For each listing, the horsepower, weight, and capacity figures are derived from real machines; closely similar models were averaged. Fuel usage, in Btu, was then estimated using Table 7.2.

These data are intended *only* for project planning and deciding on general strategies of machine use. Like most of the data in this chapter, they will seem inaccurate to manufacturers and engineers who are used to very precise, model-specific fuel consumption estimates. These figures should certainly not be confused with thorough documentation of specific machines under specific conditions. Rule-of-thumb generalizations like the Nichols and Day factors used here are what allow the *field user* to make better decisions; the ultraprecise measures that machine *designers* need are of little value in the field. Rough as they are, the estimates that follow are a first step in an important process: *gathering* and *refining* information to help construction practice change in response to sustainability concerns.

EXAMPLE OF MACHINERY EVALUATION

The example of the scraper and the workers, given at the beginning of this section, shows one way in which fuel use figures may help to encourage comparative thinking about energy options. Consider another example: excavating a particular job requires 4.0 hours with a mini-skid-steer loader and 2.25 hours with a standard-sized skid-steer. The smaller machine is 16 horsepower and gas-powered, while the larger is a 60-horsepower diesel. Table 7.3 shows that the mini-machine uses 160,000 Btu for each hour of operation, while the larger uses 336,000 Btu/hr. This gives a provisional and rough indication that although the larger machine is nearly twice as fast, it uses 756,000 Btu for the whole job, compared to the mini-machine's 640,000 Btu. Other factors could push the decision in one direction or the other; if the larger machine is slowed by tight access, its total fuel/energy consumption

will be still higher. If the mini-machine is at another job 15 miles away, while the larger machine is in the contractor's yard 2 miles from the site, the advantage may go to the larger machine. Furthermore, energy considerations could be overridden by an imperative need to avoid soil compaction, so that only the smaller machine would be appropriate.

Monetary costs will frequently appear *totally unrelated* to the energy-based comparisons. This is a symptom of a society that underprices fuel energy and overvalues speed. The decision to sacrifice some money savings to save energy is an ethical choice, and no one would argue that it is an easy one. Without considering energy, however, decisions about sustainability become complete guesswork. These figures are a first step toward informed decisions.

THE SPECIAL ROLE OF MINI-MACHINERY

For any type of landscape construction that values existing site features, small machinery makes great sense. Whether protecting a site from soil compaction or working to grade the small spaces of dispersed parking among trees, mini-machines are second only to hand labor in minimizing damage and maximizing flexibility. Compared to their heavy relatives, mini-machines

- require far less clearing for access (see Figure 10.2),
- use less fuel (though efficiency per unit of work varies),
- may produce less pollution (again, compare case by case),
- are lighter to transport, saving fuel,
- are manufactured of smaller quantities of material,
- may exert less ground pressure than a person walking (Table 1.1), and
- do tasks beyond human strength or endurance, without overkill.

Size, weight, fuel efficiency, and maneuverability are criteria for choosing among machines for site work; contact manufacturers for this information. Intelligent tool-design choices are also important, like the decision that self-propulsion isn't a requirement for all backhoes (Figure 7.6). Machines that have a wide range of

Table 7.3
Energy Consumption Estimates for Heavy Landscape Machines

Machine Type	Capacity or Rating	Operating Weight (pounds)	Horsepower	Fuel	Est. Btu per Hour
Tractors and "Tool Carriers"					
Tractor, compact (range = 16 to 40 hp)	8 cf, 1,400 lb. bucket	4,000	30	D	168,000
Lawn tractor (range = 10 to 20 hp)	light duty only	635	13	G	130,000
Backhoe-loader	5,000 lb. lift	14,000	75	D	420,000
Backhoe-loader	7,500 lb. lift	22,600	100	D	560,000
Wheel loader	0.85 cy	10,000	40	D	224,000
Wheel loader	2.0 cy	15,000	90	D	504,000
Wheel loader	5.0 cy	51,000	250	D	1,400,000
Dozer	0.75 cy	8,710	40	D	224,000
Dozer	1.4 cy	13,500	70	D	392,000
Dozer	4.0 cy	27,000	120	D	672,000
Mini-skid-steer (stand-behind)	750 lb./ 3.85 cf	1,350	16	G	160,000
Skid-steer loader	880 lb. lift	3,100	30	D	168,000
Skid-steer loader	1,750 lb. lift	6,200	60	D	336,000
Site dumper	2,500 lb. haul	1,200	13	D	72,800
Mini-excavator (track)	.03 cy	1,700	8	D	44,800
Mini-excavator (track)	1.5 cy	3,600	23	D	128,800
Mini-backhoe (wheeled, not self-propelled)	.04 cy	1,300	8	G	80,000
Road grader (small)	10' blade	11,000	35	D	196,000
Road grader (medium)	12' blade	28,000	125	D	700,000
Compactor, double drum-type	50" wide	5,400	33	D	184,800
Compactor, rubber tires	50" wide	9,300	45	D	252,000
Asphalt road reclaimer	full lane x 15"	32,000	350	D	1,960,000
Trucks					
Pickup, small/import (avg 22 mpg, or 5,700 Btu per mile)	1/2 ton	4,400	142	G	1,420,000
Pick-up, full size (avg 13 mpg, or 9,600 Btu per mile)	3/4 or 1 ton	6,400	270	G	2,700,000
Dump-truck, flatbed, etc. (avg 8 to 11 mpg, or 12,750 to 17,500 Btu/mile)	2 or 2 1/2 ton	30,000	350	D	1,960,000
Specialized Machinery					
Chain trencher	36" deep cut	720	11	G	110,000
Chain trencher	60" deep cut	4,000	32	D	179,200
Wood chipper (portable)	home use	140	5	G/O	56,250
Wood chipper (mobile)	light comml. use	1,200	20	G	200,000
Wood chipper (mobile)	heavy comml. use	7,500	116	D	649,600
Stump cutter/grinder	small	1,060	25	D	140,000
Brush mower	26" blade, cuts 1.5" stems	230	8	G	80,000
Curb-laying slipform or extruder	asphalt or concrete	2,700	20	D	112,000
Motorized wheelbarrow/ Rough terrain forklift	1,500 lb.	560	8	G	80,000

specialized attachments (for example, see Figure 7.2) are often more resource efficient than specialized machines for each job.

Several mini-machines are illustrated in Figures 7.1 through 7.6 and embody some or all of these criteria. Many other models arc available from a growing number of manufacturers.⊃

Energy Use: Small Power Equipment

"Our industry," says Jim Elmer of Tanaka America/ISM, "is where cars were twenty years ago." He is referring to handheld tools powered by tiny 2-stroke engines, of which Tanaka is a specialized and progressive manufacturer. "Up until now, manufacturers really haven't had to pay much attention to fuel consumption. We're just now getting into it."

Tanaka is one of a handful of small-engine manufacturers who met stringent emission standards from the California Air Resources Board (CARB) *before* the year 2000 deadline; their newest engines have already gained Tier-Two approval from CARB. Komatsu-Zenoah and Redmax also met the standards early.⊃

Compared with similarly rated older models, the newest handheld power tools produce 70 percent lower emissions. Moreover, although there are other ways to meet emissions requirements, redesign has also decreased fuel consumption by about 30 percent for some models. This is because much of the pollution

Figure 7.1. Some "heavy equipment" isn't. The small Bobcat excavator is about 7 feet tall by 3 feet wide. Weight and fuel use are about 10 percent of that of the larger excavator. PHOTO: Kim Sorvig.

Figure 7.2. This mini-skid-steer, from Ramrod, fits where larger machines can't and has an unusually wide range of attachments. Size generally corresponds to decreased fuel use and ground pressure. PHOTO: Ramrod Equipment⊃.

Figure 7.3. "Site dumpers" can be an efficient compromise between hand labor and full-sized tractors. PHOTO: Kim Sorvig.

Figure 7.4. Motorized wheelbarrows, like this Honda PowerWagon, can do heavy work with decreased site impact, as in Sweet Brook's restoration. PROJECT: New York DEP. PHOTO: Dean Cavallaro.

Figure 7.5. Articulated steering, as well as small size, means this roller can work around existing site features instead of obliterating them. PHOTO: Kim Sorvig.

Figure 7.6. Not all machines need to be self-propelled. Trencherman backhoes, by NorthStar, are towed to work; the bucket levers the machine around the site. PHOTO: Northern Tool and Equipment, manufacturer of NorthStar machinery⊃.

came from oil that passed through the engine unburned (for lubrication) in conventional engines and was eliminated by redesign.

Although it is easy to assume that a tiny engine with a fuel tank measured in ounces can't do much environmental harm, Elmer gives an example that puts the matter in perspective. "For most models," he says, "you produce less pollution driving your car 2,500 miles than running your chainsaw for an hour." Multiply this by the approximately 10 million such small engines sold each year, and both fuel use and pollution become significant issues. For instance, a conventional small engine used 600 hours in a year would consume 117 gallons of fuel mix; the improved engine should require only 94.[17] This savings equates to the difference between 14.6 million Btu and 11.7 million, a savings of nearly 3 million Btu for a single machine.

Companies like the ones mentioned earlier

have turned a regulatory limit into an opportunity. Efficient engines position their manufacturers very well in a competitive market of some fifty brand names of outdoor power tools. This market is rapidly changing, and tool-buyers concerned with sustainability can do a great deal to influence those changes. Seek out suppliers who are starting to pay attention to fuel consumption and are willing to give straight answers about it. With the EPA looking into stricter standards for small engines nationally, fuel and emission data ought to become much more widely available to landscape decision makers.

Today, however, that information is very difficult to obtain. Small power tools are especially difficult to rate, for several reasons. For handheld tools like chainsaws, both the throttle speed and the workload will vary widely during a single use—unlike a lawn mower, for example, which runs at a relatively constant speed once started.

Table 7.4
Energy Consumption Estimates for Small Gas Landscape Tools

Tool Type	Capacity or Rating	Operating Weight (pounds)	Horsepower	Fuel	Est. Btu per Hour
Compact stump grinder	small, full duty	180	9.0	G	90,000
Horticultural sprayer, trailer type	55 gal, 500 psi, 3 gpm	130 empty	3.5	G	35,000
Lawn aerator	26"W	200 + ballast	4.0	G	40,000
Lawn edger	heavy duty	65	3.0	G	30,000
Pressure washer	3 gpm cold water	74 to 130	5.5	G	55,000
Rototiller	26"W, 8"D	200	8.0	G	80,000
Lawn mower	30" cut	40	7.5	G	75,000
Sod cutter	18"W	325	5.5	G	55,000
Sprayer, backpack	3 gal tank	30	5.0	G	50,000
Auger, 1-person	12" max bit	19	2.0	G/O	22,500
Auger, 1-person	10" max bit	26	3.0	G/O	33,750
Auger, 2-person	10" max bit	53	3.8	G/O	42,750
Blower, backpack	405 cfm, 195 mph	28	2.8	G/O	31,500
Blower/shredder, handheld	130 mph	12 to 18	1.2	G/O	13,500
Chainsaw	12"	11	2.2	G/O	24,750
Chainsaw	24"	16	3.1	G/O	34,900
Cutoff saw, handheld	12" blade	26, plus blade	3.5	G/O	39,380
Cutoff saw, handheld	14" blade	32, plus blade	4.8	G/O	54,000
Hedge trimmer	17"	11	1.2	G/O	13,500
Lawn edger	lightweight	13	0.9	G/O	10,130
Line trimmer		8.5	1.05	G/O	11,820
Power pruner (chain-type)	10"	18	0.9	G/O	10,130
Rototiller, mini	12"W, 10"D	20	2.0	G/O	23,630

In addition, hand tools may be powered by gas, electricity, or air. Although power ratings for gas and electric are both in horsepower, the rating systems differ, with electric motors rated conservatively, and gas engines rated "as high as honestly possible."[18]

Many small-tool manufacturers are reluctant to discuss efficiency. They feel that they have been unfairly targeted, and that they have not received credit or publicity for the improvements that have been made. Lawn mower engines, once the subject of claims that they were responsible for more total pollution than all cars, have improved performance significantly since 1990; the Outdoor Power Equipment Institute shows a 70 percent decrease in emissions, for example. Handheld power tools, as seen from Elmer's examples, are making similar leaps in performance.

Given the changing market, the estimates given in Table 7.4 should be used judiciously. They are based on an average figure for 2-stroke fuel consumption per horsepower (see Table 7.2), which is fast being improved. For the time being, a conservative estimate is appropriate to sustainability concerns, since many of the tools currently in use are older models. By this book's next edition, we hope that not only will small-engine efficiency have changed considerably, but that information about these changes will be part of standard marketing literature. Until then, use Tables 7.4 to 7.8 as a *rough* guide.

The method of rating horsepower is different for electric tools, (Table 7.5). Energy-consumption estimates will have more meaning among tools of the *same* type (electrical or gas) than *between* types, though these rough figures may still have some value for basic planning.

Because air compressors are powered by either gas or electricity, and are used to power other tools in turn, they are also listed separately (Table 7.6). According to Dave Moorman of Ingersoll-Rand tool company, a basic rule of thumb for portable air compressors is that they require about 1 horsepower to produce 4 cubic feet per minute (cfm) of air. The Compressed Air & Gas Institute gives a much wider range, but this includes large stationary industrial compressors.[19] Efficiency varies considerably with altitude, since this directly affects ambient air pressure.

Table 7.5
Energy Consumption Estimates for Electric Landscape Tools

Tool Type	Capacity or Rating	Operating Weight (pounds)	Horsepower or Watts *	Power†	Est. Btu per Hour‡	
Chainsaw	12" bar	7	1,600 W	AC	(5,470)	13,675
Lawn mower	30" cut	25	6 hp	AC	(16,000)	40,000
Chop saw (stand-mounted)	14"	35	1,800 W	AC	(5,660)	14,150
Disc grinder	4.5"	5	780 W	AC	(2,450)	6,125
Horticultural sprayer, trailer-type	15 gal, 40 psi, 1.4 gpm	53 empty	180 W	DC	(570)	1,425
Power pruner (chain type)	8"	12	1.25 hp	AC	(3,190)	7,980
Submersible pump	90 gph, 2 ft head	1	5 W	AC	(16)	39
Submersible pump	1,800 gph, 20' head	10	130 W	AC	(410)	1,025
Submersible pump	300 gph, 15' head	6	220 W	AC	(690)	1,725
Submersible pump	520 gph, 15' head	7	300 W	AC	(945)	2,360
Submersible pump	2,750 gph, 15' head	10	700 W	AC	(2,200)	5,500
Winch	550 lb.	90	0.5 hp	AC	(1,275)	3,190
Winch	2,000 lb.	14	0.6 hp	DC	(1,530)	3,825
Winch	1,900 lb.	230	1.5 hp	AC	(3,825)	9,560

†All are 120V AC or 12V DC.

*Energy consumption for electrical tools is based on watts where known, or horsepower if wattage is unavailable.

‡Electrical tools show two estimates, both converted to Btu/hr: The first, in parentheses, is usage by the tool "at the plug" without transmission losses. The second factors in 60 percent losses between generation and use; that is, 2.5 times as much energy is consumed as is used at the plug. If using an on-site generator or photovoltaics, see "Tools and Their Energy Sources" on page 233.

Gas-powered electrical generators are also frequently used on landscape sites. A few examples, their rated output, and fuel consumption based on horsepower are given in Table 7.7.

Finally, for landscape maintenance, energy use can be estimated per-acre, based on work by Helen Whiffen, agricultural energy specialist with the University of Florida. Although the figures in Table 7.8 were based on Florida conditions, they can serve as a model for information that should be public knowledge in every region.[20]

Energy Use: Hand Tools and Labor

Unlike many industries, landscape construction still relies on a great deal of human labor, which is often the most efficient way to get landscape jobs done. Despite artificially low fuel prices and artificially high labor costs, hand labor is economical for landscape work where limited access, awkward terrain, irregular materials, or artistic care are involved.

As a round figure, an adult male human's base energy use is about 300 Btu per hour, or on the order of 2,500 Btu for a working day.[21] Only a few of the smallest electric motors will run for an hour on fewer than 500 Btu of energy, while almost all petroleum-fueled machines use 10,000 Btu per hour or more. Virtually all this machine energy comes from nonrenewable resources and produces varying degrees of pollution. Human (and draft animal) energy is derived from agricultural products, which are among the most

Table 7.6
Energy Consumption Estimates for Portable Air Compressors

Compressor Type	Capacity or Rating	Weight	cfm @ 90 psi	Horsepower	Fuel	Est. Btu/hr
2-stage shop model	30 gal	440	18	11.0	G	110,000
Twin tank wheeled	20 gal	167	6.5	5.0	AC	(12,750)* 31,875
Twin tank wheeled	10 gal	235	18	9.0	G	90,000
Twin tank wheeled	8 gal	139	10	5.5	G	55,000
Single tank	3 gal	25	2.9	1.5	AC	(3,825)* 9,560
Tankless	light duty	15	1.8	0.75	AC	(1,915)* 4,790

*See note on electrical ratings, Table 7.5.

Table 7.7
Fuel Consumption Estimates for Portable Electric Generators

Electrical Output		Engine Fuel Estimates		
Watts max	Amps	Horsepower	Fuel	Est. Btu/hr
1,000	7.5	2.5	G	312,500
2,700	20	5.0	G	625,000
4,400	35	8.0	G	1,000,000
10,000	80	16.0	G	2,000,000
12,000	110	20.0	G	2,500,000

Table 7.8
Energy Use in Landscape Maintenance

Maintenance Type	Energy Use per Unit	Energy Use per Acre	Annual Energy Use
Mowing, gas mower	83,350 Btu/hr.	125,000 Btu per mowing	1.25 to 2.5 million Btu per acre per year
Mowing, electric mower	40,000 Btu/hr.	60,000 Btu per mowing	600,000 to 1.2 million Btu per acre per year
Irrigation (municipal water)	18 Btu/gal	n/a	16 million Btu per acre per year
Fertilizer (for lawns)	2,700 Btu/lb.	n/a	2.16 to 7.2 million Btu per acre per year
Pesticide (for lawns)	n/a	0.625 to 2.5 million Btu per application	n/a
Trees (water + fertilzer + pesticide)	n/a	n/a	0.5 to 1.0 million Btu per tree per year

Source: Based on Whiffen, Helen H. "Landscape Maintenance Takes Energy: Use It Wisely," *Energy Efficiency and Environmental News* (U. FL Extension), Feb. 1993. Units conversion by authors. Items marked n/a were not noted by Whiffen.

quickly renewable resources; wastes from this energy source are easily biodegradable. In addition, a 180-pound worker wearing the equivalent of a man's size-10 shoe puts about 2 pounds per square inch of pressure on the soil. When a self-propelled machine has a "ground pressure" of less than 5 psi, manufacturers start advertising the fact.

Thus, although energy comparisons between human and machine are more thought-provoking than scientific, any work that can be done by hand provides a clear sustainability payoff. Some hand tools (Figure 1.17) make the most of a person's work and are worthwhile investments for sustainably minded crews. In many cases, the result is a better project and a reputation for quality work, which pay off financially, too.

A final note on human energy use: "Thinking," says energy expert Vaclav Smil, "is an enormous energy bargain." Not only does brain activity require only about 5 percent of the base energy expenditure of staying alive; that energy use stays the same whether zoning out or thinking furiously.[22] In energy terms, it costs nothing to think things through carefully—yet the result can be massive savings in both labor and equipment. Think about it!

Energy Use: Transportation

More than almost any other use of machinery, transportation touches all aspects of construction efficiency. Materials are transported to the site; so are workers and machinery. Energy use for all these movements is a significant part of the energy cost of the whole job.

Commercial trucks are often discussed very unfavorably as fuel consumers. However, they are much more efficient per ton of material moved than passenger cars or small trucks. Although many older trucks guzzle diesel at a rate of 6 miles per gallon, "for a compact car to get the equivalent mileage based on a fuel consumption *per ton mile*, the compact car would have to get almost 500 miles per gallon."[23] Passenger cars use a couple tons of machine to

haul a hundred-and-some-pound passenger—a classic example of using more power than the job requires. Large trucks running empty, however, still get 6–10 mpg while hauling only their driver, a situation that responsible companies avoid if at all possible.

Most researchers agree that one of the most important steps a construction professional can take to reduce environmental impact is to cut down transportation/fuel costs. Table 7.9 makes it clear why this is critical in materials transport.[24]

Equally if not more important is transportation of workers (see Table 7.10). The energy required is a significant part of the total energy used by the landscape professions, in part because job sites tend to be far from either the firm's offices or the workers' homes.

Compare the numbers in Table 7.10 against those for site machinery (Table 7.3), power tools (Table 7.4), or embodied energy of materials (Table 7.15). The average energy consumption for one hour's use of the large machines listed is about 65,000 Btu. A crew member who drives alone to the site in a car getting 20 mpg uses the same amount of fuel every 10 miles. Average for an hour's use of a gas-powered hand tool is around 12,000 Btu. The same employee uses that by driving 2 miles.

Notice also that getting the employee with the

Table 7.9
Transportation Energy Consumption per Ton of Material per Mile

	Btu/ton/mile	
	Low	High
Boat	350	540
Train	680	820
Truck	2,340	6,140
Plane	37,000	?

Table 7.10
Transportation Energy Consumption per Passenger Mile

	Btu per Passenger per Mile* Miles per gallon			
Number in Vehicle	20	25	30	35
1	6,250	5,000	4,000	3,500
2	3,125	2,500	2,000	1,750
3	2,000	1,700	1,350	1,175
4	1,550	1,250	1,000	875

*Gasoline vehicles. Fuel only. To allow for all energy used to make travel possible, multiply these figures by 175% (Odum, 1976).

20-mpg car to take one rider lowers the energy per passenger mile *more* than getting the employee to drive (still alone) in a new car getting 35 mpg. With construction sites frequently located on the suburban fringe, these miles add up rapidly. A *company carpooling policy* can be one of the most effective ways to save energy related to construction.

Because urban areas sprawl, it is not uncommon to have construction workers travel 20 or 30 miles each way to the site. A six-person crew, each member driving alone in a 20-mpg car, would rack up 2.25 *million* Btu per day; that equals 11,250,000 Btu per five-day workweek. That energy would power four pieces of heavy equipment all week, assuming the average noted above. It would also be enough energy to produce about 5 tons of common brick or about 500 pounds of steel, according to embodied energy per Table 7.15 (page 248). (This is *without* factoring in the energy costs of vehicle maintenance or highway infrastructure, which Odum estimated at an additional 75 percent of fuel energy.)[25]

Much of the energy "embodied" in materials comes from transportation. For example, brick used 350 miles from the factory uses as much energy in transportation as was used to produce the bricks.[26] Obviously, ignoring transportation energy distorts decisions like "Is brick appropriate as a material at this site?" For this reason, one of the most consistent recommendations from embodied energy research is to *specify local materials*.

As a society, Americans tend to overlook the costs of transportation, especially the environmental costs. It is a very difficult challenge to change this habit, even for oneself, but to move toward sustainability, everyone must rise to that challenge. No matter how well intentioned, a professional cannot truly stake his or her reputation on "green building" while commuting many miles a day in a single-occupant four-wheel-drive pickup. Transportation alternatives are hard to find but are every bit as important as the green practices adopted at the site.

Many specifiers already choose suppliers in part on the transportation distances involved. There is still plenty of room for improvement (see the quote from Pliny Fisk, page 195, for example). The financial costs of shipping are an incentive for construction specifiers to choose

local products. Rising fuel prices will also raise this incentive.

Carpooling is a different matter, and a place where green businesses have to put their money where their principles are. Fuel costs for getting to the job site are commonly borne by the worker; saving fuel saves the *company* no money, and may in fact cost money. Some companies make it a policy that all employees report to the main office and go to the site in company vehicles. This is not always the most efficient routing, however, and enforcing it may be unpopular.

One potential ally in this challenge may be the mapping software increasingly available for desktop and laptop computers. By entering employee home locations and project sites just once, such software can easily compute travel distances. Automating the process of planning the most efficient transportation day-to-day would not be a complex task. Under the name of "logistics," such programs are vital to the major transportation companies, who have saved literally billions of dollars, hours, and fuel-gallons. Simple mapping software costs are in the $100 range; the CAD systems that many design and contracting offices already have could also be modified for this purpose. The same system could provide decision-making support about suppliers as well.

Summary of Machinery and Tool Energy Guidelines

The following suggestions, although not ironclad, are a starting point for saving energy by careful planning about machinery:

1. Plan! Conventional contractors may be able to survive with seat-of-the-pants fuel-usage decisions; no one concerned with green building can afford such guesswork.

2. Cut down travel miles and fuel costs to the job by any means possible. Company-sponsored carpooling is one option. Regular tune-ups of company vehicles should be standard practice. One famous design-build architecture company, the Jersey Devil, moves onto the site in Airstream trailers for the duration. Choose your own methods, but decrease work-related transportation.

3. Use hand labor where it is reasonable to do so. Take pride in handwork's quality,

ecofriendliness, and health benefits, rather than focus only on the speed and ease of power equipment.

4. Use the most efficient tool for the job. If that tool is engine-powered, balance low horsepower and fuel consumption with speed, rather than consider speed alone.

5. Use the lightest machinery available that will do the job. Manufacturers and tool rental companies are offering more and more mini-machinery.

6. When buying or renting power tools large or small, insist on getting information about fuel consumption per hour, pollutant emissions, and ground pressure. Give your business to companies that provide this information willingly. Understand and use the information in planning jobs.

7. Look for innovative ways of generating energy at the site. Think about ways to adapt solar, wind, and fuel-cell power sources (which are usually stationary) to the needs of mobile construction crews.

Embodied Energy—Why Do We Care?[27]

Embodied energy, as discussed at the beginning of this chapter, is the total energy used to produce something—either a single material, a complex product, or a whole project. For landscape structures and plantings, fuel use by tools and machines on-site is a significant part of their embodied energy. In addition, each type of material has energy embodied in it when it arrives at the site ready for use: the energy used in manufacturing the item and transporting it to the site.

Landscape professionals need to take a closer look at embodied energy. Because the ratio of embodied energy to operating energy is so much higher for landscapes than for buildings, this topic is even more important for landscape professionals than for architects. Yet it is the architectural profession that has done the most work with embodied energy research.

A general diagram of the many energy inputs that add up to embodied energy is shown in Figure 7.7. For some materials, inputs shown in the diagram may be repeated or skipped. A simple raw material like landscape boulders or sand might involve energy only from extraction,

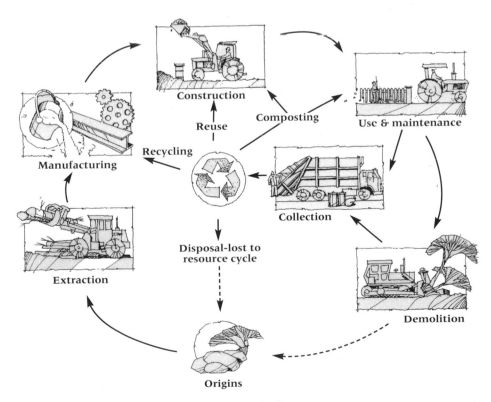

Figure 7.7. Life-cycle flowchart: landscape materials and embodied energy. ILLUSTRATION: Craig Farnsworth.

transportation, and placement on-site. The embodied energy of steel or aluminum bars would involve not only extraction, smelting the ore, and shaping the bars, but also transportation, which may occur during processing as well as from factory to site. If these bars were manufactured into tubular fencing, energy used in making the tubes and assembling the fence would be added, as would the energy to erect the fence on-site.

Embodied energy is usually expressed in terms of *energy per unit* of product, in much the same way that cost estimates are based on cost-per-unit or cost-per-quantity figures. Energy is most commonly stated in Btu or in joules (the metric/scientific standard); calories and watts are also used as energy units. Thus the embodied energy of builder's sand might be in Btu/ton or in kilojoules/cubic meter; for metal ingots, in kilocalories/pound; and for fencing, in Btu per linear foot or per panel of fence. (Conversion tables for different systems of measure can be found under "Measurements" in most dictionaries and in *Architectural Graphic Standards*.)

Examples of the embodied energy associated with building materials are shown in Tables 7.12 through 7.17. (We *strongly* recommend reading the whole chapter, not just the tables, because interpretation and comparison of these statistics requires care.)

Benefits of Embodied Energy Analysis

In concept, then, embodied energy is fairly straightforward. Embodied energy analysis has many potential benefits for designers and builders, though only part of this potential is currently feasible. In theory, embodied energy figures can be used to compare environmental impacts of widely differing materials and designs, revealing trade-offs that do not show up in economic or engineering analysis.

- Embodied energy is, ideally, much more *objective* than price as a measure of comparative product value. Accurate value comparisons in construction are critical to everyone—client, designer, and contractor—yet market prices are frequently misleading indicators of value, especially environmental value. The distorting effects of local and international markets, artificial price subsidies, inflation, and buyer psychology can be set

aside in energy analysis. (See "Adobe," page 201, as an example.) Once the underlying or intrinsic value is established by energy analysis, financial value can be better understood, too. The authors suspect that in the not too distant future, "energy accounting" will be the most accurate way to predict business expenses, profits, and losses and will be as essential a tool for contractors and designers as monetary cost-estimating is today.

- Energy is a *common denominator* in all manufacturing and construction. As such, it makes complex apples-and-oranges decisions much easier. If you need to compare the environmental impact of two functionally equivalent designs, say, a cast-in-place concrete wall built with gas-powered machines verus a wood fence made with air-powered hand tools, energy analysis is the most meaningful measure available. Questions like "steel studs verus wood framing" get a new and important perspective from knowing that steel is relatively high in embodied energy per pound, and that wood is relatively low. (Strength, durability, and recyclability must also be factored in for a complete comparison.)

- Fuels burned to produce energy are a major source of pollution, so embodied energy is a rough-and-ready *indicator* for materials that pollute. For example, about 55 kg of the greenhouse gas CO_2 is released for every gigajoule (billion joules) of energy produced by burning natural gas (a relatively clean fuel).[28] Thus, if 1 megajoule (million joules) of natural-gas-generated energy is required to produce a ton of some material, its embodied energy (1MJ/ton) also represents 0.055 kg (about 0.125 lb.) of CO_2 emissions per ton. Although fuels vary widely in how much pollution they release, and not all pollution is accounted for in fuel consumption, as a general rule, higher embodied energy means higher pollution during production.

- Since the late 1970s, Model Energy Codes have regulated *operating* energy efficiency, making dramatic changes in the work of building designers and contractors. Because of their low *operating* energy levels, landscapes have largely been ignored by such regulations. A growing need to monitor energy efficiency in *all* aspects of construction is likely to lead to *embodied* energy standards, which will affect landscape materials and construction processes. New Zealand, for instance, has already studied the feasibility of requiring embodied energy standards as part of national code (and, for the time being, rejected it as not yet practical).[29] Similarly, in 1993 the U.S. government considered a "Btu tax"; the measure was not politically acceptable, but similar initiatives are likely to succeed as both energy costs and global temperatures continue to rise.

Energy Accounting and Sustainability

Energy accounting is as complex as economics— no more and no less. There is one major difference, however. Most modern societies monitor the flow of money and trade; in industrial societies, this monitoring is a huge industry employing statisticians, economists, accountants, and many others. By contrast, accurate and detailed monitoring of energy have not yet become a mainstream priority, and the tools, methods, and institutions for this task are far from fully developed. As a result, available statistics on embodied energy are sometimes confusing and hard to compare. Is this an unavoidable limitation?

Energy accounting today *is* rather complex and inexact (see Appendix B, page 319). Critics argue that this will always be the case. The authors disagree. These limitations would be overcome if energy statistics were collected with the same diligence as that applied to monetary and trade statistics. The ability to predict, plan, and make decisions about the flow of goods and services would quickly and dramatically improve, for businesses, for individuals, and for society as a whole. The technology to collect energy data exists, at least in basic form, and the effort required would be no greater than what is now directed at economics. The results would probably be *more* accurate, with less of the "voodoo economics" that so often rules the financial world.

Construction Influence on the Energy Future

Why consider this issue in a book on construction? The reason is straightforward. Like any technological advance, energy analysis will develop only if there is a demand for it. That demand is going to come from those who are most directly affected by energy costs—those who use large amounts of energy in pursuit of their livelihoods. The construction and design industry is a major player in the future of energy, making decisions that affect more than 30 percent of the U.S. energy budget. Our professions will not single-handedly create the demand for accurate energy estimating and tracking systems—but as our industry recognizes the value of such systems, especially their value to sustainable construction, our influence will be significant.

The Athena Sustainable Materials Institute, a major embodied energy research organization, states the situation bluntly: "Building construction, renovation and operation consume more of the Earth's resources than any other human activity. This generates millions of tonnes of greenhouse gases, toxic air emissions, water pollutants, and solid wastes. No other sector has a greater impact on the global environment or faces a greater obligation to improve its environmental performance."[30]

Early in this new millennium, landscape designers and planners need to expect to choose materials at least partly on embodied energy considerations. Software to aid this process is under development. Landscape contractors will need new skills to implement energy-conscious designs and will have to understand embodied energy when proposing substitutions for specified materials. In order to stay competitive in a sustainable economy, contractors will also need to manage energy efficiently for equipment, transportation, and worker travel to and from the site. Although it is an unfamiliar concept to most landscape professionals today, embodied energy is an idea whose time is coming soon— some would say, should have come long ago— and for which there is good reason to be prepared.

Embodied Energy of Landscape Materials

More than a half dozen major studies have been published with extensive tables of embodied energy for construction materials (see Appendix B). Many others have been commissioned for in-house use, but not published.[31] None of these studies has focused specifically on *landscape* construction materials. Table 7.12 shows selected landscape materials and embodied energy values, which were derived by comparing ten published studies.

These figures are primarily included as examples, although they may be useful in rough calculations to compare energy costs of various materials, designs, or suppliers. If you intend to use these numbers directly, be sure that you

- read this *entire* chapter and Appendix B, which discusses issues of comparability, and

- base final materials decisions on life-cycle costing (page 248) and on your own good judgment, not on energy figures alone.

Appendix B, "Limits of Embodied Energy Methods Today," briefly discusses methods and assumptions used by these studies and the regional conditions that influenced the statistics. It also discusses the variability between figures for the same material in different studies, which typifies the current state of embodied energy research. Finally, it gives methods used in this compilation, which may be important in interpreting and using these figures.

EMBODIED ENERGY ESTIMATING EXAMPLE

An example of how the tables of energy statistics might be used is shown in and described below.

You have decided to build a 5-foot-high garden wall, using either adobe or straw bale construction. Footings for the wall will be the same for either material.

- Calculate the volume of the wall. Note that standard straw bales are 4 inches thicker than adobe blocks, so that the volume of the bale wall is larger. Assume a length of 100 feet for the wall.

- Convert the volume to weight, multiplying density times volume for each material (Table 7.13).

- In the Materials by Weight table (Table 7.12), unstabilized adobe (listed as earth) has embodied energy of 172 Btu/lb.; baled straw is 103 Btu/lb. Multiply these by the total weight for each material. It appears that the bale wall uses less than 2 percent of the energy required for adobe.

Table 7.11
Worked Example of Simple Embodied Energy Comparison

Wall volume

| length | 100 ft. |
| height | 5 ft. |

Standard width **(in feet) × 500 sf =**

| adobe (14 in.) | 1.2 | 600 cf |
| straw (18 in.) | 1.5 | 750 cf |

Convert to Weight

	lb./cf	× volume	total
adobe	95	600	57,000 lb.
straw	8	750	1,125 lb.

Basic Embodied Energy

	Btu/lb.	× weight	total
adobe	172	57,000	9,804,000 Btu/100 LF
straw	103	1,125	115,875 Btu/100 LF

Required for straw only

1/2" stucco	1,150 sf surface	46 cf stucco
	145 lb./cf	6,670 lbs. stucco
	860 Btu/lb.	5,736,200 Btu for stucco
wire lath	1,150 sf surface	
	52,100 Btu/sf	59,915,000 Btu for wire

Total Embodied Energy

| adobe | 9,804,000 Btu/100 LF |
| straw | 65,767,075 Btu/100 LF |

- However, straw bale construction requires stuccoing. For the stucco itself, the process is just like the other materials: calculate a volume, convert to weight, and compute embodied energy.

- Stucco requires metal wire or lath. This material is listed by area and can be looked up directly, showing 52,100 Btu/lb. Multiply the area of wire used by this amount.

- Adding the stucco and lath to the straw bale shows that adobe uses less than 15 percent of the energy required for straw bale.

The analysis could go further. Steel reinforcing is optional for low, non-load-bearing landscape walls; including it would add considerably to the embodied energy, and you might decide to substitute bamboo stakes as reinforcing.

The above example assumes that the adobes were made by hand on-site. If they were transported, you would need to look at Table 7.9, where trucking is shown to use an average of about 4,000 Btu per ton per mile. The wall weighs about 28.5 tons. If the supplier is 20 miles from the project, this adds 2,280,000 Btu to the energy for the adobe. The total is still only about 18 percent of the energy for straw bale, even without calculating transportation for the bales.

However, if someone insists on stuccoing the adobe . . .

This example shows how similar energy estimation is to money estimation, and that job- and site-specific inclusions or exclusions make a great difference in which material is most energy efficient. Factors like durability, whether there is a source of adobe soil that can be used without damage to the site, and so on must also be taken into account.

UNDERSTANDING THE EMBODIED ENERGY TABLES

For Tables 7.12 through 7.17, the estimates from ten studies were compared. The first task was to convert the measurements to comparable systems, since some were in metric, some in U.S. or U.K. units; the nonmetric studies also used different energy units. After conversion, the degree of variability did not appear as extreme as expected. Figures for any given material varied as little as ± 7 percent across the sources, and the great majority of figures agreed within ± 30 percent. While this is clearly not the kind of accu-racy that scientific energy calculations would like to achieve, it is not too different from variability accepted in construction estimation. The tables show an average, with the deviation noted up to 30 percent; where deviation exceeded this percentage, the tables show a range.

The plus-or-minus figures may be useful in customizing the numbers to a local situation. If a specific supplier is conscientious about energy efficiency, and if transportation distances are low, deduct the percentage shown; if the opposite is true, add the percentage. This ensures that the adjusted figures will not be outside the range of estimates currently available.

Most of the values are given as energy per weight, since this is the most easily converted and general way of expressing embodied energy. Weight can always be converted to or from volume using the density of the basic material. Where materials are widely specified by another type of unit, such as volume, information is also given in that form. For a few materials, this is the only form in which the original studies covered that material.

Embodied energy research is still a young discipline, and the available figures should be treated as such: surprisingly consistent, given the complexity of the subject, but at the same time, provisional and in need of improvement.⊃

Column heading notes: "CSI" column groups the materials according to CSI (Construction Specifications Institute) divisions as used in the AIA's *Environmental Resource Guide.* "AvgEst" shows the average of estimates or, if there was extreme deviation in the estimates, notes "range," followed in the "Low" and "High" columns by figures for the range of estimates for that material. "SD%" is the standard deviation among estimates, expressed as a percentage of the average. "#" shows the number of sources that gave a figure for the material; where it is blank, there was only one source.

Note: Although measurements by weight are the most widely useful, they can be perplexing at first glance. For example, Table 7.12 shows dry cement powder to have about five times as much embodied energy as ready-mix concrete. Since ready-mix is one step further along the production chain, this seems backward, but is in fact correct. The dry powder is mixed with bulky, low-energy materials (sand and aggregate) and water, all of which add weight while decreasing

Table 7.12
Embodied Energy of Selected Landscape Materials by Weight

Materials by Weight	CSI	AvgEst Btu/lb.	Low	High	SD%	#
Earth	2.3	172				
Earth, stabilized 5 concrete	2.3	241			25	2
Paving, bitum, 1.5 in. (wearing surf only)	2.7	1,242			18	2
Fertilizer (ammonia)	2.9	27,596				
Fertilizer (phosphatic)	2.9	32,373				
Fertilizer (superphosphate)	2.9	2,701				
Aggregate, crushed stone	3.0	929				
Aggregate, river stone	3.0	9				
Sand	3.0	16				
Cement, dry powder	3.1	3,062			21	5
Concrete, ready-mix	3.1	656			7	4
Lime, hydrated	3.1	4,406				
Mortar (hydrolic & masonry cements)	4.0	860				
Adobe block, bitumen stabilization	4.2	123				
Adobe block, cement stabilization	4.2	160			13	2
Adobe block, straw stabilization	4.2	202				
Brick, common	4.2	range	1,075	4,085	n/a	5
Concrete block	4.2	range	370	964	n/a	4
Concrete, aerated	4.2	1,548				
Glass	4.2	5,934			8	2
Glass block	4.2	6,200			24	3
Straw, baled	4.2	103				
Tile, quarry & paving	4.2	range	9,017	22,886	n/a	2
Tile, struct facing, 6×12×4 in.	4.2	8,385				
Stone	4.4	446			24	2
Stone, granite, cut	4.4	2,537				
Aluminum	5.1	67,368			7	5
Aluminum, anodized	5.1	87,294			6	2
Aluminum, extruded	5.1	71,380				
Aluminum, plate & sheet	5.1	93,153			25	2
Aluminum, struct shapes	5.1	92,200				
Aluminum, recycled	5.1	3,348			3	3
Aluminum, recycled, anodized	5.1	18,447				
Aluminum, recycled, extruded	5.1	7,439				
Aluminum, recycled, plate & sheet	5.1	6,364				
Brass	5.1	26,660				
Copper	5.1	32,158			23	4
Copper, pipe	5.1	73,100				
Copper, sheet	5.1	69,700				
Copper, struct shapes	5.1	46,800				
Iron, cast	5.1	14,891				
Steel, alloy, struct shapes	5.1	26,900				
Steel, carbon, galv sheets	5.1	27,800				
Steel, carbon, pipe	5.1	25,800				
Steel, carbon, sheets	5.1	16,800				
Steel, carbon, struct shapes	5.1	22,700				

Table 7.12
Continued

Materials by Weight	CSI	AvgEst Btu/lb.	Low	High	SD%	#
Steel, mild	5.1	12,214			14	5
Steel, mild, galvanized	5.1	15,652			4	2
Steel, stainless, coldroll bar	5.1	193,000				
Steel, stainless, coldroll sheet	5.1	138,000				
Steel, stainless, hotroll bar	5.1	157,000				
Steel, stainless, hotroll sheet	5.1	89,800				
Steel, recycled	5.1	4,647			7	2
Zinc	5.1	22,145			1	2
Zinc, galvanizing/kg steel	5.1	1,204				
Metal expanded lath	5.7	range	12,000	33,000	n/a	2
Steel common nails	5.9	34,000				
Steel HS bolts	5.9	26,600				
Lumber, hardwood, air-dry	6.0	range	215	602	n/a	2
Lumber, hardwood, kiln-dry	6.0	1,054			18	2
Lumber, softwood, air-dry	6.0	499				
Lumber, softwood, kiln-dry	6.0	1,269			15	2
Lumber, 3/4 in. ext. plywood	6.1	4,472				
Lumber, glue-lam beams	6.1	5,531			10	4
Lumber, plywood	6.1	4,522			10	4
Lumber, roughsawn	6.1	163			21	2
Plastics, ABS	6.5	47,715			0	2
Plastics, general	6.5	35,389			9	2
Plastics, HDPE	6.5	42,226				
Plastics, LDPE	6.5	30,560			27	2
Plastics, PET (polyethylene terephthalate)	6.5	45,800				
Plastics, polycarb glazing	6.5	68,200				
Plastics, polyester	6.5	23,091				
Plastics, polypropylene	6.5	34,260			20	2
Plastics, polystyrene	6.5	49,607			2	3
Plastics, polyurethane	6.5	31,410			1	2
Plastics, polybutylene	6.5	25,000				
Plastics, PVC	6.5	35,130			22	5
Rubber, natural latex	6.5	29,013			0	2
Rubber, synthetic	6.5	39,063			30	3
Waterproofing, asphalt	7.1	1,221				
Waterproofing, paper	7.1	10,500				
Insulation, rigid polystyrene	7.2	63,355			21	2
Shingles, cedar	7.3	3,870				
Adhesives, epoxy & resins	9.2	35,000			14	2
Adhesive, concrete	9.9	3,010				
Adhesive, phenol formaldehyde	9.9	37,410				
Adhesive, urea formaldehyde	9.9	33,626				
Paint, external oil-based	9.9	42,962			3	3
Paint, external water-based	9.9	35,672			19	4
Fabric, cotton	12.0	61,580			0	2
Fabric, polyester	12.0	23,096			0	2
Pipe, steel	15.1	25,800				

the amount of embodied energy per pound. Very light materials, like some plastics, have high embodied energy per pound because it takes so much material to make up a pound. Finally, a pound is a pound, but if a pound of copper is made into copper pipe, its embodied energy increases. If a figure seems surprising, check the specific gravity of the material, and consider whether it is mixed with other materials in use. (Corrections of real errors, of course, would be appreciated.)

NOT ENERGY ALONE

Analysis of energy requirements has the potential to be a strong baseline for comparing construction materials and methods. This baseline is potentially far more realistic than price comparison but must still be used in combination with other factors, including the following:

- *Strength* in proportion to weight or cross-section, which shows how much of a material is required to accomplish a structural function; a tiny amount of a high-energy material may be more energy-effective than a large amount of a low-energy material.

- *Durability and service life*, which tell how long a material can perform its function before being replaced or recycled, and thus, how often the investment of energy must be repeated.

- *Resource scarcity and renewability:* Glass is high-energy, but the materials to make it are more abundant than the petroleum used to make clear plastics. Neither is renewable.

- *Reusability and recyclability:* The ability to re*use* a material in its existing form means that only transportation and installation energy are required for the second use. For some materials, recycling and remanufacturing save a high proportion of the energy required for new production; aluminum, for example, can be recycled for as little as 5 percent of the energy needed to refine new ore.[32] Not all materials are equally recyclable, however. In addition, some materials are themselves recyclable, but the fasteners or adhesives used to join them interfere with reuse or recycling.

- *Toxicity:* In addition to the air and water pollution generated by energy production and use, some materials are inherently toxic or require the use of toxic chemicals in production. These issues are discussed in Principle 6.

- Other design considerations: Materials that degrade under ultraviolet light are unsuitable for exposed outdoor use, no matter how energy-efficient they may be. Another example is steel, which is energy-efficient for many uses requiring strength, but can be corroded by some soils, affecting its suitability for in-ground fittings in some regions. To overcome this, steel may be coated—but the energy cost of doing so must be accounted for.

Although it is beyond the scope of this book to give comprehensive information on each of these factors, it is clear that they must be considered in materials selection and energy analysis. A promising approach to this type of multifactor analysis is usually known as life-cycle analysis, or LCA, which is discussed on page 218. There does not appear to be any landscape-specific LCA studies at this time.

A simpler method called life-cycle costing, which can address some life-cycle issues without the extensive expertise required for LCA, is discussed in the following section.

Life-Cycle Costing: A Related Sustainability Tool

Life-cycle costing (LCC) is a relatively simple tool that makes apples-to-apples comparisons of design and construction options much easier. It was first developed for financial comparisons such as return on investment but can easily be used for energy comparisons as well. Unlike its similarly named cousin, life-cycle analysis (LCA), it does *not* deal with resource scarcity, pollution issues, or in any detail with recyclability. Nonetheless, LCC is a respected technique and ready to use today, while LCA and embodied energy analysis are still evolving. For this reason, we feel it is worth mentioning here.

Architects use LCC routinely; a rather complex explanation of the process is included in *Architectural Graphic Standards*.[33] Landscape professionals who use LCC will certainly reduce the long-term costs, both in dollars and in energy, which they pass on to their clients. The cumulative effect of such reductions is clearly a necessary step toward sustainability.

Table 7.13
Average Densities of Selected Landscape Materials

Material Type	CSI	lb./cy	lb./cf	kg./m³	Equiv.	
Soil cement 5%	2.3	2,885	107	1,710		
Aggregate	3.0	2,700	100	1,602		
Cinder or ash	3.0	1,350	50	801		
Clay, dry	3.0	1,701	63	1,009		
Cement powder	3.0	2,538	94	1,506		
Concrete	3.0	3,967	147	2,354		
Earth, loose dry	3.0	2,052	76	1,218		
Earth, packed dry	3.0	2,565	95	1,522		
Sand	3.0	3,305	122	1,961		
Mortar	4.0	2,797	104	1,659		
Adobe	4.2	2,628	97	1,559		
Bricks	4.2	2,939	109	1,744		
Concrete, aerated	4.2	1,312	49	779		
Glass	4.2	4,247	157	2,520		
Straw, baled	4.2	214	8	127		
Tile	4.2	3,646	135	2,163		
Stone (nonspecific)	4.4	4,149	154	2,462		
Stone, granite	4.4	4,455	165	2,643		
Stone, limestone	4.4	3,645	135	2,163		
Stone, marble	4.4	4,671	173	2,771		
Stone, sandstone	4.4	3,888	144	2,307		
Stone, slate	4.4	4,644	172	2,755		
Aluminum	5.1	4,503	167	2,672		
Copper	5.1	15,041	557	8,924		
Steel	5.1	13,230	490	7,850		
Zinc	5.1	11,964	443	7,098		
Lumber (nonspecific)	6.0	1,669	62	990	5.2	lb/BdFt
Lumber, hardwood	6.0	1,433	53	850	4.4	lb/BdFt
Lumber, particleboard	6.0	1,062	39	630	3.3	lb/BdFt
Lumber, plywood	6.0	1,011	37	600	3.1	lb/BdFt
Lumber, softwood	6.0	927	34	550	2.9	lb/BdFt
Polyester	6.5	243	9	144		
Polyethylene sheet	6.5	1,635	61	970		
Polypropylene	6.5	1,517	56	900		
Polyurethane	6.5	244	9	145		
PVC	6.5	2,255	84	1,338		
Rubber, natural latex	6.5	1,551	57	920		
Rubber, synthetic	6.5	2,136	79	1,267		
Bitumen	7.1	1,736	64	1,030	8.6	lb/gal
Adhesive, concrete	9.9	1,686	62	1,000		
Paint (all types, U.S.)	9.9	2,186	81	n/a	10.8	lb/gal
Paint (all types, metric)	9.9	n/a	n/a	1,300	1.3	kg/l

LCC for Better Comparative Costing

Life-cycle costing is particularly useful when comparing two or more proposed options. A simple example might be comparing the cost of two trucks for use by a landscape firm. Suppose one model costs $10,000, needs $750 maintenance every year, and gets 20 mpg, while the other costs $12,000, requires an average of $500 service every other year, and gets 30 mpg. Driving each truck 10,000 miles annually, by the end of five years the first truck costs $16,250, and the second $14,915. If the life cycle shortens to two years before trade-in, the first model costs only $12,500, the second, $13,166. The short life cycle, however, dramatically increases the cost *per year*: Keeping either truck five years costs about $3,000 a year, while keeping it only two years raises the annual price to at least $6,250.

This example shows clearly how "sticker price" alone gives a misleading comparison. The person or firm who bought the first truck, or who traded

Table 7.14
Embodied Energy of Selected Landscape Materials By Volume

Materials by Volume	CSI	AvgEst (Btu/cu.ft.)	Low	High	SD%	#
Concrete, ready cf	3.1	96,100				
Concrete, ready cy	3.1	2,590,000cy				
Lumber, hardwood	6.0	9,820				
Lumber, softwood	6.0	8,555			15	3
Lumber, glue-lam beams	6.1	15,611			10	3
Lumber, plywood	6.1	14,883				
Lumber, roughsawn	6.1	495				
Waterproofing, asphalt	7.1	8,639			22	2
Insulation, rigid polystyrene	7.2	15,300				
Paint, exterior oil-based	9.9	488,264			0	2
Paint, exterior water-based	9.9	489,032			0	2
Stains & varnishes	9.9	503,668				

Table 7.15
Embodied Energy of Selected Landscape Materials by Area

Materials by Area	CSI	AvgEst (Btu/sq.ft.)	Low	High	SD%	#
Paving brick 2.25 in. thick	2.7	133,000				
Paving, 4 in. concrete, wire reinforced	2.7	44,000				
Paving, 6 in. concrete, wire reinforced	2.7	60,000				
Paving, bitum, 1.5 in. (wearing surface only)	2.7	54,600				
Reinforced wire, welded 4×4 10/10	3.2	7,500				
Reinforced wire, welded 6×6 10/10	3.2	5,080				
Brick, common: wall 2 bricks thick, incl. mortar	4.2	281,000				
Metal expanded lath	5.7	52,100				
Lumber, 1/2 in. ext. plywood	6.1	range	2,450	7,710	n/a	3
Lumber, 3/4 in. ext. plywood	6.1	11,600				
Lumber, 3/8 in. ext. plywood	6.1	5,790				
Shingles, asphalt	7.3	26,787			8	3
Shingles, cedar	7.3	7,320				
Roofing, aluminum 0.032 in.	7.4	720,000				
Roofing, copper 20-oz.	7.4	97,700				
Roofing, plastic corrugated	7.4	50,000				
Roofing, steel 20-gauge	7.4	54,750				
Roofing, stainless steel 32-gauge.	7.4	46,900				
Paint, external oil-based	9.9	1,390				
Paint, external water-based	9.9	1,400				

in either truck early, would have to work a lot harder to make a profit. Including operating costs and specifying the duration creates a simple life-cycle costing, which gives much more accurate and useful information about the two trucks. Life-cycle costs change with length of service and amount of use.

Conventionally, many design and construction professionals have concerned themselves only with the sticker price of a project. After all, it is this up-front cost that professionals have to con-vince the client to pay, and in many cases, profits or fees are based directly on this price. Sustain-ability requires broadening this perspective. If cheap-to-build means expensive-to-maintain, up-front profits are ultimately at the expense of society and of the environment. The "cheap" truck burns more fuel and causes more pollution the longer it is on the road; trading it in after two years makes it appear cheaper, but actually doubles the annual cost. Whether looking at vehicles, buildings, or landscapes, simple sticker-price

Table 7.16
Embodied Energy of Selected Landscape Materials by Length

Materials by Linear Measure	CSI	AvgEst (Btu/lin.ft.)	Low	High	SD%	#
Rebar #2	3.2	2,620				
Rebar #3	3.2	5,900				
Rebar #4	3.2	10,500				
Rebar #5	3.2	16,400				
Rebar #6	3.2	23,600				
Masonry reinforced, 4 in. (truss or ladder)	4.0	3,670				
Pipe, ABS 2-in.	15.1	20,459			14	2
Pipe, cast iron 2-in.	15.1	86,368				
Pipe, copper 2-in.	15.1	32,107				
Pipe, PVC 2-in.	15.1	22,984				
Wire, copper insulated #10	16.1	1,740				
Wire, copper insulated #12	16.1	1,090				
Wire, copper insulated #14	16.1	688				
Wire, copper insulated #16	16.1	427				

Table 7.17
Embodied Energy of Selected Landscape Materials by Each

Materials by Each	CSI	AvgEst (Btu/each)	Low	High	SD%	#
Brick, common	4.2	14,300				
Brick, paving	4.2	25,600				
Concrete block 12 × 8 × 16 in.	4.2	49,400				
Concrete block 4 × 4 × 16 in.	4.2	9,330				
Concrete block 8 × 8 × 16 in.	4.2	27,401			16	3
Tile, structural facing, 6 × 12 × 4 in.	4.2	117,000				

estimates encourage waste and short-sightedness. LCC is a tool for designing more sustainably and more responsibly.

Basic LCC

Over a project's useful life, costs occur in five major forms. For LCC, these are referred to as Capital, Maintenance, Fuel, Replacement, and Salvage.[34] Using the first letter as an abbreviation for each, the life-cycle cost of a project, system, or piece of equipment can be written as:

LCC = C + M + F + R − S

These costs can be in terms of money, or in terms of energy, but not mixed in the same analysis. Capital costs in dollars and maintenance costs in energy would not produce a useful total, for example.

I. *Capital* costs include materials and construction work, as well as design and engineering services. Most designers and contractors are highly experienced in estimating capital costs.

Conventional bid estimates include *only* capital costs and omit the other four factors.

2. *Maintenance* costs include all anticipated *annual* operating expenses, such as routine inspection of systems, seasonal start-up and shutdown, etc. However, Maintenance does *not* include Fuel or Replacement. (Replacement in this formula refers to major system replacements that occur only a few times over the life cycle. Minor parts replaced routinely each year are included with Maintenance.)

3. Although the cost of *Fuel* to operate and maintain the project could be included in Maintenance, it is better listed separately. In monetary analysis, it is valuable to record Fuel separately because the rate of inflation is often greater for fuel prices than for other goods. In energy analysis, it can also be valuable to know how much of the total goes directly to Fuel.

4. *Replacement* represents repairs and overhauls that are not annual—for example, a photo-

voltaic system with a life span of thirty years might require replacement of storage batteries every eighth year.

5. *Salvage* (or resale) is subtracted from the money cost in conventional economic analysis, usually allowing 20 percent of the original cost of the materials. For environmental purposes, Salvage can be either a reduced cost (when materials are recycled) or an additional cost (when disposal is required).

Besides these cost amounts, it is necessary to know the predicted *useful life* of the project or equipment being evaluated. The *frequency* of routine maintenance and replacement tasks must be known, as well as fuel-consumption rates. These figures are usually obtained from manufacturers or estimated based on professional experience.

When comparing several options, use the *longest* life cycle. For example, if LCC were used to help decide on an alternative power source for a remote site, hypothetical options might be a generator (rebuild or replace every seven years), a windmill (useful life, fifteen years between rebuilds), and photovoltaic panels (thirty years before replacement). All three should be analyzed over the thirty-year period, including the costs of rebuilding the generator four times and the windmill once.

Energy LCC

For an *energy* LCC analysis, all that is necessary is to add up the energy costs for C, M, F, and R, and allow for S. Unlike the simpler forms of embodied energy study, which stop once the project is built and do not consider long-term energy costs, LCC energy analysis reveals differences in durability, operating energy, and maintenance.

From an environmental perspective, the Salvage factor is especially important. The costs of waste disposal are poorly accounted for in conventional financial analysis, as are costs of environmental cleanup. LCC using energy units has the potential to show real costs to society that are otherwise obscured.

Monetary LCC Analysis

Economic analysis also has its value for sustainable construction. Financial cost data are readily available, which cannot yet be said for energy data. Even very environmentally aware landowners and professionals must know the financial costs of proposed work, and sometimes cost is the deciding factor in approving sustainable proposals. Money savings can reflect environmental savings, although usually with considerable distortion.

LCC using dollar amounts is far preferable to simple capital cost or sticker-price analysis, for the reasons outlined earlier. As a parallel to energy costing, monetary LCC is an important tool for sustainable design and construction.

The essential formula (LCC = C + M + F + R − S) is the same, whether plugging in dollars or Btu. You must know the dollar costs of capital, maintenance, and so on. There is, however, one major difference—the term "present value," which applies only to money.

Present value is a conventional financial concept based on the idea that money in hand today is worth more than money promised later, because it can be invested. That is, if you have $100 today, in one year you will have $105 if interest is at 5 percent. If someone promises to pay you $100 in a year, you will have only $100. The promised money is thus considered to be worth 5 percent less; its present value would be about $95.

All figures used in monetary LCC must be adjusted to present value according to standard formulas. These formulas are briefly summarized here; detailed explanations and tables of "present worth factors" can be found in standard texts on financial management or engineering economics. Formulas for present value are built into many computer spreadsheets. (Although the two terms are used interchangeably, present *worth* seems to refer to the formulas or factors used to compute present *value*.)

To establish present value, it is necessary to know two things:

1. *When* the cost will be paid—at the beginning of the life cycle; annually throughout the whole life cycle; or in a specific year of the life cycle, for example, the ninth year of a twenty-year life cycle.

2. A percentage called the *discount factor*. The discount rate is the expected interest rate paid on investments, minus the predicted inflation rate. For example, if money invested today would earn an annual rate of 7 percent, and

the annual inflation rate predicted for the next few years were 4 percent, the discount rate would be 3 percent. For some products, especially fuel, price inflation is more rapid than average. Thus, general inflation might be 4 percent, while fuel-price inflation could be 6 percent. If investments were still paying 7 percent, the discount rate for fuel costs would be 1 percent instead of 3 percent. The federal government and many banks publish projections of interest and inflation.

Given the dollar amounts for each cost, its timing, and a guess at the discount rate, you are ready to prepare an LCC estimate.

The Capital cost C is always treated as a single expense, paid all at once in the first year of the life cycle. Because it is paid in the first year, it is already at present value. Even if the capital costs will be financed by an interest-bearing loan, no finance charges or interest are included in the LCC entry for capital.

All other costs are converted to present value, using one of two formulas (or you can also look them up in tables based on those formulas):

1. Costs that occur *regularly* every year (usually Maintenance and Fuel) are given a present value as follows: If the discount rate is D, and the number of years in the life cycle is L, then $[1-(1+D)^{-L}]/D$ times the *annual* cost gives the present value. For example, to give the present value of annual payments over fifteen years at a discount rate of 2 percent, compute $[1-(1+.02)^{-15}]/.02$; the computed factor in this case is 12.849. This factor is called the "uniform present worth," (UPW), referring to uniform payments over the whole period. The UPW factor is multiplied by the dollar amount of the payment. In this example, if the annual payment is $400, the present value of payments over the whole period is 12.849 × 400, or $5,139.71.

2. Costs that occur *only a few times* during the life cycle (such as Replacement and Salvage) are computed by a formula called "single present worth" (SPW). If the discount rate is represented again by D, and Y stands for the year when the cost occurs (counted from today), then the SPW factor is $1/(1+D)^Y$. Thus, the factor for a single expense paid eight years from now, and assuming a discount rate of 2 percent, would be $1/(1+.02)^8$, or 0.853. If the

actual payment in year 8 would be $400, its present value would be 400 × .853, or $341.20. If a cost occurs every eight years, it would be treated as single costs occurring in years 8, 16, 24, and so on. Thus, the present value of the same $400 replacement in year 16 is less than the present value of the payment in year 8 (SPW factor 0.728, present value $291.38).

A simplified worksheet for LCC is shown in Table 7.18. It can be used for LCC *energy* analysis by ignoring the present worth factors altogether, making sure to convert all energy costs into the same system of units. It is also easily convertible to a spreadsheet.

Summary of Guidelines for Landscape Energy Conservation

1. Transportation energy is the place where landscape professionals can probably make the most difference.

2. Cut shipping energy costs by specifying local materials as first preference, then regional products. Use products from distant suppliers sparingly—much like nonnative plants—for special accents rather than the whole landscape.

3. Cut worker transportation energy costs however possible. Make carpooling a company policy, with incentives. Track worker distances from home to each project, assign workers to short-commute projects where possible and make flexible arrangements for workers not to come to the main office when their home is nearer to their current job site.

4. Choose the right machine, tool, or labor for each task with energy consumption in mind. See detailed suggestions on page 242.

5. Improve your ability to analyze energy as part of materials selection and design, using embodied energy analysis, life-cycle costing, life-cycle analysis, or other big-picture methods.

6. Remember that saving energy is an ethical choice, not just a financial one. It will sometimes pay off in immediate dollars, but sometimes will not.

Table 7.18
Simplified Life-Cycle Costing (LCC Worksheet)

LCC Analysis of (project or equipment) _____

Expected life cycle of project or equipment _____ years "L"

For *energy* LCC analysis, ignore investment, inflation, and PW factors

    Projected return on investment during life-cycle _____% "R"

    Projected inflation during life-cycle _____% "I"

    Projected fuel inflation during life-cycle _____% "I_F"

Discount rate "D" for non-fuel items = R-I = _____

Fuel discount rate "D_F" = R–I_F = _____

Type of Cost	Amount	Year Occurring	PW Factor	Present Value
Capital	Enter full amt as Full pmt, yr 1; do the Present Value not incl. fin. chgs		NONE	_____
Annual Maint	Enter amount ⬇	each year	$[1-(1+D)^{-L}]/D$	
	_____			_____
	_____			_____
	_____			_____
	_____			_____
Annual Fuel	Enter amount ⬇	each year	$[1-(1+D_F)^{-L}]/D_F$	
	_____			_____
	_____			_____
Replacements	Enter amount ⬇	Fill in year "Y" ⬇	$1/(1+D)^Y$	
	_____	_____		_____
	_____	_____		_____
	_____	_____		_____
	_____	_____		_____
Salvage	Enter positive or negative amount ⬇	Last yr of use "Y" ⬇	$1/(1+D)^Y$	
	_____	_____		_____
			TOTAL	_____

Resources

Energy

Center for Maximum Potential Building Systems
Pliny Fisk, codirector http://www2.cmpbs.org/cmpbs/
   A source for energy, materials, and economics information concerning sustainability.

U.S. Dept. of Energy, Energy Information Clearing-house
www.eren.doe.gov
   Wide variety of info on all aspects of energy. Page /buildings/ is the most focused on construction issues. Page /femp/ focuses on contractor issues.

"Energy & Environmental Profiles" and "Technology Roadmaps" for Steel, Glass, Aluminum (1996–1998 [7 reports] U.S. Dept. of Energy, Office of Industrial Technology Washington DC)

American Institute of Architects, *Environmental Resource Guide* by Joseph A. Demkin (1994–98 [loose-leaf] Wiley)
   Loose-leaf, with annual supplements.

Energies: An Illustrated Guide to the Biosphere and Civilization by Vaclav Smil (1999 MIT Press)

Energy and Habitat: Town Planning and Design for Energy Conservation by Vinod Gupta (1984 Halsted [Wiley])

Energy Basis for Man and Nature by Howard Odum (1976 McGraw-Hill)

Environmental Costs of Electricity by Richard L. Ottinger (1991 Oceana Publications NYC)

Handbook of Energy Use for Building Construction by R. G. Stein, C. Stein, M. Buckley, & M. Green (1980 U.S. Dept. of Energy [DOE/CS/20220-1] Washington DC)

Timber Reduced Energy Efficient Homes by Ed Paschich & Paula Hendricks (1994 Sunstone Press, Santa Fe NM)

"Embodied Energy Coefficients of Building Materials" by Andrew Alcorn (1995 Building Research Association of New Zealand, Wellington NZ)

Office of Scientific and Technical Information
http://apollo.osti.gov/html/dra/
   Information on all sorts of technology, including energy.

Solistice/Crest
www.crest.org
   Long-established site for energy and sustainability information.

Energy: Site Design

Energy Conserving Site Design by E. G. McPherson (1984 ASLA, Washington DC,
800-787-2665 or www.asla.org)

Energy-Efficient and Environmental Landscaping by Ann S. Moffat & Marc Schiler (1993 Appropriate Solutions Press, Dover Rd., Box 39, South Newfane VT 05351)

Earth-Sheltered Landscapes: Site Considerations for Earth-Sheltered Environments by David Douglas DeBord & Thomas R. Dunbar (1985 Van Nostrand Reinhold)

Landscape Architecture and Energy Conservation by Coppa & Avery Consultants (1980 Vance Bibliographies *A-213*, Monticello IL)

Landscape Planning for Energy Conservation by Gary O. Robinette & Charles McClenon (1983 Van Nostrand Reinhold)

Landscaping That Saves Energy and Dollars by Ruth S. Foster (1994 Globe Pequot Press, Old Saybrook CT)

Microclimatic Landscape Design: Creating Thermal Comfort and Energy Efficiency by Robert D. Brown & Terry J. Gillespie (1995 Wiley)

"Landscaping for Energy Efficiency"
U.S. EPA
www.eren.doe.gov/erec/factsheets/landscape.html
   On landscape elements that can affect operating efficiency of adjacent buildings.

Machinery

Outdoor Power Equipment Institute (OPEI)
http://opei.mow.org/
   Industry group, largely about lawn mowers. Rather defensive on environmental issues.

MINI-EQUIPMENT

Bobcat (Melroe Co.) Fargo ND
701-241-8700 or www.bobcat.com/
Division of Ingersoll-Rand

Northstar/Northern Tool & Equipment, Burnsville MN
800-533-5545 or www.northerntool.com
   Manufacturers/distributors of Trencherman towed backhoes; wide range of grounds maintenance and other tools.

Ramrod (Leon Mfrg.), Yorkton SK Canada,
800-667-1581 or lkw@leonsmfg.com
   Manufacturers of Ramrod mini-skidsteer, illustrated.

Wacker Corp., Menomenee Falls WI
414-255-0500
   Manufacturers of small site dumpers, rollers, etc.

MINI-EQUIPMENT AND SMALL ENGINES

Komatsu and Komatsu-Zenoah/Redmax
www.komatsuutility.com/ or 847-970-4100
www.komatsu.com/zenoah/ or 770-381-5147
   Komatsu has many divisions. The Utility division (Vernon Hills IL) makes mini-excavators, etc; the Zenoah division (Norcross GA) makes power tools marketed as Redmax.

SMALL ENGINES

Tanaka engines, Kent WA
253-395-3900 or www.tanakapower equipment. com/
   Manufacturer of PureFire 2-stroke engines, an example of new fuel-efficient, less-polluting small engines.

FUEL COST ESTIMATING AND OTHER ENERGY DATA

California Energy Commission
www.energy.ca.gov/html/directory.html
> Huge directory of energy information. One page gives fuel cost and inflation statistics for LCC and other estimating, with inflation factors.

Operating Energy

Energy Conservation News
Business Communications Inc. www.buscom.com
> Monthly.

Home Energy
Energy Auditor & Retrofitter Inc.
homeenergy@envirolink.org
> Bi-monthly.

EnergyStar program
U.S. EPA and DOE
www.energystar.gov
> Efficiency ratings for various products and homes.

Embodied Energy

Athena Sustainable Materials Institute
www.athenasmi.ca/
> Lists reports on embodied energy research (not available to public through Athena, but may be in libraries).

Building Research Association of New Zealand
www.branz.org.nz/
> Cutting-edge research on embodied energy of building materials.

Embodied Energy of Building Materials
Canada Mortgage and Housing Corp (CMHC), Ottawa ON
613-748-2362

Building Materials Energy and the Environment by Bill Lawson, 1996 Royal Australian Institute of Architects

SandraM@raia.com.au or by fax
011-616-273-1953
> Concise tables on many basic building materials, plus assemblies.

CSIRO: Built Environment Sector
www.dbce.csiro.au/ind-serv/brochures
> Pages on embodied energy, sustainable construction; embodied energy software.

EMBODIED ENERGY IN PRODUCTS

www.oikos.com/

GeoNetwork—Resources for the Green Design Community
www.geonetwork.org/

GOTWH: Building Materials
http://solstice.crest.org/environment/gotwh/general/materials/index.html
> A page of the Solistice/Crest site devoted to materials and energy.

LOW EMBODIED ENERGY MATERIALS

Faculty of Architecture, University of Manitoba and Canada Mortgage and Housing Corp.
www.cadlab.umanitoba.ca/uofm/la/sustainable/design/arch/arch005.htm
> A page of the Sustainable Community Design site. Other pages include a good bibliography, case studies, and links.

3D-Cad Embodied Energy Software
CSIRO Building Construction & Engineering, Australia
www.dbce.csiro.au/ind-serv/brochures/3dcad/3dcad.htm or
information@mel.dbce.csiro.au
> Information on software under development that will calculate embodied energy directly from Cad quantity take-offs.

Celebrate Light, Respect Darkness

At night make me one with the darkness;
in the morning make me one with the light.

—Wendell Berry, 1980

Landscape lighting is a source of great pleasure, extending the use of outdoor space into nighttime hours and contributing to user safety. Outdoor lighting, however, can be either well designed and constructed or excessive or inappropriate. Extravagant lighting can be wonderful for temporary effects, but as a permanent feature of a landscape it wastes resources and causes direct damage to plant and animal species.

Lighting is the largest single use of electricity in the United States, consuming about 20 percent of all electricity used nationally.[1] Saving energy by more efficient lighting has been a major priority of most groups concerned with environmental issues. It has been estimated that by relamping older lighting with today's energy-efficient bulbs, enough energy could be saved to equal all the oil imported by the United States.[2] This immense energy savings could be accomplished without sacrificing existing levels of lighting at all. Further savings can appropriately be achieved by toning down or eliminating excessive lighting.

Landscape lighting, although a fairly small portion of the total, has been one of the fastest-*growing* sectors of the lighting industry. Because the landscape lighting industry is still developing, designers, contractors, and manufacturers have a real opportunity to ensure that efficiency and appropriate design become the standard. Without such a standard, the rapid growth of landscape lighting will contribute unnecessarily to national energy consumption. The choice between sustainable and unsustainable practices in this part of the landscape industry is clearly open to professional influence.

Respect the Need for Darkness

The impulse to fight back the night is an ancient, almost unconscious human urge, one as old as the discovery of fire. Yet although the night held primitive dangers, and still holds modern ones, it also offers mystery and is in fact biologically necessary to most species. It is important not to forget the value of darkness when current lighting technology makes it so easy to exorcise ancient fears.

Most animals and plants have seasonal or daily rhythms that are regulated by patterns of darkness and light. Excessive lighting, especially outdoors, can disrupt these patterns, causing serious harm to some species, including humans. All-night lighting can cause sleeplessness for people exposed to it and may contribute to the well-known stresses that affect shift-workers who are

Discussed in This Chapter:

- When to respect darkness and limit or eliminate lighting
- Efficiency in design of lighting fixtures
- Controllers and timers
- Low-voltage lighting
- Fiber-optic lighting
- Solar landscape lighting
- Performance evaluation

awake at night and sleep days. Most of us need darkness to sleep, and lighting outside of bedrooms should be controlled accordingly. A recent study indicates that children who sleep with constant night-lights are nearly 30 percent more likely to develop nearsightedness; the brighter the light, the greater the chances of myopia.[3] Exposure to artificial light at night has also been shown to play a major role in insomnia, which affects more than 10 million adults in America.[4]

Plants are strongly affected by day length, which at least partly controls when they bloom or leaf out. Growing under constant street lamps, there has been concern that trees could be "confused" into shedding leaves too late in the fall, risking damage from early frost, or budding too early, making them vulnerable to late-winter storms. Very little research was ever done on this topic. Saplings were shown to hold their leaves too long in the fall, but mature trees are less sensitive; the question of early budding never appears to have been addressed.[5] Thus, while nothing is proven, many observant professionals still believe that at least some species of landscape plants are stressed by extremes of artificial lighting. As with other kinds of stress, this would lead to disease and to increased landscape maintenance requirements (Principle 10). Any stress on landscape plantings may result directly in loss of plants, and indirectly in wasteful resource use, and is a sustainability issue.

Neither plants nor humans are likely to go extinct because of overlighting, but there are a few animal species for which this is a real danger. Sea turtles, for example, lay eggs in beach-sand nests, and the hatchlings emerge at night. They rely on illumination from the ocean (which always reflects light more brightly at night than does the land) to guide them back to the water. Artificial lighting on the land side of the beach will mislead the hatchlings, which follow the light onto roads and into built-up areas where they cannot survive. "A single light left on near a sea turtle nesting beach can misdirect and kill hundreds of hatchlings," according to a pamphlet by the Florida Bureau of Protected Species. Because sea turtles are already endangered by hunting and egg-gathering, many coastal communities restrict beachfront lighting during nesting season. The list of light sources that are deadly to hatchling turtles includes almost every type of outdoor and landscape light: the same

pamphlet cites "porch, pool, street, stairway, walkway, parking lot, security, . . . lighted commercial signs, . . . and even 'bug zappers,'" as well as spillover from interior lighting.

Although the sea turtle situation is unusually serious, dangers of night-lighting may also apply to other species, some of which people may not know they are harming. It is worth noting the remedies that Florida communities have found in their attempt to use lighting without environmental damage. Recommendations and regulations include keeping beachside lights off from May through October, reducing the number of lights near beaches, lowering and shielding lights, using motion-sensors rather than all-night security lights, and changing to yellow-spectrum bulbs like low-pressure sodium or yellow-coated "bug lites."

Moths are probably the creature most known for self-destructive attraction to light. Although not nearly as dramatic as sea turtles, many moths are pollinators, as are other beneficial insects. Extinction of large and unusual species like the turtle would be a tragedy, but in some ways the loss of lowly moth species may be more important: A pollinator lost can result in extinction of the pollinated plant and other creatures dependent on that plant for food or habitat.

Many urban Americans take high levels of night-lighting for granted. However, a number of communities have recently enacted "Dark Sky Ordinances." These are based on the desire to keep nighttime visibility of the heavens. Communities near research telescopes, like Tucson, and where the big brilliant sky is a tourist attraction, like Santa Fe, are the most likely places for such ordinances.[6] Although perhaps not central to sustainability, limiting the amount of unnecessary "light pollution" in the skies does affect people's quality of life and seems to the authors a worthy goal. Regulations like the dark-sky or sea-turtle laws also affect how landscape designers and contractors work and offer encouragement to those who try to use lighting in an environmentally thoughtful way.

Use Lighting Efficiently

Older lighting installations waste up to 90 percent of the energy they consume.[7] Fortunately, great strides in lighting technology have been made in the past decade, and if the new efficient bulbs were universally used, almost all that waste would be eliminated. Some newer bulbs are designed to work in existing fittings; in other cases, to save operating energy means completely replacing the old fittings.

From an environmental standpoint, lighting is an entirely artificial choice; unlike protecting food crops from pests, or taking water from natural systems in order to live, lighting is not a survival need. For this reason, it is especially important to use lighting judiciously and to know exactly what it is intended to accomplish. Only then can the technology be matched efficiently to the need.

Design for Accurate and Appropriate Light Levels

Both the individual light and the placement of lights in the landscape need to be designed to put light where it is wanted, as bright as needed, and no more. This is accomplished in several ways.

The appropriate illumination level must be established first. The Illuminating Engineering Society (IES) establishes recommended levels, which are widely published in such references as *Time-Saver Standards*. Although a more-is-better approach has often prevailed in lighting design, these illumination levels should generally be met but not exceeded. One noticeable feature of the IES levels is that light-colored surfaces on objects requiring illumination can cut the required light output by as much as two-thirds.[8] Contrast with its surroundings also makes an object easier to illuminate. For instance, light-surfaced steps require a lighting level of 200 lux (20 foot-candles); dark-surfaced, the same steps would need 500 lux (50 foot-candles). A dark-surfaced landmark in bright surroundings requires 500 lux; a bright-surfaced one against a dark backdrop needs only 50 lux (5 foot-candles). The ratio of illumination level to energy use is not one-for-one but is an important indicator of potential energy savings.

The levels set by the IES are based rationally on the human eye's ability to distinguish important objects or actions under given light levels; like many forms of engineering calculation, they err if anything on the bright side. However, light levels are sometimes set by much less justifiable means. Fast-food and all-night businesses, for instance, use very bright lighting for "curb appeal." Levels well beyond any functional need are used to attract the attention of drivers and

Figure 8.1. Modern street and road lighting usually incorporates cutoff reflectors to prevent light pollution. Landscape features may have cutoff design and should be located with care to avoid glare and spillover. PHOTO: Kim Lighting/Kevin Willmorth.

lure them to the business by giving the appearance of warmth and safety. Light as advertising takes many other forms, none of them candidates for sustainability.

Overlighting is also done on the recommendation of lawyers, who treat bright-as-day illumination as a defense against liability. Once IES standards are met, extra lighting serves no purpose in guaranteeing safety, however. Area lighting that allows people to recognize hazards can be quite dim. Proper aim is more important than extreme brightness for security lighting, which is best designed to reveal suspicious behavior rather than show every detail. In fact, excessively bright light can actually blind the "good guys" while the "bad guys" disappear into dense shadow. As a deterrent, a motion-triggered bright light is more effective than a constant one. A lawyerly preference for arguing that "my client's premises were brilliantly (not just adequately) lit" is no excuse for wasted energy and severe light pollution.

Light levels on a surface are set not only by the choice of lamp, but also by the distance and angle from lamp to surface and overlap with any other light source. Careful use of manufacturers specifications, including photometric charts that show light distribution, makes it possible to get the maximum effective lighting from the minimum energy.

Finally, good design can prevent light from spilling over in directions where it is unwanted. Carefully designed reflectors called cutoffs are used for this purpose and can cut off light on one or more sides of the fixture. Such fixtures are required by Dark Sky and similar ordinances and also help prevent glare. For some situations, spotlights can serve a similar purpose by narrowing light to a well-aimed beam.

Use Sensors and Controllers to Avoid Wasted Light

Like any electrical device, landscape lighting can be controlled by "intelligent" switches, such as timers and sensors. A typical example is the home path-light system, usually a low-voltage string of lights controlled by a photo-cell and/or a clock. These can save energy by limiting the amount of time when lighting is on. They can, of course, be abused, turning lights on mindlessly when there is no need, like irrigation in a rain-storm. Carefully used, they contribute to lighting efficiency.

Motion sensors are common in security lighting and can be installed to control almost any type of light. They save significant amounts of energy, since the light comes on only if an intruder or visitor is detected. They also decrease the annoyance and light pollution of leaving an extremely bright light on constantly. The detectors must be carefully located and adjusted when used outdoors, or false alarms will result. Remember that the sensor does not need to be located on the light fixture. Independently placing the detector requires a little more wire but often results in greater effectiveness and more flexible adjustment.

Try Low-Voltage Lighting for Flexibility

The preceding sections discuss efficiency strategies that can be used with any type of lamp, old or new. Besides good design and controllers, almost all new lamps available today are significantly more efficient in converting electricity to light than a decade ago. Several specific types of lighting may save additional energy by the ability to put a small amount of light exactly where it is wanted.

In strict theory, low-voltage (12 or 24V) wiring is *less* efficient than 110V "line voltage" supplied by utilities; higher voltage loses less during transmission, which is why power companies transmit electricity over very high voltage cables. However, low-voltage lamps were among the earliest to achieve higher light output per watt; for this kind of efficiency they compare favorably with lamps designed for line voltage. In addition, low-voltage lamps offer two advantages that *indirectly* affect their efficiency: size and safety.

A lighting fixture, or "luminaire," consists of three main parts: a lamp (the source of light, which laypeople usually call a bulb); a reflector to focus the light; and a mounting system. In most older fixtures, the reflector was the "shade," a part of the mounting system. In newer lamps, especially low-voltage systems, the light source itself is tiny, and the glass bulb contains both lamp and reflector, built in. This miniaturization has made it easier to produce a wide variety of special-purpose "self-reflectorized" lamps, from very narrow spots to very wide floods. Putting the reflector in the lamp has also made it possible to design smaller and simpler mounting systems. These in turn are easily aimed and easily located and concealed at the precise spot where light is needed.

From a sustainability perspective, miniaturization has several effects. It has significantly reduced the amount of material required to make the bulb or the fitting. (It has also made the reflector disposable; unless lamps are recycled effectively, a small amount of reflector material goes to waste with each bulb; fluorescents contain mercury and must be carefully recycled.)[9] ⊃Miniaturization has also revolutionized the field of lighting design, under the motto of "see the light, not the lamp." Precision lighting has generated a great deal of excitement for its subtle and dramatic effects. It can also be used to achieve the sustainability goal of more with less.

The second advantage of low voltage is safety. This may not seem like an environmental issue, but it has an important effect on precision lighting. Twelve-volt power's only real danger to humans is a painful but harmless shock. As a result, 12V wire can be run anywhere, even underwater, without conduit or other safety protection. Running a small wire instead of a rigid conduit allows complete flexibility in placing 12V lighting fixtures. Although 110V lamps and fixtures have also miniaturized in the past decade, the need for conduit works against flexible placement, while 12V wiring enhances the advantages of miniature bulbs.

Flexibility and precision have changed the approach of landscape lighting contractors in another important way: Because the lights are so precise, the best way to achieve an effect is to experiment in the field. Trial-and-error placement of different lights gives far better results than just drawing a paper plan, according to Jan Moyer, author of *The Landscape Lighting Book*[10] and head of the Landscape Lighting Institute.◗ This in turn encourages site-specific sensitivity, which as we have noted throughout this book, is one of the keys to sustainable landscapes.

Low-voltage systems usually rely on a transformer, which steps the power down from household current to 12V. At the lower voltage, issues like circuit overload and voltage drop become more critical than with line voltage. The size of the transformer must be matched carefully to total lighting load; the length of wiring runs must also be well planned. Voltage drop at the distant end of a wire can be enough to hurt lamp performance and life noticeably. Since both efficiency and service life are sustainability issues, it is important to pay close attention to system design. Some designers, used to the simple assumptions of line-voltage systems, consider the need to design the whole low-voltage system a drawback. Others find it an interesting and rewarding challenge, with benefits far outweighing the extra planning work.

Don't Overlook Fiber-Optic Lighting

Although primarily known for its special effects, fiber-optic landscape lighting may have environmental benefits, too. A single lamp, albeit a fairly strong one, can send its light through dozens of optical fibers spread throughout a landscape. The light may be emitted only from the end of the fiber or all along it in "side-emitting" types, which resemble neon.◗ The latter are the most common fiber optics in landscape, used primarily to line the edges of paths or other features with colored light. End-emitting fibers can be used much like spotlights or can produce remarkable twinkling points of light when drilled through any material.

It seems likely that fiber optics may offer energy efficiency benefits because they are in fact a single light with greatly extended "lenses." They are even safer than low-voltage lights, because all the power is at the light source. The fibers themselves carry no current at all, only light. The idea of precision lighting as a sustainability benefit, noted above concerning low-voltage lighting, also applies to fiber optics.

The magical ability to change color instantly is

Figure 8.2. End-emitting fiber optics in the sidewalk create a moving, color-shifting bed of stars. At Epcot Center, they attract far more attention than the floodlighting, at a fraction of the energy cost. PHOTO: Kim Sorvig.

a fiber-optic feature that designers and artists enjoy. However, it might also have uses in situations like the sea-turtle dilemma. A fiber-optic system could provide human safety by outlining paths, yet during turtle-hatching season its color and intensity could be changed without relamping to decrease its hypnotic attraction to the animals.

Fiber optics are a good example, in our opinion, of the choices involved in sustainable design and construction. Originally adopted for the delight it provokes, fiber-optic landscape lighting might seem frivolous in view of environmental worries. With careful evaluation and creativity, it may actually serve sustainable goals in ways that have not yet been considered. While not every new technology can be sustainably used, it is important not to become rigid or dismissive about the possibilities.

Use Solar Lighting

The paradoxical possibility of lighting the night with power from the sun has become a reality in recent years. Development of solar lights is closely related to advances in low-voltage lamps. Though photovoltaics can produce 120V current and may be inverted to AC, most systems produce DC, usually 12 or 24V.

For lighting, solar fixtures accentuate the characteristics of low-voltage: flexibility, economy, and the need for comprehensive evaluation of the whole system during design. While some package-system solar lights appear to avoid the need for

Figure 8.3. Solar electricity for lights and other uses saved hundreds of thousands of dollars in utility installation at Cholla Campground, near Phoenix. Operating costs are near zero. PROJECT: USFS. PHOTO: Kim Vander Hoek.

system planning, these are the weakest performers in the array of solar lighting possibilities.

The photovoltaic (PV) or solar-electric cell is a relative newcomer on the technological scene; each improvement has opened new possibilities in solar-powered applications. As recently as 1954, scientists at Bell Labs were overjoyed to get 6 percent efficiency from newly developed silicon cells—at a cost of more than $1 million—for a solar panel generating one kilowatt. (Efficiency is the percentage of available light energy a cell can convert to electricity.) Today, one-kW equipment operating at 13 percent efficiency is available retail for under $5,000, and top efficiency for experimental solar cells is 30 percent.[11]

Rising efficiency and falling cost make solar power a reality for many applications that were unthinkable a decade ago. The primary advantage of photovoltaic power is for powering sites that are remote from the utility grid. Monetary and environmental costs for transformers, wire, and trenching can be dramatically reduced by using solar power. If the distance from a project to existing utility lines is more than one-tenth mile, the capital cost of solar electric panels is usually competitive with the cost of extending the power lines. (Line extension charges vary by region and company, and are affected by terrain, so the minimum distance at which solar becomes cost-effective varies from 200 to 900 yards.)

For truly remote sites, there is an immediate cost savings; for others, higher initial costs for

photovoltaic equipment is offset by their near-zero operating costs. At Cholla Campground, a U.S. Forest Service facility near Phoenix AZ, landscape architect Kim Vander Hoek and her colleagues saved an estimated $435,000 in up-front costs by using solar power for everything: lights, water pumping and purification, and even a power hookup for the campground host's motor home. Because remote sites are the daily challenge of public-sector landscape architects, many of them are in the forefront of solar landscape design. The cost of extending powerlines is a major reason. Albuquerque's Colleen Friends, who was responsible for a Parks and Recreation solar lighting and irrigation project along that city's Tramway Road, puts it succinctly: "Without photovoltaics Tramway Trail wouldn't have been lighted."

Besides being remote, natural and historic parklands are increasingly faced with restrictions on visual disruption of the landscape. Where overhead pylons and wires are forbidden, and buried cable is impossible for reasons of geology, safety, or cost, solar panels gain an extra advantage. Photovoltaic panels can be located anywhere there is adequate sun and are often directly mounted on the facility they power; in other cases, short distribution wires run from the panels to the points of power use.

Unlike generators, photovoltaic systems are completely silent, nonpolluting, and are so reliable in unattended use that the Federal Aviation Administration and other transportation safety organizations are converting runway lights and similar signals to solar power. They have a long life span, usually in excess of twenty years; periodic cleaning of the panels and checking of storage batteries is the only routine maintenance requirement. The only environmental criticisms would be of the energy used to manufacture their glass components, hazardous "doping" chemicals, and lead, cadmium, and nickel in the batteries. With safeguards during manufacture, and proper recycling of batteries, these problems can be kept to a minimum.

No power technology is without problems. Poor performance in PV systems is usually linked to incorrect site analysis, design, or installation. For certain applications, client expectations based on unlimited high-voltage power are unachievable with PV. Because environmental and functional analysis is critical to PV design, landscape architects have much of the right training to use solar electricity successfully.

Much current site planning is deformed by the assumption that transmission lines, substations, and transformers are inevitable. Besides the environmental and aesthetic reasons in favor of photovoltaics, there is the fact that transmission losses in those same unsightly power lines are wasting much of the electricity that leaves the power plant. It seems probable that power from the sun will play an increasingly important role in landscape design.

Photovoltaic Design Considerations

To evaluate an off-the-shelf PV product or to design a custom system, it is necessary to understand the basic components of PV equipment. Detailed thought must be given to each component in relation to the whole system. The output of the cells, the storage capacity of batteries, and the size and type of each "load" or appliance must be carefully matched.

Technical assistance and supplies are available from a growing number of solar consultants and manufacturers. The Solar Energy Industries Association lists nearly 400 members nationwide. The Photovoltaic Design Assistance Center offers a clearly written handbook with step-by-step worksheets and information on designing custom systems. It is simple enough that a thoughtful homeowner could design and specify a complete system, yet detailed enough for professional use. Real Goods Trading Company offers components from many manufacturers, design assistance, and their *Alternative Energy Sourcebook*.

Photovoltaic terminology is not complicated. There are two major types of PV materials. One is called "crystalline silicone" and consists of wafers not unlike computer chips, called "cells," usually round or square and about 3 inches across. Crystalline cells are soldered together in series using foil connectors and are sandwiched under glass into a "panel," sometimes called a "module." The other type is referred to as "amorphous silicone" or "thin-film." It is the material common in solar calculators, watches, and the like and is identifiable by long stripes rather than distinct cells in its panels. Groups of panels, of either type, are referred to as "arrays." Commercial panels range in size from about 1

foot square to 4 by 4 feet and vary from a few inches thick to about half an inch. Some thin-film panels are quite flexible and resistant to breakage, a trade-off for their lower efficiency. One manufacturer has recently begun offering arrays that look and act much like shingles, mounted directly on south-facing roofs.

Each panel is rated in watts of electrical output, based on what manufacturers call Standard Test Conditions (STC) wattage. It is important to remember that actual operating conditions can be very different from the standard 1,000 watts/m² insolation and the cell temperature of 25°C (77°F). Cloudy weather conditions, which limit insolation, will decrease PV output. Most panels also lose about a half percent in performance for each degree Celsius of temperature above the standard condition. Cooler operating temperatures *increase* efficiency. It is not unusual for a 60W-rated panel to average 50W actual output.

Storage batteries stash power to be supplied at night or on cloudy days. Batteries for solar systems must be capable of supplying power in relatively small doses over long periods (car starter batteries are designed for the opposite need and are unsuitable for solar). Deep-cycle batteries, which can be fully discharged repeatedly and still hold a recharge, are a must. Such batteries are often NiCad, but several types are available. Batteries must be sized for the expected load.

Controllers to protect panels and batteries from extremes in voltage are frequently needed in PV systems. To operate AC appliances from solar panels (which produce DC), an inverter is necessary. Finally, the lamps, pumps, or other appliances attached to the system must be of the correct voltage and wattage. Even with a package system, it can be critically important for the designer to evaluate the match between site-specific insolation, PV-cell output, the battery characteristics, and the "load."

Location of the panels is critical. Crystalline panels particularly must not be even partially shaded. Panels need to be located to decrease the likelihood of vandalism; thin-film panels are somewhat less susceptible. (One enterprising California dreamer was charged with stealing roadside call-box PV panels to heat his hot tub!) Large, flat panels are susceptible to wind and must be securely mounted; some mounting systems incorporate sun-tracking mechanisms that increase the efficiency of operation.

PACKAGE PV SYSTEMS: PROMISE AND PROBLEMS

Custom PV systems, which take site conditions and user needs into very specific account, have a high success rate and can power almost anything. In offering a "package" system, whether for lighting, irrigation, or other purposes, PV manufacturers attempt to offer universality and convenience transcending site specifics. Package PV systems may work extremely well in one geographic area or for a particular application and pose problems in another.

STREET LIGHTING

Lighting, especially of an area that must be fully lit all night, is probably the most difficult test of a solar-powered system. Streetlight packages are perhaps the best-developed solar-lighting application. They combine high-efficiency lamps, an ordinary pole mounting, one or more 2-by-4 foot PV panel, and a battery system. Insulated battery cases are available with some models and improve battery life. The PV panel often acts as a photocell, automatically turning on the lamp when it ceases to receive sunlight. Controllers to prevent high and low voltage, voltage backflow, and other problems are often built in. Such products typically cost $2,000 to $3,000 per light.⊃

The panels are usually mounted above the lamp, and the aesthetics of many models could use improvement. Mounting the panels lengthways on the lamp support arm makes the panels less obtrusive. Angling the panels to maximize solar exposure increases wind loading on the structure, a design trade-off that affects both performance and appearance.

Professional-quality fixtures, like streetlamps, tend to be rugged and hard-working. Solar-powered streetlamps for the Miami community of Sorbet were the only electrical items working for nearly three weeks after Hurricane Andrew. Some residents were provoked to complain that power should have been reconnected to their homes first!

At Cholla Campground, integration of site, structure, and technology made solar power viable. Restroom facilities were designed with skylights, which cut artificial lighting needs in half. Solar electricity was used not only to power interior and exterior lights on these facilities, but also to operate motion sensors and timers to conserve energy, turning lights off when not in use. Solar power success often demands planning ahead for conservation, designing creatively, and reeducating members of the construction team as well as users.

SIGNAGE LIGHTING

Solar lighting specifically designed for billboards is also available.⊃ These systems include the PV array, controller, battery bank, and insulated battery box. They will light signs from 200 to 700 square feet for an investment in the $3,000 to $5,000 range. Each system will operate for three nights without intervening sun and provides six hours of light per night.

A growing number of federal and state highways have exit signs, steep-grade warning lights, and other signage powered by solar panels. Reliability and freedom from power lines are primary reasons for using PV systems for such applications.

GARDEN LIGHTING

Solar-powered path-lights feature prominently in mail-order catalogs and garden centers today. These small lights, available in pagoda, coach-light, or wall-mounted designs, are very similar to low-voltage landscape lights but contain a solar cell and battery. Their cost is substantially more than similar-looking low-voltage systems; at a time when LV systems with transformer and a dozen lights could be had for under $30, a single solar path-light could cost nearly triple that. In theory, each light is totally independent and self-contained and can be placed anywhere in the garden without wiring of any sort. Even more than transformer-powered low-voltage lights, solar path-lights offer flexible, movable placement and user safety.

Despite the elegance of the concept and the attractiveness of solar garden lights to landowners with environmental sensibilities, few professional landscape architects or lighting designers have fully accepted these lights. Some designers feel the low illumination levels (equivalent to 20 to 40W incandescents) serve to mark path edges but do not adequately light the path itself. (At least one model is explicitly designed as a marker light, using LED light sources that are extremely long-lasting but quite dim. The authors have seen these fail, possibly due to poor moisture seals, but in theory a working LED will outlive its owner.) High/low settings on some models allow the user to increase the illumination by reducing the operating time per night. The longest-operating lights average four to five hours per night on a full sunny day's charge; on cloudy days or in northerly regions, operating time may be far lower. While this is adequate for many residences, some users demand all-night operation.

Some early, cheaply made models suffered from mismatched battery and PV/cell capacity, or nonreplaceable batteries and bulbs, or fragile plastic fittings. Others would discharge on the supplier's shelf and fail to hold a charge when installed. The general consensus among designers and contractors interviewed is that the solar garden light is a great idea not fully supported by existing technology—but that its time will come soon, with advances in battery and PV-cell efficiency. In the meantime, using a well-planned PV panel system to power ordinary low-voltage lights (and other garden accessories) is not wire-free but is the more reliable option.

SECURITY LIGHTING

Motion-sensitive prowler lights, which require a brief blast of intense light, are far easier to power with a small PV system than is all-night lighting. Many manufacturers offer such lights, which are very similar to line-voltage models in operation but require no household power to run. Prices are up to twice the cost of line-voltage models, but there are no operating expenses.

Security of a different sort has driven up the market for another solar light—solar-charged flashlights. Once ridiculed as the proverbial "screen doors on submarines," solar flashlights became a hot item in the run-up to Y2K.

Evaluate Lamp Performance

Informed decisions about landscape lighting require some awkward comparisons. Power use and efficiency are critical in deciding which lighting is most appropriate and sustainable for a specific setting—yet efficiency comparisons are seldom apples-to-apples. Before the improvements of the past few years, it was often enough to compare lamp wattage to get a general comparative idea of light output. Today more than

ever, different lighting models operate on different voltages, have different service lives, and produce light with efficiencies that vary dramatically. A 25W PAR-36 lamp (one modernized low-voltage type) produces as much light as a 100W incandescent; yet it can be operated for one-quarter the energy cost.

One very recent entry in the efficient lamp family replaces the usual filament with a dozen or more tiny LEDs, inside a near-unbreakable polycarbonate bulb. Available in either clear or bug-light yellow, these are currently the world's most efficient bulbs: for 0.7 watts of energy, they put out light equivalent to a 10W incandescent. That is, for the same light output, the energy saved is more than 90 percent. They also give off virtually no heat. First introduced by Real Goods in summer 1999, initial cost of these bulbs is still very high: $100 for white and $40 for yellow. However, they should last for 100,000 hours (about a dozen years) of continuous use, replacing more than 100 standard bulbs. The 10-watt-equivalent output is not suitable for all uses but may well be perfect for path-lighting, assuming the 25-millimeter screw-in base fits the fixture. If experience shows these new bulbs to be as good as they sound, they will make many new designs possible—including, perhaps, the elusive stand-alone solar path-light.

The truest measure of lamp efficiency is its output in lumens per watt. Incandescent bulbs generally have the lowest efficiency (8 to 16 lumens per watt). Halogens produce 12 to 18 lumens per watt, while the best fluorescent lamps wring 50 to 80 lumens from each watt. Although inappropriate for many nonindustrial settings, sodium lamps can produce up to 1,000 lumens per watt, and metal halide, up to 1,500. Surprisingly, these industrial lamps have a range of efficiency so wide that at the lowest, it is little better than the halogens.[12]

Financial costs of lamps and fixtures also vary widely. Common low-voltage lamps, for example, may cost as much as $50 each, or as little as 50¢; fixtures vary from amazingly cheap homeowner kits to professional models with contractor prices of $200 or $300. Ballasts for fluorescents, if not built in, may be an additional cost and always require careful recycling.[13]

The useful life of common landscape lamps varies from 600 hours to more than 4,000. Fixtures vary even more widely. Some early manufacturers of outdoor lighting simply exported their interior models; corrosion from soil chemistry, temperature extremes, ultraviolet light, and other ground-level hazards soon sent them back to the drawing board. Except for the cheapest plastic fixtures, quality has improved, but service life still varies.

Because so many variables are involved, lighting evaluation is a very good candidate for life-cycle costing (page 248). LCC makes it much easier to get comparable figures on lighting's complex combination of energy inputs, efficiency, and durability.

Resources

Lighting

Coalition of Lamp Recyclers
Montpelier VT; 802-223-9000

Landscape Lighting Institute
Janet Lennox Moyer, Director
Rensselaer Polytechnic Institute, Troy NY
www.lrc.rpi.edu
> Moyer is author of *The Landscape Lighting Book*. Website has extensive links to lighting information relevant to landscape and energy.

FIBER-OPTIC LIGHTING
Lumenyte, 714-556-6655
Fiberstars, 800-327-7877
> Two manufacturers with outdoor fiber-optic experience.

The Landscape Lighting Book by
Janet Lennox Moyer (1992 Wiley)
> Detailed information on lighting hardware, design, and theory.

"Disposal of Fluorescent Lamps and Ballasts" by Alex Wilson (Oct. 1997 *Environmental Building News*)
> Detailed discussion of issues and methods for proper recycling or disposal of lighting materials.

Light Pollution

International Dark Sky Association (IDA)
Tucson AZ
www.darksky.org/ or ida@darksky.org, 520-293-3198
> Information and links concerning dark-sky ordinances and related concerns.

Solar Energy

Solar Energy Industries Association (SEIA)
Washington DC www.seia.org/main.htm or fax: 202-383-2670

Stand-Alone Photovoltaic Systems: A Handbook of Recommended Design Practices by Hal Post & Vernon Risser (1991 Photovoltaic Design Assistance Center, 505-844-2154)
> Order from National Technical Information Service, 5285 Port Royal Rd., Springfield VA 22161; ref SAND87-7023.
> The Photovoltaic Design Assistance Center is a national research lab. Data and help on all solar-electric questions. The handbook is systematic and realistic. It also includes a good primer on life-cycle costing.

Solar Sourcebook (Real Goods, 800-762-7325 or www.realgoods.com)
> Annual, both a textbook and a product catalog.

Solar Lights

SOLAR BILLBOARD LIGHTING
Zomeworks/ SoloPower, Albuquerque. NM, 505-242-5354

SOLAR GARDEN LIGHTS
Alpan, 800-325-9324
Solar Wide, 201-836-9461
Rockscapes, 310-915-8081
Intermatic, 815-675-2321
> These suppliers may also offer other solar products.

SOLAR STREET LIGHTING
Photocomm, 800-223-9580
Solar Outdoor Lighting, 407-286-9461
Scientific Analysis, 205-271-0643
> These suppliers may also offer other solar products.

Quietly Defend Silence

The day will come when man will have to fight merciless noise as the worst enemy of his health.

—Robert Koch, 1880

Gardens have traditionally been retreats where silence could be sought and savored. This feature of traditional landscapes is being eroded by the spread of technology and the increase in human population.

Is noise a sustainability issue? One research group concludes that "the most pervasive pollutant in America is noise."[1] Noise has physiological and psychological effects on living things, and the effects of constant noise are not healthy. If human lives are to be sustainable not only in basic physical needs, but psychologically sustainable, noise reduction becomes an issue much like energy consumption or toxicity.

Today there is almost nowhere on Earth where mechanical noises are truly absent. One professional "sound tracker," George Hempton, travels the world recording and studying noise; he finds it even in the most remote locations, always on the increase. In the mid-1980s, for example, he knew more than twenty places in Washington State where he could be sure to catch at least fifteen minutes of natural sounds with no motors, jets, radios, or foghorns; by 1999, there were only three.[2] Besides mechanized noise, crowd noise is almost everywhere, too.

Like the darkness of nighttime skies, silence is something worth respecting. Ironically, despite technology, darkness and silence cannot be *created*; light and noise can only be masked or excluded. In landscapes, truly excluding either is difficult, since to wall off the landscape is to make it something else than a landscape.

Be Aware of Damage Caused by Noise

Noise is frequently treated as if it were merely a matter of personal likes and dislikes, but research shows clearly that the detrimental effects of noise are quite real. Many technical volumes have been devoted to the effects of noise on health and on communities.

Continual exposure to 90 decibels or more (the level of a food blender, a noisy factory, or a small plane 1,000 feet overhead) creates a serious threat of hearing loss for most people.[3]

Complaints about noise are to be expected when the volume reaches about 30 decibels; by 40 to 45 decibels legal action is common, and in many countries anything above this level is legally unacceptable.[4] Machine noises are particularly disruptive because they contain so many conflicting harmonic overtones.

Research on negative effects of noise on endangered species is an emerging field, often called "bioacoustics." Migratory birds are a particular concern.[5] Mass beachings of whales have also been linked (controversially) to U.S. Navy use of very loud low-frequency sounds for echo-location and other military purposes.[6] It is

---

Discussed in This Chapter:

- Landscape sound barrier myths and facts
- Policy approaches to noise pollution

---

becoming increasingly clear that beyond certain thresholds, noise can truly be "toxic" to living beings, including humans.

Don't Rely on Noise "Barriers" in Most Landscapes

There is a great deal of mythology about the ability of landscapes to *stop* noise. The various methods often proposed as noise-stoppers, such as walls, berms, and plantings, are largely ineffective in that role. In a landscape setting, the only real remedy for noise is distance—a significant factor in the "get away from it all" roots of suburban sprawl and in the failure of suburbs to maintain the promised quietude as new development moves closer. Although constructed barriers can have some effect on noise, the general inability to screen noise in the landscape contributes directly to excessive consumption of space for residences—clearly a sustainability issue.

Walls

Noise walls can reflect specific noises, such as highway traffic, away from specific places. To do so, they must be quite large and massive: usually 8 feet tall or much higher, up to twice as long as the distance from the noise source to the spot being protected, and of material thick enough and/or dense enough to provide 1.3 to 2.4 pounds of material per square foot of wall surface.[7] Such walls can decrease noise levels by 5 to 10 decibels (rarely 15)—barely enough to bring air-conditioning equipment at 15 feet (60 decibels) down to the acceptable range. Larger reductions are prohibitively expensive.[8] Even "typical" noise walls cost between $1 million and $2 million per linear mile.[9]

Besides costs, walls have many drawbacks. They can make the noise *worse* somewhere else, especially if the source of noise is in a reflector-shaped bowl or valley. Second or higher stories in houses behind noise walls often derive no benefit at all. Depending on their compass orientation, tall walls can cast a permanent shadow over the very landscapes they are intended to protect. Walls also act as windbreaks, which may be desirable, but can exclude cooling breezes and may also cause snowdrifts. Noise walls are frequently set on top of earth berms. This increases their effectiveness but requires sufficiently wide

property area for the berm to be constructed. A 6 foot berm topped by a 10 foot wall tends to *appear* less massive than a 16 foot wall. However, this strategy does nothing to decrease the length of shadows thrown by the wall.

Recent research on noise walls appears to be focusing on potential benefits of randomizing the top edge and/or the surface of walls in order to disperse sound more fully. Noise walls have also been built of unusual materials: laminated glass and recycled plastic, for example.⊃

Berms

Correctly sized and shaped, earth berms and other grading can deflect or redirect some noise, with or without a noise wall on top. Putting a roadway in a cut rather than on fill can prevent part of the road noise from spreading directly outward. However, low-pitched noises like truck or train rumblings are actually transmitted through the earth itself. Living in an underground or bermed house or in a basement, people can sometimes hear trains a mile or more away, transmitted at low frequency through the soil, while higher sounds immediately outside are dampened.

The main limitation on berms is the amount of space required for their footprint. This in turn is limited by the steepest angle at which soil will hold a slope, the angle of repose. Greenwall techniques (page page 106) are frequently used to produce steep berms for noise protection.

Vegetation as Sound Barrier

Tree plantings as noise barriers are an article of faith with many landscape professionals and their clients. In fact, to cut noise significantly in terms of actual decibels, a band of planting at least one hundred feet wide is required. These plantings must include both dense shrubs and trees; trees alone are ineffective. Even in these widths and with appropriate species, a tree barrier can reduce sound by only about 3 to 5 decibels per 100 feet.[10] Any effect from a smaller planted barrier is primarily an out-of-sight, out-of-mind phenomenon—valuable in its own way, but not actually decreasing physical noise.

Except on very large properties where a "noise forest" or extensive grading might be used, neither planting nor physical landscape construction offers particularly good possibilities for decreasing the actual noise itself. This leaves two options for the landscape professional: screening or masking the perception of noise and lobbying for policies that prevent or decrease noise at its source.

Make Noise Invisible

Decreasing the psychological perception of noise is usually the main or only realistic course for landscape design and construction. Once noise is present, no amount of outdoor construction at the receiving end can eliminate it. Although few people actually see sounds,[11] "making noise invisible" is one important tactic in the landscape control of nuisance sound.

It has been shown repeatedly that a noise whose source is unseen is less annoying than noise from visible sources. Thus, coming back to walls, berms, and plantings, for most situations a visual barrier does nearly as much good for making landscapes *feel* quiet as does a massive barrier intended to stop sound. Well-known urban vest-pocket parks—for example, New York's Paley Park—rely on this as well as on the masking effects of water noise. Visual barriers generally need to be only as high as the user's eye-level. Sometimes a solid wall to about 5 feet, topped with a trellis or an open grille or fence, can increase the sense of privacy and calm without blocking sun or breeze into the landscape.

Another related factor in the perception of noise is that sounds that people feel some control over are less bothersome than sounds to which they are exposed involuntarily. The noise of cars from urban streets is as loud, in decibels, as that of a plane in a flight path overhead[12]—but the plane, over which people feel no possibility of control, is more likely to attract complaints. (Similarly, my boom box is music, while the neighbor's is noise.) This suggests that noise levels that result from community-based decisions might be less upsetting to people than those that are imposed on them by the usual approach of building roads or factories first and asking questions later.

Fight Noise with Noise

A second, relatively reliable way of dealing with noise outdoors is to add other noises. These can distract from or mask objectionable noise, even though, like other psychological methods, they do little to reduce such physical risks as hearing

loss from noise exposure. Adding noise can at least make the experience more pleasant.

Harmonious or desirable noises close at hand, like a fountain in an urban garden, can mask louder noises from further away. It is possible, though relatively uncommon, to plant or construct landscape features specifically for the sounds they produce—aspens for the shimmering rustle of their leaves or sculptures that chime or whistle musically. Designing and building such elements could be a specialty for landscape professionals, if not directly related to sustainability, at least as a service to mitigate one of the major effects of the unsustainable environments in which many people live.

A high-tech option with intriguing possibilities has recently become available, though apparently it is untested in outdoor use. This is the so-called white noise generator. White noise is sound containing all audible wavelengths, so named by comparison to white light, which contains all colors.

The simplest white noise generators emit a constant low hissing or crackling that seems to fade into the background, taking some louder and more annoying noises with it. In this sense, it acts much like a fountain, offering a sound so nondescript that it masks other sounds without calling attention to itself. Straightforward white noise sources like this have been available for some time.

The more recent development is an *interactive* white noise generator. These "listen" to ambient noises and immediately generate sounds exactly "opposite" or "complementary" to each new noise. The result is that ambient noise and generated noise add up to all wavelengths, that is, they combine to create white noise.

Limits on the area that such a device can cover may make white noise machines impractical for outdoor use—but to our knowledge, the possibility has never been explored. Like physical barriers, noise machines would not exist in an ideal world. However, until and unless policy and technology turn down the volume of civilization's many noise sources, technical fixes may be worth investigating.

Protect "Soundscapes" through Planning

What does the lack of effective noise-stopping techniques mean for landscape professionals?

271

Since we cannot wall noise out of our landscapes, we have a stake in quieting it at its source.

Architectural and engineering systems often vent their noise to the outdoors, protecting the people inside at the expense of any person or creature in the landscape. This avoids the cost of truly effective sound insulation, but its consequences are not sustainable, in the authors' view. This is not merely an abstract wish or theory. Commercial products are available to quiet noise from buildings, factories, chimneys, and exhaust stacks, as well as a wide range of ready-made highway noise barriers.⊃

Traffic noise increases with speed, at about 10 decibels per 30 mph increase.[13] Traffic calming measures (page 177) are often aimed at noise reduction as well as safety.

For a decade, the National Park Service has been struggling to manage noise in some of the nation's most beloved landscapes. Grand Canyon National Park hears more than 140,000 sightseeing flyovers, usually at low altitude, every year. Snowmobiles and jet-skis have been banned from many parks because of noise (as well as other environmental impacts, especially on wildlife). Park maintenance itself contributes to noise with leaf-blowers, chainsaws, and generators. Natural resource specialist Wes Henry, of the NPS's Washington DC office, is currently writing what is being called a "soundscape" management policy.[14]

On a day-to-day level, many communities have noise ordinances. These are difficult to enforce against individual moving sources of noise, such as cars or portable CD-players, yet most ordinances are aimed at these kinds of sources. What might make better sense would be to target long-term repeat sources, such as HVAC machinery and other architectural service equipment, as well as industrial plants and public roads.

With at-the-source noise control products available at reasonable cost, community standards could reasonably require that noises stay under a maximum level and might also require that noises cease at certain times, such as nights and weekends. Noise, like pollution, is a classic example of the democratic belief that one person's freedom to act ends where it impacts other people.

Awareness is growing that noise is harmful to human (and probably other species) health, as well as being a factor in psychological well-being. Blocking noise after it leaves its source, however, has high costs, both monetary and environmental. For these reasons, decreasing noise *by eliminating or quieting its sources* should be an issue for sustainability. Proposing to *require* noise control certainly meets with social and technical challenges. Nonetheless, as a profession, we need to be advocates for silence.

Resources

Acoustics

The International Institute of Acoustics and Vibration
www.iiav.org/
Technical papers on "outdoor acoustics," transportation noise, etc.

Acoustics for the Architect by H. G. Burris-Meyer (no date Van Nostrand Reinhold)
Overview of acoustics; little on landscape-specific issues.

Acoustics in the Built Environment by Duncan Templeton, David Saunders, & Peter Sacre (1998 Butterworth-Heinemann)

Soundscape Newsletter
World Forum for Acoustic-Ecology
http://interact.uoregon.edu/MediaLit/
WFAE HomePage#Directory
Interdisciplinary professional association studies "world soundscape as an ecologically balanced entity." Newsletter mainly on artistic aspects of designing with sound.

Outdoor Acoustics Web page
www.dat.dtu.dk/~kbr/publ.htm
Lists researchers and publications (mostly technical).

Noise

Environmental Urban Noise (Advances in Ecological Sciences) by A. Garcia (1999 Wit publisher)

The Effects of Noise on Man (1985 Academic Press)
Possibly out of print.

The Handbook of Hearing and the Effects of Noise: Physiology, Psychology, and Public Health by (1994 Academic Press)

"Human Life and Acoustics"
University of Oregon, World Forum for Acoustic Ecology
http://interact.uoregon.edu/MediaLit/FC/research/human.html
Health and social effects of noise.

Outdoor Acoustics
www.dat.dtu.dk/outpage.htm
Information on acoustics and noise control.

Noise Control

American National Standards Institute (ANSI)
> Publishes a large number of noise-related standards for power and garden tools, land-use noise levels, noise barrier types, and ways of measuring noise.

Institute of Noise Control Engineering
Poughkeepsie NY, 914-462-4006 or
http://users.aol.com/inceusa
> Web-page /books.html lists books on noise and acoustics, with links to reviews in the INCE newsletter.

Transportation Noise Control Center
http://tncc266.engr.ucdavis.edu/ or 916-752-3606
> Research center has done work on bioacoustics and threats of noise to endangered species.

NOISE WALL OF LAMINATED GLASS

Industrial Acoustics Co., Bronx NY
www.industrialacoustics.com/ or 718-931-8000
> Also offers other noise control products and consulting.

Acoustics and Noise Control Handbook for Architects and Builders by Leland K. Irvine & Roy L. Richards (1998 Krieger Publishing Company)

Dictionary of Noise and Noise Control by Robert Serre (Elsevier)

"Effects on Roadside Noise Levels of Sound Absorptive Materials in Noise Barriers" by G. R. Watts & N. S. Godfrey (1999 *Applied Acoustics*)

"Efficiency of a Noise Barrier with an Acoustically Soft Cylindrical Edge for Practical Use" by Tomonao Okubo & Kyoji Fujiwara (June 1999 *JASA* [*Journal of Acoustical Society of America*])

Engineering Noise Control: Theory and Practice by David A. Bies & Colin H. Hansen (1996 E & F Spon)

Noise and Noise Law: A Practical Approach by Mel S. Adams & Francis McManus (1995 Wiley)

Noise and Vibration Control Engineering by L. L. Beranek & Istvan L. Ver (1992 Wiley)
> Graduate level and professional reference on all aspects of noise control.

Noise Control in the Built Environment by John Roberts & Diane Fairhall (1989 Gower Publishing, Brookfield VT)

Road and Rail Noise—Effects on Housing (no date Canada Mortgage and Housing Corp [CMHC], Ottawa ON, 613-748-2362)

The Audible Landscape: A Manual for Highway, Noise and Land Use (Nov. 1974 U.S. DOT report)

Noise Reduction by a Barrier with a Random Edge Profile by Steve S. T. Ho, Ilene J. Busch-Vishniac, & David T. Blackstock
Dept. of Mechanical Engineering, University of Texas at Austin
> www.me.utexas.edu/~microbot/random.296.html
> Abstract on-line; contact for paper. A similar, slightly ungrammatical site is www.jhri.japan-highway.go.jp

"Traffic Noise Attenuation as a Function of Ground and Vegetation" by
Rudoff Hendricks, July 1995

Caltrans, Office of Materials Engineering and Testing
www.azfms.com/DocReviews/
> Recent study confirming that vegetation less than 100 feet wide can provide at most 1 decibel reduction in noise.

NOISE CONTROL COMPUTATION AND DEVICES

Brunel University, Uxbridge UK
www.brunel.ac.uk/depts/ma/resgrp/apmaths/inteqs.html or Simon.Chandler-Wilde @brunel.ac.uk
> Research into effects of terrain profile and road/ground surfaces on noise levels. Patented noise barrier designs, computer software.

Noise Pollution Clearinghouse
www.nonoise.org
> International news about noise issues of all sorts. Library, legal database, links on noise control.

Noise-barrier design software "Optima" and "Stamina"
FHWA www.fwha.com/

Maintain to Sustain

Ask rice fields and gardens for the truth;
learn from hedges and walls.

—Zen Master Dogen, 1250 A.D.

Landscapes are living things. In one important sense, they are never finished. Growth, natural succession, weathering, change of use or ownership or neighbors—all keep the landscape evolving. Except in successfully restored native landscapes, the best of which maintain themselves, evolution requires maintenance. Maintenance is the way an evolving landscape keeps pace with evolving human demands.

Most landscape professionals, and many landowners, are well aware that sustainability and careful maintenance go hand in hand. Yet the specialist structure of professional relationships often means that maintenance, construction, and design occur in totally separate compartments. At best, a conscientious maintenance contractor tries to guess the designer's intent or the builder's methods, and work accordingly. At worst, maintenance is always *somebody else's problem*, deferred until decay and disrepair take over. The landscape is then ripped up and rebuilt, and usually, the cycle starts over. This is unsatisfying to everyone involved and wastes many resources that could be more sustainably used.

Maintaining a landscape consists of three basic interlaced goals:

1. keeping the living part of the landscape healthy,

2. keeping the inanimate, constructed parts repaired, and

3. balancing the first two goals against human uses of the space.

Clearly, these goals are sometimes in conflict. Healthy vegetation can overrun the site, burying hardscape and making human access, let alone use, impossible. The processes of repairing constructed elements, like painting, repointing masonry, or fixing pipes or wiring, can cause chemical and physical damage to vegetation and inconvenience to users. Excessive or unplanned use can damage either plants or hardscape in ways that cannot be repaired without stopping those uses. The human factor also includes the financial balancing act between ideals of perfect maintenance (often based on groundskeeping practices of the rich and famous) and expenses that real owners can realistically afford.

Despite this complexity, landscape maintenance gets far less respect from society

---

Discussed (Summarized) in This Chapter:

- Designing for maintainable spaces

- Maintenance machinery, efficiency, fuel, and pollution

- Reducing pesticide use by good planning

- Sustainable use of fertilizers

- Conserving and using on-site resources

- Establishing and maintaining native plants

- Estimating the long-term costs and benefits of maintenance

- Coordinating design, construction, and maintenance

than it deserves; many people view grounds-maintenance professionals as one step up from unskilled labor. It is true that some basic landscape maintenance tasks are simple and can be done at a basic level by simple or unskilled people. Coordinating tasks and people so that their work favors the environment is by no means simple, however. Anyone who can successfully juggle the earlier stated three goals is the equal of any other professional and should be valued as such.

It has been a theme of this book that sustainable landscapes are most likely to result when there is good coordination between designers, contractors, and clients. This chapter offers an *overview* of how maintenance fits into a coordinated approach. The focus is on those maintenance practices that have the clearest *environmental* costs and benefits. A number of these practices overlap or continue sustainable techniques begun during construction or even during design.

This is *not* a complete coverage of all the issues of landscape maintenance or of published sources on the topic.⊃ Rather, it concentrates on ways in which maintenance practices can contribute to sustainability (or hinder it) and how better coordination and planning can increase the sustainability value of good maintenance.

Know the Resource Costs of Conventional Landscape Maintenance

Conventional maintenance of landscapes uses many resources, particularly fuel and petroleum-based fertilizers and pesticides. The authors have not found a comprehensive maintenance-specific figure for landscape costs. It would be very difficult to give a complete estimate of these costs, but some indicators are worth considering.

Research in 1985 indicated that the average cost for maintaining mowed grass landscapes for large institutions was about $500 per acre.[1] This included parks departments and the interstate highway system; the latter averages 8 acres of right-of-way maintenance per linear mile of road. With over 8 million lane-miles of interstate (page 173), mowing the interstates alone ranges into the billions of dollars. This source, unfortunately, does not indicate how much of this cost went for fuel, pesticides, or other specifics. The figure appears to include salaries as well as materials.

A 1999 report estimates that *25 million acres* of lawns are maintained in the United States alone. The average U.S. household spends nearly $400, as of 1999, on gardening supplies, driving a do-it-yourself landscape supply industry with total sales of $26.6 billion.[2] These figures are worth noting because a high percentage of them goes to maintenance supplies.

Mowing the lawn is perhaps the simplest item to estimate for fuel costs, yet even that work varies widely. Gas-powered mowing with home equipment averages about 125,000 Btu per acre (Table 7.4). Many of those acres would be re-mowed ten to twenty times per year. Per acre, annual mowing is in the range of 125–250 million Btu; roughly half that if electric mowers are used.

The same source estimates an annual 16 million Btu/acre for irrigation where water is supplied by municipal mains. About 2 million Btu/acre are used per year for conservatively fertilized turf; up to 7 million for some types. For pesticides, 1 million Btu per acre per application is conservative; 2.5 million is common. These figures include the embodied energy of the materials and the fuel energy for machinery to apply them.

The annual cost in energy for all these basic conventional maintenance tasks can be added up. Conservatively assume each acre is mowed only ten times per year and sprayed for weeds only twice. As shown in Table 10.1, average energy to maintain 1 *acre* conventionally lies between 21 million and 30 million Btu per year.

For the nation, the total energy is phenomenal—between 500 and 750 *trillion* Btu each year based on 25 million acres. Even though this is not a particularly accurate estimate, it gives a sense of the huge energy investments involved in conventional landscape maintenance.

Plan for Maintainable Spaces

There is a saying among horticulturists that the most common ailment of landscape plants is "lawn-mower disease." While this may not be scientifically accurate, maintenance machinery commonly inflicts serious damage on the very plants it is intended to serve. Physical wounds allow bacteria, fungi, viruses, and insects to get past the plants' first line of defense, which is the

Table 10.1
Annual Energy Used to Maintain One Acre of Lawn

Activity	One acre, one time (million Btu)	Frequency per year	Annual Total
Mowing	0.125	10 to 20	1.25 to 2.5 million Btu
Irrigation	n/a	_____	16 million Btu
Fertilization	n/a	_____	2 to 7 million Btu
Pesticides	0.625 to 2.5	2 or more	2 to 5 million Btu

bark. It is unclear how much plant disease starts in this way, but the percentage is likely quite high. Snowblowers and leaf-blowers join mowers in assaulting the bark of trees. Maintenance equipment, like construction equipment, can also stress plants by compacting soil, contributing to air pollution or soil contamination, or causing other forms of physical damage.

Landscape architects and landowners are quick to blame the maintenance contractor for all forms of "lawn-mower disease," and in some cases, contractor carelessness *is* responsible. But equally often, the design or construction of the landscape is also at fault. Maintenance machinery, and even hand maintenance, requires room to work and access to each task, and these are often forgotten in the design process.

People need room to work; average dimensions for these requirements are well known. Maintenance also uses many machines and vehicles. Like vehicles for transportation, they need specific amounts of space in which to maneuver. No competent designer would think of laying out an office or kitchen without checking human dimensions, or a street or loading dock, without checking the turning radius of each vehicle using the space. Yet in laying out landscapes, it is common to create spaces that cannot accommodate the machines to maintain them.

Figure 10.1. Design versus maintenance: To prune and remove trash, this worker had to cross the fence on his ladder; no other access was possible. PHOTO: Kim Sorvig.

As discussed in the section on page 278 we do not assume that all or even most maintenance must be done with machinery. However, when it is reasonable to expect that machinery will be used, it is shortsighted not to design for that machinery. Lawns, for example, should not have dozens of narrow extensions or acute angles where even a hand mower is awkward to use. Grass immediately under trees should be left unmowed for several inches out from the trunk;

Figure 10.2. Comparative space requirements for machine and hand digging. The more powerful the tool, the greater the required clearance. On wooded sites, these spaces have to be cleared. ILLUSTRATION: Craig Farnsworth.

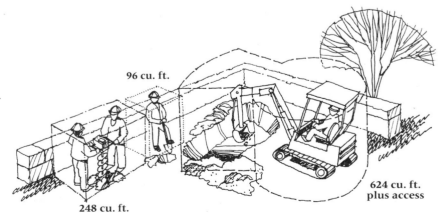

96 cu. ft.

248 cu. ft.

624 cu. ft. plus access

a bed of mulch or plantings may serve the same purpose and keeps grass from competing with tree roots. Structures that require regular painting should have a space around them in which no critically important plants are located. The concept is obvious, and the possible examples almost infinite—all the more remarkable that this important issue is so often overlooked or ignored.

Part of the problem may be that detailed information on landscape maintenance machinery is not easily available to designers. Exact dimensions for specific models are provided by manufacturers but are seldom appropriate for design use. The designer needs rule-of-thumb averages, of the sort presented for cars and trucks in *Architectural Graphic Standards* or the *Time-Saver Standards* series. These standard design sources typically do not even have an index entry for ordinary maintenance. Dimensions of garden tools are given, but only as storage-planning items, and no commercial maintenance equipment is shown. The landscape volume of *Time-Savers* does give one turning radius (36 inches) for a generic "garden tractor." By comparison, it devotes about a dozen full pages to operating-space requirements for cars and trucks of all sizes and a quarter-page to the turning radius of the Zamboni ice machine! This reflects the odd priorities and compartmentalization of conventional design training. It is quite likely that there are sources of good information on maintenance equipment, used by contractors—but seldom by designers. The authors have not found a single concise reference on this topic (and would welcome titles to list in a future edition).

Besides allowing space for maintenance, other aspects of design can make a difference in sustainability. Grouping plants together by their water requirements not only approximates natural plant associations and saves water, but also prevents over- and underwatering, which are major stresses leading to disease. Designing clear transitions between the neatest and the most naturalistic areas encourages users to accept the design and discourages unwanted mowing and pruning of the naturalistic areas. Proper plant selection, focusing on native plants, can also decrease susceptibility to pests and diseases, with a resulting decrease in maintenance. The toxic chemical treatments used as a last resort when plants become seriously ill can also be avoided if stress and damage are reduced. Specifying for durable materials, rather than the false economy of low purchase price, is another aspect of design with dramatic implications for maintenance.

In many landscapes, such as corporate headquarters, it is appropriate to interpret the maintenance *process* to the staff and to the public. Try botanic-garden-type signage explaining why and how maintenance creates the visible landscape. These and other interpretive devices can raise appreciation for the maintenance staff's work and enhance the company's commitment to sustainability.

Expect Change

Many people think of maintenance as "upkeep," keeping things the same. It is more accurate, especially in landscapes, to think of maintenance as responding to change. Plant growth and weathering are powerful forces in all landscapes and cannot be stopped (despite products that are advertised as "conquering" or "taming" these forces).

People also create change in landscapes, and it is almost as useless to resist these changes as to try to stop the tide from rising. Even well-designed and well-built landscapes change in response to user desires, which change over time or with new ownership. If a design doesn't accommodate user desires, construction and planting may be trampled as the users impose their wishes. To designers, builders, or maintenance workers, this behavior often seems unreasonable, selfish, and uncaring—and in fact it often is. But unless the entire user population can be educated to respect the original design, there is nothing to do but change it.

Use Appropriate Machinery and Fuels

Guidelines for appropriate construction machinery (see pages 50 and 242) also apply to maintenance equipment. The tendency to use the biggest machine available is even less suitable in maintenance.

Heavy construction equipment causes soil compaction and vegetation loss, but on construction sites major changes are expected, and much damage can be remedied as the job is completed. Maintenance, however, takes place in a landscape that people want to *keep as it is*. The difference is like scratching a woodworking project at the rough-cut stage, or scratching it after sanding and oiling. Minor damage to a finished landscape may be worse than the major changes made during construction. For this reason, the idea of using the lightest possible machinery may be even more important to maintenance work than it is in construction. Maintenance tools in general *are* smaller and lighter than their construction equivalents; for sustainability, use the smallest and lightest tool that can do the job. Pressure to speed up the work by using larger machinery should be evaluated very carefully, using life-cycle costing to reveal whether the savings in time are worth the trade-offs and extra costs. Principle 7 offers information on the energy costs of various machines and on life-cycle costing.

Many small machines are powered by 2-stroke engines. In general, these produce more pollution per horsepower or per unit of fuel than larger engines. This is because they are less efficient, and their combustion of fuel is less complete. Although each individual machine may contribute only a small amount of pollution, small engines are very numerous. For example, home lawn mowers alone number an estimated 40 million in the United States, consuming "several hundred million gallons" of gas/oil mix per year.[3] Add to that the many other consumer lawn and garden machines, plus professional equipment, and it becomes clear that fuel savings can have an important impact on resource use and pollution.

Very recently, significant increases have occurred in 2-stroke-engine efficiency and cleanness (page 237). Conscientious (and dollar-conscious) power tool users will switch to the newer engines sooner rather than later because of the 70 percent decrease in pollution and the 30 percent increase in fuel efficiency. It also appears to the authors that the landscape industry could benefit from sponsoring research into cleaner fuel options for small equipment. For example, natural gas conversion is widespread for warehouse machines (used indoors, where exhaust is lethal) and is becoming more common for transportation. The feasibility of converting small engines may be limited by the size of fuel tank required, but could still be investigated. Creative thinking about tools used in other industries but not widely in landscape work (for example, compressed air) might yield insights as well.

Landscape maintenance tools are increasingly available in electric models, both plug-in and

Figure 10.3. Neither wind not rain . . . but this sycamore stopped the U.S. Mail. Growth and change are inevitable landscape forces that design and maintenance must work with, not against. PHOTO: Kim Sorvig.

Figure 10.4. "Desire lines" occur at the point pedestrians see their destination. These lines can be counteracted by visual screening (barriers seldom work)—or they can be opportunities to link design to real-use patterns. PHOTO: Kim Sorvig.

cordless. Corded equipment offers the "unlimited" supply of utility power, but tangled cords and the danger of 115V shock are drawbacks. Cordless equipment solves these problems, but operating times on a single recharge are often too short for heavy-duty use. It is difficult to rate electricity as a power source, since it is clean at the point of use, but often polluting at the generating plant, and suffers up to 60 percent systemwide waste. Solar electricity panels, which avoid these losses, are now portable enough to take anywhere to recharge equipment (page 265). Improving the performance of cordless equipment, and making it easy to recharge from solar power, are sustainability research goals worthy of industry support. So is investigation of the newest offering in the alternative energy field, the fuel cell (page 41).

Many landscape maintenance tasks can actually be done best with hand tools. High-quality results, low environmental impact, and the pleasure of quiet, unmotorized work make hand labor an attractive option. Despite social pressures to mechanize every possible task, landscape maintenance remains one of the most appropriate places for craftspeople working with hand tools.

Apply Integrated Pest Management to Reduce Pesticide Use

The dangers of pesticides were among the first environmental issues to be documented, notably by Rachel Carson in *Silent Spring*. Despite forty years of concern and awareness among consumers, government, and industry, a 1995 source still estimates that Americans spread 68 million pounds of pesticides on landscapes and gardens yearly.[4] The toxicity and persistence of pesticides today have been reined in since the 1950s; many products are very specific in their target organisms. Nonetheless, they remain an automatic, unthinking response to landscape problems for many users, rather than a last resort. It is sobering to recall that, in the San Francisco Bay Area at least, gardening has been shown to be the largest single source of pollutants.[5]

Besides their toxic effects, a large percentage of pesticides is produced from nonrenewable resources, and many have significant embodied energy. Energy use in applying pesticides is also a sustainability issue.

There is little need to duplicate in this book the many detailed sources of information on how to reduce the volume and toxicity of pesticide use. Most pesticides are (or ought to be) specific to region, to species (both the plant to be protected and the species to be killed), and to weather conditions at the time of application. Encyclopedic information of that type is, of course, not included in this book. What is important to point out is that these issues are not just homeowner problems, as many books imply. In fact, the landscape most likely to be pesticide-free is one in which designer, contractor, and owner have worked together to plan for landscape health.

Healthy landscapes can fight off a high proportion of pests that would wreak havoc in a landscape under stress.

At the design stage, select plants that are well adapted to site and regional conditions, and give them the growing conditions they need. Skimpy planters or sidewalk "graves," inadequate irrigation (where it is needed), and other unfriendly hardscape all lead to unhealthy plants that must be coddled along using pesticides (see page 116). Similarly, during construction, avoid mishandling the plant stock, amend the soil appropriately, and never bury waste in planting pits.

The maintenance contractor, or the owner who gardens, is the third link in this chain. Ideally, this person needs to be part of early design reviews to spot maintenance issues that require redesign. The American tendency to build (and landscape) on speculation, before a real owner is in the picture, complicates this and many other forms of planning for sustainability. Especially where owner involvement is not possible, the designer should prepare a maintenance calendar as part of the contract documents (see page 284 and Figure 10.6). Maintenance plans, in fact, should be part of every professionally created landscape.

Use Integrated Pest Management (IPM) to control any pests that preventive health care doesn't avoid. IPM relies on a combination of biological controls (for example, predator insects or scent traps) and nontoxic chemicals such as diatomaceous earth, plus carefully targeted pesticides, as a last resort. Chemicals are usually applied with ultra-low-volume sprayers or other methods that minimize waste and drift.

Accurate timing is important in IPM. A nontoxic soap spray may kill insects in the larval stage, while the same or stronger chemicals are shrugged off by the same insects at maturity. Rather than using high-strength or high-tech solutions to bring ailing plants back from near-death, IPM treats problems when they are small. This requires more field knowledge and observation on the part of the maintenance worker and better ability to schedule treatments precisely. These are skills that the sustainability minded maintenance contractor must be willing to learn.

Some of these skills can be aided by the computer. In particular, up-to-the-minute weather information is widely Web-published. Bob Boufford, author of *The Gardener's Computer*

Companion,⊃ suggests that your computer can be programmed to use weather data for decision making. For instance, certain combinations of temperature, humidity, day-length, and precipitation trigger predictable responses from either plants, insects, or diseases: germination, blooming, insect attacks, or spreading fungi. Computers can certainly be programmed to "watch" for these combinations, using information that can be downloaded almost hourly. Once the convergence of conditions is identified, optimum times for specific maintenance tasks can in theory be scheduled automatically.

For greater accuracy, it would be possible (though expensive at present) to create site-specific computerized weather tracking stations. Sensors for irrigation systems (page 162) are more and more common and provide soil moisture, precipitation, and other information that could be relayed to any computer. In theory, sensors in the gardens of each of a contractor's clients could transmit site-specific environmental conditions and set off alerts about timely maintenance. Some large institutional irrigation systems already adjust to rainfall variations this way, using radio links to reprogram them in response to information sent by soil moisture sensors. This futuristic idea is probably a few steps ahead of most people's technology, and for all its advantages in fine-tuning landscape maintenance it may or may not prove to be sustainable. Nonetheless, like existing controllers for irrigation and lighting, computer-based maintenance scheduling may make it easier to do more with less.

Use Fertilizers Sustainably

Highly refined artificial fertilizers are sometimes likened to addictive drugs, as opposed to foods. In the chapters on construction, we have raised several concerns: that soil-amending fertilizers are overused, encouraging weak and weedy species to replace hardy natives (page 46); that artificial fertilizers involve hazardous chemicals and nonrenewable resources in production (Principle 6); and that artificial fertilizers have considerable energy costs (Principle 7). These concerns also apply to fertilizer used during maintenance.

Except for overfertilization, these problems can be avoided by using organic fertilizers, manures, and composts. Many organic products are available commercially (page 79). Their use helps solve the problems that occur when these materials are considered as "waste." The use of composts tends to decrease the need for additional fertilizer, both because the compost contains nutrients and because it helps the soil structure to retain nutrients and make them available to plants as needed.

Transportation to the site is a potential energy concern with any fertilizer, although the source of organic fertilizers is often more or less local. Much more energy is likely to be consumed in the transportation of artificial fertilizers. For example, a superphosphate fertilizer used in the American Midwest most likely originates in mines at least as far away as Wyoming or Tennessee, and possibly as distant as Morocco or the Pacific Islands.[6]

As with pest management, fertilization requirements are site-specific and species-specific. Soil analysis and foliar analysis (showing what nutrients have actually been taken up by a specific plant) are essential tools. Knowledge of local conditions—whether from a regional gardening guidebook, a local nursery, or your own experience—is required.

Don't Waste On-Site Resources

Organic fertilizers with *no* transportation cost are frequently available on-site and are often wasted. Yard waste, which accounts for about 20 percent of total landfill volume,[7] is raw material for compost. Decomposition of dead vegetation, or composting, is how natural plant communities recycle nutrients. In fact, natural communities survive almost entirely by using and reusing on-site nutrients, plus water and sunshine. Out of horticultural habit these materials are *removed*, breaking this cycle and depriving the site of nutrients. This loss of available nutrients is one main reason why imported fertilizers are ever required. The energy costs alone for removing and replacing on-site nutrients make this practice unsustainable. In addition, it takes up landfill space unnecessarily. Simply as an attitude, it devalues resources into "waste."

Compost is one of the most valuable assets for maintaining healthy landscapes. Its ability to improve soil structure, water-holding capacity, and nutrient content has made it worth mentioning in almost every chapter of this book. Any compostable material can also be used to produce biogas for energy generation, a topic beyond the scope of this book. The value of compost for landscape maintenance is so high, however, that the authors are reluctant to recommend using compost materials to produce power instead.

Lawn clippings can be left on the lawn to compost by using a mulching mower designed to shred the grass finely and spread it as it mows. For clients who find this objectionable, or if using a push-mower to save fuel, the clippings can be gathered and composted in a bin or pile for reapplication later. Leaves can also be composted, with or without pre-shredding them.

Pruned branches are another overlooked resource. They decompose very slowly if left whole, but they can be chipped to make mulch or compost. Some diseased wood, especially if it died from fungal infections, should not be composted and spread near living trees, since the fungal spores may persist. The regional Extension Service or university horticulture department can usually offer local advice on which diseases survive composting and which plants those diseases affect. They can also advise whether termites may be an issue in recycling logs and branches.

Chippers are available in a wide range of sizes. They consume energy, but certainly less than the energy costs of hauling away the wood and importing nutrients to replace it. Large branches and logs are too big for home shredders; an arborist may be willing to bring a larger machine on-site and chip these. Many communities also collect yard waste, chip it, and offer it as mulch; this reintroduces transportation energy into the equation. Logs can also be stacked to provide habitat for many types of wildlife, including butterflies. After rotting a few years, these logs usually need to be replaced and can then be broken up by hand for composting.

Composting done in piles or bins requires space that landscape designers should remember to include in site plans. The practicality of keeping the compost accessible to the kitchen is not always easy to reconcile with people's desire to hide this utilitarian function. John Lyle's attitude on the subject—that seeing such processes is part of environmental education—is worth reminding clients about.

Septic tanks and municipal sewage systems also waste valuable organic resources that could be benefiting a healthy landscape. An alternative is the composting toilet, which produces sterile compost on-site. This compost is much like municipal sewage sludge, except that it is less likely to contain heavy metals and other pollutants. Although a composting toilet is not strictly part of the landscape, it produces an on-site resource valuable enough to be considered in landscape maintenance planning.

It is still uncommon for Americans to think of sewage as a resource, preferring to put it out of sight and out of mind. The environmental and financial costs of this attitude are significant. Conventional sewage systems require massive investments in piped infrastructure, considerable maintenance and replacement for the system, energy to pump sewage, and up to 30 percent of a community's residential water supply.[8] Septic tanks return flush-water to the site through the leach-field, but the solids accumulated in the tank are simply pumped and trucked to a sewage treatment plant. (Constructed wetlands, incidentally, treat only the liquid effluent; the solids generally go to a septic tank.) In either case, the compostable resource is wasted, and a large energy and resource cost is paid for the privilege of wasting it.

Composting toilets were used in traditional communities in Japan and Europe long before they were produced commercially. Half a dozen manufacturers offer various models in the United States today. Modern composting toilets are normally odorless and clean when properly maintained; small solar fans and pumps may be used to keep the composting process active. Compost is easily removed for use, a task done every few months for most models.

For several generations of Americans, any form of composting has been somewhat unfashionable and composting toilets especially so, linked in progressive modern people's minds to rural outhouses and brush piles. As energy costs and plant health have become better understood, on-site composting has come to figure prominently in most sustainability strategies. Landscape professionals interested in sustainability will need to learn to work with on-site composting systems.

Adapt to Using Native Plants

The use of native plants has maintenance implications, too. Many people believe that native plants can produce that modern fantasy, the no-maintenance garden. Sometimes they have been told as much by overzealous advocates of native plants. Often, it is merely wishful thinking from people tired of maintenance-*intensive* landscapes, the same impulse that leads to Astroturf.

Overall, regionally adapted and native plants *do* require less maintenance than exotics. However, they may need as much care as any other planting while getting established, usually the first one to two years. Watering is almost always required at first, as well as physical protection against browsing native animals, who are of course well adapted to eat them. Once established, natives need a *different kind* of maintenance, requiring adjustments from the people who care for them.

Because many natives will be completely weaned from irrigation after the establishment period, it is wasteful to install permanent sprinklers in native landscapes. This means that watering during the initial period is done with temporary systems or by hand. To those used to fully automated irrigation, hand-watering a few natives for a couple of years may well *seem* like more maintenance than required in a conventional garden. Hand-watering may also be required in periods of extreme drought.

Pruning, another major maintenance job, is also different for native plants. Far fewer natives are as forgiving as their horticultural cousins of shearing or pollarding (also called lopping, see Figure 10.5). In fact, being tolerant of abuse is one of the criteria for a commercially successful horticultural plant: consider which species survive being sold through large home-store chains. Even when a native species is tolerant of hard clipping, the style of most native-plant landscapes makes geometric topiary trimming look out of place. Natives are usually pruned naturalistically, which requires the eye and the patience of a Japanese garden master. Properly done, such pruning is almost unnoticeable. This can disappoint people used to the showy results of European-style pruning. They may feel that they have spent hours (or paid someone to spend hours) of cautious snipping with little to show for it.

Landscape architect Jon Coe often specifies that his plantings should "prune themselves": only dead wood is to be removed, and only if really necessary. "How did magnolias," this son of a horticulturist muses, "survive 200 million years without us to prune out all that 'disease-attracting' deadwood? Do our planted trees live longer?" Especially with native plants, Coe's words are worth pondering.

These are problems of client education, or, for the homeowner, self-education. The resource conservation and habitat value of native plantings is clear, and although their beauty may be subtle, an open mind will learn to appreciate it. For the maintenance contractor, knowing how to take care of natives can be a profitable and fulfilling specialty. People who have seen their native landscapes butchered by careless conventional techniques are very loyal to the professional who can do the job right.

Evaluate Life-Cycle Costs of Maintenance Options

The same cost-cutting pressures that have made the 1990s the decade of downsizing have spread deferred maintenance throughout the land. Those who think that maintenance is expensive, however, should consider the cost of neglect.

Landscapes that are built and then neglected waste resources and have little place in a sustainable future. One of the best ways to be convinced of this, or to convey the idea to a client, is through life-cycle costing (page 248). This technique takes into account the costs of maintenance work but also shows the savings that result. Reasonable maintenance is almost always cheaper in energy costs than replacement and frequently is financially more cost-effective, too. Life-cycle costing will also reveal when a

Figure 10.5. Lopping is an example of maintenance that damages vegetation and disfigures designed landscapes. Originally a rural woodlot technique for growing poles ("pollarding"), it is unfortunately considered stylish in a few places.
PHOTO: Kim Sorvig.

landscape is so dilapidated that its maintenance is truly too expensive to justify. Maintenance work cannot be evaluated accurately simply by the sticker price. Long-term costs and benefits are clearly seen, and various options are easily compared using LCC. This technique is used by many successful professionals and takes on even more importance in pursuing resource-efficiency and sustainability.

Coordinate Design, Construction, and Maintenance

Perhaps the most important idea of all, going beyond the specifics that vary from site to site, is coordination. This has been a theme throughout the book and still bears repeating.

The most forward-thinking landscape designers prepare a site-specific maintenance plan for their clients.[9] Some firms with experience in this aspect of landscape work include Andropogon Assocs. (Philadelphia); Carol R. Johnson Assocs. (CRJA, Cambridge MA); Louise Schiller Assocs. (Princeton NJ); OLM Inc. (Atlanta GA); and Site Design & Management Systems (SDMS, Lansing MI).

Two points are key to a maintenance plan, judging by unanimous and recurring emphasis from these and other firms. One is bringing maintenance in as an issue in the very first design stages, not as an afterthought. The other is building relationships with and educating the owner and any maintenance staff or contractors. While the owner's education about maintenance starts on paper during design, maintenance personnel are craftspeople, and best results are achieved by education in the field. Since job turnover is high in the maintenance industry, this education is an ongoing process. Frequent site inspections by the designer are essential and need to be negotiated upfront as a retainer or hourly payment.

The plan schedules landscape tasks: pruning some species in spring and others in fall; replacing pond filters every five years; repointing brickwork every twenty. But it generally goes beyond just scheduling. Here are some issues that a good plan needs to address and document:

- Establish standards for maintenance—how much, what kind, and with what results, including the expected "look" of the result.

- Quantify the amount of work required—square feet of lawn or mulch, numbers of lights or sprinklers, linear feet of paths or hedges or fence. These help in-house staff plan or keep contractor bids equivalent and close in price.

- Prioritize tasks, so that staff or budget shortages can be dealt with.

- Set procedures for bidding out maintenance, or set staffing levels for in-house work.

- Reward performance, especially for contracted maintenance. Set about 25 percent of the monthly payment to the contractor as a performance payment, which depends on meeting quality standards and can be withheld if standards are not met. This requires extremely clear performance specifications but is very effective in rewarding conscientious work and avoiding carelessness.

- Provide for plan review every few years, to adapt to changes in site use.

Some large clients, such as parks departments, may have their own standard plan, keyed to public events or financial deadlines as much as to seasonal changes. Maintenance plans may cover appropriate staff and training, recommend specific products and machinery, or simply act as a reminder to do specific tasks at the right times.

The designer may write the plan or may hire a horticulturist or maintenance contractor to write it based on as-built plans. (All the firms listed on page 284 have done maintenance consulting; OLM specializes in it.) The owner can do all or part of the maintenance, pass the plan to a contractor, or in some cases, hire a branch of the designer's firm to do the work. The plan is a valuable asset if the property is sold, because it can be passed on to the next owner to ensure continuity. Such a system not only improves the long-term health of the landscape, but also increases the likelihood that the designer's vision is properly realized as the landscape matures.

Not every designer is competent to produce a maintenance plan. The need for a maintenance consultant can be an advantage if it encourages teamwork. Having a maintenance contractor on retainer as a consultant to a design firm is unusual but is an excellent way of producing

High School Park-Maintenance Plan

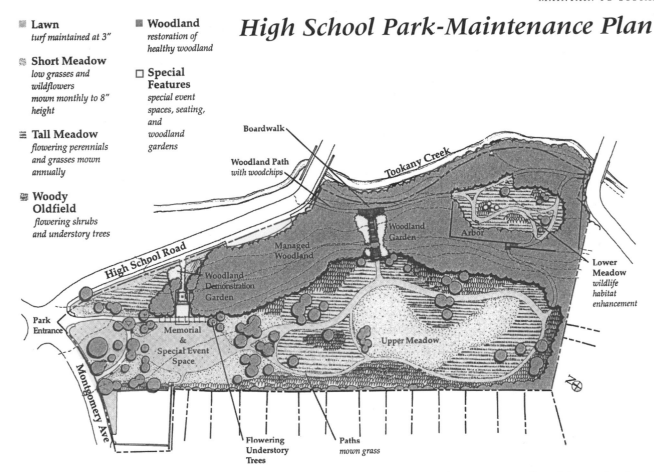

Lawn
turf maintained at 3"

Short Meadow
*low grasses and
wildflowers
mown monthly to 8"
height*

Tall Meadow
*flowering perennials
and grasses mown
annually*

**Woody
Oldfield**
*flowering shrubs
and understory trees*

Woodland
*restoration of
healthy woodland*

**Special
Features**
*special event
spaces, seating,
and
woodland
gardens*

Figure 10.6. Maintenance plans must be specific to the site and adapted to the landowner's way of working and using the place. This example graphically links tasks to specific areas of the landscape. PROJECT: Cheltenham Twp, PA. GRAPHIC: Andropogon Associates.

maintainable designs. Despite the conventional separation of trades, the ideal team for producing long-term sustainable landscapes includes an ecologist, a designer, a construction contractor, and a maintenance expert. Some design-build firms actually have such a team in-house; a consulting arrangement suits other firms better.

Two new tools can contribute directly to the accuracy of maintenance plans. These are the similarly named GPS and GIS systems—Global Positioning and Geographic Information, respectively. Their value to maintenance lies in producing and storing detailed yet cost-effective as-built plans. The GPS unit can easily measure changes during construction while they occur—a must for many landscape items like irrigation, since once buried it becomes invisible. GIS can convert GPS or other field measurements into clear diagrams and maps showing actual conditions, not just the designer's intentions. If data entry is done with foresight, GIS can also produce task-specific maps from a master file—for

example, printing an accurate location map of all shrubs of one species or all trees that need to be pruned during January.

Landscapes that do not age gracefully fall a little short of sustainability, no matter how environmentally sound their design or construction was originally. Landscapes, more than any other human construction, are about growth, change, and time. There is only one irreplaceable maintenance tool—an experienced person devoted to the place and the work. Maintenance is the task of adapting to time and change and cannot be neglected in the sustainable landscape.

Resources

Maintenance

Landscape Maintenance Association (FL)
www.lmastate.com/
  Specific to Florida, but good information; similar groups may exist in other regions.

Database of Landscape Maintenance

National Agricultural Safety Database
www.cdc.gov/niosh/nasd/video/vidhortl.html

Grounds Maintenance Handbook by Herbert S. Conover
(1977 [3ᵈ Ed.] McGraw-Hill, out of print)

*Landscape Management and Maintenance: A Guide to Its
Costing and Organization* by John Parker & Peter Bryan
(1989 Ashgate Publishing)

Professional Landscape Management by David L. Hensley
(1994 Stipes Publishing)

Landscape Operations: Management, Methods, and Material
by Leroy G. Hannebaum (1999 [3ᵈ Ed.] Prentice-Hall)

Low Maintenance Gardening (Time-Life Books, no date,
Time-Life Complete Gardener series)

Maintenance: Energy Use

"Landscape Maintenance Takes Energy: Use It
Efficiently" by Helen Whiffen (Feb. 1993 *Energy Efficiency & Environmental News*, FL Energy Extension Service, Gainesville FL) http://edis.ifas.ufl.edu or 904-392-
8535
    One of the only landscape-specific studies of energy use.

Maintenance: Organic and IPM

IPM Research Unit
University of Calf. at Davis 916-752-8350

IPM Research Center
Iowa State University www.ipm.iastate.edu/ipm/

An Illustrated Guide to Organic Gardening (1991 Sunset
Books; Lane Publishing Co., Menlo Park CA)

Gardening for a Greener Planet: A Chemical-Free Approach
by Jonathan S. Erickson (1992 Tab Books)

Rodale's All-New Encyclopedia of Organic Gardening Marshall Bradley, Barbara W. Ellis, & Fern M. Bradley
(1993 Rodale Press)

*The Organic Gardener's Handbook of Natural Insect and
Disease Control* by Barbara W. Ellis, Fern Marshall
Bradley, & Helen Atthowe (1996 Rodale Press)

Pests of the West by Whitney Cranshaw (1992 Fulcrum
Publishing, Golden CO)
    Many pest books cover only the eastern United States; this one is
    of value to half the country.

Maintenance: On-Site Waste

Composting toilets:
See Groesbeck's *Resource Guide*, section 2-15.1 for supplier listings.

The Humanure Handbook by J. C. Jenkins (1994 Jenkins
Publishing, POB 607, Grove City PA 16127)

Maintenance: Plants

*Arboriculture, Integrated Management of Landscape Trees,
Shrubs and Vines* by Richard W. Harris (1992 [2ᵈ Ed.]
Prentice-Hall)
    Author is an officer of the Council of Tree & Landscape
    Appraisers.

*Modern Arboriculture: A Systems Approach to the Care of
Trees and Their Associates*
Alex L. Shigo, 1991 Trees Associates
www.chesco.com/~treeman/treeinfo.html; Durham
NH, 603-868-7459

Tree Pruning; A Worldwide Photographic Guide by Alex L.
Shigo (1992 Trees Associates)
    Includes slide set.

Tree Maintenance by T. Pirone (1980 Oxford Press)

Turfgrass Management by A. J. Turgeon (1996 [4ᵗʰ Ed.]
Prentice-Hall)

*Urban Trees: A Guide for Selection, Maintenance, and Master
Planning* by Leonard E. Phillips Jr. (1993 McGraw-Hill)

Maintenance: Computers and Coordination

The Gardener's Computer Companion by Bob Boufford
1998 (No Starch Press, San Francisco
www.nostarch.com or 800-420-7240)
    Three hundred pages of landscape graphics software, plant selec-
    tion tools, Websites—any digital item useful in the landscape, plus
    some intriguingly wacky ones. CD-ROM with shareware for
    garden planning, seed and plant locating, weather tracking, chem-
    icals lists, etc.

Computer-Aided Facility Management by Eric Teicholz
(1992 McGraw-Hill)

Conclusions and Beginnings

If you are thinking a year ahead, sow seed. If you are thinking ten years ahead, plant trees. If you are thinking one hundred years ahead, educate the people.

—Chinese proverb

In the landscape, beginnings and endings overlap. Healthy landscapes are ecosystems, and they survive by constant change. In a self-sustaining landscape, marsh becomes meadow becomes forest, then returns to meadow after fires, or even to marsh after floods. Individual plants and animals die, but the community—the landscape—lives on through a constant "recycling" process.

Sustainability is about fitting into this endless cycle. Many conventional landscapes, and an even higher proportion of buildings, are constructed in defiance of the cycle of growth and decay. The cumulative result of thousands of sites treated this way is what one author has called a "revenge effect"[1]—*too much* success in disrupting the cycle, which spells decline or even death for the land. With current technology, it *is* possible to break the cycle temporarily, but the costs are enormous.

In this book, we have asked which approaches to landscape construction might reverse these destructive trends, or at least help to do so. What we have found is that there are *many* techniques in landscape work that contribute directly to ecosystem health or decrease damage already done. Taking the hopeful position that humanity still has a chance to live in harmony with the great cycle of life, we have called these techniques sustainable, regenerative, or environmentally responsible.

Sustainable landscape construction is not merely idealistic—it is available and feasible today. This book includes discussion of more than one hundred real projects, constructed by real people on real budgets, that include sustain-

able goals and techniques. We have found professionals doing this work in nearly every region of North America. Other countries are well ahead of the United States in some areas of sustainable construction, and we have included a few examples from abroad. Sustainable landscape construction may be a young profession, but it is no longer an orphan. A growing network of landscape professionals has adopted, tested, and adapted the methods described. A growing number of do-it-yourselfers are also involved.

Although some are experimental and all are evolving, sustainable landscape methods can and do compete successfully with conventional ones on almost any criteria—economic, functional, aesthetic. They are practical (sometimes with a learning curve), durable, and safe. Some are simply conventional methods done with extra craftsmanship, extra care in siting and scaling them to existing conditions, or extra planning and preparation. Others have been resurrected from tradition. Only a few are truly new, and even these have developed enough of a track record that they cannot be called untried.

Although we conclude that sustainable landscape methods are realistic today, the ultimate conclusion of this book depends on further growth in our field. This book reports and summarizes many green principles, but it is up to committed individuals to apply them creatively. Thus, as we end this book, we have two questions, not about what is feasible today, but about influencing the future.

The first question is, Does present sustainable practice suggest any general themes to guide and expand the landscape professions of the future?

Seven key ideas link together practical principles and techniques from earlier chapters that at first glance might not seem related. These themes or strategies are *not* essential to day-to-day work in sustainable landscape construction, though they may help. Their real value, we believe, will be for those professionals who can step back, even for a moment, and take a longer view, looking to chart a course *beyond* what can be done today.

The second question about the future of sustainable landscape construction is that of education, both professional and public. Unless new students in landscape architecture, construction and construction management, architecture, planning, and engineering are exposed to sustainable methods, they will simply perpetuate the conventional past. This chapter lists a number of specific, and we believe positive, changes for professional schools to consider. It also describes some built landscapes that educate the *public* about sustainability and natural process; in doing so, these projects argue the cause of sustainability and can also become environmental art.

This book describes a changing profession whose focus is also ever-changing. Appropriately enough, the conclusions of this book are beginnings, too.

Learning from the Landscape: Themes and Strategies

Bringing together in one place so many tested and specific methods of landscape work reveals several underlying strategies from which the specific methods have grown. We have identified seven main interlinked themes, which can be represented by these keywords:

- Decentralization
- Coordination
- Resilience
- Synergy
- Community
- Integration
- Vision

The following sections discuss each of these ideas in turn. These themes concern broad ways of dealing with the landscape—in the strict sense,

where "dealing" means negotiating, exchanging, and interacting. Themes and strategies like these, we believe, can guide future creativity and adaptation in our profession. They are also strengths that many landscape professionals already have and can build on. What our professions have learned from the landscape is in short supply— and growing demand—among related professions such as architecture and engineering. Although clearly not an exhaustive list, these themes offer a direction in which to lead.

Decentralization: Deal with Landscape Issues Near Their Source

As we have researched successful projects and methods of sustaining the land, we have heard this theme expressed time and again: *Work close to the source*. Stormwater and erosion are best managed with many small structures near the top of the watershed, the source of the runoff. Porous paving infiltrates raindrops almost literally *where they fall*—simulating the age-old relationship between healthy soil and precipitation. To keep invasive plants and animals from overrunning native ecosystems, enforcing importation and quarantine restrictions *where these aliens enter the country* is far more effective than trying to eradicate a pest that has spread across a whole continent. These examples have one thing in common: acting at the source, where the problem is smallest.

"Close to the source" rephrases E. F. Schumacher's advice that small is beautiful. Small, in dealing with landscapes, also means decentralized. Any environmental service or problem that requires an infrastructure is likely to be more cost-effective if it is decentralized. For example, constructed wastewater wetlands can be built to serve one home, or a small cluster—a significant advantage over large conventional treatment plants and their extensive infrastructure. Similarly, solar electricity and wind generation have increasingly shown potential to *place the source near the use*, eliminating not only miles of infrastructure but also major losses in long-distance transmission. Reuse is preferable to remanufacturing in part because centralized recycling requires collection and redistribution.

This, then, is the first theme that emerges from the many landscape techniques discussed in this book: Wherever possible, respond to the land in small, site-specific ways coordinated across a region rather than centralized in a single regional facility.

Coordinate Efforts

Coordination itself is a theme of this book. It applies to the multidisciplinary team doing green design and building. It applies to the well-known slogan of thinking globally while acting locally. It applies to involving a whole community, analyzing a whole watershed, or studying energy flows throughout a system.

Coordination can be lost when no one cooperates or plans ahead, but it can also be lost when all planning is centralized. In modern society, both conditions are obstacles to environmentally sound development. Extreme individualism keeps people from participating in decisions. At the other extreme, convenience for governmental or corporate decision makers can exclude citizens, while economies of scale (often false) justify centralization. Because they make such a difference to sustainable projects, coordination and cooperation should be high on the landscape professional's list of guiding values.

Rely on Resilience Rather than Strength

Another theme is that living strength comes from flexibility, not rigidity. This is most clear in bio-engineering: roots and branches are individually weaker than steel or concrete, but woven together into the soil, they outperform and outlast most rigid engineering structures. They stabilize soil not by resisting water's attack but by dissipating the flow of energy. Each small branch may deflect a few drops, each root hair holds a few soil particles—but here small is beautiful *and strong*.

The difference between conventional and sustainable pest control also involves resilience. Biological control of pests and diseases relies on living organisms to neutralize infestations (ladybugs to combat aphids, for instance). Being alive, these controls have a resilience of behavior that no chemical can match. They are often specifically targeted to a single type of pest, a quality that pesticide manufacturers have worked hard to mimic with modern chemistry. In many cases, biological control is resilient over time, too: an introduced ladybug population may regenerate itself next year, or anytime the aphid population explodes. No chemical control can do this.

Organic methods of soil fertilization also rely on the resilience and endurance of living organisms, instead of the strength of nonliving chemical inputs. It is not that chemicals are simply bad; the issue is that living organisms respond to their environment in ways more complex and interactive, more resilient, than any nonliving chemical reaction.

Almost by definition, successful landscape *maintenance* is about resilience. No matter how well-built (or even overbuilt), unmaintained outdoor structures decay sooner or later. Maintained structures, however, can be sustained almost forever—Taos Pueblo, made of mud but replastered every other year, is arguably the oldest structure still in use in America, inhabited a thousand years. Maintenance is about accepting change and growth and relying on resilience to accommodate change. Especially in landscapes, with their many living components, rigidly resisting change is not even an option.

Build for Synergy

In the landscape, multipurpose solutions *sustain*, while single-purpose solutions usually *consume*. Many of the projects we have highlighted set out to solve a single problem and found that several other functions could be met at the same time.

Natural wetlands are a clear example of diverse functions. Constructed wetlands for wastewater treatment almost automatically serve a second function as habitat. With minimal extra expense, they can also function as public parks. The same wetlands, correctly located, provide stormwater infiltration and flood control. Multiple functions make the facility easier to finance, reflecting increased social and ecological value.

Porous paving is another example of at least dual function: supporting traffic and infiltrating precipitation. By accomplishing two functions in a single space, porous paving preserves land for other purposes. Accomplishing more with less, whether space or resources, is clearly desirable for sustainability.

Synergy also means creatively turning one technique into several by noticing similarities. Structural soil and porous paving, for example, are almost identical in materials and form: crushed aggregate protects space for soil in one, for drainage in the other. Crossover concepts like this are worth exploring and may yield other regenerative, sustainable innovations.

Multipurpose also goes beyond human purposes. Landscape design and construction can and should accommodate species other than humans. Particularly in the case of plants, those species in turn provide environmental services that humans need.

Work from Community

Advocates of sustainability often quote the Iroqouis awareness that present decisions affect future generations. Similarly, individual decisions also affect the whole web of *community*. The theme of community-based action has appeared repeatedly in the most successful projects described in this book.

Watershed restoration, in particular, benefits from working with the whole human community (everyone who owns or uses land in the watershed) and with the whole biological community (all the species that use or live in the watershed). Similarly, site restoration is seldom about reinstating one species. Rather, it is about restarting a whole community, giving it time and protection to resume self-maintenance.

Community-based action takes practical form in projects driven *from the start* by public input. Simultaneously, information is gathered for an understanding of the whole site, seen as a community in a regional context. These community inputs can seldom be replaced successfully either by the wishes of an individual expert or owner or by analyzing only those site features that meet a preconceived development purpose. Truly regenerative, sustainable, or ecological design grows from roots in both human and biological communities.

Integrate Natural and Man-Built Elements

In the landscape, human presence and natural dynamics are best when integrated. Dividing the two puts humans and nature in separate jail cells. Integration is essential even in the "wilderness" preserved for scenic or scientific value—humans must fit in by obeying rules that favor the nonhuman. In the landscapes where humanity dominates, integration is also of great value. Here, it means including at least enough of nature to sustain human well-being.

In a practical sense, integration applies to landscape technology. Structural soil, for instance, is a pragmatic integration of human technology (crushed and carefully sized stone) with natural

dynamics (living soil protected by the aggregate matrix). Since humans cannot actually create life, a great many landscape technologies actually rely on integration between nonhuman organisms and human construction.

This integration is reflected visually in many of the best-loved landscapes of the world. Japanese gardens frequently mix artificially cut stones with naturally shaped ones or place dry bamboo fencing against a living bamboo grove. Examples of this are less common in European traditions, but they do exist: Luis Barragan's seamless steps in Pedregal's natural rock outcrops, or Richard Haag's formal, hedged reflecting pool amid the Bloedel Reserve woods. This integrative form of design artistry (and the superb craft required to build it) deserve more study and recognition than they have received in recent Western history. Integration is not complete until is satisfies the eye and mind.

Envision Richer Forms

Many of the techniques described in this book require the ability to envision forms more complex than those of conventional engineering. Although simplicity is a valued goal in design, simplicity in sustainable landscapes comes more appropriately from integration than from geometric minimalism.

Even a slight increase in the complexity of form can result in major improvements in function. The honeycomb structure of porous concrete is slightly more complex than solid cement—yet the increase in function is significant. In wetlands, the convoluted form of the root zone functions far better than a simple mechanical filter, and the variable depths and edges within the basin function better than an engineered, rectangular tank of even depth. The root path trench is considerably more complex in form than a simple planting pit, but it dramatically increases the odds of tree survival.

Envisioning and building these more complex forms place new demands on everyone associated with landscape work. Dreaming up and drawing a complex form, especially a truly nature-like one, is more challenging than designing a simple geometric structure. Reading the plans and building the form challenge the contractor. Understanding why he or she should pay for it is not always simple for the client.

In some ways, the will and ability to break free

from oversimplified convention and to dream with greater richness is this book's largest theme. Each of the other themes is richer and more complex than its conventional counterpart: integration is richer than overspecialization; community is richer than isolationism; resilience is more complex than rigidity; and so on. Educating ourselves, our students, and the public to understand and appreciate the richness of sustainable landscapes is an immensely important goal.

Green Education in Design and Construction

Education and training are critical to any profession, both for maintaining its standards and for enriching its vision. Landscape architecture, landscape contracting, and horticulture are no exceptions. The curriculum of today very directly influences the practices of tomorrow, as do requirements for licensing and for continuing professional education.

To make sustainable and regenerative practice a reality, teaching and training need to be in line with environmental goals. This applies to specialized training in any landscape profession or in the related professions of architecture, planning, and engineering. Anyone who has had any recent contact with these branches of education knows that sustainability is of growing interest to students—and teachers. In many cases, however, current course content and teaching methods are in conflict with the trends outlined in this book.

James Steele, in his book *Sustainable Architecture,* outlines changes in curriculum to encourage environmental knowledge and attitudes among architecture students.[2] Summarized here, these suggestions apply equally to landscape architecture; most also apply to the training of contractors, engineers, and planners.

- Assign studio problems that involve real sites, real issues, and review by real clients (or realistic role-playing).

- Simulate in studio the collaborative team approach students will encounter in their jobs.

- Emphasize holistic context (both ecological and cultural) in lectures and assignments. "Pure design" assignments should be reserved for specific teaching purposes.

- Broaden perspectives by basing class projects on appropriate technology or setting them in Third World situations.

- Require the use of local materials, energy estimates, and recycling as part of solving any design assignment.

- Encourage students to challenge policy limits during design; discuss (but don't grade) how completed projects may conflict with existing policies.

- Foster the ability to think about places from multiple perspectives: diverse cultural meanings of the same place, as well as multiple functionality.

- Expect students to plan for maintenance and constant change, both deliberate and accidental.

- Walk the talk: Encourage students and faculty to make their school and their own lives more sustainable.

These goals for education are quite similar to the 1992 Rio Earth Summit recommendations for change in the construction industry.[3] From that list and our own experience, we would add three more educational goals:

- Emphasize site selection (regional) and siting (within the property) in all design assignments.

- Include regional and vernacular traditions of design/building in the main curriculum, not merely as electives.

- Include "constructability" as part of every design review. Offer design-build classes, in which students actually construct what they design, perhaps donating it for public use.

Many teachers have already arrived at similar ideas, and some schools have made considerable strides toward greener curriculum. (An example is Brian Dunbar, a Colorado State University professor who takes landscape and interior design students to an ecotourism resort in the Virgin Islands as an intensive workshop in sustainable development and technology.[4]) There is a great deal of inertia to overcome, however, and conventional thinking still recreates itself in each graduating class. Design students still get the message, subtly or blatantly, that the most idiosyncratic and outrageous forms of creativity are the best. Engineering and contracting students are still taught no-nonsense and numerical attitudes that dismiss important social and ecological values. Sadly, accepted wisdom is often perpetuated unthinkingly, by default rather than intent.

Professional registration exams currently place relatively little emphasis on sustainability. To some extent this is understandable since the exam sets a *minimum* standard of competence. However, changes in practice, education, and the law are eventually reflected in the registration requirements. In time, we hope to see exam questions that focus on greener structures rather than on the tired old joist-sizes-for-decks or retaining-wall footing problems. Similarly, as building codes become greener, we would expect to see this reflected in professional continuing education. A number of alternative courses do exist, but too often they seem like voices crying in a wilderness.

Any change toward professional environmental awareness is, in effect, a step toward equalizing the influence of landscape compared with that of architecture. Professional registration laws today give architects and engineers (and the "hard" methods they represent) great power over site design—in some states, even registered landscape architects cannot seal a drainage plan, for example. This legislated inequality hinders landscape architects from instituting many sustainable site practices. In particular, educating architects and engineers about sustainable alternatives, and lobbying for increased authority to sign drawings for such alternatives, need to be an expanded part of the ASLA's agenda.

Educators—and students—have a special opportunity to help sustainable landscape making evolve. Many are already taking this initiative, and we hope many more will begin to do so.

Landscapes as Public Environmental Education

One often-overlooked power of the built landscape is to educate. Landscapes can tell the story—often eloquently—of a place and the people who use or used it. The story might focus on regional ecology, lost or displaced peoples, or industrial archaeology.

Methods of storytelling in landscapes are varied, limited primarily by creativity. Interpretive signs and self-guided tours are simple and effective ways of narrating site history. Educational landscapes, however, can go far beyond these basic methods.

This book describes several projects that show visitors something about ecological process. These were termed ecorevelatory. Places of this sort have also been called narrative landscapes or interpretive landscapes. Whatever they are called, and whatever methods of storytelling they use, such projects are an important tool for sustainability. They raise public awareness of landscape as a vital force in history and in contemporary life. Revealing and interpreting the landscape are ways of working against cultural tendencies that tempt people to ignore the landscape except when they are exploiting it.

Landscapes for schools, libraries, and museums are particularly suited as storytelling spaces. Gilbert AZ's Riparian Preserve (Figure 4.32), located next to the town library, is an example. Like a great number of constructed or restored wetlands, it has taken on functions traditionally associated with botanic gardens and nature centers.

Los Padillas elementary school, in Albuquerque NM's South Valley, shows how a sustainable landscape can have double value at an educational facility. When an older sewage treatment system failed odoriferously, Campbell Okuma Perkins Associates and Southwest Wetlands designed a constructed wetland on school grounds. With pathways, seating, and shelters around the wetland, the site fascinates schoolchildren and serves as an outdoor classroom for biology studies. The children of Los Padillas will grow up with fewer NIMBY and out-of-sight inhibitions than most of their peers, a direct result of familiarity with a sustainable landscape.

The Jardin Encore (Figure 6.13) performs a similar service for recycling, making it familiar, beautiful, and fun. Every year, King County WA constructs a demonstration garden of recycled materials at the regional flower show. Like the grand prize recycled-products house in the America Recycles Day contest (page 195), these gardens educate by making recycling real and attractive.

Visiting places where remarkable things happened is a fascination for many people. At memorials, monuments, and historic sites, "being right there" creates a powerful experience that no distant book or museum can match. This same experience can be used to educate people about *natural history*, too, as evidenced by Riverwalk, in Memphis TN.

Riverwalk is a topographic model of the Lower Mississippi—and what a model! Built of concrete at 1 inch to the mile, it stretches the entire length of a previously deserted island in the great river itself. Riverwalk has transformed Mud Island from waste space into a major attraction. Water flows through the modeled meanders, past street maps of major cities inset into the concrete banks. Visitors, striding 30 "miles" at a step, get a clear and unforgettable sense of how the river works, enhanced by being able to look out onto the real river only yards away.

Public environmental knowledge and awareness are key factors in whether sustainability will ever be achieved. In designing and constructing sustainable landscapes, look for opportunities to tell site visitors what is going on. Whether it is a serious interpretive project or a whimsical use of recycled materials, the *story told* may be as important as the functions fulfilled.

Thinking One Hundred Years Ahead

The twentieth century saw alarm and despair over the state of planet Earth. Documentable destruction has been so widespread that people have seriously questioned whether nature is dead, or was merely a "construct," a nostalgic cultural superstition. But nature is not a thing, it is a dynamic process. If humans ignore it, nature will simply outlive us, bloodied but unbowed. Remembering that we are part of nature, and that it deserves care, respect, and in some places even privacy, is probably our last best hope for survival as a species. May the techniques and attitudes described in this book be part of realizing that fragile and essential hope.

Figure 11.1. Landscapes and education reflect each other perfectly. Students at Los Padillas elementary (Albuquerque NM) are fascinated by the treatment wetland that serves their building—and they learn about biology, ecology, and technology in lessons held outdoors. PROJECT: Campbell Okuma Perkins Association and Southwest Wetlands. PHOTO: Kim Sorvig.

Figure 11.2. Landscapes can tell their own story eloquently. Riverwalk (Memphis TN) is a 1-inch-to-1-mile topographic model of the entire Lower Mississippi, located on a sandbar in the river itself. PROJECT: Roy P. Farrover, FAIA. PHOTO: Kim Sorvig.

The Hazards and Impacts of Landscape Materials

This appendix summarizes hazards of materials commonly used in landscape construction. Unlike toxicity listings under technical names of ingredients only a chemist could recognize, ordinary products are listed here in lay terms.

Using This List

Each entry is for a generic, common material—for example, brass or polyethylene—or for a group of materials, such as paints and coatings. No brand names are singled out, nor are the many proprietary variations on "the same" material covered here.

By looking up a material, you can get an overview of what sorts of hazards are associated with it, either as specific ingredients or as general processes in manufacturing. Names of chemical ingredients can be used for more detailed research if desired.

- "Process" listings (first section of appendix) are common to most manufacturing and distribution. Each specific material listing refers to these "general hazards"; for example, Logging processes are general hazards for any form of lumber; those for Mining affect any mineral to some degree.

- End-use issues (affecting site users and sometimes construction workers) are differentiated from Production issues (affecting manufacturing workers and the environment around processing sites).

- Related issues of energy consumption are discussed in Principle 7, not in this appendix.

- Hazards and risks can be mitigated. Risk can be controlled or contained, or it may be offset by environmental services that the material provides (brick can encapsulate some wastes, for example). The existence of a mitigating process does not mean that all manufacturers or consumers take these precautions.

- Production outside the United States is subject to different environmental regulation (if any), some stricter (Europe), some very lax (much of the Third World). Some multinational suppliers take advantage of loopholes to produce materials for the U.S. market using methods that are illegal in the United States. Besides the direct release of toxics, foreign production to avoid regulation increases long-distance shipping and associated energy and pollution problems.

- Ratings for hazards are hard to find, inconsistent, and politicized. It is beyond the scope of this book to determine whether two materials called "toxic" are equally deadly. These descriptive terms are usually direct quotes from research sources. For detailed information on the health effects of chemical components listed, refer to Material Safety Data Sheets for the chemical where available.

- Evaluation includes a decision about acceptable levels of risk. Although guided by expert advice, this choice is always at least partly subjective.

Using these summaries as starting points, contact individual manufacturers, ask persistent questions, carefully evaluate the answers, and "vote with dollars."

Information on each material comes primarily from the following sources:

1. American Institute of Architects. *Environmental Resource Guide*. Edited by Joseph A. Demkin. Loose-leaf, current through '98 Supplement ed. NYC: Wiley, 1998.

2. Hawley, Gessner G. *The Condensed Chemical Dictionary*, 10th ed. NYC: Van Nostrand Reinhold, 1981.

3. HOK Architects. *Sustainable Design Guide*. Edited by Sandra Mendler. Washington DC: HOK Architects, 1998.

Detailed page citations are not given, since each source is indexed alphabetically. Only direct quotes, or items from sources other than the above, are footnoted.

General Definitions

BOD: Biochemical Oxygen Demand, a standard measurement of water pollution involving excessive organic nutrients. The bacteria that degrade these nutrients use up oxygen in doing so, leaving little for other organisms. The higher the BOD, the more polluted the water.

CO_2: Carbon dioxide, an important greenhouse gas resulting from combustion (including the "burning" of foods during plant and animal respiration).

Leaching and leachate: The process of chemicals being carried out of solid materials by liquids; for example, chemicals originating in mine tailings leach into water. Leachate is the resulting contaminated liquid.

MCS: Multiple Chemical Sensitivity, a medical condition that makes sufferers allergic to tiny amounts of a wide range of ordinary as well as toxic chemicals.

Monomer: Any chemical molecule that can be chained together; the chains are called polymers. Most plastics are polymers.

MSDS: Material Safety Data Sheet, a standard form that lists hazards of specific chemicals. Usually specific to a single chemical and very awkward to relate to whole construction products, they are nonetheless important for detail on material hazards.

Particulates: Granular materials produced from combustion. Not all are chemically toxic, but all contribute to smog, respiratory diseases, and other problems.

Polymer: See **monomer**.

Precursor: A chemical out of which other chemicals are derived.

Reagent: A substance used to cause a reaction or to react with another chemical.

SO_x and NO_x: Sulfur and nitrogen compounds; the x stands for the number of oxygen atoms in each compound, which varies.

Thermoplastic: Describes a material that melts when heated, hardens on cooling, and can be remelted. One of the two basic types of plastics. Examples are polyethylene, polypropylene, nylon, and polyvinylchloride (PVC).

Thermosetting: Describes a material that melts once, hardens and cross-links chemically, and cannot be remelted afterward. One of the two basic types of plastics. Examples are epoxies, urethanes, and acrylics.

Turbidity: Muddiness, having sediment suspended in liquid. Turbid water excludes light and often has increased BOD; thus it is hazardous to aquatic life even if the sediment is nontoxic.

VOCs: Volatile organic compounds, carbon-containing molecules that evaporate (become gaseous) at normal outdoor temperatures. Generally measured in grams per liter, VOCs are found in many solvents and adhesives and in products based on these. They are also emitted in fuel combustion.

PROCESS LISTINGS

Process: Electrical Generation and Transmission

Production issues: CO_2 emissions (1.5 pound per kilowatt-hour).[1] Coal-fired power plants produce sulfuric and other acids; coal tailings and runoff can be toxic to plants and fish. Nuclear plants generate plutonium, pose accident hazards during use, and present severe disposal and decommissioning problems. Hydro plants disrupt watercourses; reservoirs may deform Earth's crust due to weight. Onsite generators rely on internal combustion engines, with associated pollution. Transmission losses and overcapacity generation during nonpeak hours waste almost two-thirds of commercially produced electricity.

General hazards: Mining, for coal and nuclear fuel, and for metals used in transmission. Fuel combustion, for transportation of fuels to plant.

Factors that reduce or offset risks: Commercial plants use emission control equipment and reduce pollution significantly. Solar, wind, and small water generators are available. On-site generation avoids transmission losses, somewhat offset by the need for storage batteries. Even small-engine generators on-site may produce less pollution per watt than power from centralized plants if transmission losses are included.

Renewability/recyclability: Coal and petroleum are nonrenewable. Water flow for power is renewabilble but dependent on weather patterns that large dams may affect. Alternative generation is renewable, but embodied energy of generating equipment can be high.

Associated materials in use: Copper, glass, and other insulation, heavy pressure-treated timber for poles.

Process: Fuel Combustion (engines and industrial)

Production issues: These hazards apply to almost all goods due to transport of materials, both during production and from factory to end user. All types of combustion engines produce VOCs, SO and NO compounds, CO_2, and carbon monoxide. Diesels produce particulates. Natural gas is the cleanest fuel but still produces emissions. Industrial heating processes such as calcining limestone for cement, or smelting metals, produce a range of emissions similar to engine combustion. Some heating processes rely on coal or on electricity. Spilled petroleum fuels cause soil, air, and water damage, whether spilled from a tanker or a gas can.

General hazards: Petroleum production hazards. Transportation of fuels often relies on engines using the same fuels.

Factors that reduce or offset risks: Emission controls both for vehicles and industry have improved markedly over the past decades.

Renewability/recyclability: Oil is nonrenewable, and estimates of available reserves are highly politicized. The more the present generation uses, the less remains for the future.

Associated materials in use: Metals, plastics, and rubber required for engine/vehicle construction and for fuel containers.

Process: Logging

Production issues: Soil erosion; 12,000 tons per square mile per year, compared to 24 tons/sq.mi./yr on healthy forestland. Sediment-laden runoff, causing increased turbidity and BOD in streams and lakes. Reduction in area of forests able to process CO_2 may hasten greenhouse effect. Air pollution, including VOCs, from burning of slash and waste. Habitat disruption; forests are among the most biodiverse habitats, making disruption especially serious. Some timber species, including many tropical hardwoods, have been overharvested or are harvested under conditions that damage critical habitat, especially rain forests.

General hazards: Heavy use of internal combustion machinery.

Factors that reduce or offset risks: Forestry practices vary widely, and sustainable forestry avoids many of the problems associated with clear-cut conventional logging. Wood waste is used for fuel and in secondary products; this saves energy and materials but may deprive forest soils of nutrients normally recycled by decaying wood.

Renewability/recyclability: Wood is renewable, if forest health is not compromised during logging. To keep pace with the "renewal schedule" demanded by rapid consumption of wood, trees are harvested very young. Renewal of large-log trees can require 100 years or more; keeping consumption in balance with such production is a difficult social issue. Restoration of logged lands is possible, but to bring back full biodiversity is complex.

Process: Mining

Production issues: Soil erosion; EPA est. 48,000 tons per square mile per year; this is 2,000 times the rate for stable forest, 10 times the rate for cropland, and 4 times the rate for logged forest. (It is also the rate at which construction sites erode, though usually temporary compared to mines.) Leaching in runoff can be extremely toxic, depending on type of mine; even nontoxic sediments can clog watercourses and damage aquatic life. Habitat disruption by removal and piling of overburden and tailings.

General hazards: Some of the world's largest machinery is used in mining, with colossal amounts of fuel consumed and great potential for engine-related pollution. Electric mining shovels can consume as much electricity per day as a small town.

Factors that reduce or offset risks: Few experts believe that restoration to the original condition of the land is possible. Remediation of mined lands is possible, though neither cheap nor easy. Mining and timber interests have been accustomed to avoiding the cost and responsibility of remediation. Laws that favor reclamation are slowly gaining influence.

Renewability/recyclability: Raw minerals are not renewable within a time frame useful to human commerce. Most mineral products are recyclable in a variety of forms.

Process: Petroleum Production and Refining

Production issues: Drilling muds and wastewater can contain heavy metals, caustic soda, barium sulfate, and organics that increase BOD; nontoxic sediments are also a water pollution issue. Benzene and other carcinogens, as well as VOCs, SO and NO compounds, CO_2 and carbon monoxide, are associated with oil drilling or processing. Oil-related accidents are among the most serious sources of environmental damage. Pipelines and access roads can disrupt habitat if not carefully designed and maintained.

General hazards: Fuel combustion, for site access, drilling power, and remote site uses.

Factors that reduce or offset risks: Oil production and refining are regulated, and mitigation equipment decreases emissions. Prevention of tanker spills is possible, but costs are unacceptable to industry—and perhaps to consumers accustomed to cheap oil.

Renewability/recyclability: See Fuel Combustion. Many analysts believe that oil production globally and consumer oil prices in the United States are heavily subsidized by government. Subsidies disguise true costs and thus discourage development of conservation, efficiency, and renewable alternatives.

Process: Disposal

Production issues: Many building materials cannot be (or are not in practice) reused or recycled. Building materials tend by definition to be bulky and slow to biodegrade (if at all). They have been estimated to produce 40 percent of volume sent to landfills.[2] In addition, certain building materials, such as PVC or treated lumber, are nearly impossible to dispose of without releasing toxic ingredients into air, water, or soil.

General hazards: Landfill excavation, similar to mining. Fuel combustion, for landfill operation machinery, collection, and transportation of waste to site.

Factors that reduce or offset risks: Well-managed landfills keep pollutants contained and do not accept recyclables, greenwaste, etc. Innovation in recycling and reuse continues.

Renewability/recyclability: Once dumped, materials are lost to the use cycle. Landfills can be thought of as reusable or renewable only if resource extraction methods develop to reclaim dumped materials. Landfill *space* itself is a nonrenewable resource.

PLASTICS, GLASS, AND RUBBER

Plastics are widely used in landscape construction, for pipes, geotextiles, soil-retention grids, and similar products (Table 6.1). Some of these contain recycled plastic, which is also made into plastic lumber, parking wheel-stops, etc. For many landscape uses, recycled plastic does not need to meet the same standards as for food industry, packaging, medical, or high-strength plastics. In a sense, landscape construction currently provides a "recycling service" to other industries by finding new uses for recycled materials.

Most plastics derive from petroleum in its many forms. There is wide variation in the toxicity of precursor ingredients, in toxicity of the material itself, and in the ability to recycle, reuse, or in some cases, even to dispose safely.

ABS plastic

End-use issues: ABS itself is considered nontoxic. Early ABS pipe was sometimes adulterated with scrap (some possibly toxic) in an attempt to compete with cheaper materials, esp. PVC. This resulted in wasteful failure of pipes.

Production issues: Each of ABS's three components (acrylonitrile, butadeine, and styrene) are either carcinogenic or act on the central nervous system. By-products CO_2, carbon monoxide, and hydrocarbons are released into air or mitigated. Like most plastics, ABS may release toxins when burned.

General hazards: Petroleum production.

Factors that reduce or offset risks: Factory equipment.

Renewability/recyclability: Possible, but not practiced.

Associated materials in use: Adhesives.

Acrylic glazing

End-use issues: The final product is inert and nontoxic. Flammable, producing smoke containing carbon monoxide.

Production issues: Major ingredients methacrylate and acrylic acid are regulated as hazardous irritants; they are biodegradable, but toxic to some aquatics.

General hazards: Petroleum production.

Factors that reduce or offset risks: Factory equipment.

Renewability/recyclability: Unknown.

Associated materials in use: Shipped in kraft paper or polyethylene wrapping. (Kraft, like all paper processing, is a significant pollution source, including dioxin and chlorine compounds; polyethylene, see page 301.) Sealants for installation.

Foam plastics, expanded-in-place

End-use issues: User is exposed to product ingredients (see below) until product sets. In interiors, gases may be given off for a long time. Foam as insulation material is not widely used in landscape; similar materials are used for cavity filling in tree surgery.

Production issues: Hazards are associated with both foam material and the chemicals used to expand it. In-place foams use polyurethane, polyisocyanurate, and phenol-formaldehyde (Canada only). Urea-formaldehyde was previously used. Urea production can release hydrogen sulfide, poisonous at high concentrations and irritant at lower doses. Formaldehyde is produced in a closed system; despite its toxicity, hazard to factory workers is well controlled. Formaldehyde products may outgas after placement. Phenol production requires benzene, a carcinogen. CFCs were used to expand older products; other methods of foaming were substituted. One substitute, HCFC, also damages ozone layer, although at a lesser rate.

General hazards: Petroleum production.

Factors that reduce or offset risks: Cavity filling may prolong the life of important specimen trees. Insulation saves energy, though rarely in landscapes.

Renewability/recyclability: In-place foam plastics cannot be recycled and may contaminate adjacent materials that would otherwise be recyclable. (Foams in packaging and insulating-board can be recycled.)

Alternative materials: A number of foams are now available blown with combinations of propane, isobutane, or HFC (which does not harm ozone, despite the similarity of name to HCFC). These include Convenience Products (800-325-6180); Instafoam (800-800-3626); Hilti Inc. (800-879-8000); and Todol Products (508-651-3818). The foam itself varies but may have some toxicity.[3] A low-toxic substitute may be magnesium (Mg) silicate foam (Air Krete); the foam itself is inorganic and contains no VOCs; it is expanded by CO_2 or compressed air. However, it is more fragile than other foams once set and may require a finish coating or not be suitable for landscape uses. During manufacture, Mg-silicate dust is very similar to asbestos; does not affect foam end user. Disposal hazards of Mg-silicate foam unknown; rated Poor for recyclability.[4]

Fiberglass

End-use issues: Glass fibers are not associated with significant hazards unless inhaled, which is unlikely in landscape uses of fiberglass.

Production issues: As used in outdoor furnishings and reproductions of other materials, "fiberglass" is actually plastic resin reinforced with glass fiber. Epoxy resin production uses cumene, a hazardous air pollutant and its derivatives. For other resins, see under name of plastic type, or consult supplier.

General hazards: Mining.

Factors that reduce or offset risks: Factory equipment.

Renewability/recyclability: Although solid glass and clean glass fiber from insulation are readily recyclable, fiberglass-reinforced plastics are not. Scrap glass may be recycled into glass fibers.

Glass

End-use issues: Glass is nontoxic, stable, and inert in use.

Production issues: The hazards associated with glass are primarily those listed under General Hazards, plus hazards of sealants used with glass. Energy use in glass production is a greater concern than toxicity issues. Older glass factories caused water pollution.

General hazards: Mining (sand etc.). Fuel combustion. Disposal. Centralized manufacturing means relatively long transportation to user.

Factors that reduce or offset risks: In use for solar collection, glass reduces fossil-fuel dependence. Crushed glass use may save resources in some situations.

Renewability/recyclability: Despite its inherent recyclability, glass *from buildings* is not commonly recycled. Careless demolition leaves shattered glass unsalvageable. Can be reused if carefully dismantled. Crushed glass or cullet as a substitute for sand or aggregate in landscape engineering and horticultural uses. Remelting salvaged glass does not give dramatic energy savings.

Associated materials in use: Sealants; wood, metal, and vinyl framing; metal fasteners.

Nylon

End-use issues: Nylon itself is nontoxic.

Production issues: Two major materials are used in nylon production: adipic acid, considered low in toxicity, and caprolactam, which is not carcinogenic but produces less serious toxic effects if inhaled. Both are derived from benzene, a carcinogen.

General hazards: Petroleum production. Fuel combustion.

Factors that reduce or offset risks: Factory equipment.

Renewability/recyclability: Relatively easy to recycle.

Associated materials in use: Adhesives, some with high VOC and other emissions. Some backings for nylon fabric outgas (mostly used in interiors).

Polybutylene

End-use issues: Polybutylene is considered nontoxic.

Production issues: The butene chemicals from which polybutylene is made are essentially nontoxic. They are flammable, and in gaseous form can asphyxiate. Polybutylene production was discontinued in the United States in 1996 apparently due to expensive failures of some products.[5]

General hazards: Petroleum production.

Factors that reduce or offset risks: Factory equipment.

Renewability/recyclability: No information found.

Associated materials in use: Butyl rubber is a close relative, with added isoprene (moderate irritant, flammable).

Alternative products: Appears to be replaced by polyethylene.

Polycarbonate

End-use issues: Nontoxic in use. Polycarbonate burns but is self-extinguishing, so risks from smoke are decreased.

Production issues: Although nontoxic itself, production uses phenol, acetone, carbon monoxide, and chlorine, all toxic.

General hazards: Petroleum production.

Factors that reduce or offset risks: As an extremely clear, strong, workable glazing material may decrease heating and cooling needs and resulting pollution.

Renewability/recyclability: Difficult to recycle locally, but easily ground and reformed into sheets.

Associated materials in use: Sealants, frames, fasteners.

Polyethylene (low-density LDPE, high-density HDPE, and cross-linked XLPE)

End-use issues: Polyethylene itself is nontoxic. Fumes when burned are of low toxicity.

Production issues: Catalysts, solvents. Cross-linking chemicals (for XLPE) may be hazardous. XLPE pipe is less likely to be used in landscape work than HDPE.

General hazards: Petroleum production; less refining required than for most resins.

Factors that reduce or offset risks: Factory equipment.

Renewability/recyclability: LDPE and HDPE widely accepted for recycling. XLPE cannot be recycled or reshaped.

Associated materials in use: Solvent adhesives (esp. for pipe); sealants.

Polypropylene

End-use issues: Used for artificial turf (which might itself be considered a hazard to the environment) and pipe. Considered nontoxic.

Production issues: Made from propane and ethylene, which are highly flammable but not toxic.

General hazards: Petroleum production.

Factors that reduce or offset risks: Factory equipment.

Renewability/recyclability: Recyclable, but local acceptability varies.

Associated materials in use: Adhesives.

Polystyrene

End-use issues: Nontoxic. Expanded and extruded polystyrene insulation and packaging materials are a significant litter problem because of their light weight. For the same reason, they are energy-intensive to transport. Easily flammable, smoky.

Production issues: Produced from benzene, a carcinogen, plus ethylene. CFC or HCFC to extrude polystyrene (XPS) depletes ozone; use of pentane to expand polystrene (EPS, similar to Styrofoam) contributes to ground-level smog.

General hazards: Petroleum production. Fuel combustion—transportation intensive.

Factors that reduce or offset risks: Factory equipment.

Renewability/recyclability: Technically easy to recycle, but not locally accepted in many places. Building-grade EPS contains fire retardants, so is not interchangeable with packaging products.

Associated materials in use: Adhesives.

Polyurethane and polyisocyanurate

End-use issues: Materials themselves are inert in use. Solvents in polyurethane varnishes may affect chemically sensitive people; water-based polyurethane finishes are available. The main concern with these materials is toxic cyanide fumes if burned.

Production issues: Manufacture involves several toxic ingredients: toluene, diisocyanate and phosgene, strong irritants; and hydrogen chloride, which contributes to acid rain. Isocyanates are highly toxic, requiring great care during production. Foams of these substances may be blown with HCFCs, an ozone-depleting chemical, or with CO_2, itself a greenhouse gas.

General hazards: Petroleum production.

Factors that reduce or offset risks: Factory equipment.

Renewability/recyclability: Most construction waste of these materials cannot be recycled. Polyisocyanurate bottles are recycled.

Polyvinyl chloride (PVC and CPVC)

PVC and CPVC are materials raising great contention in environmental debate. The solid polymer is relatively harmless, but other stages of PVC's life cycle raise major environmental concerns. CPVC, also known as PVDC, is a form of PVC made more heat-stable by adding extra chlorine. (Plastics industry spokespeople hotly deny much of the following information; their arguments appear hairsplitting and transparently self-serving in most cases.)

End-use issues: Chlorine compounds have been reported to leach from PVC pipe into water supply, and outgassing from some PVC products may be an indoor air quality issue. End users can also be affected by gases if PVC burns in accidental fires or, in some cases more dangerously, smolders without igniting, as when wiring insulated with PVC overheats. The state of California has recently required labeling of all "vinyl" garden hoses (vinyl is essentially PVC with plasticizers) as follows: "This product contains chemicals known to cause cancer and birth defects or reproductive harm. Do Not Drink From This Hose." PVC has been banned as a food container

PVC remains very popular despite its dangers, for several reasons. It is more rigid than many other plastics (but also easily made flexible with additives). Tensile strength is high enough to keep PVC pipes from bursting under pressure. It is easily joined by glue fittings, unlike other pipe systems, either plastic or metal. And it is relatively cheap in today's economy.

Production issues: Manufacture of PVC and CPVC poses significant problems. Ingredient vinyl chloride is a known carcinogen;

incomplete polymerization can leave leachable traces of this monomer (single molecular link in a polymer chain) in PVC. Liquid vinyl chloride is used in gluing PVC. Despite improvements, there is still potential for release of dioxins and other highly toxic chemicals during manufacture.

"The environmental community generally wants to see a phaseout or banning of [organochloride compounds, including PVC and its ingredients] except for essential uses." (National Audubon Society statement; Greenpeace makes an even stronger call for banning PVC, which appears on the same page of the *ERG*.[6])

General hazards: Petroleum production. Mining.

Factors that reduce or offset risks: Strictly regulated manufacture has dramatically reduced risks during that stage, but does not affect use and disposal or accidental hazard. There is no question that PVC has great practical and commercial value, but there is serious doubt that the risks are worth it.

Renewability/recyclability: PVC is not recyclable to any significant degree. Possible, but not practiced, is recycling of CPVC. Disposal is a serious problem. Burning PVC for disposal or in accidental fires releases chlorine compounds, dioxins, furans, and heavy metals. PVC in waste has been said to account for half of the chlorine in incineration fumes. Chlorine is a main ingredient in the organochloride and chlorofluorocarbon (CFC) groups of chemicals, which include DDT and dioxin and are strongly implicated in cancer, reproductive disorders and species loss, and ozone depletion.

Associated materials in use: Solvents used to join PVC are of concern for indoor air quality.

Alternatives: Several other plastics are less toxic in manufacture and easier to recycle or dispose of. For pipes and some other products, traditional materials like metal and clay, although less convenient and with energy and cost disadvantages, may need to be reconsidered. For garden furniture and other low-tech items, PVC should be replaced with HDPE or other plastics.

Recycled plastic products

Landscape items, from lawn edging to furniture to decking, are increasingly made of recycled plastics. These products save resources by not using new materials and by putting to use materials that would otherwise be waste, such as plastic bags and bottles. Although we applaud this present use, there is an important future issue here: these products are dependent on a supply of other plastics. This supply may fluctuate because of petroleum supply or as a result of environmental regulations aimed at primary plastic production. Too much dependence on recycled plastics may cause future difficulties for the landscape professions.

Rubber

End-use issues: Rubber (natural and various synthetics) are all nontoxic and do not leach if used underwater.

Production issues: Most synthetics—except silicone rubber—are derived primarily from petrochemicals. Sulfur (nontoxic, but part of SO compounds) is used to vulcanize all except neoprene (also called polychloroprene), where metal oxides are used. Butyl rubber is closely related to polybutylene. SBR rubber and nitrile rubber are made from different combinations of the toxic main chemicals in ABS plastic. Methyl chloride, used in silicone and butyl rubber production, is toxic in high concentrations.

General hazards: Petroleum production. Mining (sulfur, etc.).

Factors that reduce or offset risks: Important material in containment or exclusion of some pollutants.

Renewability/recyclability: Rubber can be reused by grinding. Tire dumps are a significant problem, but these tires may eventually be reused.

COATINGS, PRESERVATIVES, ADHESIVES, AND ADDITIVES

Additives and admixtures

Among construction materials, additives are most common in cement-based materials, in coatings, and in some plastics. Since additives are specific to other products, environmental and health effects of additives to a product are listed with that material. No such listing can hope to be comprehensive, but major types of additives are mentioned where possible.

Adhesives (see also products to be glued)

Adhesives are widely used for plastics including piping, for ceramic tile, stone veneer, and wood products such as glulams, plywoods, and composites. Specific products, and even specific manufacturer's versions of a product, are likely to vary from the general descriptions given later. Consult an MSDS for product-specific information. For plywood and glulam adhesives, see the wood product.

The majority of adhesives for outdoor use today are synthetic. Common types include resorcinol and phenolic glues (including those used for marine plywood), epoxies, cyanoacrylates ("super glues"), contact cements (both latex- and solvent-based), PVA (polyvinyl acetate "white glues"), silicone sealant/adhesives, and a wide range of adhesives specific to gluing plastics. So-called "construction adhesives" include a variety of types, as well as mastics (puttylike bulky adhesives that often remain flexible once set). Some traditional glues, as well as shellacs, are based on plant resins and terpenes. Animal glues, made from bones and other by-products, are not weatherproof enough for most outdoor uses.

End-use issues: Although many glues are nontoxic once set, almost all conventional synthetic adhesives have the potential to give off noxious or toxic fumes while curing, including VOCs; some, especially those containing formaldehyde, may outgas for a long time after curing. All plastic glues are poisonous and flammable. Common adhesive solvents to which users are exposed during application include toluene, xylene, methyl ethyl ketone, acetone, and mineral spirits.

Production issues: Modern adhesives are closely related to plastics and share many of the same ingredients:

- Resorcinol and phenolic glues: benzene, sulfuric acid

- Epoxies: epichlorohydrin (suspected carcinogen, toxic if inhaled, swallowed, or on skin)

- Cyanoacrylate "super glues": formaldehyde, cyanide

- Contact cements: SB latex (styrene-butadiene, see ABS plastic); solvents

- PVA (polyvinyl acetate "white glues"): vinyl acetate (toxic if inhaled)

- Silicone sealant/adhesives: hydrochloric acid, methyl chloride, coke (see Iron)

General hazards: Petroleum production and refining. Mining. Fuel combustion.

Factors that reduce or offset risks: Some manufacturers offer low-toxicity adhesives. These reduce *user* exposure; *production* hazards may be the same as for conventional formulas. Because they must resist weather, fewer exterior adhesives are available in nontoxic form.

Renewability/recyclability: Adhesives are generally not recyclable or reusable. If they perform their job, they are difficult, even impossible, to separate from the materials on which they are used. They may bond materials so strongly that the base materials are destroyed in trying to pull them apart. Adhesives may also contaminate recycling processes for otherwise recyclable materials. Some adhesives are also a source of toxic emissions when incinerated. Many builders and manufacturers actively advocate using adhesives to replace fasteners in construction. A small amount of material is saved at the time of construction by eliminating nails and screws; however, the use of adhesives often effectively ends the product's life cycle, which more than offsets any savings in materials. It is savings in time, and the fact that adhesives can be used by less-skilled workers, that account for the popularity of construction adhesives. There are occasions when adhesives can accomplish construction tasks that no other material can. For sustainability, the use of most construction adhesives should be reserved for such situations.

Associated materials in use: Plastics and metals for containers and applicators; often too contaminated to recycle.

Alternative products: Nontoxic adhesives. Fasteners.

Caulks and sealants

End-use issues: There is no clear-cut way to distinguish caulks, sealants, mastics, and adhesives, all of which share similar formulations. See acrylics, rubber (esp. neoprene), silicone, and urethane, under Adhesives or Plastics.

Traditional caulks and putties were made from linseed oil; some were based on asphalt or wax. For users other than MCS sufferers, these traditional products are low-risk.

Production issues: See similar adhesives and plastics, as above. Linseed oil can release VOCs during production.

General hazards: Petroleum production and refining. Mining. Fuel combustion.

Factors that reduce or offset risks: Caulks and sealants are important in protecting structures and the resources inside from water, weather, and solar radiation; in buildings, they contribute to energy efficiency.

Renewability/recyclability: As with adhesives, caulks and sealants are not recyclable and may cause difficulty recycling materials on which they are used.

Associated materials in use: Plastics and metals for containers and applicators; may be too contaminated to recycle.

Alternative products: A number of manufacturers now offer low-toxicity sealants, including silicones, urethanes, and penetrating oils. These protect the user but may still have production-related impacts. Always check with manufacturer about suitability for outdoor use.

PAINTS

All paints consist of pigments carried in a liquid, usually with fillers or binders that give the mix thickness. Oil, water, and "alternative" paints differ in carrier and binder/filler; the same pigments can be found in any of these, although different manufacturers use different pigment types. The main pigment used to make paints white or opaque is titanium dioxide. This is nontoxic itself, but sulfuric acid and metal sulfates are by-products; disposed of at sea or by deep injection, their environmental impact is unclear but unlikely to be good. Lead in paints has been banned for interiors but is still found in some outdoor and industrial formulations. Increased cancer risk has been shown for professional painters using conventional paints (oil or water). Both types emit benzene, and oil paints also emit xylene.

OIL-BASED (ALSO CALLED SOLVENT-BASED)

End-use issues: The solvents (or carriers) are the main concern, including toluene, xylene,

methyl ethyl ketone, and methyl isobutyl ketone. These four solvents are on the EPA's highest-priority list of seventeen toxic chemicals for which safe replacements are needed. Other oil-based solvents include mineral spirits, glycols, and acetates. All these solvents release VOCs in varying amounts. User cleanup can produce significant contamination.

Production issues: Exposure to solvents, especially long-term exposure to the four listed above, is highly dangerous to workers.

General hazards: Petroleum production and refining. Mining. Fuel combustion.

Factors that reduce or offset risks: Paints like other coatings improve durability of painted materials.

Renewability/recyclability: Some waste paint can be reprocessed to extract usable chemicals. This requires careful collection of surplus paint, separated by type.

Associated materials in use: Metal and plastic containers; oil-paint containers are regulated as hazardous materials in some places.

Alternative products: Paints based on mineral spirits are generally safer than those with other solvents. Many manufacturers have reformulated paints for lower VOC emissions.

WATER-BASED

End-use issues: Even though these paints are water-based, they contain some solvents. Typically these are glycols; propylene glycols are less toxic than ethylene glycols and are increasingly used, especially in Europe. In general, water-based paints have lower VOC levels than oil. User cleanup can produce significant contamination; carelessness may be encouraged by marketing as "easy water cleanup."

Production issues: The binders used in "latex" paints include SB rubber latex, which is produced from two toxic chemicals, styrene and butadiene. Acrylic latex and PVA (polyvinyl acetate) are also used for this purpose and include toxic ingredients; see under Adhesives.

General hazards: Petroleum production and refining. Mining. Fuel combustion.

Factors that reduce or offset risks: Paints, like other coatings, improve durability of painted materials.

Renewability/recyclability: Some waste paint can be reprocessed to extract usable chemicals.

This requires careful collection of surplus paint, separated by type.

Associated materials in use: Metal and plastic containers.

Alternative products: Check VOC ratings for any type of paint.

ALTERNATIVE

End-use issues: These paints were developed for people with chemical sensitivities. Citrus oil is the most common carrier/solvent. This emits a low level of VOCs, which are of a type that do not persist long in the air. Utterly nontoxic casein (milk) paints are not weather resistant.

Production issues: Although the ingredients of these paints are mostly natural, they require the growing of oil plants (soy, flax, castor bean) and the tapping of trees for saps. Sustainable agriculture is possible, but conventional mechanized farming can do great damage to soil and water. A few ingredients in some alternative paints are still derived from petrochemicals, specially refined.

General hazards: Fuel consumption during processing. Petroleum production and refining. Mining.

Factors that reduce or offset risks: Paints, like other coatings, improve durability of painted materials.

Renewability/recyclability: Some waste paint can be reprocessed to extract usable chemicals. This requires careful collection of surplus paint, separated by type.

Associated materials in use: Metal and plastic containers.

SWIMMING-POOL, TRAFFIC, AND OTHER SPECIALTY OUTDOOR PAINTS

End-use issues: This diverse group of paints tends not to be covered by safety standards set for indoor or building-exterior paints. Lead may be present. Toluene and other solvents, plus additives against freezing and other outdoor application conditions, may pose user hazards.[7] Get MSDS for specific products.

Production issues: Chlorinated rubber, a main ingredient, may be natural or synthetic rubber plus 65 percent chlorine, dissolved in toluene or other solvents.

Factors that reduce or offset risks: For marking, these paints have little effect on durability of painted materials. As complete coatings, they affect durability.

General hazards: Petroleum production.
Renewability/recyclability: Doubtful.

Powder coatings

As an alternative to paints, varnishes, plating, and other surface treatments, powdered plastic finishes are increasingly common. Items to be finished are sprayed or dipped with extremely fine particles of a variety of plastic resins and then heated to fuse the particles into a film. The EPA considers powder coatings a "cleaner technology" than coatings containing solvents.[8] Primarily used on metals and some ceramic, but coating for wood is being tested. Plastics used as powder vary widely, including the thermoplastics polyethylene, polypropylene, nylon, and polyvinylchloride as well as thermosetting epoxies, urethane polyesters, acrylics, triglycidyl isocyanurate (TGIC) polyesters, and many proprietary hybrids. Not very flexible for color mixing or accurate color matching.

End-use issues: Once applied, these plastic coatings are generally inert and nonhazardous. Most must be applied in a controlled factory setting, so use is limited primarily to ready-coated items. A "flame coating" method is used for large objects and has apparently been used to powder-coat bridges, so may have some application to landscape construction.

Production issues: Hazards associated with manufacturing each type of plastic apply to production of powder. Powder itself is inert, although there is a risk of airborne dust explosion (considerably less than risks for solvent explosion). If vented to outside from coating plants, these particulates may raise some issues of dust, but they are not chemically hazardous as such.

General hazards: Petroleum production and refining. Fuel combustion for heating.

Factors that reduce or offset risks: Powder coatings require no solvents during application or cleanup. They emit no VOCs. Overspray of powder can usually be recovered in factory settings so that 98 percent of the powder is used, a very low waste rate.

Renewability/recyclability: The small amount of waste powder generated is considered nonhazardous, and therefore recycling is not practiced. Coated items may be harder to recycle because the coating and coated material are hard to separate. None of the powder materials are renewable.

Associated materials in use: Liquid, solvent-based primers, precleaners, and touch-up paints raise hazards that promotional materials for these coatings gloss over.

Alternative products: This type of coating is undergoing much research. It might be worthwhile investigating whether a clear powder-coating process for outdoor wood could replace toxic preservatives.

Solder

End-use issues: Not usually considered toxic to users, given proper ventilation. Heat-produced fumes from metals may be toxic.

Production issues: Copper, zinc, tin, antimony, and silver are used in solder, flux, and brazing. See Copper and Zinc; other metals in solder have similar environmental effects during production. Antimony is toxic; tin is nontoxic, but all compounds containing tin are toxic.

General hazards: Mining.

Renewability/recyclability: Not directly recyclable, but does not interfere with recycling of soldered metals.

Solvents

End-use issues: Many solvents are highly toxic. Because they are used to clean up other materials, even low-toxicity solvents can carry toxic chemicals. Cleanup is usually the last part of a job; users are tired and want the mess out of sight. This can result in improper disposal, contaminating air, soil, and water.

Production issues: The main types of solvents are discussed under Paints, Adhesives, and Stains and Varnishes.

General hazards: Petroleum production and refining.

Factors that reduce or offset risks: Manufacturers can decrease emissions during production but have no control over how the user applies or disposes of solvents.

Renewability/recyclability: Some communities collect used solvents. It is unknown whether any of these can be remanufactured.

Associated materials in use: Metal and plastic containers.

Alternative products: A range of nontoxic or low-toxicity cleaning supplies has become available in recent years. Mostly household

cleaners, these do include products capable of cleaning up construction tools, spills, adhesives, and paints.

Varnishes, clear finishes, and stains

End-use issues: Varnishes are essentially paint without pigment. Oil- and water-based, as well as alternative formulations are available, and in most ways resemble comparable paints. VOC emission is greater for oil-based varnishes than for water-based ones. Water-based polyurethane clear finishes are favored for those with chemical sensitivities. In general, varnishes are less likely than paints to contain the most toxic solvents, such as xylene and toluene.

Stains are primarily pigments; the carrier or solvent is intended to evaporate, leaving just pigment on the surface. For oil-based stains the solvent is usually mineral spirits; toxicity varies with how this solvent is refined. Water-based stains are in general less toxic. Stains are commonly colored with iron oxides and earth pigments, which are nontoxic. A form of asphalt called gilsonite is used for dark stains; it may cause reactions in people with severe chemical sensitivities.

Production issues: Polyurethane production involves several toxic ingredients: see under Plastics. Acrylic resins and alkyd resins are used in varnishes and stains; for acrylic, see Plastics. Alkyd resin is produced using ethylene glycol, which is toxic.

General hazards: Petroleum production and refining. Mining. Fuel combustion.

Factors that reduce or offset risks: Like other coatings, improve durability of materials. Stains are viable for many landscape uses and may be preferable to paints in hazards and appearance for many uses.

Renewability/recyclability: Like paint, some waste can be reprocessed to extract usable chemicals. This requires careful collection of surplus, separated by type.

Associated materials in use: Metal and plastic containers; containers from oil-based coatings are regulated as hazardous materials in some places.

Wood preservatives

Safety of wood preservatives has been a subject of much controversy. Questions concern safety in use; potential for accidental or deliberate burning of treated wood; leaching of preservatives into soil; production dangers; and disposal problems. As with PVC, problems of disposal appear greater than direct threats to end users.

End-use issues: As Alex Wilson, editor of *Environmental Building News*, notes, there is no getting around the fact that "Preservatives are designed to kill. . . . [Preventing wood decay requires] finding the right balance between toxicity to the problem organism and safety to us and the environment."[9] The EPA has established precautions for use of all wood preservatives. Pentachlorophenol and creosote should not be used in interiors, but are fairly common outdoors, and are very common on recycled wood from industrial sources, such as railroad ties or utility poles. Both are highly toxic by inhalation. "Penta" is toxic through the skin, may be fatal if swallowed, and appears to be a cumulative toxin, with small doses building up to toxic levels over time as it moves in the food chain. Both are oilborne preservatives.

Chromated copper arsenic, or CCA, combines the wood-preserving properties of copper chromate and copper arsenite, both of which are highly toxic, the former also suspected carcinogenic. Close relatives are ACA (ammoniacal copper arsenate), ACZA (ammoniacal copper zinc arsenate), and ACC (acid copper chromate), all waterborne preservatives, usually applied under pressure. In most situations, these chemicals appear to bond very tightly with the wood; this is good for user safety but causes problems in disposal. Although gloves are recommended when handling CCA-treated wood, and the EPA requires cleaning off surface residues before indoor use, it is widely used for children's play structures and for decks. Manufacturers cite this as evidence of its safety, while consumer advocates see it as evidence of inadequate regulation. There is evidence that CCA can leach from treated wood into soil and water, especially under raised decks, in wetlands, or in marine facilities. It has been claimed that these leachates are quickly neutralized by the soil, but less so in aquatic systems.

Production issues: Pentachlorophenol is made by combining chlorine and phenol; both are hazardous, and phenol is derived from ben-

zene, a very hazardous material. Creosote and its parent material, coal tar, are both toxic, presenting hazards to workers. CCA is produced from three chemicals that are each highly toxic, capable of causing death or reproductive disorders (copper oxide, arsenic pentoxide, and chromic acid); chromic acid is also explosive and flammable. Because of this, the AIA concludes that the most serious environmental hazard of CCA is the potential for spills when materials are trucked to produce it.[10] Others believe that disposal of treated wood is even more significant.

General hazards: Petroleum production and refining. Mining. Fuel combustion.

Factors that reduce or offset risks: Preserving wood can dramatically increase its service life, thus saving resources and the energy involved in rebuilding or repairing decayed structures. Preservative treatment allows plentiful woods to be used instead of such naturally resistant but overlogged species as redwood; in many cases, the species that are treated are structurally stronger than redwood.

Renewability/recyclability: Treated wood can be reused if carefully salvaged; reused wood, such as railroad ties, is common in landscape construction. Recycling or remanufacturing is unlikely, although some attempts have been made to use shredded treated lumber as fiber in composite materials. Job-site scraps and wreckage are mostly landfilled; some are incinerated. *Environmental Building News*, after several thorough reviews of the controversy, stated flatly, "At present, there is no environmentally sound way to dispose of [CCA] treated wood . . ."[11] and went so far as to call for a phased ban on CCA. Creosote-treated wood can be incinerated; penta-treated wood *may* be possible to incinerate safely under careful controls. CCA and its relatives can only be landfilled, where the preservative means they (theoretically) never break down, thus depleting landfill space. Incineration of CCA is likely to release air pollutants; even if these are captured by stack-cleaning equipment, they end up in ash, from which they are easily leached.

Associated materials in use: Metal or plastic containers, which may be too contaminated to recycle.

Alternative products: ACQ preservative (Chemical Specialties): "Alkaline-Copper-Quat" formula is nonhazardous and has been recommended for people with chemical sensitivities. ("Quat" is quaternary ammonia.) Kodiak Inc. offers lumber pressure-treated with CDDC (copper dimethyldithiocarbamate). Osmose and Hickson, who along with Chemical Specialties are the three U.S. manufacturers of CCA, have developed alternative products but market them only in Europe where regulations on CCA make higher-priced alternatives salable.

Boron preservatives are used indoors but will not withstand wetness and may be toxic to plants. Other nontoxic preservatives based on mineral oils or pitch may be suitable for outdoor use; check with manufacturers. Further alternatives include "plastic lumber" for nonstructural use and naturally decay-resistant woods (some of which are endangered or scarce).

METALS

Aluminum
End-use issues: Although not acutely toxic to humans, aluminum can behave as a heavy metal; aluminum food containers have been implicated in Alzheimer's disease. Toxicity may be an issue with powdered chemical forms of aluminum (e.g., alum) in high concentrations, but as a metal it is difficult to ingest.

Production issues: Mining of bauxite is primarily in tropics and subtropics, resulting in removal of rain forest over large areas; land if "restored" becomes farmland, not forest. Processing alumina and aluminum results in wastewater and sludge, containing flouride, cyanide, chromium, and lead, as well as air emissions (see General hazards). Finely powdered aluminum is flammable or explosive and is a component of napalm and thermite.

General hazards: Mining. Fuel combustion.

Factors that reduce or offset risks: Factory equipment.

Renewability/recyclability: Easily and widely recycled, with major energy savings.

Associated materials in use: Plastic and metal fasteners.

Brass
End-use issues: Nontoxic to user. The EPA has reported, however, that in some underground water wells, brass parts in pumps have leached lead into drinking water; for pumps with brass parts, a significant waiting period after pump repair or replacement is recommended.

Production issues: Brass is an alloy of copper with zinc (see both); lead is added to some forms for workability. In production of most copper alloys, gases emitted contain various toxic metals.

General hazards: Mining. Fuel combustion for transport of raw materials.

Factors that reduce or offset risks: Exhaust filters and precipitators used during production.

Renewability/recyclability: Brass is reusable and recyclable, but not renewable.

Associated materials in use: Plastic and metal fasteners.

Cast iron
End-use issues: Nontoxic.

Production issues: Cast iron is defined as containing more than 2 percent carbon (cf. Steel). It shares the issues associated with other iron products but is less processed than steel. It is unclear whether this means that cast iron contributes fewer pollutants than does steel.

General hazards: See Iron. Mining. Fuel combustion.

Factors that reduce or offset risks: Cast iron can accept various impurities and thus can recycle many other iron and steel types that could not easily be recycled otherwise.

Renewability/recyclability: Recyclable, nonrenewable.

Associated materials in use: Fasteners. Paints and coatings. Specialized welding materials.

Copper
End-use issues: Copper in pure form is nontoxic and is a trace nutrient required for both plants and animals. When used in pesticide compounds, there is strong potential for contaminating the environment and harming nontargeted organisms, including people.

Production issues: Copper mining produces large amounts of waste rock and tailings, with associated habitat disruption. Copper-mine tailings are leached with solvents strong enough to dissolve remnant copper from the rock. Such solvents, along with heavy metals in runoff, can enter groundwater or surface water. Sulfur dioxide air pollution, once a major problem with copper smelting, has been greatly reduced, modern plants releasing only minor amounts. Copper dust and arsenic dust from processing can contaminate soils. More than half of common copper *compounds* are insecticides, herbicides, algicides, and fungicides, most of which have a preservative effect on wood.

General hazards: Mining.

Factors that reduce or offset risks: Containment of mine wastes. Factory equipment. Use as pesticides can increase durability of other materials, decreasing waste and thus decreasing energy use.

Renewability/recyclability: Readily and widely recycled (as metal, but not in pesticides or other compounds). Nonrenewable.

Associated materials in use: Metal and plastic fasteners. Plastics and other insulators for electrical uses.

Iron

End-use issues: Iron is itself nontoxic and is important as a plant and animal nutrient.

Production issues: Environmental concerns are primarily with mining and processing. Iron ore can contain very large amounts of mineral waste. U.S. ores are low-quality; 75 percent of the mined material is discarded as tailings. When process wastes are taken into account, 1 ton of usable iron requires nearly 6 tons of material mined. Coal mining, for fuel and for coke, and limestone mining all contribute to the environmental impact of iron. Coke (coal from which volatile gases has been driven by 2,000-degree heat) gives off fumes during production; some of these gases are burned for heat, but emissions are still a carcinogenic mix of heavy metals, hydrocarbons, and particulates. Limestone added to the molten metal floats impurities to the top; this "slag" is usually recycled. Pig iron (and often scrap) are further processed to produce steel, which has its own set of environmental impacts.

General hazards: Mining. Fuel combustion.

Factors that reduce or offset risks: Factory equipment. "Direct steel-making" uses coal, not coke, eliminating the coke emissions.

Renewability/recyclability: Recyclable. Nonrenewable.

Lead

End-use issues: Lead and virtually all lead compounds are toxic if swallowed or inhaled. More important, lead accumulates in the body, so that repeated small doses cause progressively worse damage. Lead-based paints and lead flashing may still be found on renovation jobs; lead from gasoline or vehicle exhaust contaminates many soils. Lead is a component of solder and is used in masonry fasteners. Lead-based batteries raise issues of disposal.

Production issues: Lead is an ingredient of other materials, such as brass. Still used in some specialized paints, but no longer allowed in house paints. Some lead compounds are used as reagents in processing other materials. Workers may be exposed to lead from impurities in ores of other metals. Used in storage batteries.

General hazards: Mining.

Factors that reduce or offset risks: Special precautions are required by both manufacturers and users of lead-containing products.

Renewability/recyclability: Solid lead is easily remelted. Nonrenewable.

Steel

End-use issues: Steel is nontoxic and some alloys are inert enough even for medical use.

Production issues: Steel is defined as containing less than 2 percent carbon and has many alloy forms. It is one of the most energy-intensive materials, per weight, and steel manufacturing is a major source of pollution. Depending on the process, refining of steel adds up to 100 percent to the energy required to make pig iron; shaping adds still more energy and associated air pollution. Many alloying additives, such as chromium or nickel, are toxic. Nickel smelting can produce 8 pounds of sulfur for every pound of nickel, making sulfur emissions and acid rain a serious issue in this process. Large amounts of water are required for processing steel. Liquid wastes from washing, pickling, and oils can be toxic to fish. Sludge containing a variety of toxic materials has in the past been spread on fields, which is now regulated.

General hazards: See Iron. Mining. Fuel combustion.

Factors that reduce or offset risks: Strength of steel means small amounts can do large jobs, thus reducing the energy and pollution per job. Easy to separate from other wastes magnetically for recycling. Industry has made strong efforts to reduce emissions through new technologies.

Renewability/recyclability: One of the most easily and widely recycled materials. Energy savings in recycling not as great as for aluminum. Nonrenewable.

Associated materials in use: Fasteners. Welding and brazing materials.

Zinc and galvanizing

End-use issues: Toxicity of zinc is low for humans, although higher for other species, esp. aquatics.

Production issues: Zinc in mine tailings leaches more slowly than do many other metals and tends to bond with soil or be diluted in water in ways that reduce hazards. However, zinc ores commonly contain lead and copper, whose leachates may be more toxic than those from zinc itself. Processing of zinc uses many toxic chemicals, including sulfuric acid, phosphorous pentasulfide, and sodium cyanide. Wastewater can contain heavy metals, methylene chloride, toluene, and other toxic chemicals. Chlorine in processing water may react with other toxins to form highly dangerous chlorinated compounds. Several zinc smelters are now Superfund sites. Applying galvanization to iron or steel produces wastewater and sludge similar to those from the original processing of the zinc.

General hazards: Mining. Fuel consumption.

Factors that reduce or offset risks: Control during mining operations. Factory equipment.

Renewability/recyclability: It is possible to reclaim zinc coating when recycling steel. Nonrenewable.

Alternative products: Other rust-proofing coatings, or rust-proof materials, may be more appropriate for some uses.

WOOD
Lumber

End-use issues: Woods used in construction are nontoxic. People with severe MCS may react to wood sap of softwoods—pine, cedar, spruce, etc.—but this is unlikely to be an issue outdoors. Lumber may be slightly contaminated by pesticides during growth or in storage;

again, this generally affects only MCS sufferers. For landscape use, users and designers may be faced with the choice of rot-resistant species such as redwood that are threatened by over-logging versus chemically preserved wood of other species.

Production issues: Most concerns about wood focus on forestry practices (see Logging). Overharvesting and clear-cutting of forests have had very negative effects both on the tree species themselves and on forest biodiversity. This is particularly important in the tropics but applies to forestry worldwide. Wood certified as sustainably harvested avoids or dramatically decreases these problems. Local timbers are increasingly replaced by production from distant regions such as the Pacific Northwest or Georgia, as well as foreign sources. Transportation plays a significant role in the environmental impact of lumber and may be greatly decreased by using local sources. Ordinary sawdust, if inhaled, can cause long-term lung damage; mill workers, construction crews, and finish woodworkers need to use facemasks and other dust-control equipment.

General hazards: Logging. Fuel consumption, esp. for nonlocal woods.

Factors that reduce or offset risks: Generally healthy, durable product. Low embodied energy and easily worked. Slowly biodegradable (if not treated or sheltered from weather).

Renewability/recyclability: Wood from structures can be reused if dismantled rather than demolished. Wood from old structures is often stronger and of higher quality than new lumber (unless rotted or insect damaged). Wood is recyclable as chips (and composite board), as mulch, and as pulp for paper. Wood is renewable, but probably not at the rate of current consumption. As a rule of thumb, wood structures should be built to last longer than it takes to regrow wood of the same size and quality.

Associated materials in use: Steel and galvanized fasteners. Coatings, paints, stains. Construction adhesives. Preservatives.

Alternative products: Plastic lumber resists rot and insects and may be a substitute for preservative-treated wood; it is primarily nonstructural.

Lumber, preservative-treated

See Wood preservatives, under Coatings.

Note: see also Glulam and Plywood below; some are preservative-treated.

Glulam timber

End-use issues: Glulams for wet locations are usually treated with preservatives, commonly CCA and pentachlorophenol. See Wood preservatives listing for hazards. Resorcinol/phenolic glues are most common for glulam beams; even though these incorporate formaldehyde, they are very stable once set and outgas very little. Urea-formaldehyde adhesives, occasionally used in glulams, give off some formaldehyde, but usually not enough to be a concern outdoors.

Production issues: See Adhesives, Preservatives, and Lumber.

General hazards: Logging. Petroleum production and refining. Fuel combustion.

Factors that reduce or offset risks: Like plywood and other composite wood materials, glulams make it possible to use smaller timber. This reduces the need for old-growth logging and avoids waste of small wood.

Renewability/recyclability: Glulams are reusable. If not preservative-treated, glulams are almost as recyclable as ordinary lumber. Treated glulams share the problems noted under Wood preservatives.

Associated materials in use: Metal fasteners.

Alternative products: Casein glues, used in early glulams, are nontoxic; research into improved versions might be worthwhile.

Plywood and chipboards

End-use issues: Interior-grade plywood with decorative hardwood surfaces is usually made with urea-formaldehyde adhesives, which are cheap but unstable. Emission of formaldehyde has been a concern with these plywoods and other composite-wood materials used indoors; however, these emissions have been reduced greatly over the past decade. Most softwood and exterior-grade plywoods are made with resorcinol/phenolic glues, which outgas very little, and are used in well-ventilated locations. A national standard, ANSI/HVPA HP-1, or standards set by HUD, may be used as guidelines to lowered formaldehyde emissions. Plywood outdoors sometimes delaminates, wasting resources.

Production issues: Both urea-formaldehyde and resorcinol/phenolic adhesives involve toxic materials in manufacture.

General hazards: Logging.

Factors that reduce or offset risks: Some manufactured wood products make very efficient use of small or scrap wood. Plywood produces wood panels much larger than could be sawed from any log. Sealant coatings can be used against outgassing, esp. for interior use or where user is chemically sensitive.

Renewability/recyclability: See Logging.

Associated materials in use: Same as for Lumber.

Alternative products: Usually not a landscape issue. A few interior and exterior-grade board products without formaldehyde are available.

Stone

Almost all environmental concerns about stone are part of the mining process. Differences in environmental impact between types of stone such as limestone versus sandstone are small; considerable differences may exist between specific quarries, as well as in energy usage (see Table 7.12). Stone quarries tend to be open-pit. Unlike metal ores, building stone does not generate massive amounts of tailings waste. Although this avoids many of the pollution and habitat disruption problems associated with tailings, it also means that there is little material left over to refill the pit for reclamation. Deep abandoned quarries, often filled with runoff, have been the sites of many drownings. They also serve as new habitat, however. Stone is nontoxic (although trace radioactivity can exist in some kinds). Stone dust can be a hazard to workers and can cause sediment problems in water bodies. Limestone dust can significantly change the pH of soils and water. Transportation of dimension stone varies greatly, from fieldstone used on-site to locally quarried stone to specialty stone shipped thousands of miles. Most stone is eminently reusable, though soft or porous types may not permit (or survive) attempts to remove old mortar.

CEMENT AND ASPHALT

Cement, concrete, and mortar

End-use issues: Cement once cured is normally inert. As powder or while wet, it is strongly alkaline and can burn the skin, eyes, or lungs. For chemically sensitive people, cement products may cause problems in three ways: the inclusion of additives (see Associated Materials) or contaminated aggregates; the use of some conventional form-release agents; and the absorption of irritant chemicals by the concrete, especially in CMUs (concrete masonry units) that are porous. These are primarily of concern for indoor air quality.

Improperly mixed or placed concrete is structurally unsound and deteriorates in weather. Such cement work by unskilled or dishonest contractors is unfortunately common and results in wasted resources. Concrete is so adaptable that it is often specified as "by default"; the resulting designs often weather very poorly and result in major waste. As impervious paving, concrete contributes significantly to runoff, erosion, and soil death. These misuses are not inherent in the material, but ease of use and cheapness encourage abuse.

Production issues: Cement processing is energy-intensive. Cement plants produce 1 ton of CO_2 (or more) for every ton of cement. Although this 1:1 ratio is being improved by efficiency measures, it remains a serious contribution to global warming, amounting to 2 percent of the CO_2 produced by human activity in the United States. Particulates and acid gases are also released. In 1993, about half the cement kilns in the United States burned hazardous wastes as fuel. Toxic metals, which do not burn, may be emitted into the air or into the cement. Waste as fuel was regulated by the EPA in 1993, reducing this hazard. A great majority of U.S. cement plants are foreign-owned,[12] possibly reducing motivation for environmental responsibility.

General hazards: Mining. Fuel consumption.

Factors that reduce or offset risks: Cement in porous, unpainted CMUs will absorb approximately 20 percent of its weight in CO_2. However, this does not come close to mitigating the total amount of CO_2 produced with the cement, and poured concrete, which is less porous, absorbs even less. Cement can encapsulate some hazardous materials safely, which solves a disposal problem and reuses the materials. Similarly, well-regulated use of waste for fuel may solve more problems than it creates. When well designed and constructed, concrete's durability offsets energy and pollution impacts. Can be used as binder in porous paving. Usually produced fairly close to end market, so transportation issues are lessened.

Renewability/recyclability: Limestone, aggregates, and other ingredients of cement are abundant, but not renewable. Unreinforced concrete can be crushed or broken and reused as riprap or aggregate. Manufacturers of CMUs crush and reuse broken units. Overall, however, it appears that used concrete will always be a material for which supply greatly exceeds demand, unless the rate of demolition changes dramatically.

Associated materials in use: Formwork (wood or steel). Steel reinforcing. Pigments (mostly iron oxides, from industrial by-products). Form-release agents. Additives: ingredients, usually proprietary and some mildly toxic, include sulfonic acids based on benzene, naphthalene, melamine, or lignin, as well as vegetable and animal soaps. Chemically sensitive people may exclude these from specs. Accelerators and freeze-preventing additives can be eliminated by seasonal scheduling of work. Some additives, like water-reducers and superplasticizers, may save water in arid regions.

Alternative products: Soil cement, which uses a small percentage of Portland cement mixed with native soil, is a well-tested material for outdoor paving and cast-in-place formed work. Created on-site, it lowers energy consumption, water use, and aggregate use; in naturalistic design, it has aesthetic advantages. Soil testing is essential to the correct formulation of soil cement. The compressive strength of soil cement is on the order of two-thirds that of ordinary concrete. Rammed-earth and compressed-earth block are essentially soil cement. Brick, adobe, asphalt, stone, and other materials are alternatives to concrete in some uses.

Asphalt

End-use issues: When hot, asphalt produces fumes that are moderately toxic if inhaled; modified forms of these fumes may be carcinogenic. Chemically sensitive individuals may experience problems from small amounts of asphalts in coatings and other products, as well as from obvious applications like paving. As impervious paving, asphalt contributes significantly to runoff, erosion, and soil death. Like concrete, because of its cheapness and ease of use, it is used "by default" to the point of abuse.

Production issues: Asphalt is produced as part of petroleum refining; some bitumens occur naturally. Emissions during production and storage include VOCs and particulate asphalt.

General hazards: Petroleum production and refining.

Factors that reduce or offset risks: As a sealant, can protect other materials from decay. Can serve as a binder in porous paving. Usually produced close to market, decreasing transportation energy use.

Renewability/recyclability: Asphalt paving can be ground up by paving machines and relaid on site. Other forms of asphalt, especially shingles, can theoretically be recycled if nails and other contaminants can be removed. However, roofing waste is most often landfilled or incinerated.

Associated materials in use: Aggregates. Metal containers.

Alternative products: Asphalt is too cheap and easy to use for anyone to expect it to disappear from use soon. For waterproofing large areas, and where a flexible material is required, there are few alternatives. For other uses such as paving, most alternative materials are significantly more expensive. Methods of designing for less pavement are probably more important than materials substitution in decreasing the impacts of asphalt.

Aggregates

End-use issues: The most common aggregate is gravel or crushed stone; like dimension stone, it is nontoxic. Some substitute aggregates are also used in concrete (less likely in asphalt), such as slag (from blast-furnace iron), crushed brick and concrete, and fly ash (captured from smokestacks by scrubber equipment). Advocates for MCS sufferers consider these aggregates as contaminants in concrete, of concern for indoor air quality. Used brick and concrete do absorb materials from air and water and could contain some pollutants, as may slag and fly ash. However, aggregate in concrete is normally encapsulated in a layer of cement, making it unlikely that contaminants

would be released. Aggregate contamination is unlikely to be a major issue outdoors.

Production issues: Environmental impact is primarily from mining, as well as energy used in crushing and transporting. Gravel deposits are geologically associated with present or past watercourses. Mining near or dredging in rivers is very likely to release sediments into the water. Holding ponds can control this but require land set aside for the purpose. Many deposits are shallow, which means that a large area of landscape and habitat is disturbed in mining. The closer these operations are to existing streams, the more critical their impact on wetland habitats.

General hazards: Mining. Fuel combustion.

Factors that reduce or offset risks: Without aggregate, much more cement would be required per volume of concrete, and less strength achieved. Recycling wastes as aggregate reduces disposal quantities and saves resources. Crushed aggregate is angular, an essential factor in porous paving and structural soil.

Renewability/recyclability: In theory, aggregate-bearing concrete can be crushed and reused indefinitely, at significant energy cost. The materials are abundant but not renewable.

Associated materials in use: Cement; asphalt.

Sand

End-use issues: Sand is essentially inert. Like gravel, its surface might be contaminated from air or water while in storage. As used in concrete, this is unlikely to be a hazard, but where sand is used alone, contaminants could be transferred to soil or picked up by people walking or playing. Amounts of contaminant would be limited by sand's limited ability to absorb.

Production issues: Silica sand, the most abundant and most useful type, releases silica dust during processing. Respiratory silicosis is a serious and regulated hazard to workers. Like gravel (see Aggregate), sand deposits are frequently associated with watercourses; some are windblown deposits. Mining and dredging near rivers release sediments. Some grades of sand are produced by crushing, requiring energy use.

General hazards: Mining. Fuel consumption.

Factors that reduce or offset risks: Sand is

important in construction and in soil amendment, and there are few substitutes. Some grades of sand can replace pesticides by physically deterring insects. Sand is frequently used as a filter and can help control some pollutants; as a setting bed for pavers, it allows some permeability.

Renewability/recyclability: Clean sand from paving beds can be reused on-site. Reuse or recycling that involves transporting the sand off-site is seldom feasible because of energy and labor costs.

Associated materials in use: Steel, plastic or wood edging, sheet plastic, or filter fabric is often needed to contain sand beds.

Alternative products: Crushed recycled glass is increasingly used as a sand substitute (see Glass).

Form-release agents

End-use issues: Most conventional form-release agents are petroleum-based and contain VOCs. Worse, but widely used because they are cheap, are diesel fuel and waste oils (either automotive or industrial). Sprayed on forms, these can release heavy metals and PCBs into the soil or air. Especially on foundation forms, these toxins are released directly into what will likely be landscape beds. Many individuals, not necessarily chemically sensitive, suffer from the emissions and odors of petroleum products. Such issues are less critical outdoors than when conventional release agents are used indoors. Impetus for developing alternative release agents came from manufacturers of precast concrete, whose work is done inside large buildings and whose workers experienced health problems.

Production issues: Unknown.

General hazards: Petroleum production and refining.

Factors that reduce or offset risks: Good form-release makes a form reuseable, saving form materials.

Renewability/recyclability: n/a

Alternative products: Wax, vegetable oils, biodegradable detergent, and stretched plastic sheet have been suggested. They may be practical on very small projects.

Bio-Form (Leahy-Wolff, Franklin Park IL, 888-873-5327), made from rapeseed oil with plant-based additives, is nontoxic, biodegrad-

able, and free of VOCs. Several large concrete firms use it exclusively and say it performs as well or better than petroleum-based agents. It is approximately twice as costly, but, as *Environmental Building News* points out, "Because a concrete foundation is the building element most directly in contact with soil and groundwater, this is a good place to spend a little more money on a non-polluting product."[13]

BRICK, TILE, AND ADOBE

Brick

End-use issues: Brick is essentially inert and nontoxic in use. Like concrete, waste materials are sometimes incorporated into brick. Firing is likely to render these harmless to users.

Production issues: Clay and other materials for brick are mined. Significant energy is used in firing brick, although less than for most concrete masonry equivalents. Extra dense or hard landscape brick requires extra firing energy. In addition to general hazards associated with mining, brick firing may emit particulates and gases. Depending on the materials being fired, these gases may include flouride and chlorine. These are hazardous in their own right and contribute to ozone depletion and acid rain. Wastes used as kiln fuel may be safe or unsafe.

General hazards: Mining. Fuel combustion.

Factors that reduce or offset risks: Brick is a very durable material made from plentiful raw materials. Careful inclusion of wastes in brick can reduce disposal needs.

Renewability/recyclability: Almost 100 percent of fired brick is usable. Factory rejects, as well as used brick, can be crushed and recycled or used in place of gravel or mulch. Used bricks are popular for their "character" as a building material; they should be used with some caution in structural or exposed work, since they may have lost strength during previous weathering. For MCS suffers only, used brick may absorb pollutants enough to cause reactions.

Associated materials in use: Mortar. Metal ties and fasteners.

Alternative products: Many other forms of unit masonry, not all of them significantly better or worse in environmental impacts.

Ceramic tile

End-use issues: In use, ceramic tile is essentially inert. Adhesives used for laying some types of tile contain toxic materials and may irritate chemically sensitive individuals; mortar is used instead. These issues apply mostly to indoor use. Lead glazes, uncommon in U.S. manufacture, may leach from foreign-made or old tile.

Production issues: Tile is produced in much the same way as brick and shares the problems of mining, firing energy, particulate emission, and flourine gases. Clay types differ, and materials like glass or feldspar are added. Tiles are more often glazed than bricks; a few glaze materials are seriously hazardous if not carefully handled.

General hazards: Mining. Fuel consumption.

Factors that reduce or offset risks: Tile is a very durable material made from plentiful raw materials. Addition of fillers (talc or prophyllite) can reduce the firing temperature, saving fuel.

Renewability/recyclability: Like brick, reject tile is ground and reused by manufacturers. Reusing tile on construction sites is difficult because it is fragile. Materials are abundant, but not renewable; a few glaze materials are scarce.

Associated materials in use: Adhesives. Mortar.

Adobe (stabilizers)

End-use issues: Adobe is nontoxic unless the soil from which it was made was contaminated. Stabilized adobe and other stabilized earth materials contain 3 to 5 percent asphalt or 5 to 10 percent cement, by weight. Chemically sensitive individuals may react to asphalt.

Production issues: Adobe is said to be the world's cheapest *and* most expensive building material: cheapest if produced on-site by hand, most expensive if mass-produced and shipped from off-site. Much of the expense is due to breakage during transport. Stabilization, though primarily for water resistance, may decrease breakage. However, on-site production dramatically reduces energy and pollution from transport. Straw in clay helps prevent shrinkage cracking. Adobe made from productive agricultural soils is inadvisable.

General hazards: Mining, although usually on a very small scale; soil for adobes is often taken from within the building footprint. Fuel consumption, if transported, and if mechanical adobe pressers are used.

Factors that reduce or offset risks: One of the least hazardous, and most universal, building materials.

Renewability/recyclability: Protected from weather, adobe is very stable; even when wetted, it seldom loses more than a thin surface layer per year. Neglected for twenty years (or less in wet climates), adobe begins an automatic recycling that is one of its advantages.

Associated materials in use: Asphalt. Cement. Structural supports and ties are sometimes used.

SOIL PRODUCTS

Perlite and vermiculite (soil mix)

End-use issues: Both materials are inert and nontoxic. Because of their light weight, spilled perlite and vermiculite are litter problems, unsightly but not hazardous.

Production issues: Perlite is a volcanic rock similar to obsidian; vermiculite is a silicate of magnesium, iron, and aluminum. Water bonded into the materials causes them to expand when heated, like popcorn. Emissions occur from fuel used in heating; the expanding products themselves primarily give off steam. General impacts of mining are the most significant environmental issues. The volume mined is up to twenty times less than the expanded volume, so the area disrupted per amount of final product is lower than for other types of mining. Like expanded plastics and other lightweight materials, transportation energy may be unusually high.

General hazards: Mining. Fuel consumption.

Factors that reduce or offset risks: For lightweight soil applications, these materials have few practical alternatives. Such applications may include ecoroofs (page III), which have many beneficial environmental effects.

Renewability/recyclability: As used in soil mixes, perlite and vermiculite are impractical to separate and recycle. Soil mixes can be reused, but require sterilization. The materials are abundant, but not renewable.

Fertilizers

End-use issues: Organic and artificial fertilizers pose little chemical hazard to human end users when used carefully. Nutrient deficiencies in food crops grown with artificial fertilizers are the prime reason for the organic foods movement; there is also some evidence that ornamental plants dependent on artificial fertilizers may be less healthy than those grown with organic manures. If improperly processed, organic manures may retain some pathogens, but these usually die quickly once applied. Overfertilization and leaching, from either natural or artificial fertilizers, harm surface water, groundwater, and aquatic organisms. Improperly formulated or excessive fertilization can alter soil characteristics negatively, with resulting vegetation changes.

Production issues: Artificial fertilizers are produced from petrochemicals, or from phosphate rock treated with nitric, phosphoric, or sulfuric acids, all of which are hazardous to workers. Organic or natural fertilizers imported to the site cost energy (and pollution) in transport. The site or system from which organic fertilizers are exported may suffer nutrient-cycle disruption.

General hazards: Mining. Petroleum production and refining. Fuel consumption.

Factors that reduce or offset risks: Fertilizers and soil amendments such as limestone can help restore damaged soils. Careful soil chemistry changes can sometimes substitute for use of herbicide as a way to manage undesirable plant species.

Renewability/recyclability: Organic fertilizers are almost the original recycling program, a web of reusable "wastes" as diverse as biodiversity itself. Artificial fertilizers may be accommodated in this recycling web, but because they are oversimplified in composition, often unbalance the process.

Associated materials in use: Metal and plastic containers.

THE HAZARDS AND IMPACTS OF LANDSCAPE MATERIALS

Table APX.1
Organic and Heavy-Metal Chemicals Common in Building Materials

Chemical (synonyms)	Found In
VOCs	
1,1,1-Trichloroethane (methyl chloroform)	Solvent in paints and degreasers
1,2-dichlorobenzene (ortho-dichlorobenzene)	Solvent; fumigants and insecticides; dyes; metal polishes
4-PC (4-Phelylcyclohexene)	Solvent; penetrating agent.
Acetone	Solvent; lacquers; inks; adhesives; tool cleanup.
Acrolein	Herbicides; used in polyurethane and polyester production.
Acrylonitrile (vinyl cyanide)	Paints; adhesives; dyes; pesticides; used in plastic production. Mixed with wood pulp as "synthetic soil."
Benzene	Very common in production of synthetic chemicals, esp. plastics.
Carbon tetrachloride (perchloromethane)	Metal degreasers; fumigants; rubber solvent. Banned in household-use products.
Ethylbenzene (phenylethane)	Solvent in resins; used in styrene production.
Formaldehyde (oxymethylene)	Glues, wood composites, plywoods, and glulams; plastic resins; dyes; preservative; fertilizers. Urea-formaldehyde is the least stable, and cheapest form.
Isophorone	Solvent, esp. for polyvinyl and other resins; pesticides; specialized lacquers.
Methyl ethyl ketone	Solvent in lacquers, paints, adhesives, inks, thinners, cleaners. Peroxide of MEK is fiberglass hardener.
Methyl isobutyl ketone	Solvent in paints, paint removers, lacquers, adhesives, cleaners. Acrylic and vinyl coatings.
Methylene chloride (dichloromethane)	Paint removers; degreasers; foams (blowing agent). Used in plastic production.
Naphthalene (tar camphor)	Dyes; fungicides; moth and animal repellents; cutting fluids and lubricants; coal tar; resins.
Phthalate esters	Soft plastics, as plasticizer; hardener for resins; dyes; insecticides. (Examples: DEHP; phthalic anhydride)
Styrene	Used in production of plastics, synthetic rubber, and latex (for adhesives and paints); polystyrene glazing; and Styrofoam.
Tetrachloroethane (perchloroethylene)	Degreasers for metals; paint removers; varnishes; insecticides; herbicides. Used in production of other chemicals.
Toluene (methylbenzene)	Solvent. Paints, coatings, plastics, plastic adhesives, cleaners, fuels.
Trichloroethylene	Degreasers; paints; fumigants.
Vinyl chloride	Used in plastics production, esp. PVC. Adhesives.
Xylene (dimethylbenzene) .	Solvent. Paints, lacquers, resins, rubber cements, fuels.
HEAVY METALS	
Antimony	Lead batteries; bearings; solder; pigments in paints, dyes, stains; metal alloys.
Cadmium	Pigments; metal coatings; brazing rods; ceramic glazes; NiCad batteries; electrical parts.
Chromium	Pigments for glass and paints; metal and plastic plating; alloys.
Lead	Old paints; solder; batteries.
Mercury	Mercury-vapor lamps; batteries; electrical controls; mirror plating.
Nickel	Alloys; welding; electroplating; batteries.

Sources: List from HOK *Sustainable Design Guide;* synonyms and "found in" data based on Hawley's *Chemical Dictionary.* See citations p. 296.

Limits of Embodied Energy Methods Today

The construction and design industries cannot change world patterns of energy use single-handedly, but they have a responsibility to *influence* those patterns toward sustainability. In order to meet this responsibility and use this influence successfully, it is important to understand the actual limits of embodied energy as they exist today. These limits also affect attempts to use currently available data in decisions about sustainability. These limits are briefly discussed here. Methods used to compile embodied energy statistics for this book are also noted.

Issues in Embodied Energy Research

Three main problems affect and limit embodied energy research and the availability of statistics today. These are comparability of source information, differences in analytical methods, and political issues such as proprietary secrecy.

Lack of Comparable Source Data

Energy use is recorded in a wide variety of formats. These range from very specific (miles-per-gallon data on particular models of private vehicle) to very general (Btu per dollar of product value across an entire industry). As the fine print on a new-vehicle sticker says, "actual performance may vary." Industrywide statistics may lump together (or "aggregate") such varied products or regions that they are misleading. Different operating conditions or production methods may mean that "identical" products from two different sources have very different energy histories.

Carefully collected information is more accu-

rate and easier to compare to other data. In-house records, such as those a contractor might keep on fuel consumption per machine or vehicle, can be very specific and accurate. Most data collection, however, requires larger-scale efforts, along the lines of an energy-focused Consumer Reports or Underwriters Laboratory. Lobbying in favor of nonpartisan energy studies should be a priority for sustainability minded professionals.

Understanding how published data were compiled, and under what assumptions, is something any professional can do to increase the usefulness of current information on energy. This does not require an advanced statistics degree. Energy analysis is very similar to cost estimating, a skill many construction and design professionals have. Just as estimates or bids must be scrutinized to be sure what is included and what is not, energy cost estimates require similar evaluation.

Manufacturing processes, even when they result in comparable products, may vary considerably among firms, locations, political jurisdictions, or seasons. Crushed rock versus dredged gravel, and kiln-dried versus air-dried lumber, are examples of very similar products whose embodied energy is significantly different. Fortunately, construction and design professionals already pay attention to these differences and can apply them to energy analysis.

Differences in Analytical Methods

"In practice," says energy researcher Tracy Mumma, "each individual researcher studying embodied energy has a different methodology."[1] The results of this research circulate widely in many forms—books and articles, Internet pages, and software. Knowing a little about these analytical methods and their variations can make the difference between using and misusing embodied energy in decision making. Interestingly, research for this book indicates that in many cases researchers are arriving at surprisingly similar results using very different methods.

INDUSTRY OR MARKET STUDIES

The total number of units produced by an industry (say, board feet of lumber per year or annual production of irrigation valves) is divided into the industry's total energy bill for that period. This shows an average energy use per unit. Such averages are valuable, but sustainability decisions really need to compare specific suppliers or at least regional differences. Variations caused by transportation also tend to get lost in such studies. Sometimes the number of units produced is derived from the dollar value of units sold, which can disguise many forms of normal waste and loss, such as defective items produced but never sold. Studies commissioned by the industries themselves often attempt to portray the sponsoring industry as more energy-efficient than its competitors.

MANUFACTURER-SPECIFIC *STUDIES*

Also called "process studies," these measure energy use and product output at specific facilities. Energy measurement can vary widely, however. Directly metering the flow of energy for some processes—for example, electric-powered manufacturing—is easy. For others, direct measurements are either impractical or unsafe due to extreme operating conditions. In these cases, energy use is estimated from indirect indicators. "Waste" heat, and the burning of by-products to fuel manufacturing processes, are not always consistently accounted for in different studies. For choosing materials, this level of study would be most valuable, but few are available due to the cost of data gathering. Without standardized methods and equations, the specific nature of these studies may make them hard to compare with other studies.

TRANSPORTATION

Studies differ in whether they include transportation costs at all, only transport during manufacture, or transport to the final point of use. This can be significant. For example, brick

used 350 miles (about 550 km) from the factory uses as much energy in transportation as was used to produce the bricks.[2] Either excluding or averaging transportation energy use would clearly distort a decision about whether brick was an appropriate material at that location. The authors feel that where possible for construction materials, embodied energy figures should be given at the factory gate. The final user should be the one to add actual transportation to the site, along with machine and tool energy used during installation.

INSTALLATION ENERGY

For many industrial products, such as computers or dishwashers, energy used in installing the product at the end-use site is very small. For construction, this energy use is extremely important. Some studies, like Stein's groundbreaking work in the 1980s, treat installation energy as a percentage of the total embodied energy of materials or as a factor based on square feet of floor space. Energy use per square foot of construction is clearly not comparable between building and landscape projects. As a percentage, Stein's allowance ranged from 2 percent to 3 percent of total materials energy.[3]

HUMAN ENERGY

Virtually all embodied energy studies *exclude* the energy of human labor. This is in keeping with the focus of energy studies on fossil-fuel use but does not give an inclusive picture of sustainable energy analysis. For example, grain can be made into biogas to power machines or can feed human workers. Depending on the task, human labor can be very energy-efficient and uses renewable "fuels."

In most current studies, a product made with significant human labor always appears to have less embodied energy because the human energy is left out. Since construction, and especially landscape construction, relies on large amounts of human labor, this issue assumes greater importance in relation to landscape work than in studies of energy in consumer manufacturing.

In some situations, animal power is still a viable alternative to mechanized power. The U.S. Forest Service, as recently as 1998, published research on using horse- or mule-drawn equipment for trail construction in rough terrain. Sustainable farming often involves consideration of horse-drawn equipment, as much because waste is fertilizer as for any energy reasons. Although uncommon, these possibilities should not be excluded from embodied energy research, for the same reasons that human labor needs to be reported. Stein's study set a good precedent, ignored by later studies, in giving figures on labor energy parallel to embodied energy figures.

ENVIRONMENTAL ENERGY INPUTS

Similar to the exclusion of human energy, most studies exclude any form of energy contributed to a product by nature. Botanists can approximate the amount of solar energy required to produce a pound of wood, a bowl of rice, or a barrel of oil—since all are originally plant matter. Solar energy also "pumps" water to the tops of watersheds, making it available for many uses, including hydroelectric power generation. Heat and pressure are "work" contributed by geological forces to many common mineral building materials. Yet none of these energy inputs is included in embodied energy studies today. To make a true comparison of the energy costs of living landscape materials—for instance, to compare what it really costs to shade a house with a growing tree or with a constructed shade trellis—biological energy efficiency needs to be part of the equation. The authors would suggest listing fuel energy, labor energy, and environmental energy inputs as *parallel* statistics for each material.

Political and Historical Obstacles

Politics have strongly influenced the development of energy analysis. In the 1970s, some of the world's earliest comprehensive work on embodied energy in construction was done in the United States for the Department of Energy.[4] These pioneering works remain influential, although statistically out of date. Meanwhile, energy research of all sorts fell victim to Reaganomics, and embodied energy research has received little official support in the United States in recent decades. The U.S. Department of Energy has supported several industry-specific studies of energy use, but no comprehensive comparison of materials. The impetus for embodied energy research in the United States has come from private organizations or individuals such as Pliny Fisk or Tracy Mumma, for whom official funding has been slow to come.

It is in Australia, Canada, and New Zealand that cutting-edge research has been backed by access to government data and funding, with active support of the construction industries. The American construction industry should insist on reclaiming active research support for energy studies in this country. The AIA's *Environmental Resource Guide* is a commendable step in this direction.

A second type of political obstacle to embodied energy research is proprietary secrecy. Detailed analysis of embodied energy requires tracing the manufacturing and construction process step-by-step. Many businesses fear that energy analysis will reveal trade secrets, so they refuse access to information collected for in-house use. It is unlikely, however, that energy statistics would reveal as much as the records required for a patented process. Nonetheless, this fear and resistance are sometimes obstacles. While construction practices are seldom as secretive as manufacturing, contractors and designers need to convince their suppliers that sharing energy information benefits everyone.

Methods Used in Compiling Embodied Energy Figures for This Book

The figures given in Figures 7.12 to 7.17 are based entirely on published literature in English. No new measurements or estimates were carried out for this book. Numerical information on embodied energy for construction was compiled from results of library and Internet searches.

Sources

A relatively small number of publications offer information on this topic. The following were obtained:

1. American Institute of Architects. *Environmental Resource Guide.* Edited by Joseph A. Demkin. Loose-leaf, current through '98 Supplement. NYC: Wiley, 1998.

2. Brown, Harry L., Bernard B. Hamel, and Bruce A. Hedman. *Energy Analysis of 108 Industrial Processes.* Philadelphia PA: Fairmont Press, 1985.

3. Stein, R. G., C. Stein, M. Buckley, and M. Green. *Handbook of Energy Use for Building Construction.* Vol. DOE/CS/20220-1, Energy Conservation. Washington DC: U.S. Dept. of Energy, 1980.

4. Lawson, Bill. *Building Materials Energy and the Environment.* Red Hill (Australia): Royal Australian Institute of Architects, 1996.

5. Gupta, Vinod. *Energy and Habitat: Town Planning and Design for Energy Conservation.* New Delhi: Halsted (Wiley & Sons), 1984.

6. Paschich, Ed, and Paula Hendricks. *Timber Reduced Energy Efficient Homes.* Santa Fe NM: Sunstone, 1994.

7. Anonymous. "Energy & Environmental Profiles" and "Technology Roadmaps" for steel, aluminum, glass and other industries (7 reports). Washington DC: U.S. Dept. of Energy, Office of Industrial Technology, 1996–1998.

8. Alcorn, Andrew. "Embodied Energy Coefficients of Building Materials." Wellington NZ: Building Research Association of New Zealand, 1995.

References were found to a British study for which only a partial title was known, and which thus could not be found. A Canadian study, produced by Forintek, the national forest industry research group, is also frequently cited. Unfortunately, Forintek's studies are now controlled by the Athena Sustainable Materials Institute, which despite a Web site description as a *public* source of energy data appears to treat the information as proprietary and for the benefit of the institute's industry members only. The AIA *ERG*, however, provides some statistics from this study.

Procedures

Estimates of embodied energy from each source were converted to make measurement units consistent, and then compared, using a standardized list of material names. One study, that by Brown, was dropped out at this point. Brown's presentation of data as a series of process inputs and outflows added up to values vastly different from the other studies, often by several orders of magnitude. This suggested not that the study was invalid, but that it could not be summed up into a single number without extra expertise, and thus that comparisons would be meaningless.

Of the remaining 252 estimates, 104 were for materials cited by only one source study. For the remaining materials, estimates were provided by between two and five sources. All the estimates for a given material and, where appropriate, those for closely related materials were compared. Estimates that differed by a factor of ten or more from a consistent group of estimates for the same material were eliminated; only 11 of these cases were found (about 4 percent of the total available estimates). The majority of these were industry-asserted values far lower than any other researcher's results, reported as such by the AIA along with higher values from other studies.

Estimates for each material were then averaged, and the standard deviation for each set was computed and expressed as a percentage of the average. Based on experience in construction estimating, a threshold was set at a deviation of plus or minus 30 percent—admittedly not great statistical accuracy, but adequate as a beginning for rough estimates in a complex applied field. Only 6 out of 157 materials showed deviation greater than this. These 6 were reported with high and low values rather than averages.

The resulting figures should be used judiciously, not assuming greater accuracy than is currently available. However, we feel that they justify the belief that embodied energy research is converging on reliable figures, and that future research will be able to offer energy costing that is clear, straightforward, and at least as valid for environmental decision making as is any form of financial costing.

Landscape Projects Cited in This Book

This appendix lists projects that were used to illustrate sustainable principles in this book. They are listed in order by the principle in which they first appear.

Project location, firm names, and other information found in this list are included in the main text only when the project is mentioned for the first time. If you are reading the principles out of order, and find a project mentioned without further details, scan this list to locate the principle in which it was first mentioned and to get more information about the project and the people involved in it. As noted in the acknowledgments, this list is inevitably incomplete. Those listed in it are the people or firms most directly connected to landscape aspects of the project. Nor could we possibly include all the environmentally-driven landscape projects that do exist, even if we limited the list to U.S. projects. To bring other exemplary projects to our attention, or to correct factual mistakes, please see "Contacting the Authors" on page xxi.

Introduction

Waterworks Gardens, Renton WA: Lorna Jordan, environmental artist, Seattle

Center for Regenerative Studies, Pomona CA: John Lyle, L.A., Pomona, and others

Water Pollution Control Laboratory, Portland OR: Murase Associates, L.A., Portland

Principle 1—Preservation

Le Pays de la Sangouine, Bouctouche, New Brunswick: Elide Albert, architect, New Brunswick

Loantaka Brook Reservation, Morris County NJ: Andropogon Associates, L.A., Philadelphia

High Desert, Albuquerque NM: Design Workshop, L.A., Albuquerque

McDowell Mountain Ranch, Scottsdale AZ: Design Workshop, L.A., Denver CO

Desert Highlands, Scottsdale AZ: Gage Davis Assocs., L.A., Scottsdale

Bloedel Reserve, Seattle WA: Richard Haag, L.A., Seattle

NVRPA Scenic Conservation Easement, Loudon County VA: HOH Assocs. and Rhodeside & Harwell, L.A., Alexandria VA

Thorncrown Chapel, Eureka Springs AR: Fay Jones, architect, Fayetteville AR

Anchorage Botanic Gardens, Anchorage AK: Land Design North, L.A., Anchorage

Riverside Village, Atlanta GA: Post Properties, property management, Atlanta

Fallingwater, Bear Run PA: F.L. Wright, architect.

Washington and Old Dominion trail, Washington DC & VA: Northern Virginia Regional Park Authority

Principle 2—Restoration

Spectacle Island, Boston, MA: Brown & Rowe, L.A., Boston, with Phil Craul

Danehy Park, Cambridge MA: Cambridge Dept. of Sanitation

Upper Charles River, Boston MA: Carol R. Johnson Assocs., L.A., Boston

Revival Field (Pig's Eye landfill), St. Paul MN: Mel Chin, environmental artist, New York NY

Boston Common, Boston MA

J. Paul Getty Center, Los Angeles CA

South Cove, Battery Park, New York NY: all by Phil Craul, soil scientist, Boston MA

Earth Center, South Yorkshire UK: Andrew Grant, L.A., Bath UK

Gas Works Park, Seattle WA: Richard Haag, L.A., Seattle

Roadside erosion control, Redding and other CA locations: John Haynes, Caltrans erosion specialist, Sacramento

State Fairgrounds, Tacoma WA: Lynn William Horn, L.A., Tacoma

Heritage State Parks, Massachusetts: MA Dept. of Environment

Liverpool Garden Festival, Liverpool UK: Merseyside Development Corporation, developer, Liverpool

Mountains to the Sound, Seattle WA: Mountains to Sound Greenway Trust, Seattle, www.mtsgreenway.org

Harborside International, Chicago IL: Nugent Associates, golf course architects, Long Grove IL

Fresh Kills Landfill, New York NY: NYC Sanitation Department and Rutgers University

St. Mary's Urban Youth Farm, San Francisco CA: San Francisco League of Urban Gardeners (SLUG)

Anaheim Hills, Anaheim CA: Horst Schor, restoration consultant, Anaheim

Discovery Park, Seattle WA: Seattle Parks and Recreation

National Geographic Society Headquarters, Washington DC: James Urban, L.A., Annapolis MD

Pilot phytoremediation project, Charleston SC: U.S. National Park Service, planners, Denver CO

Ebbw Vale, South Wales UK: Welsh Development Agency, developer, UK

Principle 3—Vegetation

Zoo exhibits, Seattle WA, Rochester NY, etc.: CLR Design, L.A., Philadelphia PA

Ecover Headquarters ecoroof, Oostmalle, Belgium: Ecover staff and Re-Natur Gmbh

Post Properties, Atlanta GA: Kevin Kleinhelter, L.A., Atlanta

Garage ecoroof, Portland OR: Tom Liptan, stormwater specialist, Portland

Sanders Ranch, Moraga CA: Andrea Lucas, L.A., Berkeley CA

Mudslide repair, Pacifica CA: Andrew Leiser, soil bioengineer, Berkeley CA, with Andrea Lucas

Grass Lake MN: MN State Highways

Crystal Cove State Historic Park, Newport Beach CA: Steve Musillami, L.A., CA State Parks

Cumberland Gap tunnel, Cumberland Gap VA: National Park Service

Library Square ecoroof, Vancouver BC: Cornelia Oberlander, L.A., Vancouver

Amsterdam airport ecoroof, Netherlands: Schiphol Group, developer, Amsterdam

Crestwood on the Park bank stabilization, Houston TX: Robin Sotir, bioengineering, Marietta GA

Blue Route noise and retaining walls, Philadelphia PA: Synterra Ltd., L.A., Philadelphia

Walden Pond bank restoration, Concord MA: Walker Kluesing Design Group, L.A., Boston MA

Principle 4—Water

Crosby Arboretum, Picayune MS: Ed Blake, L.A., Hattiesburg MS, with Andropogon and Fay Jones, architect

Environmental Showcase Home, Phoenix AZ: AZ Public Service

Hood Canal Wetlands Project, WA: Bruce Dees & Assocs., L.A., Tacoma WA

Residence, Santa Fe NM: Ben Haggard, permaculturist, Santa Fe

Wetlands projects, international: Donald Hammer, consultant, Norris TN

LBJ Wildflower Research Center, Austin TX: J. Robert Anderson, L.A., Austin

Riparian Reserve, Gilbert AZ: Jones & Stokes, L.A., Sacramento CA

Juanita Bay Park, WA: Jongejan Gerrard McNeal, L.A., Bellevue WA

Clark County Wetlands Park, Las Vegas NV: Las Vegas County (planned)

Mill Brook, Scarborough ME: Maine Dept. of Transportation, Portland ME

Sligo Creek watershed, Silver Spring MD: MD and Washington DC interagency team

Tree trunk revetments, MO: MO Dept. of Conservation

Indian Creek Nature Center, Cedar Rapids IA: NAWE (North American Wetland Engineering), engineers, Forest Lake MN

Staten Island Blue Belt, Staten Island NY: NY Dept. of Environmental Protection, White Plains NY, with Creative Habitats and others

Parque da Cidade, Oporto, Portugal: Sidonio Pardal, L.A., Oporto

Wheaton Branch, Silver Spring MD: Pamela Rowe, environmental planner, Metropolitan Washington Council of Governments and other agencies

Highway embankment stabilization, Portland OR: Robbin Sotir, bioengineering, Marietta GA, with OR Dept. of Transportation

Casa del Agua, Tucson AZ: Univ. of AZ

Strawberry Creek, Berkeley CA: Univ. of CA

Campus millrace restoration, Eugene OR: Univ. of OR Dept. of Landscape Architecture

Principle 5—Paving

Morris Arboretum, Philadelphia PA: Andropogon Assocs., L.A., Philadelphia

Peachtree Plaza, Atlanta GA: Henry Arnold, L.A., Princeton NJ

Impervious Surface Reduction projects, Olympia WA: City of Olympia Public Works Dept.

Riverside/Corona Resource Conservation District, Riverside CA: Conservation District staff

Westfarms Mall, Farmington CT: Invisible Structures, supplier, see Resources

Simmons Mattress Headquarters parking, Atlanta GA: Robert E. Marvin, L.A., Waterboro SC

Orange Bowl, Miami FL: Miami Community Planning and Revitalization

Oregon Museum of Science and Industry, Portland OR: Murase Associates, L.A., Portland

WA State Dept. of the Environment Headquarters parking, Lacey WA: The Berger Partnership, L.A., Seattle WA

Crushed-stone parking, Medford NJ: various

Street narrowing, Bucks County PA, Boulder CO, Kentlands MD, Seaside FL: various agencies

Heritage development, Vancouver WA

Sports Stadium parking, Portland OR

Principle 6—Materials

Earthbuilding projects, CA: Russell Beatty, L.A., CA

Toxic remediation and manufactured soils, Boston MA: Brown & Rowe, L.A., Boston

Upper Charles River, Boston MA: Carol R. Johnson Assocs., L.A., Boston

African Healing Garden, San Francisco CA: Cochran & Delaney, L.A., San Francisco

Tallulah Gorge State Park, Northern GA: GA State Parks

Earthbuilding projects, Albuquerque NM: Bill Hays, L.A., Albuquerque

Arroyo stabilization, Pima County AZ : Stuart Hoenig, agricultural engineer, Univ. of AZ, with Joshua Minyard

Jardin Encore, Seattle WA: Annual Garden Show entry by King County Commission for Marketing Recyclable Materials

Monnens Addis studio, Berkeley CA: Jeffrey Miller, L.A., San Francisco

Earthbuilding projects, Albuquerque NM: Baker Morrow, L.A., Albuquerque

Deer Creek stream stabilization, Weatherford OK: OK Dept. of Environmental Quality

Sacred Circle, Minneapolis MN: Marjorie Pitz, L.A., Minneapolis

Club de Golf, Malinalco, Mexico: Mario Schjetnan, L.A., Mexico City

Bjørnsenhagen, Oslo, Norway: Rainer Stange, L.A., Oslo

Glassphalt path at Danehy Park, Cambridge MA: Merle Ukeles, environmental artist, NYC

Airport Road Park, Spalding GA

Withlahoochee State Trail, Polk City FL

Principle 8—Lighting

Tramway Road jogging trail, Albuquerque NM: Albuquerque Parks and Recreation, L.A.

Solar street lighting, Sorbet FL: Solar Outdoor Lighting, supplier, see Resources

Cholla Campground, Phoenix AZ: U.S. Forest Service

Principle 9—Noise

Soundscape management policy, national: National Park Service

Principle 11—Conclusions and Beginnings

Los Padillas school wetland, Albuquerque NM: Campbell Okuma Perkins Assocs., L.A., and Southwest Wetlands, Albuquerque

Riverwalk, Memphis TN: Roy P. Farrover, FAIA, Memphis TN

Notes

Introduction

1. Wulff, Sonja Bisbee, and Colorado Public Interest Research Group. "Vast Open Spaces Vanishing." *Coloradoan.* 28 Dec 1998, 1, Fort Collins CO.

2. This definition is so widespread that its original author is hard to determine. It was used in the widely circulated Brundtland, Gro H., "Our Common Future." Oxford: World Commission on Environment & Development, 1987. A similar but expanded definition is given in a review of sustainability concepts in Peine, John D., ed., *Ecosystem Management for Sustainability.* Boca Raton: Lewis, 1999, p. 3: "Sustainable development integrates economic, environmental and social values during planning; distributes benefits equitably across socioeconomic strata and gender upon implementation; and ensures that opportunities for continuing development remain undiminished to future generations." The ten published sets of sustainability principles reviewed by Peine (Tables 1 through 10) stress the dynamic, boundary-crossing, and semi predictable qualities of living systems; the need for coordination and teamwork; and the value of open public involvement in sustainability decisions.

3. "There is no doubt . . . that sustainability has been taken up as a rallying cry by two completely different factions and has entirely opposite meanings for each," according to Steele, James, *Sustainable Architecture: Principles, Paradigms, and Case Studies.* NYC: McGraw-Hill, 1997, p. 22. Steele calls the concept a contradiction in terms; his two factions are, loosely, green capitalists (the Earth as resources to manage), and green socialists (the Earth as the focus of social reform).

4. BASMAA. "Grow It! The Less-Toxic Garden." San Francisco: Bay Stormwater Management Agencies Association, 1997.

5. To put things in perspective, recall that the second law of thermodynamics guarantees that over the long term nothing is sustainable!

6. These goals are reported in Cardamore, Steve, The National Construction Goals," *Southern Building,* Jan/Feb 1997, viewable at www.sbcci.org/Articles, the Web site of *Southern Building Magazine.*

7. Anonymous. "Constructability Concepts File." 99 pages. Austin TX: Construction Industries Institute, 1987. Ref: SP3-3. This and other studies of constructability (on video as well as in print) are available from the Construction Industries Institute, Austin TX, 512-232-2000 or http://construction-institute.org/.

8. Though legitimate programs are of great value, there have been problems with other green building schemes. Some programs are, in effect, merely fronts for utility companies who wish to appear green and to promote their brand of fuel or power as greener than others; others have been revamped when it was found that the criteria were "allowing one strong category [of environmental performance] to make up for others." See Wilson, Alex, "Green Builder Programs Proliferating," *Environmental Building News* 4, no. (1995): 6–7.

9. The LEED program's goal and point system is described in section L.1 of HOK Architects, *Sustainable Design Guide,* edited by Sandra Mendler. Washington DC: HOK Architects, 1998, also an excellent general reference on green architecture. The point system is being revised as of this writing, for release in 2000. Unfortunately, LEED persists in treating site selection issues as optional for "green" status.

10. Santa Fe Green Building Council, draft mission statement, 1998, drafted by Kim Sorvig with input from the group.

11. Our evaluations are not intended to be equivalent to instrumented scientific measurement (such as energy-inputs and outputs, for example), although they may be based on such studies.

12. The terms Permaculture and Xeriscape have both been trademarked to ensure that they are not abused. Like all other trademarks referenced in this book, they remain the property of their respective owners.

Successes and Challenges

1. Abrams, David. *The Spell of the Sensuous: Perception and Language in a More-Then-Human World.* NYC: Pantheon, 1996. Although its title sounds nothing like a landscape book, it offers some of this century's clearest and most beautiful thinking on the relationship between places and the human mind.
2. This is true of the Judeo-Christian tradition, too; the idea that the Bible only supports "subduing the earth" is a terrible oversimplification.
3. Thayer, Robert L. Jr. "The Experience of Sustainable Landscapes." *Landscape Journal* (Fall 1989): 101–109.
4. MacElroy, William, and Daniel Winterbottom. "Toward a New Garden." *Critiques of Built Works of Landscape Architecture, LSU School of Landscape Architecture* (Fall 1997): 10–24.
5. Thompson, William. "Cleansing Art." *Landscape Architecture,* Jan 1997, 70.
6. Participants in the ecorevelatory committee were Brenda Brown, Terry Harkness, Douglas Johnston, Beth Randall, and Robert Riley.
7. Mandelbrot, Benoit. *The Fractal Geometry of Nature,* updated ed. NYC: W. H. Freeman, 1983. Although many other books (and movies!) have built on Mandelbrot's work, this remains a classic explanation of a truly revolutionary new discipline. See esp. Chapter 1, "Theme"; for a straightforward graphic that explains the concept of fractals, see the Koch Snowflake illustrations on pages 42–44.
8. Baish, J. W., Y. Gazit, N. Safavakhsh, M. Leunig, L. T. Baxter, and R. K. Jain. "Fractal Characteristics of Tumor Vascular Architecture: Significance and Implications." *Microcirculation* 4 (1997): 395–402.
9. For an overview of this research, see Wiley, John P. Jr., "Help Is on the Way." *Smithsonian,* July 1999, 22–24.
10. "Wild" is another difficult term. Most places on Earth are in some way influenced by human management, politics, pollution, or preservation. In this sense, no place is pristine. This fact is not, in our view, an excuse for failing to preserve those places that are closest to being wild, that are most nearly self-sustaining. It is not the romance of being untouched that makes these places important, but rather what they show about the dynamics of biodiversity and how they preserve diversity lost elsewhere.
11. Hawken, Paul. *The Ecology of Commerce.* NYC: Harper, 1993. Hawken was cofounder of Smith & Hawken. Like a surprising number of others, he has used experience with the business of landscapes as the basis for leadership in thinking about a sustainable society. Another of his books, *Growing a Business* (NYC: Fireside, 1987), grew out of a seventeen-part PBS television series on alternatives to the narrowly competitive model of business management.
12. HOK Architects. *Sustainable Design Guide.* Edited by Sandra Mendler. Washington DC: HOK Architects, 1998, pp. iv–vi.
13. Ibid., iv.

Principle 1: Keep Healthy Sites Healthy

1. Associated Press. "Study: Land use affects weather." *New Mexican,* 9 Dec 1998, B-7.
2. Associated Press. "Housing construction booms; industrial out put flat in January." *New Mexican,* 18 Feb 1999, Santa Fe NM.
3. For the full visual impact of forest clearance in the United States, see comparative maps in *Smithsonian,* September 1999, p. 22, Santa Fe NM.
4. Ehrlich, Paul R., Gretchen C. Daily, Norman Myers, and James Salzman. "No Middle Way on the Environment." *Atlantic Monthly,* Dec 1997, 98–104. See esp. page 101, which lists environmental services and states, "These services operate on such a grand scale, and in such intricate and little-explored ways, that most of them could not be replaced by technology—even if no expense were spared, as Biosphere 2 showed."
5. Hard figures on this perennial subject are surprisingly rare. Federal courts have ruled that loss of a single mature tree reduced property value by 9 percent. Anonymous. *The Value of Landscaping* [Web site]. Texas A&M Horticultural Sciences, 1999. Available from http://aggie-horticulture.tamu.edu/syllabi/432/article1.html. The Urban Land Institute, in a study cosponsored by the ASLA (but involving only architects and development experts in actual research), considers the perception that landscape adds to property value as believable but unproven due to lack of quantification. Developers interviewed for the study indicated 5 percent increase in value for individual homes and 20 percent increase for public landscape amenities affecting the whole development (this increase equals six times the extra construction cost for the amenities). Presumably these figures relate to *newly installed* landscaping. Bookout, Lloyd W., Michael Beyard, and Steven W. Fader. *Value by Design.* Washington DC: Urban Land Institute and American Society of Landscape Architects, 1994. Other anecdotal evidence tends to be in this range, though the authors have heard realtors state that *mature* landscapes can add 75 percent to the sale price of a home. *Appraisers* are more likely than developers to know values for mature landscapes, and a

study of appraising formulas would probably be revealing. Some wonderfully varied estimates of the value of specific trees is shown in Table 3.2.

6. Russell, James S. "Wetland Dilemma." *Architectural Record,* Jan 1993, 36–39. Architect was Elide Albert.

7. McDonald, Stuart H. "Prospect." *Landscape Architecture,* Sept 1993, 120.

8. Campanelli, Ben. "Planning for Cellular Towers." *Planning Commissioners Journal* 28 (1997): 4.

9. Thayer, Robert. *Grey World, Green Heart.* NYC: Wiley, 1994, p. 46.

10. Frandsen, Jon. "System uses cable instead of towers." *Gannet News Service,* 22 Mar 1998.

11. Real Goods. *Solar Living Sourcebook.* Edited by John Schaeffer. 9th ed. Ukiah CA: Real Goods, 1996, pp. 374–76 and 546.

12. Knight Ridder News. "Devices will let households generate power, experts say." *New Mexican,* 7 July 1999, A-4, Santa Fe NM.

13. Center for Watershed Protection. *Model Development Principles to Protect Our Streams, Lakes, and Wetlands.* Ellicott City MD: Center for Watershed Protection 1988. The specific guideline is Principle 19; allowable clearing distance, p. 154, is based on 1991 standards from the Maryland Dept. of Natural Resources.

14. Craul, Phillip J. *Urban Soil in Landscape Design.* NYC: Wiley, 1992, pp. 135–137.

15. Ibid., p. 109.

16. Ibid., p. 45. The original gives figures per gram of soil; converted by authors.

17. Thompson, William. "A Long Road to Freedom." *Landscape Architecture,* Feb 1998, 50–55.

18. See Note 5.

19. Hauer, R. J., R. W. Miller, and D. M. Ouimet. "Street Tree Decline and Construction Damage." *Journal of Arboriculture* 20, no. 2 (1994): 94–97.

20. Craul, *Urban Soil,* p. 137.

21. Ivy, Robert Adams Jr. *Fay Jones.* Washington DC: AIA Press, 1992, p. 35.

22. Hoffmann, Donald. *Frank Lloyd Wright's Fallingwater: The House and Its History.* NYC: Dover, 1985.

23. Information from a photocopied graph attributed to AASHTO; title and date unknown.

24. Cowan, Lisa, and David Cowan. "Review of Methods for Low Impact Restoration." Paper presented at the ASLA 1997 Annual Meeting.

25. Corish, Kathleen. "Clearing and Grading: Strategies for Urban Watersheds." Washington DC: Metropolitan Washington Council of Governments, 1995.

26. Wilson, Alex. "Dewees Island: More Than Just a Green Development." *Environmental Building News,* Feb 1997, 5–7. Descriptions that follow are from this article.

Principle 2: Heal Injured Sites

1. Quoted by Alex Wilson, editor of *Environmental Building News*; personal correspondence.

2. For one U.S. example of this approach, as part of the UN's Man & the Biosphere program, see Peine, John D., ed., *Ecosystem Management for Sustainability.* Boca Raton: Lewis, 1999.

3. Gilbert, O. L. *The Ecology of Urban Habitats.* London: Chapman & Hall, 1989, p. 40.

4. Anonymous. "Activists rescue New York's community gardens." *Washington Post,* 13 May 1999.

5. Bareham, Peter. "A Brief History." *Landscape Design,* Apr 1986,

6. Lancaster, Michael, and Tom Turner. "The Sun Rises Over Liverpool." *Landscape Design,* Apr 1984, 36.

7. Beaumont, Rodney. "Focus on the Festivals." *Landscape Design,* July/Aug 1992, 18.

8. Lewis, Jon E. "How Green Is My Valley." *Landscape Design,* July/Aug 1992, 11.

9. Grant, Andrew. "Life on Earth." *Landscape Design,* May 1993, 33.

10. Porter, Jane. "The Earth Center." *Landscape Design,* Feb 1996, 12.

11. Grant, "Life on Earth," 33.

12. For an interesting look at the lives of reforestation workers, see a new book titled *Handmade Forests: The Treeplanter's Experience* by Helene Cyr. New Society Publishers. Stoney Creek CT: 1999.

13. Both quotes from Schor, Horst, "Landform Grading: Building Nature's Slopes," *Pacific Coast Builder,* June 1980, 80–83.

14. Gullying is "damage" from a conventional perspective and can literally undermine vegetation trying to reestablish a foothold. In the longer view, however, gullying is nature's first step in restoring the landform to its proper, irregular shape. The flatter and steeper a slope, the more destructively gullying attacks, until erosion and deposition begin to come back into dynamic equilibrium—something that can take far too long for human purposes. See Note 16.

15. Schor, Horst. "Landform Grading and Slope Evolution." *Journal of Geotechnical Engineering* 1995, 729–734.

16. See Nash, D B., "The Evolution of Abandoned, Wave-Cut Bluffs in Emmet County, Michigan," Ph.D. dissertation, U. Michigan, 1977. This research supports the "Diffusion Model" of slope formation, which states that natural processes optimize slope forms so that materials removed upslope balance downslope deposition. The resulting slope cross-section is an S-curve; top and toe of slope are both rounded. As Schor points out, this model strongly indicates that "a planar

slope with constant inclination, typical of conventional grading practice, is not a stable, long-term equilibrium slope" (p. 732).

17. Schor, "Landform Grading and Slope Evolution" (pp. 729–734).

18. Haynes, John. "Stepped Slopes: An Effective Answer to Roadside Erosion." *Landscape Architect and Specifier News*, Feb 1990, 31.

19. Todd, Joseph A. "Some Experiences in Stepping Slopes." Gatlinburg TN: FHWA Bureau of Public Roads, 1967.

20. Comella, William (FHWA Regional Engineer, Arlington, VA), July 28, 1971.

21. Craul, *Urban Soil*, p. 237.

22. Ibid.

23. Craul, *Urban Soil*, p. 239.

24. See, for example, Newman, P., and J. Kenworthy, *Sustainability and Cities: Overcoming Automobile Dependence.* Washington DC: Island Press, 1998.

25. Thompson, William. "Banking on a River." *Landscape Architecture*, Sept 1998, 50–55.

26. Examples of this in the megaditches of Albuquerque have been documented by Paul Lusk, former city planner, currently Professor of Architecture and Planning, UNM.

27. Bradshaw, A. D. "Landfill Sites—Outstanding Opportunities for Amenity and Wildlife." Paper presented at Design Now for the Future: End-use of Landfills, November 1992. Bradshaw is a researcher at the University of Liverpool.

28. By M. C. Dobson and A. J. Moffat. No other information available on this study.

29. William Young, "Creation of Coastal Scrubforest on Landfill," date and publication unknown.

30. Spain, Kathleen. "Get It Right at the Start." *Waste Age*, Feb 1993, 57.

31. J. G. Bockheim, quoted in Craul, *Urban Soil*, p. 86.

32. For example, see Sauer, Leslie, *The Once and Future Forest.* Washington DC: Island Press, 1998; pages 154–157 discuss soil protection and restoration. This is an excellent source for details on forest protection and restoration.

33. Based primarily on Craul, *Urban Soil*, pp. 290–291.

34. Claasen, V. P., and R. J. Zaoski. "The Effect of Topsoil Reapplications on Vegetation Reestablishment." Sacramento: California Department of Transportation, 1994.

35. Bennet, Orus L. "Land Reclamation." In *McGraw-Hill Encyclopedia of Environmental Science and Engineering*, edited by Sybil Parker and Robert Corbitt. NYC: McGraw-Hill, 1993, p. 329.

36. For a complete description of this project, see Sauer, *The Once and Future Forest* p. 159.

37. Leake, Simon. "Reuse of Site Soils." *Landscape Australia*, Aug 1995.

38. Gilbert, O. L. *The Ecology of Urban Habitats.* London: Chapman & Hall, 1989, pp. 47–51.

39. Sauer, *The Once and Future Forest*, p. 156.

40. Cranshaw, Whitney. *Pests of the West.* Golden CO: Fulcrum Publishing, 1992, Chapter 1. See also Sauer, *The Once and Future Forest*, Chapters 17 and 22.

41. Mitchell, Donna. "Compost Utilization by Departments of Transportation in the United States." Gainesville: University of Florida Dept. of Environmental Horticulture, 1997, p. 8.

42. Mitchell, "Compost . . . ," p. 9.

43. Groesbeck, Wesley A., and Jan Striefel. *Sustainable Landscape and Gardens: The Resource Guide.* 3d ed. Salt Lake City: Environmental Resources Inc., 1996, p. 59.

44. Ohio State University. "Composting factsheet." Columbus OH: Ohio State University Extension, no date.

45. Mitchell, "Compost . . . ," p. 16.

46. Ibid., p. 14.

47. Logan, Terry. "Lead Contamination in the Garden factsheet." Columbus OH: Ohio State University Extension, no date. This source also recommends peat moss; local organic material is far preferable and usually plentiful.

48. Bill Thompson, personal communication.

49. Associated Press. "Report: Toxic chemicals recycled into fertilizers." *New Mexican*, 7 July 1997, Santa Fe NM.

50. EPA, U.S. "Biosolids Recycling: Beneficial Technology for a Better Environment." Washington DC: National Center for Environmental Publications and Information, no date. Ref: EPA 832-R-94-009.

51. Craul, *Urban Soil*, p. 197.

52. Bahe, Anita. "Science and Policy: The Biological, Environmental, and Policy Implications of Organic Waste Reutilization in Urban Landscape Management." Ph.D. dissertation, North Carolina State University, 1995.

53. Leccese, Michael. "Fresh Fields." *Landscape Architecture*, Dec 1996, 44.

54. Mitchell, "Compost . . . ," p. 18.

55. Ibid., p. 17.

56. Craul, Phillip. "Designing Sustainable Soil." In *Opportunities in Sustainable Development: Strategies for the Chesapeake Bay Region*, edited by Margarita Hill. Washington DC: American Society of Landscape Architects, 1997, p. 49.

57. Ibid.

58. Federal Interagency Invasive Species Council. "Draft National Invasive Plant Management Strategy." Washington DC: U.S. Depts. of Interior and Commerce, 1996. For a clear discussion of horticultural introductions that have caused ecological havoc, see Harty, Francis M., "Exotics and Their Ecological Ramifications," *Natural Areas Journal* 6, no. 4 (1986): 20–26.

59. From DR Trimmer/Country Home Products (1-800-446-8746). Like many equipment manufacturers, DR portrays its clients as beating back unruly nature, an attitude that is problematic in itself.

60. For a discussion of the ways in which patterns change over time, known as the Shifting Mosaic Steady State, see *Sustainable Development in Forestry: An Ecological Perspective* by Bryant N. Richards, viewable at http://www.forestry.ubc.ca/schaffer/richards.html.

61. Sauer, *The Once and Future Forest*. See especially pages 298–300 and 165–193.

62. Zickefoose, J. *Enjoying Bluebirds More*. Marietta OH: Bird Watcher's Digest Press, 1993. Like many birders' books, it contains extensive lists of trees, shrubs, and vines that attract birds.

63. Adams, Amy. "Heavy Metal Garden." *Utne Reader*, May-June 1998, 86.

64. Rock, Steven. "Possibilities and Limitations of Phytoremediation." In *The Standard Handbook of Hazardous Waste Treatment and Disposal*, edited by Harry Freeman. NYC: McGraw-Hill, 1997, p. 6.

65. Rea, Philip. "Plants may clean out poisons at toxic sites." *Philadelphia Inquirer*, 12 June 1999. Rea is the primary researcher on this University of Pennsylvania project.

66. Kamnikar, Brian. "Biomounds Pass Tests in Minnesota." *Soil and Groundwater Cleanup*, May 1996, 34–43.

67. Anonymous. "Munching Microbes Make a Meal Out of Toxic Substances." *Purdue News*, Apr. 1997.

68. From "Bioremediation of Environmental Contaminants," which may be viewed at http://gw2.cciw.ca/internet/bioremediation/whatis.html.

69. Bradley, Paul. Title unknown. *Environmental Science & Technology* (June 1999). Reported by wire services, 19 June 1999.

Principle 3. Favor Living, Flexible Materials

1. Gray, Donald, and Robbin Sortir. *Biotechnical and Soil Bioengineering Slope Stabilization*. NYC: John Wiley & Sons, 1996, p. 3.

2. The history of these methods is discussed in Riley, Ann, *Restoring Streams in Cities*. Washington DC: Island Press, 1998.

3. These points were culled from USDA Natural Resource Conservation Service, *Soil Bioengineering for Upland Slope Protection and Erosion Reduction*. Washington DC: Natural Resource Conservation Service, 1992, pp. 18-1 through 18-8.

4. USDA, *Soil Bioengineering*, p. 18-5.

5. Gray and Sotir, p. 149.

6. Ibid., p. 148.

7. USDA, *Soil Bioengineering*, pp. 18-31 and 32.

8. Hough, Michael. *City Form and Natural Process*. NYC: Van Nostrand Reinhold, 1984.

9. Liptan, Tom, et al. *Integrating Stormwater into the Urban Fabric*. Portland, OR: American Society of Landscape Architects, 1997, p. 89.

10. Johnson, Jacklyn, and John Newton. *Building Green: A Guide to Using Plants on Roofs, Walls, and Pavements*. London: London Ecology Unit, no date, p. 48.

11. Ecover. *The Ecover Manual*. Oostmalle, Belgium: Ecover Publishing, 1992, p. 24.

12. Johnson and Newton, *Building Green*, p. 64.

13. Hauer, R. J., R. W. Miller, and D. M. Ouimet. "Street Tree Decline and Construction Damage." *Journal of Arboriculture* 20, no. 2 (1994): 94–97.

14. The author and date of this study are not known.

15. Pimentel's study was published in *Bioscience*; reported in Yaukey, John, "Environments output placed at $2.9 trillion," *Colorodoan*, 14 Dec 1997, Fort Collins CO.

16. The study, cited on http://www.treelink.org, is credited to Dr. Rowan Rowntree, no date.

17. Blanc's excellent lectures were compiled in Blanc, Alan, *Landscape Construction and Detailing*. NYC: McGraw-Hill, 1996.

18. Craul, Philip J. *Urban Soil in Landscape Design*. NYC: Wiley, 1992, p. 1.

19. Ibid., p. 122.

20. This quote is from Urban's contribution to Ramsey, Sleeper, and John Ray Jr. Hoke, *Architectural Graphic Standards*, 9th ed., Revised(?) ed. NYC: Wiley, 1998. Note that even the 1994 edition showed planting standards that Urban states to be actively harmful to trees.

21. The guidelines are summarized from *Architectural Graphic Standards* 1998, pp. 81–82, by James Urban.

22. Wild accusations have been made that defining plants as natives and aliens is comparable to racism against "alien" humans; see Sorvig, Kim, "Natives and Nazis: An Imaginary Conspiracy in Ecological Design," *Landscape Journal* 13, no. 1 (1994): 58–61.

23. See entries for *Abies magnifica* in Little, Elbert, *Audubon Society Field Guide to North American Trees, Western Region* (NYC: Knopf, 1980) and Kricher, John, *Ecology of Western Forests, Peterson Field Guides* (NYC: Houghton Mifflin, 1993).

24. Contact Western Polyacrylamide or the Colorado Forestry Dept. for studies on polymer use.

25. From the 1999 seed catalog of Wildseed Farms, www.wildseedfarms.com.

26. *Washington Post*. "1 out of 8 plant species faces extinction, survey says." *New Mexican*, 8 Apr 1998, B-1, Santa Fe NM.

Principle 4: Respect the Waters of Life

1. Ash, Russell. *Incredible Comparisons.* London: Dorling Kindersley, 1996, p. 23.

2. *The Devil's Dictionary*, ca. 1911.

3. Jameson, Michael. *Xeric Landscaping with Florida Native Plants.* Miami: Assoc. of Florida Native Nurseries, 1991.

4. Rubenstein, Harvey M. *A Guide to Site Planning and Landscape Construction.* 4th ed. NYC: Wiley, 1996, p. 189.

5. BASMAA. *Start at the Source.* San Francisco: Bay Area Stormwater Management Agencies Association, 1997, p 7. Italics added.

6. Rocky Mountain Institute, Studio for Creative Inquiry, and Bruce Ferguson. *Nine Mile Run Briefing Book (draft).* Snowmass CO: Rocky Mountain Institute, 1998, p. 20.

7. Hammer, Donald A. *Creating Freshwater Wetlands.* 2d ed. Boca Raton FL: Lewis Publishers (CRC Press), 1997, p. 16.

8. Berger, John. *Restoring the Earth: How Americans Are Working to Renew Our Damaged Environment.* New York: Knopf, 1985, p. 61. Constructing the marsh requires a wider strip of land than the revetment; cost of land may or may not be an issue in such projects and is not included in Berger's figures.

9. Hammer, *Creating Freshwater Wetlands*, p. 115.

10. Ibid., p. 12.

11. This list is based on Hammer, *Creating Freshwater Wetlands*, p. 139.

12. Ibid., p. 171. Further comments throughout, notably pages 137, 258, and 311.

13. Ibid., pp. 23, 337.

14. Ibid., p. 337.

15. Kentula, Mary, Robert Brooks, Stephanie Gwin, Cindy Holland, Arthur Sherman, and Jean Sifneos. *An Approach to Improving Decision Making in Wetland Restoration and Creation.* Boca Raton FL: CRC Press, 1993, pp. 17–19.

16. Galatowitsch, Susan, and Arnold van der Valk. *Restoring Prairie Wetlands: An Ecological Approach.* Ames: Iowa State University Press, 1994, p. 150; see also chart on p. 49.

17. Hammer, for example, is a strong advocate of this approach.

18. Kentula et al., see particularly pages 17–19 and 111–112. See also Galatowitsch and van der Valk, especially Chapters 1 and 3.

19. Hammer, *Creating Freshwater Wetlands*, p. 39.

20. Ibid., p. 194, is one of many who have reported this concern.

21. El Aidi, Polly. "Innovations in Wetlands Trail Construction." *Landscape Architecture*, July 1993, 120–122.

22. Design recommendations from Hammer, *Creating Freshwater Wetlands*, pp. 201, 215.

23. Ibid., p. 299.

24. Another list of invasive plants, not specific to wetlands, is found in Appendix B of Leslie Sauer's *The Once and Future Forest;* it pertains to deciduous forests of the eastern United States.

25. Hammer, *Creating Freshwater Wetlands*, pp. 264, 318–323.

26. Associated Press article, Spring 1999, no date.

27. This is a major theme of Riley, Ann, *Restoring Streams in Cities.* Washington DC: Island Press, 1998; see esp. pp. 30–31.

28. ("C.A.B."), anonymous. "Sligo Creek: Holistic Stream Restoration." *Watershed Protection Techniques* 1, no. 4 (1995): 192.

29. Ferguson, Bruce. "The Failure of Detention and the Future of Stormwater Design." *Landscape Architecture*, Dec 1991, pp. 76–79. See also Ferguson, Bruce, *Introduction to Stormwater.* NYC: Wiley & Sons, 1998, pp. 162–164.

30. Riley, *Restoring Streams*, p. 362.

31. Ibid., p. 31.

32. Rocky Mountain Institute et al., *Nine Mile Run.*

33. Wilson, Alex. "Rainwater Harvesting." *Environmental Building News,* May 1997, p. 1.

34. Mollison, Bill. *Permaculture: A Designers' Manual.* Tyalgum, NSW, Australia: Tagari Publications, 1988, esp. Chapter 7.

35. Ferguson, *Introduction to Stormwater;* see Chapter 10.

36. Marlowe, Olwen C: *Outdoor Design: A Handbook for the Architect and Planner.* NYC: Watson-Guptil (U.S. edition), 1977, pp. 102–104.

37. Ibid., p. 104.

38. Wilson, Alex, "Rainwater Harvesting," p. 12.

39. Groesbeck, Wesley, and Jan Striefel. *The Resource Guide to Sustainable Landscapes and Gardens.* 2nd ed. Salt Lake City: Environmental Resources, 1995, p. 39.

40. Brabec, Elizabeth, Jim Urban, Andropogon Association, and Oehme van Sweden Assoc. *Save Water, Save Maintenance, Save Money.* Washington DC: Anne Arundel County Dept. of Utilities, 1989, p. 5.

41. The Xeriscape council ceased to function some time ago, and the trademark reportedly passed to the University of Texas Extension.

42. Kourik, Robert. "Drip Irrigation Hardware: Selection and Use." *Landscape Architecture,* Mar 1993, pp. 74–78.

43. Kourik, Robert. "Drip Irrigation for Lawns." *Landscape Architecture,* Mar 1994, p. 40.

44. These principles are based on Kourik, "Drip . . . Hardware" and Kourik, "Drip . . . for Lawns."

45. Kourik, "Drip . . . Hardware," p. 78.

46. Groesbeck, Wesley, and Jan Striefel. *The Resource Guide to Sustainable Landscapes and Gardens.* 2nd ed. Salt Lake City: Environmental Resources, 1995, pp. 49–50.

47. Kourik, "Drip . . . for Lawns," p. 41.

48. Sole, Ricard V., and David Alonso. "Random Walks, Fractals and the Origins of Rainforest Diversity." Santa Fe NM: Santa Fe Institute, 1998. Ref: 98-08-60, Working Paper. Hordijk, Wim. "A Measure of Landscapes." Santa Fe NM: Santa Fe Institute, 1995. Ref: 95-05-049, Working Paper. These two papers are examples of such math research, primarily in ecology and molecular biology. A number of working papers are available on related topics at http://www.santafe.edu/cgi-bin/AT-publicationssearch.cgi. Use of the term "landscape" for such widely varying and nonphysical concepts as a "fitness landscape" (evolutionary theory) or "the political landscape" (journalism) make electronic information searches in our profession both difficult and entertaining.

49. Kourik, Robert. "Graywater for Residential Irrigation." *Landscape Architecture,* Jan 1995, pp. 30–33.

50. Jeppeson, Barry, and David Solley. *Domestic Greywater Reuse: Overseas Practice and Its Applicability to Australia.* Melbourne: Urban Water Research Association of Australia, 1994.

51. See Kourik, "Graywater," and Groesbeck & Streifel, *Resource Guide,* pp. 41–43.

52. Wilson, Alex. "On-site Wastewater Treatment." *Environmental Building News,* Mar/Apr 1994, pp. 1–18.

53. The project won an ASLA award and was published in *Landscape Architecture,* but never built.

54. Hammer, *Creating Freshwater Wetlands,* p. 312.

55. Patterson, Rich. "From Wasteland to Wetland." *Public Risk,* Jan 1998, p. 29.

Principle 5. Pave Less

1. Data from Web site www.bts.gov/nts/chp1/tblx5.html.

2. The number of spaces is from the International Parking Institute's Web site, www.parking.org. The area calculation assumes a standard parking space to be 10 feet by 18 feet.

3. Bruce Ferguson (Univ. of GA) estimates U.S. paving, based on volumes of asphalt and concrete sold, at a quarter-million to a half-million acres each year. This is a growth rate of 1.5 to 3.0 percent of our estimated total area—higher than the population growth rate!

4. Ash, Russel. *Incredible Comparisons.* London: Dorling Kindersley, 1996, p. 26.

5. Kelley, Ben. *The Pavers and the Paved.* NYC: Donald Brown, no date.

6. Childs, Mark. *Parking Spaces.* NYC: McGraw-Hill, 1999, p. 195.

7. Ibid., p. 197.

8. Schueler, Tom. *Site Planning for Urban Stream Protection.* Ellicott City MD: Center for Watershed Protection, 1995, p. 148.

9. Ibid.

10. These policy suggestions are based on the University of Georgia School of Environmental Design, *Land Development Provisions to Protect Georgia Water Quality,* edited by David Nichols. Athens: Georgia Dept. of Natural Resources, 1997.

11. Anonymous. "Impervious Surface Reduction Study." Olympia WA: City of Olympia Public Works Department, 1995. Ref: Final Report, pp. 84–85.

12. Center for Watershed Protection. *Model Development Principles to Protect Our Streams, Lakes, and Wetlands.* Ellicott City MD: Center for Watershed Protection, 1998, p. 76.

13. Wilson, Richard S. "Suburban Parking Requirements and the Shape of Suburbia." *Journal of the American Planning Association* 61, no. 1 (1995): 29–42.

14. Center for Watershed Protection, *Model Development Principles,* p. 73.

15. Ibid., p. 75.

16. Unterman, Richard. "Office Park Paradise." *Landscape Architecture,* Aug 1998.

17. This and following quote from R. A. White are found on his office's Web site, http://www.tlcnetwork.org/bobwhite.html

18. From the Web site Drivers.com. While many motorists associations treat traffic calming as a government conspiracy against their "rights," Drivers.com takes a very balanced view of the issues.

19. On traffic calming and scenic roads, see http://www.bts.gov/ntl/DOCS/vsb.html: "Design and Information Requirements for Travel and Tourism Needs on Scenic Byways—Final Report," by Christiana M. Briganti and Lester A. Hoel

20. This paranoic view appears in Ruane T. Peter, "Zealots Would Stop Road Work," *ENR (Engineering News-Record),* June 14 1999, p. 11. Ruane, president of ARTB, even considers urban sprawl to be "in the public interest," again for obvious and self-serving reasons.

21. FHWA's research center Web site: http://www.tfhrc.gov/

22. Center for Watershed Protection, *Model Principles,* p. 33.

23. Atkins, Crystal, and Michael Coleman. "Influence of Traffic Calming on Emergency Response Times." *ITE Journal* (Aug 1997): 42–47.

24. Sorensen, A. Ann, and J. Dixon Esseks. "Living on the Edge: The Costs and Risks of Scatter Development." *American Farmland Trust Newsletter,* Mar 1998.

25. See the Drivers.com Web site.

26. Anonymous, *Impervious Surface Reduction Study*, Executive Summary, p. 20.

27. BAASMA. *Start at the Source.* San Francisco: Bay Area Stormwater Management Agencies Association, 1997, p. 15; Bruce Ferguson was one of the consultants for this book.

28. Paine, John E. *Pervious Pavement Manual.* Orlando: Florida Concrete and Products Association, no date.

29. B. Ferguson, personal communication to Sorvig.

30. Grasspave brochure from Invisible Structures⊃.

31. Anonymous, *Impervious Surface Reduction Study*, pp. 79–80.

32. Sipes, James, and Mack Roberts. "Grass Paving Systems." *Landscape Architecture*, June 1994, p. 33.

33. Anonymous. "Henderson Field Demonstration Project Summary." Olympia WA: City of Olympia, 1996, p. 13.

34. Sipes and Roberts, "Grass Paving Systems," p. 33.

35. Anonymous, "Henderson Field . . ." pp. 7–13. A site visit in 1999 found the area fenced off for reasons unknown.

36. Evans, Matthew, Nina Bassuk, and Peter Trowbridge. "Sidewalk Design for Tree Survival." *Landscape Architecture*, Mar 1990, p. 103.

37. Akbari, Hashem; U.S. Environmental Protection Agency, Climate Change Division; Lawrence Berkeley Laboratory; and U.S. Dept. of Energy. *Cooling Our Communities: A Guidebook on Tree Planting and Light-colored Surfacing*, Lawrence Berkeley Laboratory report, LBL-31587. Washington DC. Pittsburgh PA (POB 371954, Pittsburgh 15220-7954); U.S. Environmental Protection Agency Office of Policy Analysis, Climate Change Division; for sale by the U.S. GPO. Supt. of Docs., 1992.

38. Childs, *Parking Spaces*, p. 196.

39. Information on these coatings comes from interviews with DecoAsphalt in California and Integrated Paving Concepts in Canada. Information on integral asphalt color from interviews with Asphacolor (Madera CA). See Resources for more information.

Principle 6. Consider Origin and Fate of Materials

1. Quoted in Thompson, William, "Is It Sustainable? Is It Art?" *Landscape Architecture*, May 1992, pp. 56–57. (Emphasis added.)

2. Baughman, Kathleen. "The Use of Recycled Materials in the Landscape." Unpublished, Washington State University, 1995, p. 16.

3. Reported in Pijawka, K. David, "Dozens of Activities Mark Second Annual 'Arizona Recycles Day,'" *AZ Recycling Review*, Spring 1999, p. 16.

4. Maurice Nelisher, quoted in Thompson, "Is It Sustainable? Is It Art?"

5. See Table 7.9 for these and other transportation energy rates.

6. Even the formidable AIA *Environmental Resource Guide* misuses the term renewable, making it a synonym for recyclable (p. 06118:2).

7. HOK Architects. *Sustainable Design Guide.* Edited by Sandra Mendler. Washington DC: HOK Architects, 1998, p. iii.

8. Stange, Rainer. *"Bjørnsons hage i Vika, Oslo"*; also published in German as *"Garten in Oslo," Garten und Landschaft*, November 1997.

9. Baughman, "Recycled Materials . . . ," p. 19.

10. Ibid., p. 29.

11. Ryder, Barbara. "Glass: Landscape Applications." *Landscape Architecture.* June 1995, p. 28.

12. Ibid.

13. Baughman, "Recycled Materials . . . ," p. 29.

14. Ibid., p. 39.

15. Anonymous. "Waste Tire Problem Becomes Opportunity for Erosion Control." *Land and Water*, Mar 1998, p. 36.

16. Anonymous. "Recycled Tires Turn a Problem into a Solution." *Erosion Control*, Sept 1998, pp. 18–21.

17. According to Pliny Fisk, tire surfaces pick up some pollutants from road contact, but these are removed by simple washing. Fisk notes that the EPA has tested the chemical content of tires because they are so common in playgrounds, and found them inert.

18. Anonymous. "Recycled Tires."

19. Sorvig, Kim. "Brave New Landscape." *Landscape Architecture*, July 1992, pp. 75–77.

20. Wilson, Alex. "Test Methods Approved for Plastic Lumber." *Environmental Building News*, Oct 1997, p. 4. (Includes contacts for further information.)

21. Winterbottom, Daniel. "Plastic Lumber." *Landscape Architecture*, Jan 1995, p. 34.

22. Anonymous. "Where the Rubber Meets the Trail." *Rails to Trails*, Winter 1999, p. 5.

23. *San Jose Mercury News.* "Old-growth forests get a break from Home Depot." *New Mexican*, 29 Aug 1999, p. D-1, Santa Fe NM.

24. Chiras, Daniel D. *Environmental Science: Action for a Sustainable Future.* 4th ed. Redwood City CA: Benjamin/Cummings, 1994, pp. 203–209.

25. Fisk, Pliny. "Comparison of Available Wastes and Production of Wood Products." Austin TX: Center for Maximum Potential Building Systems, 1993. This information is graphed from data by the U.S. Dept. of Commerce, Natural Resources Research Institute, U.S. EPA, and the Institute for Local Self-Reliance.

26. Information on AERT thanks to Pliny Fisk.

27. The EPA's recommendation for maximum indoor concentration of radon, 4 picocuries, was set at the average amount of radon found naturally in outdoor air.

28. Craul, Philip J. *Urban Soil in Landscape Design.* NYC: Wiley, 1992. Based on Table 6.1, p. 186.

29. Baker, Paula, Erica Elliot, and John Banta. *Prescriptions for a Healthy House.* Santa Fe NM: InWord Publishers, 1998, pp. xv–xvi.

30. Ibid., pp. 55–59.

31. Real Goods. *Solar Living Sourcebook.* Edited by John Schaeffer. 9th ed. Ukiah CA: Real Goods, 1996. Cites Lovins on pp. 374–376 and presents related information on p. 546.

32. This figure, and the following ones for logging and construction, originate with the U.S. EPA, cited in van der Leeden, Frits, *Water Encyclopedia.* Boca Raton FL: Lewis Publishers, 1990. Other experts have claimed increases up to 40,000 times the baseline.

33. Malin, Nadav, and Alex Wilson. "Material Selection: Tools, Resources, and Techniques for Choosing Green." *Environmental Building News,* Jan 1997, pp. 10–14; American Institute of Architects. *Environmental Resource Guide.* Edited by Joseph A. Demkin. Looseleaf, current through '98 Supplement ed. NYC: Wiley, 1998; Mumma, Tracy, and CRBT staff. *Guide to Resource Efficient Building Elements.* Missoula MT: Center for Resourceful Building Technology, 1995 and later.

34. EPA/625/R-94/006, September 1994, "Guide to Cleaner Technologies: Organic Coating Replacements." Viewable at http://es.epa.gov/program/epaorgs/ord/orgcoat.html.

35. On PVC, see AIA *Environmental Resource Guide,* p. Mat-09652:35–37. On wood preservatives, see Wilson, Alex, "A Call for CCA Phaseout." *Environmental Building News,* Mar 1997, p. 2, and other articles in *EBN.*

36. AIA *Environmental Resource Guide,* p. Mat-09652:36. For further information, see under PVC in Appendix A.

37. Wilson, Alex. "Using Wood Outdoors." *Landscape Architecture,* Quoted from manuscript.

38. AIA *Environmental Resource Guide,* p. MAT-06180:14.

39. Wilson, "CCA Phaseout." See v. 2, no. 1, Jan/Feb 1993, p. 10 for earlier research backing up the phaseout proposal.

40. Associated Press. "Report: Toxic chemicals recycled into fertilizers." *New Mexican,* 7 July 1997, and other reports subsequently, Santa Fe NM.

Principle 7: Know the Costs of Energy Over Time

1. American Institute of Architects. *Environmental Resource Guide.* Edited by Joseph A. Demkin. Looseleaf, current through '98 Supplement ed. NYC: Wiley, 1998.

2. Stein, R. G., C. Stein, M. Buckley, and M. Green. *Handbook of Energy Use for Building Construction.* Vol. DOE/CS/20220-1, *Energy Conservation.* Washington DC: US Dept. of Energy, 1980. Statistics from pages 10 and 9, respectively. These statistics are based on conditions in the 1970s and are probably not exactly comparable to the AIA figures.

3. Mumma, Tracy. "Reducing the Embodied Energy of Buildings." *Home Energy,* Jan 1995, pp. 19–22.

4. Swezey, Kenneth M. *Formulas, Methods, Tips, and Data.* NYC: Harper & Row, 1969, pp. 620 and 595; based on an average density for different species of pine of 37.5 lbs./cf and an average of 12.5 million Btu per cord (128 cf).

5. Both statistics from AIA-ERG, closely comparable to Stein.

6. This use of the term is scattered throughout the several informative publications of the DOE's Office of Industrial Technology.

7. HOK Architects. *Sustainable Design Guide.* Edited by Sandra Mendler. Washington DC: HOK Architects, 1998, p 2.21, for example.

8. Mumma, "Reducing Embodied Energy . . . ," p. 19.

9. Ibid., p. 20. Costs are in energy terms, not in dollars paid for energy.

10. Work and time comparison from Bruun, Erik, and Buzzy Keith, *Heavy Equipment.* NYC: Black Dog & Leventhal, 1997, p. 10 (assume a full workday means eight hours in this context). Horsepower of scraper from pp. 22–23 (a bulldozer or second scraper is often required to push the working scraper in hard soils; this doubles the energy consumption, but is not included here). Horsepower to gallons/hr per Nichols, Herbert L. Jr., and David A. Day, *Moving the Earth: The Workbook of Excavation,* 4th ed. NYC: McGraw-Hill, 1998, p. 12.III. Gallons to Btu based on Table 7.1 . Human energy expenditure per workday based on Dorf, Richard C., *The Energy Factbook.* NYC: McGraw-Hill, 1981, p 10, ca. 0.7 Kw, converted to Btu; some sources give much higher energy use for human labor, which is very variable and, in a mechanical sense, inefficient.

11. Malin, Nadav. "Battery Fanatic." *Environmental Building News,* Mar 1993, p. 4.

12. These are the 1997 record-holders for largest truck and largest hydraulic excavator in the world, both built by Komatsu. Even these, picked because they resemble familiar equipment types, are far from the world's largest or heaviest equipment, since bucket-wheel excavators range up to nearly 15,000 tons, moving 10,000 or more cubic yards of soil per hour. Bruun and Keith, *Heavy Equipment.*

13. These are rough figures within what is actually a range of energy, influenced especially by temperature and elevation at the site. Diesel, for example, can produce between 132,000 and 152,000 Btu per gallon. For fine detailed information on this topic,

see Haywood, John B., *Internal Combustion Engine Fundamentals*. NYC: McGraw-Hill, 1988.

14. Nichols and Day, *Moving the Earth*, p. 12.111. Figures for 2-stroke are from Haywood, *Fundamentals*, p. 887.

15. Properly speaking, the horsepower figure should be actual, tested horsepower. For *rough* estimating and comparison of different machine *types*, using the rated or theoretical horsepower is probably accurate enough and is often the only figure available.

16. Nichols and Day, *Moving the Earth*, pp. 12.110–12.111, give the basic figures; conversion to Btu and to light/heavy percentages by authors.

17. The two engines on which these comparisons are based are Tanaka's conventional TBC-3010, at 29cc or 1.6 hp, and the new "Pure-Fire" TBC-270PF at 26cc or 1.4 hp.

18. Post, Irwin. "Horsepower: Is Bigger Really Better?" *Independent Sawmill & Woodlot Management.* Apr 1999, pp. 15–17.

19. Rollins, John P., and Compressed Air and Gas Institute. *Compressed Air and Gas Handbook.* 5 ed. Engelwood Cliffs NJ: Prentice-Hall, 1989, p. 846, Table 13.31.

20. Whiffen, Helen H. "Landscape Maintenance Takes Energy: Use It Wisely." *Energy Efficiency and Environmental News* (U. FL Extension), Feb 1993. This newsletter is viewable at http://edis.ifas.ufl.edu/.

21. Based on Dorf, *Energy Factbook*, p. 11. Human metabolism and energy output are notoriously variable. Other experts consider 300 Btu per hour an average for light labor, like desk jobs or driving a truck, and rate very heavy labor up to 1,500 Btu per hour.

22. Smil, Vaclav. *Energies: An Illustrated Guide to the Biosphere and Civilization.* Cambridge MA: MIT Press, 1999, p. 90.

23. From a very interesting and unusually objective Web site on all matters truck-related: www.yondar.com/yondar/faq.htm. The calculation is based on the tonnage hauled by an 18-wheeler, but similar ton-mile efficiency is achieved by some large construction trucks.

24. Figures in table based on Lawson, Bill, *Building Materials Energy and the Environment* (Red Hill (Australia): Royal Australian Institute of Architects, 1996), p. 12, and Dorf, *Energy Factbook*, p. 79.

25. Odum, Howard T., and Elizabeth C. Odum. *Energy Basis for Man and Nature.* NYC: McGraw-Hill, 1976 p. 34, Figure 2–5.

26. Based on Lawson, *Building Materials*, Tables 1.2 (road transport) and 1.3 (brick embodied energy).

27. This heading is borrowed from one of the first articles on embodied energy in construction: Malin, Nadav, "Embodied Energy—Just What Is It and Why Do We Care?" *Environmental Building News,* May/June 1993, pp. 8–9.

28. Lawson, *Building Materials*, p. 12, Table 1.1.

29. Baird, G., R. Jacques, A. Alcorn, P. Wood, and J. B. Storey. "Progress toward the specification of embodied energy performance criteria for New Zealand buildings." Ponrua NZ: Building Research Association of New Zealand, 1998.

30. ASMI Web site, click heading "The Challenge."

31. Malin, "Embodied Energy," p. 9.

32. Mumma, "Reducing Embodied Energy," p. 22.

33. 1994 edition, pp. 122–123.

34. Based on Post, Hal, and Vernon Risser. "Stand-Alone Photovoltaic Systems: A Handbook of Recommended Design Practices." Albuquerque: Sandia National Laboratory, 1991. Ref. SAND87-7023 revised. Available from National Technical Information Service. Pages 59–64 and worksheet on B-57.

Principle 8. Celebrate Light, Respect Darkness

1. Schaeffer, John, and Real Goods staff. *The Book of Light.* Ukiah CA: Real Goods, 1996; pp. 4–11 discuss energy use and lighting.

2. Real Goods *Book of Light*; the original source of this information appears to be Amory Lovins and the Rocky Mountain Institute.

3. Stone, Richard A. "Infant Myopia and Night Lighting." *Nature,* 13 May 1999.

4. Associated Press. "Study gives new directions for insomnia research." *New Mexican,* 25 June 1999, A-4, Santa Fe NM; this reports work by researchers Charles Czeisler and Richard Kronauer at Harvard University Medical School.

5. Bassuk, Nina. 1978. This literature review, and the information that no other research has been done since the 1970s, was kindly shared by the author.

6. Peterson, Karen. "Night-sky law needs to be tougher, researchers say." *New Mexican,* 8 Apr 1999, B-4, Santa Fe NM. Exemptions, from prisons to ordinary billboards, are commonly pushed through by lobbyists.

7. Based on the fact that new lamps *save* up to 90 percent; see multi-LED bulb description in this chapter.

8. Harris, Charles W., and Nicholas T. Dines. *Timesaver Standards for Landscape Architecture.* NYC: McGraw-Hill, 1988, pp. 540-11 to 540-13.

9. Wilson, Alex. "Disposal of Flourescent Lamps and Ballasts." *Environmental Building News,* Oct 1997, 1, 9–14.

10. Moyer, Janet Lennox. *The Landscape Lighting Book.* NYC: Wiley, 1992. This has a truly remarkable amount of detail on materials, operation, and design.

11. Smil, Vaclav. *Energies: An Illustrated Guide to the Biosphere and Civilization.* Cambridge MA: MIT Press, 1999, p. xvi, Table 7.
12. Harris & Dines, *Time-Saver.*
13. Wilson, "Disposal of Flourescent."

Principle 9. Quietly Defend Silence

1. Rosenburg, Eric, and Ilene J. Busch-Vishniac. "Continued Investigation of Noise Reduction by a Random-Edge Noise Barrier." Paper presented at the 133rd Acoustical Society of America Meeting, State College PA, June 17 1997.
2. Associated Press. "Population boom makes for a noisy planet." *New Mexican,* 27 June 1999, pp. A-1 and A-3, Santa Fe NM. Ironically, the next item on the page with this article was a small ad headed "Hearing Loss? 24-hour recorded message."
3. Ramsey, Charles G., Harold R. Sleeper, and John Ray Hoke Jr. *Architectural Graphics Standards.* 9th ed. NYC: Wiley, 1994, p. 59, tables.
4. Harris, Charles W., and Nicholas T. Dines. *Time-saver Standards for Landscape Architecture.* NYC: McGraw-Hill, 1988, p. 660-5, tables.
5. Some research on the subject of bioacoustics, related to endangered birds and legislation to protect them from excessive noise, has been done at the Transportation Noise Control Center, a research institute at UC Davis.
6. For those interested in this topic, search the Web for LFAS (Low Frequency Active Sonar).
7. Harris and Dines, *Time-Saver,* p. 660-6.3.
8. Ibid.
9. Rosenburg and Busch-Vishniac.
10. Harris and Dines, *Time-Saver,* p. 660-6.6.
11. There is, however, a rare psychological gift called synasthesia in which people see specific colors simultaneous with hearing certain sounds. Does noise torment them like an allergy?
12. Ramsey and Hoke, *Architectural Graphic Standards,* p. 59, table.
13. This statistic from the Web site of Industrial Acoustics Co., www.industrialacoustics.com.
14. Associated Press. "Park Service officials want to get a word in: 'Quiet.'" *New Mexican,* 3 July 1999, A-1, A-2, Santa Fe NM.

Principle 10. Maintain to Sustain

1. Research by University of Wisconsin landscape architecture professor Darrel Morrison, reported in Berger, John, *Restoring the Earth: How Americans Are Working to Renew Our Damaged Environment.* New York: Knopf, 1985, p. 124.
2. MacIntyre, John. "Facts of Life: Gardening." *Spirit,* May 1999, p. 158; a compilation of miscellaneous garden statistics in the tradition of the Harper's Index.
3. Groesbeck, Wesley, and Jan Striefel. *The Resource Guide to Sustainable Landscapes and Gardens,* 2d ed. Salt Lake City: Environmental Resources, 1995, p. 39.
4. Ibid.
5. BASMAA (Bay Area Stormwater Management Agencies Association, from its executive director, Geoff Brosseau.
6. Hawley, Gessner G. *The Condensed Chemical Dictionary,* 10th ed. NYC: Van Nostrand Reinhold, 1981; entry for Phosphate Rock, p. 809.
7. Groesbeck and Streifel, *Resource Guide,* p. 39.
8. Ibid.
9. Information on current practice with maintenance plans is from interviews with Leslie Sauer of Andropogon and/or summarized from Kellum, Jo, "The Legacy of Design," *Landscape Architecture,* Sept 1999, p. 108. Jo Kellum refers to the difficulty of maintenance coordination as being similar to herding cats.

Conclusions and Beginnings

1. Tenner, Edward. *Why Things Bite Back: Technology and the Revenge of Unintended Consequences.* NYC: Vintage, 1996. Tenner is former science and history editor at Princeton University Press. His lively account of technology proves you should be careful what you wish for.
2. Steele, James. *Sustainable Architecture: Principles, Paradigms and Case Studies.* NYC: McGraw-Hill, 1997, p. 244.
3. For a summary, see Steele, Chapter 1. Construction-specific recommendations were Section 4 of the original report.
4. Wulff, Sonja Bisbee. "CSU students learn sustainable landscape design at tropical resort." *Coloradoan,* 12 July 1999, A5, Fort Collins CO.

Appendix A

1. Amory Lovins, cited in Real Goods. *Solar Living Sourcebook.* Edited by John Schaeffer. 9th ed. Ukiah CA: Real Goods, 1996, pp. 374–376 and 546.
2. HOK Architects. *Sustainable Design Guide.* Edited by Sandra Mendler. Washington DC: HOK Architects, 1998, p. ii.
3. Wilson, Alex. "Non ozone-depleting foam sealants." *Environmental Building News* 6, no. 9 (1997): 8.
4. American Institute of Architects. *Environmental Resource Guide.* Edited by Joseph A. Demkin. Looseleaf, current through '98 Supplement ed. NYC: Wiley, 1998, p. Ap-2:2.
5. Ibid., p. Ap-10:20.

6. Ibid., p. Mat-09652:36. For further information, see under PVC in Appendix A.

7. Sonner, Scott. "Paint is hazardous, Forest Service workers say." *Associated Press/New Mexican,* 18 Mar 1999, B-5.

8. EPA/625/R-94/006, September 1994, "Guide to Cleaner Technologies: Organic Coating Replacements." Viewable at http://es.epa.gov/program/epaorgs/ord/orgcoat.html.

9. Wilson, Alex. "Using Wood Outdoors." *Landscape Architecture,* Sept 1999. Quoted from manuscript.

10. AIA *Environmental Resource Guide,* p. Mat-06180:14.

11. Wilson, Alex. "A Call for CCA Phase-out." *Environmental Building News,* Mar 1997, p. 2. See v. 2 no. 1, Jan/Feb 1993, p. 10 for earlier research backing up the phaseout proposal.

12. Pliny Fisk, personal correspondence.

13. Short note in *EBN* v. 6, no. 1, Jan 1997, pp. 7–8.

Appendix B

1. Mumma, Tracy. "Reducing the Embodied Energy of Buildings." *Home Energy,* Jan 1995, pp. 19–22. p. 21

2. Based on Lawson, Bill. *Building Materials Energy and the Environment.* Red Hill (Australia): Royal Australian Institute of Architects, 1996, Tables 1.2 (road transport) and 1.3 (brick embodied energy).

3. Stein, R. G., C. Stein, M. Buckley, and M. Green. *Handbook of Energy Use for Building Construction.* Vol. DOE/CS/20220-1, *Energy Conservation.* Washington DC: U.S. Dept. of Energy, 1980, p. 43.

4. Ibid.

Index